NEW
WEBSTER'S
DICTIONARY

NEW WEBSTER'S DICTIONARY

Vest Pocket Edition

Delair

ISBN: 0-8326-0036-9
Lib. of Cong. Catalog Card Number: 75-18560

STAFF

EXECUTIVE EDITOR
Edward G. Finnegan

EDITORS
Marilyn Finnegan
Rhonda Heisler
Judy Van Wie
McVey Associates

ABBREVIATIONS USED IN THIS DICTIONARY

a.	adjective
adv.	adverb
conj.	conjunction
esp.	especially
fem.	feminine form
inf.	informal
int.	interjection
n.	noun
pl.	plural
prep.	preposition
pron.	pronoun
usu.	usually
v.	verb
v.i.	verb (intransitive)
v.t.	verb (transitive)

A

a, *indef. art.* one; each.

aard·vark, *n.* African mammal that feeds on ants.

a·back, *adv.* backward. **taken aback**, taken by surprise.

ab·a·cus, *n. pl.*, **ab·a·cus·es**, **ab·a·ci**. frame of beads used for counting.

a·ban·don, *v.* give up wholly; surrender; desert. *n.* a letting go. **a·ban·doned**, *a.* **a·ban·don·er**, *n.* **a·ban·don·ment**, *n.*

a·base, *v.* **a·based**, **a·bas·ing**. humble. **a·base·ment**, *n.*

a·bash, *v.* confuse. **a·bash·ment**, *n.*

a·bate, *v.* **a·bat·ed**, **a·bat·ing**. diminish. **a·bate·ment**, *n.*

ab·bey, *n. pl.*, **ab·beys**. monastery or convent. **ab·bess**, *fem.* **ab·bot**, *n.*

ab·bre·vi·a·tion, *n.* shortened form. **ab·bre·vi·ate**, *v.*

ab·di·cate, *v.* **-cat·ed**, **-cat·ing**. renounce, as a throne. **ab·di·ca·tion**, *n.*

ab·do·men, *n.* part of the body between the chest and hips. **ab·dom·i·nal**, *a.*

ab·duct, *v.* kidnap. **ab·duc·tion**, *n.* **ab·duc·tor**, *n.*

ab·er·ra·tion, *n.* deviation.

a·bet, *v.* **a·bet·ted**, **a·bet·ting**. encourage. **a·bet·tor**, *n.*

ab·hor, *v.* **ab·horred**, **ab·hor·ring**. hate. **ab·hor·rence**, *n.* **ab·hor·rer**, *n.* **ab·hor·rent**, *a.*

a·bide, *v.i.* **a·bode** or **a·bid·ed**, **a·bid·ing**. reside. *v.t.* await; endure; remain. **a·bid·ance**, *n.*

a·bil·i·ty, *n. pl.*, **-ties**. competence; capability. *pl.* talents.

ab·ject, *a.* low. **ab·jec·tion**, *n.* low state. **ab·ject·ly**, *adv.*

ab·jure, *v.* **ab·jured**, **ab·jur·ing**. renounce upon oath. **ab·ju·ra·tion**, *n.* **ab·jur·er**, *n.*

a·ble, *a.* competent; qualified; **a·bly**, *adv.*

ab·ne·gate, *v.*, **-gat·ed**, **-gat·ing**. deny; renounce.

ab·nor·mal, *a.* unnatural. **ab·nor·mal·ly**, *adv.* **ab·nor·mal·i·ty**, *n. pl.*, **-ties**.

a·board, *adv.*, *prep.* on board.

a·bode, *n.* place of residence.

a·bol·ish, *v.* do away with. **a·bol·ish·a·ble**, *a.* **a·bol·ish·er**, *n.* **a·bol·ish·ment**, *n.* **ab·o·li·tion**, *n.* **ab·o·li·tion·ist**, *n.*

a·bom·i·nate, *v.*, **-nat·ed**, **-nat·ing**. abhor. **a·bom·i·na·tion**, *n.*

ab·o·rig·i·ne, *n.* early native of a country.

a·bor·tion, *n.* miscarriage.

a·bound, *v.* have in great quantity.

a·bout, *prep.* around; concerning; *adv.* around, near to.

a·bove, *prep.* higher than. *adv.* overhead. *a.* preceding.

a·brade, *v.* **a·brad·ed**, **a·brad·ing**. rub or wear down; irritate. **a·bra·sive**, *a.*, *n.*

a·bra·sion, *n.* scraped area.

a·breast, *adv.*, *a.* side by side.

a·bridge, *v.*, **a·bridged**, **a·bridg·ing**. shorten; condense. **a·bridg·a·ble**, **a·bridge·a·ble**, *a.* **a·bridg·ment**, **a·bridge·ment**, *n.*

a·broad, *adv.* at large; out of doors; in foreign countries.

ab·ro·gate, *v.*, **-gat·ed**, **-gat·ing**. repeal; annul.

ab·rupt, *a.* steep; sudden; brusque; disconnected.

ab·scess, *n.* pus in body tissue. **ab·scessed**, *a.*

ab·scond, *v.* flee from the law.

ab·sent, *a.* not present; keep away. **ab·sence**, *n.*

ab·so·lute, *a.* perfect; positive; despotic; ultimate. **ab·so·lute·ly**, *adv.* **ab·so·lut·ism**, *n.*

ab·solve, *v.*, **ab·solved**, **ab·solv·ing**. acquit; forgive. **ab·solv·a·ble**, *a.* **ab·solv·er**, *n.* **ab·so·lu·tion**, *n.*

ab·sorb, *v.* suck up; engage attention. **ab·sorb·en·cy**, *n.* **ab·sorb·ent**, *a.* **ab·sorp·tion**, *n.*

ab·stain, *v.* keep from doing. **ab·sten·tion**, *n.* **ab·sti·nence**, *n.* **ab·sti·nent**, *a.*

ab·ste·mi·ous, *a.* temperate.

ab·stract, *v.* summarize. *a.* not concrete; based on theory. *n.* summary. **ab·strac·tion**, *n.*

ab·surd, *a.* ridiculous. **ab·surd·i·ty**, *n. pl.*, **-ties**.

a·bun·dant, *a.* plentiful.

a·buse, *v.*, **a·bused**, **a·bus·ing**. misuse. *n.* misuse; insulting language.

a·bu·sive, *a.* insulting.

a·but, *v.*, **a·but·ted**, **a·but·ting**. border.

a·byss, *n.* bottomless opening.

ac·a·dem·ic, *a.* relating to schools; theoretical; not practical. **ac·a·dem·i·cal·ly**, *adv.*

a·cad·e·my, *n. pl.*, **-mies**. private or military school; association.

ac·cede, *v.*, **ac·ced·ed**, **ac·ced·ing**. agree or assent; join.

ac·cel·er·ate, v., -at·ed, -at·ing. increase speed. **ac·cel·er·a·tion**, n. **ac·cel·er·a·tor**, n.

ac·cent, n. stress; stress mark; distinctive pronunciation. v. emphasize.

ac·cen·tu·ate, v., -at·ed, -at·ing. mark with an accent; emphasize. **ac·cen·tu·a·tion**, n.

ac·cept, v. take; assent to; understand. **ac·cept·ance**, n. **ac·cept·a·ble**, a.

ac·cess, n. means of approach. **ac·ces·si·ble**, a. easy of access. **ac·ces·si·bil·i·ty**, n.

ac·ces·so·ry, a. contributing; accompanying. n. pl., -ries. one who aids or allows a crime; accompaniment.

ac·ci·dent, n. chance; unforeseen injury; unexpected happening. **ac·ci·den·tal**, a.

ac·claim, v. applaud; acknowledge. n. approval.

ac·cla·ma·tion, n. applause; oral vote showing acceptance.

ac·cli·mate, v., -mat·ed, -mat·ing. adapt to a new place or climate. **ac·cli·ma·tion**, n.

ac·co·lade, n. honor; praise.

ac·com·mo·date, v.t., -dat·ed, -dat·ing. adapt; oblige; have or make room for. v.i. agree. **ac·com·mo·da·tion**, n.

ac·com·pa·ny, v., -nied, -ny·ing. go with; play a subordinate musical part to. **ac·com·pa·ni·ment**, n. **ac·com·pa·nist**, n.

ac·com·plice, n. helper in a crime.

ac·com·plish, v. complete; execute. **ac·com·plish·ment**, n.

ac·cord, n. agreement; harmony. v.t. grant. v.i. be in harmony. **ac·cor·dance**, n. **ac·cord·ing**, a.

ac·cor·di·on, n. portable, bellowslike musical instrument.

ac·count, v. consider. v.i. furnish explanations. n. business statement; description; reason; advantage; behalf. **ac·count·a·ble**, a. responsible.

ac·cre·tion, n. growth.

ac·crue, v. result as an addition. **ac·cru·al**, n.

ac·cu·mu·late, v.t., -lat·ed, -lat·ing. heap or pile up. v.i. collect. **ac·cu·mu·la·tion**, n.

ac·cu·ra·cy, n. correctness.

ac·cu·rate, a. exact. **ac·cu·rate·ly**, adv. **ac·cu·rate·ness**, n.

ac·cuse, v., -cused, -cus·ing. charge with a crime; blame.

ac·cu·sa·tion, n. **ac·cu·sa·to·ry**, a. **ac·cus·ing·ly**, adv.

ac·cus·tom, v. familiarize by use or habit.

a·cer·bi·ty, n. sourness; severity.

a·ce·tic, a. like vinegar; sour.

ac·e·tone, n. liquid solvent.

a·cet·y·lene, n. gas used as a fuel in welding.

ache, n. pain. v., ached, ach·ing. suffer from pain.

a·chieve, v., a·chieved, a·chiev·ing. accomplish.

ac·id, a. sour. n. compound that combines with bases to form salts. **a·cid·i·ty**, n.

a·cid·i·fy, v., -fied, -fy·ing. make acid. **a·cid·i·fi·er**, n.

ac·knowl·edge, v., -edged, -edg·ing. own or recognize; thank. **ac·knowl·edg·ment**, n.

ac·me, n. highest point.

ac·ne, n. pimples.

ac·o·lyte, n. altar boy.

a·corn, n. nut of an oak.

a·cous·tics, n. study of sound.

ac·quaint, v. make familiar.

ac·quaint·ance, n. person slightly known.

ac·qui·esce, v., -esced, -esc·ing. agree quietly or passively. **ac·qui·es·cent**, a.

ac·quire, v., ac·quired, ac·quir·ing. get. **ac·qui·si·tion**, n. **ac·quis·i·tive**, a.

ac·quit, v., ac·quit·ted, ac·quit·ting. release from obligation; conduct. **ac·quit·tal**, n.

a·cre, n. unit of land, 43,560 sq. ft. **a·cre·age**, n.

ac·rid, a. sharp; bitter. **a·crid·i·ty**, n.

ac·ri·mo·ny, n. sharpness; bitterness. **ac·ri·mo·ni·ous**, a.

ac·ro·bat, n. performer on a trapeze, trampoline, etc. **ac·ro·bat·ic**, a. **ac·ro·bat·ics**, n. pl.

a·cross, adv. from side to side; on the other side. prep.

act, v. exert power; do; behave; perform; feign. n. deed; division of a plan; law. **act·ing**, a.

ac·tion, n. activity; deed; battle; lawsuit.

ac·ti·vate, v., -vat·ed, -vat·ing. make active. **ac·ti·va·tion**, n. **ac·ti·va·tor**, n.

ac·tive, a. effective; quick; agile. **ac·tive·ly**, adv. **ac·tive·ness**, n. **ac·tiv·i·ty**, n.

ac·tor, n. performer.

ac·tress, n. female actor.

ac·tu·al, a. real; present; current. **ac·tu·al·ly,** *adv.*

ac·tu·al·ize, *v.,* -ized, -iz·ing. realize. **ac·tu·al·i·za·tion,** *n.*

ac·tu·ate, *v.,* -at·ed, -at·ing. put into action. **ac·tu·a·tion,** *n.*

a·cu·i·ty, *n.* acuteness.

a·cu·men, *n.* keenness of mind.

a·cute, *a.* keen; crucial; sharp; less than a right angle. **a·cute·ly,** *adv.* **a·cute·ness,** *n.*

ad·age, *n.* proverb.

ad·a·mant, *a.* set and unchanging. **ad·a·mant·ly,** *adv.*

a·dapt, *v.* make fit; adjust. **a·dap·tive,** *a.* **ad·ap·ta·tion,** *a.*

add, *v.t.* join or unite. *v.i.* perform addition. **add·a·ble, add·i·ble,** *a.*

ad·den·dum, *n. pl.,* **ad·den·da.** addition; appendix.

ad·dict, *v.* habituate. *n.* one addicted to a practice or habit. **ad·dic·tion,** *n.* **ad·dict·ed,** *a.* **ad·dic·tive,** *a.*

ad·di·tion, *n.* act or process of adding; increase. **ad·di·tion·al,** *a.* **ad·di·tion·al·ly,** *adv.*

ad·dress, *v.* speak to; direct in writing. *n.* speech; person's name and direction.

ad·e·noid, *n. usu. pl.* mass of tissue in the pharynx.

a·dept, *n.* expert. *a.* skilled.

ad·e·quate, *a.* enough. **ad·e·quate·ly,** *adv.* **ad·e·qua·cy,** *n.*

ad·here, *v.,* -hered, -her·ing. cling; be attached to. **ad·her·ence,** *n.* **ad·her·ent,** *a.*

ad·he·sive, *a.* gummy. *n.* substance like glue. **ad·he·sive·ness,** *n.*

ad·ja·cent, *a.* adjoining.

ad·jec·tive, *n.* word that modifies a noun. **ad·jec·ti·val,** *a.*

ad·join, *v.* be next to; annex.

ad·journ, *v.t.* postpone. *v.i.* end a meeting. **ad·journ·ment,** *n.*

ad·judge, *v.,* -judged, -judg·ing. judge; sentence.

ad·jure, *v.,* -jured, -jur·ing. charge or ask solemnly. **ad·ju·ra·tion,** *n.* **ad·jur·er,** *n.*

ad·just, *v.t.* fix; settle. *v.i.* adapt. **ad·just·ment,** *n.*

ad·ju·tant, *n.* assistant (officer). **ad·ju·tan·cy,** *n.*

ad·lib, *v.* improvise words, etc.

ad·min·is·ter, *v.* manage; direct; distribute.

ad·min·is·tra·tion, *n.* management; executive. **ad·min·is·tra·tive,** *a.*

ad·mire, *v.,* -mired, -mir·ing. look up to. **ad·mi·ra·ble,**

adj. n. **ad·mi·ra·tion,** *n.*

ad·mis·si·ble, *a.* allowed.

ad·mis·sion, *n.* entrance; entrance fee; confession.

ad·mit, *v.t.,* **ad·mit·ted, ad·mit·ting.** allow to enter; confess. *v.i.* permit. **ad·mit·tance,** *n.*

ad·mon·ish, *v.* reprove; advise. **ad·mo·ni·tion,** *n.*

a·do·be, *n.* sun-dried brick.

ad·o·les·cence, *n.* youth. **ad·o·les·cent,** *a.*

a·dopt, *v.* take as one's own. **a·dop·tion,** *n.* **a/dop/tive,** *a.*

a·dore, *v.,* **a·dored, a·dor·ing.** worship. **ad·o·ra·tion,** *n.*

a·dorn, *v.* decorate.

a·dren·a·line, *n.* heart stimulating hormone.

a·droit, *a.* nimble.

ad·u·la·tion, *n.* high praise.

a·dult, *a.* mature. *n.* full-grown person. **a·dult·hood,** *n.*

a·dul·ter·y, *n.* extramarital sexual intercourse. **a·dul·ter·ous,** *a.*

ad·vance, *v.,* **ad·vanced, ad·vanc·ing.** move forward; rise in rank. *a.* placed before. *n.* moving forward; *pl.* personal approaches for gain.

ad·van·tage, *n.* favorable factor; benefit. **ad·van·ta·geous,** *a.*

ad·ven·ture, *n.* exciting or dangerous experience. *v.,* -tured, -tur·ing. risk or hazard. **ad·ven·tur·er,** *n.* **ad·ven·tur·ess,** *n. fem.* **ad·ven·tur·ous,** *a.*

ad·ven·ture·some, *a.* daring.

ad·verb, *n.* word that modifies a verb, adjective, or adverb. **ad·ver·bi·al,** *a.*

ad·ver·sar·y, *n., pl.,* -ies. foe.

ad·verse, *a.* opposing; hostile. **ad·verse·ly,** *adv.*

ad·ver·si·ty, *n. pl.,* -ties. distress; misfortune.

ad·ver·tise, *v.,* -tised, -tis·ing. bring to public attention. **ad·ver·tise·ment,** *n.* **ad·ver·tis·ing,** *n.*

ad·vice, *n.* counsel.

ad·vise, *v.t.,* **ad·vised, ad·vis·ing.** give advice. *v.i.* take counsel. **ad·vis·a·ble,** *a.* **ad·vis·er, ad·vi·sor,** *n.*

ad·vo·cate, *n.* one who pleads a case. *v.,* -cat·ed, -cat·ing. plead in favor of; recommend.

adz, adze, *n.* tool like an ax.

ae·gis, *n.* protecting power.

aer·ate, *v.,* -at·ed, -at·ing. expose to air. **aer·a·tion,** *n.*

aer·i·al, *a.* pertaining to air or

aircraft. *n.* antenna.

aer·o·naut·ics, *n. pl.* study of aircraft. **aer·o·naut·ic,** *a.*

aero·space, *n.* atmosphere.

aes·thete, *n.* lover of beauty.

aes·thet·ic, *a.* pertaining to taste or beauty. **aes·thet·i·cal·ly,** *adv.*

a·far, *adv.* from a distance.

af·fa·ble, *a.* courteous.

af·fair, *n.* matter; happening; romance.

af·fect, *v.* act upon; influence; pretend. **af·fect·ing,** *a.*

af·fec·ta·tion, *n.* pretense.

af·fec·tion, *n.* fondness; love.

af·fec·tion·ate, *a.* tender. **af·fec·tion·ate·ly,** *adv.*

af·fi·ance, *v.,* **-anced, -anc·ing.** betroth.

af·fi·da·vit, *n.* written declaration.

af·fil·i·ate, *v.,* **-at·ed, -at·ing.** associate. *n.* affiliated member. **af·fil·i·a·tion,** *n.*

af·fin·i·ty, *n. pl.,* **-ties.** relation; similarity; attraction.

af·firm, *v.* assert; confirm. **af·fir·ma·tion,** *n.*

af·firm·a·tive, *n.* assent. *a.* affirming.

af·fix, *v.* append; fasten. *n.* prefix or suffix.

af·flict, *v.* give pain to; distress.

af·flic·tion, *n.*

af·flu·ence, *n.* wealth. **af·flu·ent,** *a.* **af·flu·ent·ly,** *adv.*

af·ford, *v.* able to bear the expense; yield; supply.

af·front, *v.* offend; insult; confront. *n.* insult.

a·fire, *a., adv.* on fire.

a·flame, *a., adv.* flaming.

a·float, *a., adv.* floating.

a·foot, *a., adv.* on foot.

a·foul, *a., adv.* fouled, tangled.

a·fraid, *a.* fearful.

a·fresh, *adv.* anew; again.

aft, *a., adv.* near the stern.

af·ter, *a.* later. *conj.* later than. *adv.* afterward. *prep.* behind; in search of.

af·ter·birth, *n.* placenta.

af·ter·noon, *n.* time between noon and evening.

af·ter·ward, *adv.* or **af·ter·wards,** *adv.* later.

a·gain, *adv.* once more; besides.

a·gainst, *prep.* in opposition to; toward; resting upon.

a·gape, *a., adv.* openmouthed.

age, *n.* time which a person has lived; state of being old; life expectancy; legal maturity; historical period. *v.,* **aged,** *ag-*

ing or **age·ing.** grow old.

a·ged, *a.* very old.

a·gen·cy, *n. pl.,* **-cies.** action; means; office or business.

a·gen·da, *n. pl.* memoranda.

a·gent, *n.* active power, cause; one who acts for another.

ag·glom·er·ate, *v.,* **-at·ed, -at·ing.** collect together. *a.* massed together. **ag·glom·er·a·tion,** *n.* **ag·glom·er·a·tive,** *a.*

ag·gran·dize, *v.,* **-dized, -diz·ing.** make greater; extend. **ag·gran·dize·ment,** *n.*

ag·gra·vate, *v.,* **-vat·ed, -vat·ing.** make worse; provoke. **ag·gra·va·tion,** *n.*

ag·gre·gate, *v.,* **-gat·ed, -gat·ing.** bring together. *n.* mass. *a.* total. **ag·gre·ga·tive,** *a.*

ag·gres·sion, *n.* first attack or act of hostility.

ag·gress, *v.* commit aggression. **ag·gres·sive,** *a.* **ag·gres·sor,** *n.*

ag·grieve, *v.,* **ag·grieved, ag·griev·ing.** give pain; oppress.

a·ghast, *a.* struck with horror.

ag·ile, *a.* nimble; quick; alert. **a·gil·i·ty,** *n.* nimbleness.

ag·i·tate, *v.,* **-tat·ed, -tat·ing.** force into action; shake; debate. **ag·i·ta·tion,** *n.*

a·glow, *a.* glowing.

ag·nos·tic, *n.* person who disclaims God. **ag·nos·ti·cism,** *n.*

a·go, *a., adv.* past; gone.

ag·o·nize, *v.i.,* **-nized, -niz·ing.** be in extreme pain; strain. *v.t.* distress. **ag·o·ny,** *n. pl.,* **-nies.**

a·grar·i·an, *a.* relating to lands or farmers.

a·gree, *v.,* **a·greed, a·gree·ing.** consent; harmonize; tally; suit. **a·gree·ment,** *n.*

a·gree·a·ble, *a.* suitable; pleasing. **a·gree·a·ble·ness,** *n.*

ag·ri·cul·ture, *n.* cultivation of land; farming. **ag·ri·cul·tur·al,** *a.* **ag·ri·cul·tur·ist,** *n.*

a·gron·o·my, *n.* agriculture. **a·gron·o·mist,** *n.*

a·ground, *a., adv.* run ashore.

a·head, *adv.* in front; before.

aid, *v.* help. *n.* assistance.

aide, *n.* assistant.

ail, *v.* be in pain, ill health, or trouble. **ail·ing,** *a.*

ail·ment, *n.* disease.

aim, *v.* direct; endeavor. *v.t.* intend (to). *n.* directing of a missile; target; purpose; scheme. **aim·less,** *a.*

air, *n.* gases surrounding the earth; tune; manner. **airs,** *af-*

fected manner. *v.* expose to air; ventilate; state publicly. **air·less,** *a.*

air-con·di·tion, *v.* regulate the quality, temperature, etc. of air indoors. **air-con·di·tioned,** *a.* **air con·di·tion·er,** *n.* **air con·di·tion·ing,** *n.*

air·craft, *n. pl.* **air·craft.** machine or craft for flying.

air·field, *n.* airport.

air·ing, *n.* exposure to air.

air·lift, *n.* supply line operated by aircraft. *v.* transport by air.

air·line, *n.* aerial transportation company.

air·mail, *n.* mail sent by airplane. *v.* send by airmail.

air·plane, *n.* power-driven aircraft.

air·port, *n.* airfield.

air raid, *n.* attack by enemy aircraft.

air·sick·ness, *n.* nausea caused by flying. **air·sick,** *a.*

air·way, *n.* route for air traffic.

air·wor·thy, *a.* adapted or safe for service in the air. **air·wor·thi·ness,** *n.*

air·y, *a.,* **-i·er, -i·est.** like air; gay; lively. **air·i·ness,** *n.* **air·i·ly,** *adv.*

aisle, *n.* passageway. **aisled,** *a.*

a·jar, *a., adv.* partly opened.

a·kin, *a.* showing similarity; related by blood.

al·a·bas·ter, *n.* white marblelike mineral. **al·a·bas·trine,** *a.*

a·lac·ri·ty, *n.* cheerful willingness; briskness.

a·larm, *n.* sound or device to awaken or warn; apprehension. *v.* disturb with terror. **a·larm·ing,** *a.* **a·larm·ing·ly,** *adv.*

a·larm·ist, *n.* one who excites alarm. **a·larm·ism,** *n.*

al·ba·tross, *n.* large web-footed sea bird.

al·be·it, *conj.* although.

al·bi·no, *n. pl.,* **-nos.** person or animal lacking pigmentation or color. **al·bin·ic,** *a.*

al·bum, *n.* book for pictures; jacketed phonograph record.

al·bu·men, *n.* white of an egg.

al·bu·min, *n.* water-soluble protein. **al·bu·mi·nous,** *a.*

al·che·my, *n.* medieval chemistry. **al·che·mist,** *n.*

al·co·hol, *n.* intoxicating ingredient of liquor. **al·co·hol·ic,** *a.*

al·cove, *n.* recess.

ale, *n.* beer-like liquor.

a·lee, *adv.* on the lee side.

a·lert, *a.* vigilant; lively. *n.* warning of danger. *v.* warn. **a·lert·ness,** *n.*

al·fal·fa, *n.* plant grown as fodder.

al·ga, *n. pl.,* **al·gae,** water plant without stems, roots, or leaves.

al·ge·bra, *n.* mathematics using signs and letters. **al·ge·bra·ic,** *a.* **al·ge·bra·i·cal,** *a.*

a·li·as, *n. pl.,* **a·li·as·es,** adopted or false name.

al·i·bi, *n.* evidence of innocence; excuse.

al·ien, *a.* foreign; different in nature. *n.* foreigner. **al·ien·a·ble,** *a.* **al·ien·a·bil·i·ty,** *n.*

al·ien·ate, *v.,* **-at·ed, -at·ing.** estrange. **al·ien·a·tion,** *n.*

a·light, *v.,* **a·light·ed** or **a·lit,** **a·light·ing.** get off; settle; happen upon.

a·lign, *v.t.* form in line. *v.i.* ally oneself. **a·lign·ment,** *n.*

a·like, *a.* similar. *adv.* equally; resembling exactly.

al·i·ment, *n.* food. *v.* nourish. **al·i·men·tal,** *a.* **al·i·men·ta·tion,** *n.* **al·i·men·ta·ry,** *a.*

al·i·mo·ny, *n.* money paid for the support of one's former spouse.

a·live, *a.* living; aware; sprightly; sensitive to.

al·ka·li, *n. pl.,* **-lies,** or **-lis.** hydroxide which neutralizes acids. **al·ka·line,** *a.*

al·ka·lize, *v.,* **-lized, -liz·ing.** make alkaline.

all, *a.* every one of; during the whole. *n.* whole number; total. **above all,** firstly. *adv.* completely. **all but,** nearly.

all-a·round, *a.* versatile.

al·lay, *v.,* **al·layed, al·lay·ing.** quiet; lessen. **al·lay·er,** *n.*

al·le·ga·tion, *n.* assertion without proof.

al·lege, *v.,* **al·leged, al·leg·ing.** assert, esp. without proof. **al·lege·a·ble,** *a.*

al·leged, *a.* declared to be true. **al·leg·ed·ly,** *a.*

al·le·giance, *n.* loyalty.

al·le·go·ry, *n. pl.,* **-ries.** symbolic representation. **al·le·gor·i·cal,** *a.* **al·le·gor·ist,** *n.*

al·ler·gy, *n. pl.,* **-gies.** bodily reaction to pollen, foods, etc.

al·le·vi·ate, *v.,* **-at·ed, -at·ing.** make easier to be endured. **al·le·vi·a·tion,** *n.* **al·le·vi·a·tor,**

n. **al·le·vi·a·tive,** a.

al·ley, n. pl., **al·leys.** narrow passageway; bowling lane.

al·li·ance, n. union of interests; compact.

al·li·ga·tor, n. reptile like a crocodile.

al·lo·cate, v., **-cat·ed, -cat·ing.** allot; apportion. **al·lo·ca·tion,** n.

al·lot, v., **al·lot·ted, al·lot·ting.** divide; assign; set apart. **al·lot·ment,** n.

al·low, v. grant; admit; set apart; permit. **al·low·a·ble,** a.

al·low·ance, n. permission; money; v., **-anced, -anc·ing.** put on an allowance.

al·loy, n. metal composition. v. impair by mixture.

al·lude, v., **al·lud·ed, al·lud·ing.** hint at.

al·lure, v., **al·lured, al·lur·ing.** tempt; entice. n. charm; appeal. **al·lure·ment,** n.

al·lu·sion, n. hint; suggestion. **al·lu·sive,** a. **al·lu·sive·ly,** adv. **al·lu·sive·ness,** n.

al·lu·vi·um, n. pl., **-vi·ums, -vi·a.** soil deposited by flowing water.

al·ly, v.t., **al·lied, al·ly·ing.** unite; bind together; v.i. form an alliance. **al·lied,** a.

al·ly, n. pl., **al·lies.** confederate; supporter.

al·ma·nac, n. yearly publication of various statistical information.

al·might·y, a. all-powerful.

al·mond, n. nutlike fruit of the almond tree.

al·most, adv. nearly.

alms, n. pl., sing. charity.

a·loft, adv. on high.

a·lone, a. solitary. adv. only; solely; without help.

a·long, adv. lengthwise; in company. prep. in accord with.

a·loof, adv. at a distance. a. uninvolved; reserved. **a·loof·ly,** adv. **a·loof·ness,** n.

a·loud, adv. not whispered.

al·pha·bet, n. letters of a written language in order. a. **al·pha·bet·i·cal,** a. **al·pha·bet·ize,** v.

al·read·y, adv. previously; so soon.

al·so, adv. likewise; too.

al·tar, n. sacred table in a church.

al·ter, v. change; modify; vary. **al·ter·a·ble,** a. **al·ter·a·bly,** adv. **al·ter·a·tion,** n.

al·ter·ca·tion, n. dispute; fight.

al·ter e·go, n. second self; exact substitute.

al·ter·nate, v., **-nat·ed, -nat·ing.** take turns; interchange. n. official substitute. a. appearing in turn or as every other. **al·ter·nate·ly,** adv. **al·ter·na·tion,** n.

al·ter·na·tive, n. choice between two things.

al·though, conj. even though.

al·tim·e·ter, n. instrument for measuring altitude.

al·ti·tude, n. height.

al·to, n. contralto.

al·to·geth·er, adv. wholly; completely; n. whole.

al·tru·ism, n. devotion to others. **al·tru·is·tic,** a.

a·lu·mi·num, n. oxidation-resistant metal.

a·lum·nus, n. pl., **-ni.** graduate of a college or university. **a·lum·na,** n. fem. pl. **-nae.**

al·ways, adv. perpetually; forever.

a.m. before noon.

a·mal·gam, n. alloy of mercury with another metal.

a·mal·gam·ate, v., **-at·ed, -at·ing.** combine. **a·mal·gam·a·tion,** n.

a·mass, v. accumulate.

am·a·teur, n. non-professional. **am·a·teur·ish,** a.

am·a·to·ry, a. of love.

a·maze, v., **a·mazed, a·maz·ing.** astound; astonish. **a·maz·ed·ly,** adv. **a·maze·ment,** n. **a·maz·ing,** a.

am·a·zon, n. tall, strong woman.

am·bas·sa·dor, n. highest rank official representative.

am·ber, n. pale-yellow fossil resin; color of amber.

am·bi·dex·trous, a. able to use both hands with equal ease.

am·big·u·ous, a. equivocal; indefinite. **am·bi·gu·i·ty,** n.

am·bi·tion, n. desire for; distinction or success; aspiration. **am·bi·tious,** a.

am·biv·a·lence, n. state of having contradictory feelings. **am·biv·a·lent,** a.

am·ble, v., **am·bled, am·bling.** move easily and unhurriedly. n. gentle pace; **am·bler,** n.

am·bu·la·to·ry, a. able to walk; movable. n. cloister.

am·bu·late, v., **-lat·ed, -lat·ing.** walk; move. **am·bu·lant,** a. a.

am·bus·cade, n. ambush. v., **-cad·ed, -cad·ing.** ambush.

am·bush, n. surprise attack; position or attacking force itself. *v.* attack from ambush; waylay. **am·bush·er**, *n.*

a·me·ba, *n.* amoeba.

a·mel·io·rate, *v.*, **-rat·ed**, **-rat·ing**. improve. **a·mel·io·ra·tion**, *n.* **a·mel·ior·a·tive**, *a.*

a·men, *interj.* so be it.

a·me·na·ble, *a.* ready to yield to advice. **a·me·na·bil·i·ty**, *n.* **a·me·na·bly**, *adv.*

a·mend, *v.* make better; revise; correct. **a·mend·a·ble**, *a.* **a·mend·ment**, *n.*

a·mends, *n. pl.* compensation.

a·men·i·ty, *n.* agreeableness. *pl.* civilities.

A·mer·i·can, *a.* of America; native of America esp. a citizen of the U.S.

am·e·thyst, *n.* violet-blue quartz. **am·e·thys·tine**, *a.*

a·mi·a·ble, *a.* pleasing; friendly. **a·mi·a·bil·i·ty**, *n.*

am·i·ca·ble, *a.* friendly; peaceable. **am·i·ca·bil·i·ty**, *n.*

a·mid, *prep.* in the midst of; among. Also **amidst**.

a·mid·ships, *adv.* in or toward the middle of a ship.

a·mi·no ac·id, *n.* basic building block of protein.

a·miss, *adv.*, *a.* improperly.

am·mo·nia, *n.* gas of nitrogen and hydrogen. **am·mon·ic**, *a.*

am·mu·ni·tion, *n.* projectiles for guns.

am·ne·sia, *n.* loss of memory. **am·ne·sic**, *a.* **am·nes·tic**, *a.*

am·nes·ty, *n. pl.*, **-ties**. pardon. *v.*, **-tied**, **-ty·ing**. pardon.

a·moe·ba, *n. pl.*, **-moe·bae**, **a·moe·bas**. one-celled protozoan.

a·mong, *prep.* in or into the midst or number of.

a·mongst, *prep.* among.

a·mor·al, *a.* without morals.

am·o·rous, *a.* loving.

a·mor·phous, *a.* formless.

am·or·tize, *v.*, **-tized**, **-tiz·ing**. make gradual payments. **am·or·ti·za·tion**, *n.*

a·mount, *n.* sum. *v.* total; result in.

am·pere, *n.* unit of electric current.

am·phib·i·an, *a. n.* amphibian animal; seaplane.

am·phib·i·ous, *a.* able to live on land or water.

am·phi·the·a·ter, *n.* arena.

am·ple, *a.*, **am·pler**, **am·plest**. large; abundant. **am·ply**, *adv.*

am·pli·fy, *v.*, **-fied**, **-fy·ing**. increase; elaborate. **am·pli·fi·ca·tion**, *n.* **am·pli·fi·er**, *n.*

am·pli·tude, *n.* abundance; extent; greatness.

am·pu·tate, *v.*, **-tat·ed**, **-tat·ing**. cut off, as a limb. **am·pu·ta·tion**, *n.* **am·pu·tee**, *n.*

a·muck, *adv.* in a frenzy.

am·u·let, *n.* charm against evil.

a·muse, *v.*, **a·mused**, **a·mus·ing**. entertain; divert. **a·mus·ing**, *a.* **a·muse·ment**, *n.*

an, *a. indef. art.* one; each.

a·nach·ro·nism, *n.* misplacement of persons or events in time. **a·nach·ro·nis·tic**, *a.*

an·a·con·da, *n.* large boa snake.

a·nae·mi·a, *n.* anemia.

an·a·gram, *n.* word formed by transposing the letters of another word.

a·nal, *a.* of the anus.

an·al·ge·sic, *a.*, *n.* drug or other remedy to remove pain.

a·nal·o·gize, *v.*, **-gized**, **-giz·ing**. explain by analogy.

a·nal·o·gy, *n. pl.*, **-gies**. parallelism; likeness. **a·nal·o·gous**, *a.*

a·na·lyze, *v.*, **-lyzed**, **-lyz·ing**. resolve into its important parts; study critically; psychoanalyze. **an·a·ly·za·tion**, *n.* **a·nal·y·sis**, *n. pl.*, **-ses**. **an·a·lyst**, *n.* **an·a·lyt·ic**, *a.*

an·ar·chism, *n.* lawlessness. **an·ar·chist**, *n.*

an·ar·chy, *n.* lack of government and law. **an·ar·chic**, *a.*

a·nath·e·ma, *n. pl.*, **-mas**. that which is hated or avoided; curse. **a·nath·e·ma·tize**, *v.*, **-ized**, **-iz·ing**.

a·nat·o·my, *n. pl.*, **-mies**. study of the internal structure of bodies; physique.

an·ces·tor, *n.* forefather. **an·ces·tress**, *n. fem.* **an·ces·tral**, *a.*

an·ces·try, *n. pl.*, **-tries**. lineage.

an·chor, *n.* iron weight which holds a ship at rest. *v.* hold fast. **at an·chor**, anchored. **an·chor·age**, *n.*

an·cho·vy, *n. pl.*, **-vies**. tiny fish of the herring family.

an·cient, *a.* of times long past; old. *n.* very old person; **the ancients**, people of ancient times. **an·cient·ly**, *adv.*

and, *conj.* plus; also.

an·ec·dote, *n.* short story. **an·ec·do·tal**, *a.*

a·ne·mi·a, *n.* lack of red corpuscles. **a·ne·mic**, *a.*

an·e·mom·e·ter, *n.* instrument that measures wind velocity.

an·es·the·sia, *n.* lost sense of feeling, pain, etc.

an·es·thet·ic, *n.* substance causing anesthesia. **an·es·the·tist,** *n.*

an·es·the·tize, *v.,* -tized, -tiz·ing.

a·new, *adv.* again; afresh.

an·gel, *n.* messenger of God. **an·gel·ic,** *a.*

an·ger, *n.* ire; wrath. *v.* excite to anger.

an·gle, *n.* space within two or more sides diverging from a common point. *v.t.,* **an·gled, an·gling.** bend in angles. *v.i.* fish with hook and line; seek (*for*) by any artful means; slant. **an·gled,** *a.* **an·gler,** *n.*

an·gle·worm, *n.* earthworm.

An·gli·cize, *v.,* -cized, -ciz·ing. make English. **An·gli·ci·za·tion,** *n.*

an·gling, *n.* rod fishing.

An·glo-Sax·on, *n.* early settler in Britain. one of the English race; Old English.

an·go·ra, *n.* wool of the Angora goat.

an·gry, *a.* showing anger; raging. **an·gri·ly,** *adv.*

an·guish, *n.* extreme pain or distress. *v.t.* cause acute distress. *v.i.* suffer intensely.

an·gu·lar, *a.* having angles; pointed; bony. **an·gu·lar·i·ty,** *n.*

an·hy·drous, *a.* without water.

an·i·mad·vert, *v.* criticize. **an·i·mad·ver·sion,** *n.*

an·i·mal, *n.* living being that can move voluntarily; beast; brute. *a.* of animals.

an·i·mal·ize, *v.,* -ized, -iz·ing. make like an animal; brutalize.

an·i·mate, *v.,* -mat·ed, -mat·ing. make alive; stimulate. *a.* alive. **an·i·ma·tion,** *n.* **an·i·mat·ed,** *a.*

an·i·mos·i·ty, *n.* bitter feeling; hatred.

an·ise, *n.* plant whose seeds are used for flavoring.

an·kle, *n.* joint between the foot and leg.

an·nals, *n. pl.* chronological historical records.

an·neal, *v.* temper; toughen.

an·nex, *v.* unite; attach. *n.* addition. **an·nex·a·tion,** *n.*

an·ni·hi·late, *v.,* -lat·ed, -lat·ing. destroy. **an·ni·hi·la·tion,** *n.*

an·ni·ver·sa·ry, *n. pl.,* -ries. day on which some event is annu-

ally celebrated.

an·no·tate, *v.,* -tat·ed, -tat·ing. make notes. **an·no·ta·tion,** *n.*

an·nounce, *v.,* **an·nounced, an·nounc·ing.** proclaim; make known. **an·nounce·ment,** *n.*

an·noy, *v.* bother; vex. **an·noy·ance,** *n.* **an·noy·ing,** *a.*

an·nu·al, *a.* yearly. *n.* plant that lives one year or season.

an·nu·i·ty, *n.* yearly payment one receives.

an·nul, *v.,* **an·nulled, an·nul·ling.** make void. **an·nul·ment,** *n.*

an·nun·ci·ate, *v.,* -at·ed, -at·ing. announce. **an·nun·ci·a·tion,** *n.*

an·ode, *n.* positive electrode.

a·noint, *v.* pour oil on; consecrate. **a·noint·ment,** *n.*

a·nom·a·ly, *n.* something abnormal; irregularity. **a·nom·a·lism,** *n.* **a·nom/al·lous,** *a.*

a·non·y·mous, *a.* without any name acknowledged. **an·o·nym·i·ty,** *n.* **a·non·y·mous·ly,** *adv.*

an·oth·er, *a.* different; any other. *pron.* one more.

an·swer, *v.* reply; respond; suit. *n.* reply; response; solution. **an·swer·a·ble,** *a.*

ant, *n.* small insect living in a colony.

ant·ac·id, *n.* alkali.

an·tag·o·nize, *v.,* -nized, -niz·ing. act in opposition; provoke. **an·tag·o·nist,** *n.*

ant·arc·tic, *a.* of the southern pole.

an·te, *n.* poker stake. *v.,* **an·ted, an·te·ing.**

ant·eat·er, *n.* mammal that eats ants.

an·te·cede, *v.,* -ced·ed, -ced·ing. go before. **an·te·ced·ent,** *n.*

an·te·date, *v.,* -dat·ed, -dat·ing. date before; precede.

an·te·di·lu·vi·an, *a.* before the flood; very old.

an·te·lope, *n. pl.,* -lopes, -lope. mammal resembling the deer.

an·ten·na, *n. pl.,* -nae, -nas. feeler on an insect; transmitter and intercepter of radio waves.

an·te·ri·or, *a.* prior.

an·te·room, *n.* small room leading into a larger one.

an·them, *n.* sacred or patriotic song.

an·ther, *n.* part of a plant stamen containing pollen.

an·thol·o·gy, *n. pl.,* -gies. collection of literary material. **an-**

thol·o·gist, *n.*

an·thra·cite, *n.* hard coal.

an·thrax, *n. pl.,* **an·thra·ces,** disease of cattle.

an·thro·poid, *a.* resembling man. *n.* large ape.

an·thro·pol·o·gy, *n.* study of man. **an·thro·pol·o·gist,** *n.*

an·ti-, *prefix.* against.

an·ti·bi·ot·ic, *n.* substance that inhibits or kills bacteria.

an·ti·bod·y, *n. pl.,* **-bod·ies.** substance in the blood that counteracts toxins.

an·tic, *n.* caper; trick.

an·tic·i·pate, *v.,* **-pat·ed,** **-pat·ing.** look forward to; expect. **an·tic·i·pa·tion,** *n.*

an·ti·cli·max, *n.* abrupt descent from the important to the trivial.

an·ti·dote, *n.* remedy to counteract the effects of poison.

an·ti·his·ta·mine, *n.* compound used for the treatment of allergies and colds.

an·ti·pas·to, *n.* appetizer course of fish, olives, etc.

an·tip·a·thy, *n. pl.,* **-thies.** natural instinctive dislike. **an·ti·pa·thet·ic,** *a.*

an·tip·o·des, *n. pl.* exact opposite side of the earth. **an·tip·o·dal,** *a.*

an·ti·quate, *v.,* **-quat·ed,** **-quat·ing.** make outdated. **an·ti·quat·ed,** *a.*

an·tique, *a.* ancient. *n.* thing very old, usually 100 yrs. *v.,* **an·tiqued,** **an·tiqu·ing.** cause to appear antique; emboss.

an·tiq·ui·ty, *n. pl.,* **-ties.** ancient times. *pl.* relics.

an·ti·Sem·i·tism, *n.* hatred of Jews.

an·ti·sep·tic, *a.* lacking germs. *n.* substance that kills germs.

an·ti·so·cial, *a.* opposed to social contact or order.

an·tith·e·sis, *n. pl.,* **-ses,** opposition; contrast.

an·ti·tox·in, *n.* serum.

an·ti·trust, *a.* referring to rules against monopoly.

ant·ler, *n.* bonelike horn of a deer. **ant·lered,** *a.*

an·to·nym, *n.* word opposite in meaning to another.

a·nus, *n.* opening at the lower end of the digestive canal.

an·vil, *n.* block for hammering metal objects.

anx·i·e·ty, *n. pl.,* **-ties.** worry.

anx·ious, *a.* worried.

an·y, *a., pron.* one; some; every. *adv.* at all.

an·y·bod·y, *pron.* anyone.

an·y·how, *adv.* in any way.

an·y·one, *pron.* any person.

an·y·place, *adv.* in or to any place.

an·y·thing, *n., pron.* any thing. *adv.* at all.

an·y·way, *adv.* in any way.

an·y·where, *adv.* any place.

a·or·ta, *n. pl.,* **-tas, -tae.** main artery of the body.

a·part, *adv.* separately. *a.* in pieces. **apart from,** besides.

a·part·ment, *n.* room or rooms where people live.

ap·a·thy, *n. pl.,* **-thies.** indifference. **ap·a·thet·ic,** *a.*

ape, *n.* tailless primate. *v.,* **aped, ap·ing.** mimic. **ap·ish,** *a.*

ap·er·ture, *n.* opening; hole.

a·pex, *n. pl.,* **a·pex·es, a·pi·ces.** highest point. **ap·i·cal,** *a.*

a·phid, *n.* plant louse.

aph·o·rism, *n.* maxim.

aph·ro·dis·i·ac, *n.* drug, etc., exciting sexual desire.

a·pi·a·rist, *n.* beekeeper.

a·pi·ar·y, *n. pl.,* **-ies.** place where bees are kept.

a·piece, *adv.* to each; for each.

a·plomb, *n.* self-confidence.

a·poc·a·lypse, *n.* revelation.

a·pol·o·gize, *v.,* **-gized, -giz·ing.** make an apology.

a·pol·o·gy, *n. pl.,* **-gies.** expression of regret; poor substitute. **a·pol·o·get·ic,** *a.*

ap·o·plec·tic, *a.* of apoplexy. *n.* person who has apoplexy.

ap·o·plex·y, *n.* paralysis caused by a stroke.

a·port, *adv.* to port.

a·pos·ta·tize, *v.,* **-tized, -tiz·ing.** abandon principles, faith, or party. **a·pos·tate,** *n.*

a·pos·tle, *n.* disciple. **ap·os·tol·ic,** *a.*

a·pos·tro·phe, *n.* sign (') indicating the omission of a letter in a word, or the possessive case.

a·poth·e·car·y, *n. pl.,* **-ies.** druggist.

ap·pall, ap·pal, *v.,* **ap·palled, ap·pal·ling.** dismay.

ap·pa·ra·tus, *n. pl.,* **-tus, ap·pa·rat·us, ap·pa·rat·us·es.** device or tool.

ap·par·el, *n.* clothing. *v.,* **-eled, -el·ing.** dress.

ap·par·ent, *a.* evident; seeming.

ap·pa·ri·tion, *n.* ghost.

ap·peal, *v.* make an appeal; attract. *n.* call for sympathy, help, etc.; referral of a case to a superior court. **ap·peal·a·ble**, *a.* **ap·peal·er**, *n.*

ap·pear, *v.* come in sight; perform publicly; seem. **ap·pear·ance**, *n.*

ap·pease, *v.*, **ap·peased**, **ap·peas·ing**. quiet; assuage; satisfy. **ap·pease·ment**, *n.* **ap·peas·er**, *n.*

ap·pel·lant, *n.* one who appeals.

ap·pel·la·tion, *n.* name.

ap·pend, *v.* attach.

ap·pen·dage, *n.* thing attached.

ap·pen·dec·to·my, *n.* removal of the appendix.

ap·pen·di·ci·tis, *n.* inflammation of the appendix.

ap·pen·dix, *n. pl.*, **ap·pen·dix·es**, **ap·pen·di·ces**, part added to a book; vermiform appendix.

ap·per·tain, *v.* pertain.

ap·pe·tite, *n.* desire for food; eagerness or longing.

ap·pe·tiz·ing, *a.* exciting the appetite.

ap·plaud, *v.* show approval by clapping the hands; praise. **ap·plause**, *n.*

ap·ple, *n.* fleshy, red or yellow fruit.

ap·pli·cant, *n.* one who applies.

ap·pli·ca·tion, *n.* act of applying thing applied; request; close study; form.

ap·ply, *v.t.*, **ap·plied**, **ap·ply·ing**. put, refer, or use as suitable; study hard. *v.i.* make a request. **ap·pli·ca·ble**, *a.*

ap·point, *v.* assign; designate. **ap·point·ee**, *n.* **ap·poin·tive**, *a.* **ap·point·ment**, *n.*

ap·por·tion, *v.* allot. **ap·por·tion·ment**, *n.*

ap·pose, *v.*, **ap·posed**, **ap·pos·ing**. put one thing next to another. **ap·po·si·tion**, *n.* **ap·pos·i·tive**, *a., n.*

ap·praise, *v.*, **ap·praised**, **ap·prais·ing**. estimate the value of. **ap·prais·al**, *n.*

ap·pre·ci·ate, *v.t.*, **-at·ed**, **-at·ing**. be grateful for; regard highly; value properly. *v.i.* rise in value. **ap·pre·ci·a·tion**, *n.*

ap·pre·hend, *v.* arrest; understand; expect with fear. **ap·pre·hen·si·ble**, *a.* **ap·pre·hen·sion**, *n.* **ap·pre·hen·sive**, *a.*

ap·pren·tice, *n.* person being taught a trade; *v.*, **-ticed**, **-tic·ing**. become or accept as an apprentice.

ap·prise, **ap·prize**, *v.*, **ap·prised** or **ap·prized**, **ap·pris·ing** or **ap·priz·ing**. inform.

ap·proach, *v.* come or go near. *n.* act of drawing near; way to come. **ap·proach·a·ble**, *a.*

ap·pro·ba·tion, *n.* approval.

ap·pro·pri·ate, *v.*, **-at·ed**, **-at·ing**. take for oneself; set apart; provide; *a.* set apart; belonging to; fit. **ap·pro·pri·ate·ly**, *adv.* **ap·pro·pri·a·tion**, *n.* **ap·pro·pri·a·tive**, *a.*

ap·prov·al, *n.* official permission.

ap·prove, *v.*, **ap·proved**, **ap·prov·ing**. think or judge well of; give permission to.

ap·prox·i·mate, *a.* nearly equal; *v.* come near; estimate. **ap·prox·i·ma·tion**, *n.*

ap·ri·cot, *n.* peachlike fruit.

A·pril, *n.* fourth month.

a·pron, *n.* garment worn over the front to protect clothes.

a·pro·pos·of, *prep.* concerning.

apt, *a.* fit; quick to learn; liable. **apt·ly**, *adv.*

ap·ti·tude, *n.* natural ability; readiness in learning.

aq·ua, *n. pl.*, **aq·uas**, **aq·uae**. water. *a.* bluish-green.

a·quar·i·um, *n. pl.*, **-i·ums**, **-i·a**. glass fish tank.

a·quat·ic, *a.* of water. *n.* water-growing plant. *pl.* water sports.

aq·ue·duct, *n.* pipe or channel for carrying water.

a·que·ous, *a.* watery.

aq·ui·line, *a.* like an eagle's beak; curving; hooked.

Ar·ab, *n.* native of Arabia, or a member of a Semitic people. **A·ra·bi·an**, *a.* **Ar·a·bic**, *a., n.*

Ar·a·bic nu·mer·als, *n.* figures 1 through 9, and 0.

ar·a·ble, *a.* fit for plowing.

ar·bi·ter, *n.* judge.

ar·bi·trar·y, *a.* according to one's will or desires. **ar·bi·trar·i·ly**, *adv.* **ar·bi·trar·i·ness**, *n.*

ar·bi·trate, *v.*, **-trat·ed**, **-trat·ing**. judge; determine. **ar·bi·tra·tor**, *n.* **ar·bi·tra·tion**, *n.*

ar·bor, *n.* tree-shaded place.

ar·bo·re·al, *a.* of trees.

ar·bo·re·tum, *n. pl.*, **-tums**, **-ta**. botanical garden.

arc, *n.* thing bow-shaped; part of a circle. *v.*, **arced** or **arcked**, **arc·ing** or **arck·ing**. form an electric arc.

ar·cade, *n.* series of arches on

pillars; covered passageway.

arch, *n.* curved covering, or structure. *v.* form an arch.

arch, *a.* sly; chief. **arch·ly,** *adv.*

arch-, *prefix.* chief; principal.

ar·chae·ol·o·gy, ar·che·ol·o·gy, *n.* study of ancient peoples and their remains.

ar·cha·ic, *a.* old-fashioned.

arch·an·gel, *n.* angel of the highest rank.

arch·bish·op, *n.* bishop of the highest rank.

arch·duke, *n.* prince. **arch·duch·ess,** *n. fem.*

ar·cher·y, *n.* shooting with a bow and arrow. **arch·er,** *n.*

ar·che·type, *n.* model or first form. **ar·che·typ·i·cal,** *a.*

ar·chi·pel·a·go, *n. pl.,* **-goes, -gos.** group of many islands.

ar·chi·tect, *n.* designer of buildings.

ar·chi·tec·ture, *n.* design and construction of buildings. **ar·chi·tec·tur·al,** *a.*

ar·chive, *n.* public records; their location. **ar·chi·val,** *a.*

arch·priest, *n.* chief priest.

arc·tic, *a.* area of the North Pole; cold, frigid.

ar·dent, *a.* passionate; fervent; burning; hot. **ar·dent·ly,** *adv.*

ar·dor, *n.* eagerness; zeal.

ar·du·ous, *a.* difficult; steep.

ar·e·a, *n.* region; surface, as given in square units; range.

a·re·na, *n.* place for contests, games, etc.

ar·gon, *n.* inert gas.

ar·go·sy, *n. pl.,* **ar·go·sies.** merchant ship; fleet.

ar·got, *n.* jargon; slang.

ar·gue, *v.,* **ar·gued, ar·gu·ing.** offer reasons for or against; dispute. **ar·gu·a·ble,** *a.* **ar·gu·er,** *n.* **ar·gu·ment,** *n.* **ar·gu·men·ta·tive,** *a.*

a·ri·a, *n.* song; solo, as in an opera.

ar·id, *a.* dry; unimaginative. **a·rid·i·ty,** *n.*

a·rise, *v.,* **a·rose, a·ris·en, a·ris·ing.** come up; rise.

ar·is·toc·ra·cy, *n. pl.,* **ar·is·toc·ra·cies.** nobility or upper class. **a·ris·to·crat,** *n.* **a·ris·to·crat·ic,** *a.*

a·rith·me·tic, *n.* computation by numbers. **a·rith·met·i·cal,** *a.* **a·rith·me·ti·cian,** *n.*

ark, *n. Bible:* ship of Noah.

arm, *n.* upper limb of the body; anything that extends from a

main body; weapon. *v.* furnish with weapons. **arm·er,** *n.*

ar·ma·da, *n.* fleet of armed ships.

ar·ma·dil·lo, *n. pl.,* **ar·ma·dil·los.** mammal covered with a shell of bony plates.

ar·ma·ment, *n.* nation's military forces or equipment.

arm·ful, *n. pl.,* **arm·fuls.** as much as both arms can hold.

ar·mi·stice, *n.* truce.

ar·moire, *n.* wardrobe.

ar·mor, *n.* defensive covering. **ar·mored,** *a.*

ar·mor·y, *n. pl.,* **ar·mor·ies.** place to store arms.

arm·pit, *n.* hollow under the upper arm.

ar·my, *n. pl.,* **ar·mies.** military land force; vast number.

a·ro·ma, *n.* fragrance. **ar·o·mat·ic,** *a.*

a·round, *adv., prep.* in a circle; on every side; in the opposite direction.

a·rouse, *v.,* **a·roused, a·rous·ing.** excite into action; awaken.

ar·range, *v.,* **ar·ranged, ar·rang·ing.** put in proper order; adapt; make plans. **ar·rang·er,** *n.* **ar·range·ment,** *n.*

ar·rant, *a.* thorough going.

ar·ray, *n.* things in regular order; raiment. *v.* arrange in order; adorn or dress.

ar·rest, *v.* check; seize by legal authority. *n.* seizure.

ar·rive, *v.,* **ar·rived, ar·riv·ing.** come to a place; get to a destination. **ar·riv·al,** *n.*

ar·ro·gate, *v.,* **-gat·ed, -gat·ing.** make unreasonable claims.

ar·ro·gant, *a.* **ar·ro·gance,** *n.*

ar·row, *n.* pointed shaft used for shooting from a bow; mark like an arrow.

ar·row·head, *n.* tip of an arrow.

ar·se·nal, *n.* place for storing arms.

ar·se·nic, *n.* poisonous grayish-white element.

ar·son, *n.* crime of intentionally burning property.

art, *n.* meaningful or beautiful object; any of the fine arts, esp. painting, drawing, or sculpture; craft; skill.

ar·ter·y, *n. pl.,* **ar·ter·ies.** tube conveying blood from the heart. **ar·te·ri·al,** *a.*

art·ful, *a.* sly; skillful.

ar·thri·tis, *n.* inflammation of the joints. **ar·thrit·ic,** *a.*

ar·ti·cle, *n.* single item; provision of a document; prose contribution; part of speech: *a*, *an*, or *the*.

ar·tic·u·late, *a.* jointed; expressed clearly. *v.*, **-lat·ed**, **-lat·ing**. joint; speak clearly. **ar·tic·u·la·tion**, *n.*

ar·ti·fi·cial, *a.* man-made; not genuine; affected. **ar·ti·fi·cial·ness**, *n.*

ar·til·ler·y, *n.* mounted guns.

art·ist, *n.* one skilled in the arts, esp. the fine arts.

ar·tis·tic, *a.* of art or artists. **ar·tis·ti·cal·ly**, *adv.*

as, *adv.* to such a degree or extent; for example. *conj.* while; because. *prep.* like; in the role of. *pron.* that.

as·bes·tos, **as·bes·tus**, *n.* fibrous mineral used to make fireproof cloth, paper, etc.

as·cend, *v.* climb or go upward. **as·cend·an·cy**, **as·cend·en·cy**, *n.* **as·cend·ant**, **as·cend·ent**, *a.* **as·cen·sion**, *n.*

as·cent, *n.* act of rising; upward slope.

as·cer·tain, *v.* find out; make certain.

as·cet·ic, *n.* one who practices self-denial. *a.* very self-denying. **as·cet·i·cism**, *n.*

as·cot, *n.* wide neck scarf.

as·cribe, *v.* **as·cribed**, **as·crib·ing**. attribute; assign.

a·sex·u·al, *a.* not sexual.

ash, *n.* (often pl.) powdery remains burned material; tree. **ash·en**, *a.* ash·y, **-i·er**, **-i·est**, *a.*

a·shamed, *a.* feeling shame.

a·side, *adv.* on or to one side; apart. *n.* actor's lines spoken to the audience.

as·i·nine, *a.* obstinate; silly.

ask, *v.* request; question; inquire about; invite. **ask·er**, *n.*

a·skance, *adv.* sideways; with suspicion. Also **a·skant**.

a·skew, *adv.*, *a.* awry.

a·slant, *adv.* at a slant. *prep.* slantingly across. *a.* slanting.

a·sleep, *a.*, *adv.* sleeping; numb.

a·so·cial, *a.* withdrawn.

asp, *n.* deadly viper.

as·par·a·gus, *n.* herb grown for its edible shoots.

as·pect, *n.* look; view; mien.

as·per·i·ty, *n.*, *pl.*, **-ties**. roughness or harshness.

as·perse, *v.* **as·persed**, **as·pers·ing**. slander. **as·per·sion**, *n.*

as·phalt, *n.* black substance used for pavements.

as·phyx·i·ate, *v.*, **-at·ed**, **-at·ing**. suffocate. **as·phyx·i·a·tion**, *n.*

as·pi·ra·tion, *n.* ardent desire.

as·pire, *v.*, **as·pired**, **as·pir·ing**. desire; aim for. **as·pir·ant**, *n.*

as·pi·rin, *n.* white crystalline derivative used to relieve pain and reduce fever.

ass, *n.* donkey; dolt.

as·sail, *v.* set upon; assault. **as·sail·a·ble**, *a.* **as·sail·ant**, *n.*

as·sas·sin, *n.* murderer.

as·sas·si·nate, *v.*, **-nat·ed**, **-nat·ing**. kill. **as·sas·si·na·tion**, *n.* **as·sas·si·na·tor**, *n.*

as·sault, *n.*, *v.* attack.

as·sem·ble, *v.*, **-bled**, **-bling**. bring or call together. **as·sem·blage**, *n.* **as·sem·bly**, *n.*, *pl.*, **-blies**.

as·sent, *n.* consent. *v.* concur.

as·sert, *v.* affirm positively; assert. **ser·tion**, *n.* **as·ser·tive**, *a.*

as·sess, *v.* tax; fine; evaluate. **as·sess·ment**, *n.* **as·ses·sor**, *n.*

as·set, *n.* item having value; property.

as·sev·er·ate, *v.*, **-at·ed**, **-at·ing**. affirm positively.

as·sid·u·ous, *a.* devoted; diligent. **as·sid·u·ous·ness**, *n.*

as·sign, *v.* apportion; fix; appoint; refer. **as·sign·ment**, *n.*

as·sig·na·tion, *n.* meeting.

as·sim·i·late, *v.*, **-lat·ed**, **-lat·ing**. liken; absorb. **as·sim·i·la·tion**, *n.*

as·sist, *v.*, *n.* aid; help. **as·sist·ance**, *n.* **as·sist·ant**, *a.*

as·so·ci·ate, *v.*, **-at·ed**, **-at·ing**. join; connect mentally; unite in company. *a.* combined. *n.* ally; partner. **as·so·ci·a·tion**, *n.*

as·so·nance, *n.* resemblance of sounds. **as·so·nant**, *a.*

as·sort·ed, *a.* varied.

as·sort·ment, *n.* mixed collection.

as·suage, *v.*, **as·suaged**, **as·suag·ing**. lessen; moderate.

as·sume, *v.*, **as·sumed**, **as·sum·ing**. undertake; take for granted; put on. **as·sump·tion**, *n.*

as·sure, *v.*, **as·sured**, **as·sur·ing**. make sure or certain; convince. **as·sur·ance**, *n.*

as·ter, *n.* plant with starlike flowers.

as·ter·isk, *n.* figure (*).

a·stern, *adv.* at or toward the stern of a ship; backward.

asth·ma, *n.* chronic disorder of respiration. **asth·mat·ic**, *a.*

a·stir, *adv.*, *a.* moving.

as·ton·ish, *v.* amaze; surprise. **as·ton·ish·ment**, *n.*

as·tound, *v.* astonish.

a·stray, *adv.*, *a.* off the correct path.

a·stride, *a.*, *adv.*, *prep.* with one leg on each side.

as·trol·o·gy, *n.* supposed science of the effect of celestial bodies on human affairs. **as·trol·o·ger**, *n.*

as·tro·naut, *n.* traveler in interplanetary space.

as·tron·o·my, *n.* science of celestial bodies. **as·tron·o·mer**, *n.* **as·tro·nom·ic**, *a.*

as·tute, *a.* shrewd; keen.

a·sun·der, *adv.*, *a.* apart.

a·sy·lum, *n.* sanctuary; institution for the insane, the blind, etc.

at, *prep.* showing position, state or location.

at·el·ier, *n.* workshop; studio.

a·the·ism, *n.* disbelief in God. **a·the·ist**, *n.*

ath·lete, *n.* one trained for sports of agility and strength. **ath·let·ic**, *a.*

ath·lete's foot, *n.* ringworm of the feet, caused by fungus.

a·thwart, *adv.*, *prep.* across; in opposition to.

at·las, *n. pl.*, **at·las·es.** collection of maps in a volume.

at·mos·phere, *n.* gases surrounding the earth; general feeling; aura. **at·mos·pher·ic**, *a.*

at·oll, *n.* coral island surrounding a central lagoon.

at·om, *n.* smallest particle of an element. **a·tom·ic**, *a.*

a·tom·ic pile, *n.* nuclear reactor.

at·om·ize, *v.*, **-ized, -iz·ing.** reduce to atoms; reduce to a spray. **at·om·iz·er**, *n.*

a·tone, *v.*, **a·toned, a·ton·ing.** make amends. **a·tone·ment**, *n.*

a·top, *adv.* on or at the top. *prep.* on the top of.

a·tro·cious, *a.* wicked; cruel. *inf.* very bad. **a·troc·i·ty**, *n. pl.*, **-troc·i·ties.**

at·ro·phy, *n. pl.*, **-phies.** wasting away or shriveling up. *v.*, **-phied, -phy·ing.** affect with atrophy. **a·troph·ic**, *a.*

at·tach, *v.* fasten; join; affix. **at·tach·ment**, *n.*

at·tack, *v.* assault; assail; seize, as disease. *n.* assault.

at·tain, *v.* achieve; acquire;

gain; reach. **at·tain·ment**, *n.*

at·tempt, *v.* make an effort; try. *n.* endeavor.

at·tend, *v.* accompany; be present at; pay attention to. **at·tend·ance**, *n.* **at·tend·ant**, *a.*, *n.*

at·ten·tion, *n.* heedfulness; care; readiness. **at·ten·tive**, *a.*

at·test, *v.* bear witness to; declare the truth of. **at·tes·ta·tion**, *n.*

at·tic, *n.* garret.

at·tire, *v.*, **at·tired, at·tir·ing.** dress; adorn. *n.* clothing.

at·ti·tude, *n.* posture of a person; manner.

at·tor·ney, *n. pl.*, **-neys.** legal agent; lawyer.

at·tract, *v.* draw toward; entice. **at·trac·tion**, *n.* **at·trac·tor**, *n.* **at·trac·tive**, *a.*

at·trib·ute, *v.*, **-but·ed, -but·ing.** ascribe; impute. *n.* property or characteristic. **at·tri·bu·tion**, *n.* **at·trib·u·tive**, *a.*

a·typ·i·cal, *a.* not typical.

au·burn, *n.*, *a.* reddish-brown.

auc·tion, *n.* public sale of property to the highest bidder. *v.* sell by auction. **auc·tion·eer**, *n.*

au·da·cious, *a.* daring; bold; insolent. **au·dac·i·ty**, *n.*

au·di·ble, *a.* capable of being heard. **au·di·bly**, *adv.*

au·di·ence, *n.* formal interview; people reached by a magazine, television show, etc.

au·dit, *n.* examination of accounts. *v.* make an audit of. **au·di·tor**, *n.*

au·di·tion, *n.* hearing; trial performance. *v.* give an audition.

au·di·to·ri·um, *n.* hall used for public gatherings.

au·di·to·ry, *a.* of hearing.

aught, *n.* zero.

aug·ment, *v.* increase; enlarge. **aug·men·ta·tion**, *n.*

Au·gust, *n.* eighth month.

aunt, *n.* sister of one's father or mother; uncle's wife.

au·ra, *n. pl.*, **au·ras, au·rae.** subtle influence or quality about a person or object.

au·re·ate, *a.* golden.

au·ri·cle, *n.* external ear; cavity in the heart.

au·ro·ra, *n.* polar lights. **au·ro·ral**, *a.*

aus·pice, *n. pl.*, **aus·pic·es.** omen. *usu. pl.* protection.

aus·pi·cious, *a.* propitious; favorable.

aus·tere, *a.* harsh; severe; rigorous. **aus·ter·i·ty,** *n.*

au·then·tic, *a.* genuine.

au·then·ti·cate, *v.,* **-cat·ed, -cat·ing.** prove authentic. **au·then·ti·ca·tion,** *n.* **au·then·tic·i·ty,** *n.*

au·thor, *n.* originator or creator; writer.

au·thor·i·ta·tive, *a.* having authority; dictatorial.

au·thor·i·ty, *n. pl.,* **-ties.** right to command. *pl.* persons exercising power; reference source or expert.

au·thor·ize, *v.,* **-ized, -iz·ing.** give authority to; empower. **au·thor·i·za·tion,** *n.*

au·to, *n. inf.* automobile.

au·to·bi·og·ra·phy, *n. pl.,* **-phies.** biography of a person's life written by himself. **au·to·bi·og·ra·pher,** *n.*

au·to·crat, *n.* absolute ruler. **au·toc·ra·cy,** *n. pl.,* **-cies.** **au·to·crat·ic,** *a.*

au·to·graph, *n.* signature. *v.* write one's signature on.

au·to·mat·ic, *a.* involuntary or reflexive; self-regulating.

au·to·ma·tion, *n.* technique of making a machine operate more automatically.

au·tom·a·ton, *n. pl.,* **-tons, -ta.** robot.

au·to·mo·bile, *n.* car. **au·to·mo·tive,** *a.*

au·ton·o·mous, *a.* self-governing. **au·ton·o·mous·ly,** *adv.* **au·ton·o·my,** *n. pl.,* **-mies.**

au·top·sy, *n.* examination of a body, to determine cause of death.

au·tumn, *n.* season between summer and winter.

aux·il·ia·ry, *a.* helping; subsidiary. *n. pl.,* **aux·il·ia·ries.** aid; subordinate group.

a·vail, *v.t.* assist; benefit. *v.i.* be of use. *n.* effective use.

a·vail·able, *a.* accessible. **a·vail·a·bil·i·ty,** *n.*

av·a·lanche, *n.* vast body of snow, rock, or earth sliding down a mountain.

a·vant-garde, *n.* people with the newest ideas.

av·a·rice, *n.* desire for wealth. **av·a·ri·cious,** *a.*

a·ve, *interj.* hail! farewell!

a·venge, *v.,* **a·venged, a·veng·ing.** revenge. **a·veng·er,** *n.*

av·e·nue, *n.* street; means of access.

a·ver, *v.,* **a·verred, a·ver·ring.**

affirm with confidence.

av·er·age, *n.* arithmetic mean; typical example. *v.,* **-aged, -ag·ing.** find the average of; have as an average. *a.* ordinary.

a·verse, *a.* opposed. **a·verse·ly,** *adv.* **a·ver·sion,** *n.*

a·vert, *v.* turn away; prevent.

a·vi·a·tion, *n.* operation, design of airplanes. **a·vi·a·tor,** *n.* **a·vi·a·trix,** *n.*

av·id, *a.* eager; greedy.

av·o·ca·do, *n. pl.,* **-dos.** edible, tropical fruit.

av·o·ca·tion, *n.* hobby; job.

a·void, *v.* shun; keep away from. **a·void·a·ble,** *a.*

av·oir·du·pois, *n.* system of weights in which 1 lb. contains 16 oz.

a·vow, *v.* declare openly; own. **a·vow·al,** *n.* **a·vowed,** *a.*

a·wait, *v.* wait for; expect.

a·wake, *a.* not sleeping; alert. *v.,* **a·woke, a·wak·ing; a·waked, a·wak·ing.** arouse.

a·wak·en, *v.* awake.

a·ward, *v.* adjudge; give as a prize. *n.* judgment; prize.

a·ware, *a.* cognizant; conscious. **a·ware·ness,** *n.*

a·way, *adv.* at a distance; apart. *a.* not present; afar.

awe, *n.* reverential fear. *v.,* **awed, aw·ing.** strike with awe.

aw·ful, *a.* dreadful; ugly; objectionable. **aw·ful·ly,** *adv.*

a·while, *adv.* for some time.

awk·ward, *a.* clumsy; inconvenient; embarrassing. **awk·ward·ly,** *adv.* **awk·ward·ness,** *n.*

awn·ing, *n.* covered frame hanging over a window, deck, etc.

a·wry, *a., adv.* crooked.

ax, axe, *n. pl.,* **ax·es.** bladed tool for chopping, hewing, etc.

ax·i·om, *n.* self-evident truth. **ax·i·o·mat·ic,** *a.*

ax·is, *n. pl.,* **ax·es.** straight line about which a body revolves; alliance.

ax·le, *n.* shaft on which wheels rotate. **ax·i·al,** *a.*

aye, ay, *interj.,n.* yes; yea.

az·ure, *a.* sky blue. *n.* blue color.

B

baa, *n.* bleating of a sheep. *v.,* **baaed, baa·ing.** bleat.

bab·ble, *v.,* **-bled, -bling.** utter words imperfectly; murmur; tell secrets. *n.* senseless prattle. **bab·bler,** *n.*

babe, *n.* baby.

ba·bel, *n.* confusion of sounds. Also **Babel.**

ba·boon, *n.* long-muzzled primate.

ba·bush·ka, *n.* head scarf.

ba·by, *n., pl.,* **ba·bies.** very young child; infant. *a. v.,* **ba·bied, ba·by·ing.** pamper. **ba·by·hood,** *n.* **ba·by·ish,** *a.*

bac·ca·lau·re·ate, *n.* degree of Bachelor of Arts; commencement speech.

bac·cha·nal, *n.* drunken orgy; reveler. **bac·cha·na·li·an,** *a.*

bach·e·lor, *n.* unmarried man. **bach·e·lor·hood,** *n.*

ba·cil·lus, *n., pl.,* **ba·cil·li.** bacterium. **bac·il·lar·y,** *a.*

back, *n.* region of the spine; rear. *v.i.* move or go back. *v.t.* support. *a.* in the rear; in a backward direction. *adv.* to or toward the rear or past. **back·er,** *n.* **back·ing,** *n.*

back·bone, *n.* spine; fortitude.

back·drop, *n.* curtain used as the background of a stage setting.

back·fire, *n.* premature explosion in the cylinder of an engine; unexpected result. *v.,* **-fired, -fir·ing.**

back·gam·mon, *n.* board game played with pieces and dice.

back·ground, *n.* ground behind an object or representation; past happenings, conditions, events.

back·hand, *n.* hand turned backward in making a stroke; handwriting sloping to the left. **back·hand·ed,** *a.*

back·lash, *n.* reaction.

back·log, *n.* stock, work, etc., awaiting processing.

back·side, *n.* back part of anything; posterior.

back·slide, *v.,* **-slid; -slid** or **-slid·den; -slid·ing.** turn away from religion or morality. **back·slid·er,** *n.*

back·stage, *adv.* in the dressing rooms.

back·track, *v.* retrace one's steps; retreat.

back·ward, *adv.* toward the back, rear, or past; with the back foremost. Also **backwards.** *a.* in reverse; retarded; bashful. **back·ward·ness,** *n.*

ba·con, *n.* cured back and sides of a hog.

bac·te·ri·a, *n. pl.* of bacterium. microscopic organism causing fermentation, putrefaction, disease, etc. **bac·te·ri·al,** *a.* **bac·te·ri·al·ly,** *adv.*

bac·te·ri·ol·o·gy, *n.* study of bacteria. **bac·te·ri·ol·o·gist,** *n.*

bad, *a.,* **worse, worst.** not good; wicked, rotten; defective; severe. *n.* that which is bad. **bad·ly,** *adv.* **bad·ness,** *n.*

badge, *n.* emblem; symbol.

badg·er, *n.* burrowing mammal. *v.* harass; pester.

bad·min·ton, *n.* game using shuttlecocks and rackets.

baf·fle, *v.,* **-fled, -fling.** elude; bewilder, perplex. **baf·fler,** *n.* **baf·fling,** *a.*

bag, *n.* receptacle of leather, cloth, etc.; sack; valise; purse. *v.i.,* **bagged, bag·ging.** hang loosely. *v.t.* put into a bag; kill or catch. **bag·gy,** *a.*

bag·gage, *n.* luggage.

bag·nio, *n., pl.,* **-ios.** brothel.

bag·pipe, *n. usu. pl.* musical instrument with a leather bag and pipes. **bag·pip·er,** *n.*

bail, *v.* empty (a boat) of water; free from arrest by giving bail. *n.* amount guaranteed for a prisoner's release.

bail·iff, *n.* sheriff's deputy; court officer.

bait, *n.* lure; enticement. *v.* lure; annoy; persecute.

bake, *v.,* **baked, bak·ing.** cook by dry heat; harden bricks, etc., by heat. **bak·er,** *n.*

bak·er's doz·en, *n.* thirteen.

bak·er·y, *n., pl.,* **-ies.** place for baking bread and cakes.

bal·ance, *n.* instrument for weighing; equilibrium; harmonious arrangement; mental stability; excess or equality of debits or credits. *v.,* **-anced, -anc·ing.** weigh; adjust evenly; offset; reckon up or settle. **bal·anc·e·a·ble,** *a.*

bal·co·ny, *n., pl.,* **-nies.** projecting platform or gallery of a building.

bald, *a.* having no hair on the head; unconcealed. **bald·ly,** *adv.* **bald·ness,** *n.*

bal·der·dash, *n.* nonsense.

bale, *n.* bundle. *v.,* **baled, bal·ing.** make into a bale.

ba·leen, *n.* whalebone.

bale·ful, *a.* destructive; portending evil. **bale·ful·ly.**

balk, *n.* check or hindrance. *v.t.* hinder. *v.i.* stop short and refuse to go on. **balk·y,** *a.*

ball, *n.* spherical body; round body use in games; dance. *v.* form or make into a ball.

bal·lad, *n.* simple song; narrative poem.

bal·lad·ry, *n.* ballad poetry.

bal·last, *n.* heavy matter carried in a ship to steady it. *v.* place ballast in or on.

bal·le·ri·na, *n.* female ballet dancer.

bal·let, *n.* elaborate story-telling dance.

bal·lis·tics, *n. pl.* study of projectiles in flight. **bal·lis·tic,** *a.* **bal·lis·ti·cian,** *n.*

bal·loon, *n.* bag filled with a gas lighter than air causing it to rise. *v.* expand.

bal·lot, *n.* paper used to vote.

ball·room, *n.* large room for balls or dancing.

balm, *n.* fragrant ointment.

balm·y, *a.,* **-i·er, -i·est.** aromatic; healing. *inf.* crazy. **balm·i·ly** *adv.* **balm·i·ness,** *n.*

ba·lo·ney, *n. inf.* nonsense; bologna sausage.

bal·sa, *n.* light wood; tree.

bal·sam, *n.* oleoresin; plant or tree yielding a balsam.

bal·us·trade, *n.* row of posts joined by a rail.

bam·boo, *n.* woody plant; hollow stem of this plant.

ban, *v.,* **banned, ban·ning.** prohibit. *n.* authoritative prohibition.

ba·nal, *a.* commonplace; trite. **ba·nal·i·ty,** *n.*

ba·nan·a, *n.* long, pulpy, usu. yellow fruit.

band, *n.* group; body of musicians; fetter; strip; range of radio frequencies. *v.* tie or mark with a band; unite.

band·age, *n.* strip of cloth used to dress wounds. *v.,* **-aged, -ag·ing.** dress wounds.

ban·dit, *n. pl.,* **-dits, -dit·ti.** robber. **ban·dit·ry,** *n.*

ban·dy, *v.,* **-died, -dy·ing.** toss back and forth. *a.* bowed. **ban·dy·leg·ged,** *a.*

bane, *n.* cause of destruction; curse. **bane·ful,** *a.*

bang, *v.* beat noisily. *n.* loud, sudden sound.

ban·ish, *v.* exile; expel. **ban·ish·er,** *n.* **ban·ish·ment,** *n.*

ban·is·ter, *n.* handrail.

ban·jo, *n.* stringed musical instrument having a body like a tambourine.

bank, *n.* mound; heap; steep acclivity; tier; row; establishment for the deposit and lending of money. *v.* embank; cover (a fire) with ashes; do business with. **bank·a·ble,** *a.*

bank·er, *n.* **bank·ing,** *n.*

bank·rupt, *a.* legally adjudged unable to pay one's debts. *v.* make bankrupt. **bank·rupt·cy,** *n. pl.,* **-cies.**

ban·ner, *n.* flag. *a.* leading.

ban·nis·ter, *n.* banister.

ban·quet, *n.* formal dinner. *v.* feast. **ban·quet·er,** *n.*

ban·ter, *v.* raillery; joking. *v.* speak teasingly.

bap·tism, *n.* ritual initiation ceremony of a Christian church of immersing in or sprinkling of water. **bap·tis·mal,** *a.* **bap·tist,** *n.*

bap·tize, *v.,* **-tized, -tiz·ing.** administer baptism to; purify.

bar, *n.* long piece of wood or metal; obstruction; legal profession; counter where liquor is served; band or stripe. *v.,* **barred, bar·ring.** obstruct; exclude. *prep.* except. **barred,** *a.*

barb, *n.* point projecting backward from a main point, critical remark. **barbed,** *a.*

bar·bar·i·an, *n.* uncivilized person; savage. *a.* **bar·bar·ic,** *a.*

bar·ba·rous, *a.* rude and ignorant; barbaric; cruel. **bar·ba·rism,** *n.* **bar·bar·i·ty,** *n. pl.,* **-ties.**

bar·be·cue, *n.* meat roasted over an open fire. *v.,* **-cued, -cu·ing.** broil (food) over an open fire; prepare in a well-seasoned sauce.

barbed wire, *n.* fence wire having barbs. Also **barb·wire.**

bar·ber, *n.* one who shaves beards or cuts and dresses hair. **bar·ber·shop,** *n.*

bar·bi·tu·rate, *n.* drug used as a sedative or hypnotic.

bard, *n.* poet. **bard·ic,** *a.*

bare, *a.,* **bar·er, bar·est.** naked; plain; empty; mere. *v.* reveal; uncover. **bare·ness,** *n.* **bare·ly,**

adv.

bare·faced, *a.* audacious.

bar·gain, *n.* agreement; thing bought at a low price. *v.* make a bargain. **bar·gain·er**, *n.*

barge, *n.* flat-bottomed boat.

bar·i·tone, *n.* male voice between bass and tenor; brass instrument.

bar·i·um, *n.* soft, whitish metallic element.

bark, *n.* covering of trees; cry of a dog; ship. *v.* scrape or rub off; make a barking sound. **bark·er**, *n.*

bar·keep·er, *n.* bartender.

bar·ley, *n. pl.,* **-leys.** cereal grain.

bar·maid, *n.* female bartender.

bar mitz·vah, a ceremony recognizing a Jewish boy as adult.

barn, *n.* farm building used for storage.

bar·na·cle, *n.* crustacean.

barn·yard, *n.* yard of a barn.

ba·rom·et·er, *n.* instrument for measuring atmospheric pressure. **bar·o·met·ric**, *a.*

bar·on, *n.* lowest-ranking nobleman. **bar·on·age**, *n.* **bar·on·ess**, *n.* **ba·ro·ni·al**, *a.*

ba·roque, *a.* ornate; grotesque.

bar·rack, *n. usu. pl.* building for lodging soldiers.

bar·ra·cu·da, *n. pl.,* **-da, -das.** voracious tropical fish.

bar·rage, *n.* barrier of artillery fire.

bar·rel, *n.* cylindrical wooden vessel, with bulging sides; firing tube of a gun.

bar·rel or·gan, *n.* hand organ.

bar·ren, *a.* unfruitful; sterile. **bar·ren·ness**, *n.*

bar·rette, *n.* clasp for holding hair.

bar·ri·cade, *n.* barrier.

bar·ri·er, *n.* natural or manmade obstruction.

bar·room, *n.* bar; tavern.

bar·row, *n.* wheelbarrow.

bar·ten·der, *n.* one who serves alcoholic drinks at a bar.

bar·ter, *v.* trade by exchanging. **bar·ter·er**, *n.*

ba·salt, *n.* heavy, dark volcanic rock.

base, *n.* bottom of anything; fundamental principle or element; center of authority; compound which reacts with acid to form salt. *v.,* **based, bas·ing.** make or form a base for. *a.,* **bas·er, bas·est.** morally low; mean. **ba·sal**, *a.*

base·ball, *n.* game played with bat and ball by two teams; ball used.

base·born, *a.* of humble birth.

base·less, *a.* groundless.

base·ment, *n.* story of a building below ground.

bash, *v. inf.* beat violently.

bash·ful, *a.* shy. **bash·ful·ly**, *adv.* **bash·ful·ness**, *n.*

ba·sic, *a.* fundamental. **ba·si·cal·ly**, *adv.*

ba·sil, *n.* aromatic plant.

ba·sil·i·ca, *n.* church of an ancient building design.

ba·sin, *n.* round, shallow vessel used for holding liquids; reservoir; tract of country drained by a river.

ba·sis, *n. pl.,* **ba·ses.** bottom or base of anything.

bask, *v.* enjoy warmth.

bas·ket, *n.* container made of straw, thin strips of wood, etc.

bas·ket·ry, *n.*

bas·ket·ball, *n.* team game played with a ball and basket-like goals; ball used.

bass, *n.* lowest male voice; such a singer; deeptoned instrument. *a.* low; deep; grave.

bass, *n. pl.,* **bass, bass·es.** fish.

bas·si·net, *n.* basket used as an infant's bed.

bas·soon, *n.* bass woodwind instrument.

bas·tard, *n.* illegitimate child. *a.* illegitimate; not genuine. **bas·tard·ize**, *v.*

baste, *v.,* **bast·ed, bast·ing.** sew with long stitches; drip fat, etc. upon while cooking.

bas·ti·on, *n.* stronghold.

bat, *n.* flying mammal; stick used to hit a ball in games. *v.,* **bat·ted, bat·ting.** hit; wink. **bat·ter**, *n.*

batch, *n.* quantity of a thing made at once.

bath, *n. pl.,* **baths.** dipping in water for cleansing; water for this; bathtub or room.

bathe, *v.,* **bathed, bath·ing.** wash; swim. **bath·er**, *n.*

bat·on, *n.* staff; wand.

bat·tal·ion, *n.* army unit; any large group or force.

bat·ter, *v.* beat with continuous blows; wear out, by long service. *n.* mixture of ingredients, used in baking.

bat·ter·y, *n.* unlawful beating; pieces of artillery used togeth-

er; dry cell.

bat·tle, *n.* combat; conflict. *v.,* **-tled, -tling.** join in battle.

bat·ty, *a.,* **-ti·er, -ti·est.** *inf.* insane; odd.

bau·ble, *n.* trifle.

bawd·y, *a.,* **-i·er, -i·est.** obscene; suggestive. **bawd,** *n.*

bawl, *v.* cry out; weep loudly.

bay, *n.* bay window; gulf; horse of reddish-brown color; laurel tree; howl; cornered and forced to fight. *v.* howl; hold at bay.

bay·o·net, *n.* sword fixed to a rifle muzzle.

bay·ou, *n.* inlet or outlet of a lake, river, etc.

ba·zaar, *n.* Oriental market; charity sale.

ba·zoo·ka, *n.* portable rocket gun.

be, *v.* pres. sing. **am, are, is;** pres. pl. **are;** past sing. **was, were, was;** past pl. **were;** pp. **been;** ppr. **being.** exist; live; occupy a position; take place; remain as before.

beach, *n.* shore.

bea·con, *n.* guiding signal.

bead, *n.* small, perforated, usu. round object threaded on string; drop; globule. *v.* furnish with beads. **bead·ed,** *a.* **bead·y,** *a.,* **-i·er, -i·est.**

beak, *n.* bird's bill. **beaked,** *a.*

beak·er, *n.* open-mouthed vessel of glass, etc.

beam, *n.* straight, heavy piece of timber, iron, etc.; width of a vessel; ray of light; constant radio signal. *v.* shine.

bean, *n.* edible seed contained in a pod.

bear, *n. pl.,* **bears, bear.** massive mammal having shaggy hair; gruff person. *v.,* **bore.** carry or bring; endure; have a name, aspect, etc.; bring forth or produce. **bear·a·ble,** *a.* **bear·a·bly,** *adv.* **bear·er,** *n.* **bear·ing,** *n.* **bear·ish,** *a.*

beard, *n.* hair that grows on the face of men. **beard·ed,** *a.* **beard·less,** *a.*

bear·skin, *n.* skin of a bear.

beast, *n.* four-footed animal; brutal man. **beast·li·ness,** *n.* **beast·ly,** *a.* **-li·er, -li·est.**

beat, *v.,* **beat·en, beat·ing.** strike repeatedly; stir with vigor; overcome; flutter. *n.* rhythmical blow; musical emphasis; patrolled area. **beat·en,** *a.*

beat·er, *n.*

be·a·tif·ic, *a.* making happy.

be·at·i·tude, *n.* blessedness; bliss.

beau·ty, *n. pl.,* **-ties.** loveliness; elegance; grace; beautiful person or thing. **beau·te·ous,** *a.* **beau·ti·ful,** *a.* **beau·ti·ful·ly,** *adv.* **beau·ti·fy,** *v.*

bea·ver, *n.* amphibious rodent with soft brown fur and a broad flat tail.

be·cause, *conj.* for the reason that; since.

beck, *n.* beckoning gesture.

beck·on, *v.* summon by a motion of the hand or head.

be·come, *v.,* **be·came, be·come, be·com·ing.** come, change, or grow to be; be suitable to. **be·com·ing,** *a.*

bed, *n.* piece of furniture on which to sleep; plot of ground in which plants are grown; layer; foundation. *v.,* **bed·ded, bed·ding.** put to bed; go to bed. **bed·ding,** *n.*

bed·clothes, *n. pl.* bedding.

be·deck, *v.* deck out; adorn.

be·dev·il, *v.,* **-iled, -il·ing.** torment; muddle.

bed·lam, *n.* uproar and confusion; insane asylum.

be·drag·gle, *v.,* **-gled, -gling.** soil or soak.

bed·rid·den, *a.* confined to bed, esp. for a long time.

bed·room, *n.* sleeping room.

bed·stead, *n.* framework to support a bed.

bee, *n.* insect that produces honey and wax.

beech, *n.* tree bearing edible nuts.

beef, *n. pl.,* **beefs, beeves.** adult bovine animal; flesh of such an animal; *inf.* muscle; complaint. *v. inf.* complain. **beef·y,** *a.,* **-i·er, -i·est.**

bee·hive, *n.* hive for bees.

beer, *n.* alcoholic beverage made of fermented malted barley and hops. **beer·y,** *a.*

bees·wax, *n.* wax secreted by bees.

beet, *n.* plant which has a fleshy edible root.

bee·tle, *n.* insect having hard outer wings.

be·fall, *v.,* **be·fell, be·fall·en, be·fall·ing.** happen (to).

be·fit, *v.,* **be·fit·ted, be·fit·ting.** suit. **be·fit·ting,** *a.*

be·fore, *adv.* in front; previously; earlier. *prep.* ahead of; earlier than; rather than; in the presence of. *conj.* previous to the time when.

be-fore-hand, *adv.* in advance.

be-friend, *v.* make friends with; assist.

beg, *v.,* **begged, beg-ging.** ask for charity; beseech. **beg-gar,** *n.* **beg-gar-ly,** *a.*

be-gin, *v.,* **be-gan, be-gun, be-gin-ning.** start; originate. **be-gin-ner,** *n.* **be-gin-ning,** *n.*

be-guile, *v.,* **be-guiled, be-guil-ing.** deceive; charm; amuse; while away (time).

be-half, *n.* interest; support.

be-have, *v.,* **be-haved, be-hav-ing.** act properly. **be-hav-ior,** *n.*

be-head, *v.* decapitate.

be-hind, *prep.* at the back of; in support of; remaining after; later in time than. *adv.* out of sight; backward; slow.

be-hind-hand, *adv., a.* in arrears; late.

beige, *n.* light brownish-gray.

be-ing, *n.* existence; life; creature.

be-lat-ed, *a.* late; too late. **be-lat-ed-ly,** *adv.*

belch, *v.* eject wind noisily from the stomach; issue out violently. *n.* belching.

be-lea-guer, *v.* besiege.

bel-fry, *n. pl.,* **-fries.** bell tower.

be-lief, *n.* trust; confidence; faith.

be-lieve, *v.,* **be-lieved, be-liev-ing.** accept the truth of; trust; have faith; suppose. **be-liev-a-ble,** *a.*

bell, *n.* hollow metallic object, which gives forth a ringing sound when struck.

bell-boy, *n.* in a hotel, one who carries luggage, runs errands, etc. Also **bell-hop.**

bel-li-cose, *a.* warlike.

bel-lig-er-ence, *n.* warfare; warlike nature. **bel-lig-er-en-cy,** *n.* **bel-lig-er-ent,** *a.*

bel-low, *n., v.* roar.

bel-lows, *n. pl.* folding instrument which produces a strong current of air.

bel-ly, *n. pl.,* **-lies.** abdomen. *v.,* **-lied, -ly-ing.** swell; bulge.

bel-ly-ache, *n.* pain in the belly. *v.,* **-ached, -ach-ing.** *inf.* complain.

be-long, *v.* have a proper place; be suitable. **be-long-ings,** *n. pl.* possessions.

be-loved, *a.* greatly loved. *n.* one

greatly loved.

be-low, *prep.* lower; beneath. *adv.* in a lower place.

belt, *n.* band worn around the waist; strip. *v.* strike with a belt. **belt-ed,** *a.*

be-moan, *v.* lament.

be-muse, *v.,* **be-mused, be-mus-ing.** bewilder. **be-mused,** *a.*

bench, *n.* long seat; court of justice; work table. *v.* remove a player from a game.

bend, *v.,* **bent, bend-ing.** render curved; flex; crook; incline. *n.* bending; curve. **bend-er,** *n.*

be-neath, *adv.* below. *prep.* under.

ben-e-dic-tion, *n.* blessing.

ben-e-fac-tion, *n.* benefit. **ben-e-fac-tor,** *n.*

be-nef-i-cent, *a.* doing good.

ben-e-fi-cial, *a.* conferring benefit. **ben-e-fi-cial-ly,** *adv.*

ben-e-fi-ci-ar-y, *n. pl.,* **-ar-ies.** one who receives benefits provided by insurance, a trust fund, etc.

ben-e-fit, *n.* advantage or profit. *v.t.,* **-fit-ed, -fit-ing.** do good to. *v.i.* derive benefit.

be-nev-o-lence, *n.* good will; kindness. **be-nev-o-lent,** *a.*

be-nign, *a.* kind; gracious; not malignant. **be-nig-ni-ty,** *n. pl.,* **-ties. be-nign-ly,** *adv.*

be-nig-nant, *a.* kind; benign. **be-nig-nan-cy,** *n. pl.,* **-cies.**

bent, *a.* not straight; determined. *n.* inclination.

be-queath, *v.* give or leave by will.

be-quest, *n.* legacy.

be-rate, *v.* **be-rat-ed, be-rat-ing.** chide; to scold.

be-reave, *v.,* **be-reaved** or **be-reft, be-reav-ing.** deprive of someone loved. **be-reave-ment,** *n.*

be-ret, *n.* soft, visorless, cloth cap.

berg, *n.* iceberg.

ber-ga-mot, *n.* citrus fruit.

ber-i-ber-i, *n.* disease of the nerves caused by lack of vitamin B_1.

ber-ry, *n. pl.,* **ber-ries.** small, juicy or pulpy fruit, containing many seeds.

ber-serk, *a.* frenzied. *adv.* into a violent frenzy.

berth, *n.* station for a vessel at anchor; sleeping place in a ship, etc.

be-seech, *v.,* **be-sought** or **be-**

seeched, be·seech·ing. beg eagerly for.

be·set, v., be·set, be·set·ting. hem in; attack on all sides. be·set·ting, a.

be·side, prep. at the side of; in comparison with; in addition to; near to; apart from.

be·sides, adv. moreover. prep. in addition to.

be·siege, v., be·sieged, be·sieg·ing. lay seige to.

be·smirch, v. sully; tarnish.

be·speak, v., be·spoke, be·spoke or be·spok·en, be·speak·ing. order or engage.

best, a., irreg. superl. of good. largest; most. adv. in the highest degree; most excellently. n. highest possible state of excellence. v. defeat; outdo.

bes·tial, a. like a beast; brutish. bes·tial·ly, adv. bes·tial·i·ty, n. pl., -ties.

be·stow, v. give; confer.

bet, v. wager. v., bet or bet·ted, bet·ting. wager.

be·ta, n. second letter of the Greek alphabet.

be·tray, v. deliver to an enemy by treachery; seduce; reveal. be·tray·al, n.

be·troth, v. affiance. be·troth·al, n. be·trothed, n.

bet·ter, a., compar. of good. superior; of a higher quality. adv., compar. of well. in a more excellent manner. usu. pl. one's superiors. v. improve.

bet·ter·ment, n. improvement.

be·tween, prep. in the space or time separating; intermediate to; involving both of. adv. in the intervening space, time, position, etc.

bev·er·age, n. drink.

bev·y, n. pl., bev·ies. flock of birds; group, esp. of women.

be·wail, v. lament.

be·ware, v. be wary of; look out for.

be·wil·der, v. puzzle; confuse. be·wil·der·ment, n.

be·witch, v. cast a spell over; fascinate. be·witch·er·y, n. be·witch·ing, a.

be·yond, adv. farther away. prep. later than; out of reach of; more than.

bi·as, n. oblique line across a fabric; bent; prejudice. a. diagonal. adv. obliquely. v., bi·ased, bi·as·ing, bi·assed, bi·as-

sing. prejudice.

bib, n. cloth worn under a child's chin while eating.

Bi·ble, n. sacred writings of the Christian religion; Old Testament in the form received by the Jews. Bib·li·cal, a. Bib·li·cal·ly, adv.

bib·li·og·ra·phy, n. pl., -phies. list of book, articles, etc. bib·li·og·ra·pher, n.

bi·cen·ten·ni·al, n. second hundredth anniversary.

bi·ceps, n. pl. two muscles of the upper arm.

bick·er, v. quarrel.

bi·cy·cle, n. two-wheeled vehicle. v., -cled, -cling. ride a bicycle. bi·cy·clist, n.

bid, v., bid or bade, bid, bid·den, bid·ding. ask; command; offer (a price). n. offer of a price; amount of a bid. bid·da·ble. a. bid·der, n.

bid·dy, n. pl., bid·dies. hen.

bide, v., bid·ed, bid·ing. abide.

bi·en·ni·al, a. once in two years; lasting for two years. n. plant that lives for two years. bi·en·ni·al·ly, adv.

bier, n. frame on which a corpse or coffin is laid.

big, a., big·ger, big·gest. great; important; large. adv. boastfully.

big·a·my, n. pl., big·a·mies. crime of marrying another while still married. big·a·mist, n. big·a·mous, a.

bight, n. bend; bay.

big·ot, n. opinionated and intolerant person. big·ot·ed, a. big·ot·ry, n. pl., -ries.

bike, n., v. inf. bicycle.

bi·lat·er·al, a. two-sided.

bile, n. bitter liquid secreted by the liver; ill humor. bil·i·ar·y, a. bil·ious, a.

bilge, n. lowest part of a ship's hull. inf. nonsense.

bilk, v. defraud.

bill, n. account of money due; piece of paper money; draft of a proposed statute; beak. v. charge in a bill.

bill·board, n. signboard.

bil·let, n. quarters for a soldier. v. place in lodgings.

bill·fold, n. wallet.

bil·liards, n. pl. game played on a cloth-covered table with balls and a cue.

bil·lion, n. thousand millions. bil·lionth, a., n. bil·lion·aire, n.

bill of fare, *n.* menu.

bil·low, *n.* great wave. **bil·low·y**, *a.,* **-i·er, -i·est.** *v.* swell.

bil·ly goat, *n.* male goat.

bi·month·ly, *a., adv.* every two months; twice a month. *n. pl.,* **-lies.** bimonthly publication.

bin, *n.* box or enclosed place used as a storage place.

bi·na·ry, *a.* paired; double.

bind, *v.,* **bound, bind·ing.** tie; fasten; bandage; confine; sew together and cover (a book); be obligatory. **bind·er**, *n.* **bind·ing**, *a., n.*

bind·er·y, *n. pl.,* **-er·ies.** place where books are bound.

binge, *n. inf.* spree.

bin·go, *n.* game like lotto.

bi·noc·u·lar, *n. usu. pl.* field glass.

bi·og·ra·phy, *n. pl.,* **-phies.** life story of another person. **bi·og·ra·pher**, *n.* **bi·o·graph·i·cal**, **bi·o·graph·ic**, *a.*

bi·ol·o·gy, *n.* science of plants and animals. **bi·o·log·i·cal**, *a.* **bi·ol·o·gist**, *n.*

bi·op·sy, *n. pl.,* **bi·op·sies.** examination of tissue from a living subject.

bi·par·ti·san, *a.* of two parties.

bi·ped, *n.* animal having two feet. **bi·ped·al**, *a.*

birch, *n.* tree of whitish bark and hard wood.

bird, *n.* warm-blooded vertebrate having feathers and wings.

bird·ie, *n.* golf score of one under par on a hole.

bird's-eye, *a.* seen comprehensively; general.

birth, *n.* act of being born; parturition; lineage.

birth·day, *n.* day or anniversary of birth.

birth·mark, *n.* congenital mark on a person's body.

birth·right, *n.* right of a person entitled by birth.

bis·cuit, *n.* bread baked in small pieces. *Brit.* cracker.

bi·sect, *v.* divide into two equal parts. **bi·sec·tion**, *n.*

bi·sex·u·al, *a.* of both sexes.

bish·op, *n.* prelate who governs a diocese. **bish·op·ric**, *n.*

bis·muth, *n.* metallic element used in medicine.

bi·son, *n.* American buffalo.

bis·tro, *n. pl.,* **bis·tros.** small bar or night club.

bit, *n.* small piece or quantity;

inf. short time; cutting or drilling part of a tool; mouthpiece of a bridle.

bitch, *n.* female canine animal. *v. slang.* complain.

bite, *v.,* **bit, bit, bit·ten, bit·ing.** cut, break or seize with the teeth; cause a sharp pain in; seize a bait. *n.* a biting; morsel of food; wound. **bit·ing**, *a.* **bit·ing·ly**, *adv.*

bit·ter, *a.* having a harsh taste; painful; distressful; harsh. **bit·ter·ish**, *a.* **bit·ter·ness**, *n.*

bit·tern, *n.* wading bird of the heron family.

bi·tu·mi·nous coal, *n.* soft, impure coal.

bi·valve, *n.* mollusk, as the oyster, clam, mussel, etc.

biv·ou·ac, *n.* temporary encampment. *v.,* **-acked, -ack·ing.** encamp in bivouac.

bi·zarre, *a.* odd; fantastic. **bi·zarre·ness**, *n.*

blab, *v.,* **blabbed, blab·bing.** let out (secrets); prattle.

black, *a.* of the darkest possible color; dismal; evil. *n.* black pigment. *v.* blacken. **black·ly**, *adv.*

black·ber·ry, *n. pl.,* **-ries.** juicy, dark fruit of certain bushes and vines.

black·bird, *n.* black bird of the thrush family.

black·board, *n.* smooth hard surface for writing on with chalk.

black·en, *v.* make black.

black·guard, *n.* scoundrel.

black·head, *n.* skin blemish.

black-heart·ed, *a.* evil.

black·jack, *n.* pirate's flag; small club; card game.

black mag·ic, *n.* witchcraft.

black·mail, *n.* extortion by threats of exposure.

black·out, *n.* period of darkness; temporary loss of consciousness.

black·smith, *n.* person who shoes horses.

blad·der, *n.* sac which stores and secretes urine.

blade, *n.* leaf of grass; flat part of something; cutting part of a weapon or tool.

blame, *v.,* **blamed, blam·ing.** place the responsibility on; find fault with. *n.* censure. **blame·ful**, *a.* **blame·less**, *a.* **blame·wor·thy**, *a.* deserving blame. **blame·wor·thi·ness**, *n.*

blanch, v. bleach; turn pale.

bland, a. gentle; mild. **bland·ly**, adv. **bland·ness**, n.

blan·dish, v. coax; cajole.

blank, a. free from marks; empty. n. thing left blank. **blank·ly**, adv. **blank·ness**, n.

blan·ket, n. cover. a. covering a wide range of things.

blare, v., **blared**, **blar·ing**. sound loudly. n. loud sound.

blar·ney, n. gross flattery.

blas·pheme, v. speak impiously of God. **blas·phem·ous**, a. **blas·phem·y**, n. pl., **-phem·ies**.

blast, n. forcible stream of air; explosive. v. destroy; explode. **blast·ed**, a.

bla·tant, a. clamorous; brazenly obvious. **bla·tan·cy**, n.

blaze, n. flame; brilliance. v., **blazed**, **blaz·ing**. burn brightly; shine; mark.

bleach, v. whiten. n. any agent used for bleaching.

bleach·ers, n. pl. outdoor seats for spectators.

bleak, a. desolate; dreary. **bleak·ly**, adv. **bleak·ness**, n.

blear, v. make dim or blurred. **blear·y**, a., **-i·er**, **-i·est**.

bleat, v. utter the cry of a sheep. n. the sound.

bleed, v., **bled**, **bleed·ing**. lose blood.

blem·ish, v. mar; sully. n. defect; blot.

blend, v., **blend·ed** or **blent**, **blend·ing**. mix; come together. n. mixture. **blend·er**, n.

bless, v., **blessed** or **blest**, **bless·ing**. invoke divine favor; bestow happiness; make holy. **bless·ed**, a. **bless·ed·ness**, n. **bles·sing**, n.

blight, n. destructive disease or influence. v. destroy; ruin.

blimp, n. small dirigible.

blind, a. not having sight. v. make unable to see; dazzle. n. thing to hinder sight or keep out light. **blind·ness**, n. **blind·ing**, a. **blind·ly**, adv.

blind·fold, v. cover the eyes of. n. cloth placed over the eyes. **blind·fold·ed**, a.

blink, v. wink rapidly; twinkle. n. act of blinking.

bliss, n. highest degree of happiness. **bliss·ful**, a.

blis·ter, n. fluid-filled vesicle on the skin. v. raise a blister on. **blis·ter·y**, a.

blithe, a. gay. **blithe·ly**, adv.

bliz·zard, n. violent snowstorm.

bloat, v. swell or puff up.

bloc, n. groups, nations, etc., united to further their joint interests.

block, n. solid mass; portion of a city street; obstacle; obstruction. v. shape; obstruct. **block·age**, n. **block·er**, n.

block·ade, n. obstruction of passage. v., **-ad·ed**, **-ad·ing**. subject to a blockade.

blond, **blonde**, a. of a fair color of hair. n. person with blond hair.

blood, n. red fluid that circulates in the body; lineage; family. **blood·hound**, n. large dog; inf. relentless pursuer.

blood·shed, n. slaughter.

blood·shot, a. red and inflamed, said of the eye.

blood·thirst·y, a. murderous.

blood·y, a., **-i·er**, **-i·est**. of blood; stained with blood; bloodthirsty. v., **blood·ied**, **blood·y·ing**. stain with blood. **blood·i·ness**, n.

bloom, n. blossom; glow of health or beauty. v. flower; glow with health. **bloom·ing**, a.

bloom·ers, n. pl. loose undergarments.

blos·som, n. flower. v. bloom.

blot, n. spot or stain. v., **blot·ted**, **blot·ting**. stain; dry with blotting paper. **blot·ter**, n.

blotch, n. discolored patch on the skin. v. cover or mark with blotches. **blotch·y**, a.

blouse, n. woman's garment extending to the waist.

blow, v., **blew**, **blown**, **blow·ing**. move, as wind or air; give out sound by being blown; burst. n. blast of air; knock; shock. **blow·er**, n.

blow·torch, n. torch used for soldering.

blow·up, n. explosion; inf. outburst of anger; enlarged photograph.

blub·ber, n. fat of whales. v. sob noisily. **blub·ber·y**, a.

bludg·eon, n. short, heavy club. v. beat.

blue, a., **blu·er**, **blue·est**. azure; low in spirits. n. azure; blue pigment. v., **blued**, **blu·ing**. make blue. **blue·ness**, n.

blue·bell, n. plant with blue, bell-shaped flowers.

blue·ber·ry, n. pl., **-ries**. shrub with edible, bluish berries.

blue·bird, *n.* small, blue song-bird.

blue jay, *n.* bird having a blue crest and back.

blue jeans, *n.* pants of blue denim.

blue·print, *n.* detailed plan of white lines on a blue ground.

blues, *n. pl.* melancholy; slow style of jazz; spell of mental depression.

bluff, *a.* rough; plain; frank. *n.* steep bank; bold pretense. *v.* mislead or daunt.

blu·ing, *n.* rinse used in laundering to offset yellow tinge.

blun·der, *v.* move or do clumsily; bungle. *n.* stupid mistake. **blun·der·er,** *n.*

blunt, *a.* dull; abrupt; plain. *v.* make blunt. **blunt·ness,** *n.*

blur, *v.,* blurred, blur·ring. render indistinct. *n.* smear; blurred condition. **blur·ry,** *a.*

blurt, *v.* utter unthinkingly.

blush, *v.* flush, as from shame. *n.* reddening of the face. **blush·ful,** *a.* **blush·ing·ly,** *adv.*

blus·ter, *v.* roar as wind; be loud or swaggering. *n.* noisy talk. **blus·ter·ous,** *a.*

boar, *n.* male of swine, wild or tame.

board, *n.* piece of timber; flat slab or surface; daily meals provided for pay; body of directors. *v.* cover with boards; go on board of. **board·er,** *n.*

boast, *v.* brag; take pride in. *n.* boastful statement. **boast·ful,** *a.* **boast·ful·ness,** *n.*

boat, *n.* small waterborne vessel.

boat·swain, *n.* ship's officer in charge of rigging, etc.

bob, *v.,* bobbed, bob·bing. move up and down; cut (the hair) short.

bob·by pin, *n.* metal hair pin.

bob·cat, *n.* wildcat; lynx.

bob·o·link, *n.* songbird.

bob·sled, *n.* racing sled.

bob·white, *n.* quail.

bode, *v.,* bod·ed, bod·ing. *v.* portend.

bod·ice, *n.* woman's laced outer garment covering the waist and bust.

bod·y, *n.* torso; corpse; mass; main part; group of persons; substance. *v.,* bod·ied, bod·y·ing. embody. **bod·ied,** *a.* **bod·i·ly,** *a., adv.*

bod·y·guard, *n.* guard who pro-tects one's person.

bog, *n.* quagmire; marsh. *v.,* bogged, bog·ging. sink in or as in a bog. **bog·gy,** *a.*

bo·gus, *a.* counterfeit.

bo·gy, bo·gey, bog·ie, hobgoblin.

boil, *v.* bubble up and emit vapor by heating; seethe; cook in a boiling liquid. *n.* state of boiling; suppurating sore. **boil·er,** *n.*

bois·ter·ous, *a.* rowdy; violent; rough. **bois·ter·ous·ly,** *adv.* **bois·ter·ous·ness,** *n.*

bold, *a.* daring; fearless; impudent; striking to the eye. **bold·ly,** *adv.* **bold·ness,** *n.*

bo·lo·gna, *n.* sausage made of beef, veal, and pork. Also **bo·lo·gna sau·sage.**

bol·ster, *n.* long pillow. *v.* support. **bol·ster·er,** *n.*

bolt, *n.* stroke of lightning; metallic pin; movable bar for fastening a door; roll of fabric. *v.* fasten with a bolt; swallow hurriedly; shoot forth suddenly. **bolt·er,** *n.*

bomb, *n.* explosive projectile. *v.* drop bombs upon.

bom·bard, *v.* attack with bombs; shell. **bom·bar·dier,** *n.* **bom·bard·ment,** *n.*

bom·bast, *n.* inflated language. **bom·bas·tic,** *a.*

bomb·er, *n.* plane or person that drops bombs.

bond, *n.* anything that binds; obligation; interest-bearing certificate. *v.* bind; put under a legal bond. **bond·ed,** *a.*

bond·age, *n.* slavery.

bone, *n.* hard material which forms the skeleton. *v.,* boned, bon·ing. remove the bones from.

bon·fire, *n.* outdoor fire.

bon·net, *n.* hat.

bo·nus, *n. pl.* bo·nus·es. sum paid over what is required.

bon·y, *a., -i·er, -i·est.* of bone; having prominent bones.

boo, *interj.,* *v.* exclamation of dislike or to frighten. *v.,* booed, boo·ing. cry "boo" (at).

boo-boo, *n. inf.* blunder.

boo·by, *n. pl., -bies.* dunce.

boo·by trap, *n.* camouflaged trap.

book, *n.* printed work on sheets bound together. *v.* record; make a reservation. **book·bind·er,** *n.* **book·ish,** *a.*

book·keep·ing, *n.* art of recording transactions in a book. **book·keep·er,** *n.*

book·let, *n.* little book.

boom, *n.* deep hollow noise; vigorous growth; spar. *v.* make a booming sound; develop rapidly.

boo·me·rang, *n.* curved piece of wood which returns to the thrower. *v.* recoil.

boon, *n.* great benefit.

boor, *n.* rude or insensitive person. **boor·ish,** *a.*

boost, *v.* push up; advance or aid. *n.* push from behind. **boost·er,** *n.*

boot, *n.* shoe that reaches above the ankle; sharp kick. *v.* kick. **boot·ee,** *n.* baby's knitted sock.

booth, *n.* covered stall; seating compartment.

boot·leg, *v.,* **-legged, -leg·ging,** sell goods illegally, esp. liquor. *a.* illegal. **boot·leg·ger,** *n.*

boo·ty, *n. pl.,* **-ties,** plunder.

booze, *n.* any alcoholic drink. *v.* drink excessively. **booz·er,** *n.* **booz·y,** *a.,* **-i·er, -i·est.**

bo·rax, *n.* white crystalline salt.

bor·der, *n.* margin; frontier. *v.* be adjacent; form a border to. **bor·dered,** *a.*

bore, *v.,* **bored, bor·ing.** make a hole by piercing; weary by dullness. *n.* dull, tiresome person or thing; cylindrical cavity of a tube. **bore·dom,** *n.*

bo·ric ac·id, *n.* white acid, used as a weak antiseptic.

born, *a.* brought into being.

bor·row, *v.* obtain, with the intention of returning; appropriate. **bor·row·er,** *n.*

bos·om, *n.* breast of a human being. *a.* intimate.

boss, *n.* manager or employer. *v.* manage; domineer. **boss·y,** *a.,* **-i·er, -i·est.** *inf.* domineering. **boss·i·ness,** *n.*

bo·sun, *n.* boatswain. Also **bos'n, bo's'n, bo'sun.**

bot·a·ny, *n.* study of plants. **bo·tan·ic, bo·tan·i·cal,** *a.* **bot·a·nist,** *n.*

botch, *n.* poorly done work. *v.* perform in a bungling manner. **botch·y,** *a.,* **-i·er, -i·est.**

both, *a., pron.* two considered together. *conj.* equally; alike. **both·er,** *v.* worry; trouble; fuss. *n.* annoy; trouble. **both·er·some,** *a.*

bot·tle, *n.* vessel for holding liquids. *v.,* **-tled, -tling.** put into

bottles. **bot·tler,** *n.*

bot·tom, *n.* foot, base, or foundation. *a.* undermost.

bou·doir, *n.* lady's bedroom.

bough, *n.* branch of a tree.

bought, pt. and pp. of **buy.**

bouil·lon, *n.* clear broth.

boul·der, *n.* large rock.

boul·e·vard, *n.* broad avenue.

bounce, *v.,* **bounced, bounc·ing.** strike a surface and rebound. *n.* bound; sudden leap. **bounc·er,** *n.* **bounc·ing,** *a.*

bound, *n. usu. pl.* boundary; leap. *v.* abut; set limits; leap. *a.* tied; under obligation; destined.

bound·a·ry, *n. pl.,* **-ries.** bound; limits.

boun·te·ous, *a.* generous; abundant. **boun·te·ous·ness,** *n.*

boun·ty, *n. pl.,* **-ties.** generosity; gift.

bou·quet, *n.* bunch of flowers; distinct aroma.

bour·bon, *n.* whiskey.

bour·geois, *n. pl.,* **-geois.** member of the middle class. *a.* middle-class.

bour·geoi·sie, *n. pl.,* **-sie.** middle class.

bout, *n.* contest.

bo·vine, *a.* oxlike; dull. *n.* bovine animal.

bow, *n.* wood bent by a string for shooting arrows; implement with horsehairs for playing a violin; decorative knot. *v.* bend or curve.

bow, *v.* bend, as in respect. *n.* bodily inclination; forward part of a ship.

bow·el, *n. usu. pl.* part of the intestines; interior part.

bow·er, *n.* shady recess.

bowl, *n.* round, deep dish. *v.* play at bowling. **bowl·er,** *n.*

bow·leg, *n.* leg curved outward. **bow·leg·ged,** *a.*

bowl·ing, *n.* game in which heavy balls are rolled at a set of pins.

box, *n.* case or receptacle; chest; compartment. *v.* enclose, as in a box; fight with the fists. **box·er,** *n.* **box·ing,** *n.*

box·car, *n.* enclosed freight car.

boy, *n.* male child. **boy·hood,** *n.* **boy·ish,** *a.* **boy·ish·ness,** *n.*

boy·cott, *v.* refuse to work for, or deal with. *n.* refusal to buy, deal with, etc.

bra, *n. inf.* brassiere.

brace, *n.* support; clasp. *v.,*

braced, brac·ing. strengthen; give firmness to; acquire vigor. **brac·er,** *n.* **brac·ing,** *n.*

brace·let, *n.* ornamental band for the wrist. **brace·let·ed,** *a.*

brack·et, *n.* projecting support; one of two marks, []. *v.* support with or enclose in brackets.

brack·ish, *a.* slightly salt.

brad, *n.* thin wire nail.

brag, *v.,* **bragged, brag·ging.** boast. *n.* boast.

brag·gart, *n.* boaster.

braid, *v.* weave; plait. *n.* braided thing. **braid·ing,** *n.*

braille, *n.* printing for the blind, in which raised dots represent letters.

brain, *n.* nerve tissue that fills the cranium; *pl.* intellectual power. *v.* beat severely about the head.

brain·less, *a.* stupid.

brain·y, *a.,* **-i·er, -i·est.** having brains; intellectual.

braise, *v.,* **braised, brais·ing.** brown (meat) then simmer.

brake, *n.* mechanical device for stopping. *v.,* **braked, brak·ing.** stop.

bram·ble, *n.* prickly shrub; its berry. **bram·bly,** *a.*

bran, *n.* outer coat of grain.

branch, *n.* limb; extension; subdivision. *v.* put forth branches. **branch·ed,** *a.*

brand, *n.* instrument used to brand cattle; mark; trademark; class of goods. *v.* burn a mark upon; mark permanently.

bran·dish, *v.* shake or wave.

bran·dy, *n. pl.,* **bran·dies.** liquor distilled from wine, or from fermented juice. *v.,* **bran·died, bran·dy·ing.** preserve with brandy. **bran·died,** *a.*

brash, *a.* rash; impudent.

brass, *n.* soft yellow alloy. *a.* made of brass; brazen.

bras·siere, *n.* undergarment worn to support the breasts.

brass·y, *a.,* **-i·er, -i·est.** impudent; harsh.

brat, *n.* spoiled child.

bra·va·do, *n.* swaggering defiance.

brave, *a.* courageous; fearless. *v.,* **braved, brav·ing.** meet, with courage. **brav·er·y,** *n. pl.,* **-ies.**

bra·vo, *interj.* excellent!

brawl, *v.* quarrel or fight noisily.

n. noisy quarrel. **brawl·er,** *n.*

brawn, *n.* muscular strength. **brawn·y,** *a.,* **-i·er, -i·est.**

bray, *v.* utter the cry of a donkey. *n.* sound of donkeys.

bra·zen, *a.* impudent. *v.* behave with insolence.

breach, *n.* break or rupture; gap. *v.* make a breach or opening in; break.

bread, *n.* baked food made of flour, milk, etc. *v.* cover with bread crumbs.

breadth, *n.* width.

break, *v.,* **broke, bro·ken, break·ing.** shatter; violate; annul; crack; interrupt; ruin financially; tame. *n.* breaking; gap; stoppage. **break·a·ble,** *a.* **break·age,** *n.*

break·down, *n.* breaking down; analysis.

break·fast, *n.* morning meal. *v.* take breakfast.

break·wa·ter, *n.* structure serving to break the force of waves.

breast, *n.* milk-secreting organ; front of the chest.

breast·bone, *n.* sternum.

breath, *n.* air inhaled and exhaled; pause; light current of air. **breath·less,** *a.*

breathe, *v.,* **breathed, breath·ing.** inhale and exhale air; exist; take a rest; whisper. **breath·er,** *n.* **breath·ing,** *n.*

breech, *n.* hinder part.

breech·es, *n. pl.* short trousers.

breed, *v.,* **bred, breed·ing.** produce (offspring); raise; rear. *n.* lineage; kind. **breed·er,** *n.*

breeze, *n.* light wind. *v.* blow a breeze; hurry. **breez·y,** *a.,* **-i·er, -i·est. breez·i·ness,** *n.*

breth·ren, *n. pl.* of **brother.**

brev·i·ty, *n.* state of being brief; conciseness.

brew, *v.* prepare beer, tea, etc.; plot. *n.* that which is brewed. **brew·er,** *n.* **brew·er·y,** *n. pl.,* **-ies.**

bribe, *n.* price, favor, etc. to corrupt. *v.,* **bribed, brib·ing.** give a bribe. **brib·a·ble,** *a.* **brib·er·y,** *n. pl.,* **-ies.**

brick, *n.* hardened block of clay for building. *v.* lay or build with brick.

bride, *n.* woman newly married, or about to be. **brid·al,** *a.*

bride·groom, *n.* man newly married, or about to be.

brides·maid, *n.* woman who attends the bride at a wedding.

bridge, *n.* structure spanning a river, road, etc.; link; mounting for artificial teeth; card game. *v.* span.

bri·dle, *n.* part of the harness of a horse about the head. *v.,* **bri·dled, bri·dling.** restrain.

brief, *a.* short; concise. *n.* summary. *v.* summarize; instruct. **brief·ly,** *adv.* **brief·ing,** *n.*

bri·er, *n.* prickly shrub.

brig, *n.* prison on a ship; two-masted vessel.

bri·gade, *n.* large body of troops.

bright, *a.* shining; quick-witted. **bright·ness,** *n.*

bright·en, *v.* make bright.

bril·liance, *n.* great brightness; striking achievement. **bril·lian·cy,** *n.* **bril·liant,** *a.*

brim, *n.* upper edge as a cup; projecting rim as of a hat. *v.,* **brimmed, brim·ming.** fill to the brim.

brim·stone, *n.* sulfur.

brine, *n.* salt water. **brin·y,** *a.*

bring, *v.,* **brought, bring·ing.** fetch; carry; accompany; change in state or condition.

brink, *n.* edge of a steep place.

brisk, *a.* quick; lively; bracing. **brisk·ly,** *adv.* **brisk·ness,** *n.*

bris·tle, *n.* short, stiff hair. *v.,* **bris·tled, bris·tling.** erect the bristles. **bris·tly,** *a.*

brit·tle, *a.* hard, but breaking readily.

broach, *v.* suggest a subject for the first time.

broad, *a.* wide; large; not limited; general; blunt.

broad·cast, *v.,* **-cast** or **-cast·ed, -cast·ing.** send out by radio or television; spread widely. *n.* radio or television program.

broad·cloth, *n.* smooth, closely woven fabric.

broad·mind·ed, *a.* liberal; tolerant.

broad·side, *n.* comprehensive attack. *adv.* with the side turned toward.

bro·cade, *n.* material woven in an elaborate pattern. *v.,* **-cad·ed, -cad·ing.** weave with a design.

broc·co·li, *n.* vegetable with edible florets and stalks.

bro·chure, *n.* pamphlet.

broil, *v.* cook by putting close to a fire. **broil·er,** *n.*

bro·ken, *a.* in pieces; uneven;

fragmentary; ruined; tamed.

bro·ker, *n.* one who buys and sells, on commission. **bro·ker·age,** *n.*

bro·mide, *n.* compound used as sedative.

bron·chi·al tubes, *n.* bronchi.

bronze, *n.* alloy of copper and tin. *v.,* **bronzed, bronz·ing.** give the color of bronze to.

brooch, *n.* ornamental pin or clasp.

brood, *n.* family of young birds; family's children. *v.* think about for a long time; incubate.

brook, *n.* small stream.

broom, *n.* sweeping tool. *v.* sweep.

broth, *n.* thin soup.

broth·el, *n.* house of prostitution.

broth·er, *n. pl.,* **broth·ers, breth·ren.** son of the same parents; male member; monk. **broth·er·hood,** *n.*

broth·er·in·law, *n. pl.,* **brothers·in·law.** brother of one's husband or wife; sister's husband.

brow, *n.* forehead; edge.

brow·beat, *v.,* **-beat, -beat·en, -beat·ing.** bully.

brown, *a.* of a dusky color between red and yellow. *v.* become or cause to become brown.

browse, *v.,* **browsed, brows·ing.** graze; leisurely inspect.

bru·in, *n.* bear.

bruise, *v.,* **bruised, bruis·ing.** injure without cutting; discolor the skin. *n.* injury or discoloration of the skin.

bru·net, *a.* brown or black-haired. *n.* person having dark complexion, hair, and eyes.

brunt, *n.* chief stress, force, or violence.

brush, *n.* bristled instrument used for dusting, painting, etc.; brushing; dense growth of bushes. *v.* pass a brush over; wet or paint lightly.

brusque, brusk, *a.* abrupt; rude.

bru·tal, *a.* inhuman, savage, or cruel. **bru·tal·i·ty,** *n.*

bru·tal·ize, *v.,* **-ized, -iz·ing.** treat in a brutal manner.

brute, *n.* resembling an animal. *n.* brute creature. **brut·ish,** *a.*

bub·ble, *n.* film of liquid inflated with air or gas; globule of air or gas in a liquid. *v.,* **-bled,**

-bling. gurgle; form bubbles.

buc·ca·neer, n. pirate.

buck, n. male deer, goat, etc. v. throw by bucking.

buck·et, n. pail. v., **-et·ed, -et·ing.** lift or carry in buckets.

buck·le, n. fastening clasp, as on a belt. v., **-led, -ling.** fasten with a buckle; warp.

buck·shot, n. leaden pellet.

buck·skin, n. soft leather.

buck·wheat, n. plant grown for its dark flour.

bud, n. undeveloped plant stem, leaf or flower. v., **bud·ded, bud·ding.** produce buds; begin to grow.

bud·dy, bud·die, n. pl., **-dies.** pal.

budge, v. move slightly; stir.

budg·et, n. plan for financing. v. provide for or confine to a budget. **budg·et·ar·y,** a.

buff, n. fuzzy leather; fan. v. polish. **buff·er,** n.

buf·fa·lo, n. pl., **-loes, -los.** bison.

buf·fet, n. blow. v., **-fet·ed, -fet·ing.** batter; struggle.

buf·fet, n. cabinet for china, table linen, etc.; counter for serving.

buf·foon, n. clown. **buf·foon·er·y,** n. pl., **-ies.**

bug, n. insect; inf. germ or virus; hidden microphone. v., **bugged, bug·ging.** inf. plant a hidden device; pester. **bug·gy,** a., **-gi·er, -gi·est.**

bug·gy, n. pl., **-gies.** one-horse carriage; baby carriage.

bu·gle, n. instrument like a trumpet. v., **-gled, -gling.** sound a bugle. **bu·gler,** n.

build, v., **built, build·ing.** construct or erect; make. n. physique. **build·er,** n.

build·ing, n. structure.

bulb, n. underground leaf bud; round part of an electric light. **bul·bous,** a.

bulge, n. swelling; hump. v., **bulged, bulg·ing.** swell out. **bulg·y,** a.

bulk, n. large mass; main body; volume. v. be of great size. **bulk·y,** a., **-i·er, -i·est.**

bull, n. male of domestic beef cattle or of various other animals.

bul·let, n. projectile shot from rifles or pistols.

bul·le·tin, n. brief news statement.

bul·lion, n. gold or silver in the mass.

bull·ock, n. castrated bull.

bull's-eye, n. center of a target, or a shot that hits it.

bul·ly, n. pl., **-lies.** person who bothers others weaker than himself. v., **-lied, -ly·ing.** threaten.

bul·rush, n. large rush.

bul·wark, n. wall against injury or danger. v. protect.

bum, n. loafer; drunk. v. live off others; live idly. a., **bum·mer, bum·mest.** inf. of poor quality.

bum·ble·bee, n. large bee.

bump, v. strike heavily against. n. sudden heavy blow; sudden rise on a surface. **bump·y,** a., **-i·er, -i·est.**

bump·er, n. device for absorbing shock. a. unusually plentiful.

bun, n. bread-roll.

bunch, n. cluster; collected mass. v. form a bunch. **bunch·y,** a., **-i·er, -i·est.**

bun·dle, n. things tied together; parcel. v., **-dled, -dling.** bind into a bundle.

bun·ga·low, n. small house.

bun·gle, n. blunder. v., **-gled, -gling.** botch. **bun·gler,** n.

bun·ion, n. knob on the side of the big toe.

bunk, n. built-in bed. v. inf. occupy a bunk.

bun·ny, n. pl., **-nies.** rabbit.

bunt·ing, n. fabric used for flags; sleeping bag for babies.

bu·oy, n. float fixed in a place to mark. v. keep afloat.

buoy·an·cy, n. power to float or rise; cheerfulness. **buoy·ant,** a. **buoy·ant·ly,** adv.

bur, n. burr.

bur·den, n. load; responsibility; heavy lot or fate. v. place a load on; oppress. **bur·den·some,** a.

bu·reau, n. pl., **bu·reaus, bu·reaux.** dresser; commercial or administrative agency.

bu·reauc·ra·cy, n. pl., **-cies.** government by bureaus; body of officials. **bu·reau·crat,** n.

bur·geon, n. bud. v. bud.

bur·glar·ize, v., **-ized, -iz·ing.** rob by breaking and entering. **bur·glar,** n. **bur·gla·ry,** n. pl., **-ries.**

bur·i·al, n. burying a deceased person.

bur·lap, n. coarse fabric.

bur·lesque, n. caricature; entertainment with skits, bawdy humor, etc. *a.* comical. *v.*, **-lesqued**, **-les·qu·ing.** caricature. **bur·les·quer**, *n.*

bur·ly, *a.*, **-li·er**, **-li·est.** great in size; forceful.

burn, *v.*, **burned** or **burnt**, **burn·ing.** be or set on fire; glow like fire; injure or change by fire or heat. *n.* injury caused by burning; sunburn. **burn·a·ble**, *a.* **burn·ing**, *a.* **burn·er**, *n.*

bur·nish, *n.* gloss. *v.* shine or buff. **bur·nish·er**, *n.*

burnt, *a.* affected by burning.

burr, **bur**, *n.* prickly seed-vessel; rough edge.

bur·ro, *n. pl.*, **-ros.** donkey.

bur·row, *n.* hole made by an animal. *v.* make a burrow.

burst, *v.*, **burst**, **burst·ing.** break suddenly; explode; issue forth suddenly. *n.* act or result of bursting. **burst·er**, *n.*

bur·y, *v.*, **bur·ied**, **bur·y·ing.** inter; cover up.

bus, *n. pl.*, **bus·es**, **bus·ses.** motor-driven vehicle for public transportation. *v.*, **bused** or **bussed**, **bus·ing** or **bus·sing.** go by bus.

bush, *n.* low shrub; thicket; uncleared country. **bush·y**, *a.*, **-i·er**, **-i·est.**

bush·el, *n.* dry measure of 4 pecks; vessel of this capacity.

busi·ness, *n.* commercial activity; trade; profession; task; affair; firm, factory, or store.

bust, *n.* breast; sculpture of the head, shoulders, and breast.

bus·tle, *v.*, **-tled**, **-tling.** move or act with a great show of energy. *n.* activity with noise; pad beneath the skirt of a dress. **bus·tling**, *a.*

bus·y, *a.*, **-i·er**, **-i·est.** actively or attentively engaged; full of activity. *v.*, **bus·ied**, **bus·y·ing.** be occupied. **bus·i·ly**, *adv.*

bus·y·bod·y, *n. pl.*, **-ies.** prying person.

but, *conj.* except; unless; on the contrary; only or merely. *prep.* except.

butch·er, *n.* one who slaughters animals, or dresses their flesh; brutal killer. *v.* slaughter.

but·ler, *n.* manservant.

butt, *n.* object of ridicule; thick, large, or blunt end; stub. *v.* join at the end; strike with head; jut.

but·ter, *n.* churned, fatty portion of milk. *v.* spread with butter. **but·ter·y**, *n.*

but·ter·fin·gered, *a.* apt to drop things.

but·ter·fly, *n. pl.*, **-flies.** insect with broad, colored wings.

but·ter·milk, *n.* liquid remaining after butter has been churned from milk.

but·ter·scotch, *n.* hard candy deriving its flavor from butter and brown sugar.

but·tocks, *n. pl.* rump.

but·ton, *n.* knob or disk with holes. *v.* fasten with buttons.

but·tress, *n.* supporting structure; prop. *v.* support; prop up.

bux·om, *a.* full-bosomed.

buy, *v.*, **bought**, **buy·ing.** purchase. *n.* something bought. **buy·a·ble**, *a.* **buy·er**, *n.*

buzz, *v.* make a humming sound, like bees; utter in a murmur; signal with a buzzer. *n.* humming sound. **buzz·er**, *n.*

buz·zard, *n.* bird of the hawk family.

by, *prep.* beside or near; not later than; through the means of; in relation to. *adv.* near; past.

by·gone, *a.* past; former. *n. pl.* that which is past.

by·law, *n.* standing rule of a group.

by·pass, *n.* detour; secondary route. *v.* detour.

by·prod·uct, *n.* secondary product; minor consequence.

by·stand·er, *n.* spectator.

by·way, *n.* side road.

by·word, *n.* proverb.

C

cab, *n.* taxicab; in a truck, etc., the roofed compartment for the driver.

ca·bal, *n.* persons secretly united in some intrigue. *v.*, **ca·balled**, **ca·ball·ing.** intrigue.

cab·a·ret, *n.* restaurant providing entertainment.

cab·bage, *n.* plant with a compact, edible head.

cab·by, *n. pl.*, **-bies.** *inf.* cab driver.

cab·in, *n.* small rude house; room in a plane or ship.

cab·i·net, *n.* cupboard with shelves and doors. (*often cap.*) body of ministers who direct government.

ca·ble, n. thick, hemp or wire rope; chain; cablegram. v., **ca·bled, ca·bling.** send a cable.

ca·ble·gram, n. telegram sent by underwater cable.

ca·boose, n. last car of a freight train, for the crew.

cache, n. hiding place, esp. for provisions; items so hidden. v., **cached, cach·ing.** conceal or hide away.

cack·le, v., **-led, -ling.** utter a shrill noisy cry. n. shrill cry of a goose. **cack·ler,** n.

ca·coph·o·y, n. pl., **-nies.** harsh sound.

cac·tus, n. pl., **-tus·es, -ti.** spiny plant of dry regions.

cad, n. ungentlemanly person. **cad·dish,** a.

ca·dav·er, n. dead body. **ca·dav·er·ous,** a.

cad·die, cad·dy, n. person who carries clubs for a golfer. v., **-died, -dying.** serve as a caddy.

ca·dence, n. rhythmic succession of words; beat of a rhythmical movement.

ca·det, n. student of officer training.

ca·fe, ca·fé, n. restaurant; tavern.

caf·e·te·ri·a, n. self-service restaurant.

caf·feine, n. stimulant found in coffee, tea, etc.

cage, n. barred enclosure. v., **caged, cag·ing.** confine.

ca·jole, v., **ca·joled, ca·jol·ing.** persuade by flattery. **ca·jol·er·y,** n. pl., **-ies.**

cake, n. sweet food of baked batter; shaped or molded mass. v., **caked, cak·ing.** form into a compact mass.

cal·a·boose, n. inf. jail.

ca·lam·i·ty, n. pl., **-ties.** disaster; misfortune; mishap. **ca·lam·i·tous,** a.

cal·ci·fy, v., **-fied·fy·ing.** change into a stony condition. **cal·ci·fi·ca·tion,** n.

cal·ci·um, n. alkaline element found in bones and teeth.

cal·cu·late, v., **-lat·ed, -lat·ing.** compute; estimate; plan in advance. **cal·cu·lat·ed,** a. **cal·cu·la·tion,** n. **cal·cu·la·tor,** n.

cal·cu·lat·ing, a. scheming.

cal·cu·lus, n. pl., **-li, -lus·es.** study of mathematic functions.

cal·dron, n. cauldron.

cal·en·dar, n. register of the year; list.

calf, n. pl., **calves.** young of the cow, elephant, seal, etc.; back of the leg below the knee.

cal·i·ber, cal·i·bre, n. diameter of a gun barrel or bullet; degree of quality.

cal·i·brate, v., **-brat·ed, -brat·ing.** measure the caliber of. **cal·i·bra·tion,** n.

cal·i·co, n. pl., **-coes, -cos.** cotton cloth printed on one side.

ca·liph, ca·lif, n. muslim religious and civil leader. **cal·iph·ate, cal·if·ate,** n.

cal·is·then·ics, n. exercises.

call, v. utter in a loud voice; request to come; telephone; name; summon; halt. n. shout or cry; communication by telephone; short visit.

call·ing, n. vocation.

cal·lous, a. hardened; unfeeling. **cal·loused,** a.

cal·low, a. lacking maturity; inexperienced.

cal·lus, n. pl., **cal·lus·es.** hardened portion of skin.

calm, n. stillness. a. still; tranquil. v. quiet.

ca·lor·ic, a. of or having to do with heat.

cal·o·rie, n. pl., **-ries.** unit of heat; unit of food measurement.

cal·um·ny, n. pl., **-nies.** slander. **ca·lum·ni·ate,** v., **-at·ed, -at·ing. ca·lum·ni·a·tion,** n.

ca·lyp·so, n. pl., **ca·lyp·sos.** music of the West Indies.

ca·lyx, n. pl., **ca·lyx·es, cal·y·ces.** outside of a flower; sepals.

cam, n. device for making irregular rotary motion.

cam·el, n. one or two-humped animal.

ca·mel·lia, n. plant with roselike flowers.

cam·e·o, n. precious stone carved with a raised design.

cam·er·a, n. device for making photographs.

cam·ou·flage, n. disguise or plan used as a false front. v., **-flaged, -flag·ing.** disguise or conceal.

camp, n. temporary living place or shelter. v. set up or stay in a camp. **camp·er,** n.

cam·paign, n. military operation; organized activity. v. serve in or go on a campaign. **cam·paign·er,** n.

cam·pus, n. pl., **cam·pus·es.**

grounds of a college.

can, *aux. v.,* **could.** have the ability to.

can, *n.* airtight metal container. *v.,* **canned, can·ning.** preserve in a can or jar.

ca·nal, *n.* man-made waterway; body tube. *v.,* **-naled, -nal·ing** or **-nalled, -nall·ing.** make a canal through.

ca·nar·y, *n.* small singing bird often kept as a pet.

can·cel, *v.,* **-celed, -cel·ing** or **-celled, -cell·ing.** annul; call off; strike out; counterbalance. **can·cel·la·tion,** *n.*

can·cer, *n.* malignant growth.

can·de·la·brum, *n. pl.,* **-bra, -brums.** branched candlestick.

can·did, *a.* frank; sincere.

can·di·da·cy, *n. pl.,* **-cies.** A candidate.

can·di·date, *n.* one proposed for an office. **can·di·da·cy,** *n. pl.,* **-cies.**

can·dle, *n.* wax enclosing a wick, burned for light.

can·dor, *n.* frankness.

can·dy, *n. pl.,* **-dies.** sweet made from sugar syrup. *v.* coat with sugar. **can·died,** *a.*

cane, *n.* stem of some palms and grasses; walking stick. *v.,* **caned, can·ing.** beat with a cane; build with cane.

ca·nine, *a.* of or like a dog. *n.* dog.

can·is·ter, *n.* small box for tea, coffee, etc.

can·ker, *n.* open sore.

can·na·bis, *n.* marijuana.

can·ner·y, *n. pl.,* **-ies.** canning plant.

can·ni·bal, *n.* one who eats human flesh. **can·ni·bal·ism,** *n.*

can·non, *n. pl.,* **can·nons,** or **can·non.** mounted gun.

can·ny, *a.,* **-i·er, -i·est.** shrewd; frugal. **can·ni·ly,** *adv.*

ca·noe, *n.* slender boat, propelled by paddles. *v.,* **ca·noed, ca·noe·ing.** travel by canoe.

can·on, *n.* church law; standard or criterion.

can·on·ize, *v.,* **-ized, -iz·ing.** raise to sainthood. **can·on·i·za·tion,** *n.*

can·o·py, *n. pl.,* **-pies.** overhanging protection.

cant, *n.* insincere talk; slanting position. *v.* bevel; tilt.

can·ta·loup, **can·ta·loupe,** **can·ta·lope,** *n.* sweet melon.

can·tan·ker·ous, *a.* cross.

can·teen, *n.* army store; small water container.

can·ter, *n.* horse's gait. *v.* ride at a moderate gallop.

can·tor, *n.* singer in a synagogue.

can·vas, *n.* heavy cloth, used for artwork, tents. etc.

can·vass, *v.* ask for opinions, votes, etc. *n.* act of canvassing. **can·vass·er,** *n.*

can·yon, *n.* narrow valley with steep sides.

cap, *n.* brimless hat; small, tight-fitting lid. *v.,* **capped, cap·ping.** put a cap on.

ca·pa·ble, *a.* able; competent.

ca·pa·bly, *adv.* **ca·pa·bil·i·ty,** *n. pl.,* **-ties.**

ca·pac·i·ty, *n. pl.,* **-ties.** power of receiving or containing; ability.

cape, *n.* headland; sleeveless outer garment.

ca·per, *n.* frolicsome leap; prank. *v.* skip playfully.

cap·il·lar·y, *a.* having a very small bore. *n. pl.,* **-lar·ies.** minute blood vessels.

cap·i·tal, *a.* involving the loss of life; principal. *n.* capital letter; official seat of government; any form of wealth.

cap·i·tal·ism, *n.* free enterprise. **cap·i·tal·is·tic,** *a.* **cap·i·tal·ist,** *n.*

cap·i·tal·ize, *v.,* **-ized, -iz·ing.** write in capital letters; use to one's advantage.

cap·i·tol, *n.* statehouse.

ca·pit·u·late, *v.,* **-lat·ed, -lat·ing.** yield; surrender.

ca·price, *n.* whim. **ca·pri·cious,** *a.* **ca·pri·cious·ness,** *n.*

cap·size, *v.,* **-sized, -siz·ing.** upset or overturn.

cap·sule, *n.* small case, esp. a dose of medicine. *a.* very brief; summarized. **—cap·su·lar,** *a.*

cap·tain, *n.* leader; officer; ship's commander. *v.* lead.

cap·tion, *n.* heading; title.

cap·ti·vate, *v.,* **-vat·ed, -vat·ing.** charm. **cap·ti·va·tion,** *n.*

cap·tive, *a.* held prisoner. *n.* prisoner. **cap·tiv·i·ty,** *n. pl.,* **-ties.**

cap·tor, *n.* one who captures.

cap·ture, *v.,* **-tured, -tur·ing.** take by force. **cap·tur·er,** *n.*

car, *n.* automobile; wheeled vehicle.

car·a·mel, *n.* burnt sugar; chewy candy.

car·at, *n.* standard unit, for weighing precious stones.

car·a·van, *n.* company of travelers.

car·a·way, *n.* plant having seeds used to flavoring.

car·bine, *n.* light, short rifle. Also **car·a·bine.**

car·bo·hy·drate, *n.* compound of carbon, hydrogen, and oxygen.

car·bon, *n.* nonmetallic element.

car·bo·nate, *n.* salt of carbonic acid. **car·bo·na·tion,** *n.*

car·bon di·ox·ide, *n.* colorless, odorless, gas.

car·bon mon·ox·ide, *n.* odorless, very poisonous gas.

car·bon pa·per, *n.* paper for making a copy.

car·bun·cle, *n.* painful swelling under the skin.

car·bu·re·tor, *n.* device which mixes fuel with air.

car·cass, car·case, *n.* dead body of an animal.

car·ci·no·ma, *n. pl., -mas, -ma·ta,* cancer.

card, *n.* piece of stiff paper; playing card; *pl.* cardplaying.

card·board, *n.* stiff pasteboard.

car·di·ac, *a.* of the heart.

car·di·gan, *n.* knitted jacket.

car·di·nal, *n.* prince of the Roman Catholic Church; red finch. *a.* chief.

care, *v.,* **cared, car·ing.** be concerned. *n.* anxiety; concern; caution; charge. **care·free,** *a.* **care·ful,** *a.* **care·less,** *a.*

ca·reer, *n.* one's life's work; progress.

ca·ress, *n.* expression of affection by touch. *v.* show affection with caresses.

care·tak·er, *n.* custodian.

car·go, *n. pl., -goes or -gos.* goods loaded on a ship, etc.

car·i·bou, *n. pl., -bous or -bou.* N. American reindeer.

car·i·ca·ture, *n.* absurd imitation. *v.,* **-tured, -tur·ing.** make a caricature of .

car·il·lon, *n.* set of bells.

car·nage, *n.* slaughter.

car·nal, *a.* of the body; sensual. **car·nal·i·ty,** *n.*

car·na·tion, *n.* plant with flowers of various colors.

car·ni·val, *n.* merrymaking; travelling show with side-shows, rides, etc.

car·niv·o·rous, *a.* flesh-eating.

car·ol, *n.* Christmas song. *v.,*

-oled, -ol·ing. sing.

ca·rouse, *n.* drinking bout. *v.,* **-roused, -rous·ing.** go on a drinking spree. **ca·rous·er,** *n.*

carp, *n. pl.,* **carp, carps.** freshwater fish. *v.* complain.

car·pen·ter, *n.* one who builds with wood. **car·pen·try,** *n.*

car·pet, *n.* thick fabric floor covering. *v.* cover with a carpet. **car·pet·ing,** *n.*

car·riage, *n.* conveyance; wheeled vehicle; bearing.

car·ri·er, *n.* one who or that which carries.

car·ri·on, *n.* rotting flesh.

car·rot, *n.* long, edible plant root. **car·rot·y,** *a.*

car·ry, *v.,* **-ried, -ry·ing.** bear; convey or transport an object; stock merchandise; gain victory.

cart, *n.* two-wheeled vehicle used for conveyance or pleasure. *v.* carry in a cart. **car·ter,** *n.* **cart·age,** *n.*

car·tel, *n.* international monopolistic control.

car·ti·lage, *n.* elastic tissue of the skeleton.

car·tog·ra·phy, *n.* map making. **car·tog·ra·pher,** *n.*

car·ton, *n.* pasteboard box.

car·toon, *n.* caricature; comic strips. **car·toon·ist,** *n.*

car·tridge, *n.* tube holding a bullet, shot, etc., for a firearm.

carve, *v.,* **carved, carv·ing.** make or shape by cutting; cut up meat. **carv·ing,** *n.*

cas·cade, *n.* waterfall. *v.,* **-cad·ed, -cad·ing.** fall in a cascade.

case, *n.* instance; situation; suit; receptacle; sheath. *v.,* **cased, cas·ing.** encase.

case·ment, *n.* window opening by swinging on hinges.

cash, *n.* ready money. *v.* give or obtain cash for.

cash·ew, *n.* edible, kidney-shaped nut.

cash·ier, *n.* one who collects money in a bank, store, etc.

cash·mere, *n.* fabric of fine, soft goat's under-wool.

cas·ing, *n.* protective covering; door or window frame.

ca·si·no, *n. pl., -nos.* building for gambling.

cask, *n.* barrel.

cas·ket, *n.* coffin.

cas·se·role, *n.* covered baking dish.

cas·sette, *n.* tape cartridge.

cas·sock, *n.* long garment worn by clergymen.

cast, *v.*, **cast**, **cast·ing**. throw; deposit, as a vote; assign (a part); mold. *n.* actors in a play; mold; casting; tinge.

cas·ta·nets, *n.* pieces of hard wood clicked together.

caste, *n.* social class.

cast·er, *n.* small wheel.

cas·ti·gate, *v.*, **-gat·ed**, **-gat·ing**. censure; criticize. **cas·ti·ga·tion**, *n.* **cas·ti·ga·tor**, *n.*

cast i·ron, *n.* hard, impure iron. **cast-iron**, *a.* of cast iron; inflexible.

cas·tle, *n.* fortified residence; *chess*. rook.

cast-off, *a.* discarded. *n.* thing discarded.

cas·tor, *n.* oil substance used in medicine.

cas·trate, *v.*, **-trat·ed**, **-trat·ing**. deprive of the testicles. **cas·tra·tion**, *n.*

cas·u·al, *a.* accidental; careless; offhand. **cas·u·al·ly**, *adv.*

cas·u·al·ty, *n. pl.*, **-ties**. chance or accident; one injured or killed.

cat, *n.* small, tame mammal; lions, tigers, leopards, etc.

cat·a·clysm, *n.* sudden, violent change. **cat·a·clys·mal**, *a.*

cat·a·comb, *n. usu. pl.* underground burial place.

cat·a·log, **cat·a·logue**, *n.* methodical list or register. *v.*, **-loged**, **-log·ing**, or **-logued**, **-logu·ing**. list.

cat·a·lyst, *n.* substance causing a chemical change.

cat·a·pult, *n.* weapon for hurling missiles; device for launching. *v.* shoot from, or as if from, a catapult.

cat·a·ract, *n.* waterfall; opacity of the eye lens.

ca·tarrh, *n.* cold.

ca·tas·tro·phe, *n.* overwhelming misfortune. **cat·as·troph·ic**, *a.*

catch, *v.*, **caught**, **catch·ing**. capture, seize, or take captive; grab; get. *n.* anything that catches; that which is caught; hidden condition. **catch·er**, *n.*

catch·ing, *a.* infectious.

catch·y, *a.* **-i·er**, **-i·est**. attractive and easily recalled.

cat·e·chism, *n.* religious instruction. **cat·e·chis·mal**, *a.*

cat·e·gor·i·cal, *a.* positive. **cat·e·gor·i·cal·ly**, *adv.*

cat·e·go·ry, *n. pl.*, **-ries**. class.

cat·e·gor·ize, *v.*, **-rized**, **-riz·ing**. class.

ca·ter, *v.* give special attention; provide food for. **ca·ter·er**, *n.*

cat·er·pil·lar, *n.* larva of a butterfly, moth, etc.

cat·gut, *n.* tough cord made from animal intestines.

ca·thar·sis, *n. pl.*, **-ses**. purgation. **ca·thar·tic**, *a.*, *n.*

ca·the·dral, *n.* large or important church.

cath·o·lic, *a.* universal; liberal; (*cap.*) Roman Catholic. *n.* (*cap.*) Roman Catholic. **ca·thol·i·cism**, *n.*

cat·kin, *n.* spikelike blossom.

cat·nap, *n.* short nap. *v.*, **-napped**, **-nap·ping**. doze.

cat·nip, *n.* mint plant.

cat·sup, *n.* ketchup.

cat·tail, *n.* tall marsh plant.

cat·tle, *n.* cows, steers, etc. **cat·tle·man**, *n. pl.*, **-men**.

cat·ty, *a.*, **-ti·er**, **-ti·est**. spiteful. **cat·ti·ness**, *n.*

cau·cus, *n. pl.*, **-cus·es**. political meeting to nominate candidates, elect delegates, etc. *v.*, **-cused**, **-cus·ing**. hold or meet in a caucus.

caul·dron, **cal·dron**, *n.* large metal kettle.

cau·li·flow·er, *n.* plant related to the cabbage family with a compact, white head.

caulk, **calk**, *v.* fill the seams of to make watertight.

cause, *n.* that which produces an effect; reason; ideal or movement. *v.*, **caused**, **caus·ing**. bring about.

cause·way, *n.* raised and paved roadway.

caus·tic, *a.* capable of destroying animal tissue; critical. *n.* caustic substance.

cau·ter·ize, *v.*, **-ized**, **-iz·ing**. burn to avoid infection.

cau·tion, *n.* cautious behavior. *v.* warn. **cau·tious**, *a.*

cav·al·cade, *n.* procession.

cav·a·lier, *n.* knight; courtly gentleman. *a.* disdainful.

cav·al·ry, *n. pl.*, **-ries**. mounted soldiers. **cav·al·ry·man**, *n. pl.*, **-men**.

cave, *n.* hollow in the earth. *v.*, caved, cav·ing. fall in.

cav·ern, *n.* large cave. **cav·ern·ous**, *a.*

cav·i·ar, **cav·i·are**, *n.* salted fish eggs.

cav·il, *v.*, **-iled**, **-il·ing**. raise trivial objections; find fault. **cav·il·er,** *n.*

cav·i·ty, *n. pl.,* **-ties.** hollow place; void.

ca·vort, *v. inf.* prance.

cay·enne, *n.* hot, red pepper.

cease, *v.,* **ceased, ceas·ing.** stop; end. **cease·less,** *a.*

cease-fire, *n.* truce.

ce·dar, *n.* evergreen tree.

cede, *v.,* **ced·ed, ced·ing.** yield to another.

ceil·ing, *n.* overhead inner lining of a room; topmost limit.

cel·e·brate, *v.,* **-brat·ed, -brat·ing.** solemnize; commemorate with ceremonies; extol. **cel·e·bra·tion,** *n.*

cel·e·brat·ed, *a.* famous.

ce·leb·ri·ty, *n. pl.,* **-ties.** famous person; fame.

ce·ler·i·ty, *n.* swiftness.

cel·er·y, *n.* stalky vegetable.

ce·les·tial, *a.* heavenly.

cel·i·ba·cy, *n.* state of being unmarried. **cel·i·bate,** *n.*

cell, *n.* small room in a prison, monastery, etc.; basic unit of all living things; device which generates electricity. **cel·lu·lar,** *a.*

cel·lar, *n.* basement.

cel·lo, 'cel·lo, *n. pl.,* **-los.** violoncello. **cel·list,** *n.*

cel·lo·phane, *n.* transparent, cellulose film.

cel·lu·lose, *n.* main part of the cell walls of plants.

ce·ment, *n.* mixture of lime, silica, and water, used to make sidewalks, walls, etc.; glue. *v.* unite by cement.

cem·e·ter·y, *n. pl.,* **-ies.** graveyard.

cen·sor, *n.* official who prohibits objectionable books, plays, etc. *v.* prohibit; suppress. **cen·sor·ship,** *n.*

cen·sure, *n.* criticism. *v.,* **-sured, -sur·ing.** criticize; blame. **cen·sur·a·ble,** *a.*

cen·sus, *n. pl.,* **cen·sus·es.** official count of inhabitants.

cent, *n.* hundredth part of a dollar.

cen·taur, *n.* fabulous being, half man and half horse.

cen·ten·ni·al, *a.* of a 100-year period. *n.* its anniversary.

cen·ter, *n.* middle section of anything; central place. *v.* place in a center.

cen·ti·grade, *a.* of a thermometer where the freezing point of water is 0°; and the boiling point is 100°. Also **Celsius.**

cen·ti·me·ter, *n.* hundredth part of a meter.

cen·tral, *a.* in, at, or near the center.

cen·tral·ize, *v.,* **-ized, -iz·ing.** draw to a center; bring under one's control.

cen·tu·ri·on, *n.* in ancient Rome, a military officer.

cen·tu·ry, *n. pl.,* **cen·tu·ries.** period of a hundred years.

ce·ram·ics, *n.* art of shaping and baking clay articles. **ce·ram·ic,** *a.*

ce·re·al, *n.* edible grain, as wheat, oats, barley, rice, etc.

ce·re·bral, *a.* of the brain.

cer·e·mo·ni·al, *n.* system of rites. *a.* ritual.

cer·e·mo·ny, *n. pl.,* **-nies.** formal rite or observance. **cer·e·mo·ni·ous,** *a.*

ce·rise, *n., a.* cherry-red.

cer·tain, *a.* sure; true; not specifically named. **cer·tain·ly,** *adv.* **cer·tain·ty,** *n. pl.,* **-ties.**

cer·tif·i·cate, *n.* written proof of certain facts.

cer·ti·fy, *v.,* **-fied. -fy·ing.** testify to in writing; establish as a fact. **cer·ti·fi·a·ble,** *a.* **cer·ti·fi·ca·tion,** *n.*

cer·ti·tude, *n.* certainty.

ces·sa·tion, *n.* ceasing; stop.

ces·sion, *n.* giving up.

cess·pool, *n.* pit for sewage.

chafe, *v.,* **chafed, chaf·ing.** stimulate warmth by rubbing; anger.

chaff, *n.* husks of grain separated by thrashing. *v.* tease.

cha·grin, *n.* disappointment; humiliation. *v.* **-grined, -grin·ing.** mortify.

chain, *n.* fetter; series of linked things. *v.* unite.

chair, *n.* seat with a back.

chair·man, *n. pl.,* **-men.** presiding officer of a meeting.

chaise longue, *n. pl.,* **chaise longues, chais·es longues.** chair with a long seat.

chal·et, *n.* Swiss house.

chal·ice, *n.* cup.

chalk, *n.* limestone; marking chalk. **chalk·y,** *n., a. v.*

chal·lenge, *n.* dare. *v.,* **chal·lenged, chal·leng·ing.** call to a contest; object to.

cham·ber, *n.* room; compartment in the cartridge of a revolver.

cham·ber·maid, *n.* person who cleans bedrooms.

cha·me·le·on, *n.* lizard with the ability to change color.

cham·ois, *n. pl.*, **cham·ois**. goatlike antelope; soft leather.

cham·pagne, *n.* effervescent wine.

cham·pi·on, *n.* one who fights for a cause or wins first place.

chance, *n.* luck; risk. *v.i.* happen. *v.t.* risk.

chan·cel·lor, *n.* high ranking administrative person.

chan·de·lier, *n.* lighting fixture hung from the ceiling.

change, *v.t.*, **changed, changing**. make or become different; substitute; exchange; place fresh linen on. *v.i.* be altered.

chan·nel, *n.* waterway; broadcasting band.

chant, *v.* sing. *n.* short, repetitive melody.

chan·ti·cleer, *n.* rooster.

cha·os, *n.* utter confusion or disorder. **cha·ot·ic**, *a.*

chap, *v.*, **chapped, chapping**. crack; make rough, esp. the skin. *n.* crack in the skin.

chap, *n.* fellow.

chap·el, *n.* room or building for worship.

chap·e·ron, chap·er·one, *n.* supervisor of single persons.

chap·lain, *n.* clergyman.

chap·ter, *n.* division of a book; branch of a society.

char, *v.*, **charred, charring**. burn; scorch.

char·ac·ter, *n.* symbol; letter; distinguishing mark; moral constitution; person in a drama or novel.

char·ac·ter·is·tic, *a.* typical. *n.* distinguishing feature.

char·ac·ter·ize, *v.*, **-ized, -iz·ing**. portray. **char·ac·ter·i·za·tion**, *n.* **char·ac·ter·iz·er**, *n.*

cha·rade, *n.* pantomime, word-guessing game.

char·coal, *n.* partly burned material used as fuel.

charge, *v.*, **charged, charg·ing**. load; impose a task; accuse formally; impose or ask a price; defer payment; attack violently. *n.* full load; duty; accusation; expense; attack.

char·i·ot, *n.* two-wheeled horse-drawn vehicle. **char·i·ot·eer**, *n.*

char·i·ta·ble, *a.* generous.

char·i·ty, *n. pl.*, **-ties**. leniency; relief of the poor.

char·la·tan, *n.* quack.

charm, *n.* magical saying; trinket; ability to please and attract. *v.t.* fascinate; enchant. *v.i.* act as a charm. **charm·er**, *n.*

chart, *n.* graph or table; marine map. *v.* plan.

char·ter, *n.* deed. *v.* hire; grant.

char·treuse, *n.* light green color.

chase, *v.*, chased, chas·ing. pursue; hunt. *n.* pursuit. **chas·er**, *n.*

chasm, *n.* gaping opening in the earth.

chas·sis, *n.* framework of a car.

chaste, *a.* virtuous. **chaste·ly**, *adv.* **chas·ti·ty**, *n.*

chas·tise, *v.*, **-tised, -tis·ing**. punish by physical means. **chas·tise·ment**, *n.*

chat, *v.*, **chat·ted, chat·ting**. talk casually. *n.* friendly talk.

chat·tel, *n.* personal property.

chat·ter, *v.* talk rapidly; make a rapid clicking noise; *n.* a chattering; idle conversation.

chauf·feur, *n.* one hired to drive a car. *v.* act as a chauffeur.

chau·vin·ist, *n.* one having an exaggerated enthusiasm for a country, sex, etc. **chau·vin·ism**, *n.*

cheap, *a.* priced low; inferior; stingy. *adv.* at a low price; in a cheap way. **cheap·ly**, *adv.*

cheap·en, *v.* make cheap.

cheat, *v.t.* deceive. *v.i.* act dishonestly. *n.* deception; fraud.

check, *n.* sudden stop; control; written order for money drawn on a bank; bill; mark put against items on a list; pattern of squares. *v.* stop; restrain; investigate; verify; leave temporarily; designate with a check; decorate with a pattern of squares.

check·mate, *n.* position of a king in chess when he cannot move; defeat. *v.*, **-mat·ed, -mat·ing**. put in check.

cheek, *n.* either side of the face below the eye.

cheek·y, *a.*, **-i·er, -i·est**. impudent. **cheek·i·ly**, *adv.*

cheer, *n.* gladness; shout of acclamation. *v.t.* gladden; encourage. *v.i.* utter a cheer.

cheer·ful, *a.* gay; willing.

cheer·less, *a.* gloomy.

cheese, *n.* pressed curd of milk.

chee·tah, *n.* cat like the leopard.

chef, *n.* cook.

chem·i·cal, *n.* substance of a chemical process. *a.* of chemistry. **chem·i·cal·ly**, *adv.*

chem·is·try, *n.* scientific study of compounds and elements. **chem·ist**, *n.*

cher·ish, *v.* hold dear.

cher·ry, *n. pl.*, **-ries.** small, red, pitted fruit; tree itself.

cher·ub, *n. pl.*, **cher·ubs**, **cher·u·bim.** winged child-like angel. **che·ru·bic**, *a.*

chess, *n.* game for two players using 16 pieces on a checkerboard. **chess·man**, *n. pl.*, **-men.**

chest, *n.* part of the body from neck to abdomen; box with a lid.

chest·y, *a.*, **-i·er**, **-i·est.** having a large chest.

chew, *v.* grind with the teeth. *n.* that which is chewed.

chic, *a.* smart; stylish.

chi·can·er·y, *n. pl.*, **-ies.** trickery.

chick, *n.* young chicken.

chicken, *n.* common barnyard fowl; its meat.

chic·o·ry, *n. pl.*, **-ries.** herb used in salads, and as a coffee substitute.

chide, *v.*, **chid·ed** or **chid**, **chid·ed** or **chid·den**, **chid·ing.** scold.

chief, *a.* leading. *n.* head or leader. **chief·ly**, *adv.*

chief·tain, *n.* chief.

chif·fon, *n.* soft, thin fabric.

chil·blain, *n.* inflamed sore produced by cold.

child, *n. pl.*, **chil·dren.** son or daughter; very young person. **child·hood**, *n.* **child·ish**, *a.* **child·like**, *a.*

chil·i, **chil·li**, **chil·e**, *n. pl.*, **chil·ies**, **chil·lies**, **chil·es.** hot pepper.

chill, *n.* moderate coldness; sensation of cold. *v.* become cold. *a.* shivering with cold.

chill·y, *a.*, **-i·er**, **-i·est.** feeling cold. **chill·i·ness**, *n.*

chime, *n.* set of tuned bells. *v.* sound as a set of bells.

chi·me·ra, **chi·mae·ra**, *n.* phantom. **chi·mer·ic**, *a.*

chim·ney, *n.* passage for the smoke of a fire or furnace.

chim·pan·zee, *n.* small anthropoid ape of Africa. Also **chimp.**

chin, *n.* face below the mouth.

chi·na, *n.* porcelain.

chin·chil·la, *n.* rodent of S. America; its fur.

chink, *n.* crack. *v.* crack.

chintz·y, *a.*, **-zi·er**, **-zi·est.** cheap.

chip, *v.*, **chipped**, **chipping.** cut away or break off in small pieces. *n.* fragment.

chip·munk, *n.* ground squirrel.

chi·rop·o·dist, *n.* podiatrist. **chi·rop·o·dy**, *n.*

chi·ro·prac·tic, *n.* treatment by stretching or bending the spine. **chi·ro·prac·tor**, *n.*

chirp, *v.* make short, sharp sounds. *n.* short, shrill sound.

chis·el, *n.* tool for shaping wood, stone, etc. *v.*, **-led**, **-lled**, **-ling**, **-lling.** cut with a chisel; cheat. **chis·el·er**, *n.*

chit·chat, *n.* friendly talk.

chiv·al·ry, *n. pl.*, **-ries.** bravery, honor and courtesy of knights. **chiv·al·ric**, *a.* **chiv·al·rous**, *a.*

chlo·rine, *n.* chemical disinfectant.

chlo·ro·phyll, **chlorophyl**, *n.* green coloring in plants.

choc·o·late, *n.* ground cocoa seeds; beverage or candy made of chocolate.

choice, *n.* selection. *a.* carefully selected. **choice·ly**, *adv.*

choir, *n.* group of singers.

choke, *v.t.*, **choked**, **choking.** strangle. *v.i.* be clogged. *n.* act or sound of choking.

chol·er, *n.* nager.

chol·er·a, *n.* disease of the stomach and intestines.

chol·er·ic, *a.* quick-tempered.

cho·les·te·rol, *n.* substance in animal tissue.

choose, *v.t.*, **chose**, **chosen**, **choosing.** select. *v.i.* make a choice.

chop, *v.*, **chopped**, **chopping.** cut with a quick, heavy blow. *n.* cutting blow; slice of meat.

chop·py, *a.*, **-pier**, **-piest.** rough; moving in short broken waves. **chop·pi·ness**, *n.*

cho·ral, *a.* of or sung by a chorus or choir.

cho·rale, *n.* hymn.

chord, *n.* three or more tones sounded together. **chord·al**, *a.*

cho·re·og·ra·phy, *n.* dance arrangement. **cho·re·og·ra·pher**, *n.*

chor·is·ter, *n.* choir singer.

chor·tle, *v.*, **-tled**, **-tling.** chuckle or utter with glee. *n.*

cho·rus, *n. pl.*, **-rus·es.** dancing and singing ensemble; composition in parts; body of vocalists; refrain. *v.*, **-rused**, **-rusing.**

sing or speak in concert.

chos·en, a. selected; preferred.

chow·der, n. clam or fish stew.

Christ, n. Jesus as Messiah.

chris·ten, v. baptize; name. **chris·ten·ing**, n.

Chris·ten·dom, n. Christian lands; all Christians.

Chris·ti·an·i·ty, n. pl., -ties. religion of the doctrines taught by Christ. **Chris·tian**, n., a.

Christ·mas, n. Dec. 25; celebration of the birth of Christ.

chro·mat·ic, a. of color; mus. of semitones.

chrome, n. chromium.

chro·mi·um, n. hard, metallic element used in alloys.

chro·mo·some, n. bodies in cell nuclei that carry genes.

chron·ic, a. long-lasting or recurring. **chron·i·cal·ly**, adv.

chron·i·cle, n. record of events in the order of occurrence. v., -cled, -cling. record in a chronicle. **chron·i·cler**, n.

chron·o·log·i·cal, a. containing an account of events in order of time. **chro·nol·o·gist**, n. **chro·nol·o·gy**, n. pl., -gies.

chro·nom·e·ter, n. highly precise timepiece.

chrys·a·lis, n. pl., -lis·es, **chry·sal·i·des**. pupa; cocoon.

chry·san·the·mum, n. autumnal flower and plant.

chub·by, a., -bier, -biest. plump. **chub·bi·ness**, n.

chuck, v. give an affectionate tap; toss. n. cut of beef; clamp.

chuck·le, v., -led, -ling. laugh in an easy manner. n.

chug, n. short, coughlike noise. v. make such a sound.

chum, n. pal.

chum·my, a., -mier, -miest. intimate. **chum·mi·ly**, adv.

chump, n. blockhead; dolt.

chunk, n. thick mass. **chunk·y**, a.

church, n. edifice for public worship; denomination.

churl·ish, a. rude; surly.

churn, n. vessel for making butter. v. make butter in a churn; agitate.

chute, n. rapid; inclined channel for sliding things.

ci·der, n. apple juice.

ci·gar, n. tight roll of tobacco leaves for smoking.

cig·a·rette, **cig·a·ret**, n. papered roll of finely cut tobacco for smoking.

cil·i·a, n. pl. of **cilium**. microscopic, hairlike processes.

cinch, n. girth for a saddle; thing sure or easy. v. bind firmly.

cinc·ture, n. belt; enclosure.

cin·der, n. burned-out coal, wood, etc. pl., ashes.

cin·e·ma, n. pl., -mas. motion-picture theater; motion picture.

cin·na·mon, n. spice from tree bark.

ci·pher, n. zero; code; key to a code. v. figure; write in code.

cir·ca, adv., prep. about.

cir·cle, n. figure formed by a curved line, having every point equally distant from center; cycle; sphere of influence; orb. v., -cled, -cling. surround; revolve. **cir·cler**, n.

cir·cuit, n. periodical journey; line bounding a space; path of an electric current; theater chain. v. go in a circuit.

cir·cu·lar, a. round; indirect. n. notice for general distribution. **cir·cu·lar·i·ty**, n.

cir·cu·late, v., -lated, -lating. move around; spread; distribute. **cir·cu·la·tion**, n.

cir·cum·cise, v., -cised, -cising. cut off the foreskin of the penis. **cir·cum·ci·sion**, n.

cir·cum·fer·ence, n. line around a circle; distance around.

cir·cum·lo·cu·tion, n. roundabout talk.

cir·cum·nav·i·gate, v., -gated, -gating. sail around.

cir·cum·scribe, v., -scribed, -scribing. encircle; limit.

cir·cum·spect, a. wary; prudent.

cir·cum·stance, n. related fact or event; pl., financial condition. **cir·cum·stan·tial**, a.

cir·cum·vent, v. outwit.

cir·cus, n. pl., -cus·es. traveling show of acrobats, clowns, wild animals, etc.

cir·rho·sis, n. disease of the liver. **cir·rhot·ic**, a.

cir·rus, n. pl., **cir·ri**. fleecy cloud at high altitude.

cis·tern, n. reservoir.

cit·a·del, n. fortress.

cite, v., -cited, -citing. summon; quote; mention. **ci·ta·tion**, n.

cit·i·zen, n. member of a nation. **cit·i·zen·ry**, n. pl., -ries.

cit·ric ac·id, n. acid derived from citrus fruits.

cit·ron·el·la, n. oil used in making insect repellent.

cit·rus, n. pl., **cit·rus, cit·rus·es.** genus of trees and shrubs of lemons, oranges, etc.

cit·y, n. pl., **cit·ies.** large and important population center.

civ·ic, a. of a city or citizen.

civ·il, a. pertaining to citizens; not ecclesiastical or military; polite. **civ·il·ly,** adv.

ci·vil·ian, n. one not in military life. a. of civilians.

ci·vil·i·ty, n. pl., **-ties.** act of politeness; courtesy.

civ·i·li·za·tion, n. advanced social development; culture of a definite group.

civ·i·lize, v., **-lized, -lizing.** bring out of a savage state.

civ·il war, n. war between people of the same country.

clad, a. clothed; adorned.

claim, v. assert; demand as due. n. assertion; just title to anything; thing claimed. **claim·a·ble,** a. **claim·ant,** n.

clair·voy·ance, n. power to discern objects not in sight. **clair·voy·ant,** a.

clam, n. edible shellfish.

clam·my, a., **-mier, -miest.** cool and moist. **clam·mi·ness,** n.

clam·or, n. loud outcry; din. v. make a clamor. **clam·or·ous,** a.

clamp, n. device that holds objects together. v. fasten with clamps.

clan, n. group of related persons. **clan·nish,** a.

clan·des·tine, a. secret.

clang, n. loud, ringing, metallic sound. v. make this sound.

clap, v., **clapped** or **clapt, clapping.** strike together to produce a sharp sound; applaud. n. loud, percussive noise.

clar·et, n. dry red wine.

clar·i·fy, v.t., **-fied -fying.** make clear. v.i. become clear. **clar·i·fi·ca·tion,** n.

clar·i·net, n. single-reed woodwind instrument.

clar·i·ty, n. lucidity.

clash, v. collide; disagree. n. harsh sound; collision.

clasp, n. device for holding things together; grasp; close embrace. v. fasten; embrace.

class, n. division of society or school; style; sort. v. classify. **class·a·ble,** a.

clas·sic, a. of the highest class; in the style of Greek and Roman antiquity. n. author or

work of the first rank; pl. literature of ancient Greece and Rome.

clas·si·cal, a. classic; pertaining to serious music.

clas·si·fy, v., **-fied, -fying.** arrange in classes; restrict circulation of. **clas·si·fi·ca·tion,** n. **clas·si·fied,** a.

class·y, a., **-ier, -iest.** stylish.

clat·ter, v. make rattling sounds; prattle. n. abrupt, rattling sounds; noisy chatter.

clause, n. word group having both subject and predicate; part of a document.

claw, n. sharp hooked nail on the foot of a bird or animal. v. scratch as with nails.

clay, n. plastic earthy material.

clean, a. pure; free from dirt; complete. v. make clean. adv. wholly. **clean·er,** n. **clean·li·ness,** n. **clean·ly,** a.

cleanse, v., **cleansed, cleansing.** make clean; purify. **cleans·er,** n.

clear, a. bright; transparent; distinct; evident; innocent; open; free. v.t. make clear; pass; gain. v.i. become clear. **clear·ly,** adv. **clear·ness,** n.

clear·ance, n. clear space; sale.

clear·ing, n. tract of land cleared of wood.

cleat, n. piece used to provide traction.

cleave, v., **cleft, cleaved, clove; cleft, cleaved, cloven; cleaving.** part; split; adhere; cling.

clef, n. musical character that indicates pitch.

cleft, n. crack.a. split.

clem·en·cy, n. mildness; mercy; leniency. **clem·ent,** a.

clench, v. close tightly; grip.

cler·gy, n. pl., **-gies.** ministers, pastors, and priests.

cler·i·cal, a. of the clergy or clerks.

clerk, n. general office worker; salesperson; minor official. v. serve as a clerk.

clev·er, a. intelligent; ingenious. **clev·er·ness,** n.

click, n. slight, sharp sound. v. make a small sharp sound.

cli·ent, n. one who resorts to another, esp. a lawyer, for services; customer.

cliff, n. precipice.

cli·mate, n. weather of a region. **cli·mat·ic,** a.

cli·max, n. highest point; culmi-

nation. *v.* come to a climax.

climb, *v.* rise; ascend. *n.* a climbing. **climber,** *n.* **climb·a·ble,** *a.*

clinch, *v.* secure; grapple.

cling, *v.,* **clung, clinging.** adhere; hold fast. **cling·er,** *n.*

clin·ic, *n.* place to examine patients. **clin·i·cal,** *a.*

clip, *v.,* **clipped, clipping.** cut; shear; cut short; fasten. *n.* act of clipping; metal clasp.

clique, *n.* exclusive set of persons. **cliqu·ish,** *a.*

cloak, *n.* loose outer garment; disguise. *v.* cover with a cloak; disguise.

clock, *n.* timepiece. *v.* time with a stopwatch.

clock·wise, *adv., a.* in the direction of rotation of the hands of a clock.

clog, *v.,* **clogged, clogging.** impede; choke up. *n.* hinderance; shoe with a wooden sole.

clois·ter, *n.* covered walk; monastery; convent. *v.* confine in a cloister. **clois·tral,** *a.*

close, *v.,* **closed, closing.** shut; end; fill up. *n.* end.

close, *a.,* **closer, closest.** shut in; lacking fresh air; stingy; near; intimate; nearly even. *adv.* tightly. **close·ness,** *n.*

clos·et, *n.* small room for storage. *v.,* **-eted, -eting.** shut in a place for secret talk.

clot, *n.* coagulated mass. *v.,* **clotted, clotting.** coagulate.

cloth, *n. pl.,* **cloths.** fabric formed by weaving.

clothe, *v.,* **clothed** or **clad, clothing.** dress. **cloth·ing,** *n.*

clothes, *n. pl.* apparel.

cloud, *n.* mass of water particles in the air; any similar mass; thing that darken0s or threatens. *v.* cover with clouds; obscure; darken; render gloomy. **cloud·y,** *a.* **cloud·i·ness,** *n.*

clove, *n.* aromatic spice; small bulb as in garlic.

clo·ver, *n.* three-leaved herb.

clown, *n.* comic performer in a circus or play. *v.* act like a clown. **clown·ish,** *a.*

cloy, *v.* surfeit.

club, *n.* stick, used as a weapon; *pl.* playing card suit; social organization. *v.t.* beat with a club; *v.i.* form a club.

cluck, *n.* sound uttered by a hen. *v.* make such a sound.

clue, *n.* information that helps solve a mystery.

clum·sy, *a.,* **-sier, -siest.** awkward. **clum·si·ness,** *n.*

clus·ter, *n.* bunch; group. *v.* grow or collect in clusters.

clutch, *v.* hold tightly; seize. *n.* grip; *usu. pl.* power; device for connecting and disconnecting shafts with wheels.

clut·ter, *n.* confusion; litter. *v.* put in a clutter.

coach, *n.* enclosed carriage; railroad passenger-car; bus; private tutor; athletic instructor. *v.* act as a coach.

co·ag·u·late, *v.,* **-lated, -lating.** congeal; clot. **co·ag·u·la·tion,** *n.*

coal, *n.* mineral burned for its heat; ember.

co·a·lesce, *v.,* **-lesced, -lescing.** fuse. **co·a·les·cence,** *n.*

co·a·li·tion, *n.* union into one body; alliance.

coarse, *a.,* **coarser, coarsest.** rough; vulgar. **coars·en,** *v.*

coast, *n.* seashore. *v.* slide down a slope. **coast·er,** *n.*

coast·line, *n.* shoreline.

coat, *n.* outer garment with sleeves; layer; external covering. *v.* cover with a coat. **coat·ing,** *n.*

coax, *v.* wheedle.

cob, *n.* corncob.

co·balt, *n.* silver-white, magnetic metallic element.

cob·ble, *v.,* **-bled, -bling.** make or repair, as shoes. **cob·bler,** *n.*

co·bra, *n.* hooded snake.

cob·web, *n.* spiderweb.

co·caine, *n.* alkaloid used as an anesthetic and narcotic.

cock, *n.* male of any bird; faucet. *v.* raise the hammer of a firearm; tilt upward.

cock·a·too, *n. pl.,* **-toos.** crested parrot.

cock·le, *n.* edible mollusk.

cock·roach, *n.* nocturnal insect.

cock·tail, *n.* mixed drink; appetizer.

cock·y, *a.,* **-i·er, -i·est.** *inf.* conceited. **cock·i·ness,** *n.*

co·coa, *n.* powdered chocolate, used to make a hot drink.

co·co·nut, co·coa·nut, *n.* hardshelled fruit with a white edible meat.

co·coon, *n.* silky covering for insect larvae.

cod, *n. pl.,* **cod, cods.** large food fish. Also **cod·fish.**

cod·dle, *v.,* **-dled, -dling.** pamper.

code, *n.* system of rules and regulations; communication signals; cipher. *v.,* **cod·ed, cod·ing.** arrange in a code.

cod·i·fy, *v.,* **-fied, -fy·ing.** reduce to a code, as laws.

co·ed, *n.* female student.

co·ed·u·ca·tion, *n.* education of both sexes together.

co·erce, *v.,* **co·erced, co·erc·ing.** repress; compel. **co·er·cion,** *n.* **co·er·cive,** *a.*

cof·fee, *n.* drink made from ground coffee beans.

cof·fin, *n.* casket.

cog, *n.* tooth on a wheel.

co·gent, *a.* compelling; convincing. **co·gen·cy,** *n.*

cog·i·tate, *v.,* **-tat·ed, -tat·ing.** ponder; think about.

cog·nac, *n.* French brandy.

cog·ni·zance, *n.* knowledge or notice. **cog·ni·zant,** *a.*

co·here, *v.,* **co·hered, co·her·ing.** stick together.

co·her·ent, *a.* sticking together; logical. **co·her·ence,** *n.*

co·he·sive, *a.* cohering.

co·hort, *n.* companion.

coif·fure, *n.* hair style.

coil, *n.* ring or series of spirals. *v.* form rings or coils.

coin, *n.* piece of metal money. *v.* make into money by stamping; invent. **coin·age,** *n.*

co·in·cide, *v.,* **-cid·ed, -cid·ing.** happen the same place or time; agree. **co·in·ci·dence,** *n.* **co·in·ci·den·tal,** *a.*

co·i·tus, *n.* sexual intercourse. **co·i·tal,** *a.*

coke, *n.* fuel obtained by heating coal.

col·an·der, *n.* strainer.

cold, *a.* chilly; frigid; indifferent. *n.* absence of heat; viral infection. **cold·ness,** *n.*

cold-blood·ed, *a.* having cold blood; cruel.

cole-slaw, *n.* salad made of raw, sliced cabbage leaves.

col·ic, *n.* painful spasm of the intestines. **col·ick·y,** *a.*

col·i·se·um, *n.* large stadium.

col·lab·o·rate, *v.,* **-rat·ed, -rat·ing.** work together; cooperate with the enemy. **col·lab·o·ra·tion,** *n.*

col·lapse, *v.,* **col·lapsed, col·laps·ing.** fall in. *n.* falling inward; failure. **col·laps·i·ble,** *a.*

col·lar, *n.* part of a shirt or coat worn around the neck.

col·lat·er·al, *a.* secondary. *n.* property pledged as a guarantee of payment.

col·league, *n.* associate.

col·lect, *v.* gather; obtain payment of. **col·lec·tion,** *n.*

col·lec·tive, *a.* combined.

col·lege, *n.* school of higher learning. **col·le·gi·ate,** *a.*

col·lide, *v.,* **-lid·ed, -lid·ing.** strike against. **col·li·sion,** *n.*

col·lo·qui·al, *a.* of common conversation. **col·lo·qui·al·ly,** *adv.* **col·lo·qui·al·ism,** *n.*

col·lu·sion, *n.* secret agreement for deceit.

co·logne, *n.* scented toilet water.

co·lon, *n. pl.,* **-lons, co·la.** part of the large intestine; punctuation mark (:).

colo·nel, *n.* commissioned officer.

col·on·nade, *n.* series of columns.

colo·ny, *n. pl.,* **-nies.** settlers in a new country remaining subjects of the parent state; country colonized. **co·lo·ni·al,** *a.* **col·o·nist,** *n.* **col·o·ni·za·tion,** *n.*

col·or, *n.* hue or tint; pigment. *usu. pl.* flag. *v.* tinge; paint; distort. **col·or·ed,** *a.* **col·or·ful,** *a.* **col·or·ing,** *n.*

co·los·sal, *a.* very large.

co·los·sus, *n. pl.,* **co·los·si, co·los·sus·es.** object of gigantic size.

colour, see **color**.

col·umn, *n.* pillar; supporting, column-like object; vertical row of lines. **col·umn·ist,** *n.*

co·ma, *n. pl.,* **co·mas.** unconsciousness. **co·ma·tose,** *a.*

comb, *n.* toothed instrument, for arranging hair. *v.* dress the hair with a comb.

com·bat, *v.,* **-bat·ed, -bat·ing** or **-bat·ted, -bat·ting.** fight. *n.* battle. **com·bat·ant,** *a.*

com·bi·na·tion, *n.* things combined; series of numbers.

com·bine, *v.,* **-bined, -bin·ing.** join; unite. *n.* controlling group; harvesting machine.

com·bo, *n. pl.,* **com·bos.** small group of musicians.

com·bus·ti·ble, *a.* flammable.

com·bus·tion, *n.* act or process of burning.

come, *v.,* **came, come, com·ing.** approach; arrive; appear; extend or reach; occur.

come-back, *n. inf.* recovery of

skill or public acceptance; clever response.

co·me·di·an, n. actor in comedy. **co·me·di·enne,** n. fem.

com·e·dy, n. pl., **-dies.** funny dramatic composition.

come·ly, a. handsome.

com·et, n. heavenly body orbiting the sun in eccentric paths.

com·fort, v. soothe; cheer. n. relief in affliction; consolation. **com·fort·a·ble,** a.

com·fort·er, n. light bedcover.

com·fy, a., **-fi·er, -fi·est.** inf. comfortable.

com·ic, a. funny. n. comic actor. **com·i·cal,** a.

com·ic strip, n. series of cartoons.

com·ma, n. pl., **com·mas.** punctuation mark (,).

com·mand, v. direct with authority; order. n. authority; order; ability to control. **com·mand·er,** n.

com·man·deer, v. seize for military or other public use.

com·mand·ment, n. command or mandate.

com·mem·o·rate, v., **-rat·ed, -rat·ing.** honor the memory of. **com·mem·o·ra·tion,** n.

com·mence, v., **-menced, -menc·ing.** begin; start.

com·mence·ment, n. start; graduation ceremony.

com·mend, v. praise; approve. **com·men·da·tion,** n.

com·ment, v. remark upon. n. expression of opinion; remark.

com·men·tar·y, n. pl., **-ies.** series of comments.

com·men·ta·tor, n. one who reports news, weather, etc.

com·merce, n. trade; business.

com·mer·cial, n. radio or television advertisement. a. of commerce.

com·mis·sar·y, n. pl., **-ies.** military or camp store.

com·mis·sion, n. authority; rank of an officer; group authorized to act; agent's service percentage. v. authorize; delegate. **com·mis·sioned,** a. **com·mis·sion·er,** n.

com·mit, v., **-mit·ted, -mit·ting.** give in trust or charge; do; bind by pledge. **com·mit·ment,** n.

com·mit·tee, n. group appointed to report or act on something.

com·mod·i·ty, n. pl., **-ties.** article

of trade or commerce.

com·mon, a. usual; ordinary; joint or united; widespread; vulgar.

com·mon·place, n. common subject or remark. a. ordinary.

com·mon·wealth, n. nation where the people rule.

com·mo·tion, n. disturbance.

com·mune, v., **-muned, -mun·ing.** converse.

com·mu·ni·cate, v., **-cat·ed, -cat·ing.** transmit; make known. **com·mu·ni·ca·ble,** a. **com·mu·ni·ca·tion,** n.

com·mun·ion, n. act of sharing; (often cap.) Eucharist.

com·mun·ism, n. social system based on common ownership. **com·mun·ist,** n.

com·mu·ni·ty, n. pl., **-ties.** body of people of a place.

com·mute, v., **-mut·ed, -mut·ing.** interchange; travel from the suburbs to the city to work. **com·mut·er,** n.

com·pact, n. agreement; face powder case. a. solid; not verbose.

com·pan·ion, n. one who accompanies another; match for a thing.

com·pa·ny, n. pl., **-nies.** individuals associated together; guests; companionship; commercial association.

com·pa·ra·ble, a. Capable of being compared. **com·pa·ra·bil·i·ty.**

com·par·a·tive, a. estimated by comparison.

com·pare, v., **-pared, -par·ing.** contrast one thing with another. **com·pa·ra·ble,** a. **com·par·i·son,** n.

com·part·ment, n. separate part of a general design. v. partition.

com·pass, n. instrument for determining directions; instrument for drawing circles, etc.; range.

com·pas·sion, n. mercy. **com·pas·sion·ate,** a.

com·pat·i·ble, a. in harmony.

com·pa·tri·ot, n. fellow countryman.

com·pel, v., **-pelled, -pel·ling.** urge with force; oblige.

com·pen·sate, v., **-sat·ed, -sat·ing.** make up for; pay for. **com·pen·sa·tion,** n.

com·pete, v., **-pet·ed, -pet·ing.** vie. **com·pet·i·tor,** n.

com·pe·tence, *n.* adequacy.

com·pe·tent, *a.* suitable.

com·pe·ti·tion, *n.* rivalry; trial of skill. **com·pet·i·tive**, *a.*

com·pile, *v.*, -piled, -pil·ing. put (various materials) together. **com·pi·la·tion**, *n.*

com·pla·cence, *n.* self-satisfied. Also **complacency**. **com·pla·cent**, *a.*

com·plain, *v.* express pain, censure, resentment. **com·plaint**, *n.*

com·ple·ment, *n.* that which completes or makes perfect; full quantity. *v.* complete.

com·plete, *a.* having no lack; thorough; finished. *v.*, -plet·ed, -plet·ing. make whole; finish. **com·ple·tion**, *n.*

com·plex, *a.* complicated. *n.* structural whole of many parts; *inf.* fixed idea. **com·plex·i·ty**, *n. pl.*, -ties.

com·plex·ion, *n.* color or hue of the skin.

com·pli·cate, *v.*, -cat·ed, -cat·ing. make complex, or involved. **com·pli·cat·ed**, *a.* **com·pli·ca·tion**, *n.*

com·pli·ment, *n.* expression of admiration; *pl.* good wishes. *v.* praise.

com·pli·men·ta·ry, *a.* expressing a compliment; free.

com·ply, *v.*, -plied, -ply·ing. fulfill; execute; conform. **com·pli·ance**, *n.* **com·pli·ant**, *a.*

com·po·nent, *n.* part.

com·pose, *v.*, -posed, -pos·ing. form by uniting; write; calm. **com·po·si·tion**, *n.*

com·pos·ite, *a.* made up of various parts. *n.* something compound.

com·po·sure, *n.* calmness.

com·pound, *v.* combine. *a.* composite. *n.* thing formed by combining parts.

com·pre·hend, *v.* understand; include. **com·pre·hen·sion**, *n.* **com·pre·hen·sive**, *a.*

com·press, *v.* press together; condense. *n.* soft pad of cloth. **com·pres·sion**, *n.*

com·prise, *v.*, -prised, -pris·ing. include; be made up of.

com·pro·mise, *n.* settlement by concessions. *v.*, -mised, -mis·ing. settle by a compromise; endanger.

comp·trol·ler, *n.* controller.

com·pul·sion, *n.* act of compelling; impulse. **com·pul·sive**, *a.*

com·pul·so·ry, *a.*

com·punc·tion, *n.* qualm.

com·pute, *v.*, -put·ed, -put·ing. calculate. **com·pu·ta·tion**, *n.*

com·put·er, *n.* electronic calculating machine.

com·rade, *n.* companion.

con, *adv.* against.

con·cave, *a.* incurved.

con·ceal, *v.* hide.

con·cede, *v.*, -ced·ed, -ced·ing. admit as true; grant.

con·ceit, *n.* exaggerated opinion of one's own worth.

con·ceit·ed, *a.* vain.

con·ceive, *v.*, -ceived, -ceiv·ing. become pregnant; imagine; think. **con·ceiv·a·ble**, *a.*

con·cen·trate, *v.*, -trat·ed, -trat·ing. direct toward one object; strengthen. **con·cen·tra·tion**, *n.*

con·cept, *n.* general notion or idea. **con·cep·tu·al**, *a.*

con·cep·tion, *n.* inception of life; concept.

con·cern, *v.* interest; involve. *n.* solicitude; anxiety; commercial firm. **con·cerned**, *a.*

con·cern·ing, *prep.* relating to; about.

con·cert, *n.* musical performance; accord or harmony.

con·ces·sion, *n.* act of conceding; that which is conceded.

con·cil·i·ate, *v.*, -at·ed, -at·ing. placate; reconcile. **con·cil·i·a·tion**, *n.*

con·cise, *a.* brief; succinct.

con·clude, *v.*, -clud·ed, -clud·ing. resolve; end. **con·clu·sion**, *n.*

con·coct, *v.* devise; plot; mix. **con·coc·tion**, *n.*

con·cord, *n.* agreement; peace.

con·course, *n.* broad thoroughfare; open space.

con·crete, *a.* not abstract; specific. *n.* artificial stonelike material.

con·cu·bine, *n.* mistress; secondary wife.

con·cur, *v.*, -curred, -cur·ring. agree; coincide. **con·cur·rence**, *n.* **con·cur·rent**, *a.*

con·cus·sion, *n.* shock occasioned by a blow; brain injury. **con·cus·sive**, *a.*

con·demn, *v.* pronounce to be guilty or unfit; doom. **con·dem·na·tion**, *n.*

con·dense, *v.*, -densed, -dens·ing. make more dense; abridge. **con·den·sa·tion**, *n.*

con·de·scend, *v.* lower oneself; patronize. **con·de·scen·sion**, *n.*

con·di·ment, *n.* seasoning.

con·di·tion, *n.* state of being; *pl.* circumstances. *v.* stipulate; subject to particular conditions; put in fit state. **con·di·tion·al**, *a.*

con·do·lence, *n.* sympathy.

con·do·min·i·um, *n.* individually owned apartment.

con·done, *v.*, **-doned**, **-don·ing.** pardon. **con·do·na·tion**, *n.*

con·du·cive, *a.* promoting, or furthering.

con·duct, *v.* lead; manage; direct; behave. *n.* behavior; direction. **con·duc·tor**, *n.*

con·duit, *n.* pipe; tube.

cone, *n.* figure having a circular base, tapering to a point.

con·fec·tion, *n.* candy or preserve. **con·fec·tion·a·ry**, *a.*

con·fed·er·a·cy, *n. pl.*, **-cies.** league or alliance; (cap.) southern states during the U.S. Civil War.

con·fed·er·ate, *a.* united. *n.* ally. **con·fed·er·a·tion**, *n.*

con·fer, *v.*, **-ferred**, **-fer·ring.** bestow; consult. **con·fer·ral**, *n.* **con·fer·ence**, *n.*

con·fess, *v.* admit, as a crime; own to. **con·fes·sion**, *n.* **con·fes·sion·al**, *n.* **con·fes·sor**, *n.*

con·fet·ti, *n. pl.* bits of colored paper thrown at weddings, parties, parades, etc.

con·fide, *v.*, **-fid·ed**, **-fid·ing.** show trust by imparting secrets.

con·fi·dence, *n.* belief in a person or thing; self-reliance; confidential communication. **con·fi·dent**, *a.*

con·fi·den·tial, *a.* secret.

con·fig·u·ra·tion, *n.* external form; conformation.

con·fine, *n. usu. pl.* border; limit. *v.*, **-fined**, **-fin·ing.** limit; imprison. **con·fined**, *a.* **con·fine·ment**, *n.*

con·firm, *v.* strengthen; verify; admit to membership in a church. **con·fir·ma·tion**, *n.*

con·firmed, *a.* fixed; settled.

con·fis·cate, *v.*, **-cat·ed**, **-cat·ing.** appropriate summarily. **con·fis·ca·tion**, *n.*

con·fla·gra·tion, *n.* great fire.

con·flict, *n.* fight; opposition. *v.* struggle; clash.

con·form, *v.* make like; bring into harmony; adapt. **con·form·i·ty**, *n. pl.*, **-ties.**

con·found, *v.* confuse.

con·found·ed, *a. inf.* damned. **con·front**, *v.* face; bring together. **con·fron·ta·tion**, *n.*

con·fuse, *v.*, **-fused**, **-fus·ing.** mix up; bewilder. **con·fus·ed·ly**, *adv.* **con·fu·sion**, *n.*

con·fute, *v.*, **-fut·ed**, **-fut·ing.** prove to be false.

con·geal, *v.* coagulate.

con·gen·ial, *a.* compatible; agreeable.

con·gen·i·tal, *a.* existing from birth.

con·gest, *v.* collect together in undue quantity. **con·ges·tion**, *n.* **con·ges·tive**, *a.*

con·glom·er·ate, *n.* anything composed of heterogeneous elements. **con·glom·er·a·tion**, *n.*

con·grat·u·late, *v.*, **-lat·ed**, **-lat·ing.** express pleasure on some good fortune of another. **con·grat·u·la·tion**, *n. usu. pl.*

con·gre·gate, *v.*, **-gat·ed**, **-gat·ing.** bring together in a crowd; assemble. **con·gre·ga·tion**, *n.*

con·gress, *n.* meeting of representatives; (cap.) U.S. national legislative body. **con·gres·sion·al**, *a.* **con·gress·man**, *n. pl.*, **-men.**

con·ic, *a.* like a cone. **con·i·cal**, *a.*

co·ni·fer, *n.* cone-bearing tree, as the pine, fir, etc.

con·jec·ture, *n.* guess. *v.*, **-tured**, **-tur·ing.** surmise; guess. **con·jec·tur·al**, *a.*

con·ju·gate, *v.*, **-gat·ed**, **-gat·ing.** inflect (a verb).

con·junc·tion, *n.* union; word serving to unite words.

con·jure, *v.*, **-jured**, **-jur·ing.** adjure; affect or effect by magic. **con·jur·er**, **con·jur·or**, *n.*

con·nect, *v.* link; bring into relation; join. **con·nec·tion**, *n.*

con·nive, *v.*, **-nived**, **-niv·ing.** cooperate secretly.

con·nois·seur, *n.* one competent to judge in an art or in matters of taste.

con·note, *v.*, **-not·ed**, **-not·ing.** denote secondarily; imply. **con·no·ta·tion**, *n.*

con·quer, *v.* be victorious. **con·quer·or**, *n.* **con·quest**, *n.*

con·science, *n.* faculty which decides right and wrong.

con·sci·en·tious, *a.* painstaking; careful.

con·scious, *a.* aware; mentally alert; intentional.

con·se·crate, *v.*, **-crat·ed**, **-crat·**

ing. hallow. **con·se·cra·tive**, *a.*
con·se·cra·tion, *n.*

con·sec·u·tive, *a.* successive.
con·sec·u·tive·ly, *adv.*

con·sen·sus, *n.* majority of opinion.

con·sent, *v.* agree. *n.* permission; agreement.

con·se·quence, *n.* result.

con·se·quent, *a.* resulting. **con·se·quent·ly**, *adv.*

con·serv·a·tive, *a.* opposed to radical changes; moderate. *n.* conservative person.

con·serv·a·to·ry, *n. pl.*, **-ries.** greenhouse; school for the arts.

con·serve, *v.*, **-served, -serv·ing.** keep safe; preserve. **con·ser·va·tion**, *n.*

con·sid·er, *v.* think on with care; respect; take into account; judge to be. **con·sid·er·ate**, *a.* **con·sid·er·a·tion**, *n.*

con·sid·er·a·ble, *a.* important; large. **con·sid·er·a·bly**, *adv.*

con·sid·er·ing, *prep.* taking into account; in view of.

con·sign, *v.* transfer; deliver; entrust. **con·sign·ment**, *n.*

con·sist, *v.* be composed or to be made up (with *of*).

con·sist·en·cy, *n. pl.*, **-cies.** coherence; degree of density; agreement. **con·sist·ent**, *a.*

con·sole, *v.*, **-soled, -sol·ing.** comfort; solace. **con·sol·a·ble**, *a.* **con·so·la·tion**, *n.*

con·sol·i·date, *v.*, **-dat·ed, -dat·ing.** unite; combine. **con·sol·i·da·tion**, *n.*

con·so·nant, *n.* letter representing a speech sound produced by partial closure of the breath canal.

con·sort, *n.* intimate associate. *v.* associate.

con·spic·u·ous, *a.* easy to be seen; noteworthy.

con·spire, *v.*, **-spired, -spir·ing.** plot. **con·spir·a·cy**, *n. pl.*, **-cies.** **con·spir·a·tor**, *n.*, *a.*

con·sta·ble, *n.* policeman. **con·stab·u·lar·y**, *n. pl.*, **-ies.**

con·stant, *a.* invariable; continuing; steadfast. *n.* something constant. **con·stan·cy**, *n.* **con·stant·ly**, *adv.*

con·stel·la·tion, *n.* group of fixed stars.

con·ster·na·tion, *n.* dismay.

con·sti·pa·tion, *n.* difficult evacuation of the bowels. **con·sti·pate**, *v.*

con·stit·u·ent, *a.* constituting. *n.* essential part; voter.

con·sti·tute, *v.* compose; form.

con·sti·tu·tion, *n.* make·up; fundamental principles. **con·sti·tu·tion·al**, *a.*

con·strain, *v.* force; confine. **con·straint**, *n.*

con·struct, *v.* form; build. **con·struc·tive**, *a.* **con·struc·tion**, *n.*

con·strue, *v.*, **-strued, -stru·ing.** interpret; infer.

con·sul, *n.* country's agent residing in a foreign city. **con·su·late**, *n.*

con·sult, *v.* seek advice; take counsel together. **con·sult·ant**, *n.* **con·sul·ta·tion**, *n.*

con·sume, *v.*, **-sumed, -sum·ing.** destroy; use up; eat up. **con·sum·er**, *n.*

con·sum·mate, *v.*, **-mat·ed, -mat·ing.** fulfill; complete. **con·sum·ma·tion**, *n.*

con·sump·tion, *n.* act of consuming; that consumed.

con·tact, *n.* touch; connection.

con·ta·gion, *n.* communication of disease. **con·ta·gious**, *a.*

con·tain, *v.* have within itself; be capable of holding; restrain. **con·tain·er**, *n.*

con·tam·i·nate, *v.*, **-nat·ed, -nat·ing.** defile; pollute. **con·tam·i·na·tion**, *n.*

con·tem·plate, *v.*, **-plat·ed, -plat·ing.** observe; consider; intend; expect. **con·tem·pla·tion**, *n.* **con·tem·pla·tive**, *a.*

con·tem·po·rar·y, *a.* existing at the same time. *n. pl.*, **-rar·ies.** those living at the same time.

con·tempt, *n.* disdain; scorn; disgrace; disrespect. **con·tempt·i·ble**, *a.*

con·temp·tu·ous, *a.* scornful.

con·tend, *v.* struggle; strive in rivalry; assert.

con·tent, *a.* satisfied; easy in mind. *n.* satisfaction; *usu. pl.* that which is contained; capacity. **con·tent·ed**, *a.*

con·test, *v.* dispute; struggle for; compete. *n.* struggle; dispute. **con·test·ant**, *n.*

con·ti·nent, *n.* main land mass. **con·ti·nen·tal**, *a.*

con·tin·gent, *a.* accidental; uncertain. *n.* quota. **con·tin·gen·cy**, *n. pl.*, **-cies.**

con·tin·ue, *v.*, **-ued, -u·ing.** endure; keep on; go on after interruption. **con·tin·u·al**, *a.* **con·tin·u·a·tion**, *n.* **con·tin·u·**

ous, *a.*

con·tort, *v.* bend out of shape. **con·tor·tion,** *n.*

con·tour, *n.* outline of a figure or body.

con·tra·band, *n.* illegal traffic; smuggling.

con·tra·cep·tive, *a.* preventing impregnation. *n.* contraceptive agent. **con·tra·cep·tion,** *n.*

con·tract, *v.* reduce; acquire; shrink; make a mutual agreement. *n.* enforceable pact. **con·trac·tion,** *n.* **con·trac·tor,** *n.*

con·tra·dict, *v.* assert to be contrary to what has been asserted. **con·tra·dic·tion,** *n.* **con·tra·dic·to·ry,** *a.*

con·tral·to, *n. pl.,* **-tos** or **-ti.** lowest female voice.

con·trap·tion, *n. inf.* contrivance; gadget.

con·tra·ry, *a.* opposite; different; stubborn. *n. pl.,* **-ries.** that which is opposite.

con·trast, *v.* compare by observing differences; set off. *n.* difference.

con·trib·ute, *v.,* **-ut·ed, -ut·ing.** give; pay as a share. **con·tri·bu·tion,** *n.*

con·trite, *a.* penitent. **con·trite·ly,** *adv.* **con·tri·tion,** *n.*

con·trive, *v.,* **-trived, -triv·ing.** plan; invent; manage. **con·triv·ance,** *n.*

con·trol, *v.,* **-trolled, -trol·ling.** regulate; dominate; curb. *n.* act or power of controlling. **con·trol·ler,** *n.*

con·tro·ver·sy, *n. pl.,* **-sies.** dispute; quarrel. **con·tro·ver·sial,** *a.*

con·fuse, *v.,* **-fused, -fus·ing.** bruise. **con·tu·sion,** *n.*

con·va·lesce, *v.,* **-lesced, -lesc·ing.** grow better after sickness. **con·va·les·cence,** *n.* **con·va·les·cent,** *a.*

con·vene, *v.,* **-vened, -ven·ing.** assemble. **con·ven·er,** *n.*

con·ven·ience, *n.* quality of being convenient.

con·ven·ient, *a.* agreeable to the needs or purpose; easily done; near.

con·vent, *n.* dwelling for nuns.

con·ven·tion, *n.* assembly; rule. **con·ven·tion·al,** *a.*

con·verge, *v.,* **-verged, -verg·ing.** meet in a point. **con·ver·gence,** *n.* **con·ver·gent,** *a.*

con·ver·sant, *a.* knowledgeable or experienced.

con·ver·sa·tion, *n.* informal talk. **con·ver·sa·tion·al,** *a.*

con·verse, *v.,* **-versed, -vers·ing.** talk. *n.* conversation; opposite or contrary.

con·vert, *v.* change from one condition, belief, etc., to another. *n.* one converted. **con·ver·sion,** *n.*

con·vert·i·ble, *n.* car with a collapsible top.

con·vex, *a.* denoting a surface that is curved outward.

con·vey, *v.* carry or transport; transmit. **con·vey·ance,** *n.*

con·vict, *v.* prove guilty. *n.* person serving a prison term.

con·vic·tion, *n.* state of being convicted; fixed belief.

con·vince, *v.,* **-vinced, -vinc·ing.** satisfy by argument, proof, etc. **con·vinc·ing,** *a.*

con·viv·i·al, *a.* jovial.

con·vo·ca·tion, *n.* assembly.

con·voy, *v.* escort. *n.* escort, esp. for protection.

con·vulse, *v.,* **-vulsed, -vuls·ing.** shake violently. **con·vul·sion,** *n.* **con·vul·sive,** *a.*

coo, *v.,* **cooed, coo·ing.** utter the soft sound of pigeons or doves. *n.* cooing sound.

cook, *v.* prepare food by the action of heat. *n.* chef.

cook·ie, cook·y, *n. pl.,* **cook·ies.** small, flat, sweet cake.

cool, *a.* moderately cold; calm; unmoved. *v.* make or become cool. **cool·ness,** *n.* **cool·er,** *n.*

coop, *n.* pen for poultry. *v.* confine.

co·op·er·ate, *v.,* **-at·ed, -at·ing.** work or act together. **co·op·er·a·tion,** *n.* **co·op·er·a·tive,** *a.*

co·or·di·nate, *v.,* **-nat·ed, -nat·ing.** arrange; act in harmonious combination. **co·or·di·na·tion,** *n.*

coot·ie, *n. inf.* louse.

cop, *v.,* **copped, cop·ping.** *inf.* catch; steal. *n.* policeman.

cope, *v.,* **coped, cop·ing.** deal with successfully.

co·pi·ous, *a.* abundant; plentiful. **co·pi·ous·ness,** *n.*

cop·per, *n.* malleable, reddish-brown metal. **cop·per·y,** *a.*

copse, *n.* wood of small trees.

cop·u·late, *v.,* **-lat·ed, -lat·ing.** have sexual intercourse. **cop·u·la·tion,** *n.*

cop·y, *n. pl.,* **cop·ies.** reproduction of an original (book, engraving, etc.). *v.,* **cop·ied, cop-**

y·ing. imitate.

cop·y·right, n. author's exclusive right of property to his work.

co·quette, n. flirt.

cor·al, n. hard, limy skeletons of sea animals forming reefs.

cord, n. string or small rope; measure of cut wood 128 cu. ft. **corded,** a.

cor·dial, a. courteous; warm. **cor·dial·i·ty,** n.

cor·do·van, a. designating a kind of fine leather.

cor·du·roy, n. thick, ribbed cotton fabric. a. of corduroy.

core, n. central part, as of fruit. v., **cored, cor·ing.** remove the core.

cork, n. outer bark of an oak; stopper. v. stop with a cork.

cork·screw, n. device used to draw corks from bottles. a. spiral.

corn, n. tall cereal plant grown for its edible kernels borne on ears; horny thickening of the skin.

cor·ner, n. meeting place of two converging lines or surfaces; region. v. force into an awkward position.

cor·net, n. brass wind instrument related to the trumpet.

cor·nice, n. horizontal molded projection which crowns a wall or building.

corn·starch, n. starchy flour made from corn.

cor·nu·co·pi·a, n. horn overflowing with flowers and fruit, symbolizing plenty.

co·rol·la, n. part of a flower, composed of petals.

cor·ol·lar·y, n. pl., **-ies.** inference; natural consequence or result.

co·ro·na, n. pl., **-nas, -nae.** circle of light; crown, as of a tooth.

cor·o·nar·y, a. referring to the arteries supplying blood to the heart. n. coronary thrombosis.

cor·o·na·tion, n. crowning of a sovereign.

cor·o·ner, n. local officer who investigates, by inquest before a jury (coroner's jury) unnatural deaths.

cor·po·ral, a. of the body.

cor·po·ral, n. noncommissioned officer.

cor·po·rate, a. united in one body. **cor·po·ra·tive,** a.

cor·po·ra·tion, n. number of persons under authority of law, operating as a single person in business.

corps, n. pl., **corps.** organized (military) group.

corpse, n. dead body.

cor·pu·lent, a. portly. **cor·pulence, cor·pu·len·cy,** n.

cor·pus·cle, n. particle of the blood. **cor·pus·cu·lar,** a.

cor·ral, n. pen for horses and cattle. v., **-ralled, -ral·ling.** confine in a corral; seize.

cor·rect, v. set right; mark the errors in; punish. a. proper; accurate. **cor·rec·tion,** n.

cor·re·late, v., **-lat·ed, -lat·ing.** place in or bring into mutual relation. **cor·re·la·tion,** n.

cor·re·spond, v. be in agreement; exchange letters. **cor·re·spond·ing,** a. **cor·re·spond·ence,** n. **cor·re·spond·ent,** a., n.

cor·ri·dor, n. hall.

cor·rob·o·rate, v., **-rat·ed, -rat·ing.** confirm. **cor·rob·o·ra·tion,** n.

cor·rode, v., **-rod·ed, -rod·ing.** eat or wear away. **cor·ro·sion,** n. **cor·ro·sive,** a.

cor·ru·gate, v., **-gat·ed, -gat·ing.** bend into folds. **cor·ru·ga·tion,** n.

cor·rupt, v. contaminate; weaken morally; bribe. a. corrupted. **cor·rup·tion,** n.

cor·sage, n. bouquet worn by a woman.

cor·set, n. supporting undergarment. **cor·set·ed,** a.

cos·met·ic, a. beautifying. n. beautifying preparation.

cos·mic, a. of the cosmos; immeasurably large.

cos·mo·pol·i·tan, a. belonging to all parts of the world. n. person who feels at home everywhere.

cos·mos, n. universe thought of as a system of order and harmony.

cost, n. price; loss or penalty. v., **cost or cost·ed, cost·ing.** require an expenditure.

cost·ly, a., **-li·er, -li·est.** costing much. **cost·li·ness,** n.

cos·tume, n. dress belonging to another period or place.

cot, n. light portable bed.

cot·tage, n. small dwelling.

cot·ton, n. soft white fibers of the cotton plant; cloth or thread made of this. a. of cotton. **cot·ton·y,** a.

couch, n. sofa.

cough, n. loud expulsion of air from the lungs. v. expel air from the lungs.

could, past form of can.

could·n't, could not.

coun·cil, n. governing body. **coun·cil·or, coun·cil·man,** n.

coun·sel, n. advice; lawyer. v., **-seled, -sel·ing.** advise. **coun·sel·ing,** n. **coun·se·lor,** n.

count, v. reach a total; name (numerals) in order; consider; be of value. n. act of counting; result of counting; nobleman. **count·a·ble,** a.

coun·te·nance, n. face; appearance or expression of the face. v., **-nanced, -nanc·ing.** allow; support.

count·er, n. table on which goods are laid; flat serving area; working space. a., adv. contrary. v. oppose.

coun·ter·act, v. oppose; withstand. **coun·ter·ac·tive,** a.

coun·ter·feit, a. not genuine; forged. n. imitation; forgery. v. imitate with intent to defraud. **coun·ter·feit·er,** n.

coun·ter·part, n. copy; thing which fits together.

coun·ter·sign, n. signature added to another signature, as for authentication. v. ratify.

coun·tess, n. wife of a count.

count·less, a. innumerable.

coun·tri·fied, a. rustic.

coun·try, n. pl., **-tries.** land; nation; rural districts. a. rural.

coun·ty, n. pl., **-ties.** administrative division of a state.

coup, n. pl., **coups.** stroke.

cou·ple, n. pair; man and wife; partners; inf. few. v., **-pled, -pling.** unite.

cou·pon, n. ticket which gives something of value when redeemed.

cour·age, n. fearlessness; bravery. **cou·ra·geous,** a.

cour·i·er, n. messenger.

course, n. path along which anything moves; customary manner of procedure; prescribed series, as of studies; part of a meal.

court, n. courtyard; retinue of a sovereign; place where justice is administered; any judicial body; space for games. v. woo.

cour·te·ous, a. polite.

cour·te·sy, n. pl., **-sies.** politeness; favor.

court·ly, a., **-li·er, -li·est.** dignified. **court·li·ness,** n.

court-mar·tial, n. pl., **courts-mar·tial.** trial in a military court. v., **-mar·tialed, -mar·tial·ing.** try by court-martial.

court·ship, n. period during which wooing takes place.

cous·in, n. son or daughter of an uncle or aunt.

cove, n. small sheltered bay.

cov·e·nant, n. agreement.

cov·er, v. put something over or upon as for protection or concealment. n. that which covers. **cov·ered,** a.

cov·er·let, n. bedspread.

cov·ert, a. concealed. **cov·ert·ly,** adv. **cov·ert·ness,** n.

cov·et, v. wish for eagerly.

cov·et·ous, a. eager to possess that to which one has no right. **cov·et·ous·ness,** n.

cow, n. pl., **cows.** female of a bovine animal, or of other animals, as the elephant. v. intimidate.

cow·ard, n. one who lacks courage. **cow·ard·ice,** n.

cow·boy, n. man who looks after cattle.

cow·er, v. stoop, as from fear.

cowl, n. hooded garment worn by monks; hood. **cowl·ed,** a.

coy, a. shy; modest. **coy·ly,** adv. **coy·ness,** n.

coy·o·te, n. prairie wolf.

co·zy, a., **-zi·er, -zi·est.** snug; comfortable. **co·zi·ness,** n.

crab, n. short, broad crustacean; ill-tempered person. v., **crabbed, crab·bing.** grumble. **crab·by,** a.

crab ap·ple, n. small, sour wild apple.

crack, v. break; snap; cause to make a sharp sudden noise. n. chink; burst of sound; flaw.

crack·er, n. crisp biscuit.

crack·le, v., **-led, -ling.** make slight, sharp noises; change by forming tiny surface cracks. n. act of crackling.

cra·dle, n. baby's bed that rocks. v., **-dled, -dling.** rock, as in a cradle.

craft, n. skill; trade; vessel.

crafts·man, n. pl., **-men.** artisan. **crafts·man·ship,** n.

craft·y, a., **-i·er, -i·est.** cunning; sly. **craft·i·ness,** n.

crag, n. steep, rugged rock. **crag·ged,** a. **crag·gy,** a.

cram, *v.*, **crammed**, **cram·ming**. stuff hastily; prepare hurriedly for a test.

cramp, *v.* restrict. *n.* painful contraction of a muscle; violent abdominal pain; *pl.* continuing abdominal pain.

cran·ber·ry, *n. pl.*, **-ries**. plant with a red, acid fruit.

crane, *n.* large wading bird; device for moving heavy weights. *v.*, **craned**, **cran·ing**. stretch (the neck).

crank, *n.* device for conveying motion; *inf.* eccentric. *v.* move with a crank.

crank·y, *a.*, **-i·er**, **-i·est**. ill-tempered. **crank·i·ness**, *n.*

craps, *n.* dice game.

crash, *v.* shatter. *n.* breaking with loud noise; falling to ruin.

crass, *a.* gross. **crass·ness**, *n.*

crate, *n.* openwork casing.

cra·ter, *n.* hole, pit, etc., in the ground. **cra·tered**, *a.*

cra·vat, *n.* necktie.

crave, *v.*, **craved**, **crav·ing**. long for; beg. **crav·ing**, *n.*

cra·ven, *a.* cowardly. *n.* coward. **cra·ven·ly**, *adv.*

crawl, *v.* move slowly on the hands and knees; creep along the ground. *n.* slow creeping motion. **crawl·y**, *a.*

cray·fish, *n. pl.*, **-fish·es**, **-fish**. small crustacean.

cray·on, *n.* pencil of colored wax.

cra·zy, *a.*, **-zi·er**, **-zi·est**. *inf.* insane; eccentric.

creak, *v.* make a sharp, grating sound. *n.*

cream, *n.* fatty part of milk; emulsified cosmetic; best part. **cream·y**, *a.*, **-i·er**, **-i·est**.

crease, *n.* line or mark made by folding. *v.*, **creased**, **creas·ing**. make a crease in.

cre·ate, *v.*, **cre·at·ed**, **cre·at·ing**. bring into being. **cre·a·tion**, *n.* **cre·a·tive**, *a.* **cre·a·tor**, *n.*

crea·ture, *n.* animate being.

cre·den·tial, *n.* claim to confidence; *pl.* documents giving a person belief.

cred·it, *v.* believe; give credit for. *n.* approval or honor; selling or lending on the basis of future payment; recorded acknowledgment. **cred·it·a·ble**, *a.* **cred·i·tor**, *n.*

cre·do, *n. pl.*, **-dos**. creed.

cred·u·lous, *a.* apt to believe without evidence.

creed, *n.* formula of belief.

creek, *n.* small stream.

creep, *v.*, **crept**, **creep·ing**. move along the ground; move slowly. *n. slang.* obnoxious person. **creep·y**, *a.*

cre·mate, *v.*, **-mat·ed**, **-mat·ing**. burn a corpse. **cre·ma·tion**, *n.*

crêpe, *n.* thin, crinkled fabric of silk, cotton, etc.

cres·cent, *n.* crescent moon.

crest, *n.* head; top; summit; ridgelike formation.

cre·vasse, *n.* fissure.

crev·ice, *n.* crack.

crew, *n.* persons engaged upon a particular work.

crib, *n.* child's bed; pen.

crick·et, *n.* chirping insect.

crime, *n.* serious violation of human law; sin.

crim·i·nal, *a.* of crime. *n.* person guilty of crime.

crim·son, *a.*, *n.* deep red.

cringe, *v.*, **cringed**, **cring·ing**. shrink, from fear; cower.

crin·kle, *v.*, **-kled**, **-kling**. wrinkle; rustle. **crin·kly**, *a.*, **-i·er**, **-i·est**.

crip·ple, *n.* partially disabled person. *v.*, **-pled**, **-pling**. disable.

cri·sis, *n. pl.*, **cri·ses**. turning point.

crisp, *a.* brittle; fresh; brisk. **crisp·ness**, *n.*

cri·te·ri·on, *n. pl.*, **-ri·a**, **cri·te·ri·ons**. standard.

crit·ic, *n.* reviewer.

crit·i·cal, *a.* inclined to find fault; pertaining to crisis; important.

crit·i·cize, *v.*, **-cized**, **-ciz·ing**. judge critically; find faults. **crit·i·cism**, *n.*

croak, *v.* make the noise of a frog. *n.* low, harsh sound.

cro·chet, *v.*, **-cheted**, **-chet·ing**. knit with a small hook.

crock·er·y, *n.* earthenware.

croc·o·dile, *n.* reptile similar to an alligator.

cro·cus, *n. pl.*, **-cus·es**, **-ci**. small bulbous plant with a solitary flower.

crook, *n.* hook; *inf.* swindler, or thief. **crook·ed**, *a.*

croon, *v.* sing softly.

crop, *n.* cultivated produce; riding whip. *v.*, **cropped**, **crop·ping**. cut off; clip.

cro·quet, *n.* lawn game played by knocking wooden balls through wickets.

cro·quette, *n.* ball of fried meat or fish.

cross, *n.* figure formed by two lines crossing; hybrid. *a.* ill-humored. *v.* draw or run across; pass from side to side of; clash with. **cross·ly**, *adv.*

cross·ex·am·ine, *v.*, **-ined**, **-in·ing**. examine (a witness).

cross·road, *n.* road that crosses another; *pl.* place where roads intersect.

cross·wise, *a., adv.* across. Also **cross·ways**.

crotch, *n.* part where the legs are joined.

crouch, *v.* bend or stoop low.

crow, *n.* black bird; cry of a rooster. *v.* make the sound of a cock; gloat.

crow·bar, *n.* metal bar, used as a lever.

crowd, *n.* throng. *v.* push or shove; fill full.

crown, *n.* decorative covering for the head of a monarch; exalting attribute; top. *v.* invest with regal dignity and power.

cru·cial, *a.* critical.

cru·ci·ble, *n.* vessel for melting or heating metals.

cru·ci·fix, *n.* cross.

cru·ci·fy, *v.*, **-fied**, **-fy·ing**. put to death by nailing to a cross. **cru·ci·fix·ion**, *n.*

crude, *a.*, **crud·er**, **crud·est**. raw; lacking in culture.

cru·el, *a.* causing pain, grief, etc. **cru·el·ty**, *n.*

cruise, *v.*, **cruised**, **cruis·ing**. sail from place to place. **cruis·er**, *n.*

crumb, *n.* small particle.

crum·ble, *v.*, **-bled**, **-bling**. break into crumbs; fragment. **crum·bly**, *a.*, **-bli·er**, **-bli·est**.

crum·ple, *v.*, **-pled**, **-pling**. rumple. **crum·ply**, *a.*

crunch, *v.* crush or grind noisily. *n.* act or sound of crunching. **crunch·y**, *a.*, **-i·er**, **-i·est**.

cru·sade, *n.* aggressive movement for the defense of an idea or cause. *v.*, **-sad·ed**, **-sad·ing**. go on a crusade. **cru·sad·er**, *n.*

crush, *v.* crumple; overpower. *n.* crushing; *inf.* intense infatuation. **crush·ing**, *a.*

crust, *n.* hard outer portion of bread or pie. *v.* form a crust. **crus·tal**, *a.*

crus·ta·cean, *n.* hard-shelled (aquatic) animal.

crust·y, *a.*, **-i·er**, **-i·est**. of crust; surly. **crust·i·ness**, *n.*

crutch, *n.* forked support.

cry, *v.*, **cried**, **cry·ing**. call loudly; shout; shed tears. *n. pl.*, **cries**. act or sound of crying; shout; fit of weeping; call of an animal. **cry·ing**, *a.*

crypt, *n.* burial vault.

cryp·tic, *a.* hidden; secret.

crys·tal, *n.* clear, transparent mineral; glass of a high degree of brilliance. *a.* of crystal.

crys·tal·lize, *v.*, **-lized**, **-liz·ing**. form crystals; *fig.* give definite form to. **crys·tal·li·za·tion**, *n.*

cub, *n.* young of the fox, bear, etc.

cube, *n.* solid bounded by six equal squares; third power of a quantity. *v.*, **cubed**, **cub·ing**. raise to the third power; find the cube of. **cu·bic**, *a.*

cuck·oo, *n. pl.*, **-oos**. migratory bird, noted for its call.

cu·cum·ber, *n.* plant, yielding a long fleshy fruit.

cud, *n.* regurgitated food.

cud·dle, *v.*, **-dled**, **-dling**. hug tenderly; nestle. **cud·dle·some**, *a.* **cud·dly**, *a.*

cudg·el, *n.* club. *v.*, **-eled**, **-eling**. beat.

cue, *n.* guiding hint or suggestion; long line of people; rod used in pool.

cuff, *n.* fold or band on a garment; blow with the fist. *v.* strike with the fist.

cu·li·nar·y, *a.* of cooking.

cull, *v.* pick; gather.

cul·mi·nate, *v.*, **-nat·ed**, **-nat·ing**. reach the highest point; finish; end. **cul·mi·na·tion**, *n.*

cul·prit, *n.* person charged with a crime; one guilty of an offense.

cult, *n.* system of religious worship; sect. **cul·tic**, *a.*

cul·ti·vate, *v.*, **-vat·ed**, **-vat·ing**. prepare land for raising a crop; train; refine. **cul·ti·va·tion**, *n.*

cul·ture, *n.* behavior and technology of any people; acquired ability of appreciating excellence; civilization. *v.*, **-tured**, **-tur·ing**. cultivate; develop. **cul·tur·al**, *a.*

cul·vert, *n.* drain; sewer.

cum·ber, *v.* overload; obstruct. **cum·ber·some**, *a.*

cu·mu·late, *v.*, **-lat·ed**, **-lat·ing**. heap up; amass. **cu·mu·la·tion**, *n.*

cun·ning, *n.* craftiness; guile. *a.* showing ingenuity; crafty.

cup, *n.* small, open vessel, used to drink from; quantity of a cup. *v.*, **cupped**, **cup·ping**. take or place in or as in a cup. **cupped**, *a.*

cup·cake, *n.* cup-shaped cake.

cup·ful, *n. pl.*, **-fuls**. amount that a cup holds.

cu·pid·i·ty, *n.* avarice.

cur, *n.* worthless dog.

curb, *n.* restraint; border along a street. *v.* check.

curd, *n.* (*often pl.*) coagulat sour milk.

cur·dle, *v.*, **-dled**, **-dling**. thicken into curd; go bad.

cure, *v.*, **cured**, **cur·ing**. restore to health; prepare for preservation. *n.* healing.

cur·few, *n.* order for being inside at a specified hour.

cu·ri·os·i·ty, *n. pl.*, **-ties**. inquisitiveness. **cu·ri·ous**, *a.*

curl, *v.* form curls, as the hair; coil. *n.* ringlet; coil.

curl·y, *a.*, **-i·er**, **-i·est**. having curls. **curl·i·ness**, *n.*

cur·rant, *n.* small, round fruit of certain shrubs.

cur·ren·cy, *n. pl.*, **-cies**. circulation; money.

cur·rent, *a.* generally accepted; of the present time. *n.* that which flows.

cur·ric·u·lum, *n. pl.*, **-lums**, **-la**. course of study.

cur·ry, *n. pl.*, **-ries**. curry powder. *v.*, **-ried**, **-ry·ing**. rub and clean (a horse).

curse, *v.*, **cursed** or **curst**, **cursing**. utter a wish of evil against; swear. *n.* malediction; torment.

cur·so·ry, *a.* rapidly done.

curt, *a.* brief or terse. **curt·ly**, *adv.* **curt·ness**, *n.*

cur·tail, *v.* cut short; diminish. **cur·tail·ment**, *n.*

cur·tain, *n.* movable hanging piece of material. *v.* provide, shut off, or adorn with a curtain.

curt·sy, *n. pl.*, **-sies**. bow, of a bending of the knees. *v.*, **-sied**, **-sy·ing**. make a curtsy.

curve, *n.* continuously bending line; any curved outline. *v.*, **curved**, **curv·ing**. bend in a curve. *a.* curved.

cush·ion, *n.* baglike case; pillow. *v.* furnish with a cushion.

cus·tard, *n.* mixture of milk, eggs, and sweetening.

cus·to·di·an, *n.* caretaker.

cus·to·dy, *n. pl.*, **-dies**. guardianship; imprisonment.

cus·tom, *n.* habitual practice; convention; duty. *a.* made to order. **cus·tom·ar·y**, *a.*

cus·tom·er, *n.* one who shops.

cut, *v.*, **cut**, **cut·ting**. divide; sever; shorten; carve; wound the feelings of; cross. *n.* cutting; wound caused by cutting; manner. *a.* that has been cut; diluted. **cut·ting**, *a.*, *n.*

cute, *a.*, **cut·er**, **cut·est**. *inf.* pleasing or attractive; clever. **cute·ness**, *n.*

cu·ti·cle, *n.* non-living skin around the nails.

cut·ler·y, *n.* knives and other cutting instruments.

cut·let, *n.* slice of meat for broiling or frying.

cut·rate, *a.* sold or selling below the usual price.

cut·throat, *n.* murderer. *a.* murderous; cruel; ruthless.

cy·a·nide, *n.* poison.

cyc·la·men, *n.* plant of the primrose family, with very handsome flowers.

cy·cle, *n.* complete recurring course or series; bicycle, tricycle, or the like. *v.*, **cy·cled**, **cy·cling**. move in cycles; ride a bicycle. **cy·clic**, *a.* **cy·cli·cal·ly**, *adv.*

cy·clist, *n.* one who rides a cycle.

cy·clone, *n.* violent windstorm or tornado.

cy·clo·tron, *n.* accelerator which whirls charged particles at very high speeds.

cyg·net, *n.* young swan.

cyl·in·der, *n.* figure having curved sides and two parallel circular bases. **cy·lin·dric**, **cy·lin·dri·cal**, *a.*

cym·bal, *n.* circular, brass musical instrument. **cym·bal·ist**, *n.*

cyn·ic, *n.* one who disbelieves in goodness. **cyn·i·cism**, *n.* **cyn·i·cal**, *a.*

cy·press, *n.* evergreen tree; its hard wood.

cyst, *n.* abnormal sac containing fluid. **cys·tic**, *a.*

czar, *n.* Russian emperor; autocrat. Also **tsar**, **tzar**.

cza·ri·na, *n.* czar's wife.

D

dab, *v.t.*, **dabbed**, **dab·bing**. apply lightly. *n.* quick, light blow. **dab·ber**, *n.*

dab·ble, *v.*, **-bled**, **-bling**. spatter. **dab·bler**, *n.*

dad, *n. Inf.* father. Also **dad·dy**, *pl.* **dad·dies**.

daft, *a.* crazy.

dag·ger, *n.* weapon with a short, sharp-pointed blade.

dai·ly, *a.* each day. *adv.* every day.

dain·ty, *a.*, **-ti·er**, **-ti·est**. delicately beautiful. *n. pl.*, **-ties.** a delicacy. **dain·ti·ly**, *adv.* **dain·ti·ness**, *n.*

dair·y, *n. pl.* **dair·ies**. where milk and cream are made and sold. **dair·y·man**, *n. pl.*, **-men.**

da·is, *n.* platform.

dale, *n.* valley.

dal·ly, *v.i.*, **-lied**, **-ly·ing**. waste time; flirt. **dal·li·ance**, *n.*

dam, *n.* barrier to obstruct the flow of a liquid. *v.t.*, **dammed**, **dam·ming**.

dam·age, *n.* injury to person, property, character, etc. *v.*, **-aged**, **-aging**. injure. **dam·age·a·ble**, *a.*

damn, *v.* condemn. *adv.*, *adj.* damned. **dam·na·ble**, *a.* **dam·na·ble·ness**, *n.* **dam·na·bly**, *adv.* **dam·na·tion**, *n.*

damned, *a.* condemned.

damp, *a.* moist. humid. **damp·en**, *v.*

dance, *v.*, **danced**, **danc·ing**. move rhythmically. **dan·cer**, *n.*

dan·der, *n.* temper.

dan·druff, *n.* scurf on the scalp.

dan·ger, *n.* exposure to ruin; a cause of risk. **dan·ger·ous**, *a.* **dan·ger·ous·ly**, *adv.* **dan·ger·ous·ness**, *n.*

dan·gle, *v.*, **-gled**, **-gling**. hang loose. **dan·gler**, *n.*

dank, *a.* humid. **dank·ly**, *adv.* **dank·ness**, *n.*

dap·ple, *n.* spots of coloring. *v.*, **-pled**, **-pling**. **dap·pled**, *a.*

dare, *v.*, **dared**, **dared**, **daring**. have the necessary courage. **dar·ing**, *n.* **dar·ing·ly**, *adv.*

dark, *a.* devoid of light.

dark·en, *v.* make or become dark. **dark·ish**, *a.* **dark·ly**, *adv.* **dark·ness**, *n.*

dar·ling, *n.* a person very dear. **dar·ling·ly**, *adv.* **dar·ling·ness**, *n.*

darn, *v.* mend or sew. **darn·er**, *n.*

dash, *v.* strike violently. *n.* violent stroke; a mark of punctuation.

dash·board, *n.* instrument panel of an automobile or airplane.

das·tard, *n.* a coward. **das·tard·li·ness**, *n.* **das·tard·ly**, *a.*

date, *n.* a statement of time. *v.t.*, **dat·ed**, **dat·ing**. append the date to. *v.i.* reckon time. **dat·a·ble**, *a.* **dat·er**, *n.*

daub, *v.* besmear. **daub·er**, *n.*

daugh·ter, *n.* in relation to her real or adopted parents, a female child. **daugh·ter·ly**, *a.*

daugh·ter-in-law, *n. pl.*, **daugh·ters-in-law**. a son's wife.

daunt·less, *a.* bold. **daunt·less·ly**, *adv.* **daunt·less·ness**, *n.*

daw·dle, *v.*, **-dled**, **-dling**. waste time. **daw·dler**, *n.*

dawn, *v.i.* grow light; begin to develop. *n.* daybreak.

day, *n.* time between sunrise and sunset.

day·break, *n.* dawn.

day-dream, *n.* reverie. **day-dream·er**, *n.*

day·light, *n.* light of day.

day·time, *n.* time of daylight.

daze, *v.t.*, **dazed**, **daz·ing**. stun. *n.* state of being dazed. **daz·ed·ly**, *adv.*

daz·zle, *v.*, **-zled**, **-zling**. overpower by intense light. **daz·zler**, *n.* **daz·zling·ly**, *adv.*

dea·con, *n.* lay church official; member of the clerical order below a priest. **dea·con·ry**, *n.* **dea·con·ship**, *n. fem.* **dea·con·ess**.

dead, *a.* devoid of life.

dead·en, *v.* dull. **dead·en·er**, *n.*

dead-end, *a.* closed at one end.

dead end, *n.* impasse.

dead·ly, *a.*, **-lier**, **-liest**. fatal. **dead·li·ness**, *n.*

deaf, *a.* lacking sense of hearing. **deaf·ly**, *adv.* **deaf·ness**, *n.*

deaf·en, *v.t.* make deaf. **deaf·en·ing·ly**, *adv.*

deaf-mute, *n.* a person both deaf and dumb.

deal, *n.* a quantity; distribution of cards. *v.*, **dealt**, **deal·er**, *n.*

dean, *n.* administrative officer of a college or church. **dean·ship**, *n.*

dear, *a.* beloved; high-priced. **dear·ly**, *adv.* **dear·ness**, *n.*

death, *n.* act or fact of dying. **death·less**, *a.* **death·ly**, *a.*, *adv.*

de·ba·cle, *n.* rout.

de·bar, v.t., de·barred, de·bar·ring. to prohibit. **de·bar·ment**, n.

de·bate, v., de·bat·ed, de·bat·ing. engage in discussion. **de·bat·a·ble**, a. **de·bat·er**, n.

de·bauch, v. corrupt. **de·bauch·er**, n. **de·bauch·ment**, n. **de·bauch·er·y**, n. pl., -ies.

de·bil·i·tate, v.t., -tat·ed, -tat·ing. weaken. **de·bil·i·ta·tion**, n.

de·bil·i·ty, n. pl., -ties. feebleness.

deb·it, n. debt. v.t.

deb·o·nair, a. pleasant. Also **deb·o·naire**, **deb·on·naire**.

de·bris, n. fragments.

debt, n. obligation.

debt·or, n. person in debt.

de·but, dé·but, n. first appearance in society. **deb·u·tante**, **deb·u·tante**, n.

dec·ade, n. group of ten.

dec·a·dent, a. deteriorating. **dec·a·dence**, n. **dec·a·dent·ly**, adv.

de·cant·er, n. decorative bottle for serving wine, etc.

de·cay, v. deteriorate.

de·cease, v.i. die. **de·ceased**, a., n.

de·ceit, n. fraud. **de·ceit·ful**, a. **de·ceit·ful·ly**, adv.

de·ceive, v., de·ceived, de·ceiving. mislead.

De·cem·ber, n. twelfth month.

de·cen·cy, n. pl., -cies. propriety. **de·cent**, a. **de·cent·ly**, adv.

de·cep·tion, n. fraud. **de·cep·tive**, a. **de·cep·tive·ly**, adv.

de·cide, v., de·cid·ed, de·cid·ing. settle. **de·ci·sion**, n.

de·cid·ed, a. resolute. **de·cid·ed·ly**, adv.

dec·i·mal, a. of tens.

de·ci·pher, v.t. decode.

de·ci·sive, a. final. **de·ci·sive·ly**, adv. **de·ci·sive·ness**, n.

deck, v.t. adorn. n. flooring of a ship; pack of playing cards.

de·clare, v.t., de·clared, de·claring. announce officially. **dec·la·ra·tion**, n.

de·cline, v., de·clined, de·clining. lean or slope downward. n.

de·com·pose, v., -posed, -posing. decay. **de·com·po·si·tion**, n.

dec·o·rate, v.t., -rat·ed, -rat·ing. embellish; confer distinction. **dec·o·ra·tion**, n. **dec·o·ra·tive**, a. **dec·o·ra·tor**, n.

de·coy, n. a thing or person intended to lead into a snare.

de·crease, v., de·creased, de·creas·ing. grow or make less. **de·creas·ing·ly**, adv.

de·cree, n. authoritative decision. v., de·creed, de·cree·ing.

de·crep·it, a. weakened by long use.

de·cry, v.t., de·cried, de·cry·ing. censure.

de·duce, v.t., de·duced, de·duc·ing. infer.

de·duct, v.t. subtract. **de·duct·i·ble**, a. **de·duc·tion**, n.

deed, n. an act.

deem, v. judge.

deep, a. far down; not superficial. **deep·en**, v.

de·face, v.t., de·faced, de·fac·ing. to disfigure.

de·fame, v.t., de·famed, de·fam·ing. slander. **def·a·ma·tion**, n.

de·fault, n. failure to perform an obligatory act. v. **de·fault·er**, n.

de·feat, n. overthrow. v.t.

de·fect, n. fault. v.i. desert. **de·fec·tion**, n. **de·fec·tor**, n. **de·fec·tive**, a.

de·fend, v. protect.

de·fend·ant, n. one charged in a lawsuit.

de·fense, de·fence, n. protection. **de·fen·sive**, a. **de·fen·sive·ly**, adv.

de·fer, v., de·ferred, de·fer·ring. delay; yield. **de·fer·ment**, n.

def·er·ence, n. respect.

de·fi·ance, n. a challenge. **de·fi·ant**, a. **de·fi·ant·ly**, adv.

de·fi·cient, a. lacking. **de·fi·cien·cy**, n. pl., -cies. **de·fi·cient·ly**, adv.

def·i·cit, n. a falling short.

de·file, v.t., de·filed, de·fil·ing. sully.

de·fine, v.t., de·fined, de·fin·ing. state the meaning; specify distinctly. **def·i·ni·tion**, n.

def·i·nite, a. clearly defined. **def·i·nite·ly**, adv.

de·fin·i·tive, a. final. **de·fin·i·tive·ly**, adv.

de·flate, v., de·flat·ed, de·flat·ing. release gas or air from; lower. **de·fla·tion**, n. **de·fla·tion·ar·y**, a.

de·flect, v. turn aside.

de·form, v.t. disfigure. n. **de·formed**, a. **de·form·i·ty**, n. pl., -ties.

de·fraud, v.t. cheat.

de·fray, v.t. pay.

deft, a. apt. **deft·ly**, adv. **deft·ness**, n.

de·funct, a. dead.

de·fy, v.t., de·fied, de·fy·ing.

dare. **de·fi·er**, *n.*

de·gen·er·ate, *v.i.*, -ated, -ating. deteriorate.

de·grade, *v.t.*, **de·grad·ed**, **de·grad·ing**. reduce in rank. **deg·ra·da·tion**, *n.*

de·gree, *n.* step in a process, scale, order, etc.

de·hy·drate, *v.t.*, -drat·ed, -drat·ing. remove water from. *v.i.* lose water. **de·hy·dra·tion**, *n.*

de·i·fy, *v.t.*, -fied, -fy·ing. make a god of.

deign, *v.* condescend.

de·i·ty, *n. pl.*, -ties. godhood.

de·ject·ed, *a.* sad. **de·ject·ed·ly**, *adv.* **de·jec·tion**, *n.*

de·lay, *v.* put off.

de·lec·ta·ble, *a.* delightful.

del·e·gate, *v.t.*, -gat·ed, -gat·ing. assign to another. *n.* representative. **del·e·ga·tion**, *n.*

de·lete, *v.t.*, **de·let·ed**, **de·let·ing**. blot out. **de·le·tion**, *n.*

de·lib·er·ate, *v.*, -at·ed, -at·ing. consider. *a.* carefully weighed. **de·lib·er·ate·ly**, *adv.* **de·lib·er·a·tion**, *n.*

del·i·ca·cy, *n. pl.*, -cies. exquisite quality.

del·i·cate, *a.* fine. **del·i·cate·ly**, *adv.* **del·i·cate·ness**, *n.*

del·i·ca·tes·sen, *n.* a store which sells prepared foods.

de·li·cious, *a.* highly pleasing to the taste.

de·light, *v.* provide great pleasure. *n.* **de·light·ed**, *a.* **de·light·ed·ly**, *adv.* **de·light·ful**, *a.* **de·light·ful·ly**, *adv.* **de·light·ful·ness**, *n.*

de·lin·e·ate, *v.t.*, -at·ed, -at·ing. describe the form of. **de·lin·e·a·tion**, *n.* **de·lin·e·a·tor**, *n.*

de·lin·quent, *a.* neglectful. *n.* **de·lin·quen·cy**, *n. pl.*, -cies.

de·lir·i·um, *n. pl.*, -i·ums, -i·a. temporary disorder of mental faculties. **de·lir·i·ous**, *a.* **de·lir·i·ous·ly**, *adv.*

de·liv·er, *v.t.* carry and turn over to; utter; aid in birth. **de·liv·er·a·ble**, *a.* **de·liv·er·er**, *n.* **de·liv·er·ance**, *n.* **de·liv·er·y**, *n.*

del·ta, *n.* alluvial land between diverging branches of the mouth of a river.

de·lude, *v.t.*, **de·lud·ed**, **de·lud·ing**. mislead. **de·lu·sive**, *a.* **de·lu·sion**, *n.*

del·uge, *n.* great flood. *v.t.*, -uged, -ug·ing. inundate.

de·luxe, *a.*, *adv.* of superior quality.

delve, *v.i.*, delved, delv·ing.

carry on research.

dem·a·gogue, dem·a·gog, *n.* one who makes use of popular emotions for personal power. **dem·a·gogu·er·y**, *n.* **dem·a·gog·ic**, *a.*

de·mand, *v.* ask for with authority.

de·mar·ca·tion, *n.* separation. Also **de·mar·ka·tion**.

de·mean, *v.t.* degrade.

de·mean·or, *n.* behavior.

de·ment·ed, *a.* insane.

de·mer·it, *n.* defect.

de·mise, *n.* termination.

de·moc·ra·cy, *n. pl.*, -cies. government by the people. **dem·o·crat**, *n.* **dem·o·crat·ic**, *a.* **dem·o·crat·i·cal·ly**, *adv.*

de·mol·ish, *v.t.* raze. **de·mo·li·tion**, *n.*

de·mon, *n.* devil. **de·mon·ic**, *a.*

dem·on·strate, *v.*, -strat·ed, -strat·ing. show clearly. **dem·on·stra·tion**, *n.* **de·mon·stra·tive**, *a.* **dem·on·stra·tor**, *n.*

de·mor·al·ize, *v.t.*, -ized, -iz·ing. deprive of spirit.

de·mote, *v.t.*, **de·mot·ed**, **de·mot·ing**. reduce to lower rank. **de·mo·tion**, *n.*

den, *n.* cave; small, cozy room.

den·im, *n.* heavy cotton fabric.

de·nom·i·na·tion, *n.* name for a class of things. **de·nom·i·na·tion·al**, *a.*

de·nom·i·na·tor, *n.* term of a fraction, usually written under the line.

de·note, *v.t.*, **de·not·ed**, **de·not·ing**. indicate.

de·nounce, *v.t.*, **de·nounced**, **de·nounc·ing**. condemn openly. **de·nounce·ment**, *n.* **de·nun·ci·a·tion**, *n.*

dense, *a.*, **den·ser**, **den·sest**. compact; obtuse. **dense·ly**, *adv.* **den·si·ty**, *n. pl.*, -ties.

dent, *n.* a hollow or depression. *v.t.* make a dent in.

den·tal, *a.* of or pertaining to the teeth.

den·tist, *n.* a doctor who practices dentistry.

den·ture, *n.* a set of teeth.

de·nude, *v.t.*, **de·nud·ed**, **de·nud·ing**. strip.

de·nun·ci·ate, *v.*, -at·ed, -at·ing. denounce. **de·nun·ci·a·tion**, *n.* **de·nun·ci·a·to·ry**, *a.*

de·ny, *v.t.*, **de·nied**, **de·ny·ing**. declare not true; refuse. **de·ni·al**, *n.*

de·o·dor·ant, *n.* agent for de-

stroying odors. *a.* **de·o·dor·ize,**
v.t., **-ized, -iz·ing.**

de·part, *v.* leave. **de·par·ture,** *n.*

de·part·ment, *n.* division of a
complex whole. **de·part·men·tal,** *a.*

de·pend, *v.i.* be controlled or
conditioned (*on* or *upon*). **de·pend·ence, de·pend·ance,** *n.*
de·pend·a·ble, *a.* **de·pend·a·bly,**
adv. **de·pend·a·bil·i·ty,** *n.* **de·pend·en·cy, de·pend·an·cy,** *n.,
pl.,* **-cies. de·pend·ent, de·pend·ant,** *n.*

de·pict, *v.t.* to portray. **de·pic·tion,** *n.*

de·plete, *v.t.*, **de·plet·ed, de·plet·ing.** reduce. **de·ple·tion,** *n.*

de·plore, *v.t.*, **de·plored, de·plor·ing.** lament. **de·plor·a·ble,**
a. **de·plor·a·bly,** *adv.*

de·port, *v.t.* eject from a country. **de·por·ta·tion,** *n.*

de·port·ment, *n.* behavior.

de·pose, *v.t.*, **de·posed, de·pos·ing.** remove high office.

de·pos·it, *v.* set down with care;
entrust for safekeeping; *n.*
that which is laid down. **de·pos·i·tor,** *n.*

de·pot, *n.* a station.

de·prave, *v.t.*, **de·praved, de·prav·ing.** corrupt. **de·praved,**
a. **de·prav·i·ty,** *n., pl.,* **-ties.**

de·pre·ci·ate, *v.t.*, **-ated, -ating.** reduce in value; belittle. **de·pre·ci·a·tion,** *n.* **de·pre·ci·a·to·ry,** *a.*

de·press, *v.t.* lower; make sad.
de·pres·sant, *n.* **de·pressed,** *a.*
de·pres·sion, *n.*

de·prive, *v.t.*, **de·prived, de·priv·ing.** divest of something.
dep·ri·va·tion, *n.*

depth, *n.* deepness.

dep·u·ty, *n., pl.,* **-ties.** person appointed to act for another.

de·range, *v.t.*, **de·ranged, de·rang·ing.** disturb the order of.
de·ranged, *a.* **de·range·ment,** *n.*

der·e·lict, *a.* delinquent. **der·e·lic·tion,** *n.*

de·ride, *v.t.*, **de·rid·ed, de·rid·ing.** mock. **de·ri·sion,** *n.* **de·ri·sive,** *a.*

de·rive, *v.t.*, **de·rived, de·riv·ing.**
draw from a source; deduce.
de·riv·a·ble, *a.* **der·i·va·tion,** *n.*
de·riv·a·tive, *a.*

de·rog·a·to·ry, *a.* belittling. **de·rog·a·to·ri·ly,** *adv.*

der·rick, *n.* apparatus for hoisting heavy weights.

de·scend, *v.* move from a higher
to a lower place. **de·scend·ent,**

de·scend·ant, *a.*

de·scend·ant, *n.* an offspring.

de·scribe, *v.t.*, **de·scribed, de·scrib·ing.** portray orally or in
writing. **de·scrib·a·ble,** *a.* **de·scrip·tion,** *n.* **de·scrip·tive,** *a.*
de·scrip·tive·ly, *adv.*

de·seg·re·gate, *v.*, **-gated, -gat·ing.** abolish racial segregation
in. **de·seg·re·ga·tion,** *n.*

des·ert, *n.* a wilderness. *v.* abandon. **de·sert·er,** *n.*

de·serve, *v.*, **de·served, de·serv·ing.** merit. **de·serv·ing,** *a.*

de·sign, *v.* plan. *n.* **de·sign·er,** *n.*

des·ig·nate, *v.t.*, **-nated, -nat·ing.** appoint. **des·ig·na·tion,** *n.*

de·sire, *v.t.*, **de·sired, de·sir·ing.**
want. **de·sir·a·ble,** *a.*

de·sist, *v.i.* cease.

desk, *n.* table for writing.

des·o·late, *v.t.*, **-lated, -lat·ing.**
lay waste. *a.* barren. **des·o·la·tion,** *n.*

de·spair, *v.i.* be without hope.
de·spair·ing, *a.*

des·per·ate, *a.* frantic. **des·per·ate·ly,** *adv.* **des·per·a·tion,** *n.*

des·pi·ca·ble, *a.* contemptible.
des·pi·ca·bly, *adv.*

de·spise, *v.t.*, **de·spised, de·spis·ing.** scorn.

de·spite, *prep.* in spite of.

de·spoil, *v.t.* rob.

de·spond, *v.i.* lose heart. **de·spond·en·cy,** *n.* **de·spond·ent,** *a.*

des·pot, *n.* absolute ruler. **des·pot·ic,** *a.* **des·pot·ism,** *n.*

des·sert, *n.* dish served at the
end of a meal.

des·ti·na·tion, *n.* predetermined
end of a journey.

des·tine, *v.t.*, **-tined, -tin·ing.** intend.

des·ti·ny, *n., pl.,* **-nies.** fate.

des·ti·tute, *a.* in abject poverty.
des·ti·tu·tion, *n.*

de·stroy, *v.t.* ruin.

de·struc·tion, *n.* ruin. **de·struct·i·ble,** *a.*

de·tach, *v.t.* disengage. **de·tach·a·ble,** *a.* **de·tached,** *a.*

de·tail, *v.t.* enumerate. *n.* an
item. **de·tailed,** *a.*

de·tain, *v.t.* restrain from proceeding.

de·tect, *v.t.* discover. **de·tect·a·ble,** *a.*

de·tec·tive, *n.* individual whose
function is to detect and investigate crimes.

dé·tente, *n.* thaw in tension.

de·ter, *v.t.*, **de·terred, de·ter·ring.** discourage from acting.

de·ter·rent, *n.*

de·ter·gent, *n.* cleansing agent.

de·te·ri·o·rate, *v.,* **-rated, -rating.** depreciate. **de·te·ri·o·ra·tion,** *n.*

de·ter·mine, *v.,* **-mined, -min·ing.** settle, fix, establish. **de·ter·mi·na·tion,** *n.*

de·ter·mined, *a.* resolute.

de·test, *v.t.* abhor. **de·test·a·ble,** *a.*

de·tour, *n.* a roundabout way. *v.*

de·tract, *v.* take away. **de·trac·tion,** *n.* **de·trac·tor,** *n.*

det·ri·ment, *n.* damage. **det·ri·men·tal,** *a.*

de·val·u·ate, *v.t.,* **-ated, -ating.** reduce the value of. **de·val·u·a·tion,** *n.*

dev·as·tate, *v.t.,* **-tated, -tating.** ravage. **dev·as·ta·tion,** *n.* **dev·as·ta·ting,** *a.*

de·vel·op, *v.* gradually acquire; to unfold gradually. **de·vel·op·ment,** *n.*

de·vi·ate, *v.,* **-ated, -ating.** turn aside. **de·vi·ant.** **de·vi·a·tion,** *n.*

de·vice, *n.* invented for a specific use; a scheme.

dev·il, *n.* evil spirit; mischievous person. **dev·il·ish,** *a.*

de·vi·ous, *a.* indirect.

de·vise, *v.,* **-vised, -vis·ing.** to scheme.

de·void, *a.* void (of).

de·vote, *v.t.,* **-vot·ed, -vot·ing.** give (one's complete attention) to.

de·vot·ed, *a.* loyal. **de·vot·ed·ly,** *adv.*

dev·o·tee, *n.* one who is wholly devoted.

de·vo·tion, *n.* loyalty. **de·vo·tion·al,** *a., n.*

de·vour, *v.t.* eat up voraciously.

de·vout, *a.* warmly devoted; sincere. **de·vout·ly,** *adv.* **de·vout·ness,** *n.*

dew, *n.* moisture deposited in small drops, especially during the night, on the surfaces of bodies.

dex·ter·ous, *a.* having skill with the hands. **dex·ter·i·ty,** *n.*

di·a·be·tes, *n.* disease marked by excessive sugar in the blood. **di·a·bet·ic,** *a., n.*

di·a·bol·ic, *a.* devilish. Also **di·a·bol·i·cal. di·a·bol·i·cal·ly,** *adv.*

di·a·dem, *n.* crown.

di·ag·nose, *v.t.,* **-nosed, -nos·ing.** ascertain the cause by studying symptoms. **di·ag·no·sis,** *n. pl.,* **-ses. di·ag·nos·tic,** *a.* **di·ag-**

nos·ti·cian, *n.*

di·ag·o·nal, *a.* extending from one angle to the opposite. **di·ag·o·nal·ly,** *adv.*

di·a·gram, *n.* figure, outline. *v.t.,* **-gramed, -gram·ing** or **-grammed, -gram·ming.**

di·al, *n.* any plate with graduations on which a pointer moves to indicate a measurement. *v.t.,* **di·aled, di·al·ing.** regulate by turning a dial; call by means of a dial telephone.

di·a·lect, *n.* form of a language prevailing in a particular district. **di·a·lec·tal,** *a.*

di·a·logue, *n.* conversation between two or more persons.

di·am·e·ter, *n.* straight line passing from one side to the other through the center of a curvilinear figure. **di·a·met·ric,** *a.* Also, **diametrical. di·a·met·ric·al·ly,** *adv.*

di·a·mond, *n.* naturally crystallized carbon. *baseball,* the infield or entire playing field.

di·a·per, *n.* soft cloth used as a breechcloth for infants. *v.t.* put a diaper on.

di·a·phragm, *n.* partition or septum; vibrating disk; a device placed over the uterine cervix for contraception.

di·ar·rhe·a, *n.* abnormally frequent and fluid evacuation of the bowels. Also **di·ar·rhoea.**

di·a·ry, *n. pl.,* **-ries.** daily record. **di·a·rist,** *n.*

dice, *n. pl., sing.* **die.** small cubes. *v.i.,* **-diced, -dicing.** *v.t.* cut into small cubes.

dick·er, *v.* haggle.

dic·tate, *v.,* **-tat·ed, -tat·ing.** give orders; read aloud for recording. *n.* a command. **dic·ta·tion,** *n.*

dic·ta·tor, *n.* person exercising absolute authority. **dic·ta·tor·ship,** *n.* **dic·ta·to·ri·al,** *a.*

dic·tion, *n.* enunciation.

dic·tion·ar·y, *n. pl.,* **-ar·ies.** book containing alphabetically arranged words of a language.

did, *v.t.* past tense of do.

die, *v.i.* **died, dy·ing.** cease to live. *n.* metal device for cutting, stamping, etc.

di·et, *n.* regular food and drink; food and drink chosen for health reasons, esp. to lose weight. *v.i.* eat according to a diet. **di·e·tar·y,** *a. n. pl.,* **-tar·ies. di·e·ti·cian,** *n.*

dif-fer, *v.i.* be unlike; disagree. *n.*

dif-fer-ence, *n.* state of being different; dispute; remainder in subtraction.

dif-fer-ent, *a.* unlike; novel. **dif-fer-ent-ly**, *adv.*

dif-fi-cult, *a.* hard to make, do, understand, or please. **dif-fi-cul-ty**, *n. pl.*, **-ties.**

dif-fuse, *v.t.*, **-fused, -fusing.** disseminate. *a.* widely spread. **dif-fuse-ly**, *adv.* **dif-fu-sion**, *n.* **dif-fu-sive-ly**, *adv.*

dig, *v.t.*, **dug, dig-ging.** remove, as with a sharp instrument. **dig-ger**, *n.* **dig-gings**, *n. pl.*

di-gest, *v.* convert, food into a form absorbable by the body. *n.* systematic compilation. **di-gest-i-ble**, *a.* **di-gest-i-bil-i-ty**, *n.* **di-ges-tion**, *n.*

dig-it, *n.* finger or toe; any positive integer under 10, usu. including 0.

dig-ni-fy, *v.t.*, **-fied, -fy-ing.** honor. **dig-ni-fied**, *a.*

dig-ni-ty, *n. pl.*, **-ties.** formal deportment; self-respect; elevated rank.

di-gress, *v.i.* depart from the main subject of a discourse. **di-gres-sion**, *n.* **di-gres-sive**, *a.* **di-gres-sive-ly**, *adv.*

dike, *n.* embankment constructed to restrain flood waters.

di-lap-i-dat-ed, *a.* run-down. **di-lap-i-da-tion**, *n.*

di-late, *v.*, **-lat-ed, -lat-ing.** expand. *adv.* **di-la-tion**, *n.* **di-la-ta-tion**, *n.*

di-lem-ma, *n.* predicament.

dil-i-gence, *n.* constant effort; care. **dil-i-gent**, *a.* **dil-i-gent-ly**, *adv.*

dill, *n.* herb with aromatic seeds and foliage.

di-lute, *v.t.*, **-lut-ed, -lut-ing.** weaken by admixture. **di-lute-ness**, *n.* **di-lu-tion**, *n.*

dim, *a.*, **dim-mer, dim-mest.** somewhat dark; obscure. *v.*, **dimmed, dim-ming.** render or become dim. **dim-ly**, *adv.* **dim-ness**, *n.*

dime, *n.* coin equal to ten cents.

di-men-sion, *n.* magnitude of length, breadth, thickness, or time. **di-men-sion-less**, *a.* **di-men-sion-al**, *a.*

di-min-ish, *v.t.* cause to be or appear less. *v.i.* decrease. **di-min-ish-a-ble**, *a.*

di-min-u-tive, *a.* tiny. **di-min-u-tive-ly**, *adv.* **di-min-u-tive-ness**, *n.*

dim-ple, *n.* small natural depression in the human body.

din, *n.* loud sound.

dine, *v.i.*, **dined, din-ing.** eat.

din-er, *n.* restaurant.

di-nette, *n.* small dining area.

din-gy, *a.*, **-gi-er, -gi-est.** dirty; soiled. **din-gi-ness**, *n.*

din-ner, *n.* chief meal of the day.

di-no-saur, *n.* extinct reptile.

dint, *n.* means; force.

di-o-cese, *n.* circuit of a bishop's jurisdiction. **di-oc-e-san**, *a.*

dip, *v.t.*, **dipped, dip-ping.** plunge temporarily into a liquid.

diph-the-ri-a, *n.* epidemic inflammatory disease of the air passages.

diph-thong, *n.* sound made by gliding from the sound of one vowel into the sound of another.

di-plo-ma, *n.* document conferring power, privilege, or honor.

di-plo-ma-cy, *n. pl.*, **-cies.** art of conducting negotiations; tact. **dip-lo-mat**, *n.* **dip-lo-mat-ic**, *a.* **dip-lo-mat-i-cal-ly**, *adv.*

dire, *a.*, **dir-er, dir-est.** dreadful. **dire-ly**, *adv.* **dire-ness**, *n.*

di-rect, *a.* shortest way; candid. *v.* guide. **di-rect-ness**, *n.* **di-rect-ly**, *adv.* **di-rec-tor**, *n.*

di-rec-tion, *n.* course or line along which anything moves. **di-rec-tion-al**, *a.*

dirge, *n.* funeral hymn.

dirt, *n.* any foul substance; loose soil. **dirt-y**, *a.*, *v.t.*

dis-a-ble, *v.t.*, **-bled, -bling.** incapacitate. **dis-a-bil-i-ty**, *n. pl.*, **-ties.**

dis-ad-van-tage, *n.* drawback. *v.t.*, **-taged, -taging.** subject to a disadvantage. **dis-ad-van-ta-geous**, *a.*

dis-a-gree, *v.i.*, **-greed, -greeing.** differ. **dis-a-gree-ment**, *n.*

dis-a-gree-a-ble, *a.* unpleasant.

dis-ap-pear, *v.i.* vanish. **dis-ap-pear-ance**, *n.*

dis-ap-point, *v.t.* fall short of expectations. **dis-ap-point-ment**, *n.*

dis-ap-prove, *v.i.*, **-proved, -prov-ing.** censure. **dis-ap-prov-al**, *n.* **dis-ap-prov-ing-ly**, *adv.*

dis-arm, *v.t.* take weapons from.

dis-ar-ray, *n.* disorder.

dis·as·ter, n. calamity. dis·as·trous, a. dis·as·trous·ly, adv.

dis·a·vow, v.t. deny; reject. dis·a·vow·al, n.

dis·band, v. disperse.

dis·bar, v.t., -barred, -bar·ring. expel from the legal profession.

dis·burse, v.t., -bursed, -bursing. pay out. dis·burse·ment, n. dis·burs·er, n.

disc, disk, n., v.t. disk.

dis·card, v.t. cast aside.

dis·cern, v. perceive as being different. dis·cern·i·ble, a. dis·cern·i·bly, adv. dis·cern·ing, a. dis·cern·ment, n.

dis·charge, v., -charged, -charging. relieve or free of anything.

dis·ci·ple, n. follower.

dis·ci·pline, n. order; punishment; branch of learning. v.t., -plined, -plining. chastise. dis·ci·pli·nar·y, a.

dis·claim, v.t. deny responsibility for. dis·claim·er, n.

dis·close, v.t., -closed, -closing. reveal. dis·clo·sure, n.

dis·com·fort, n. minor pain.

dis·con·cert, v.t. throw into confusion. dis·con·cert·ing, a. dis·con·cert·ed, a.

dis·con·nect, v.t. separate or sever the connection. dis·con·nec·tion, n. dis·con·nect·ed, a.

dis·con·so·late, a. inconsolable. dis·con·so·late·ly, adv.

dis·con·tent, n. dissatisfaction. dis·con·tent·ed, a. dis·con·tent·ed·ly, adv.

dis·con·tin·ue, v., -ued, -u·ing. terminate. dis·con·tin·u·ance, n. dis·con·tin·u·a·tion, n. dis·con·tin·u·ous, a.

dis·cord, n. disagreement.

dis·count, n. deduction from the customary price.

dis·cour·age, v.t., -aged, -ag·ing. dishearten. dis·cour·age·ment, n.

dis·cour·te·ous, a. rude. dis·cour·te·ous·ly, adv.

dis·cov·er, v.t. come upon. dis·cov·er·y, n. pl., -ies.

dis·cred·it, v.t. withhold belief.

dis·creet, a. prudent. dis·creet·ly, adv. dis·cre·tion, n.

dis·crep·an·cy, n. pl., -cies. inconsistency.

dis·crim·i·nate, v., -nated, -nat·ing. differentiate. dis·crim·i·na·tion, n.

dis·cuss, v.t. talk over. dis·cus·sion, n.

dis·dain, v.t. scorn. n. dis·dain·ful, a. dis·dain·ful·ly, adv.

dis·ease, n. sickness. dis·eased, a.

dis·en·chant, v.t. disillusion. dis·en·chant·ment, n.

dis·fig·ure, v.t., -ured, -ur·ing. spoil in appearance.

dis·grace, n. dishonor. v.t., -graced -grac·ing. dis·grace·ful, a. dis·grace·ful·ly, adv.

dis·guise, v.t., -guised, -guis·ing. alter the ordinary appearance of. n. mask.

dis·gust, n. distaste; loathing. v.t. cause to feel aversion. dis·gust·ed, a. dis·gust·ing, a.

dish, n. open vessel used esp. for serving food.

dis·heart·en, v.t. discourage. dis·heart·en·ing, a.

dis·hon·est, a. not honest. dis·hon·es·ty, n. pl., -ties.

dis·hon·or, n. disgrace. v.t. dis·hon·or·a·ble, a.

dis·il·lu·sion, v.t. free from illusion.

dis·in·fect, v.t. cleanse of disease germs. dis·in·fect·ant, n., a.

dis·in·her·it, v.t. deprive of inheritance.

dis·in·te·grate, v., -grated, -grating. reduce to fragments. dis·in·te·gra·tion, n.

dis·in·ter·est, n. indifference. dis·in·ter·es·ted, a.

disk, disc, n. flat, circular object.

dis·like, n. distaste.

dis·lo·cate, v.t., -cated, -cating. move out of place. dis·lo·ca·tion, n.

dis·loy·al, a. not loyal. dis·loy·al·ty, n.

dis·mal, a. dark, gloomy.

dis·man·tle, v.t., -tled, -tling. take apart.

dis·may, v.t. distress.

dis·mem·ber, v.t. separate the members of.

dis·miss, v.t. send away.

dis·o·bey, v. refuse to obey. dis·o·be·di·ence, n.

dis·or·der, n. confusion; sickness. dis·or·der·ly, a. dis·or·der·li·ness, n.

dis·or·gan·ize, v.t., -ized, -izing. throw into disorder. dis·or·gan·i·za·tion, n.

dis·own, v.t. refuse to acknowledge as one's own.

dis·par·age, v.t., -aged, -ag·ing.

belittle. **dis·par·ag·ing·ly,** *adv.* well-known.

dis·par·i·ty, *n.* inequality.

dis·patch, *v.t.* send; *n.* haste.

dis·pel, *v.t.,* **-pelled, -pelling.** scatter.

dis·pense, *v.t.,* **-pensed, -pensing.** distribute; excuse. **dis·pen·sa·tion,** *n.*

dis·perse, *v.t.,* **-persed, -persing.** scatter; drive off.

dis·place, *v.t.,* **-placed, -placing.** remove from usual position.

dis·play, *v.t.* show.

dis·please, *v.t.,* **-pleased, -pleasing.** annoy. **dis·pleas·ure,** *n.*

dis·pose, *v.t.,* **-posed, -posing.** put in a certain position; get rid of. **dis·pos·a·ble,** *a.* **dis·po·si·tion,** *n.*

dis·prove, *v.t.,* **-proved, -proving.** prove to be false.

dis·pute, *v.i.,* **-puted, -puting.** argue over.

dis·qual·i·fy, *v.t.,* **-fied, -fying.** make unable to do something because of a violation of a rule. **dis·qual·i·fi·ca·tion,** *n.*

dis·re·gard, *n.* lack of attention. *v.t.* pay no attention to.

dis·rep·u·ta·ble, *a.* not respectable.

dis·re·spect, *n.* discourtesy. **dis·re·spect·ful,** *a.*

dis·rupt, *v.t.* upset.

dis·sat·is·fy, *v.t.,* **-fied, -fying.** fail to satisfy. **dis·sat·is·fac·tion,** *n.*

dis·sect, *v.t.* divide; cut apart.

dis·sent, *v.i.* disagree in opinion. *n. a.* **dis·sen·sion,** *n.* **dis·sent·er,** *n.*

dis·si·pate, *v.,* **-pated, -pating.** scatter.

dis·solve, *v.,* **-solved, -solving.** melt; slowly disappear.

dis·so·nance, *n.* mixture of harsh sounds.

dis·suade, *v.t.,* **-suaded, -suading.** persuade not to do something. **dis·sua·sion,** *n.*

dis·tance, *n.* space or length between two points.

dis·tant, *a.* far away.

dis·taste, *n.* dislike. **dis·taste·ful,** *a.* **dis·taste·ful·ly,** *adv.*

dis·till, *v.t.,* **-tilled, -till·ing.** heat liquid until it becomes steam and then catch the cooled drops. **dis·till·er·y,** *n.*

dis·tinct, *a.* not alike.

dis·tinc·tion, *n.* sign of honor.

dis·tin·guish, *v.t.* set apart; recognize as different. **dis·tin·guish·a·ble,** *a.*

dis·tin·guished, *a.* famous;

dis·tort, *v.t.* twist out of shape; change the true meaning.

dis·tract, *v.t.* draw attention from. **dis·tract·ed,** *a.* **dis·trac·tion,** *n.*

dis·traught, *a.* disturbed.

dis·tress, *n.* pain. *v.t.* **dis·tress·ing,** *a.*

dis·trib·ute, *v.t.,* **-uted, -uting.** divide in shares; arrange. **dis·tri·bu·tion,** *n.*

dis·trict, *n.* portion of a country, state or city.

dis·trust, *v.t.* doubt. *n.*

dis·turb, *v.t.* destroy quiet or rest. **dis·turb·ance,** *n.*

dis·u·nite, *v.t.,* disunited, disuniting. separate.

ditch, *n.* a trench. *v.t.* abandon.

dive, *v.i.,* dived or dove, diving. plunge head-first into water. **div·er,** *n.*

di·verge, *v.,* **-verged, -verg·ing.** differ or vary. **di·ver·gence,** *n.*

di·verse, *a.* different. **di·ver·si·fy,** *v.t.,* **-fied, -fying. di·ver·si·fied,** *a.*

di·vert, *v.t.* turn off from any course; entertain. **di·ver·sion,** *n.* **di·ver·sion·ar·y,** *a.* **di·ver·si·ty,** *n.*

di·vide, *v.t.,* **-vided, -viding.** separate. **di·vis·i·ble,** *a.* **di·vi·sion,** *n.* **di·vi·sive,** *a.*

div·i·dend, *n.* number to be divided; something unexpected; profit divided among stockholders. *n.*

di·vine, *a.* pertaining to God. *v.t.,* divined, divining. foretell. **di·vin·i·ty,** *n. pl.,* **-ties.**

di·vorce, *n.* legal dissolution of a marriage. *v.t.,* **-vorced, -vorc·ing.**

di·vulge, *v.t.,* divulged, divulging. reveal. **di·vul·gence,** *n.*

diz·zy, *a.,* **-zi·er, -zi·est.** unstable; giddy; dazed. **diz·zi·ness,** *n.*

do, *v.,* **did, done, doing.** perform; complete; cause; give; suffice; fare; suffice.

doc·ile, *a.* teachable.

dock, *n.* a wharf; shipping or loading platform. *v.* bring or come into dock; join orbiting objects in outer space.

doc·tor, *n.* person licensed to practice medicine; a physician, dentist, or veterinarian; one who has received the degree of this name from a university.

doc·trine, *n.* body or system of teachings; dogma. **doc·tri·nal**, *a.*

doc·u·ment, *n.* legal or official paper. *v.t.* support by evidence.

doc·u·men·ta·ry, *a.* derived from documents. *n., pl.,* **-ries.**

dodge, *v.,* **dodged, dodg·ing.** move back and forth or to and fro; evade.

doe, *n. pl.,* **does, doe.** female of the deer, goat, antelope, and rabbit.

doff, *v.t.* take off.

dog, *n.* any animal belonging to the same family which includes the wolves, jackals and foxes.

dog·ged, *a.* tenacious. **dog·ged·ly**, *adv.* **dog·ged·ness**, *n.*

dog·ma, *n., pl.,* **-mas.** settled belief; a tenet. **dog·mat·ic**, *a.* **dog·mat·i·cal·ly**, *adv.*

dog·ma·tize, *v.i.* **-tized, -tiz·ing.** express oneself in a dogmatic way.

doi·ly, *n. pl.,* **-lies.** small cloth mat.

dol·drums, *n. pl.* low spirits; period of inactivity.

dole, *n.* that which is distributed; given in charity. *v.t.,* **doled, dol·ing.**

doll, *n.* toy representing a human being.

dol·lar, *n.* monetary unit of the U.S.

dol·ly, *n. pl.,* **-lies.** low platform on rollers.

dol·or·ous, *a.* sorrowful.

dolt, *n.* dull person.

do·main, *n.* realm; field of action.

dome, *n.* hemispherical roof. *v.,* **domed, dom·ing.**

do·mes·tic, *a.* pertaining to the home. *n.* hired servant. **do·mes·ti·cal·ly**, *adv.*

do·mes·ti·cate, *v.t.* **-cat·ed, -cat·ing.** tame.

dom·i·nate, *v.,* **-nat·ed, -nat·ing.** have power over. **dom·i·nance**, *n.* **dom·i·nant**, *a.* **dom·i·na·tion**, *n.*

dom·i·neer, *v.* rule arbitrarily. **dom·i·neer·ing**, *a.*

do·min·ion, *n.* right of governing.

don, *v.t.,* **donned, don·ing.** put on.

do·nate, *v.,* **-nat·ed, -nat·ing.** contribute. **do·na·tion**, *n.* **do·nor**, *n.*

done, *a.* completed.

doom, *n.* judgment; fate. *v.t.* condemn to punishment.

door, *n.* opening or passage into a room, etc.

dope, *n.* any addictive drug; unintelligent person. *v.t.,* **doped, dop·ing.** affect with drugs.

dor·mer, *n.* section that sticks out from a sloping roof.

dor·mi·to·ry, *n., pl.,* **-ties.** large sleeping room.

dor·sal, *a.* of the back of the body.

dor·y, *n. pl.,* **dor·ies.** small flat bottomed boat.

dose, *n.* quantity of medicine prescribed to be taken at one time. **dos·age**, *n.*

dot, *n.* small point or spot. *v.,* **dot·ted, dot·ting.** mark with dots.

dot·age, *n.* feebleness in old age.

dou·ble, *a.* twofold; a fold. *v.,* **-bled, -bling.** make twice as great in number, size, etc.; fold.

doubt, *v.* waver in opinion. *n.* indecision. **doubt·ful**, *a.* **doubt·less**, *adv., a.*

dough, *n.* pasty mixture. *Inf.* money.

dough·nut, *n.* small roundish cake.

dour, *a.* sullen.

douse, *v.t.,* **doused, dous·ing.** plunge into water.

dow·a·ger, *n.* widow who has property inherited from her deceased husband.

dow·dy, *a.,* **-di·er, -di·est.** shabby.

down, *adv.* from higher to lower. *prep.* in a descending direction on, over, or along. *a.* downward; dejected. *n.* fine soft plumage of birds.

down·cast, *a.* dejected.

down·fall, *n.* ruin.

down·grade, *v.t.,* **-grad·ed, grad·ing.** reduce in salary, status, etc.

down·heart·ed, *a.* discouraged.

down·ward, *adv.* in a descending course. Also **down·wards.**

doze, *v.i.,* **dozed, doz·ing.** sleep lightly.

doz·en, *n. pl.,* **doz·ens.** group of twelve.

drab, *a.,* **drab·ber, drab·best.** dull. **drab·ly**, *adv.* **drab·ness**, *n.*

draft, *n.* act of pulling loads; a current of air; the selecting of persons; written order for the payment of money; design. **draft·y**, *a.*, **-i·er**, **-i·est**.

drag, *v.*, **dragged**, **drag·ging**. pull heavily along; pass tediously.

drag·on, *n.* mythical, monstrous animal.

drain, *v.* draw off gradually; exhaust. *n.* that by which anything is drained. **drain·age**, *n.*

dra·ma, *n.* a play; series of climactic events. **dra·mat·ic**, *a.* **dra·mat·i·cal·ly**, *adv.* **dram·a·tize**, *v.t.*, **-tized**, **-tiz·ing**. **dram·a·ti·za·tion**, *n.*

dra·mat·ics, *n. pl.* excessive emotional behavior.

dram·a·tist, *n.* playwright.

drape, *v.*, **draped**, **drap·ing**. cover or hang with some fabric. *n.* a curtain. **dra·per·y**, *n. pl.*, **-per·ies**.

dras·tic, *a.* severe. **drast·i·cal·ly**, *adv.*

draw, *v.*, **drew**, **drawn**, **draw·ing**. pull; take money from a bank; take out a pistol, etc.; sketch. **draw·ing**, *n.*

draw·back, *n.* disadvantage.

draw·bridge, *n.* bridge which can be raised.

draw·er, *n.* sliding storage compartment.

drawl, *v.* utter in a slow manner. *n.*

drawn, *a.* haggard.

dread, *v.t* anticipate with terror. *n.* apprehension. **dread·ful**, *a.* **dread·ful·ly**, *adv.*

dream, *n.* images in the mind during sleep. *v.*, **dreamed** or **dreamt**, **dream·ing**. have a dream. **dream·er**, *n.* **dream·y**, *a.*, **-i·er**, **-i·est**.

drear·y, *a.*, **-i·er**, **-i·est**. dismal. **drear·i·ly**, *adv.*

dredge, *n.* contrivance for gathering objects from the bed of a river, etc. *v.*, **dredged**, **dredg·ing**. clear with a dredge.

dreg, *n. Usu. pl.* sediment of liquors.

drench, *v.t.* soak.

dress, *v.*, **dressed** or **drest**, **dres·sing**. put clothes on; to trim. *n.* clothing.

dress·er, *n.* chest of drawers.

drib·ble, *v.*, **-bled**, **-bling**. fall in drops.

drift, *n.* act of moving something along by; something piled into masses by currents. *v.* be heaped up; move along aimlessly.

drift·wood, *n.* wood cast ashore by the water.

drill, *v.* bore with a drill; teach by repetition. *n.* tool for drilling holes; instruction by repetition.

drink, *v.*, **drank**, **drunk**, **drink·ing**. swallow liquid. *n.* any liquid which is swallowed.

drip, *v.*, **dripped** or **dript**, **drip·ping**. fall in drops. *n.* the falling of drops.

drive, *v.*, **drove**, **driv·en**, **driv·ing**. propel onward; move along. *n.* act of driving; any strong motivating force; organized effort.

driv·el, *v.*, **-eled**, **-el·ing**. utter nonsense. *n.*

driz·zle, *v.i.*, **-zled**, **-zling**. rain in small drops.

droll, *a.* comical. **droll·er·y**, *n. pl.*, **-er·ies**.

drone, *n.* male bee; hum. *v.i.*, **droned**, **dron·ing**. talk in a monotonous tone.

drool, *v.i.* water at the mouth.

droop, *v.i.* hang down. **droop·y**, *a.*, **droop·i·er**, **droop·i·est**.

drop, *n.* a liquid globule; depth to which anything drops. *v.*, **dropped** or **dropt**, **drop·ping**. fall.

drop·sy, *n.* edema.

dross, *n.* waste matter.

drought, *n.* long period of dry weather.

drown, *v.* die or be killed by immersion in fluid.

drowse, *v.*, **drowsed**, **drows·ing**. be sleepy. **drow·sy**, *a.*, **-si·er**, **-si·est**. **drow·si·ly**, *adv.* **drow·si·ness**, *n.*

drudg·er·y, *n. pl.*, **-er·ies**. hard, boring work.

drug, *n.* any medicinal substance; a narcotic. *v.t.*, **drugged**, **drug·ging**. administer drugs to.

drug·gist, *n.* pharmacist.

drum, *n.* percussion instrument; metal barrel. *v.*, **drummed**, **drum·ming**. tap rhythmically.

drum·stick, *n.* stick for beating a drum.

drunk, *a.* intoxicated with strong drink.

drunk·ard, *n.* an inebriate.

drunk·en, *a.* intoxicated. **drunk·en·ly**, *adv.* **drunk·en·ness**, *n.*

dry, *a.*, **dri·er**, **dri·est**. free from moisture; thirsty; free from sweetness. *v.* make or become dry. **dry·ly,** *adv.* **dry·ness,** *n.*

du·al, *a.* of or indicating two. **du·al·i·ty,** *n.*

dub, *v.t.,* **dubbed, dub·bing.** strike lightly with a sword; name.

du·bi·ous, *a.* doubtful. **du·bi·ous·ly,** *adv.*

duch·ess, *n.* wife or widow of a duke.

duck, *v.* plunge under water for a brief period of time; stoop; evade.

duct, *n.* conduit. **duct·less,** *a.*

dude, *n.* a dandy.

due, *a.* owed or payable as an obligation; proper; expected. *n.*

du·el, *n.* any contest between two persons or parties. *v.i.,* **du·eled, du·el·ing. du·el·ist,** *n.*

du·et, *n.* music for two voices or instruments.

duke, *n.* nobleman of the highest rank after a prince. **duke·dom,** *n.*

dull, *a.* deficient intelligence; uninteresting; not sharp; not bright; muffled. *v.* make or become dull. **dull·ness, dul·ness,** *n.*

du·ly, *adv.* properly.

dumb, *a. Inf.* slow-witted. Mute; silent.

dum·found, *v.t.* astound. Also **dumb·found.**

dum·my, *n. pl.,* **-mies.** exposed hand in bridge; mannequin.

dump, *v.* throw down in a mass; cast off. *n.* place where a mass of rubbish is put.

dump·ling, *n.* rounded mass of dough.

dunce, *n.* an ignoramus.

dune, *n.* hill of sand formed by wind.

dung, *n.* excrement of animals.

dun·ga·ree, *n.* coarse, durable cotton.

dun·geon, *n.* strong, close prison.

dupe, *n.* person easily cheated. *v.t.,* **duped, dup·ing.** deceive.

du·pli·cate, *v.t.,* **-cat·ed, -cat·ing.** copy exactly. *a.* exactly like something else. *n.* copy exactly like an original. **du·pli·ca·tion,** *n.* **du·pli·ca·tor,** *n.*

du·plic·i·ty, *n. pl.,* **-ties.** double-dealing.

du·ra·ble, *a.* lasting.

du·ra·tion, *n.* time which anything lasts.

du·ress, *n.* coercion.

dur·ing, *prep.* throughout; at a point in.

dusk, *n.* darker stage of twilight.

dusk·y, *a.,* **-i·er, -i·est. dusk·i·ly,** *adv.*

dust, *n.* any finely powdered substance. *v.* free from dust. **dust·y,** *a.,* **-i·er, -i·est.**

du·ty, *n. pl.,* **-ties.** obligation; import tax. **du·ti·ful,** *a.*

dwarf, *n.* being smaller than ordinary stature or size; stunted. *v.t.*

dwell, *v.i.,* **dwelt** or **dwelled, dwell·ing.** reside. **dwell·ing,** *n.*

dwin·dle, *v.,* **-dled, -dling.** diminish gradually.

dye, *n.* hue. *v.t.,* **dyed, dye·ing.** color. **dye·ing,** *n.*

dy·nam·ic, *a.* active; forceful. **dy·nam·i·cal,** *a.*

dy·na·mite, *n.* an explosive. *v.t.* shatter with dynamite.

dy·na·mo, *n. pl.,* **-mos.** dynamo-electric machine.

dy·nas·ty, *n. pl.,* **-ties.** succession of rulers of the same line; period during which they rule.

dys·en·ter·y, *n., Inf.* diarrhea.

E

each, *a.* every one of. *pron.* each one. *adv.* apiece.

ea·ger, *a.* enthusiastic; keen; impatient. **ea·ger·ly,** *adv.* **ea·ger·ness,** *n.*

ea·gle, *n.* large, strong bird of prey.

ea·glet, *n.* young eagle.

ear, *n.* organ of hearing; power to distinguish sounds; attention; spike of corn or other grain. **eared,** *a.*

ear·drum, *n.* tympanic membrane of the ear.

earl, *n.* nobleman, the third in rank. **earl·dom,** *n.*

ear·ly, *adv., a.,* **-li·er, -li·est.** in or during the first part of; before the usual time. **ear·li·ness,** *n.*

earn, *v.* gain by service rendered; get as one's desert or due. **earn·er,** *n.*

ear·nest, *a.* serious; sincerely zealous. **ear·nest·ly,** *adv.*

earn·ings, *n. pl.* that which is earned; wages; profit.

ear·ring, *n.* ornament worn on the lobe of the ear.

ear·shot, *n.* range of hearing.

earth, *n.* (*often cap.*) planet on

which we live; soil or dirt; ground.

earth·en·ware, *n.* pottery, dishes, etc., of baked clay.

earth·ly, *a.,* **-li·er, -li·est.** of the earth or this world.

earth·quake, *n.* trembling of the earth's crust.

earth·y, *a.,* **-i·er, -i·est.** of earth or soil; natural. **earth·i·ness,** *n.*

ease, *n.* freedom from labor, pain, formality, etc.; repose. *v.,* **eased, eas·ing.** relieve; render less difficult; lessen tension, pain, etc.

ea·sel, *n.* frame for supporting an artist's canvas.

eas·i·ly, *adv.* in an easy manner; beyond question. **eas·i·ness,** *n.*

east, *n.* direction of the sunrise; areas lying east. *a., adv.* in an easterly direction; in the east. **east·ern,** *a.*

east·ward, *a., adv.* toward the east. Also **east·wards.**

eas·y, *a.,* **-i·er, -i·est.** comfortable; free from anxiety or care; not difficult; lenient.

eas·y·go·ing, *a.* calm, relaxed.

eat, *v.,* **ate, eat·en, eat·ing.** consume food; wear or waste away. **eat·a·ble,** *a., n.*

eaves, *n. pl.* overhanging lower edge of a roof.

eaves·drop, *v.,* **-dropped, -dropping.** listen clandestinely. **eaves·drop·per,** *n.*

ebb, *n.* return of tidewater toward the sea; decline. *v.* recede; decay; decline.

eb·on·y, *n. pl.,* **-ies.** hard, black wood. *a.* of ebony.

ec·cen·tric, *a.* odd; off center. *n.* eccentric person. **ec·cen·tric·i·ty,** *n. pl.,* **-ties.**

ec·cle·si·as·tic, *a.* of the church or clergy. *n.* clergyman. **ec·cle·si·as·ti·cal,** *a.*

ech·o, *n. pl.,* **ech·oes.** repetition of sound, produced by the reflection of sound waves. *v.,* **ech·oed, ech·o·ing.** repeat. **ech·o·er,** *n.*

e·clipse, *n.* obscuration of the light of the sun, moon, etc., by the intervention of another heavenly body. *v.,* **e·clipsed, e·clips·ing.** obscure; surpass. **e·clip·tic,** *a.*

e·col·o·gy, *n.* study of organisms and their environment. **e·co·log·ic,** *a.* **e·col·o·gist,** *n.*

e·co·nom·i·cal, *a.* frugal.

e·co·nom·ics, *n. pl.* science of

the production, distribution, and consumption of wealth.

e·co·nom·ic, *a.* **e·con·o·mist,** *n.*

e·con·o·mize, *v.,* **-mized, -miz·ing.** manage frugally.

e·con·o·my, *n. pl.,* **-mies.** thrifty management; management and productivity of the resources of a country.

ec·sta·sy, *n. pl.,* **-sies.** rapture. **ec·stat·ic,** *a.*

ec·u·men·i·cal, *a.* universal; fostering worldwide Christian unity. **ec·u·men·ism,** *n.*

ec·ze·ma, *n.* inflammatory disease of the skin.

ed·dy, *n. pl.,* **-dies.** small whirlpool.

e·den·tate, *a.* toothless.

edge, *n.* sharp side of a blade; keenness; border; brink. *v.,* **edged, edg·ing.** put an edge on; move edgeways. **edged,** *a.*

edg·y, *a.,* **edg·i·er, edg·i·est.** irritable; nervous.

ed·i·ble, *a.* fit to be eaten. *n. usu. pl.* anything fit to eat.

e·dict, *n.* decree.

ed·i·fice, *n.* building.

ed·i·fy, *v.,* **-fied, -fy·ing.** instruct and improve. **ed·i·fi·ca·tion,** *n.*

ed·it, *v.* prepare or revise (literary matter) for publication; supervise the publication of. **ed·i·tor,** *n.*

e·di·tion, *n.* form in which a literary work is published.

ed·i·to·ri·al, *a.* of editors. *n.* article, as in a newspaper, setting forth the opinion of the editor. **ed·i·to·ri·al·ize,** *v.,* **-ized, -iz·ing.**

ed·u·cate, *v.,* **-cat·ed, -cat·ing.** advance development of, esp. by teaching or schooling. **ed·u·ca·tion,** *n.*

eel, *n. pl.,* **eels, eel.** fish having a serpent-like body.

ee·rie, *a.,* **ee·ri·er, ee·ri·est.** frightening; strange.

ef·face, *v.,* **-faced, -fac·ing.** obliterate; render inconspicuous. **ef·face·ment,** *n.*

ef·fect, *n.* result; power to produce results; purport; *pl.* property. *v.* bring about; produce. **ef·fec·tive,** *a.* **ef·fec·tu·al,** *a.*

ef·fem·i·nate, *a.* having qualities unsuitable to a man.

ef·fer·vesce, *v.,* **-vesced, -vesc·ing.** bubble. **ef·fer·ves·cence,** *n.* **ef·fer·ves·cent,** *a.*

ef·fi·ca·cious, *a.* effectual.

ef·fi·cient, *a.* able to be used with satisfaction and economy; competent. **ef·fi·cien·cy**, *n. pl.*, **-cies**.

ef·fi·gy, *n. pl.*, **-gies**. image, esp. a sculptured likeness of a person.

ef·fort, *n.* exertion; endeavor. **ef·fort·less**, *a.*

ef·fuse, *v.*, **-fused, -fus·ing**. pour out; flow. **ef·fu·sion**, *n.* **ef·fu·sive**, *a.*

egg, *n.* roundish reproductive body in a shell or membrane. *v.* incite, urge, or provoke.

egg·nog, *n.* drink of eggs, sugar, milk, and nutmeg.

e·go, *n. pl.*, **-gos**. individual self. **e·go·tism**, *n.* self-centeredness. **e·go·tist**, *n.*

e·gress, *n.* act of going or issuing out; exit.

e·gret, *n.* heron having white, flowing plumes.

eight, *a.* one more than seven in number. *n.* symbol for this. **eighth**, *a., n.*

eight·een, *a.* eight plus ten. *n.* symbol for this. **eight·eenth**, *a., n.*

eight·y, *a., n. pl.*, **eight·ies**. eight times ten. **eight·i·eth**, *a., n.*

ei·ther, *a., pron.* one or the other; each of two. *adv.* too; also; likewise.

e·ject, *v.* throw out; expel. **e·jec·tion**, *n.* **e·jec·tor**, *n.*

eke, *v.*, **eked, ek·ing**. increase. **eke out**, supplement; make (a living) laboriously.

e·lab·o·rate, *v.*, **-rat·ed, -rat·ing**. work out or complete with great detail. *a.* marked by great detail. **e·lab·o·ra·tion**, *n.*

e·lapse, *v.*, **-lapsed, -laps·ing**. slip away; pass, said of time.

e·las·tic, *a.* adaptable; flexible. **e·las·tic·i·ty**, *n.*

e·late, *v.*, **e·lat·ed, e·lat·ing**. put in high spirits; make happy. **e·la·tion**, *n.*

el·bow, *n.* bend or joint of the arm. *v.* jostle.

eld·er, *a.* older; senior. *n.* one who is older. **eld·er·ly**, *a.* quite old. **eld·est**, *a.* oldest.

e·lect, *v.* select for an office by vote; choose. *a.* chosen. **e·lec·tion**, *n.* **e·lec·tive**, *a., n.* **e·lec·tor**, *n.*

e·lec·tor·ate, *n.* whole body of voters or electors.

e·lec·tric, *a.* of electricity; stir-

ring. Also **e·lec·tri·cal**.

e·lec·tri·cian, *n.* one who works with electric devices.

e·lec·tric·i·ty, *n.* basic energy of the movement of subatomic particles.

e·lec·tri·fy, *v.*, **-fied, -fy·ing**. equip with or affect by electricity; thrill.

e·lec·tro·cute, *v.*, **-cut·ed, -cut·ing**. execute by means of an electric current. **e·lec·tro·cu·tion**, *n.*

e·lec·trode, *n.* electric current terminal.

e·lec·tron, *n.* particle of negative charge of an atom.

e·lec·tron·ics, *n. pl.* study of the behavior of electrons. **e·lec·tron·ic**, *a.*

el·e·gant, *a.* tastefully fine; gracefully refined. **el·e·gance**, **el·e·gan·cy**, *n.*

el·e·gy, *n. pl.*, **-gies**. mournful poem. **el·e·gize**, *v.*

el·e·ment, *n.* component part; natural habitat; substance of atoms of the same atomic number.

el·e·men·ta·ry, *a.* of first principles or rudiments; simple; primary.

el·e·phant, *n.* large mammal with a long trunk and tusks of ivory. **el·e·phan·tine**, *a.*

el·e·vate, *v.*, **-vat·ed, -vat·ing**. raise; cheer; elate. **el·e·va·tion**, *n.*

el·e·va·tor, *n.* mechanical device for raising and lowering passengers or goods.

e·lev·en, *n., a.* number between 10 and 12. **e·lev·enth**, *a.*

elf, *n. pl.*, **elves**. small imaginary being with magical powers. **elf·in**, *a., n.* **elf·ish**, *a.*

e·lic·it, *v.* bring out; evoke.

el·i·gi·ble, *a.* fit to be chosen. **el·i·gi·bil·i·ty**, *n.*

e·lim·i·nate, *v.*, **-nat·ed, -nat·ing**. omit; discharge wastes; remove. **e·lim·i·na·tion**, *n.*

e·lite, *n.* best. **e·lit·ist**, *n.*

e·lix·ir, *n.* alcoholic liquid containing medicinal agents.

elk, *n. pl.*, **elks, elk**. wapiti.

e·lipse, *n.* oval figure. **el·lip·ti·cal**, *a.*

elm, *n.* shade tree.

el·o·cu·tion, *n.* art of speaking effectively in public. **el·o·cu·tion·ist**, *n.*

e·lon·gate, *v.*, **-gat·ed, -gat·ing**. lengthen; extend.

e·lope, v., **e·loped, e·lop·ing.** run away to be married. **e·lope·ment,** n. **e·lop·er,** n.

el·o·quence, n. art of using language with fluency, force, etc. **el·o·quent,** a.

else, a. other; in addition. adv. otherwise.

else·where, adv. in, at, or to another place.

e·lu·ci·date, v., **-dat·ed, -dat·ing.** make clear; explain.

e·lude, v., **e·lud·ed, e·lud·ing.** baffle; evade. **e·lu·sive,** a.

e·ma·ci·ate, v., **-at·ed, -at·ing.** lose flesh gradually. **e·ma·ci·a·tion,** n.

em·a·nate, v., **-nat·ed, -nat·ing.** flow forth; issue.

e·man·ci·pate, v., **-pat·ed, -pat·ing.** free from bondage. **e·man·ci·pa·tion,** n.

em·balm, v. preserve from loss or decay. **em·balm·er,** n.

em·bar·go, n. pl., **-goes.** authoritative stoppage of freight or commerce.

em·bark, v. board a ship; engage in an enterprise.

em·bar·rass, v. feel self-conscious; disconcert.

em·bas·sy, n. pl., **-sies.** official office and residence of an ambassador.

em·bel·lish, v. adorn.

em·ber, n. live coal or glowing piece of wood.

em·bez·zle, v., **-zled, -zling.** appropriate that entrusted, as money, etc. **em·bez·zler,** n.

em·blem, n. symbol; distinctive badge.

em·boss, v. fashion relief or raised work on.

em·brace, v., **-braced, -brac·ing.** hug; accept; take in; surround. n. embracing.

em·broi·der, v. adorn with needlework; embellish. **em·broi·der·y,** n. pl., **-der·ies.**

em·bry·o, n. pl., **-bry·os.** organism at any stage in development before birth or hatching, esp. the early stages.

em·er·ald, n. green gem. a. of a clear deep green color.

e·merge, v., **-merged, -merg·ing.** come forth. **e·mer·gence,** n.

e·mer·gen·cy, n. pl., **-cies.** sudden, usu. unexpected occasion calling for immediate action.

em·er·y, n. substance used for grinding and polishing.

em·i·grate, v., **-grat·ed, -grat·ing.** quit one country and settle in another. **em·i·grant,** n. **em·i·gra·tion,** n.

em·i·nent, a. high; noteworthy. **em·i·nence,** n.

em·is·sar·y, n. pl., **-sar·ies.** person sent on a mission.

e·mit, v., **e·mit·ted, e·mit·ting.** throw or give out; utter; issue. **e·mis·sion,** n. **e·mit·ter,** n.

e·mo·tion, n. feelings of joy, fear, love, etc.

em·per·or, n. highest person in an empire. **em·press,** n. fem.

em·pha·sis, n. pl., **-ses,** importance or significance; stress.

em·phat·ic, a.

em·pha·size, v., **-sized, -siz·ing.** give emphasis to.

em·pire, n. area governed by an emperor; imperial power and dominion.

em·ploy, v. engage the services of; keep busy; make use of; n. **em·ploy·ee, em·ploy·e,** n. **em·ploy·er,** n. **em·ploy·ment,** n.

em·pow·er, v. authorize.

emp·ty, a. containing nothing; meaningless. v., **-tied, -ty·ing.** remove the contents from; discharge. **emp·ti·ness,** n. **emp·ti·ly,** adv.

em·u·late, v., **-lat·ed, -lat·ing.** strive to equal or excel by imitating.

e·mul·sion, n. mixture of two liquids kept in suspension. **e·mul·sive,** a.

en·a·ble, v., **-bled, -bling.** give means, ability, etc.

en·act, v. make into a law; act the part of.

e·nam·el, n. glossy paint or varnish; hard covering of a tooth. v., **-eled, -el·ing.** lay enamel on. **e·nam·el·ware,** n.

en·am·or, v. inflame with love. **en·am·ored·ness,** n.

en·case, v., **-cased, -cas·ing.** enclose in or as in a case.

en·chant, v. bewitch; charm. **en·chant·ing,** a. **en·chant·ment,** n. **en·chant·ress,** n.

en·cir·cle, v., **-cled, -cling.** surround.

en·close, v., **-closed, -clos·ing.** surround; put in. **en·clo·sure,** n.

en·com·pass, v. envelop; include. **en·com·pass·ment,** n.

en·core, n. demand for an additional performance.

en·coun·ter, n. accidental meeting; meet suddenly; engage in battle.

en·cour·age, v., -aged, -ag·ing. inspire with courage, hope, etc. en·cour·ag·ing, a.

en·croach, v. trespass; intrude. en·croach·ment, n.

en·cum·ber, v. impede; burden.

en·cy·clo·pe·di·a, n. book or set of books of articles on all subjects. Also en·cy·clo·pae·di·a.

end, n. conclusion; death; result; purpose; bounds. v. put an end to; conclude. end·ing, n.

en·dan·ger, v. imperil.

en·dear, v. make beloved.

en·deav·or, n. serious effort. v. try; attempt.

en·dorse, v., -dorsed, -dors·ing. write one's signature on the back (of a check); lend support to. en·dorse·ment, n.

en·dow, v. furnish with any gift, quality, talent.

en·dur·ance, n. a bearing up under pain or distress without yielding; fortitude.

en·dure, v., -dured, -dur·ing. undergo; suffer without yielding; last; put up with. en·dur·ance, n. en·dur·ing, a.

en·e·my, n. pl., -mies. foe; adversary.

en·er·gy, n. pl., -gies. inherent power; power of operating. en·er·get·ic, a.

en·force, v., -forced, -forc·ing. force compliance with laws; compel. en·forc·er, n.

en·gage, v., -gaged, -gag·ing. hire; betroth; attract; do battle with; mesh. en·gaged, a. en·gage·ment, n. en·gag·ing, a.

en·gen·der, v. produce; cause to exist.

en·gine, n. machine that uses thermal energy to do work; locomotive.

en·gi·neer, n. one who practices engineering.

en·gi·neer·ing, n. practical application of scientific knowledge.

Eng·lish, a. of England or the English language. n. English language or people.

en·grave, v., -graved, -grav·ing. cut figures, letters, etc., into a hard substance. en·grav·er, n. en·grav·ing, n.

en·gross, v. absorb; monopolize. en·gross·ing, a.

en·gulf, v. swallow up; overwhelm. en·gulf·ment, n.

en·hance, v., -hanced, -hanc·ing. increase.

e·nig·ma, n. riddle. en·ig·mat·ic, en·ig·mat·i·cal, a.

en·join, v. admonish; command.

en·joy, v. receive pleasure from; have and use with satisfaction. en·joy·ment, n.

en·large, v., -larged, -larg·ing. make larger. en·larg·er, n. en·large·ment, n.

en·light·en, v. give insight to; instruct.

en·list, v. join the military; employ. en·list·ment, n.

en·liv·en, v. make gay.

en·mi·ty, n. pl., -ties. ill will.

en·no·ble, v., -bled, -bling. dignify.

e·nor·mi·ty, n. pl., -ties. atrocity.

e·nor·mous, a. great in size.

e·nough, a., n. adequate (quantity). adv. sufficiently.

en·rage, v., -raged, -rag·ing. make furious.

en·rich, v. make rich; improve the quality of.

en·roll, v. register; enlist; record. en·roll·ment, n.

en·sem·ble, n. complete outfit; fun group of singers, etc.

en·shrine, v., -shrined, -shrin·ing. place in a shrine; cherish.

en·sign, n. flag; banner; milit. lowest officer in the navy.

en·slave, v., -slaved, -slav·ing. make a slave of.

en·sue, v., -sued, -su·ing. follow as a consequence.

en·tail, v. limit an inheritance of property; bring on.

en·tan·gle, v., -gled, -gling. make tangled; involve.

en·ter, v. come or go into; begin; join; set down in a record; enroll.

en·ter·prise, n. project attempted; adventurous spirit; firm. en·ter·pris·ing, a.

en·ter·tain, v. treat with hospitality; amuse; take into consideration. en·ter·tain·er, n. en·ter·tain·ment, n.

en·thrall, v., -thralled, -thrall·ing. charm or captivate. Also en·thral.

en·thu·si·asm, n. keen and active interest. en·thu·si·ast, n.

en·tice, v., -ticed, -tic·ing. lure. en·tice·ment, n.

en·tire, a. whole; full; intact. en·tire·ly, adv. en·tire·ty, n.

en·ti·tle, v., -tled, -tling. give a right; give a name or title to.

en·ti·tle·ment, *n.*

en·ti·ty, *n. pl.*, **-ties**. being.

en·trails, *n. pl.* bowels.

en·trance, *n.* act of entering; admission; doorway or passage. Also **en·trance·way**.

en·trance, *v.*, **-tranced**, **-tranc·ing**. fill with delight.

en·treat, *v.* ask earnestly; plead for. **en·treat·y**, *n.*

en·tree, *n.* entry; main course of a meal.

en·trench, *v.* dig a trench around; place in a strong position. **en·trench·ment**, *n.*

en·trust, *v.* trust to the care of; consign.

en·try, *n. pl.*, **-tries**. act of entering; entrance; contestant item entered.

e·nu·mer·ate, *v.* **-at·ed**, **-at·ing**. name one by one; count. **e·nu·mer·a·tion**, *n.*

e·nun·ci·ate, *v.*, **-at·ed**, **-at·ing**. pronounce; state definitely.

en·vel·op, *v.*, **-oped**, **-op·ing**. surround entirely.

en·ve·lope, *n.* paper cover, usu. for a letter.

en·vi·ron·ment, *n.* factors and conditions influencing an organism; surroundings.

en·voy, *n.* one sent on a mission; diplomatic agent.

en·vy, *n. pl.*, **-vies**. resentment or jealously. *v.*, **-vied**, **-vy·ing**. feel envy toward. **en·vi·er**, *n.* **en·vi·ous**, *a.*

en·zyme, *n.* substance in living cells acting as a catalyst in the metabolism.

e·phem·er·al, *a.* short-lived.

ep·ic, *a.* heroic; majestic. *n.* long poem describing extraordinary events.

ep·i·dem·ic, *a.* affecting a great number. *n.* outbreak which spreads rapidly.

ep·i·der·mis, *n.* outer layer of the skin.

ep·i·lep·sy, *n.* nervous disease characterized by convulsive seizures. **ep·i·lep·tic**, *a., n.*

ep·i·logue, **ep·i·log**, *n.* section ending a piece of literature.

e·pis·co·pal, *a.* of a bishop.

ep·i·sode, *n.* incident; one of the parts of a serial.

e·pis·tle, *n.* letter.

ep·i·taph, *n.* inscription on a tomb. **ep·i·taph·ic**, *a.*

ep·i·thet, *n.* word or phrase about a person; term of abuse. **ep·i·thet·ic**, *a.*

e·pit·o·me, *n.* summary; person or thing that typifies the whole. **e·pit·o·mize**, *v.*

ep·och, *n.* particular period of time. **ep·och·al**, *a.*

ep·ox·y, *n.* resin.

e·qua·ble, *a.* fair; uniform; steady. **e·qua·bil·i·ty**, *n.*

e·qual, *a.* alike in quantity, value, rank, ability, etc.; even. *n.* one who or that which is equal. *v.*, **e·qualed**, **e·qual·ing**. match. **e·qual·ly**, *adv.* **e·qual·i·ty**, *n. pl.*, **-ties**.

e·qual·ize, *v.*, **-ized**, **-iz·ing**. make equal. **e·qual·iz·er**, *n.*

e·qua·nim·i·ty, *n.* calmness.

e·quate, *v.*, **e·quat·ed**, **e·quat·ing**. state the equality of or between; make equal. **e·qua·tion**, *n.*

e·qua·tor, *n.* that circle dividing the earth into the N. and S. hemispheres.

e·ques·tri·an, *a.* of horses or horsemanship. *n.* rider on horseback. **e·ques·tri·enne**, *n.*

e·qui·lib·ri·um, *n. pl.*, **-ums**, **-a**. equal balance.

e·qui·nox, *n.* time when day and night are of equal length.

e·quip, *v.*, **e·quipped**, **e·quip·ping**. provide with everything necessary for. **e·quip·per**, *n.* **e·quip·ment**, *n.*

eq·ui·ta·ble, *a.* just; fair. **eq·ui·ty**, *n. pl.*, **-ties**.

e·quiv·a·lent, *a.* equal. *n.* that which is equivalent.

e·quiv·o·cal, *a.* ambiguous; doubtful. **e·quiv·o·cate**, *v.*

e·ra, *n.* period of time marked by special events.

e·rad·i·cate, *v.*, **-cat·ed**, **-cat·ing**. destroy thoroughly. **e·rad·i·ca·tion**, *n.*

e·rase, *v.*, **e·rased**, **e·ras·ing**. rub out; eliminate. **e·ras·er**, *n.*

ere, *conj., prep.* poet. before.

e·rect, *v.* set in an upright position; build; cause to come into being. *a.* upright. **e·rec·tive**, *a.* **e·rec·tion**, *n.*

er·mine, *n. pl.*, **-mine**, **-mines**. small mammal with a white winter coat.

e·rode, *v.*, **e·rod·ed**, **e·rod·ing**. eat away; slowly wear away. **e·ro·sion**, *n.*

e·rot·ic, *a.* sexual love; increasing sexual desire. **e·rot·i·cism**, *n.*

err, *v.* wander; be wrong; blunder. **err·ing·ly**, *adv.*

er·rand, *n.* trip to carry a message or to do a job.

er·rant, *a.* traveling; wandering. **er·rant·ly,** *adv.*

er·rat·ic, *a.* wandering; deviating; queer.

er·ro·ne·ous, *a.* wrong; false.

er·ror, *n.* mistake; inaccuracy.

erst·while, *a.* former.

er·u·dite, *a.* learned; scholarly. **er·u·di·tion,** *n.*

e·rupt, *v.* burst forth; eject; break out. **e·rup·tion,** *n.*

es·ca·la·tor, *n.* moving staircase.

es·cal·lop, *n., v.* scallop.

es·ca·pade, *n.* adventurous or thoughtless action.

es·cape, *v.,* **-caped, -cap·ing.** get away; avoid capture; fade away; slip out. *n.* act of escaping; leakage; means of escaping.

es·chew, *v.* shun; avoid.

es·cort, *n.* woman's date; body of persons accompanying others for protection. *v.* attend as an escort.

es·crow, *n.* deed, bond, etc. held in custody until the fulfillment of some condition.

e·soph·a·gus, oe·soph·a·gus, *n. pl.,* **-gi, -ji.** gullet.

es·o·ter·ic, *a.* understood only by those few with special knowledge.

es·pe·cial, *a.* special; particular. **es·pe·cial·ly,** *adv.*

es·pi·o·nage, *n.* practice of spying.

es·pouse, *v.,* **-poused, -pous·ing.** adopt; marry. **es·pous·er,** *n.* **es·pous·al,** *n.*

es·py, *v.,* **-pied, -py·ing.** see; discover.

es·say, *n.* trial; test; short, literary piece. *v.* attempt; try. **es·say·ist,** *n.*

es·sence, *n.* intrinsic value; extract; perfume.

es·sen·tial, *a.* important; basic; absolutely necessary. *n.* basic; necessary.

es·tab·lish, *v.* install on a permanent basis; prove; found. **es·tab·lish·ment,** *n.*

es·tate, *n.* property with a manor house on it; property or possessions.

es·teem, *v.* respect; admire. *n.* high regard.

es·thet·ic, *a.* aesthetic.

es·ti·ma·ble, *a.* valued; worthy of esteem.

es·ti·mate, *v.,* **-mat·ed, -mat·ing.** calculate approximately; judge. *n.* approximate judgment or calculation. **es·ti·ma·tor,** *n.* **es·ti·ma·tion,** *n.*

es·trange, *v.,* **-tranged, -trang·ing.** turn away in feeling or affection.

es·tu·ar·y, *n. pl.,* **-ies.** wide mouth of a river.

et cet·er·a, *n.* and so forth.

etch, *v.* engrave by the action of an acid; impress firmly on the mind. **etch·ing,** *n.*

e·ter·nal, *a.* everlasting; endless **e·ter·nal·ly,** *adv.*

e·ter·ni·ty, *n. pl.,* **-ties.** being without beginning or end; endless time.

e·ther, *n.* liquid used mainly as an anesthetic and a solvent.

e·the·re·al, *a.* delicate and airy; heavenly; celestial

eth·ics, *n. pl.* principles of morality, or the study of morals. **eth·i·cal,** *a.*

eth·nic, *a.* of those groups sharing a common language or customs. Also **eth·ni·cal.**

eth·nol·o·gy, *n.* study of the various groups of mankind.

et·i·quette, *n.* accepted code of social behavior.

é·tude, *n.* study.

et·y·mol·o·gy, *n. pl.,* **-gies.** explanation of the origin and changes of a word. **et·y·mol·o·gist,** *n.*

eu·gen·ics, *n. pl.* science of improving the qualities of the human species.

eu·lo·gize, *v.,* **-gized, -giz·ing.** speak or write in praise of. **eu·lo·gy,** *n. pl.,* **-gies.**

eu·nuch, *n.* castrated male.

eu·phe·mism, *n.* inoffensive word substituted for an unpleasant term. **eu·phe·mist,** *n.*

eu·pho·ny, *n.* agreeableness of sound. **eu·phon·ic,** *a.*

eu·pho·ri·a, *n.* mood of elation. **eu·phor·ic,** *a.*

eu·tha·na·sia, *n.* mercy killing.

e·vac·u·ate, *v.,* **-at·ed, -at·ing.** make empty; vacate; quit. **e·vac·u·a·tion,** *n.*

e·vade, *v.,* **-vad·ed, -vad·ing.** avoid; escape from or elude.

e·val·u·ate, *v.,* **-at·ed, -at·ing.** determine the value of; appraise. **e·val·u·a·tion,** *n.*

e·van·gel·i·cal, *a.* of the gospel; seeking the conversion of sinners.

e·van·ge·list, *n.* (often cap.) gospel writer; preacher of the gospel; revivalist. e·van·ge·lism, n.

e·vap·o·rate, v., -rat·ed, -rat·ing. change to vapor; disappear. e·vap·o·ra·tion, n.

e·va·sion, n. act of avoiding; excuse. e·va·sive, a.

eve, n. period just preceding some event; evening.

even, a. level; smooth; uniform; fair; equal; of a number, divisible by two. adv. evenly. v. make even. e·ven·ly, adv.

eve·ning, n. time from sunset until night. a. of evening.

e·vent, n. anything that happens; occurrence. e·vent·ful, a.

e·ven·tu·al, a. coming later or as a result.

e·ven·tu·al·i·ty, n. pl., -ties. that which may happen.

ev·er, adv. at any time; always; continually.

ev·er·green, a. always green. n. evergreen plant.

eve·ry, a. each; all conceivable; total.

e·vict, v. expel by force; expel from property by a legal process. e·vic·tion, n.

ev·i·dence, n. proof; testimony. v., -denced, -denc·ing. prove; indicate.

ev·i·dent, a. obvious; plain.

e·vil, a. morally wrong; wicked; bad. adv. badly; ill. n. that which is evil. e·vil·do·er, n.

e·voke, v., e·voked, e·vok·ing. call up; elicit.

ev·o·lu·tion, n. development; something evolved.

e·volve, v., e·volved, e·volv·ing. develop by degrees.

ewe, n. female sheep, etc.

ew·er, n. large pitcher.

ex·act, v. call for; demand. a. strictly accurate or correct. ex·act·ing, a.

ex·ag·ger·ate, v., -at·ed, -at·ing. magnify; overstate. ex·ag·ger·a·tion, n.

ex·alt, v. raise up in rank, honor, etc.; dignify; praise. ex·al·ter. n. ex·al·ta·tion, n.

ex·am·ine, v., -ined, -in·ing. inspect or observe; question, as a witness. ex·am·i·na·tion, n. ex·am·in·er, n.

ex·am·ple, n. sample; model.

ex·as·per·ate, v., -at·ed, -at·ing. irritate; anger. ex·as·per·a·tion, n.

ex·ca·vate, v., -vat·ing. make a

hole in; unearth. ex·ca·va·tion, n.

ex·ceed, v. pass beyond; surpass; excel.

ex·ceed·ing, a. great; exceptional. ex·ceed·ing·ly, adv.

ex·cel, v., -celled, -cell·ing. surpass; outdo.

ex·cel·lent, a. extremely good; choice. ex·cel·lence, n.

ex·cept, v. exclude; object. prep. with exception of. conj. unless. ex·cep·tion, n.

ex·cep·tion·al, a. out of the ordinary.

ex·cerpt, v. pick out from for quotation. n. extract.

ex·cess, n. extreme; amount by which one thing exceeds another. ex·ces·sive, a.

ex·change, v., -changed, -chang·ing. interchange. n. act of exchanging.

ex·cise, n. tax on certain items. Also ex·cise tax.

ex·cite, v., -cit·ed, -cit·ing. call into action; stir up. ex·cit·a·ble, a. ex·cite·ment, n. ex·cit·ing, a.

ex·claim, v. cry out. ex·cla·ma·tion, n.

ex·clude, v., -clud·ed, -clud·ing. shut or keep out. ex·clu·sion, n. ex·clu·sive, a.

ex·com·mu·ni·cate, v., -cat·ed, -cat·ing. expel from the church. ex·com·mu·ni·ca·tion, n.

ex·cre·ment, n. refuse matter discharged from the body.

ex·cur·sion, n. trip; trip made at reduced fares.

ex·cuse, v., -cused, -cus·ing. seek to remove the blame from; pardon; dispense with. n. reason; explanation.

ex·e·cute, v., -cut·ed, -cut·ing. inflict capital punishment on; perform or do; put into effect. ex·e·cu·tion, n.

ex·ec·u·tive, a. suited for executing. n. person or body charged with administrative work. ex·ec·u·tive·ly, adv.

ex·ec·u·tor, n. law. person appointed to carry out the provisions of a will.

ex·em·pla·ry, a. serving as a model; worthy of imitation.

ex·empt, v. free from any duty; grant immunity to. a. not included. ex·emp·tion, n.

ex·er·cise, n. bodily activity; putting into action; something done as practice or training.

v., **-cised, -cis·ing.** put through exercises.

ex·ert, *v.* put in action. **ex·er·tion,** *n.*

ex·hale, *v.*, **-haled, -hal·ing.** breath out; emit.

ex·haust, *v.* use up; drain of resources; wear out; discharge contents. **ex·haus·tion,** *n.* **ex·haus·tive,** *a.*

ex·hib·it, *v.* expose to view; place on display. *n.* that which is exhibited. **ex·hib·i·tor,** *n.* **ex·hi·bi·tion,** *n.*

ex·hil·a·rate, *v.*, **-rat·ed, -rat·ing.** make cheerful.

ex·hort, *v.* encourage. **ex·hor·ta·tion,** *n.*

ex·i·gent, *a.* urgent.

ex·ile, *n.* separation from one's country; person exiled. *v.*, **exiled, ex·il·ing.** banish.

ex·ist, *v.* have being; live. **ex·ist·ence,** *n.*

ex·it, *n.* passage out of. *v.* leave.

ex·o·dus, *n.* mass migration.

ex·or·bi·tant, *a.* excessive.

ex·ot·ic, *a.* of foreign origin or character; unusual.

ex·pand, *v.* spread out or unfold; increase; enlarge. **ex·pan·sion,** *n.* **ex·pan·sive,** *a.*

ex·panse, *n.* wide extent of anything.

ex·pect, *v.* await; regard as likely to occur; suppose. **ex·pect·an·cy,** *n. pl.*, **-cies. ex·pect·ant,** *a.* **ex·pect·ant·ly,** *adv.* **ex·pec·ta·tion,** *n.*

ex·pe·di·en·cy, *n.* seeking of selfish gain at the expense of principle. **ex·pe·di·ent,** *a.*, *n.* help the progress of; hasten. **ex·pe·dit·er,** *n.*

ex·pe·dite, *v.*, **-dit·ed, -dit·ing.**

ex·pe·di·tion, *n.* excursion made for some specific purpose; persons engaged in it.

ex·pel, *v.*, **ex·pelled, ex·pel·ling.** drive away; cut off from membership.

ex·pend, *v.* pay out; use up. **ex·pend·i·ture,** *n.*

ex·pense, *n.* cost or charge; *pl.* charges incurred.

ex·pen·sive, *a.* costly.

ex·pe·ri·ence, *n.* instance of personally undergoing something; knowledge gained from what one has undergone. *v.*, **-enced, -enc·ing.** have experience of; undergo.

ex·per·i·ment, *n.* test or trial. **ex·per·i·men·tal,** *a.*

ex·pert, *a.* experienced; skillful. *n.* skillful or practiced person. **ex·pert·ly,** *adv.*

ex·per·tise, *n.* specialized knowledge.

ex·pire, *v.*, **ex·pired, ex·pir·ing.** exhale; die; come to an end.

ex·plain, *v.* make clear or evident; give or show the meaning or reason for. **ex·plain·er,** *n.*

ex·pla·na·tion, *n.*

ex·plic·it, *a.* precise in expression. **ex·plic·it·ly,** *adv.*

ex·plode, *v.*, **ex·plod·ed, ex·plod·ing.** blow up break up noisily. **ex·plo·sion,** *n.*

ex·ploit, *n.* notable deed; heroic act. *v.* use for profit or selfishly. **ex·ploi·ta·tion,** *n.* **ex·ploit·er,** *n.*

ex·plore, *v.* travel with the intent of making discovery; investigate. **ex·plo·ra·tion,** *n.* **ex·plor·er,** *n.*

ex·po·nent, *n.* one who explains anything; one who stands as a symbol.

ex·port, *v.* send, as goods, for sale in foreign countries. *n.* item exported. *a.* of goods exported. **ex·por·ta·tion,** *n.*

ex·pose, *v.*, **ex·posed, ex·pos·ing.** leave unprotected; uncover; display. **ex·po·sure,** *n.*

ex·po·si·tion, *n.* laying open; explanation; show.

ex·pound, *v.* explain; argue the defense of.

ex·press, *v.* declare; make known; send by a fast system. *a.* clearly stated; fast. *n.* rapid and direct vehicle or other conveyance. *adv.* by way of express. **ex·press·er,** *n.*

ex·pres·sion, *n.* manner in which a thing is put into words; word, phrase, etc.; ability of expressing emotion. **ex·pres·sive,** *a.*

ex·pul·sion, *n.* act of driving out. **ex·pul·sive,** *a.*

ex·qui·site, *a.* of exceptionally choice quality; of uncommon beauty; keen. **ex·qui·site·ly,** *adv.*

ex·tant, *a.* still existing.

ex·tem·po·ra·ne·ous, *a.* offhand; improvised.

ex·tend, *v.* stretch out; pull out; enlarge; offer. **ex·ten·sion,** *n.*

ex·ten·sive, *a.* of great extent. **ex·ten·sive·ly,** *adv.*

ex·tent, *n.* space or degree to which a thing extends; scope;

extended space.

ex·te·ri·or, a. external; outer. n. outer surface.

ex·ter·mi·nate, v., -nat·ed, -nat·ing. destroy utterly. **ex·ter·mi·na·tion**, n.

ex·ter·nal, a. exterior; of or coming from without.

ex·tinct, a. having died out.

ex·tinc·tion, n. dying out as of a species.

ex·tin·guish, v. put out; quench; put an end to.

ex·tol, v., **ex·tolled**, **ex·toll·ing.** praise; applaud.

ex·tort, v. obtain from a person by force. **ex·tor·tion**, n.

ex·tra, a. more than what is usual or necessary. n. something additional. adv. beyond the ordinary.

ex·tract, v. pull out by force; take out. n. something extracted; passage selected from a book, etc.; concentrate. **ex·trac·tion**, n.

ex·tra·or·di·nar·y, a. beyond the usual.

ex·trav·a·gant, a. spending more money than necessary; wasteful. **ex·trav·a·gance**, n.

ex·treme, a. utmost in degree; going to great lengths; final. n. highest degree; excessive length. **ex·treme·ly**, adv.

ex·trem·i·ty, n. pl., -ties. extreme point or part; moment of danger; usu. pl. end part of a limb.

ex·tri·cate, v., -cat·ed, -cat·ing. disengage; distentangle.

ex·tro·vert, n. one who is outgoing, active, etc. **ex·tro·ver·sion**, n.

ex·u·ber·ant, a. high-spirited; overflowing. **ex·u·ber·ance**, n.

ex·ude, v., **ex·ud·ed**, **ex·ud·ing.** ooze; discharge; give off.

ex·ult, v. rejoice in triumph. **ex·ult·ant**, a. **ex·ul·ta·tion**, n.

eye, n. organ of sight; sight; view; regard. v., **eyed**, **ey·ing** or **eye·ing.** view; watch narrowly.

eye·ful, n. pl., -fuls. complete view of something.

eye·let, n. hole; metal ring to line such a hole.

eye·sight, n. vision; view.

eye·sore, n. something offensive to look at.

eye·tooth, n. pl., -teeth. upper canine tooth.

eye·wit·ness, n. one who sees an act and can report on it. v.

witness.

F

fa·ble, n. brief moral tale; a myth.

fab·ric, n. cloth.

fab·ri·cate, v., -cat·ed, -cat·ing. make, form; make up.

fab·u·lous, a. remarkably good; not real.

fa·cade, n. main face of a building.

face, n. front of the head; appearance; self-respect. v., **faced**, **fac·ing.** turn face toward; confront. **fa·cial**, a.

fac·et, n. surface gem of a cut; aspect.

fa·ce·tious, a. without serious intent.

fac·ile, a. easy.

fa·cil·i·tate, v.t., -tat·ed, -tat·ing. make easy.

fa·cil·i·ty, n. pl., -ties. ease or skill. often pl. something for a particular purpose.

fac·sim·i·le, n. exact copy.

fact, n. actually happening; truth.

fac·tion, n. group opposing the main group. **fac·tion·al**, a.

fac·tor, n. causal element.

fac·to·ry, n. pl., -ries. building used for manufacturing goods.

fac·tu·al, a. of facts; real.

fac·ul·ty, n. natural ability; teaching staff.

fad, n. passing fashion.

fade, v., **fad·ed**, **fad·ing.** lose color, strength.

fag, v., **fagged**, **fag·ging.** exhaust, make tired.

fag·ot, n. bundle of wood.

Fahr·en·heit, a. of a thermometer on which the boiling point of water is 212°, the freezing point is 32°.

fail, v. fall short; weaken; not succeed; become bankrupt; neglect; disappoint. **fail·ure**, n.

faint, v. become unconscious. n. a momentary loss of consciousness. a. feeble; weak. **faint·ness**, n.

fair, a. pretty; blond; bright, sunny; honest, just; mediocre. **fair·ly**, adv. impartially; moderately. **fair**, n. exposition, carnival.

fair·y, n. pl., -ies. tiny imaginary being with human form and superhuman powers.

faith, n. loyalty; belief in God;

trust.

faith·ful, *a.* loyal; exact. **faith·ful·ly**, *adv.*

faith·less, *a.* disloyal.

fake, *v.* **faked, fak·ing**, pretend; counterfeit; sham. *n., a.*

fal·con, *n.* hawk trained to hunt.

fall, *v.*, **fell, fall·en, fall·ing.** drop down suddenly; occur. *n.* a falling; autumn; decline or overthrow; *usu. pl.* a waterfall. **fall back**, retreat; **fall off**, diminish; **fall out**, quarrel; **fall through**, fail; **fall to**, begin.

fal·la·cy, *n.* misleading, false. **fal·la·cious**, *a.*

fal·li·ble, *a.* liable to error.

fall·out, *n.* radioactive particles from a nuclear explosion; descent of such particles.

fal·low, *a.* plowed but unseeded; inactive.

false, untrue; faithless; not genuine. **false, false·ly**, *adv.* **fal·si·fy**, *v.*, **fal·si·ty**, *n.*

false·hood, *n.* a lie.

fal·ter, *v.* stumble; stammer; waver.

fame, *n.* widespread public renown.

fa·mil·iar, *a.* well-known; friendly; intimate. **fa·mil·iar·i·ty**, *n.*, **fa·mil·iar·ize**, *v.*

fam·i·ly, *n. pl.*, **-lies.** parents and their children; relatives; lineage; group of related things.

fam·ine, *n.* widespread scarcity of food.

fam·ish, *v.* suffer from hunger or thirst.

fa·mous, *a.* widely known.

fan, *n.* implement for producing cooling air currents; admirer; avid supporter. *v.*, **fanned, fan·ning.** move air with a fan; stir up; spread out.

fa·nat·ic, *n., a.* marked by extreme, uncritical zeal. Also **fa·nat·i·cal**, *a.*, **fa·nat·i·cism**, *n.*

fan·ci·er, *n.* one having a specialized interest in something.

fan·cy, *n. pl.*, **-cies.** imagination; a whim; a fondness; a notion. **fan·ci·ful**, *a.* Also *a.*, **-ci·er**, **-ci·est**, ornamental; extra fine. *v.*, **-cied, -cy·ing.** imagine; like.

fan·fare, *n.* flourish of trumpets; publicity.

fang, *n.* long, pointed tooth.

fan·tas·tic, *a.* unreal; grotesque; outstanding.

fan·ta·sy, *n. pl.*, **-sies.** a creation of the imagination.

far, *a., adv.* **far·ther** or **fur·ther**,

far·thest or **fur·thest.** distant; to an advanced degree.

far·a·way, *a.* distant; dreamy.

farce, *n.* exaggerated comedy; absurd pretense; mere show. **far·ci·cal**, *a.*

fare, *v.* **fared, far·ing.** get along. *n.* price of transportation; food and drink.

farewell, *int.* good-bye. *n., a.* parting.

far-fetched, *a.* improbable.

farm, *n.* land for raising crops, livestock. *v.* cultivate (land). **farm·er**, *n.*, **farm·house**, *n.*, **farm·ing**, *n.*

far-off, *a.* distant.

far·sight·ed, *a.* seeing far objects best; planning ahead.

fas·ci·nate, *v.*, **-nat·ed, -nat·ing.** attract; captivate.

fas·cism, *n.* militaristic dictatorship. **fas·cist**, *n.*

fash·ion, *n.* kind or form of anything; mode or way; current style. *v.* form; make. **fash·ion·a·ble**, *a.* stylish.

fast, *a.* rapid; fixed; faithful; lasting; of questionable morals. *adv.* rapidly; deeply. *v.* abstain from food. *n.* period of fasting.

fas·ten, *v.* to secure; to attach.

fas·tid·i·ous, *a.* hard to please; squeamish.

fat, *a.*, **fat·ter, fat·test.** plump; oily, greasy; rich; *n.* oily animal substance.

fa·tal, *a.* causing death.

fa·tal·ism, *n.* belief that all things are predetermined. **fa·tal·ist**, *n.*

fa·tal·i·ty, *n. pl.*, **-ties.** a violent death.

fate, *n.* destiny; one's appointed lot; outcome; death; ruin. **fate·ful**, *a.*

fa·ther, *n.* male parent; a priest. originator or founder. *v.* beget. **fa·ther·hood**, *n.*

fa·ther-in-law, *n. pl.*, **fa·thers-in-law.** father of one's husband or wife.

fath·om, *n. pl.*, **-oms, -om.** depth of six feet. *v.* comprehend; penetrate.

fa·tigue, *n.* weariness. *v.* to tire or wear out.

fat·ten, *v.* make or get fat.

fau·cet, *n.* device with a valve to control flow of liquid from a pipe.

fault, *n.* defect; error; cause for blame; break in rock forma-

tion. *v.* find fault with. **fault·y,
-i·er, -i·est,** *a.* **fault·less,** *a.*

fau·na, *n. pl.,* **-nas, -nae.** animal
life of a certain region.

faux pas, *n. pl.,* **faux pas.** social
blunder.

fa·vor, *n.* kind act; approval;
token of good will; show
favor. *v.* toward; resemble.
fa·vor·a·ble, *a.* **fa·vored,** *n.*

fa·vor·ite, *n., a.* preferred (one).
fa·vor·it·ism, *n.*

fawn, *n.* young deer. *v.*

faze, *v.,* **fazed, faz·ing.** disturb.

fear, *n.* emotion caused by expectation of evil, danger; awe;
dread. *v.* to feel fear. **fear·ful,**
a. afraid. **fear·less,** *a.* bold.
fear·some, *a.* frightening.

fea·si·ble, *a.* possible; likely.
fea·si·bil·i·ty, *n.*

feast, *n.* large meal; festival. *v.*
have a feast; delight.

feat, *n.* bold act.

feath·er, *n.* outgrowth covering
a bird's body; kindred. **feath-
ered, feath·er·y,** *a.*

fea·ture, *n.* facial part; characteristic; special attraction. *v.,*
-tured, -tur·ing. make a feature of.

Feb·ru·ar·y, *n.* second month.

fe·ces, *n. pl.* excrement.

fe·cund, *a.* fertile.

fed·er·al, *a.* of a union of states
under a central government.

fed·er·a·tion, *n.* act of uniting in
a league. **fed·er·ate,** *v.*

fee, *n.* payment for service.

fee·ble, *a.* weak. **fee·bly,** *adv.*

feed, *v.,* **fed, feed·ing.** give food
to; take food or eat. *n.* fodder.

feel, *v.,* **felt, feel·ing.** touch; have
a sense of; be aware of; be-
lieve in; appear; seem; *n.*
sense of touch; way a thing
feels.

feel·er, *n.* organ of touch.

feel·ing, *a.* sensitivity. *n.* sense
of touch; sensation; emotion;
opinion.

feign, *v.* pretend.

feint, *n.* a deceiving movement.

fe·lic·i·tate, *v.,* **-tat·ed, -tat·ing.**
congratulate. **fe·lic·i·ta·tion,** *n.*

fe·lic·i·tous, *a.* appropriate.

fe·lic·i·ty, *n.* happiness.

fe·line, *a., n.* like a cat.

fell, *v.* to knock or cut down.

fel·low, *n.* man or boy; companion; an equal. *a.* associate.
fel·low·ship, *n.*

fel·on, *n.* criminal.

fel·o·ny, *n.* major crime.

felt, *n.* fabric made of pressed
fibers.

fe·male, *a., n.* of the sex that
conceives and gives birth; girl
or woman.

fem·i·nine, *a.* womanly. **fem·i-
nin·i·ty,** *n.*

fem·i·nism, *n.* doctrine of equal
rights for women.

fe·mur, *n.* thighbone.

fen, *n.* boggy land; a marsh.

fence, *n.* barrier of posts, wire,
etc. *v.* enclose with a fence;
fight with swords. **fenc·ing,** *n.*

fend, *v.* ward off or avert. **fend
for oneself,** manage alone.

fen·der, *n.* that part of a vehicle
covering each wheel.

fer·ment, *v.* agitate; excite; undergo fermentation. *n.* fer-
menting agent; agitation. **fer-
men·ta·tion,** *n.*

fern, *n.* flowerless plant with
feathery leaves.

fe·ro·cious, *a.* savage; intense.
fe·ro·ci·ty, *n.*

fer·ret, *n.* kind of weasel. *v.*
search out.

fer·ry, *v.* carry across water by
boat; travel by ferry. *n.* a fer-
ryboat.

fer·tile, *a.* producing or able to
produce crops, offspring; inventive. **fer·til·i·ty,** *n.*

fer·ti·lize, *v.* make fertile.

fer·ti·liz·er, *n.* substance used to
enrich soil.

fer·vor, *n.* intense feeling; zeal.
fer·vent, fer·vid, *a.*

fes·ter, *v.* form pus; decay; ran-
kle.

fes·ti·val, *n.* celebration; program of cultural events.

fes·tive, *a.* joyous. **fes·tiv·i·ty,** *n.
pl.,* **-ties,** joyous events.

fes·toon, *v., n.* (adorn with) a
looped garland.

fetch, *v.* go and bring back.

fetch·ing, *a.* charming; attractive.

fete, fête, *n.* holiday; lavish party. *v.* honor with a fete.

fet·id, *a.* stinking.

fet·ish, *n.* object thought to have
mysterious powers.

fet·ter, *n.* foot shackle; restraint. *v.* restrain.

fet·tle, *n.* state or condition.

fe·tus, *n.* unborn young.

feud, *n., v.* (engage in) a quarrel.

feu·dal·ism, *n.* medieval social
system. **feu·dal,** *a.*

fe·ver, *n.* high body temperature. **fe·ver·ish**, *a.*

few, *a.* of small number; not many.

fi·an·ce, *n.* man engaged to be married. **fi·an·cee**, *fem.*

fi·as·co, *n. pl.*, **-cos, -coes.** complete, humiliating failure.

fi·at, *n.* a decree.

fib, *n.* petty lie. *v.* **fibbed, fib·bing.**

fiber, **fi·bre**, *n.* threadlike part; character. **fi·brous**, *a.*

fi·ber·glass, *n.* material made of fine, flexible glass filaments.

fick·le, *a.* changeable.

fic·tion, *n.* literature of imagined events. **fic·tion·al**, **fic·ti·tious**, *a.*

fid·dle, *v.*, *n.* (to play) a violin. *v.* to fidget; meddle. **fid·dler**, *n.*

fi·del·i·ty, *n.* faithfulness.

fidg·et, *v.* make nervous movements. **fidg·et·y**, *a.*

fie, *int.* shame!

field, *n.* piece of cleared land; sphere of interest; expanse; all entrants in a contest. *v.* respond to well; handle.

fiend, *n.* demon; addict. **fiend·ish**, *a.*

fierce, *a.* savage; hostile. **fierce·ly**, *adv.*

fier·y, *a.* like a fire; intensely hot; inflamed.

fif·teen, *a.*, *n.* one more than 14.

fif·teenth, *a.*, *n.*

fifth, *a.*, *n.* following the fourth; one of five equal parts.

fif·ty, *a.* five times ten. **fif·ti·eth**, *a.* **fif·ties**, *n. pl.* numbers, years between 50 and 60.

fig, *n.* small sweet pear-shaped fruit.

fight, *n.*, *v.* **fought, fight·ing.** battle; struggle; contest. **fight·er**, *n.*

fig·ment, *n.* thing imagined.

fig·ur·a·tive, *a.* metaphorical, not literal.

fig·ure, *n.* shape; person; likeness of a person or thing; emblem; number symbol; pattern or design. *v.* compute; imagine; consider; be conspicuous. **fig·ure out**, solve.

fig·ure·head, *n.* leader with no real power.

fig·ur·ine, *n.* small statue.

fil·a·ment, *n.* fine thread or fiber.

filch, *v.* steal; pilfer.

file, *n.* ridged rool for cutting, scraping; cabinet or folder for orderly storage of papers; ver-

tical row. *v.* reduce; rub smooth; arrange; move in a file.

fi·let, *n.* boneless piece of meat, fish. Also **fil·let**. *v.* slice into filets.

fil·i·bus·ter, *v.*, *n.* delay legislation by obstructionist tactics, esp. by long speeches.

fil·i·gree, *n.* lacy work of fine wire.

fil·ings, *n. pl.* particles removed by a file.

fill, *v.* make or become full; close or repair; hold or put into (a position); satisfy; complete. *n.* anything that fills. **fill·in**, *n.* replacement. **fill out**, *v.* enlarge; complete.

fill·ing, *n.* that which fills something.

fil·lip, *n.* stimulus; tonic.

fil·ly, *n. pl.*, **-lies.** young female horse.

film, *n.* thin coating; haze or blur; flexible cellulose material used in photography; motion picture. *v.* to make a motion picture of.

fil·ter, *n.* thing for straining out impurities. *v.* to pass through a filter.

filth, *n.* foul matter; obscenity. **filth·y**, *a.*, **-i·er, -i·est. filth·i·ness**, *n.*

fin, *n.* winglike organ attached to fishes.

fi·na·gle, *v.*, **-gled, -gling.** acquire through intrigue. **fi·na·gler**, *n.*

fi·nal, *a.* last; conclusive. *n. usu. pl.* the last and decisive in a series. **fi·nal·ist**, **fi·nal·i·ty**, *n.* **fi·nal·ly**, *adv.*

fi·na·le, *n.* last section of a musical work.

fi·nance, *n.* money management; *pl.* funds. *v.*, **-nanced, -nanc·ing.** to manage finances of; provide capital for. **fi·nan·cial**, *a.* **fin·an·cier**, *n.*

finch, *n.* small songbird.

find, *v.*, **found, find·ing.** come upon; discover; learn; recover; judge. *n.* act of finding; something found.

fine, *a.*, **fin·er, fin·est.** excellent; sharp; delicate in texture. *n.* payment exacted as punishment. *v.* cause to pay a fine.

fine art, *n. usu. pl.*, **fine arts.** art concerned with beauty.

fin·er·y, *n.* showy clothes.

fi·nesse, *n.* delicacy in handling a difficult situation.

fin·ger, *n.* any of the members of the hand, usu. excluding thumb. *v.* to touch. **fin·ger·nail,** *n.*

fin·ger·print, *n.* impression of the markings of the fingertip.

fin·ish, *v.* end, complete; use up; prepare the surface of. *n.* the end; surface quality.

fi·nite, *a.* having limits.

fir, *n.* evergreen tree.

fire, *n.* rapid combustion with heat, light, flame; discharge of firearms; ardor; *v.,* **fired, fir·ing.** add fuel to; to discharge (a gun), (from a job). **on fire,** burning.

fire·arm, *n.* gunpowder-charged weapon.

fire·crack·er, *n.* paper-enclosed explosive.

fire en·gine, *n.* truck equipped to extinguish fires.

fire·fly, *n.* winged insect which gives off light.

fire·man, *n.* one who fights or tends fires.

fire·place, *n.* lower part of a chimney in which fuel is burned.

fire·plug, *n.* water hydrant.

fire·works, *n. pl.* devices for brilliant displays of light or loud noise.

firm, *a.* business company. *a.* stiff; fixed; steady. *v.* make or become firm. **firm·ly,** *adv.* **firm·ness,** *n.*

fir·ma·ment, *n.* sky.

first, *a.* before all others. *n.* first one; the beginning.

first aid, *n.* emergency care for injuries, illness.

first class, *n.* first, best, or highest rank. **first-class,** *a., adv.*

first-hand, first-hand, *a., adv.* from the source; direct.

first-rate, *a.* excellent.

fis·cal, *a.* financial.

fish, *n. pl.,* **fish, fish·es.** cold-blooded, aquatic animal (often) with scales, and with fins, gills. *v.* catch fish; seek indirectly. **fish·er·man, fish·er·y,** *n.*

fish·y, *a.* of fish; dubious.

fis·sion, *n.* splitting into parts.

fis·sure, *n.* narrow opening.

fist, *n.* hand closed tightly.

fist·i·cuff, *n. pl.* combat with the fists.

fit, *n.* convulsion; outburst; way of fitting. *a.,* **fit·ter, fit·test.** suitable; healthy. *v.,* **fit·ted or**

fit, fit·ting. be proper for; to put into place exactly; prepare; supply.

fit·ful, *a.* irregular.

fit·ting, *n.* adjustment; *pl.* furnishings, fixtures. *a.* appropriate.

five, *a.* one more than four.

fix, *v.* make fast, firm, or stable; determine; repair; prepare, as food. *inf.* influence by bribery. *n.* a predicament. **fixed,** *a.*

fix·a·tion, *n.* morbid preoccupation.

fix·ture, *n.* person, thing securely fixed in position.

fiz·zle, *v.,* **-zled, -zling.** hissing, sputtering. *inf.* fail. *n.* hissing sound. *inf.* fiasco.

flab·by, *a.,* **-bi·er, -bi·est.** limp; feeble.

flag, *n.* cloth symbolic of a country, a club, etc. *v.,* **flagged, flag·ging.** decorate or signal with a flag; decline.

flag·on, *n.* container for liquids.

fla·grant, *a.* notorious.

flag·stone, *n.* paving stone.

flail, *n.* tool to thresh grain. *v.* use a flail; beat.

flair, *n.* natural skill.

flake, *n.* a scale; a small, flat piece. **flaked, flak·ing.** form into flakes. **flak·y,** *a.*

flam·boy·ant, *a.* showy.

flame, *n.* (send out) tongues of fire. **flam·ing,** *a.*

flam·ma·ble, *a.* easily ignited.

flank, *n.* side. *v.* be at or pass around the side of.

flap, *v.,* **flapped, flapping.** swing or sway loosely, esp. with noise. *n.* loose, flat piece.

flare, *v.,* **flared, flar·ing.** blaze up; spread outward. *v.* signal by flares. *n.* blaze of fire or light used to signal; a sudden burst; spreading outward.

flash, *n.* sudden brief outburst of flame, light; an instant; bit of news. *v.* burst suddenly into view; move suddenly. **flash·y,** *a.,* **-i·er, -i·est.** sparkling; gaudy.

flash·back, *n.* recall of previous action, thoughts, events alongside existing action.

flash·light, *n.* hand-held electric light.

flask, *n.* type of bottle.

flat, *a.* level; broad and thin; lying spread out; dull; tasteless; *mus.* below the true pitch. *adv.* in a flat way; precisely. Also **flat·ly.** n. flat part; deflated tire; apartment; mus. note ½ step below another. v. make or become flat.

flat·ter, v. praise insincerely; make more attractive. **flat·ter·y,** n.

flaunt, v. make a brazen display.

fla·vor, n. taste. v. give flavor to.

fla·vor·ing, n. substance that adds, increases flavor.

flaw, n. imperfection. v. make a flaw in.

flax, n. plant with fiber spun into linen thread.

flay, v. to skin; criticize ruthlessly.

flea, n. small, wingless, bloodsucking insect.

fleck, n. a spot.

flee, v., **fled, flee·ing.** to run away.

fleece, n. sheep's wool. v. swindle. **fleec·y,** a. fluffy.

fleet, a. swift. n. group of boats, vehicles.

fleet·ing, a. passing rapidly.

flesh, n. body tissue; fruit or vegetable pulp.

flex, v. bend; contract.

flex·i·ble, a. easily bent; adaptable.

flick, v., n. (move with) a sudden light blow or stroke.

flick·er, v. shine, move unsteadily. n. flutter.

fli·er, n. aviator.

flight, n. act, manner, or power of flying; swift movement; a fleeing; set of stairs.

flim·sy, a., **-si·er, -si·est.** Lacking strength, solidity.

flinch, v. draw back from pain, danger.

fling, v., **flung, fling·ing.** throw with force; discard. n. brief, wild time.

flint, n. hard fine-grained rock.

flip, v., **flipped, flip·ping.** toss with a sudden movement; turn over.

flip·pant, a. disrespectful.

flirt, v. to play at love. **flir·ta·tion,** n.

flit, v., **flit·ted, flit·ting.** move quickly and lightly.

float, v. rest or move gently on the surface of liquid or in air; launch. n. thing that stays on the surface of a liquid; decorated parade vehicle.

flock, n. group of animals of the same kind. v. gather in a flock.

floe, n. large mass of floating ice.

flog, v., **flogged, flog·ging.** beat or whip.

flood, n. great flow of water, esp. rising over land; superabundance. v. to overflow.

floor, n. bottom surface of a room, story of a building; the right to speak. v. furnish with a floor; knock down.

flop, v., **flopped, flop·ping.** fall or flap suddenly, heavily, or clumsily; fail. **flop·py,** a.

flo·ra, n. pl., **-ras, -rae.** plants of a district, region, or period.

flo·ral, a. of or like flowers.

flor·id, a. showy; ruddy.

flo·rist, n. one who grows or sells flowers.

floss, n. silklike fiber.

flo·til·la, n. a little fleet.

flot·sam, n. floating cargo or wreckage of a shipwreck.

flounce, v., **flounced, flounc·ing.** throw the body about. n. a ruffle.

floun·der, v. slip or stumble about.

flour, n. finely ground meal of grain.

flour·ish, v. to be in good health, thrive, at prime; brandish. v. n. ostentatious display.

flout, v. mock or insult.

flow, v. move continuously and smoothly. n. a flowing.

flow·er, n. blossom of a plant; plant in bloom; best part. v. to blossom.

flu, n. inf. influenza.

flub, v., **flubbed, flub·bing.** inf. blunder.

fluc·tu·ate, v., **-at·ed, -at·ing.** shift irregularly.

flue, n. chimney shaft.

flu·ent, a. easy in writing, speech. **flu·en·cy,** n.

fluff, n. light, downy particles. v. make or become fluffy. **fluff·y,** a.

flu·id, a. capable of flowing. n. substance that flows, esp. liquid or gas.

fluke, n. stroke of luck.

flunk, v. inf. fail a course or exam.

flu·o·res·cent, a. giving off a cool light.

fluor·i·da·tion, n. addition of fluoride to drinking water.

fluor·o·scope, n. type of X-ray machine.

flur·ry, n. pl., **-ries.** gust of wind, rain, snow; sudden agitation.

flush, v. wash out; redden; fly out or start up suddenly. n. blush, glow. a. even, level; wealthy.

flus·ter, v. agitate; become confused.

flute, n. tubelike woodwind instrument.

flut·ter, v. wave or flap rapidly. n. quick, irregular motion.

flux, n. constant change; flow. v. fuse by melting.

fly, n., pl., **flies.** winged insect; flap covering zipper, etc.; baseball batted high. v. **flew, flown, fly·ing.** move through the air on wings; move swiftly; flee; transport by aircraft. **fly·er,** n. flier.

fly·wheel, n. wheel that regulates a machine's speed.

foal, n. young horse.

foam, n. bubbles formed on liquids. **foam·y,** a.

fo·cus, n., pl., **fo·cus·es, fo·ci,** point at which rays of light meet; adjustment of lens distance to get a clear image; a central point. v., **-cused** or **-cussed, cus·ing, -cus·sing.** bring into focus; concentrate.

fod·der, n. livestock feed.

foe, n. an enemy.

fog, n. dense mist; mental confusion. v., **fogged, fog·ging.** make or become foggy.

fo·gy, fo·gey, n., pl., **-gies, -geys.** old-fashioned person.

foi·ble, n. minor fault.

foil, n. thin metal sheeting; one that sets off another by contrast; fencing sword. v. thwart.

foist, v. pass off by deception.

fold, v. double over upon itself; intertwine; enclose or wrap. n. a folded part; a pen for sheep. **fold·er,** n. folded printed sheet; protective covering for papers.

fo·li·age, n. leaves of plants.

folk, n., pl., **folk** or **folks.** people in general. a. of the common people. **folks,** n., pl. one's own family.

folk·lore, n. traditional beliefs, customs, legends, songs of a people.

fol·li·cle, n. small cavity, sac, or gland.

fol·low, v. go or come after; accept the authority of; go along; result from; take up, pursue; understand. **fol·low·er,** n.

fol·low·ing, n. group of followers. a. next after.

fol·ly, n., pl., **-lies.** foolishness.

fo·ment, v. to instigate.

fond, a. loving or tender. **fond·ly,** adv.

fon·dle, v., **-dled, -dling.** caress.

food, n. substance absorbed by an organism to sustain life and enable growth.

fool, n. silly person; dupe; clown. v. jest; trick; waste foolishly.

fool·har·dy, a. recklessly bold.

fool·ish, a. silly; unwise.

fool·proof, a. infallible.

foot, n. pl. **feet.** end part of the vertebrate leg; measure of 12 inches; bottom or base.

foot·ball, n. (game played with) an inflated ball.

foot·hold, n. firm standing.

foot·ing, n. secure position or basis.

foot·note, n. note at the bottom of a page.

foot·print, n. impression left by a foot.

foot·step, n. act of taking a step; distance or sound of one step; footprint.

fop, n. vain man.

for, prep. in the interest of; in place of; in favor of; with the purpose of; meant to be used with, by; regarding; as far or as long as. conj. because.

for·age, n. food for horses, cattle. v. search for food.

for·ay, n., v. raid.

for·bear, v., **-bore, -borne, -bear·ing.** refrain from; withhold.

for·bid, v., **-bade** or **-bad, -bidden, -bid·ding.** prohibit. **for·bid·den,** a. **for·bid·ding,** a. threatening.

force, n. strength; group combined for joint action. v., **forced, forc·ing.** compel; to break open. **force·ful,** a.

for·ceps, n. instrument for seizing and holding objects.

for·ci·ble, a. marked by force; effective.

ford, n., v. (cross at) a shallow place.

fore, a., n. front.

fore·arm, n. arm between elbow and wrist.

fore·bode, for·bode, v. foretell; warn. **fore·bod·ing,** n., a.

fore·cast, v. predict. n. prediction.

fore-close, *v.* deprive of right to redeem mortgaged property.

fore-fa-ther, *n.* ancestor.

fore-fin-ger, *n.* finger next to thumb.

fore-go, *v.,* **-went, -gone, -going.** go before; precede. **fore-go-ing, fore-gone,** *a.*

fore-ground, *n.* part of a scene nearest the observer.

fore-head, *n.* part ot the face above the eyebrows.

for-eign, *a.* of another country; alien; strange. **for-eign-er,** *n.*

fore-man, *n. pl.,* **-men.** person who supervises others; chairman of a jury.

fore-most, *a., adv.* first.

fore-noon, *n.* morning hours before noon.

fore-run-ner, *n.* sign or omen of something to follow; ancestor.

fore-see, *v.,* **-saw, -seen, -see-ing.** see or know in advance.

fore-sight, *n.* insight; act or power of foreseeing.

fore-skin, *n.* fold of skin over the glans of the penis.

for-est, *n.* tract of land covered with trees.

fore-stall, *v.* prevent by advance action.

for-est-ry, *n.* science of managing forests.

fore-tell, *v.,* **-told, -tell-ing.** predict.

for-ev-er, *adv.* eternally; continually.

fore-word, *n.* preface.

for-feit, *v.* lose the right to by some fault. **for-fei-ture,** *n.* penalty.

forge, *n.* furnace or workshop to heat metal before shaping. *v.* heat in a forge and shape by hammering; imitate a signature; move forward slowly. **forg-er-y,** *n.*

for-get, *v.,* **-got, -got-ten** or **-got, -get-ting.** unable to recall; omit; neglect. **for-get-ful,** *a.*

for-give, *v.,* **-gave, -given, -giv-ing.** cease to feel resentment against; pardon. **for-give-ness,** *n.* **for-giv-ing,** *a.*

for-go, *v.,* **-went, -gone, -going.** do without.

fork, *n.* pronged tool; point of branching. *v.* to use a fork; to branch.

for-lorn, *a.* abandoned; wretched.

form, *n.* shape; mold; style;

document to be filled in. *v.* give form, shape to; to assume form; constitute.

for-mal, *a.* customary; marked by ceremony; elegant. **for-mal-i-ty,** *n. pl.,* **-ties.**

for-mat, *n.* general plan or arrangement.

for-ma-tion, *n.* process or state of forming; arrangement. **form-a-tive,** *a.*

for-mer, *a.* long past; first mentioned. **for-mer-ly,** *adv.*

for-mi-da-ble, *a.* exciting fear, awe; discouraging approach.

for-mu-la, *n. pl.,* **-las, -lae.** rule, concept, principle expressed in algebraic symbols. **for-mu-late,** *v.*

for-ni-ca-tion, *n.* voluntary sexual intercourse between unmarried persons. **for-ni-cate,** *v.*

for-sake, *v.,* **-sook, -sak-en, -sak-ing.** desert; abandon.

for-swear, *v.,* **-swore, -sworn, -swear-ing.** reject, renounce upon oath; swear falsely.

fort, *n.* fortified place.

forth, *adv.* forward; out into view.

forth-com-ing, *a.* soon to appear, arrive, occur.

forth-right, *a.* direct; frank.

forth-with, *adv.* immediately.

for-ti-fi-ca-tion, *n.* the act of fortifying; a fort.

for-ti-fy, *v.,* **-fied, -fy-ing.** strengthen.

for-ti-tude, *n.* calm courage.

fort-night, *n.* two weeks.

for-tress, *n.* fortified place.

for-tu-i-tous, *a.* accidental; lucky.

for-tu-nate, *a.* lucky.

for-tune, *n.* great wealth; luck, good or bad; fate.

for-ty, *n. pl.,* **-ties.** four times ten. **for-ti-eth,** *n., a.*

fo-rum, *n.* public discussion.

for-ward, *adv.* onward; ahead. Also **for-wards.** *a.* in the front; precocious; bold. *v.* send on; promote.

fos-sil, *n.* animal or plant remains found in earth's crust or strata.

fos-ter, *v.* promote; bring up.

foul, *a.* unclean; stormy; morally repugnant; unfair or unlawful. *n.* an act contrary to rules. *v.* to make or become dirty; entangled.

found, *v.,* pt. and pp. of **find;** set up or establish. **found-er,** *n.*

foun·da·tion, *n.* establishment or basis; lowest division of a building or wall; endowed institution.

found·er, *v.* fall in or sink down; stumble or go lame; fail utterly.

found·ling, *n.* child found after abandonment.

found·ry, *n. pl.*, **-ries.** place for casting metals.

fount, *n.* fountain; source.

foun·tain, *n.* spring or source of water; a jet of water.

four, *a.* one more than three. *n.*

fourth, *a., n.*

four·score, *a.* four times twenty; eighty.

four·teen, *a.* one more than 13.

four·teenth, *a., n.*

fowl, *n.* a bird, esp. one used as food.

fox, *n. pl.*, **fox·es**, wild doglike animal. *v.* outwit, deceive. **fox·y**, *a.* cunning.

foy·er, *n.* entrance hall.

fra·cas, *n.* uproar; brawl.

frac·tion, *n.* part of a whole; a very small portion.

frac·tious, *a.* unruly.

frac·ture, *n.* a break, breach, or split. *v.* to break or crack.

frag·ile, *a.* easily broken.

frag·ment, *n.* a part broken off.

fra·grance, *n.* pleasing scent. **fra·grant**, *a.*

frail, *a.* weak; delicate; fragile. **frail·ty**, *n. pl.*, **-ties.**

frame, *n.* structure; border; mood; *inf.* plot to determine outcome. *v.* surround; fashion, shape. *inf.* prearrange results of.

frame·work, *n.* supportive or enclosing structure.

franc, *n.* French monetary unit.

fran·chise, *n.* right to vote; special privilege.

frank, *a.* candid; outspoken. *v.* mark or send a letter free. **frank·ly**, *adv.* **frank·ness**, *n.*

frank·furt·er, *n.* small linked sausage.

frank·in·cense, *n.* aromatic gum-resin.

fran·tic, *a.* overcome by fear, anxiety, grief. **fran·ti·cal·ly**, *adv.*

fra·ter·nal, *a.* brotherly: of a society of men.

fra·ter·ni·ty, *n. pl.*, **-ties.** brotherliness; men's college social club.

frat·er·nize, *v.* associate in a brotherly way.

fraud, *n.* deceit, trickery; an imposter. **fraud·u·lent**, *a.*

fraught, *a.* filled (with).

fray, *v.* cause to ravel or tear. *n.* quarrel; brawl.

fraz·zle, *v.* fray; to tire out. *n.* tired state.

freak, *n.* abnormal person or thing.

freck·le, *n.* small brownish spot on the skin.

free, *a.*, **fre·er**, **fre·est.** not subject to the will of others; unconfined; acquitted; without charge; loose. *v.* make free. **free·dom**, *n.*

free·boot·er, *n.* pirate.

free-for-all, *n.* brawl.

free·way, *n.* toll-free multiple-lane expressway that moves traffic without interruption.

freeze, *v.*, **froze, fro·zen, freez·ing.** to harden into ice; become extremely cold; damage by cold; become rigid; fix wages, rents, prices at a specific level.

freight, *n.* goods transported; price paid for such cargo; train for freight.

freight·er, *n.* cargo ship.

French, *a.* of the people or language of France.

French horn, *n.* musical wind instrument of brass with coiled tube.

fre·net·ic, *a.* frantic.

fren·zy, *n. pl.*, **-zies.** wild excitement.

fre·quen·cy, *n. pl.*, **-cies.** frequent occurrence; rate of occurrence.

fre·quent, *a.* happening often. *v.* visit often.

fres·co, *n. pl.*, **-coes, -cos.** painting on moist plaster.

fresh, *a.* not stale, smoked, frozen, preserved; in good condition; new. **fresh·en**, *v.*

fresh·man, *n. pl.*, **-men.** first-year student.

fret, *v.* worry. **fret·ful**, *a.*

fret·work, *n.* ornamental open-work.

fri·a·ble, *a.* easily crumbled.

fri·ar, *n.* man belonging to a religious order.

fric·as·see, *n.* stewed meat.

fric·tion, *n.* rubbing together of two surfaces. **fric·tion·al**, *a.*

Fri·day, *n.* sixth day of the week.

friend, *n.* person known well

and liked. **friendship,** n.

friend·ly, a., **-li·er, -li·est.** helpful; supportive.

frieze, n. decorated horizontal band around a room, building, etc.

fright, n. sudden, violent fear.

fright·en, v. scare; drive away by scaring; become afraid.

fright·ful, a. causing fright; dreadful.

frig·id, a. very cold.

frill, n. ruffle; a nonessential.

fringe, n. decorative border of threads; something marginal.

frisk, v. to frolic. *inf.* search by feeling over clothing.

frisky, a., **-i·er, -i·est.** lively.

frit·ter, v. waste (away) little by little. n. small fried cake.

friv·o·lous, a. of little importance; silly.

frizz, v. form tufts, curls, knots.

fro, adv. from; away; back.

frock, n. dress; loose outer garment.

frog, n. web-footed, tailless amphibian.

frol·ic, n. merry prank. v. play, romp. **frol·ic·some,** a.

from, prep. starting at; originating with; out of; not like; a place away; because of.

frond, n. large leaf, esp. of a palm or fern.

front, n. foremost part or surface; line of battle; movement to achieve a common goal. a. of or at the front. v. to face, confront. **front·age,** n. **fron·tal,** a.

fron·tier, n. a country's border; a new, unexplored area. **fron·tiers·man,** n. pl., **-men.**

frost, n. freezing temperature; frozen vapor. v. cover with frost or icing.

frost·bite, n. injury from severe cold. **frost·bit·ten,** a.

frost·ing, n. icing.

froth, n. foam.

fro·ward, a. perverse; ungovernable.

frown, v. show displeasure by wrinkling the brow. n. stern look.

frow·zy, a., **-zi·er, -zi·est.** slovenly; unkempt.

fru·gal, a. thrifty.

fruit, n. pulpy edible substance covering the seeds of various flowering plants and trees; an offspring. **fruit·ful,** a. abundant. **fruit·less,** a. unproductive.

fru·i·tion, n. fulfillment, accomplishment.

frus·trate, v., **-trat·ed, -trat·ing.** disappoint; thwart. **frus·tra·tion,** n.

fry, v., **fried, fry·ing.** cook in heated fat.

fudge, v. cheat; falsify. n. a soft candy.

fu·el, n. combustible matter to maintain fire. v. supply with or get fuel.

fu·gi·tive, a. fleeing, or tending to flee. n. a runaway.

ful·crum, n. pl., **-crums, -cra.** support by which a lever is sustained or turns.

ful·fill, ful·fil, v., **-filled, -fil·ling.** accomplish; perform; complete. **ful·fill·ment, ful·fil·ment,** n.

full, a. containing much or all that can be held; complete; satisfied; rounded out; adv. exactly; very. n. utmost extent. **full·ness,** n. **ful·ly,** adv.

full-blown, a. mature.

full-fledged, a. completely developed; of full status.

ful·mi·nate, v. explode; denounce vehemently.

ful·some, a. offensively insincere.

fum·ble, v. grope or handle awkwardly. n. an act of fumbling.

fume, n. offensive smoke, gas, or vapor; irritable mood. v. emit fumes; show anger.

fu·mi·gate, v. expose to fumes, esp. for disinfection.

fun, n. that which is diverting, amusing, mirthful. a. full of fun.

func·tion, n. normal or proper activity; formal social occasion. v. perform specified activity. **func·tion·al,** a.

fund, n. a stock of money. pl. cash. v. to provide money for.

fun·da·men·tal, a. essential; basic. n. something essential.

fu·ner·al, n. burial rites.

fu·ne·re·al, a. gloomy; mournful.

fun·gus, n. pl., **-gi, -gus·es.** any of a group of plants with no flowers, leaves, chlorophyll.

fun·nel, n. slim tube with a cone-shaped mouth; flue, chimney. v., **-neled, -nel·ing.** shape like a funnel; move as if through a funnel.

fun·ny, *a.,* **-ni·er, -ni·est.** amusing.

fur, *n.* soft, thick, hairy coating of certain animals. **fur·ry,** *a.*

fu·ri·ous, *a.* full of fury.

furl, *v.* wrap or roll.

fur·long, *n.* one-eighth of a mile.

fur·lough, *n.* permission given to be absent from military service. *v.* grant a furlough.

fur·nace, *n.* structure for generating heat.

fur·nish, *v.* supply with something necessary, useful, desired.

fur·nish·ings, *n. pl.* furniture; men's accessories.

fur·ni·ture, *n.* movable articles in a room.

fu·ror, *n.* outburst of enthusiasm, excitement.

fur·row, *n.* groove made by a plow; wrinkle. *v.* make or become furrowed.

fur·ther, *adv.* to a greater extent; in addition. *a.* additional; farther. *v.* advance; promote.

fur·ther·more, *adv.* besides.

fur·thest, *a., adv.* most distant.

fur·tive, *a.* taken or done stealthily.

fu·ry, *n. pl.,* **-ries.** unrestrained anger, energy, speed.

fuse, *n.* safety device in an electric circuit; wick used to ignite an explosive. *v.* melt together.

fu·se·lage, *n.* body or hull of an airplane.

fuss, *n.* excessive anxiety over trifles. *v.* bother with trifles. **fuss·y,** *a.,* **-i·er, -i·est.** anxious, elaborate.

fu·tile, *a.* of no purpose; unsuccessful. **fu·til·i·ty,** *n.*

fu·ture, *a.* any time or state that is to come.

fuzz, *n.* loose, light, fibrous matter. **fuzz·y,** *a.* covered with fuzz; indistinct.

G

gab·ar·dine, *n.* fabric with fine diagonal ribs.

ga·ble, *n.* triangular wall enclosed by sloping ends of a ridged roof.

gad, *v.,* **gad·ded, gad·ding.** ramble restlessly. **gad·a·bout,** *n.*

gad·fly, *n.* large stinging fly; bothersome person.

gad·get, *n.* small device.

gaff, *n.* strong hook; *inf.* ordeal; abuse.

gag, *v.,* **gagged, gag·ging.** stop up to prevent speech or sound; cause to vomit; choke. *n.* something which limits speech; *inf.* joke.

gage, *n.* a pledge; a token of challenge to combat; gauge.

gai·e·ty, *n.* state of being cheerful.

gai·ly, *adv.* cheerfully.

gain, *v.* win; attain; increase; profit; make progress. *n.* profit; increase.

gain·say, *v.,* **-said, -say·ing.** contradict; deny.

gait, *n.* manner of walking or stepping.

ga·la, *a.* festive. *n.* festive occasion.

gal·ax·y, *n. pl.,* **-ies.** system of stars.

gale, *n.* strong wind.

gall, *n.* bitterness of spirit; impudence; plant tumor. *v.* make sore by rubbing; annoy.

gal·lant, *a.* brave, high-spirited, chivalrous. **gal·lant·ry,** *n.*

gal·ler·y, *n. pl.,* **-ies.** long covered walkway area used for public displays; balcony.

gal·ley, *n.* early form of ship; ship's kitchen.

gal·lon, *n.* four quarts.

gal·lop, *v.,* *n.* (ride at) a horse's full speed.

gal·lows, *n.* wooden frame for hanging condemned persons.

ga·losh, *n. usu. pl.* overshoe worn to keep feet dry.

gal·va·nize, *v.,* **-nized, -niz·ing.** stimulate by or as by electric current; coat metal with zinc.

gam·bit, *n.* strategy to gain an initial advantage, as in chess.

gam·ble, *v.,* **-bled, -bling.** play game of chance for stakes; risk. *n.* venture involving risk; chance.

gam·bol, *v., n.* frolic; leap.

game, *n.* amusement, pastime; wild animals hunted for sport or profit; *a.* lame. *v.* play games of chance.

gam·in, *n.* street urchin.

gam·ut, *n.* whole range or series.

gan·der, *n.* male goose; *inf.* glance.

gang, *n.* group working together or associated socially.

gan·gling, *a.* awkwardly tall and slender.

gang·plank, *n.* ramp for getting on and off a ship.

gan·grene, *n.* the dying of tissue.

gang·ster, *n.* member of a criminal gang.

gang·way, *n.* passageway; gangplank.

gap, *n.* opening; wide divergence; blank.

ga·rage, *n.* place for sheltering, repairing motor vehicles.

garb, *n.* mode of dress.

gar·bage, *n.* table waste; worthless goods.

gar·ble, *v.,* **-bled, -bling.** distort; jumble.

gar·den, *n.* plot of ground for growing vegetables, fruits, flowers.

gar·gan·tu·an, *a.* gigantic.

gar·gle, *n., v.* (liquid to) wash or rinse the mouth or throat.

gar·ish, *a.* gaudy.

gar·land, *n.* wreath of leaves, twigs, flowers.

gar·ment, *n.* article of clothing.

gar·ner, *n.* a store of anything. *v.* collect; store.

gar·net, *n.* deep red gem.

gar·nish, *v.* decorate; *n.* decoration.

gar·ret, *n.* part of a house immediately under the roof.

gar·ri·son, *n.* troops stationed in a fort. *a* fort.

gar·ru·lous, *a.* very talkative.

gar·ter, *n.* band or supporter to hold up a stocking.

gas, *n.* vapor-like state of matter; gasoline. *v.* overcome with gas. **gas·e·ous,** *a.*

gash, *v., n.* (make a) deep, long cut.

gas·ket, *n.* ring used to make a joint watertight.

gas·o·line, *n.* liquid fuel made from petroleum.

gasp, *v.* labor for breath. *n.* short, convulsive effort to breathe.

gas·tric, *a.* of the stomach.

gas·tron·o·my, *n.* art of good eating.

gate, *n.* movable structure to open or close any passageway; total of paid admission.

gate·way, *n.* a means of entry.

gath·er, *v.* bring together; gather in folds; acquire; infer. *n.* fold in cloth.

gauche, *a.* awkward.

gaud·y, *a.,* **-i·er, -i·est.** garish; tastelessly showy. **gaud·i·ly,** *adv.*

gauge, *n.* a standard of measure; tool used for measuring. *v.,* **gauged, gaug·ing.** to measure; estimate.

gaunt, *a.* haggard.

gaunt·let, *n.* type of protective glove. **throw down the gauntlet,** challenge.

gauze, *n.* thin transparent fabric of meshlike weave. **gauz·y,** *a.*

gav·el, *n.* presiding officer's mallet.

gawk, *v.* stare idly or stupidly.

gawk·y, *a.,* **-i·er, -i·est.** awkward; clumsy.

gay, *a.* cheerfully lively; brilliantly colored. *inf.* homosexual.

gaze, *v.,* **gazed, gaz·ing.** look steadily, intently. *n.* a fixed look.

ga·zelle, *n.* small Asian and African antelope.

ga·zette, *n.* a newspaper.

gaz·et·teer, *n.* geographical dictionary.

gear, *n.* a toothed wheel; equipment. *v.* connect by gearing; adjust; fit exactly.

gel·a·tin, *n.* glutinous protein obtained from animal tissues. **ge·lat·i·nous,** *a.*

geld, *v.,* **geld·ed** or **gelt, geld·ing.** castrate. **geld·ing,** *n.*

gem, *n.* precious or semiprecious stone.

gen·der, *n.* classification of words as masculine, feminine, neuter.

gene, *n.* element of a chromosome that transmits an inherited characteristic.

ge·ne·al·o·gy, *n.* study of family history.

gen·er·al, *a.* of the whole; usual; not specialized; indefinite; having extended command; **in gen·er·al,** commonly.

gen·er·al·i·ty, *n.* vague statement. **gen·er·al·ize,** *v.*

gen·er·ate, *v.* to cause to be; produce. **gen·er·a·tive,** *a.*

gen·er·a·tion, *n.* people born and living at same time; act of generating.

gen·er·a·tor, *n.* apparatus for converting mechanical into electrical energy.

ge·ner·ic, *a.* referring to a genus, kind, or class; not registered as a trademark.

gen·er·ous, *a.* unselfish; ample.

gen·er·os·i·ty, *n.*

gen·e·sis, *n.* creation (*cap.*) first book of Old Testament.

ge·net·ics, *n. pl.* science of hereditary. **ge·net·ic**, *a.*

gen·ial, *a.* kindly.

ge·nie, *n.* spirit of Islamic mythology.

gen·i·tals, *n. pl:* sex organs. **gen·i·tal**, *a.*

gen·ius, *n.* (person with) unusual ability and very high intelligence.

gen·o·cide, *n.* deliberate mass murder of a people.

gen·teel, *a.* well-bred; polite.

gen·tile, *a., n. (often cap.)* non-Jewish (person).

gen·til·i·ty, *n.* refinement; elegance.

gen·tle, *a.* kind in manner; mild; gradual. **gen·tly**, *adv.*

gen·tle·man, *n. pl.,* **-men.** man of good breeding, politeness, courtesy.

gen·try, *n.* the class next below the nobility.

gen·u·ine, *a.* authentic; sincere.

ge·nus, *n.* a kind, class, or sort.

ge·og·ra·phy, *n.* science of the surface of the earth. **ge·o·gra·phic, ge·o·graph·i·cal**, *a.* **ge·og·ra·pher**, *n.*

ge·ol·o·gy, *n.* science of physical history and structure of the earth. **ge·o·log·ic, ge·o·log·i·cal**, *a.* **ge·ol·o·gist**, *n.*

ge·om·e·try, *n.* branch of mathematics studying points, lines, angles, surfaces, solids. **ge·o·met·ric**, *a.*

ge·o·phys·ics, *n. pl.* science of effects of weather, earthquakes, tides, etc. on the earth's features. **ge·o·phys·i·cal**, *a.*

ger·i·at·rics, *n. pl.* area of medicine dealing with diseases and care of aging persons. **ger·i·at·ric**, *a.*

germ, *n.* disease-producing microorganism; seed.

ger·mane, *a.* appropriate; relevant.

ger·mi·nate, *v.* begin or cause to develop, sprout. **ger·mi·na·tion**, *n.*

ger·und, *n.* *-ing* form of a verb used as a noun.

ges·tic·u·late, *v.* express by gestures.

ges·ture, *n.* motion or action that expresses an idea or feeling. *v.* make gestures.

get, *v.,* got, got or gotten, getting. acquire; come to have; capture; achieve power over; grasp the meaning of. **get a·long**, manage. **get a·way**, escape; start. **get at**, to reach. **get e·ven with**, to be revenged. **get o·ver**, to recover. **get up**, to rise.

gey·ser, *n.* gushing spring of hot water and steam.

ghast·ly, *a.,* **-lier, -liest.** frightful; dreadful.

gher·kin, *n.* small cucumber used for pickles.

ghet·to, *n.* city area populated by a minority group.

ghost, *n.* disembodied spirit of a dead person; mere shadow or semblance. **ghost·ly**, *a.*

ghoul, *n.* evil demon who robs graves and feeds on corpses.

GI, *n. pl.,* **GI's** or **GIs.** U.S. serviceman, esp. an enlisted man. Also **G.I.**

gi·ant, *n., a.* (person or thing) of unusually great size.

gib·ber·ish, *n.* rapid, inarticulate talk.

gib·bon, *n.* small, tailless ape.

gibe, jibe, *v., n.* taunt; jeer.

gib·let, *n. usu. pl.* edible internal part of a fowl.

gid·dy, *a.* dizzy; flighty. **gid·di·ness**, *n.*

gift, *n.* a present; a natural quality.

gi·gan·tic, *a.* colossal; huge.

gig·gle, *v.* laugh in a silly way.

gild, *v.* overlay with gold. **gilt**, *a.*

gill, *n.* respiratory organ of fishes.

gim·mick, *n.* crafty device; trick.

gimp, *n.* person who limps; a hobbling gait.

gin, *n.* machine for separating cotton from its seeds; alcoholic liquor.

gin·ger, *n.* spice from pungent root of ginger plant; this plant.

gin·ger ale, *n.* non-alcoholic drink flavored with ginger.

gin·ger·bread, *n.* cake flavored with ginger.

gin·ger·ly, *adv.* cautiously. *a.* wary.

ging·ham, *n.* cotton fabric in striped or checked patterns.

gip·sy, *n. pl.,* **gip·sies.** gypsy.

gi·raffe, *n.* long-necked; spotted African animal.

gird, *v.* encircle; *fig.* equip oneself for action.

gird·er, *n.* horizontal supporting beam.

gir·dle, *n.* that which girds or

enclos*es*; light corset.

girl, *n.* female child. **girl·ish,** *a.*

girth, *n.* band passed under horse's belly; circumference.

gist, *n.* essential part.

give, *v.,* **gave, giv·en, giv·ing.** place into another's grasp; donate; trade; permit; perform; sacrifice; to be the cause of; transmit; yield under pressure. **give in,** yield. **give off,** emit. **give out,** break down; distribute. **give up,** surrender.

giv·en, *a.* bestowed; stated.

giz·zard, *n.* bird's second stomach.

gla·cia, *n.* vast ice mass slowly descending from mountains. **gla·cial,** *a.*

glad, *a.* cheerful. **glad·ly,** *adv.* **glad·ness,** *n.* **glad·den,** *v.*

glade, *n.* forest clearing.

glad·i·o·lus, *n.* plant with swordlike leaves and spikes of flowers. Also **glad·i·o·la.**

glam·our, or **glam·or,** *n.* excitement and allure. **glam·our·ous,** *a.*

glance, *v.* look quickly; hit and glide off. *n.* brief look.

gland, *n.* organ that secretes bodily substances. **glan·du·lar,** *a.*

glare, *v.,* **glared, glar·ing.** shine with a strong, dazzling light; stare piercingly. *n.* dazzling light; angry look.

glar·ing, *a.* plainly obvious.

glass, *n.* hard, brittle, transparent substance; something made of glass; optical instrument; *pl.* spectacles.

glass·y, *a.,* **-i·er, -i·est.** resembling glass; expressionless.

glau·co·ma, *n.* eye disease.

glaze, *v., n.* (cover with) a smooth, lustrous coating; furnish with glass.

gleam, *n.* beam of light; *v.* shine softly.

glean, *v.* collect slowly and arduously.

glee, *n.* joy. **glee·ful,** *a.*

glen, *n.* secluded narrow valley.

glib, *a.* fluent.

glide, *v.* move smoothly, without effort. *n.* a gliding movement.

glim·mer, *v.* shine faintly. *n.* faint, unsteady light.

glimpse, *n.* quick look. *v.* get a quick view of.

glint, *n., v.* flash; gleam.

glis·ten, *v., n.* sparkle.

glit·ter, *v., n.* (shine with) bright sparkling light.

gloat, *v.* contemplate with evil satisfaction.

globe, *n.* the earth; spherical solid body. **glob·al,** *a.*

glob·ule, *n.* small spherical particle.

gloom, *n.* darkness; dejection. **gloom·y,** *a.*

glo·ry, *n.* praise; blessings of heaven. *v.* rejoice. **glo·ri·fy,** *v.* **glo·ri·ous,** *adj.*

gloss, *n.* luster; false appearance. **gloss·y,** *a.*

glos·sa·ry, *n.* specialized dictionary.

glot·tis, *n.* opening at top of windpipe between vocal chords.

glove, *n.* covering for the hand.

glow, *v.* emit bright light and heat without flame. *n.* state of glowing.

glow·er, *v.* look angrily, with sullen dislike.

glow·worm, *n.* luminous insect.

glue, *v., n.* (join with) strong adhesive.

glum, *a.* frowning; sullen.

glut, *v.* feed or fill to excess. *n.* excessive supply.

glut·ton, *n.* one who overindulges in eating. **glut·ton·y,** *n.*

gnarl, *n.* knot. *v.* twist. **gnarled,** *a.*

gnash, *v.* strike or grind together.

gnat, *n.* small biting fly.

gnaw, *v.* wear away by biting.

gnome, *n.* imaginary dwarfed person.

gnu, *n.* type of African antelope.

go, *v.,* **went, gone, go·ing.** move; proceed; depart; suit or fit; result; be or become. *n.* success; energy; an attempt. **go af·ter,** pursue. **go off,** explode. **go o·ver,** reexamine. **go with,** accompany; harmonize with.

goad, *n.* animal prod. *v.* incite.

goal, *n.* aim or objective; area where the players attempt to place the ball to score.

goat, *n.* agile, hollow-horned cud-chewing mammal.

goat·ee, *n.* small, neat-pointed beard.

gob·ble, *v.* swallow hastily. *n.* noise made by a male turkey.

gob·let, *n.* stemmed drinking glass.

gob·lin, *n.* evil sprite.

God, *n.* creator and ruler of the universe.

god, *n.* person, spirit, or object, worshipped and adored. **god-dess**, *n. fem.*

god-child, *n. pl.*, **-chil-dren.** child sponsored by a godparent. **god-daugh-ter, god-son**, *n.*

god-ly, *a.*, **-lier, -liest.** pious.

god-par-ent, *n.* sponsor of a child at its baptism. **god-fa-ther, god-moth-er**, *n.*

god-send, *n.* unexpected piece of good fortune.

gog-gle, *n.* wide-eyed. *pl.* protective spectacles.

go-ing, *n.* departure; conditions for travel; progressing toward a goal. *a.* functioning standard.

goi-ter, *n.* enlargement of thyroid gland.

gold, *n.* valuable, yellow metallic element; money; bright yellow color. **gold, gold-en**, *a.* made of, colored like gold; favorable.

golf, *n.* game played with clubs and a small ball on a grassy course.

gon-do-la, *n.* long, narrow boat used on Venetian canals. **gon-do-lier**, *n.* boatman.

gong, *n.* saucer-shaped bell sounded by a hammer.

gon-or-rhe-a, *n.* venereal disease.

goo-ber, *n.* a peanut.

good, *n.* that which is good; *pl.* possessions. *a.* **bet-ter, best.** of favorable quality; virtuous; right, proper; pleasant; valid; pleasant; ample. **good-ness**, *n.*

good-by, good-bye, *a. int.* farewell.

good-heart-ed, *a.* charitable; kind.

good-look-ing, *a.* handsome.

good-ly, *a.*, **-li-er, -li-est.** pleasing; large.

good-y, *n. pl.*, **-ies.** *inf.* something good to eat.

goose, *n. pl.*, **geese.** large, web-footed, long-necked water bird; silly person.

goose-ber-ry, *n. pl.*, **-ries.** small, edible, acid, berry.

gore, *n.* blood that is shed; panel of cloth. *v.* pierce with a horn.

gorge, *n.* narrow ravine. *v.* stuff with food.

gor-geous, *a.* splendid in appearance.

gosh, *int.* expression of surprise.

gos-ling, *n.* young goose.

gos-pel, *n.* doctrine taught by Christ and apostles.

gos-sa-mer, *n.* fine, filmy substance or fabric. *a.* filmy.

gos-sip, *n.* rumors; person given to idle talk; talk idly.

gouge, *n.* chisel; groove. *v.* make grooves in; *fig.* cheat.

gourd, *n.* fruit of melons, pumpkins, etc.

gour-mand, *n.* one who enjoys good eating.

gour-met, *n.* connoisseur of food and drink.

gout, *n.* disease characterized by inflamed joints.

gov-ern, *v.* control; influence; restrain.

gov-ern-ess, *n.* female teacher hired to instruct children at home.

gov-ern-ment, *n.* exercise of political authority; governing organization; system by which power is vested and exercised.

gov-er-nor, *n.* one who governs; head of a state in U.S.

gown, *n.* woman's dress; official robe.

grab, *v.* seize suddenly and eagerly. *n.* sudden snatch.

grace, *n.* elegance of form; favor; mercy or pardon; short mealtime prayer. *v.* adorn; dignify. **grace-ful**, *a.*

gra-cious, *a.* kind; courteous; charming.

gra-da-tion, *n.* succession by gradual steps.

grade, *n.* a degree in any series; one year of schoolwork; a mark rating a pupil's work; slope. *v.* arrange in order according to size, quality, rank; give a rating to.

grad-u-al, *a.* proceeding little by little. **grad-u-al-ly**, *adv.*

grad-u-ate, *v.* confer or receive a degree or diploma after a course of study; mark with degrees for measuring. *n.* one who has received an academic degree. **grad-u-a-tion**, *n.*

graf-fi-to, *n. pl.*, **-ti**, inscription scrawled in public view.

graft, *n.* plant shoot inserted in another plant to grow there; transplanted body tissue; dishonest gain by public officials. *v.* transplant by grafting.

gra·ham flour, *n.* wholewheat flour.

grain, *n.* seeds of cereal grasses; particle; tiny amount; pattern of fibers in wood.

gram, *n.* metric unit of weight, about .035 oz.

gram·mar, *n.* study of forms and rules of a language. **gram·mat·i·cal,** *a.*

gra·na·ry, *n. pl.,* **-ries.** storehouse for grain.

grand, *a.* vast in scope or size; illustrious; splendid; principal.

grand·child, *n.* a son's or daughter's child. **grand·daugh·ter, grand·son,** *n.*

gran·dil·o·quence, *n.* high-sounding words.

gran·di·ose, *a.* impressive; imposing.

grand ju·ry, *n.* jury that hears accusations, studies evidence, and has power to indict for trial.

grand·par·ent, *n.* a parent of a parent. **grand·fa·ther, grand·moth·er,** *n.*

grand·stand, *n.* elevated seats for sports spectators.

grange, *n.* farm, with its buildings.

gran·ite, *n.* igneous rock abundant in earth's crust.

grant, *v.* give; bestow; admit. *n.* act of granting; thing granted.

gran·u·late, *v.* form into grains.

gran·ule, *n.* small particle. **gran·u·lar,** *a.*

grape, *n.* edible, pulpy, smooth-skinned fruit which grows on vines.

grape·fruit, *n.* large, round, yellow fruit with an acid, flavorful pulp.

graph, *n.* diagram of a system of connections between two or more things.

graph·ic, *a.* vividly described; pertaining to graphs, writing. **graph·i·cal·ly,** *adv.*

graph·ite, *n.* soft carbon used in lead pencils.

grap·nel, *n.* instrument with hooks or clamps for seizing, holding objects.

grap·ple, *n.* grapnel; grip. *v.* seize; struggle.

grasp, *v.* seize and hold; comprehend. *n.* grip; power to grasp; mastery.

grasp·ing, *a.* greedy.

grass, *n.* plants on which grazing animals pasture; plant with jointed stems, long, narrow leaves, flower spikelets; lawn. **grass·y,** *a.*

grass·hop·per, *n.* leaping insect.

grate, *n.* framework of metal bars. *v.* grind into particles; scrape with a harsh noise; irritate.

grate·ful, *a.* thankful.

grat·i·fy, *v.* give pleasure to; satisfy; indulge. **grat·i·fi·ca·tion,** *n.*

grat·ing, *n.* framework of bars.

gra·tis, *a., adv.* without charge.

grat·i·tude, *n.* thankfulness.

gra·tu·i·tous, *a.* free; unjustified.

gra·tu·i·ty, *n. pl.,* **-ties.** gift; tip.

grave, *n.* burial place. *a.* solemn; serious.

grav·el, *n.* mix of small stones and pebbles.

grav·en, *a.* sculptured; carved.

grave·yard, *n.* cemetery.

grav·i·tate, *v.* move toward some attracting influence.

grav·i·ta·tion, *n.* force by which all masses are mutually attracted to each other.

grav·i·ty, *n. pl.,* **-ties.** seriousness; weightiness; gravitation.

gra·vy, *n.* meat juices.

gray, grey, *n.* color between white and black; dismal.

graze, *v.* feed on growing grass; touch lightly in passing.

grease, *n.* melted animal fat; oily matter in general. *v.* smear with grease. **greas·y,** *a.*

great, *a.* beyond what is ordinary in extent, scope, character; first-rate.

greed, *n.* desire for possessing more than one needs. **greed·y,** *a.*

green, *a.* color of growing grass; covered with grass; unripe; inexperienced.

green·er·y, *n.* vegetation.

greet, *v.* meet; salute.

greet·ing, *n.* salutation at meeting.

gre·gar·i·ous, *a.* sociable.

gre·nade, *n.* small explosive shell.

grey, *n., a., v.* gray.

grid, *n.* grating; gridiron.

grid·dle, *n.* flat rimless frying pan.

grid·i·ron, *n.* football field; grill.

grief, *n.* deep sadness.

griev·ance, *n.* complaint.

grieve, *v.* feel or cause to feel sorrowful.

griev·ous, *a.* serious; full of grief.

grif·fin, grif·fon, *n.* mythical creature, part eagle, part lion.

grill, *v.* broil on a grate; *inf.* question relentlessly. *n.* grate for broiling food.

grille, grill, *n.* metal lattice or grating.

grim, *a.* fierce; sullen.

grim·ace, *n.* facial distortion expressing scorn, pain, disgust, etc. *v.* twist the face.

grime, *n.* deeply ingrained dirt. **grim·y**, *a.*

grin, *v.*, *n.* (give) a broad smile.

grind, *v.*, **ground**, **grind·ing**. reduce to fine particles or wear smooth by friction; rub harshly; operate by turning a crank; work laboriously.

grind·stone, *n.* revolving stone for sharpening tools.

grip, *n.* seizing and holding fast; handclasp; control; small valise. *v.* grasp firmly.

grippe, *n.* influenza.

gris·ly, *a.* frightful; horrible.

grist, *n.* grain ground or to be ground in a mill.

gris·tle, *n.* cartilage.

grit, *n.* fine, hard grains of sand; firmness of character. *v.* grate; grind. **grit·ty**, *a.*

griz·zled, griz·zly, *a.* gray.

groan, *v.* utter a deep sound of grief, pain, disapproval. *n.* a moan.

gro·cer, *n.* food merchant.

gro·cer·y, *n. pl.*, **-ies**. retail food store. *pl.* goods sold by such stores.

grog·gy, *a.* exhausted from lack of sleep; dizzy.

groin, *n.* fold where thigh joins abdomen.

groom, *n.* bridegroom; person in charge of horses or stable. *v.* make clean, neat; prepare for a specific purpose.

groove, *n.* narrow channel; fixed routine.

grope, *v.* search out by feeling one's way.

gross, *a.* total prior to deductions; flagrant; unrefined; enormous. *n.* twelve dozen.

gro·tesque, *a.* unnatural; bizarre.

grot·to, *n. pl.*, **-toes, -tos**. cave.

grouch, *v. inf.* show discontent. *n.* morose, irritable person. **grouch·y**, *a.*

ground, *n. sometimes pl.* land; basis; support; dregs. *v.* restricted to the ground; connect to a ground.

ground hog, *n.* woodchuck.

ground·work, *n.* basis; foundation.

group, *n.* assemblage of persons or things; *v.* arrange in or form a group.

grouse, *v.* grumble. *n.* complaint.

grove, *n.* a cluster of trees.

grov·el, *v.*, **-eled, -el·ing**. to humble oneself.

grow, *v.*, **grew, grown, grow·ing**. develop toward maturity; survive; arise; increase.

growl, *v.* (utter) a deep guttural sound of anger, hostility.

grown-up, *n.* an adult. **grown-up**, *a.*

growth, *n.* act, process, of growing; something that has grown.

grub, *v.*, **grubbed, grub·bing**. dig up; drudge. *n.* insect larva.

grub·by, *a.*, **-bi·er, -bi·est**. dirty; slovenly.

grudge, *v.* permit reluctantly. *n.* ill will; envy.

gru·el·ing, *a.* causing strain.

grue·some, *a.* horrible, frightening.

gruff, *a.* surly; harsh.

grum·ble, *v.* complain; utter in a low voice.

grump·y, *a.* irritable.

grunt, *v.* (utter) a deep guttural sound.

guar·an·tee, *n.*, *v.* pledge that specifications or obligations will be met. Also **guar·an·ty**.

guard, *v.* protect; watch over; take precautions. *n.* sentry.

guard·house, *n.* military jail.

guard·i·an, *n.* one who has charge or custody of any person or thing. *a.* protecting.

gu·ber·na·to·ri·al, *a.* pertaining to a governor.

guer·ril·la, *n.* independent soldier who harasses, attacks behind the lines.

guess, *v.* deduce; estimate; suppose. *n.* conjecture.

guest, *n.* person shown hospitality in another's home or place of business.

guf·faw, *n.* loud, sudden laughter.

guide, *v.* lead, direct. *n.* person or thing that guides. **guid·ance**, *n.*

guild, *n.* business association for mutual aid.

guile, *n.* craft; deceit.

guil·lo·tine, *n.* instrument for beheading.

guilt, *n.* fact of having performed a wrong act; remorse for an offense.

guilt·y, *a.,* **-i·er, -i·est.** showing guilt; judged responsible for an offense.

guin·ea pig, *n.* rodent used in experiments.

guise, *n.* outward appearance; pretense.

gui·tar, *n.* musical instrument with violinlike body and (usu.) 6 strings.

gulch, *n.* deep ravine.

gulf, *n.* portion of ocean extending into the land; wide separation.

gull, *n.* sea bird; person easily cheated. *v.* make a fool of.

gul·let, *n.* esophagus.

gul·li·ble, *a.* easily cheated.

gul·ly, *n., pl.,* **-lies.** ravine.

gulp, *v.* swallow eagerly; gasp. *n.* large swallow.

gum, *n.* fleshy tissue around the teeth.

gum, sticky substance; chewing gum. *v.* stick with gum; become sticky.

gun, *n.* portable firearm. *v.* shoot, hunt with a gun.

gun·ner·y, *n.* art of firing or managing guns.

gun·ny, *n.* strong coarse cloth (sac) of jute.

gun·pow·der, *n.* explosive mixture for fireworks, guns.

gun·smith, *n.* one who makes, repairs small firearms.

gun·wale, gun·nel, *n.* upper edge of a boat's side.

gup·py, *n.* small tropical fish.

gur·gle, *v.* (utter) a bubbling sound.

gush, *v.* rush forth; be extravagantly sentimental.

gust, *n.* violent blast of wind.

gus·ta·to·ry, *a.* pertaining to the sense of taste.

gus·to, *n.* relish; zest.

gut, *n.* intestinal canal; cord made of intestine. *pl. inf.* courage. *v.* destroy the inside of.

gut·ter, *n.* channel for carrying off water.

gut·tur·al, *a.* harsh; rasping.

guy, *n.* guiding rope. *inf.* fellow.

guz·zle, *v.* drink greedily.

gym, *n. inf.* gymnasium.

gym·na·si·um, *n.* place for athletic exercises, contests.

gym·nas·tics, *n. pl.* athletic exercises. **gym·nas·tic,** *a.* **gymnast,** *n.*

gy·ne·col·o·gy, *n.* medical science dealing with functions, diseases of women.

gyp, *n., v. inf.* cheat.

gyp·sum, *n.* chalky mineral.

gyp·sy, *n. pl.,* **-sies.** wanderer.

gy·rate, *v.* rotate; whirl.

gy·ro·scope, *n.* rotating wheel mounted to turn freely, used to maintain equilibrium, determine direction.

H

ha, hah, *interj.* exclamation, surprise, wonder, etc.

hab·it, *n.* tendency to act constantly in a certain manner; custom; costume.

hab·it·a·ble, *a.* suitable for habitation.

hab·i·tat, *n.* natural abode or locality.

hab·i·ta·tion, *n.* dwelling.

ha·bit·u·al, *a.* constantly practiced; customary; regular. **ha·bit·u·al·ly,** *adv.*

ha·bit·u·ate, *v.,* **-at·ed, -at·ing.** accustom; familiarize.

hack, *v.* make rough cuts; emit short coughs. *n.* short, broken cough; worn-out horse; rough cut.

hack·neyed, *a.* trite.

had, *v.* pt. and pp. of **have.**

haft, *n.* handle of an implement or weapon.

hag, *n.* ugly old woman.

hag·gard, *a.* appearing wasted or worn; gaunt.

hag·gle, *v.,* **-gled, -gling.** bargain with; dispute over small points. **hag·gler,** *n.*

hail, *v.* salute; greet; call out to; cast down like hail. *int.* salutation. *n.* greeting; small pellets of ice which fall during showers.

hail·stone, *n.* a single pellet of hail.

hair, *n.* fine filament which grows from the skin; mass of such fibers, as on the head; slight measure. *a.* of or for hair. **hair·y,** *a.,* **-i·er, -i·est.**

hair·breadth, *n.* minute distance. *a.* very narrow. Also **hair's·breadth, hairs·breadth.**

hair·dress·er, *n.* one who styles hair, esp. women's hair.

hair·pin, *n.* doubled pin, used to hold hair in place. *a.* U-shaped.

hale, *v.,* **haled, hal·ing.** compel to comply. *a.,* **hal·er, hal·est.** robust; vigorous.

half, *n. pl.,* **halves.** one of two equal parts; *a.* being one of the half parts; partial. *adv.* to the extent of half; in part.

half-heart·ed, *a.* lacking eagerness or enthusiasm. **half-heart·ed·ly,** *adv.*

half-way, *a.* to or at half the full extent. *adv.* midway between two points; partial.

half-wit, *n.* feebleminded person. **half-wit·ted,** *a.*

hal·i·but, *n. pl.,* **-but, -buts.** edible flatfish.

hall, *n.* large room for public assembly; passageway.

hal·le·lu·jah, *int.* praise the lord!

hal·low, *v.* consecrate.

hal·lu·ci·na·tion, *n.* apparent perception. **hal·lu·ci·na·to·ry,** *a.*

hal·lu·ci·no·gen, *n.* drug that causes hallucinations.

hall·way, *n.* corridor.

ha·lo, *n. pl.,* **-los, -loes.** circle of light.

halt, *n.* stop. *v.* stop; restrain; hesitate. **halt·ing,** *a.* **halt·ing·ly,** *adv.*

hal·ter, *n.* noosed rope for tying beasts; woman's backless sports top.

halve, *v.,* **halved, halv·ing.** divide into halves.

ham, *n.* meat of a hog's thigh. **ham·my,** *a.*

ham·burg·er, *n.* ground beef; patty.

ham·let, *n.* small village.

ham·mer, *n.* tool for beating or driving. *v.* beat, drive, or form with a hammer.

ham·mock, *n.* hanging canvas bed.

ham·per, *v.* impede. *n.* kind of basket.

hand, *n.* extremity of the arm; side; person employed in manual labor; applause; *cards.* cards held by each player. *a.* by, using, or for the hand. *v.* grasp, touch, or work with the hands; pass. **hand·ful,** *n. pl.,* **-fuls. hand·i·ly,** *adv.*

hand-bag, *n.* pocketbook.

hand-book, *n.* manual.

hand-cuff, *n. usu. pl.* metal bracelet with lock. *v.* put handcuffs on.

hand·i·cap, *n.* disadvantage or advantage. *v.* **-capped, -cap·ping.** assign a handicap.

hand·i·craft, *n.* skill of one's hands; work of an artisan, tradesman, etc.

hand·i·work, *n.* work done by the hands.

hand·ker·chief, *n.* hemmed square of cloth for personal use.

han·dle, *n.* part intended to be grasped by the hand. *v.,* **-dled, -dling.** touch or use the hands on; manage; deal with; trade in. **han·dler,** *n.*

hand-maid·en, *n.* female attendant. Also **hand-maid.**

hand·some, *a.,* **-som·er, -som·est.** goodlooking; generous.

hand·y, *a.,* **-i·er, -i·est.** convenient; near; skilled in using the hands.

hand·y·man, *n. pl.,* **-men.** one hired to do odd jobs.

hang, *v.,* **hung** or **hanged.** fasten from above; swing freely; suspend by the neck until dead; droop; attach to walls; hold fast. *n.* way in which a thing hangs. **hang·ing,** *a., n.*

hang·ar, *n.* shelter for airplanes.

hang·er-on, *n. pl.,* **-ers-on** follower; parasite.

hank, *n.* definite length or weight of yarn.

hank·er, *v.* long for. **hank·er·ing,** *n.*

hap·haz·ard, *a.* accidental. **hap·haz·ard·ly,** *adv.*

hap·less, *a.* luckless. **hap·less·ly,** *adv.*

hap·pen, *v.* take place; come to pass by chance; have the fortune.

hap·pen·ing, *n.* event.

hap·py, *a.,* **-pi·er, -pi·est.** joyful; lucky; apt. **hap·pi·ly,** *adv.* **hap·pi·ness,** *n.*

ha·rangue, *n.* loud speech; tirade. *v.,* **-rangued, -rangu·ing.** deliver a harangue.

har·ass, *v.* annoy by repeated attacks. **har·ass·ment,** *n.*

har·bor, *n.* port; haven or refuge. *v.* shelter; entertain within the mind.

hard, *a.* solid and firm; difficult; harsh or severe. *adv.* firmly or tightly; with great vigor. **hard·ness,** *n.*

hard-core, *a.* unyielding.

hard·en, *v.* make or become

hard. **hard·en·er**, *n.*

hard-heart·ed, *a.* pitiless.

har·di·ness, *n.* quality or state of being hardy.

hard·ly, *adv.* scarcely; barely; unlikely; harshly.

hard·ship, *n.* condition that is hard to bear.

hard·ware, *n.* metalware.

har·dy, *a.*, **-di·er**, **-di·est.** robust; bold. **har·di·ly**, *adv.*

hare, *n. pl.*, **hares, hare.** rabbit.

har·em, *n.* area for women in a Muslim family; these women.

hark, *v.* listen.

har·lot, *n.* prostitute. **har·lot·ry**, *n.*

harm, *n.* injury; damage. *v.* hurt; damage. **harm·ful**, *a.* **harm·ful·ness**, *n.* **harm·less**, *a.*

har·mon·i·ca, *n.* mouth organ.

har·mo·nize, *v.*, **-nized**, **-niz·ing.** be or set in harmony.

har·mo·ny, *n. pl.*, **-nies.** accord; friendship. **har·mo·ni·ous**, *a.*

har·ness, *n.* working gear of a draft animal. *v.* put a harness on; *fig.* bring under conditions for working.

harp, *n.* musical instrument with strings. *v. inf.* dwell on a subject. **harp·ist**, *n.*

har·poon, *n.* spear used to kill whales. *v.* strike with a harpoon.

har·ri·den, *n.* hag.

har·row, *n.* spiked implement for leveling plowed soil. *v.* draw a harrow over; harass.

har·row·ing, *a.* distressing.

har·ry, *v.*, **-ried**, **-ry·ing.** harass; torment; worry.

harsh, *a.* unpleasant; crude; severe. **harsh·ness**, *n.*

hart, *n. pl.*, **harts, hart.** stag.

har·vest, *n.* gathering of any crop; that which is reaped. *v.* reap.
  har·ves·ter, *n.*

has, *v.* third person, pres. sing., of **have.**

hash, *n.* chopped meat cooked with potatoes, etc.

hasp, *n.* clasp.

has·sle, *n. inf.* fight. *v.*, **-sled**, **-sling.** vex.

has·sock, *n.* footstool.

haste, *n.* speed; rashness.

has·ten, *v.* hurry.

hast·y, *a.*, **-i·er**, **-i·est.** moving with haste; rash. **hast·i·ly**, *adv.* **hast·i·ness**, *n.*

hat, *n.* head covering. *v.* **hat·ted**, **hat·ting.** provide with a hat.

hatch, *n.* hatchway; cover for it. *v.* bring forth, as young, from the egg; devise.

hatch·et, *n.* small ax.

hatch·way, *n.* opening in a ship's deck; hatch.

hate, *v.*, **hat·ed**, **hat·ing.** dislike greatly; detest. *n.* great dislike. **hat·er**, *n.* **hate·ful**, *a.*

ha·tred, *n.* great dislike.

haugh·ty, *a.*, **-ti·er**, **-ti·est.** proud; disdainful. **haugh·ti·ly**, *adv.* **haugh·ti·ness**, *n.*

haul, *v.* pull; transport; drag. *n.* pulling; that hauled; distance carried. **haul·age**, *n.*

haunch, *n.* hip; flank.

haunt, *v.* frequent; appear as a ghost. *n.* place one frequents. **haunt·ed**, *a.*

haunt·ing, *a.* lingering.

hau·teur, *n.* haughtiness.

have, *v.*, **have, has**; **had**; **hav·ing.** possess; hold; be impelled; experience; conduct; bring about or cause to be; allow; bear.

ha·ven, *n.* port; refuge.

hav·er·sack, *n.* cloth bag worn over the shoulder.

hav·oc, *n.* devastation; disorder.

hawk, *n.* bird of prey; swindler. *v.* peddle; cough; clear the throat. **hawk·ish**, *a.*

haw·ser, *n.* rope used in towing or securing a ship.

hay, *n.* cut and dried grass.

hay·stack, *n.* hay pile.

haz·ard, *n.* risk; peril; chance; obstacle on a golf course. *v.* risk. **haz·ard·ous**, *a.*

haze, *n.* mist, smoke, or dusky vapor; mental fog.

ha·zel, *n.* tree producing edible nuts; reddish-brown color.

ha·zy, *a.*, **-zi·er**, **-zi·est.** misty; vague. **ha·zi·ness**, *n.*

he, *pron.*, *sing. nom.* **he**, *poss.* **his**, *obj.* **him**; *intens. and refl.* **himself**; *pl. nom.* **they**, *poss.* **their** or **theirs**, *obj.* **them.** male being in question or last mentioned; anyone.

head, *n.* upper part of the body; mind; leader or chief; crisis; top part. *v.* lead. *a.* chief; principal. **head·ship**, *n.*

head·ache, *n.* pain in the head; *inf.* annoyance.

head·ing, *n.* title.

head·land, *n.* promontory.

head·light, *n.* light on the front of a vehicle.

head·line, *n.* title line over a

newspaper article.

head·long, *adv.* headfirst; rashly. *a.* hasty.

head·most, *a.* foremost.

head·quar·ters, *n. pl.* central office.

head·strong, *a.* obstinate.

head·way, *n.* advance; progress.

head·y, *a.,* **-i·er, -i·est.** strongly intoxicating; rash. **head·i·ness,** *n.*

heal, *v.* make sound; cure. **heal·er,** *n.*

health, *n.* physical or mental vigor; absence of ailments. **health·ful,** *a.* **health·y,** *a.,* **-i·er, -i·est.** **health·i·ness,** *n.*

heap, *n.* pile. *v.* put in a heap; cast in great quantity.

hear, *v.,* **heard, hear·ing.** perceive by the ear; heed. **hear·er,** *n.* **hear·ing,** *n.*

hark·en, *v.* harken.

hear·say, *n.* rumor.

hearse, *n.* funeral vehicle.

heart, *n.* organ that circulates blood; seat of emotion and passions; core; playing card marked with a heart-shaped figure.

heart·ache, *n.* grief.

heart·break, *n.* overwhelming sorrow. **heart·break·ing,** *a.*

heart·en, *v.* encourage.

heart·felt, *a.* deeply felt.

hearth, *n.* floor of a fireplace; fireside.

heart·less, *a.* cruel.

heart·rend·ing, *a.* grievous.

heart·sick, *a.* deeply grieved.

heart·y, *a.,* **-i·er, -i·est.** sincere; cordial; healthy; substantial. **heart·i·ness,** *n.*

heat, *n.* hotness; ardor; stress; single effort as in a race. *v.* make hot; become excited. **heat·ed,** *a.* **heat·er,** *n.*

heath, *n.* open wasteland.

hea·then, *a., n.* pagan.

heave, *v.,* **heaved** or **hove, heav·ing.** lift or hurl with effort; breathe with effort. *n.* rhythmical rise and fall.

heav·en, *n. rel.* place where the blessed go after death; *usu. pl.* sky. **heav·en·ly,** *a.*

heav·y, *a.,* **-i·er, -i·est.** of great weight; of great force or intensity; grievous. **heav·i·ly,** *adv.* **heav·i·ness,** *n.*

heav·y-hand·ed, *a.* harsh.

heav·y-heart·ed, *a.* mournful.

heck·le, *v.,* **-led, -ling.** harass by interrupting.

hec·tic, *a.* of undue turmoil. **hec·ti·cal·ly,** *adv.*

hedge, *n.* line of shrubbery. *v.* **hedged, hedg·ing.** plant a hedge; avoid a direct statement. **hedg·er,** *n.*

heed, *v.* listen to with care; attend to. *n.* care; attention.

heel, *v.* incline; tilt; add a heel to; follow closely. *n.* hind part of the foot, shoe; etc.; crust of bread.

heft, *n.* weight; bulk. **heft·y,** *a.,* **-i·er, -i·est.**

heif·er, *n.* young cow.

height, *n.* state of being tall; altitude; *pl.* highest point.

height·en, *v.* make or raise higher; become greater.

hei·nous, *a.* completely abominable. **hei·nous·ness,** *n.*

heir, *n.* one who inherits. **heir·ess,** *n. fem.*

heir·loom, *n.* possession passed from generation to generation.

hel·i·cop·ter, *n.* aircraft held in the air by blades rotating on a vertical axis.

he·li·um, *n.* gaseous element.

he·lix, *n. pl.,* **hel·i·ces, hel·ix·es.** spiral.

hell, *n.* place of punishment of the wicked after death; torment. **hell·ish,** *a.*

hel·lo, *int.* greeting.

helm, *n.* steering instrument of a ship. **helms·man,** *n. pl.,* **-men.**

hel·met, *n.* head armor.

help, *v.* assist; aid; remedy; be of use to. *n.* aid; hired servants. **help·er,** *n.* **help·ful,** *a.*

help·ing, *n.* single serving of food.

help·less, *a.* defenseless. **help·less·ness,** *n.*

hem, *n.* border. *v.* **hemmed, hem·ming.** double over the edge and sew down; enclose.

hem·i·sphere, *n.* one half of a sphere or globe. **hem·i·spher·ic, hem·i·spher·i·cal,** *a.*

hem·lock, *n.* evergreen tree; poisonous plant.

hem·or·rhage, *n.* heavy flow of blood. *v.,* **-rhaged, -rhag·ing.** bleed heavily.

hem·or·rhoid, haem·or·rhoid, *n. usu. pl.* swelling of a blood vessel at the anus.

hemp, *n.* tall herb producing hashish, marijuana, and fibers for making rope.

hen, *n.* female fowl, bird, etc.

hence, *adv.* from this place or

time; therefore; thus.

hence·forth, *adv.* from this time forward. Also **hence·for·ward**.

hench·man, *n. pl.*, **-men.** trusted attendant. **hench·man·ship**, *n.*

hep·a·ti·tis, *n.* inflammation of the liver.

her, *pron. obj.* and *poss.* case of **she**.

her·ald, *n.* bearer of messages; forerunner. *v.* proclaim. **he·ral·dic**, *a.*

her·ald·ry, *n. pl.*, **-ries.** science of armorial bearings.

herb, *n.* plant used in medicines, scents, or seasonings. **her·ba·ceous**, *a.* **her·bage**, *n.*

her·cu·le·an, *a.* very great in strength, courage, etc. very difficult to perform.

herd, *n.* group of animals traveling or feeding together. *v.* gather together. **herd·er**, *n.* **herds·man**, *n. pl.*, **-men.**

here, *adv.* in, at, or towards this place; now; at this point. *int.* present. *n.* this place; this world.

here·af·ter, *adv.* after this. *n.* life after death.

he·red·i·tar·y, *a.* inherited.

he·red·i·ty, *n. pl.*, **-ties.** transmission of characteristics of parents to offspring.

here·in, *adv.* in this.

her·e·sy, *n. pl.*, **-sies.** belief opposed to accepted doctrine. **her·e·tic**, *n.* **he·ret·i·cal**, *a.* **he·ret·i·cal·ly**, *adv.*

here·to·fore, *adv.* up to now.

her·it·age, *n.* legacy, as a culture or tradition.

her·met·ic, *a.* airtight. Also **her·met·i·cal**, **her·met·i·cal·ly**, *adv.*

her·mit, *n.* recluse. **her·mit·age**, *n.*

her·ni·a, *n.* rupture.

he·ro, *n. pl.*, **he·roes.** courageous, noble man. **he·ro·ic**, *a.* **her·o·ine**, *n. fem.* **her·o·ism**, *n.*

her·o·in, *n.* narcotic.

her·on, *n.* wading bird.

hers, *pron. poss.* case of **she.**

her·self, *pron.* form of **her.**

hes·i·tate, *v.*, **-tat·ed**, **-tat·ing.** pause; be doubtful. **hes·i·tant**, *a.* **hes·i·tan·cy**, *n. pl.*, **-cies.** **hes·i·ta·tion**, *n.*

het·er·o·ge·ne·ous, *a.* having dissimilar elements.

hew, *v.*, **hewed**, **hewed** or **hewn**, **hew·ing.** chop. **hew·er**, *n.*

hex·a·gon, *n.* figure having six angles and six sides. **hex·ag·o-**

nal, *a.*

hey, *int.* exclamation to express joy or call attention.

hey·day, **hey·dey**, *n.* prime.

hi·ber·nate, *v.*, **-nated**, **-nat·ing.** pass the winter in a dormant condition. **hi·ber·na·tion**, *n.*

hic·cup, *n.* quick, involuntary intake of breath. *v.*, **-cuped** or **-cupped**, **-cup·ing** or **-cup·ping.** be affected with hiccups. Also **hic·cough.**

hide, *v.*, **hid**, **hid·den** or **hid**, **hid·ing.** conceal intentionally. *n.* animal pelt. **hid·er**, *n.*

hid·e·ous, *a.* extremely ugly. **hid·e·ous·ness**, *n.*

hie, *v.*, **-hied**, **hie·ing** or **hy·ing.** hasten.

hi·er·ar·chy, *n. pl.*, **-chies.** ranking according to authority in a church or government.

hi·er·o·glyph·ic, *a.* of pictographic inscriptions. *n.* picture representing a word or idea. Also **hi·er·o·glyph.**

high, *a.* lofty; elevated; tall; shrill. *adv.* at or to a high point. *n.* position of height.

high·fa·lu·tin, *a. int.* pompous. Also **high·fa·lu·ting.**

high·flown, *a.* pretentious.

high·hat, *a. inf.* condescending. *v.*, **-hat·ted**, **-hat·ting.** snub.

high·way, *n.* public road.

hi·jack, **high·jack**, *v.* rob in transit. **hi·jack·ing**, *n.*

hike, *v.*, **hiked**, **hik·ing.** walk a long distance; *inf.* raise; increase. *n.* march. **hik·er**, *n.*

hi·lar·i·ous, *a.* very funny. **hi·lar·i·ty**, *n.*

hill, *n.* small elevation of land. **hill·y**, *a.*, **-i·er**, **-i·est**, *a.*

hill·ock, *n.* small hill.

hilt, *n.* handle of a sword, tool, etc.

him, *pron. obj.* case of **he.**

him·self, *pron.* reflexive or emphatic form of **he.**

hind, *a.*, **hind·er**, **hind·most** or **hind·er·most.** rear.

hin·der, *v.* impede; thwart.

hind·er·er, *n.* **hin·drance**, *n.*

hind·most, *a.* farthest behind.

hinge, *n.* joint on which a door, gate, etc., turns. Also **hinge joint.** *v.*, **hinged**, **hing·ing.** attach by a hinge; depend.

hint, *n.* suggestion; clue. *v.* allude indirectly. **hint·er**, *n.*

hip, *n.* haunch; hip joint.

hip·pie, *n.* young adult, usu. nonconformist in dress and behavior.

hip·po·pot·a·mus, *n. pl.*, **-mus·es**, **-mi**. thick-skinned, hairless animal.

hire, *v.* engage the services of for pay. *n.* price paid for this. **hir·er**, *n.*

hire·ling, *n.* mercenary.

his, *pron.* of or belonging to him.

hiss, *v.* make a sound like the letter s; express disapproval. *n.* such a sound.

his·to·ry, *n. pl.*, **-ries**. account of past events. **his·to·ri·an**, *n.* **his·tor·ic**, **his·tor·i·cal**, *a.*

his·tri·on·ic, *a.* theatrical; affected. Also **his·tri·on·i·cal**. **his·tri·on·i·cal·ly**, *adv.*

hit, *v.*, **hit**, **hit·ting**. deal a blow; come into collision; strike; affect severely. *n.* impact; blow; success.

hitch, *v.* fasten by a knot or hook; jerk. *n.* jerk; catch; hindrance. **hitch·er**, *n.*

hitch·hike, *v.*, **-hiked**, **-hik·ing**. travel by obtaining free rides. **hitch·hik·er**, *n.*

hith·er, *adv.* to this place.

hith·er·to, *adv.* until now.

hive, *n.* shelter for a swarm of bees; *pl.* skin eruption.

hoard, *n.* articles preserved for future use. *v.* collect and lay up. **hoard·ing**, *n.*

hoarse, *a.* sounding husky or gruff. **hoarse·ness**, *n.*

hoax, *n.* trick. *v.* play a trick upon. **hoax·er**, *n.*

hob·ble, *v.*, **-bled**, **-bl·ing**. limp. *n.* limp; fetter.

hob·by, *n. pl.*, **-bies**. activity carried on for pleasure.

hob·nob, *v.*, **-nobbed**, **-nob·bing**. be on a familiar basis.

ho·bo, *n. pl.*, **-boes**, **-bos**. tramp. **ho·bo·ism**, *n.*

hock, *n.* joint in the hind leg. *v.* *inf.* pawn. **hock·er**, *n.*

hock·ey, *n.* team game played on ice.

hod, *n.* trough for carrying mortar and bricks.

hodge·podge, *n.* jumble.

hoe, *n.* tool used for breaking up the surface of the ground. *v.*, **hoed**, **hoe·ing**. work with a hoe. **ho·er**, *n.*

hog, *n.* swine. *v.*, **hogged**, **hog·ging**. take more than one's share of. **hog·gish**, *a.*

hoi pol·loi, *n.* multitude.

hoist, *v.* raise; lift. *n.* apparatus for hoisting. **hoist·er**, *n.*

hold, *v.*, **held**, **hold·ing**. have in the hand; keep in a certain position; contain; keep; adhere. *n.* interior of a ship. **hold·er**, *n.*

hold·ing, *n.* tenure of land; *often pl.* property.

hole, *n.* hollow place; cavity; gap or rent. *v.*, **holed**, **hol·ing**. make a hole; hide away. **hole·y**, *a.*

hol·i·day, *n.* day of rest; holy day; *pl.* vacation.

ho·li·ness, *n.* being holy.

hol·ler, *v. inf.* cry out; shout. *n. inf.* loud wail.

hol·low, *a.* not solid; sunken; deep or low; meaningless. *n.* cavity. **hol·low·ness**, *n.*

hol·ly, *n. pl.*, **-lies**. trees or shrubs having red berries.

hol·ly·hock, *n.* plant with showy flowers.

hol·o·caust, *n.* vast destruction, usu. by fire.

hol·ster, *n.* leather case for a pistol.

ho·ly, *a.*, **-li·er**, **-li·est** consecrated to God; saintly.

hom·age, *n.* respect.

home, *n.* dwelling; residence of a person or family. *a.* domestic; being the headquarters. *adv.* to or toward home; to the point. **home·less**, *a.*

home·ly, *a.*, **-li·er**, **-li·est**. unattractive.

home·made, *a.* made at home.

home run, *n. baseball.* scoring run.

home·sick, *a.* longing for home. **home·sick·ness**, *n.*

home·spun, *a.* plain. *n.* cloth of a plain weave made at home.

home·ward, *a.*, *adv.* toward home. Also **home·wards**.

home·y, **hom·y**, *a.*, **-i·er**, **-i·est** *inf.* cozy.

hom·i·cide, *a.* killing of one human being by another. **hom·i·cid·al**, *a.*

hom·i·ly, *n. pl.*, **-lies**. discourse or sermon.

hom·i·ny, *n.* edible hulled corn.

ho·mo·gen·e·ous, *a.* uniform in structure; similar.

ho·mog·e·nize, *v.*, **-nized**, **-niz·ing**. make homogeneous.

hone, *n.* stone used for sharpening instruments. *v.*, **honed**, **hon·ing**. sharpen on a hone.

hon·est, *a.* without deceit or fraud; upright; sincere. **hon-**

es·ty, *n. pl.,* **-ties.**

hon·ey, *n. pl.,* **-eys.** sweet fluid made by bees. *v.,* **-eyed** or **-ied,** **ey·ing.** flatter.

hon·ey·comb, *n.* structure of wax formed by bees for storing honey. *v.* pierce with many holes.

hon·ey·moon, *n.* holiday spent by a newly married couple.

hon·ey·suck·le, *n.* climbing shrub having flowers.

honk, *n.* cry of a goose; any similar sound.

hon·or, *n.* high public esteem, credit, fame, or glory; sense of moral standards; (*usu. cap.*) title; *pl.* civilities. *v.* confer honor; fulfill.

hon·or·a·ble, *a.* worthy of honor. **hon·or·a·bly,** *adv.*

hon·or·ar·y, *a.* bestowed in honor; indicative of honor.

hood, *n.* cowl; anything that resembles a hood in form or in use. **hood·ed,** *a.*

hood·lum, *n.* thug.

hood·wink, *v.* deceive; cheat. **hood·wink·er,** *n.*

hoof, *n. pl.,* **hoofs, hooves.** horny covering encasing the foot in certain animals.

hook, *n.* curved piece of metal adapted to catch, hold, or pull something. *v.* fasten or catch with a hook; curve like a hook. **hooked,** *a.*

hook·up, *n.* connection.

hoop, *n.* circular band. **hooped, hoop·like,** *a.*

hoot, *v.* cry out or shout, esp. in derision; utter the cry of an owl. *n.* cry of an owl; shout. **hoot·ing·ly,** *adv.*

hop, *v.,* **hopped, hop·ping.** leap on one foot or by lifting all feet. *n.* hopping.

hope, *n.* belief that one's desires may be attained; thing hoped for. *v.,* **hoped, hop·ing.** long for. **hop·er,** *n.* **hope·ful,** *a.* **hope·less,** *a.*

hop·per, *n.* large chamber for temporarily storing grain or coal.

horde, *n.* mob; pack.

ho·ri·zon, *n.* apparent boundary between earth and sky.

hor·i·zon·tal, *a.* parallel to the horizon; level.

hor·mone, *n.* secretion of an endocrine gland. **hor·mo·nal,** *a.*

horn, *n.* hard appendage on the heads of cattle, goats, etc.

wind instrument. **horned,** *a.,* **horn·y,** *a.,* **-i·er, -i·est.**

hor·net, *n.* large wasp.

hor·o·scope, *n.* diagram of the heavens used by astrologers.

hor·ren·dous, *a.* dreadful. **hor·ren·dous·ly,** *adv.*

hor·ri·ble, *a.* exciting horror; terrible. **hor·ri·bly,** *adv.*

hor·rid, *a.* exciting horror; hideous. **hor·rid·ness,** *n.*

hor·ri·fy, *v.,* **-fied, -fy·ing.** strike with horror; appall. **hor·ri·fi·ca·tion,** *n.*

hor·ror, *n.* powerful feeling of fear or abhorrence.

horse, *n. pl.,* **hors·es, horse.** large domesticated quadruped; trestle.

horse·back, *n.* back of a horse. *adv.* on horseback.

horse·man, *n. pl.,* **-men.** person skilled in horseback riding. **horse·man·ship,** *n.*

horse·pow·er, *n.* unit for measuring power.

horse·rad·ish, *n.* herb root, used as a hot condiment.

horse·shoe, *n.* U-shaped metal plate attached to a horse's hoof; *pl.* form of quoits.

hor·ti·cul·ture, *n.* cultivation of flowers, shrubs, etc. **hor·ti·cul·tur·ist,** *n.*

ho·san·na, *int.* exclamation of praise to God.

hose, *n. pl.,* **hose.** stockings.

hose, *n. pl.,* **hos·es.** flexible tube. *v.,* **hosed, hos·ing.** water by means of a hose.

ho·sier·y, *n.* stockings.

hos·pi·ta·ble, *a.* being gracious to guests. **hos·pi·tal·i·ty,** *n. pl.,* **-ties.**

hos·pi·tal, *n.* institution in which persons are given medical care.

hos·pi·tal·ize, *v.,* **-ized, -iz·ing.** place in a hospital. **hos·pi·tal·i·za·tion,** *n.*

host, *n.* one who receives and entertains guests; multitude. **host·ess,** *n. fem.*

hos·tage, *n.* person handed over or held as a pledge.

hos·tile, *a.* antagonistic; of an enemy or like an enemy; unfriendly. **hos·tile·ly,** *adv.* **hos·til·i·ty,** *n. pl.,* **-ties.**

hot, *a.,* **hot·ter, hot·test.** having heat, esp. in a high degree; very warm; pungent; passionate, inflamed.

hot-blood·ed, *a.* excitable.

ho·tel, *n.* place with living accommodations for transient visitors.

hot·house, *n.* greenhouse.

hound, *n.* hunting dog. *v.* pursue relentlessly. **hound·er**, *n.*

hour, *n.* 60 minutes; specific time; customary time. **hour·ly**, *a.*, *adv.*

house, *n. pl.*, **hous·es.** building where people live; legislative body; business establishment. *v.*, housed, hous·ing. lodge.

house·bro·ken, *a.* trained, as dogs, to excrete only in the proper place. **house·break**, *v.*, -broke, -brok·en, -break·ing.

house·hold, *n.* house; family.

house·keep·er, *n.* one who maintains a home. **house·keep·ing**, *n.*

house·work, *n.* tasks involved in housekeeping.

hous·ing, *n.* shelter; lodging; houses.

hov·el, *n.* shed; mean dwelling. *v.*, hov·eled, hov·el·ing. shelter or lodge as in a hovel.

hov·er, *v.* hang fluttering in the air; move near vigilantly. **hov·er·ing**, *a.*

how, *adv.* in what manner; to what extent; in what condition; why.

how·ev·er, *adv.* notwithstanding; yet. *conj.* in whatever manner or degree.

howl, *v.* utter a loud, mournful cry, as of a dog; wail. *n.* loud cry or wail. **howl·er**, *n.*

how·so·ev·er, *adv.* in whatever way; to whatever extent.

hub, *n.* central part of a wheel; center of activity.

hub·bub, *n.* tumult; uproar.

huck·le·ber·ry, *n. pl.*, -ries. black edible berry.

hud·dle, *v.*, hud·dled, hud·dling. crowd together; hunch one's body together. *n.* crowd.

hue, *n.* color; shade, tint.

huff, *n.* feeling of petulant anger. *v.* puff. **huff·y**, *a.*, huf·fi·er, huf·fi·est.

hug, *v.*, hugged, hug·ging. embrace; keep close to. *n.* close embrace. **hug·ger**, *n.*

huge, *a.*, hug·er, hug·est. very large in area; enormous. **huge·ly**, *adv.* **huge·ness**, *n.*

hulk, *n.* body of an old ship; something or someone bulky. **hulk·ing**, *a.*

hull, *n.* husk or outer covering

of a seed or fruit; body of a ship.

hum, *v.*, hummed, hum·ming. make a sound like that of a bee; sing with the lips closed. *n.* murmuring sound. **hum·mer**, *n.*

hu·man, *a.* of mankind or man. *n.* human being. **hu·man·ness**, *n.*

hu·mane, *a.* kind; merciful. **hu·mane·ly**, *adv.* **hu·mane·ness**, *n.*

hu·man·i·tar·i·an, *a.* philanthropic. *n.* one who promotes the welfare of mankind.

hu·man·i·ty, *n. pl.*, -ties. mankind; quality of being human or humane.

hum·ble, *a.*, -bler, -blest. modest; low in rank. *v.*, -bled, -bling. render humble. **hum·ble·ness**, *n.* **hum·bly**, *adv.*

hum·bug, *n.* hoax, fraud. *v.*, -bugged, -bug·ging. deceive; trick. **hum·bug·ger·y**, *n.*

hum·drum, *a.* dull; monotonous.

hu·mid, *a.* moist; damp. **hu·mid·ly**, *adv.*

hu·mid·i·fy, *v.*, -fied, -fy·ing. make humid. **hu·mid·i·fi·er**, *n.*

hu·mid·i·ty, *n.* moistness. relative **hu·mid·i·ty.** percentage of water vapor in the air.

hu·mil·i·ate, *v.*, -at·ed, -at·ing. humble; disgrace. **hu·mil·i·at·ing**, *a.* **hu·mil·i·a·tion**, *n.*

hu·mil·i·ty, *n.* state of being humble.

hum·ming·bird, *n.* tiny bird.

hu·mor, *n.* that quality which tends to excite laughter; quality for perceiving the ludicrous; temperament. *v.* comply with the inclination of. **hu·mor·ist**, *n.* **hu·mor·ous**, *a.*

hump, *n.* rounded protuberance. *v.* raise in a hump. **humped**, *a.* **hump·y**, -ier, -iest.

hu·mus, *n.* organic constituent of soil.

hunch, *v.* thrust out or up in a hump. *n.* hump; *inf.* premonition.

hunch·back, *n.* back deformed by a curvature of the spine; humpback. **hunch·backed**, *a.*

hun·dred, *a.*, *n. pl.*, -dred or dreds. number between 99 and 101. **hun·dredth**, *n.*, *a.*

hun·ger, *n.* need or craving for food; eager desire. *v.* feel hunger. **hun·gry**, *a.*, -gri·er, -griest. **hun·gri·ness**, n.

hunk, n. inf. large portion.

hunt, v. chase or search for; pursue. n. chase; search. **hunt·er**, n. **hunt·ing**, n.

hur·dle, n. barrier to be jumped over; fig. barrier. v., **hur·dled**, **hur·dling**. jump over, as in racing; overcome.

hurl, v. throw or fling away forecefully. **hurl·er**, n.

hur·rah, int. exclamation joy, applause, etc. Also **hur·ray**.

hur·ri·cane, n. violent cyclonic storm.

hur·ry, v., **hur·ried**, **hur·ry·ing**. impel to greater speed or haste. n. hurrying; urgency. **hur·ried**, a. **hur·ried·ly**, adv.

hurt, v., hurt, **hurt·ing**. cause or feel pain; harm; damage. n. anguish; damage.

hur·tle, v., **hur·tled**, **hur·tling**. move rapidly; hurl.

hus·band, n. married man. v. manage with prudence.

hus·band·ry, n. agricultural cultivation and the breeding of animals for food.

hush, v. silence; calm. n. stillness; quiet.

husk, n. covering of certain fruits or seeds. v. deprive of the husk. **husk·er**, n.

husk·y, a., -i·er, -i·est. hoarse; burly. **husk·i·ness**, n.

hus·sy, n. pl., **huss·ies**. disreputable, brazen woman.

hus·tle, v., -tled, -tling. shove; jostle; force hurriedly. n. hustling. **hus·tler**, n.

hut, n. shack; cabin.

hy·a·cinth, n. bulbous plant with bell-shaped flowers.

hy·brid, n. offspring of two animals or plants of different races, etc. **hy·brid·ism**, n.

hy·drant, n. upright pipe with valves and an outlet for water.

hy·drau·lic, a. pertaining to water or other liquid in motion. **hy·drau·li·cal·ly**, adv.

hy·dro·chlo·ric·ac·id, n. strong, corrosive acid. Also **mu·ri·at·ic acid**.

hy·dro·e·lec·tric, a. of production of electric current by moving water.

hy·dro·gen, n. colorless, gaseous element.

hy·dro·gen bomb, n. bomb using the fusion of light nuclei to produce a powerful explosion. Also **H-bomb**.

hy·dro·pho·bi·a, n. fear of water; rabies.

hy·drous, a. containing water.

hy·e·na, n. large animal recognized by its piercing cry. Also **hy·ae·na**.

hy·giene, n. principles for health and cleanliness. **hy·gi·en·ic**, a. **hy·gi·en·i·cal·ly**, adv. **hy·gien·ist**, n.

hymn, n. song in adoration of God.

hym·nal, n. book of hymns. Also **hymn·book**.

hy·per·sen·si·tive, a. excessively sensitive. **hy·per·sen·si·tiv·i·ty**, n.

hy·per·ten·sion, n. high blood pressure.

hy·phen, n. short line (-) used in punctuation.

hy·phen·ate, v., -at·ed, -at·ing. join by a hyphen.

hyp·no·sis, n. pl., -ses. artificially induced state marked by susceptibility to suggestion. **hyp·not·ic**, a.

hyp·no·tize, v., -tized, -tiz·ing. put into a hypnotic state. **hyp·no·tism**, n. **hyp·no·tist**, n.

hy·po·chon·dri·ac, n. person who fancies himself ill.

hy·poc·ri·sy, n. pl., -sies. act of feigning feelings or beliefs. **hyp·o·crite**, n.

hy·po·der·mic, a. concerning the injection of medical preparations under the skin.

hy·pot·e·nuse, n. side of a right triangle which is opposite the right angle.

hy·poth·e·sis, n. pl., -ses. supposition; temporary explanation. **hy·poth·e·size**, v., -sized, -siz·ing. **hy·po·thet·i·cal**, a.

hys·te·ri·a, n. emotional frenzy. **hys·ter·ic**, **hys·ter·i·cal**, a.

hys·ter·ics, n. pl. fit of hysteria.

I

I, pron. pron. by which a speaker or writer denotes himself.

i·bis, n. pl., -bis·es, i·bis. large wading bird.

ice, n. solid form of frozen water; dessert made of frozen fruit juice. v., **iced**, **ic·ing**. cover with ice; frost.

ice·berg, n. large floating mass of ice.

ice cream, n. frozen dessert food made of cream.

i·ci·cle, n. hanging mass of ice.

i·ci·ly, *adv.* in an icy manner.

ic·ing, *n.* sugary frosting for cakes.

i·con, *n.* religious image.

i·con·o·clast, *n.* one who attacks cherished beliefs. **i·con·o·clasm,** *n.*

i·cy, *a.,* **i·ci·er, i·ci·est.** of ice; slippery; very cold.

i·de·a, *n.* thought; notion; conviction; plan; inkling.

i·de·al, *a.* achieving a standard of perfection. *n.* conception or standard of perfection; model person or thing. **i·de·al·ism,** *n.* **i·de·al·ist,** *n.*

i·de·al·ize, *v.,* **-ized, -iz·ing.** imagine or form an ideal. **i·de·al·i·za·tion,** *n.*

i·den·ti·cal, *a.* same. **i·den·ti·cal·ly,** *adv.* **i·den·ti·cal·ness,** *n.*

i·den·ti·fy, *v.,* **-fied, -fy·ing.** recognize; prove. **i·den·ti·fi·ca·tion,** *n.*

i·den·ti·ty, *n. pl.,* **-ties.** being the same one; individuality.

i·de·ol·o·gy, *n. pl.,* **-gies.** system of ideas.

id·i·om, *n.* form of expression peculiar to one language; dialect. **id·i·o·mat·ic,** *a.*

id·i·o·syn·cra·sy, *n. pl.,* **-sies.** quirk.

id·i·ot, *n.* mentally retarded person. **id·i·ot·ic,** *a.* **id·i·o·cy,** *n. pl.,* **-cies.**

i·dle, *a.,* **-dler, -dlest.** doing nothing; useless. *v.,* **i·dled, i·dling.** spend time inactively. **i·dle·ness,** *n.* **i·dly,** *adv.*

i·dol, *n.* object of worship.

i·dol·a·try, *n. pl.,* **-tries.** worship of idols. **i·dol·a·ter,** *n.* **i·dol·a·trous,** *a.*

i·dol·ize, *v.,* **-ized, -iz·ing.** worship as an idol.

i·dyll, i·dyl, *n.* short poem of rustic life. **i·dyl·lic,** *a.*

if, *conj.* in case that; even though; whether.

ig·loo, *n. pl.,* **-loos.** Eskimo hut of blocks of hard snow.

ig·nite, *v.,* **-nit·ed, -nit·ing.** set on fire; take fire. **ig·ni·tion,** *n.*

ig·no·ble, *a.* mean; base.

ig·no·min·y, *n. pl.,* **-ies.** public disgrace; shame.

ig·no·rant, *a.* lacking in knowledge; uninformed. **ig·no·rant·ly,** *adv.* **ig·no·rance,** *n.*

ig·nore, *v.,* **-nored, -nor·ing.** refuse to notice.

ill, *a.,* **worse, worst.** sick; unfortunate; bad. **ill·ness,** *n.*

il·le·gal, *a.* unlawful.

il·leg·i·ble, *a.* incapable of being read. **il·leg·i·bly,** *adv.*

il·le·git·i·mate, *a.* illegal; born out of wedlock. **il·le·git·i·ma·cy,** *n. pl.,* **-cies.**

il·lic·it, *a.* unlawful.

il·lit·er·ate, *a.* unable to read or write. *n.* (one) **il·lit·er·a·cy,** *n. pl.,* **-cies.**

il·log·i·cal, *a.* contrary to logic. **il·log·ic,** *n.*

il·lu·mi·nate, *v.,* **-nat·ed, -nat·ing.** light up; make clear; decorate. **il·lu·mi·na·tion,** *n.*

il·lu·mine, *v.,* **-mined, -min·ing.** illuminate.

il·lu·sion, *n.* false impression or belief. **il·lu·so·ry,** *a.*

il·lus·trate, *v.,* **-trat·ed, -trat·ing.** make clear by examples; ornament by pictures. **il·lus·tra·tion,** *n.*

il·lus·tri·ous, *a.* renowned.

im·age, *n.* representation of a person or thing; likeness; mental picture. **im·ag·er,** *n.*

im·ag·i·nar·y, *a.* not real.

im·ag·i·na·tion, *n.* action of forming mental images. **im·ag·i·na·tive,** *a.*

i·mag·ine, *v.,* **-ined, -in·ing.** conceive; suppose.

im·be·cile, *n.* one who is mentally deficient. *a.* mentally feeble.

im·bibe, *v.,* **-bibed, -bib·ing.** drink; absorb. **im·bib·er,** *n.*

im·bue, *v.,* **-bued, -bu·ing.** soak with moisture; inspire.

im·i·tate, *v.,* **-tat·ed, -tat·ing.** copy. **im·i·ta·tion,** *n.*

im·mac·u·late, *a.* free from stain; clean.

im·ma·te·ri·al, *a.* unimportant.

im·ma·ture, *a.* not mature. **im·ma·tu·ri·ty,** *n.*

im·meas·ur·a·ble, *a.* incapable of being measured.

im·me·di·ate, *a.* instant; in closest relation; direct.

im·me·mo·ri·al, *a.* beyond memory or record.

im·mense, *a.* vast; very great; huge. **im·men·si·ty,** *n.*

im·merse, *n.,* **-mersed, -mers·ing.** plunge into. **im·mer·sion,** *n.*

im·mi·grate, *v.,* **-grat·ed, -grat·ing.** move to a country to reside there. **im·mi·grant,** *n.* **im·mi·gra·tion,** *n.*

im·mi·nent, *a.* impending.

im·mo·bile, *a.* immovable.

im·mod·er·ate, a. without restraint; excessive.

im·mod·est, a. lacking modesty or propriety.

im·mor·al, a. not moral.

im·mor·tal, a. not subject to death. **im·mor·tal·i·ty**, n.

im·mov·a·ble, a. unalterable.

im·mune, a. exempt; free from. **im·mu·ni·ty**, n. pl., -ties.

im·mu·ta·ble, a. unchangeable. **im·mu·ta·bil·i·ty**, n.

imp, n. mischievous child.

im·pact, n. collision; force of a collision.

im·pair, v. make worse; deteriorate. **im·pair·ment**, n.

im·part, v. make known; give.

im·par·tial, a. not partial.

im·pas·sion, v. move with passion. **im·pas·sioned**, a.

im·pas·sive, a. unmoved.

im·pa·tient, a. not patient. **im·pa·tience**, n.

im·peach, v. charge with wrongdoing; accuse an official of misconduct. **im·peach·a·ble**, a. **im·peach·ment**, n.

im·pec·ca·ble, a. faultless.

im·pede, v., -ped·ed, -ped·ing. obstruct; hinder.

im·ped·i·ment, n. hindrance; handicap, esp. a speech defect.

im·pel, v., -pelled, -pel·ing. drive or urge forward.

im·pend, v. be ready to happen. **im·pend·ing**, a.

im·per·a·tive, a. urgent; obligatory.

im·per·fect, a. not perfect. **im·per·fec·tion**, n. defectiveness; defect or fault.

im·pe·ri·al, a. of an empire.

im·per·il, v., -iled, -il·ing. endanger. **im·per·il·ment**, n.

im·pe·ri·ous, a. dictatorial.

im·per·son·al, a. without personal reference or connection. **im·per·son·al·ly**, adv.

im·per·son·ate, v., -at·ed, -at·ing. assume the appearance, speech, etc., of someone. **im·per·son·a·tion**, n.

im·per·ti·nent, a. rude; insolent; not pertinent.

im·per·vi·ous, a. incapable of being passed through, or emotionally affected.

im·pet·u·ous, a. impulsive.

im·pe·tus, n. pl., -tus·es. force of motion; stimulus.

im·pi·ous, a. not pious. **im·pi·e·ty**, n. pl., -ties.

im·plac·a·ble, a. not to be appeased; stubborn.

im·plant, v. fix firmly; plant deeply. **im·plan·ta·tion**, n.

im·ple·ment, n. tool; utensil.

im·pli·cate, v., -cat·ed, -cat·ing. involve in a matter.

im·pli·ca·tion, n. act of implying; something implied.

im·plic·it, a. understood; implied; absolute.

im·plore, v., -plored, -plor·ing. entreat; beg.

im·ply, v., -plied, -ply·ing. hint; signify.

im·po·lite, a. not polite.

im·port, v. bring in, esp. goods from a foreign country; mean. n. thing imported.

im·por·tance, n. significance; consequence. **im·por·tant**, a.

im·por·tune, v., -tuned, -tun·ing. make solicitations.

im·pose, v., -posed, -pos·ing. set by authority; lay on; foist. **im·po·si·tion**, n.

im·pos·ing, a. making an impression. **im·pos·ing·ly**, adv.

im·pos·si·ble, a. not possible. **im·pos·si·bil·i·ty**, n. pl., -ties. **im·pos·si·bly**, adv.

im·pos·tor, n. person who assumes the character or name of another.

im·po·tent, a. lacking strength; powerless. **im·po·tence**, **im·po·ten·cy**, n.

im·pound, v. seize and retain.

im·pov·er·ish, v. reduce to poverty.

im·prac·ti·ca·ble, a. not practicable; unfeasible.

im·prac·ti·cal, a. not practical.

im·preg·na·ble, a. not able to be taken by force.

im·preg·nate, v., -nat·ed, -nat·ing. make pregnant; fill or saturate; imbue.

im·press, v. stamp or imprint; fix firmly on the mind; urge; influence. **im·pres·sion**, n.

im·print, v. mark; impress.

im·pris·on, v. incarcerate.

im·prob·a·ble, a. unlikely.

im·promp·tu, a., adv. offhand.

im·prop·er, a. not proper.

im·prove, v., -proved, -prov·ing. better. **im·prove·ment**, n.

im·pro·vise, v., -vised, -vis·ing. extemporize. **im·prov·i·sa·tion**, n.

im·pru·dent, a. not prudent.

im·pu·dent, a. impertinent.

im·pulse, n. impelling action or

force; involuntary inclination.
im·pul·sive, *a.*

im·pu·ni·ty, *n.* exemption from punishment, injury, etc.

im·pure, *a.* foul; not morally pure; corrupt. **im·pure·ly**, *adv.* **im·pu·ri·ty**, *n. pl.*, **-ties.**

im·pute, *v.,* **-put·ed**, **-put·ing.** attribute; blame.

in, *prep.* inclusion within; during; indication of action, relation, or respect. *adv.* into; on the inside. *n.* one of those who are in power.

in·a·bil·i·ty, *n.* lack of power, means, or ability.

in·ac·tive, *a.* not active.

in·ad·e·quate, *a.* not adequate; insufficient; inept.

in·ane, *a.* empty; foolish. **in·an·i·ty**, *n. pl.,* **-ties.**

in·an·i·mate, *a.* not animate.

in·as·much as, *conj.* insofar as; seeing that; since.

in·au·gu·rate, *v.,* **-rat·ed**, **-rat·ing.** induct into office; install; initiate; begin. **in·au·gu·ra·tion**, *n.*

in·born, *a.* innate; inherent.

in·cal·cu·la·ble, *a.* beyond calculation; unpredictable.

in·can·des·cent, *a.* glowing with heat; brilliant. **in·can·des·cence**, *n.*

in·ca·pa·ble, *a.* not capable; unable; **in·ca·pa·bly**, *adv.*

in·ca·pac·i·tate, *v.,* **-tat·ed**, **-tat·ing.** make unable or unfit; disqualify.

in·car·nate, *v.,* **-nat·ed**, **-nat·ing.** invest with a form; be the embodiment of. **in·car·na·tion**, *n.*

in·cen·di·ar·y, *a.* setting on fire; tending to arouse strife, riot, or rebellion.

in·cense, *n.* substance producing a sweet odor when burned; fragrance. *v.,* **-censed**, **-cens·ing.** make angry.

in·cen·tive, *n.* motive.

in·cep·tion, *n.* beginning; origin.

in·ces·sant, *a.* continual.

in·cest, *n.* sexual intercourse between close blood relations. **in·ces·tu·ous**, *a.*

inch, *n.* measure of length, the twelfth part of a foot. *v.* move slowly by inches.

in·ci·dence, *n.* range; extent.

in·ci·dent, *n.* occurrence; event.

in·ci·den·tal, *a.* occurring with; casual. *n. pl.* incidental items. **in·ci·den·tal·ly**, *adv.*

in·cin·er·ate, *v.,* **-at·ed**, **-at·ing.** burn. **in·cin·er·a·tor**, *n.*

in·cip·i·ent, *a.* in the beginning stage.

in·ci·sion, *n.* cut; gash.

in·cite, *v.,* **-cit·ed**, **-cit·ing.** move to action; stir up.

in·clem·ent, *a.* severe; harsh.

in·cline, *v.,* **-clined**, **-clin·ing.** cause to lean or bend; slant; tend. *n.* slope. **in·cli·na·tion**, *n.* **in·clined**, *a.*

in·clude, *v.,* **-clud·ed**, **-clud·ing.** put within limits; contain. **in·clu·sion**, *n.* **in·clu·sive**, *a.*

in·cog·ni·to, *a.* having a concealed identity. *adv.* with the real identity concealed.

in·come, *n.* money accruing from labor, property, etc.

in·com·pa·ra·ble, *a.* unequaled.

in·com·pe·tent, *a.* unable; inadequate.

in·com·plete, *a.* not finished.

in·com·pre·hen·si·ble, *a.* not to be understood.

in·con·ceiv·a·ble, *a.* unimaginable; unthinkable.

in·con·gru·ous, *a.* out of place; inappropriate.

in·con·se·quen·tial, *a.* of no consequence; trivial.

in·con·sid·er·ate, *a.* thoughtless.

in·con·sis·tent, *a.* not consistent; lacking agreement.

in·con·spic·u·ous, *a.* not readily noticed.

in·con·ven·ience, *n.* trouble; discomfort. *v.,* **-ienced**, **-ienc·ing.** put to inconvenience. **in·con·ven·ient**, *a.*

in·cor·po·rate, *v.,* **-rat·ed**, **-rat·ing.** form a corporation; combine so as to form one body. **in·cor·po·ra·tion**, *n.*

in·cor·rect, *a.* not correct; not exact; improper. **in·cor·rect·ly**, *adv.*

in·cor·ri·gi·ble, *a.* incapable of being reformed.

in·crease, *v.,* **-creased**, **-creas·ing.** become greater; grow; add to. *n.* growing larger; amount augmented. **in·creas·a·ble**, *a.*

in·cred·i·ble, *a.* too extraordinary to be believed.

in·cred·u·lous, *a.* skeptical.

in·crim·i·nate, *v.,* **-nat·ed**, **-nat·ing.** accuse; implicate.

in·cu·ba·tor, *n.* temperature-controlled apparatus for hatching eggs or for premature babies.

in·cum·bent, *a.* lying or resting upon; person holding an office.

in·cur, *v.,* -**curred**, -**cur·ring**. become liable to.

in·cur·a·ble, *a.* not curable.

in·debt·ed, *a.* in debt; beholden. **in·debt·ed·ness**, *n.*

in·de·cent, *a.* offensive; vulgar. **in·de·cen·cy**, *n. pl.,* -**cies.**

in·deed, *adv.* in fact. *int.* expression of surprise.

in·def·i·nite, *a.* without fixed limit; not clearly defined. **in·def·i·nite·ly**, *adv.*

in·del·i·ble, *a.* incapable of being obliterated. **in·del·i·bly**, *adv.*

in·dem·ni·fy, *v.,* -**fied**, -**fy·ing**. secure against loss; reimburse for damages. **in·dem·ni·ty**, *n. pl.,* -**ties.**

in·dent, *v.* begin a line of type in from the margin; notch. *n.* blank space at the beginning of a paragraph; notch. **in·den·ta·tion**, *n.*

in·de·pend·ent, *a.* not subject to the control of others. **in·de·pend·ence**, *n.*

in·de·scrib·a·ble, *a.* beyond description.

in·de·struct·i·ble, *a.* incapable of being destroyed. **in·de·struct·i·bly**, *adv.*

in·dex, *n. pl.,* -**dex·es**, -**di·ces**. alphabetical list, as in a book, for facilitating reference; forefinger; indication.

In·di·an corn, *n.* maize; corn.

in·di·cate, *v.,* -**cat·ed**, -**cat·ing**. point out; suggest; signify. **in·di·ca·tion**, *n.* **in·dic·a·tive**, *a.*

in·dict, *v.* accuse or charge with a crime. **in·dict·ment**, *n.*

in·dif·fer·ent, *a.* without concern; unbiased. **in·dif·fer·ence**, *n.*

in·dig·e·nous, *a.* native.

in·di·gent, *a., n.* needy; poor. **in·di·gence**, *n.*

in·di·gest·i·ble, *a.* not digestible.

in·di·ges·tion, *n.* difficulty in digesting food; stomach discomfort caused by this.

in·dig·nant, *a.* exhibiting displeasure at what seems unjust or unworthy. **in·dig·nant·ly**, *adv.* **in·dig·na·tion**, *n.*

in·dig·ni·ty, *n. pl.,* -**ties**. insult; outrage.

in·di·go, *n. pl.,* -**gos**, -**goes**. deep violet blue; blue dye.

in·di·rect, *a.* deviating from a direct course.

in·dis·creet, *a.* lacking sound judgment. **in·dis·cre·tion**, *n.*

in·dis·crim·i·nate, *a.* random. **in·dis·crim·i·nat·ing**, *a.*

in·dis·pen·sa·ble, *a.* absolutely necessary.

in·dis·posed, *a.* mildly ill; unwilling. **in·dis·po·si·tion**, *n.*

in·dis·sol·u·ble, *a.* stable.

in·di·vid·u·al, *a.* single; peculiar to a person or thing. *n.* single person or thing; particular person. **in·di·vid·u·al·i·ty**, *n. pl.,* -**ties.**

in·doc·tri·nate, *v.,* -**nat·ed**, -**nat·ing**. instruct in any doctrine. **in·doc·tri·na·tion**, *n.*

in·do·lent, *a.* lazy; idle.

in·door, *a.* occurring, used, or belonging in a building.

in·doors, *adv.* in or into a house or building.

in·duce, *v.,* -**duced**, -**duc·ing**. persuade; bring on, produce, or cause. **in·duce·ment**, *n.*

in·duct, *v.* bring in as a member; call into military service. **in·duct·ee**, *n.* **in·duc·tion**, *n.* **in·duc·tive**, *a.*

in·dulge, *v.,* -**dulged**, -**dulg·ing**. gratify the wishes of; humor. **in·dul·gence**, *n.*

in·dus·tri·al, *a.* of industry.

in·dus·tri·ous, *a.* hardworking. **in·dus·tri·ous·ly**, *adv.*

in·dus·try, *n. pl.,* -**tries**. trade or manufacturing; diligence in employment.

in·e·bri·ate, *v.,* -**at·ed**, -**at·ing**. intoxicate. *n.* drunkard. **in·e·bri·a·tion**, *n.*

in·ef·fec·tive, *a.* not effective. **in·ef·fec·tive·ness**, *n.*

in·el·i·gi·ble, *a.* not eligible. **in·el·i·gi·bil·i·ty**, *n.*

in·ept, *a.* not suitable; awkward. **in·ept·i·tude**, *n.*

in·ert, *a.* having no power of action or resistance; sluggish. **in·ert·ness**, *n.*

in·er·tia, *n.* property of matter by which it retains its state of rest or of motion. **in·er·tial**, *a.*

in·ev·i·ta·ble, *a.* certain to happen.

in·ex·o·ra·ble, *a.* unyielding.

in·ex·pert, *a.* not skilled.

in·ex·pli·ca·ble, *a.* incapable of being explained.

in·fal·li·ble, *a.* absolutely trustworthy or certain.

in·fa·my, *n. pl.,* -**mies**. shameful notoriety; evilness. **in·fa·**

mous, *a.*

in·fant, *n.* baby. *a.* being in the earliest period or stage. **in·fan·cy,** *n. pl.,* **-cies.**

in·fan·tile, *a.* of infants.

in·fan·try, *n. pl.,* **-tries.** foot soldiers. **in·fan·try·man,** *n. pl.,* **-men.**

in·fat·u·ate, *v.,* **-at·ed, -at·ing.** inspire or possess with passion. **in·fat·u·a·tion,** *n.*

in·fect, *v.* contaminate with disease. **in·fec·tion,** *n.* **in·fec·tious,** *a.*

in·fer, *v.,* **-ferred, -fer·ring.** conclude by reasoning; imply. **in·fer·ence,** *n.*

in·fe·ri·or, *a.* lower in place or position; of lower grade. *n.* one inferior to others. **in·fe·ri·or·i·ty,** *n.*

in·fer·nal, *a.* hellish.

in·fest, *v.* overrun; be numerous in. **in·fes·ta·tion,** *n.*

in·fi·del, *n.* disbeliever.

in·fi·del·i·ty, *n. pl.,* **-ties.** skepticism; unfaithfulness.

in·fil·trate, *v.,* **-trat·ed, -trat·ing.** permeate.

in·fi·nite, *a.* without limits.

in·fin·i·tes·i·mal, *a.* infinitely small.

in·fin·i·tive, *n.* verb form which expresses meaning without specifying person or number. **in·fin·i·ty,** *n. pl.,* **-ties.** unlimited extent or number.

in·firm, *a.* feeble, weak; not steadfast. **in·firm·ness,** *n.*

in·fir·ma·ry, *n. pl.,* **-ries.** small hospital.

in·flame, *v.,* **-flamed, flam·ing.** set afire; excite; rouse; cause redness and swelling. **in·flam·ma·tion,** *n.*

in·flam·ma·ble, *a.* flammable.

in·flate, *v.,* **-flat·ed, -flat·ing.** distend, swell, or puff out; raise. **in·fla·tion,** *n.*

in·flect, *v.* modulate, as the voice; decline or conjugate. **in·flec·tion,** *n.*

in·flict, *v.* cause to bear or suffer from; impose on. **in·flic·tion,** *n.* **in·flic·tive,** *a.*

in·flu·ence, *n.* power of affecting others; person or thing that exerts such force. *v.,* **-enced, -enc·ing.** exert influence.

in·flu·en·za, *n.* highly contagious virus disease.

in·flux, *n.* act of flowing in.

in·form, *v.* give information.

in·formed, *a.* **in·form·er,** *n.*

in·for·mal, *a.* unofficial; casual. **in·for·mal·ly,** *adv.*

in·for·ma·tion, *n.* news; facts; knowledge. **in·for·ma·tive,** *a.*

in·fre·quent, *a.* seldom; rare.

in·fringe, *v.,* **-fringed, -fring·ing.** violate; encroach. **in·fringe·ment,** *n.*

in·fu·ri·ate, *v.,* **-at·ed, -at·ing.** enrage. **in·fu·ri·a·tion,** *n.*

in·fuse, *v.,* **-fused, -fus·ing.** pour into; instill. **in·fu·sive,** *a.* **in·fu·sion,** *n.*

in·gen·ious, *a.* clever; inventive. **in·ge·nu·i·ty,** *n.*

in·got, *n.* mass of molded metal.

in·grain, *v.* fix deeply and firmly; infuse. **in·grained,** *a.*

in·grat·i·tude, *n.* want of gratitude; unthankfulness.

in·gre·di·ent, *n.* element of any mixture. *n.*

in·hab·it, *v.* live in. **in·hab·it·ed,** *a.* **in·hab·it·ant,** *n.*

in·hale, *v.,* **-haled, -hal·ing.** breathe in.

in·here, *v.,* **-hered, -her·ing.** exist in; be innate. **in·her·ent,** *a.*

in·her·it, *v.* acquire through heredity; receive a legacy. **in·her·it·ance,** *n.*

in·hib·it, *v.* restrain; hinder. **in·hi·bi·tion,** *n.*

in·hu·man, *a.* not human; brutal; cruel.

in·iq·ui·ty, *n. pl.,* **-ties.** gross injustice; sin.

in·i·tial, *a.* of the beginning. *n.* first letter of a word or name. *v.* **-tialed, -tial·ing.** put one's initials on. **in·i·tial·ly,** *adv.*

in·i·ti·ate, *v.,* **-at·ed, -at·ing.** begin; guide by instruction in rudiments. **in·i·ti·a·tion,** *n.* **in·i·ti·a·tor,** *n.*

in·i·ti·a·tive, *n.* introductory act; ability to originate action.

in·ject, *v.* force a fluid into; interject. **in·jec·tion,** *n.*

in·junc·tion, *n.* act of ordering or directing; writ.

in·jure, *v.,* **-jured, -jur·ing.** do harm to; hurt; offend. **in·ju·ry,** *n. pl.,* **-ries.**

in·jus·tice, *n.* wrong.

ink, *n.* colored liquid used for writing, printing, etc. **ink·y,** *a.,* **-i·er, -i·est.**

ink·ling, *n.* hint or whisper.

in·let, *n.* narrow passage or strip of water.

in·mate, *n.* occupant of an asylum, prison, etc.

inn, *n.* public house or restaurant.

in·nate, *a.* inborn; native.

in·ner, *a.* interior; private.

in·ner·most, *a.* farthest inward.

in·no·cent, *a.* free from sin, guilt, etc. **in·no·cence,** *n.*

in·noc·u·ous, *a.* inoffensive.

in·no·vate, *v.,* **-vat·ed, -vat·ing.** change by introducing something new. **in·no·va·tion,** *n.* **in·no·va·tive,** *a.*

in·nu·en·do, *n. pl.,* **-dos, -does.** insinuation.

in·nu·mer·a·ble, *a.* countless.

in·oc·u·late, *v.,* **-lat·ed, -lat·ing.** vaccinate. **in·oc·u·la·tion,** *n.* **in·oc·u·la·tor,** *n.*

in·quest, *n.* legal or judicial inquiry.

in·quire, *v.,* **-quired, -quir·ing.** ask for information. **in·quir·y,** *n. pl.,* **-ies.**

in·qui·si·tion, *n.* act of investigating; an inquiry.

in·quis·i·tive, *a.* overly curious.

in·road, *n. usu. pl.* encroachment; raid; invasion.

in·sane, *a.* not sane; mad. **in·san·i·ty,** *n. pl.,* **-ties.**

in·scribe, *v.,* **-scribed, -scrib·ing.** write down or engrave. **in·scrip·tion,** *n.*

in·sect, *n.* small arthropod having three pairs of legs and wings.

in·se·cure, *a.* prone to fear or anxiety; unsafe.

in·sen·si·ble, *a.* unconscious; numb to pain.

in·sep·a·ra·ble, *a.* incapable of being parted. **in·sep·a·ra·bly,** *adv.*

in·sert, *v.* put or set in in. something inserted. **in·ser·tion,** *n.*

in·side, *n.* inner side, surface, or part. *a.* within; internal. *adv.* on the inside. *prep.* within.

in·sid·i·ous, *a.* deceitful.

in·sight, *n.* understanding; discernment; perception.

in·sig·ni·a, *n. pl.* badges of office, honor, etc.

in·sig·nif·i·cant, *a.* having little importance. **in·sig·nif·i·cance,** *n.*

in·sin·u·ate, *v.,* **-at·ed, -at·ing.** hint or suggest subtly; imply. **in·sin·u·a·tion,** *n.*

in·sip·id, *a.* tasteless; dull.

in·sist, *v.* demand firmly; assert. **in·sist·ence,** *n.* **in·sist·ent,** *a.*

in·so·lent, *a.* disrespectful; rude.

in·so·lence, *n.*

in·sol·u·ble, *a.* incapable of being dissolved or solved. *n.*

in·som·ni·a, *n.* inability to sleep. **in·som·ni·ac,** *n., a.*

in·spect, *v.* examine closely. **in·spec·tion,** *n.* **in·spec·tor,** *n.*

in·spire, *v.,* **-spired, -spir·ing.** arouse; prompt creative action. **in·spi·ra·tion,** *n.*

in·stall, *v.* set up for use; appoint to an office. **in·stal·la·tion,** *n.*

in·stall·ment, *n.* any of the specified parts of a debt, story, etc.

in·stance, *n.* example.

in·stant, *a.* immediate; *inf.* of foods, readily prepared. *n.* very short space of time. *adv.* at once.

in·stan·ta·ne·ous, *a.* occurring or completed within a very short time.

in·stead, *adv.* rather than; in lieu.

in·step, *n.* arched upper part of the foot.

in·sti·gate, *v.,* **-gat·ed, -gat·ing.** incite. **in·sti·ga·tion,** *n.*

in·still, *v.,* **-stilled, -still·ling.** introduce drop by drop. **in·stil·la·tion,** *n.*

in·stinct, *n.* innate impulse; natural aptitude. **in·stinc·tive,** *a.* also **in·stinc·tu·al.**

in·sti·tute, *v.,* **-tut·ed, -tut·ing.** establish. *n.* society for carrying on a particular work. **in·sti·tu·tion,** *n.*

in·struct, *v.* teach. **in·struc·tion,** *n.* **in·struc·tor,** *n.*

in·stru·ment, *n.* tool; means; device for producing music. **in·stru·men·tal,** *a.*

in·suf·fer·a·ble, *a.* intolerable; unendurable.

in·suf·fi·cient, *a.* not sufficient. **in·suf·fi·cien·cy,** *n.*

in·su·lar, *a.* of an island.

in·su·late, *v.,* **-lat·ed, -lat·ing.** isolate; prevent the passage of electricity, heat, etc. **in·su·la·tion,** *n.*

in·su·lin, *n.* preparation used for treating diabetes.

in·sult, *v.* affront or indignity. *v.* treat with abuse, insolence, etc.

in·sure, *v.,* **-sured, -sur·ing.** guarantee against risk or loss. **in·sur·ance,** *n.*

in·sur·rec·tion, *n.* revolt.

in·tact, *a.* untouched or unaffected.

in·te·ger, *n.* whole number.

in·te·gral, *a.* whole; necessary. **in·te·gral·ly,** *adv.*

in·te·grate, *v.,* **-grat·ed, -grat·ing.** bring into a whole; make available equally to all. **in·te·gra·tion,** *n.*

in·teg·ri·ty, *n.* honesty; soundness.

in·tel·lect, *n.* power to learn and to think; intelligence. **in·tel·lec·tu·al,** *a.*

in·tel·li·gence, *n.* ability to reason; intellectual power; information. **in·tel·li·gent,** *a.*

in·tel·li·gi·ble, *a.* capable of being understood.

in·tend, *v.* design or mean. **in·tend·er,** *n.* **in·tend·ed,** *a.*

in·tense, *a.* very great or strong. **in·ten·sive,** *a.* **in·ten·si·ty,** *n. pl.,* **-ties.**

in·ten·si·fy, *v.,* **-fied, -fy·ing.** render intense.

in·tent, *a.* fixed with attention; earnest; fixed with some purpose in view. *n.* intention or design.

in·ten·tion, *n.* purpose or design; end intended. **in·ten·tion·al,** *a.*

in·ter, *v.,* **in·terred, in·ter·ring.** bury. **in·ter·ment,** *n.*

in·ter·act, *v.* act on each other. **in·ter·ac·tion,** *n.*

in·ter·breed, *v.,* **-bred, -breed·ing.** crossbreed.

in·ter·cede, *v.,* **-ced·ed, -ced·ing.** mediate; plead on behalf of. **in·ter·ces·sion,** *n.*

in·ter·cept, *v.* take or stop while on the way. **in·ter·cep·tion,** *n.* **in·ter·cep·tive,** *a.*

in·ter·change, *v.,* **-changed, -chang·ing.** change reciprocally. *n.* exchange; alternate succession; intersection of highways.

in·ter·course, *n.* reciprocal dealings between persons or nations; sexual union.

in·ter·est, *n.* attentiveness or curiosity; benefit; self-interest; share; money paid for the use of money borrowed. *v.* concern. **in·ter·est·ed,** *a.* **in·ter·est·ing,** *a.*

in·ter·fere, *v.,* **-fered, -fer·ing.** intervene; meddle. **in·ter·fer·ence,** *n.*

in·ter·im, *n.* intervening time; *a.* temporary.

in·te·ri·or, *a.* inner; situated inland; internal. *n.* inside; inside

of a building or room.

in·ter·jec·tion, *n.* expression of emotion or passion.

in·ter·lock, *v.* lock one in another firmly.

in·ter·lop·er, *n.* trespasser.

in·ter·lude, *n.* intervening episode or period.

in·ter·mar·ry, *v.,* **-mar·ried, -mar·ry·ing.** marry, as two families, castes, etc., or within the limits of the family. **in·ter·mar·riage,** *n.*

in·ter·me·di·ate, *a.* between two points. *v.* **-at·ed, -at·ing.** intervene.

in·ter·mi·na·ble, *a.* unending.

in·ter·mis·sion, *n.* space of time between periods of action.

in·ter·mit, *v.,* **-mit·ted, -mit·ting.** cease for a time. **in·ter·mit·tent,** *a.*

in·tern, *n.* medical graduate in a hospital for training. *v.* confine within an area. **in·tern·ship,** *n.*

in·ter·nal, *a.* of the inside; interior; inner. **in·ter·nal·ly,** *adv.*

in·ter·na·tion·al, *a.* between or among nations; affecting different nations. **in·ter·na·tion·al·ize,** *v.,* **-ized, -iz·ing.**

in·ter·plan·e·tar·y, *a.* existing between the planets.

in·ter·play, *n.* interaction.

in·ter·po·late, *v.,* **-lat·ed, -lat·ing.** insert, as new or spurious matter. **in·ter·po·la·tion,** *n.*

in·ter·pose, *v.,* **-posed, -pos·ing.** put between; come between. **in·ter·po·si·tion,** *n.*

in·ter·pret, *v.* explain; translate; construe. **in·ter·pre·ta·tion,** *n.*

in·ter·ro·gate, *v.,* **-gat·ed, -gat·ing.** examine by asking questions. **in·ter·ro·ga·tion,** *n.*

in·ter·rupt, *v.* make a break in; hinder. **in·ter·rup·tion,** *n.* **in·ter·rup·tive,** *a.*

in·ter·sect, *v.* cut into; divide by crossing; cross each other. **in·ter·sec·tion,** *n.*

in·ter·sperse, *v.,* **-spersed, -spers·ing.** scatter; diversify. **in·ter·sper·sion,** *n.*

in·ter·state, *a.* between states.

in·ter·twine, *v.,* **-twined, -twin·ing.** twine, as one with another.

in·ter·val, *n.* intervening period of time; gap.

in·ter·vene, *v.,* **-vened, -ven·ing.** come between; intercede. **in·ter·ven·tion,** *n.*

in·ter·view, *n.* meeting for a conference or evaluation; conversation at such a meeting. *v.* have an interview with. **in·ter·view·er,** *n.*

in·tes·tine, *n. often pl.* lower part of the alimentary canal. **in·tes·ti·nal,** *a.*

in·ti·mate, *a.* private; personal. *v.,* **-mat·ed, -mat·ing.** make known by hint or indication. **in·ti·ma·tion,** *n.*

in·tim·i·date, *v.,* **-dat·ed, -dat·ing.** make timid; fill with fear. **in·tim·i·da·tor,** *n.*

in·to, *prep.* toward the inner part; to the condition, etc., of.

in·tol·er·a·ble, *a.* not able to be tolerated.

in·tol·er·ant, *a.* bigoted; prejudiced. **in·tol·er·ance,** *n.*

in·to·na·tion, *n.* change in pitch of the voice.

in·tox·i·cate, *v.,* **-cat·ed, -cat·ing.** make drunk; excite. **in·tox·i·ca·tion,** *n.*

in·tra·mu·ral, *a.* within the limits of an institution.

in·tran·si·tive, *a.* of a verb which does not take a direct object.

in·tra·ve·nous, *a.* occurring or introduced within a vein.

in·trep·id, *a.* fearless.

in·tri·cate, *a.* entangled; complicated. **in·tri·ca·cy,** *n. pl.,* **-cies.** **in·tri·cate·ly,** *adv.*

in·trigue, *v.,* **-trigued, -tri·guing.** excite the curiosity of; scheme. *n.* plot; secret love affair. **in·tri·guing,** *a.*

in·trin·sic, *a.* inherent; essential. Also **in·trin·si·cal.**

in·tro·duce, *v.,* **-duced, -duc·ing.** make acquainted; present; bring before; begin. **in·tro·duc·tion,** *n.*

in·tro·vert, *v.* direct the mind upon itself. *n.* shy person. **in·tro·vert·ed,** *a.*

in·trude, *v.,* **-trud·ed, -trud·ing.** force oneself upon others. **in·trud·er,** *n.*

in·tu·i·tion, *n.* knowledge discerned without reasoning; insight. **in·tu·i·tive,** *a.*

in·ure, *v.,* **in·ured, in·ur·ing.** become accustomed to pain, etc.

in·vade, *v.,* **-vad·ed, -vad·ing.** enter with force. **in·va·sion,** *n.* **in·vad·er,** *n.*

in·va·lid, *n.* person suffering from ill health.

in·val·id, *a.* not valid.

in·val·u·a·ble, *a.* priceless.

in·var·i·a·ble, *a.* constant.

in·vent, *v.* originate; contrive. **in·ven·tion,** *n.*

in·ven·to·ry, *n. pl.,* **-ries.** list of goods.

in·verse, *a.* opposite in order or relation.

in·vert, *v.* turn upside down; reverse. **in·ver·sion,** *n.*

in·ver·te·brate, *a.* without a backbone. *n.* animal having no backbone.

in·vest, *v.* clothe; install; put, as money, into, for a profitable return. **in·ves·tor,** *n.* **in·vest·ment,** *n.*

in·ves·ti·gate, *v.,* **-gat·ed, -gat·ing.** inquire into and examine. **in·ves·ti·ga·tion,** *n.* **in·ves·ti·ga·tor,** *n.*

in·vet·er·ate, *a.* ingrained.

in·vig·or·ate, *v.,* **-at·ed, -at·ing.** give life and energy to.

in·vin·ci·ble, *a.* unconquerable.

in·vis·i·ble, *a.* imperceptible.

in·vite, *v.,* **-vit·ed, -vit·ing.** ask, as a person, to come to a place; give occasion for. **in·vi·ta·tion,** *n.*

in·vo·ca·tion, *n.* act of invoking.

in·voice, *n.* list of items sent to a purchaser; bill.

in·voke, *v.,* **in·voked, in·vok·ing.** call upon in prayer; appeal to.

in·vol·un·tar·y, *a.* not voluntary.

in·volve, *v.,* **-volved, -volv·ing.** include as necessary; affect; entangle. **in·volve·ment,** *n.*

in·ward, *adv.* toward the inside. *a.* internal. Also **in·wards. in·ward·ness,** *n.*

i·o·dine, *n.* nonmetallic element. used in medicine and photography.

i·on, *n.* electrified atom or group of atoms. **i·on·ic,** *a.*

i·o·ta, *n.* jot.

i·rate, *a.* enraged.

ire, *n.* anger.

ir·i·des·cent, *a.* displaying colors like those of the rainbow. **ir·i·des·cence,** *n.*

i·ris, *n. pl.,* **i·ris·es, ir·i·ses.** colored portion of the eye; plant having handsome flowers.

irk, *v.* annoy. **irk·some,** *a.*

i·ron, *n.* metallic element; appliance for pressing cloth; *pl.* fetters. *a.* of iron. *v.* press clothing. **i·ron·er,** *n.*

i·ron·clad, *a.* covered with iron; fixed.

i·ro·ny, *n. pl.,* **-nies.** figure of

speech in which the literal meaning is the opposite of the intended meaning. **i·ron·ic**, *a.* Also **i·ron·i·cal**.

ir·ra·di·ate, *v.*, **-at·ed**, **-at·ing**. shed light on; heal by radiation. **ir·ra·di·a·tion**, *n.*

ir·ra·tion·al, *a.* void of reason. **ir·ra·tion·al·i·ty**, *n.*

ir·rec·on·cil·a·ble, *a.* not to be reconciled.

ir·re·deem·a·ble, *a.* not redeemable.

ir·ref·u·ta·ble, *a.* incapable of being refuted.

ir·reg·u·lar, *a.* not regular; uneven; not in accordance with rules or customs. **ir·reg·u·lar·i·ty**, *n.*

ir·rel·e·vant, *a.* not pertinent. **ir·rel·e·vance**, *n.*

ir·rep·a·ra·ble, *a.* not reparable.

ir·re·press·i·ble, *a.* incapable of being repressed.

ir·re·proach·a·ble, *a.* innocent; faultless.

ir·re·sist·i·ble, *a.* not resistible; tempting.

ir·res·o·lute, *a.* undecided.

ir·re·spec·tive, *a.* without regard to circumstances.

ir·re·spon·si·ble, *a.* unreliable.

ir·rev·er·ence, *n.* lack of reverence; irreverent conduct, words, etc. **ir·rev·er·ent**, *a.*

ir·rev·o·ca·ble, *a.* irreversible.

ir·ri·gate, *v.*, **-gat·ed**, **-gat·ing**. water by artificial means. **ir·ri·ga·tion**, *n.*

ir·ri·ta·ble, *a.* capable of being irritated.

ir·ri·tate, *v.*, **-tat·ed**, **-tat·ing**. provoke; vex; inflame. **ir·ri·ta·tion**, *n.*

is, *v.* third person pres. sing. of the verb **be**.

is·land, *n.* land surrounded by water.

isle, *n.* small island.

i·so·late, *v.*, **-lat·ed**, **-lat·ing**. place apart; insulate. **i·so·la·tion**, *n.*

i·sos·ce·les, *a.* having two equal sides.

is·sue, *n.* outflow; offspring; point in question; quantity issed at one time. *v.*, **-sued**, **-su·ing**. send out; give forth; distribute; publish.

isth·mus, *n. pl.* **isth·mus·es**, **isth·mi**. strip of land connecting larger bodies of land.

it, *pron.* third person sing. neuter pron. corresponding to **he**

and **she**.

i·tal·ic, *n. usu. pl.* printing in which the letters slope to the right.

i·tal·i·cize, *v.*, **-cized**, **-ciz·ing**. use italics. **i·tal·i·ci·za·tion**, *n.*

itch, *v.* have an irritation of the skin which causes a desire to scratch. *n.* itching; uneasy desire. **itch·y**, *a.*

i·tem, *n.* article; single detail of any list.

i·tem·ize, *v.*, **-ized**, **-iz·ing**. set down by items.

i·tin·er·ant, *a.* traveling about. *n.* traveler.

i·tin·er·ar·y, *n. pl.*, **-ies**. travel route; plan of a journey.

its, *pron.* *a.* poss. case of it.

it·self, *pron.* reflexive or emphatic form of it.

i·vo·ry, *n. pl.*, **-ries**. hard dentine from the tusks of elephants, etc.; yellow to creamy-white color. *a.* of ivory.

i·vy, *n. pl.*, **i/vies**. climbing plant. **i·vied**, *a.*

J

jab, *v.* strike. *n.*, thrust. **jabbed**, **jab·bing**.

jab·ber, *v.* talk rapidly, indistinctly, foolishly. *n.* chatter.

jack, *n.* a fellow; workman; sailor; machine for raising weights; card picturing a boy or knave; tool useful in some task; *inf.* money; electric plug-in receptacle. *a.* male. *v.* raise as with a jack.

jack·al, *n.* wild dog of Asia and Africa.

jack·ass, *n.* male donkey; fool.

jack·et, *n.* short protective outer covering; coat.

jack·knife, *n. pl.*, **-knives**. strong pocketknife. *v.*, **-knifed**, **-knif·ing**. bend in the middle like a jackknife.

jack·pot, *n.* the stakes which accumulate during card play; highest prize.

jack rab·bit, *n.* large hare of western N. America.

jade, *n.* hard green gemstone. **jad·ed**, *a.* worn-out horse; loose woman. *v.*, **jad·ed**, **jad·ing**. weary or wear out.

jag·uar, *n.* large, powerful, black-spotted feline.

jail, *n.* prison. *v.* imprison.

ja·lop·y, *n. pl.*, **-ies**. *inf.* old, unpretentious car.

jal·ou·sie, *n.* window blind with adjustable horizontal louvers.

jam, *v.,* jammed, jam·ming. squeeze tightly between surfaces; render unworkable by wedging, displacement. *n.* act or state of jamming; obstruction. *inf.* predicament; fruit preserve.

jamb, *n.* side piece of a doorway.

jam·bo·ree, *n. inf.* noisy gathering.

jan·gle, *v.,* -gled, -gling. *n.* (make or cause to make) harsh, discordant sounds.

jan·i·tor, *n.* caretaker of a building.

Jan·u·ar·y, *n.* first month of the year.

Jap·a·nese, *a.* pertaining to Japan.

jar, *n.* wide-mouthed vessel. *v.* jarred, jar·ing. make a harsh sound; jolt. *n.* harsh sound; jolt.

jar·gon, *n.* special vocabulary of a class, trade, or profession.

jas·mine, jas·min, *n.* fragrant-flowered shrub.

jaun·dice, *n.* disease that turns the skin yellow; *v.* envy.

jaunt, *v. n.* (make) a short pleasure trip.

jaun·ty, *a.,* -ti·er, -ti·est. brisk; perky.

jave·lin, *n.* light spear.

jaw, *n.* one of two bones that form the mouth framework; *v.* talk, gossip.

jay, *n.* noisy bird of the crow family.

jay·walk, *v.* cross a street amid traffic. **jay·walk·er,** *n.*

jazz, *n.* popular American music with strong rhythms.

jazz·y, *a.,* -i·er, -i·est. *inf.* lively; flashy.

jeal·ous·y, *n. pl.,* -ies. envious resentment or watchfulness. **jeal·ous,** *a.*

jean, *n. pl.* trousers made of denim.

Jeep, *n. trademark.* small, sturdy automobile.

jeer, *v. n.* ridicule, scoff.

Je·ho·vah, *n.* God.

jell, *v.* become definite in shape or form.

jel·ly, *n. pl.,* -lies. soft, gelatinous food product of boiled fruit juice and sugar.

jel·ly·fish, *n. pl.,* -fish, -fish·es.

jellylike sea animal with tentacles.

jeop·ar·dy, *n.* exposure to death, hazard. **jeop·ar·dize,** *v.,* -dized, -diz·ing.

jerk, *v., n.* (give a) short sudden thrust, push, or twitch. **jerk·y,** *a.*, -i·er, -i·est.

jer·kin, *n.* snug, sleeveless, hip-length jacket.

jer·sey, *n.* soft, elastic knitted fabric.

jest, *n.* joke; jeer.

Je·sus, *n.* founder of Christianity.

jet, *n.* a shooting forth; spout that shoots a jet; jet engine; jet plane; a hard, black mineral. *v.,* jet·ted, jet·ting. to issue in a jet; travel by jet propulsion.

jet pro·pul·sion, *n.* propulsion by means of a jet of gas or fluid. **jet-pro·pelled,** *a.*

jet·sam, *n.* goods thrown overboard to lighten a ship.

jet·ti·son, *n.* cargo thrown overboard to lighten a vessel. *v.* discard.

jet·ty, *n. pl.,* -ties. landing pier extending into the water.

Jew, *n.* believer in Judaism; descendant of the Hebrews.

jew·el, *n.* gem; precious possession.

jew·el·er, *n.* one who makes, repairs, deals in jewelry.

jew·el·ry, *n.* articles for personal ornament.

jib, *n.* triangular sail ahead of the foremast.

jibe, *v.,* jibed, jib·ing. *inf.* agree.

jif·fy, *n. pl.,* -fies. *inf.* a moment.

jig, *n.* lively dance; device which guides a tool. *v.,* jigged, jig·ging. dance a jig.

jig·ger, *n.* measure of about 1½ oz. of liquor.

jig·gle, *v.,* -gled, -gling. move with short, quick jerks.

jig saw, *n.* narrow saw for curved cuts.

jig·saw puz·zle, *n.* puzzle of cut pieces that form a picture when assembled.

jilt, *v.* discard or cast off (a lover).

jim·my, *n. pl.,* -mies. short crowbar. *v.,* -mied, -my·ing. force open with a jimmy.

jin·gle, *v., n.,* -gled, -gling. (make or cause) a tinkling sound. *n.* short, catchy tune.

jinx, *n. inf.* thing that brings bad

luck. v. bring bad luck to.

jit·ter, v. inf. behave nervously. **jit·ters,** n. pl. inf. uneasiness. **jit·ter·y,** a.

jive, n. swing or jazz music. v. inf. tease; confuse.

job, n. piece of work; the object worked on. v., **jobbed, jobbing.** work by the piece; buy and sell as a middle man. **job·ber,** n.

job lot, n. assorted goods sold in a single dealing.

jock·ey, n. pl., **-eys.** race-horse rider. v., **-eyed, -ey·ing.** maneuver for advantage.

jo·cose, a. joking.

joc·u·lar, a. joking; playful. **joc·u·lar·i·ty,** n.

joc·und, a. cheerful.

jodh·pur, n. pl. riding breeches.

jog, v., **jogged, jog·ging.** push or shake suddenly; pace at a regular gait. **jog·ger,** n.

join, v. connect; bring together. n. seam.

joint, n. junction; the joining of two or more bones; inf. place of low reputation. a. shared by two or more. v. unite with a joint. **joint·ed,** a. **joint·ly,** adv.

joist, n. horizontal timber supporting floor boards.

joke, n. thing said or done to evoke laughter. v. make jokes. **jok·er,** n.

jol·ly, a., **-li·er, -li·est.** merry; gay.

jolt, v. shake up roughly; start suddenly. n. a sudden blow, upset.

jon·quil, n. a species of narcissus.

josh, v. inf. banter in a teasing way.

jos·tle, v., **-tled, -tling.** bump, strike, or push.

jot, n. a tiny amount. v., **-ted, -ting.** write down quickly.

jour·nal, n. a diary; a record of transactions; periodical or magazine; the part of an axle that moves on bearings.

jour·nal·ism, n. occupation of conducting a news medium. **jour·nal·ist,** n.

jour·ney, n. a trip. v. travel.

jour·ney·man, n. pl., **-men.** workman who has completed his apprenticeship.

joust, n., v., fight with lances between mounted knights.

jo·vi·al, a. merry; good-humored.

jowl, n. the under jaw; the cheek.

joy, n. gladness; pleasure; delight. **joy·ful, joy·ous,** a.

ju·bi·la·tion, n. a rejoicing; a triumph. **ju·bi·lant,** a.

ju·bi·lee, n. celebration of a 25th or 50th anniversary.

Ju·da·ism, n. Jewish religion.

judge, v., **judged, judg·ing.** hear, examine, and decide, as a court case; form an opinion of; infer, think. n. one who judges.

judg·ment, n. the act of judging; decision; legal sentence; good sense.

ju·di·cial, a. relating to courts of justice or judges.

ju·di·ci·ar·y, a. judicial; n. court system; judges.

ju·di·cious, a. showing good judgment.

ju·do, n. method of self-defense.

jug, n. vessel, with handle and narrow neck, for holding liquids.

jug·gle, v. perform feats of manual or bodily dexterity.

jug·u·lar, a. relating to two large veins of the neck.

juice, n. fluid part of animal or plant substances. **juic·y,** a.

ju·jit·su, n. a style of Japanese wrestling.

juke·box, n. coin-operated record player.

Ju·ly, n. seventh month.

jum·ble, v., n. (mix) in a confused mass.

jum·bo, a. unusually large.

jump, v. spring clear of the ground; move suddenly; leap over. n. sudden move; distance jumped. **jump at,** accept eagerly.

jump·er, n. one who jumps; a sleeveless dress.

junc·tion, n. act or place of joining.

junc·ture, n. point of joining; point of time.

June, n. sixth month.

jun·gle, n. tropical forest.

jun·ior, a. lower or younger in standing; third year of a four year course of study.

ju·ni·per, n. evergreen tree or shrub.

junk, n. old, discarded material; flat-bottomed Oriental ship.

jun·ket, n. sweetened, flavored, curdled milk; pleasure trip.

ju·ris·dic·tion, *n.* range of authority; court system.

ju·ris·pru·dence, *n.* science of law; body of court decisions.

ju·rist, *n.* one versed in law.

ju·ror, *n.* member of a jury.

ju·ry, *n. pl.*, **-ries.** group selected to give a decision.

just, *a.* fair; proper; legal. *adv.* exact in time; exactly; barely.

jus·tice, *n.* impartiality; lawfulness; a judge.

jus·ti·fy, *v.*, **-fied, -fy·ing.** show to be just, right, warranted. **jus·ti·fi·ca·tion**, *n.* **jus·ti·fi·a·ble**, *a.*

jut, *v.* project beyond the main body.

jute, *n.* strong, coarse fiber.

ju·ve·nile, *a.* young; immature. *n.* young person.

K

kale, *n.* curly-leafed cabbage.

ka·lei·do·scope, *n.* tube that shows various colors and symmetrical forms with aid of mirrors.

kan·ga·roo, *n. pl.*, **-roos, roo.** pouched, leaping Australian mammal.

kar·at, *n.* measure of fineness of gold or weight of gems.

ka·ra·te, *n.* method of combat and self-defense.

ka·ty·did, *n.* type of grasshopper.

kay·ak, kai·ak, *n.* arctic canoe.

keel, *n.* center piece stretching along bottom of a vessel from stem to stern. **keel o·ver**, capsize; fall over.

keen, *a.* mentally acute; extremely perceptive; intense; enthusiastic. **keen·ly**, *adv.*

keep, *v.*, **kept, keep·ing.** retain; fulfill; protect; preserve; hold in custody; continue. *n.* food and shelter; care.

keep·ing, *n.* possession; just proportion.

keg, *n.* small barrel.

kelp, *n.* type of seaweed.

ken, *v.* to know. *n.* range of knowledge.

ken·nel, *n.* doghouse; place where dogs are bred or boarded.

ker·chief, *n.* cloth covering head or neck; handkerchief.

ker·nel, *n.* substance inside a nutshell, seed, fruit stone; essential part.

ker·o·sene, ker·o·sine, *n.* coal oil.

ketch, *n.* sailing vessel with two masts.

ketch·up, *n.* thick, seasoned tomato sauce.

ket·tle, *n.* vessel used in cooking; teakettle.

ket·tle·drum, *n.* drum of brass or copper, with a parchment head.

key, *n.* instrument for working a lock; essential person or thing; a means of understanding or solving; a lever or part pressed in operating a piano, typewriter, etc.; scale of tones; coral reef. *a.* controlling; fundamental. *v.* adjust. **key up**, excite.

key·board, *n.* series of keys of a piano, typewriter, etc.

key·note, *n.* note on which a system of tones is founded; main idea.

key·stone, *n.* stone at apex of an arch which locks the whole.

khak·i, *n.*, *a.* (cloth of) yellowish-brown color.

kick, *v.* strike out with the foot; recoil; *inf.* complain. *n.* an act of kicking; *inf.* thrill; complaint.

kick·off, *n.* kicking the ball to begin play in football; beginning.

kid, *n.* young goat, or its skin; *inf.* child. *v. inf.* tease.

kid·nap, *v.* seize and forcibly carry away, usu. for ransom.

kid·ney, *n.* organ which excretes urine.

kill, *v.*, deprive of life; put an end to. *n.* act of killing.

kiln, *n.* oven used to bake, dry, or burn clay.

kil·o·cy·cle, *n.* 1000 cycles per second.

kil·o·gram, *n. weight of 1000 grams.*

kil·o·me·ter, *n.* distance of 1000 meters.

kil·o·watt, *n.* 1000 watts of electric power.

kilt, *n.* knee-length pleated skirt worn. esp. by men in Scotland.

kin, *n.* relatives.

kind, *n.* variety, sort. **in kind**, in the same way. *a.* good, benevolent. **kind·ly**, *a.*, *adv.* **kindness**, *n.*

kin·der·gar·ten, *n.* class for pre-school children.

kind·heart·ed, *a.* kindly.

kin·dle, v. set on fire.

kin·dling, n. materials for lighting a fire.

kin·dred, n. relatives. a. related; similar.

king, n. male ruler of a nation; playing card with king's picture; chief piece in chess.

king·dom, n. domain of a king, queen.

king·fish·er, n. crested, bright-colored bird.

kink, n. twist or tight curl; mental quirk. **kink·y**, a.

kin·ship, n. family relationship; close bond.

kins·man, n. pl., -men. male relative.

kiss, v. touch with the lips in greeting or affection.

kit, n. set of tools, supplies, for a special purpose; case to contain these objects; set of parts to be assembled.

kitch·en, n. place appropriated to cooking.

kitch·en·ette, n. small kitchen.

kite, n. light paper-covered frame to fly in the wind.

kith, n. archaic, friends.

kit·ten, n. young cat. Also **kit·ty**.

kit·ty, n. stakes in a card game.

knack, n. ability; aptitude.

knap·sack, n. supply bag strapped to the back of travelers.

knave, n. dishonest, tricky person.

knead, v. press and squeeze into a mass.

knee, n. joint between thigh and lower leg.

kneel, v., knelt or kneeled, **kneel·ing**. rest on the knees.

knell, n. funeral bell.

knick·knack, n. a trifle; a trinket.

knife, n. pl., knives. a thin blade attached to a handle, for cutting. v. cut or stab with a knife.

knight, n. medieval soldier; Br. man holding honorary title Sir; chess piece. v. to dub a knight.

knit, v., knit·ted or knit, knit·ting. weave by looping or knotting yarn, using needles; join closely. n. a knitted fabric. **knit·ting**, n.

knob, n. rounded handle.

knock, v. strike a blow; to rap; make a pounding noise; inf. criticize. n. a rap. **knock down**, take apart. **knock off** inf. stop work; deduct. **knock out**, make unconscious.

knoll, n. small round hill.

knot, n. intertwined material that fastens or binds; group of people or objects; perplexing situation; lump in wood where a branch has grown; a nautical mile per hour. v., knot·ted, **knot·ting**. make or become entangled.

know, v., knew, known, know·ing. understand as fact or truth; to be aware of, familiar with, skilled in.

know-how, n. inf. technical skill.

know·ing, a. wise; shrewd.

knowl·edge, n. what is known or may be learned.

knowl·edge·a·ble, a. intelligent; well-informed.

knuck·le, n. joint of a finger.

kohl·ra·bi, n. pl., -bies. variety of cabbage.

Ko·ran, n. sacred book of the Moslems.

ko·sher, a. right, lawful, clean according to Jewish dietary laws.

kum·quat, n. yellow-orange citrus fruit.

L

lab, n. inf. laboratory.

la·bel, n. paper slip on an object to indicate its owner, contents, etc.; brand. v., -beled, -bel·ing. attach a label to. **la·bel·er**, n.

la·bi·al, a. of the lips.

la·bor, n. work; those engaged in work; task; process of childbirth. v. work; toil; move with effort. **la·bor·er**, n.

lab·o·ra·to·ry, n. pl., -ries. room equipped for scientific investigation.

la·bored, a. produced with labor; forced; too elaborate.

la·bo·ri·ous, a. toilsome; not easy.

la·bor un·ion, n. trade union.

lab·y·rinth, n. maze.

lace, n. string used for fastening shoes, etc.; delicate fabric. v. fasten with lace; intertwine; adorn with lace. laced, a. lac·ing, n. lac·y, a.

lac·er·ate, v., -at·ed, -at·ing. tear; make a ragged wound in. **lac·er·a·tion**, n.

lack, n. deficiency; that wanted or needed. v. be deficient in.

lack·ing, a., prep.

lack·ey, n. male servant; servile follower.

la·con·ic, a. brief; terse.

lac·quer, n. varnish producing a hard, glossy finish. v. coat with lacquer.

lac·tic, a. of or from milk.

la·cu·na, n. pl., -nas, -nae. gap or hiatus; pit; cavity.

lad, n. young man or boy.

lad·der, n. frame of wood, metal, etc., with crosspieces forming steps for climbing and descending.

lad·en, a. loaded; burdened.

la·dle, n. long-handled utensil with a cuplike bowl. v., la·dled, la·dling. dip or convey with a ladle.

la·dy, n. polite term for any woman; wife; noblewoman.

lag, v., lagged, lag·ging. fall behind; hand back; n. lagging; amount of retardation.

la·ger, n. beer aged after brewing. Also la·ger beer.

lag·gard, a. lagging; slow. n. backward person.

la·goon, n. shallow body of water; water within an atoll. Also la·gune.

la·ic, a. secular. n. layman.

laid, pt. and pp. of lay.

lain, pp. of lie.

lair, n. den of a wild beast.

la·i·ty, n. pl., -ties. lay persons collectively.

lake, n. sizable inland body of water.

lam, v., lammed, lam·ming. inf. beat; run off. n. inf. escape.

la·ma, n. Lamaist priest.

lamb, n. young sheep, or the meat from it; meek person.

lam·baste, v., -bast·ed, -bast·ing. inf. beat; censure.

lame, a., lam·er, lam·est. crippled, esp. in the legs or feet; sore; weak. v., lamed, lam·ing. make lame. lame·ly, adv.

la·mé, n. fabric of metallic, esp. gold or silver, threads.

la·ment, v. mourn; regret. n. elegy. lam·en·ta·tion, n.

lam·i·nate, v., -nat·ed, -nat·ing. divide into thin layers; form by placing layer upon layer. lam·i·na·tion, n.

lamp, n. device, often decorative, for providing light.

lam·poon, n. abusive satire in prose, verse, etc. v. satirize in a lampoon.

lam·prey, n. pl., -preys. eellike animal.

lance, n. sharp-pointed shaft. v., lanced, lanc·ing. pierce; make an incision in.

lan·cet, n. small surgical instrument.

land, n. solid substance of the earth's surface; soil; country; realm. v. come to land or shore; reach; come down upon the surface. land·ed, a. land·ing, n.

land·la·dy, n. pl., -dies. female landlord.

land·locked, a. enclosed by land; shut off from the sea.

land·lord, n. owner of land or real estate; innkeeper.

land·mark, n. fixed object that distinguishes a locality; turning point.

land·scape, n. natural scene of land forms; picture of such a scene. v., -scaped, -scap·ing. design by gardening. land·scap·er, n.

land·slide, n. sliding of soil or rock from a higher to a lower level; overwhelming victory.

lane, n. narrow way or passage; fixed route.

lan·guage, n. communication, esp. through written and vocal symbols.

lan·guid, a. drooping; weak; listless; slow.

lan·guish, v. be or become dull, feeble, or spiritless; pine. lan·guish·ing, a.

lan·guor, n. lassitude; feebleness; apathy.

lank, a. lean, tall, and bony; long and limp. lank·ness, n.

lank·y, a., -i·er, -i·est. awkwardly thin and tall.

lan·o·lin, n. oily substance obtained from wool.

lan·tern, n. portable case which is transparent, for enclosing a light.

lap, v., lapped, lap·ping. fold; overlap; take up with the tongue. n. part from the waist to the knees when sitting. lap·per, n.

la·pel, n. fold of the front facings of a garment.

lapse, n. error, usu. trivial; unnoticed passage of time; slipping downward. v., lapsed, lapsing. err; slip into ruin.

lar·ce·ny, n. pl., -nies. theft. lar·ce·nous, a.

larch, *n.* tree of the pine family; its wood.

lard, *n.* fat of hogs after rendering.

lar·der, *n.* pantry.

large, *a.*, **larg·er**, **larg·est.** of great size, extent, or capacity. *adv.* in a greater than usual size. **large·ness**, *n.*

large·ly, *adv.* to a great extent; mainly.

lar·gess, **lar·gesse**, *n.* charitable giving.

lar·i·at, *n.* lasso.

lark, *n.* singing bird; frolic; sport; prank.

lar·va, *n. pl.*, **-vae.** stage following the egg in the life cycle of an insect. **lar·val**, *a.*

lar·yn·gi·tis, *n.* inflammation of the larynx.

lar·ynx, *n. pl.*, **-lar·ynx·es** or **la·ryn·ges**, structure of the trachea containing vocal cords. **la·ryn·ge·al**, *a.*

las·civ·i·ous, *a.* lustful; lewd. **las·civ·i·ous·ly**, *adv.*

la·ser, *n.* device emitting an intense, direct light beam.

lash, *n.* whip; blow with a whip; cutting remark. *v.* whip; goad; tie or bind. **lash·ing**, **lash·er**, *n.*

lass, *n.* girl.

las·si·tude, *n.* weariness or weakness; listlessness.

las·so, *n. pl.*, **-sos** or **-soes.** long rope with a running noose. *v.* catch with a lasso.

last, *a.* happening or coming after all the others; utmost. *adv.* finally. *v.* endure.

last·ing, *a.* enduring.

last·ly, *adv.* finally.

latch, *n.* device for securing a door or gate.

late, *a.*, **lat·er** or **lat·ter**, **lat·est** or **last.** after the usual time; far advanced; departed; recent. *adv.* lately. **late·ness**, *n.* **lat·er**, *a.*, *adv.*

late·ly, *adv.* recently.

la·tent, *a.* not manifested; undeveloped. **la·ten·cy**, *n.*

lat·er·al, *a.* of or toward a side. **lat·er·al·ly**, *adv.*

la·tex, *n. pl.*, **la·tex·es** or **lat·i·ces.** milky juice of certain plants, the source of natural rubber.

lath, *n.* supporting board. **lath·er**, **lath·ing**, *n.*

lathe, *n.* machine for shaping wood, metal, etc.

lath·er, *n.* foam made from water and soap or sweat. *v.*

apply lather to, become lathered. **lath·er·y**, *a.*

lat·i·tude, *n.* distance north or south of the equator measured in degrees.

lat·ter, *a.* more recent; second of two.

lat·tice, *n.* crisscrossed structure. **lat·ticed**, *a.*

laud·a·ble, *a.* praiseworthy. **laud·a·to·ry**, *a.*

laugh, *v.* express amusement, etc., with a chuckling noise. *n.* act or sound of laughing. **laugh·a·ble**, *a.* **laugh·ter**, *n.*

launch, *v.* propel into the air or the water; set afloat; initiate. *n.* kind of motorboat.

laun·der, *v.* wash as clothes; wash and iron. **laun·der·er**, *fem.* **laun·dress**, *n.*

laun·dry, *n. pl.*, **-dries.** place for laundering; articles to be washed or already washed.

lau·rel, *n.* small evergreen tree; *pl.* honor.

la·va, *n.* molten rock.

lav·a·to·ry, *n. pl.*, **-ries.** room with a sink and often with a toilet.

lav·en·der, *n.* mint yielding a fragrant oil. *a.* pale, delicate purple.

lav·ish, *a.* liberal; extravagant. *v.* bestow in great abundance. **lav·ish·ness**, *n.*

law, *n.* body of binding rules or principles; rule; injunction; legal profession; governing force.

law·a·bid·ing, *a.* observant of the law.

law·ful, *a.* allowed by law.

law·less, *a.* not controlled by law. **law·less·ness**, *n.*

lawn, *n.* mown grass around a house.

law·suit, *n.* action in a court of justice.

law·yer, *n.* attorney-at-law.

lax, *a.* loose or slack; loose in morals. **lax·i·ty**, *n.*

lax·a·tive, *a.* having the quality of loosening the intestines. *n.* purgative.

lay, *v.*, **laid**, **lay·ing.** put in a position of rest; place; set; arrange; bet; present; impose; lay eggs. *a.* laic.

lay, *v.* past tense of **lie**.

lay·er, *n.* thickness; stratum.

lay·ette, *n.* clothing, blankets, etc., for a newborn child.

lay·man, *n. pl.*, **-men.** person

who is not a clergyman or of a profession.

lay-out, *n.* plan or arrangement.

la-zy, *a.*, **-zi-er**, **-zi-est**. reluctant to work; indolent; sluggish. **la-zi-ly**, *adv.* **la-zi-ness**, *n.*

lead, *n.* heavy, soft, malleable metal; bullets or shot; graphite. **lead-en**, *a.* **lead-ing**, *n.*

lead, *v.*, **led**, **lead-ing**. guide by showing the way; command; be first among; induce; direct; *n.* guidance; first or foremost place. **lead-er**, *n.* **lead-er-ship**, *n.*

lead-ing, *a.* guiding; chief.

leaf, *n. pl.*, **leaves**. lateral outgrowth of a stem; lamina; single thickness of paper. *v.* produce leaves; flip or turn, as pages. **leaf-less**, *a.*

leaf-age, *n.* leaves; foliage.

leaf-let, *n.* folded sheet of printed matter; young leaf.

leaf-y, *a.*, **-i-er**, **-i-est**. abounding in leaves.

league, *n.* association of parties, states, etc.; about 3 miles. *v.*, **leagued**, **lea-guing**. unite in a league.

leak, *v.* let air, water, etc., enter or escape; divulge. *n.* opening. **leak-age**, *n.* **leak-y**, *a.*, **-i-er**, **-i-est**.

lean, *v.*, **leaned** or **leant**, **lean-ing**. slope; slant; tend toward; rely; *a.* spare; containing little fat. **lean-ness**, *n.*

lean-ing, *n.* bias; tendency.

leap, *v.*, **leaped** or **leapt**, **leap-ing**. spring; pass over. *n.* jump. **leap-er**, *n.*

learn, *v.*, **learned** or **learnt**, **learn-ing**. gain knowledge, skill, etc. **learn-er**, *n.*

learn-ed, *a.* erudite. **learn-ed-ly**, *adv.* **learn-ed-ness**, *n.*

lease, *n.* contract or specified time for rental. *v.*, **leased**, **leas-ing**. grant by lease.

leash, *n.* line by which a dog is held; control.

least, *a.* smallest in size, etc. *n.* least amount. *adv.* to the least extent.

leath-er, *n.* tanned hide. *a.* of leather. **leath-er-y**, *a.*

leave, *v.*, **left**, **leav-ing**. go away; quit; allow to remain; bequeath. *n.* liberty granted to act; permission, esp. to be absent. **leav-er**, *n.*

leav-en, *n.* yeast or a mass of fermented dough. Also **leav-**

en-ing.

leaves, *n.* plural of **leaf**.

lec-ture, *n.* discourse delivered instruction; reprimand. *v.*, **-tured**, **-tur-ing**. give a lecture to. **lec-tur-er**, *n.*

ledge, *n.* projecting shelf.

ledg-er, *n.* account book.

lee, *n.* shelter, esp. the side turned away from the wind. *a.* *naut.* of the lee.

leech, *n.* bloodsucking aquatic worm.

leek, *n.* herb, allied to the onion.

leer, *v.*, cast a sly, malicious, or lascivious look. *n.* such a look. **leer-ing-ly**, *adv.*

leer-y, *a.* *inf.* wary (of).

lee-way, *n.* degree of freedom; additional time, space, etc.

left, *a.* side turned toward the west when one faces north. *n.* left side. *adv.* on or to the left side. **left-ist**, *n.*, *a.*

leg, *n.* limb which supports and moves the body; something resembling a leg. *v.*, **legged**, **leg-ging**, *inf.* run.

leg-a-cy, *n. pl.*, **-cies**. bequest.

le-gal, *a.* of or pertaining to law; lawful. **le-gal-ly**, *adv.*

le-gal-i-ty, *n. pl.*, **-ties**. lawfulness.

le-gal-ize, *v.*, **-ized**, **-iz-ing**. make legal. **le-gal-i-za-tion**, *n.*

le-ga-tion, *n.* diplomatic minister, his assistants, and residence.

leg-end, *n.* unverifiable story handed down by tradition; caption or inscription. **leg-end-ar-y**, *a.*

leg-ging, *n.* covering for the leg; *usu. pl.* pants worn over trousers.

leg-gy, *a.*, **-gi-er**, **-gi-est**. *inf.* having shapely or overly long legs.

leg-i-ble, *a.* capable of being read. **leg-i-bil-i-ty**, *n.*

le-gion, *n.* large body of troops; great number. *a.* innumerable. **le-gion-naire**, *n.*

leg-is-late, *v.*, **-lat-ed**, **-lat-ing**. make or enact laws. **leg-is-la-tive**, *a.* **leg-is-la-tor**, *n.* **leg-is-la-tion**, *n.*

leg-is-la-ture, *n.* body of persons who make laws.

le-git-i-mate, *a.* lawful; born of parents legally married. *v.*, **-mat-ed**, **-mat-ing**. authorize or justify. **le-git-i-ma-cy**, *n.*

le-git-i-mize, *v.*, **-mized**, **-miz-ing**.

legitimate.

leg·ume, *n.* plant with a podlike fruit.

lei·sure, *n.* free or unoccupied time; ease. *a.* free.

lei·sure·ly, *a., adv.* acting without hurrying.

lem·on, *n.* yellow, acid fruit of a subtropical tree. *a.* light yellow color.

lem·on·ade, *n.* drink of lemon juice, water, etc.

lend, *v.*, lent, lend·ing. grant for temporary use; adapt. **lend·er**, *n.*

length, *n.* linear measure from end to end; extent; long continuance. **length·en**, *v.* lengthwise, *adv.*, *a.*

length·y, -i·er, -i·est. long. **length·i·ness**, *n.*

le·ni·ent, *a.* mild; merciful. **le·ni·ence**, **le·ni·en·cy**, *n.*

lens, *n. pl.*, lenses. curved piece usu. of glass, used for changing the direction of light rays.

leop·ard, *n.* large, ferocious spotted cat.

lep·er, *n.* person affected with leprosy.

lep·ro·sy, *n.* Hansen's disease. **lep·rous**, *a.*

less. *a.* fewer or smaller; lower in importance. *n.* smaller amount. *adv.* to a smaller degree. *prep.* minus. **less·er**, *a.*

less·en, *v.* make less; become less.

les·son, *n.* assignment to be learned by a student; instructive experience.

lest, *conj.* for fear that.

let, *v.*, let, let·ting. permit; rent.

le·thal, *a.* deadly; fatal.

leth·ar·gy, *n. pl.*, -gies. sluggish inactivity; drowsiness. **le·thar·gic**, **le·thar·gi·cal**, *a.*

let·ter, *n.* symbol representing a speech sound; written message; *pl.* learning; literature. *v.* inscribe. **let·tered**, *a.* **let·ter·er**, *n.* **let·ter·ing**, *n.*

let·ter·head, *n.* printed heading on stationery.

let·tuce, *n.* vegetable having edible leaves.

leu·ke·mi·a, *n.* fatal disease of the blood.

lev·ee, *n.* embankment; quay; reception.

lev·el, *n.* device for determining the horizontal plane; elevation; flat surface; status. *a.* even. *v.*, -eled, -el·ing. make

level; lay low; direct. **lev·el·er**, *n.* **lev·el·ly**, *adv.*

lev·er, *n.* bar used for lifting or prying.

lev·er·age, *n.* action of a lever; increased power of acting.

lev·i·tate, *v.*, -tat·ed, -tat·ing. rise or float in the air. **lev·i·ta·tion**, *n.*

lev·i·ty, *n.* excessive frivolity.

lev·y, *n. pl.*, -ies. raising or collecting. *v.*, -ied, -y·ing. impose, as an assessment; enlist.

lewd, *a.* lascivious; obscene. **lewd·ly**, *adv.* **lewd·ness**, *n.*

lex·i·con, *n.* dictionary.

li·a·bil·i·ty, *n. pl.*, -ties. extent to which one is liable, as for a debt; drawback.

li·a·ble, *a.* under obligation; likely to incur; susceptible.

li·ai·son, *n.* intercommunication; illicit affair.

li·ar, *n.* one who lies.

li·bel, *n.* defamatory writing. *v.*, -beled, -bel·ing. defame by libel. **li·bel·er**, *n.* **li·bel·ous**, *a.*

lib·er·al, *a.* generous; tolerant; favoring progress and reforms. *n.* one who is liberal. **lib·er·al·ism**, *n.* **lib·er·al·i·ty**, *n. pl.*, -ties.

lib·er·al·ize, *v.*, -ized, -iz·ing. render liberal.

lib·er·ate, *v.*, -at·ed, -at·ing. set at liberty. **lib·er·a·tion**, *n.* **lib·er·a·tor**, *n.*

lib·er·ty, *n. pl.*, -ties. freedom; independence; immunity; privilege.

li·bi·do, *n.* sexual instinct.

li·brar·y, *n. pl.*, -ies. place set apart for literary material; collection of books. **li·brar·i·an**, *n.*

li·bret·to, *n. pl.*, -tos, -ti. words of an opera; book containing the words.

lice, *n.* plural of louse.

li·cense, *n.* formal permission; official permit; freedom of action, etc.; laxity. *v.* li·censed, li·cens·ing. authorize. **li·cen·see**, *n.*

li·cen·tious, *a.* unrestrained by law; lascivious.

li·chen, *n.* plant growing in patches on rocks, trees, etc.

lick, *v.* pass the tongue over; *inf.* beat or defeat. *n.* stroke of the tongue over. **lick·er**, *n.* **lick·ing**, *n.*

lic·o·rice, **li·quo·rice**, *n.* sweet-tasting plant extract.

lid, *n.* movable piece for closing the opening of a container.

lid·ded, *a.*

lie, *v.*, **lay**, **lain**, **ly·ing**. be in or assume a recumbent position; be placed; be inherent or to exist.

lie, *v.*, **lied**, **ly·ing**. speak falsely or utter untruth knowingly. *n.* intentional untruth.

lien, *n.* legal claim.

lieu, *n. archaic.* stead. **in lieu of**, in place of.

lieu·ten·an·cy, *n. pl.*, **-cies.** rank, or authority of a lieutenant.

lieu·ten·ant, *n.* officer, civil or military.

life, *n. pl.*, **lives.** quality of being alive; period during which anything exists; person's history; course of living; animation; living beings; *a.* lifelong.

life·boat, *n.* boat for saving persons.

life·guard, *n.* one employed to save bathers from drowning.

life·less, *a.* dead; dull. **life·less·ness**, *n.*

life·long, *a.* lasting or continuing through life.

life·size, *a.* of the size of the original object or living person. Also **life·sized**.

life·time, *n.* period of time that life continues.

lift, *v.* move upward; raise; elate. *n.* act of lifting; ride in a vehicle. **lift·er**, *n.*

lig·a·ment, *n.* fibrous tissue connecting bones at a joint.

lig·a·ture, *n.* anything that binds; thread, wire, etc., for tying blood vessels. *v.*, **-tured**, **-tur·ing.** bind.

light, *n.* radiant energy; illuminating source; aspect; means of kindling. *a.* pale, whitish; not heavy; trifling. *adv.* lightly. *v.*, **light·ed** or **lit**, **light·ing.** kindle; land. **light·er**, *n.*, *a.* **light·ness**, *n.*

light·en, *v.* grow brighter; make light; make less heavy; lessen.

light·foot·ed, *a.* nimble.

light·head·ed, *a.* dizzy.

light·heart·ed, **light·heart·ed**, *a.* cheerful; optimistic.

light·house, *n.* tower with a light to warn navigators.

light·ly, *adv.* in a light manner; gently; easily.

light·ning, *n.* discharge of atmospheric electricity resulting in a flash of light. *v.*, **-ninged**,

-ning. release a flash of lightning.

light·ning bug, *n.* firefly.

light·ning rod, *n.* metallic rod protecting structures from lightning.

light-year, *n.* distance traversed by light in one year.

like, *a.* similar. *prep.* in the manner of. *conj.* **nonstandard.** just as; as if. *v.*, **liked**, **lik·ing.** find to one's taste; regard with favor. *n. usu. pl.* liking. **lik·a·ble**, **like·a·ble**, *a.*

like·ly, *a.*, **-li·er**, **-li·est.** credible; probable. promising. *adv.* probably. **like·li·hood**, *n.*

lik·en, *v.* compare.

like·ness, *n.* close resemblance, esp. a portrait.

like·wise, *adv.* in like manner; also; too.

li·lac, *n.* shrub with large clusters of purple flowers. *a.* light purple color.

lilt, *n.* springing step; sprightly song or tune. **lilt·ing**, *a.*

lil·y, *n. pl.*, **-ies.** plant with showy funnel-shaped flowers.

limb, *n.* appendage, as an arm; large branch of a tree.

lim·ber, *a.* flexible; supple.

lim·bo, *n.* place or state of things forgotten or no longer wanted.

lime, *n.* calcium oxide; greenish-yellow fruit. **lim·y**, *a.*

lime·light, *n.* spotlight; center of public interest.

lim·er·ick, *n.* amusing verse of five lines.

lime·stone, *n.* rock chiefly of calcium carbonate.

lim·it, *n.* final or furthest point; boundary; *v.* restrict. **lim·i·ta·tion**, *n.* **lim·it·ed**, *a.*

lim·ou·sine, *n.* large automobile.

limp, *v.* walk lamely. *n.* act of limping. *a.* lacking stiffness. **limp·ness**, *n.*

line, *n.* long mark or stroke; row or series; business and the merchandise peculiar to it; system of public conveyances. *v.*, **lined**, **lin·ing.** mark with a line or lines; form a line; cover on the inside.

lin·e·age, *n.* line of descent; race; family.

lin·e·al, *a.* hereditary.

lin·e·ar, *a.* of a line or lines; pertaining to length. **lin·e·ar·ly**, *adv.*

lin·en, *n.* cloth, or thread of

flax. *a.* of flax.

lin·er, *n.* steamship or airplane; lining.

line-up, line·up, *n.* formation of persons or things into a line.

lin·ger, *v.* stay longer than usual; loiter. **lin·ger·er,** *n.*

lin·ge·rie, *n.* women's underwear.

lin·go, *n. pl.,* -goes. inf. language one does not understand.

lin·guist, *n.* person skilled in languages. **lin·guis·tics,** *n. pl.*

lin·i·ment, *n.* preparation for rubbing on the skin.

link, *n.* ring of a chain. *v.* join. linked, *a.* link·er, *n.*

li·no·le·um, *n.* floor covering.

lin·seed, *n.* flaxseed.

lint, *n.* fluff or fuzz or fabric ravelings. **lint·y,** *a.,* **-i·er, -i·est.**

li·on, *n.* large, tawny animal of the cat family. **li·on·ness,** *n. fem.* **li·on·like,** *a.*

lip, *n.* either of two parts forming the margins of the mouth; edge of a vessel.

lip·py, *a.,* -pi·er, -pi·est. *inf.* impudent in speech.

lip·stick, *n.* cosmetic for coloring the lips.

liq·ue·fy, *v.,* -fied, -fy·ing. convert from a solid form to a liquid. **liq·ue·fi·er,** *n.*

li·queur, *n.* strong, sweet liquor.

liq·uid, *a.* able to flow like water. *n.* fluid substance.

liq·ui·date, *v.,* -dat·ed, -dat·ing. settle or pay, as a debt or claim; do away with. **liq·ui·da·tion,** *n.* **liq·ui·da·tor,** *n.*

liq·uor, *n.* distilled alcoholic beverage.

lisp, *v.* pronounce imperfectly. *n.* lisping.

list, *n.* record of a series of names, words, etc. *v.* make a list of; careen to one side. **list·ed,** *a.* **list·ing,** *n.*

lis·ten, *v.* give ear. **lis·ten·er,** *n.*

list·less, *a.* lacking of interest or energy.

lit·er·al, *a.* exact; factual. **lit·er·al·ly,** *adv.*

lit·er·ar·y, *a.* pertaining to literature; well-read. **lit·er·ar·i·ly,** *adv.*

lit·er·ate, *a.* able to read and write. **lit·er·a·cy,** *n.*

lit·er·a·ture, *n.* fiction, poetry, etc. writings of a country or period.

lithe, *a.* pliant; limber. Also **lithe·some, lithe·ly,** *adv.*

lit·i·gate, *v.,* -gat·ed, -gat·ing. make the subject of a lawsuit. **lit·i·ga·tion,** *n.*

lit·ter, *n.* scattered rubbish; young produced at one birth; stretcher. *v.* scatter about.

lit·tle, *a.,* **lit·tler** or less or less·er; **lit·tlest** or least. small; short; petty. *n.* short time; small quantity. *adv.,* less, least. in a small degree.

lit·ur·gy, *n. pl.,* -gies. ritual for worship.

live, *v.,* lived, liv·ing. have life; abide. *v.* pass or spend. **liv·er,** *n.* **liv·ing,** *a., n.*

live, *a.* being alive; full of life; burning.

live·li·hood, *n.* means of maintaining life.

live·long, *a.* lasting a long time.

live·ly, *a.,* -li·er, -li·est. active; spirited. **live·li·ness,** *n.*

liv·en, *v.* put life into; cheer. **liv·en·er,** *n.*

liv·er, *n.* glandular organ.

liv·er·wurst, *n.* liver sausage.

live·stock, *n.* domestic animals.

liv·id, *a.* black and blue; of a lead or ashen color. **liv·id·ness,** *n.*

liz·ard, *n.* four-legged reptile.

lla·ma, *n.* mammal related to the camel.

lo, *int.* look; see; behold.

load, *n.* burden; quantity that can be or usu. is carried; *v.* put a load on or in; burden. **load·ed,** *a.* **load·er,** *n.*

loaf, *n. pl.,* **loaves.** molded mass of bread or other food. *v.* lounge. **loaf·er,** *n.*

loam, *n.* rich soil. **loam·y,** *a.*

loan, *n.* that which is lent. *v.* lend.

loath, loth, *a.* very averse.

loathe, *v.,* loathed, loath·ing. abhor. **loath·ing,** *n.* **loath·some,** *a.*

lob·by, *n. pl.,* -bies. entrance hall used as a waiting room; persons who try to influence legislators. *v.* try to influence. **lob·by·ist,** *n.*

lobe, *n.* lower part of the external ear. **lobed,** *a.*

lob·ster, *n.* edible crustacean having two claws.

lo·cal, *a.* particular place; limited or confined. *n.* one living in a particular place. **lo·cal·i·ty,** *n. pl.,* -ties.

lo·cate, *v.,* -cat·ed, -cat·ing. place; ascertain the whereabouts of. **lo·ca·tion,** *n.*

lock, *n.* tuft of hair; device for fastening or securing something. *v.* fasten or secure by a lock; join. **lock·er,** *n.*

lo·co·mo·tive, *a., n.* self-propelled engine used for moving trains.

lo·cust, *n.* destructive migratory grasshopper.

lode, *n.* vein of metallic ore.

lodge, *v.,* **lodged, lodg·ing.** shelter; live in hired quarters; be fixed in a position. *n.* habitation used as a temporary abode; meeting place of a branch of a society. **lodg·er,** *n.* **lodg·ing,** *n.*

loft, *n.* hayloft; gallery.

loft·y, *a.,* **-i·er, -i·est.** extremely high; haughty.

log, *n.* piece of unhewed timber; record. *v.* cut into logs; record. **log·ger,** *n.*

log·ic, *n.* science of formal reasoning. **lo·gi·cian,** *n.* **log·i·cal,** *a.*

lo·gy, *a.,* **-gi·er, -gi·est.** *inf.* heavy; sluggish; dull.

loin, *n. usu. pl.* part between the false ribs and the hipbone; cut of meat.

loi·ter, *v.* linger idly about a place. **loi·ter·er,** *n.*

loll, *v.* lounge; let hang.

lol·li·pop, lol·ly·pop, *n.* sucker.

lone, *a.* solitary.

lon·er, *n.* person who chooses to be alone.

lone·ly, *a.,* **-li·er, -li·est.** deserted; sad from want of companionship. **lone·li·ness,** *n.*

lone·some, *a.* lonely.

long, *a.* not short; having many items; lengthy; having a long time to run. *adv.* for a great extent of space or time. *v.* desire earnestly.

lon·gev·i·ty, *n.* long life.

long·ing, *n.* yearning.

lon·gi·tude, *n.* distance east or west of the prime meridian.

lon·gi·tu·di·nal, *a.* lengthwise; of longitude.

long·shore·man, *n. pl.,* **-men.** dock laborer.

long·suf·fer·ing, *a.* bearing injuries for along time.

long·wise, *adv.* lengthwise. Also **long·ways.**

look, *v.* direct the eyes toward an object; seem to the mind. *n.* act of looking; *usu. pl.* outward aspect or appearance. **look·er,** *n.*

look·ing glass, *n.* mirror.

look·out, *n.* watch kept; person keeping such a watch.

loom, *n.* machine for weaving. *v.* appear indistinctly; threaten.

loon, *n.* waterfowl having a laughterlike call.

loon·y, *a.,* **-i·er, -i·est.** *inf.* crazy. **loon·i·ness,** *n.*

loop, *n.* doubling of a portion of a cord, etc., upon itself, leaving an opening. *v.* form loops; encircle.

loop·hole, *n.* small aperture; opportunity for escape or evasion.

loose, *a.,* **loos·er, loos·est.** free; not tight; lax; not firmly fixed. *v.,* **loosed, loos·ing.** let loose; release. *adv.* loosely. **loos·en,** *v.*

loot, *n.* spoils; *inf.* money. *v.* plunder. **loot·er,** *n.*

lop, *v.,* **lopped, lop·ping.** remove or cut off.

lope, *v.,* **loped, lop·ing.** move with a long easy stride. *n.* act or the gait of loping.

lop·sid·ed, *a.* larger at one side than the other.

lord, *n.* ruler, governor, etc.; (*cap.*) God; (*cap.*) *Brit.* nobleman. *v.* domineer. **lord·ly,** *a.,* **-li·er, -li·est.**

lore, *n.* store of knowledge.

lose, *v.,* **lost, los·ing.** mislay; cease to have; miss; fail to win. **los·er,** *n.* **los·ing,** *a., n.*

loss, *n.* that which is lost; deprivation of.

lost, *a.* no longer possessed or to be found; having gone astray; that which one has failed to win.

lot, *n.* marked objects used to decide a question, etc.; casting of such objects; decision so made; alloted portion. *v.,* **lot·ted, lot·ting.** cast or draw lots for; allot.

lo·tion, *n.* liquid applied to the skin.

lot·ter·y, *n. pl.,* **-ies.** game of fund raising by sale of numbered tickets.

loud, *a.* strongly heard; making very audible sounds. **loud·ly,** *adv.* **loud·ness,** *n.*

loud·speak·er, *n.* device for amplifying.

lounge, *v.,* **lounged, loung·ing.** loll; *n.* kind of sofa; place for lounging. **loung·er,** *n.*

louse, *n. pl.*, **lice**. wingless, parasitic insect.

lout, *n.* awkward person.

lou·ver, *n.* slats covering an opening so as to admit air but exclude rain.

love, *n.* feeling of deep affection; object of love. *v.*, **loved, lov·ing**. have deep affection for; be in love; caress. **love·less**, *a.* **lov·a·ble, love·a·ble**, *a.* **lov·er**, *n.*

love·ly, *a.*, **-li·er**, **-li·est**. beautiful. **love·li·ness**, *n.*

lov·ing, *a.* affectionate. **lov·ing·ness**, *n.*

low, *a.* of small extent upward; lying or being below the general level; humble; vulgar; near depletion. *adv.* in or to a low position. *n.* that which is low. **low·ness**, *n.*

low·er, *a.* in an inferior position. *v.* let down; reduce; humble. **low·er·ing**, *a.*

low·ly, *a.*, **-li·er**, **-li·est**. low or humble; meek. *adv.* in a low position. **low·li·ness**, *n.*

loy·al, *a.* faithful to. **loy·al·ist**, *n.* **loy·al·ty**, *n. pl.*, **-ties**.

loz·enge, *n.* small tablet, usu. medicated.

lu·au, *n.* Hawaiian feast.

lub·ber, *n.* clumsy individual; one unskilled in seamanship. **lub·ber·li·ness**, *n.*

lu·bri·cate, *v.*, **-cat·ed**, **-cat·ing**. apply an oily or greasy substance to. **lu·bri·cant**, *n.* **lu·bri·ca·tion**, *n.*

lu·cid, *a.* clear, intelligible; sane. **lu·cid·i·ty**, *n.*

luck, *n.* chance; fate; good fortune. **luck·i·ness**, *n.*

luck·y, *a.*, **-i·er**, **-i·est**. favored by luck; believed capable of bringing success.

lu·cra·tive, *a.* profitable. **lu·cra·tive·ness**, *n.*

lu·cre, *n.* money.

lu·di·crous, *a.* comical; very ridiculous.

lug, *v.*, **lugged, lug·ging**. drag; pull along or carry. *n.* projecting part resembling the ear, as a handle.

lug·gage, *n.* hand baggage.

luke·warm, *a.* tepid; indifferent. **luke·warm·ness**, *n.*

lull, *v.* cause to rest by soothing means; subside; become calm. *n.* temporary quiet before or after a storm.

lull·a·by, *n. pl.*, **-bies**. song to lull or quiet babies.

lum·ber, *v.* move clumsily or heavily. *n.* sawed timber or logs. **lum·ber·ing**, *n.*, *a.*

lu·mi·nar·y, *n. pl.*, **-ies**. person of eminence; body that gives light.

lu·mi·nous, *a.* radiating or reflecting light. **lu·mi·nos·i·ty**, *n.* **lu·mi·nous·ness**, *n.*

lump, *n.* shapeless mass; swelling. *v.* unite into one mass; form lumps. **lump·y**, *a.*, **-i·er**, **-i·est**. **lump·i·ness**, *n.*

lu·nar, *a.* of the moon.

lu·na·tic, *n.* insane person. *a.* mad. **lu·na·cy**, *n. pl.*, **-cies**.

lunch, *n.* light midday meal. *v.* eat lunch. **lunch·er**, *n.*

lunch·eon, *n.* midday meal, usu. formal.

lung, *n.* saclike respiratory organ.

lure, *n.* enticement; bait. *v.*, **lured, lur·ing**. attract.

lu·rid, *a.* sensational; shining with an unnatural glare.

lurk, *v.* lie in wait.

lus·cious, *a.* highly pleasing.

lush, *a.* having luxuriant foliage; opulent. **lush·ness**, *n.*

lust, *n.* sexual appetite; longing. *v.* desire. **lust·ful**, *a.*

lus·ter, *n.* sheen; brilliance; fame. **lus·trous**, *a.*

lus·ty, *a.*, **-i·er**, **-i·est**. robust; hearty. **lust·i·ness**, *n.*

lute, *n.* stringed instrument, having a pear-shaped body.

lux·u·ri·ant, *a.* richly abundant; profuse. **lux·u·ri·ance**, *n.*

lux·u·ri·ous, *a.* opulent; furnished with luxuries.

lux·u·ry, *n. pl.*, **-ries**. nonessential, usu. costly; indulgence in such nonessentials.

lye, *n.* strong alkaline solution used in making soap.

lymph, *n.* clear, bodily fluid. **lum·phat·ic**, *a.*

lynch, *v.* put to death by mob action, esp. by hanging. **lynch·er**, *n.* **lynch·ing**, *n.*

lynx, *n. pl.*, **lynx, lynx·es**. wildcat.

lyre, *n.* harplike musical instrument.

lyr·ic, *a.* having the form of a song; expressing personal feelings. *n.* lyric poem; *usu.* pl. text of a song. **lyr·i·cal**, *a.* **lyr·i·cist**, *n.*

M

ma, *n. inf.* mother.

ma'am, *n. inf.* madam.

ma·ca·bre, *a.* gruesome.

mac·ad·am, *n.* (road made of) small broken stones.

mac·a·ro·ni, *n.* flour dough in tubular form.

mac·a·roon, *n.* cooky made with almond meal or coconut.

ma·caw, *n.* large parrot.

mace, *n.* medieval spiked weapon; official's staff; spice.

ma·chet·e, *n.* large knife.

mach·i·nate, *v.* devise with evil purpose. **mach·i·na·tion,** *n.*

ma·chine, *n.* apparatus used to perform work; group controlling political activity. *v.* make, finish by machine.

ma·chin·er·y, *n.* mechanical apparatus; working parts of a machine.

ma·chin·ist, *n.* one who operates machinery or machine tools.

mack·er·el, *n.* edible ocean fish.

mack·i·naw, *n.* short woolen coat.

mack·in·tosh, mac·in·tosh, *n.* rubberized waterproof coat.

mac·ro·cosm, *n.* the great world; universe.

mad, *a.,* **mad·der, mad·dest.** insane; foolish; frenzied; furious. **mad·ly,** *adv.* **mad·ness,** *n.* **mad·den,** *v.*

mad·am, *n.* polite term of address for a woman.

mad·ame, *n.* French title of respect for a married woman.

mad·cap, *a.* impulsive; reckless.

mad·e·moi·selle, *n.* French title of respect for unmarried woman.

mad·house, *n.* chaotic situation or place.

mad·man, *n.* lunatic.

Ma·don·na, *n.* the Virgin Mary.

mad·ras, *n.* striped, patterned cotton cloth.

maes·tro, *n.* master (of music).

mag·a·zine, *n.* periodical publication; storage room for military supplies.

ma·gen·ta, *n.* purplish-red color.

mag·got, *n.* wormlike insect larva.

mag·ic, *n.* sorcery; sleight of hand to create illusions, perform tricks. *a.* of magic. **mag·i·cal,** *a.* **mag·i·cal·ly,** *adv.*

ma·gi·cian, *n.* one skilled in magic.

mag·is·trate, *n.* civil officer who administers law.

mag·nan·i·mous, *a.* generous.

mag·nate, *n.* person of rank, influence.

mag·ne·sia, *n.* white powder used in manufacturing, and as an antacid, laxative.

mag·ne·si·um, *n.* silver-white metallic element.

mag·net, *n.* body that attracts certain substances. **mag·net·ic,** *a.* **mag·net·ism,** *n.* **mag·net·ize,** *v.*

mag·nif·i·cent, *a.* extraordinarily superb; impressive. **mag·nif·i·cence,** *n.*

mag·ni·fy, *v.,* **-fied, -fy·ing.** make seem greater or larger, as by use of a lens. **mag·ni·fi·ca·tion,** *n.*

mag·ni·tude, *n.* greatness of size, amount, or extent.

mag·no·lia, *n.* flowery tree or shrub; its blossom.

mag·pie, *n.* large, noisy, black-and-white bird.

ma·ha·ra·jah, ma·ha·ra·ja, *n.* Indian prince. **ma·ha·ra·ni, ma·ha·ra·nee,** *n. fem.*

mah-jongg, mah-jong, *n.* game of Chinese origin played with 144 dominolike pieces.

ma·hog·a·ny, *n.* reddish-brown hard wood of a tropical tree.

maid, *n.* female servant; young unmarried woman.

maid·en, *n.* young unmarried woman. *a.* unmarried; virgin; fresh, unused.

mail, *n.* letters, papers, packages sent and delivered through post office; postal system; armor made of metal mesh. *v.* send through the mail. **mail·box,** *n.* **mail·man,** *n. pl.* **-men.**

maim, *v.* mutilate; disable.

main, *a.* principal; chief. *n.* chief portion; principal gas or water conduit; the ocean. **main·ly,** *adv.*

main·land, *n.* principal section of a country or continent.

main·spring, *n.* principal spring in a watch.

main·tain, *v.* preserve; support; keep possession of; continue; assert. **main·te·nance,** *n.*

mai·tre d'hôtel, *n.* hotel steward; headwaiter.

maize, *n.* Indian corn; yellow.

maj·es·ty, *n.* grandeur. (*usu. cap.*) title of royalty. **ma·jes·tic,** *a.*

ma·jor, *a.* greater; *mus.* half step higher than the minor. *n.* one of superior rank; course of academic specialization; commissioned military officer. *v.* pursue a principal subject.

ma·jor·i·ty *n. pl.,* **-ties.** number which is over half of the total.

make, *v.,* **made, mak·ing.** bring into existence; form; manufacture; cause; establish; gain; compel; do, perform. *n.* style, form. **make be·lieve,** pretend. **make do,** manage. **make out,** succeed. **make sure,** ascertain. **make up,** reconcile; consist of; put on cosmetics. **make way,** allow to pass. **ma·ker,** *n.* a substitute.

make-shift, *n., a.* temporary substitute.

make-up, *n.* cosmetics; physical, mental constitution.

mal·ad·just·ment, *n.* unsatisfactory adjustment. **mal·ad·just·ed,** *a.*

mal·a·dy, *n. pl.,* **-dies.** ailment.

ma·lar·i·a, *n.* disease with chills and fever, transmitted by mosquitoes.

mal·con·tent, *a., n.* dissatisfied (person).

male, *a.* of the sex which produces sperm; masculine. *n.* a male animal.

male·dic·tion, *n.* curse.

male·fac·tor, *n.* evildoer. **mal·e·fac·tion,** *n.*

ma·lev·o·lent, *a.* malicious. **ma·lev·o·lence,** *n.*

mal·fea·sance, *n.* illegal, detrimental conduct, esp. in public office.

mal·for·ma·tion, *n.* abnormal structure. **mal·formed,** *a.*

mal·ice, *n.* active or vindictive ill will. **ma·li·cious,** *a.*

ma·lign, *v.* speak evil of. *a.* evil; harmful.

ma·lig·nant, *a.* having extreme malevolence; tending to cause death. **ma·lig·nan·cy,** *n.*

ma·lin·ger, *v.* feign illness to avoid duty.

mall, *n.* landscaped public area for walking.

mal·lard, *n.* wild duck.

mal·le·a·ble, *a.* capable of being shaped by hammering, pressure; adaptable.

mal·let, *n.* hammer used for driving another tool.

mal·nu·tri·tion, *n.* faulty, insufficient nutrition.

mal·o·dor, *n.* offensive odor. **mal·o·dor·ous,** *a.*

mal·prac·tice, *n.* improper, neglectful performance of public or professional duty.

malt, *n.* grain, usu. barley, used in brewing and distilling; beverage produced from malt.

mam·ma, ma·ma, *n.* mother.

mam·mal, *n.* vertebrate animal characterized by sucking of young, presence of hair, live births.

mam·mon, *n.* evil riches.

mam·moth, *n.* extinct, long-tusked, hairy elephant. *a.* very large.

man, *n. pl.,* **men.** human being, particularly a male adult; human race; game piece. *v.* supply with men.

man·a·cle, *n. often pl.* handcuffs.

man·age, *v.* control; direct, carry on. **man·age·a·ble,** *a.* **man·ag·er, man·age·ment,** *n.*

man·da·rin, *n.* official of the Chinese Empire.

man·date, *n.* command; policy direction dictated by electorate; territory controlled by another nation. **man·da·to·ry,** *a.*

man·do·lin, *n.* pear-shaped, stringed musical instrument.

mane, *n.* long neck hair of some animals.

ma·neu·ver, *n.* regulated movement; scheme. *v.* perform military maneuvers; handle skillfully; scheme.

man·ga·nese, *n.* grayish metallic element used as an alloy.

mange, *n.* skin disease.

man·ger, *n.* feedbox, trough for horses or cattle.

man·gle, *v.* destroy or badly damage. *n.* machine to iron fabrics using heated rollers.

man·go, *n.* edible tropical fruit; the tree itself.

man·gy, *a.,* **-gi·er, -gi·est.** squalid; shabby.

man·han·dle, *v.* handle roughly.

man·hole, *n.* circular hole serving as a sewer entrance.

man·hood, *n.* state of being an adult male; manly qualities; men collectively.

ma·ni·a, *n.* intense excitement, enthusiasm. **man·ic,** *a.*

ma·ni·ac, *n.* wildly insane person.

man·i·cure, *n.* care of the nails,

hands. *v.* trim or care for.

man·i·fest, *a.* clearly visible; obviously understood. *v.* reveal. *n.* shipper's document. **man·i·fes·ta·tion,** *n.*

man·i·fes·to, *n.* public declaration.

man·i·fold, *a.* having many different parts, features. *n.* exhaust pipe.

ma·nip·u·late, *v.* handle, manage, or use with skill. **ma·nip·u·la·tion,** *n.* **ma·nip·u·la·tive,** *a.*

man·kind, *n.* human race collectively.

man·ly, *a.,* **-li·er, -li·est.** of or appropriate to a man. **man·li·ness,** *n.*

man·na, *n.* divine or spiritual food.

man·ne·quin, *n.* life-sized human model; fashion model.

man·ner, *n.* way, style of performing or behaving; *pl.* polite social conduct; sort, kind.

man·ner·ism, *n.* characteristic trait, style.

man·ner·ly, *a., adv.* polite.

man·or, *n.* landed estate; mansion.

man·pow·er, *n.* power of a man; collective strength.

man·sard, *n.* curb roof.

man·sion, *n.* large dwelling.

man·slaugh·ter, *n.* unlawful, unplanned killing of a person.

man·tel, *n.* ornamental work surrounding and above a fireplace.

man·tle, *n.* loose, sleeveless cloak; cover. *v.* conceal; envelop.

man·u·al, *a.* made, operated, used by the hands. *n.* handbook.

man·u·fac·ture, *n.* making of goods by manual labor or machinery. *v.* make by hand or machinery; invent fictitiously.

ma·nure, *n.* animal waste used as fertilizer.

man·u·script, *n.* handwritten or typewritten work.

man·y, *a.,* **more, most.** numerous. *n., pron.* a great number.

map, *n.* charting of the earth's surface. *v.* show in a map; plan.

ma·ple, *n.* shade tree important for lumber, syrup.

mar, *v.,* **marred, mar·ring.** injure; spoil.

mar·a·schi·no, *n.* liqueur made from sour cherries.

mar·a·thon, *n.* long-distance (foot) race; contest requiring great stamina.

ma·raud, *v.* raid for plunder. **ma·raud·er,** *n.*

mar·ble, *n.* hard limestone; little ball used in play. *a.* hard or veined like marble.

march, *v.* walk with steady, measured pace; advance steadily. *n.* measured, uniform walk; progress; marching music.

mare, *n.* female horse.

mar·ga·rine, *n.* butter substitute of fats extracted from vegetable oils.

mar·gin, *n.* border; edge; limit, condition; difference between cost and selling price; security money deposited against loss. **mar·gi·nal,** *a.*

mar·i·gold, *n.* golden-flowered garden plant.

mar·i·jua·na, *n.* narcotic, from hemp plant; plant itself.

ma·ri·na, *n.* small boat basin where moorings, supplies are available.

mar·i·nate, *v.* soak in seasoned brine before cooking.

ma·rine, *a.* of the sea. *n.* member of U.S. Marine Corps.

mar·i·ner, *n.* seaman.

mar·i·on·ette, *n.* jointed, stringed puppet.

mar·i·tal, *a.* pertaining to marriage.

mar·i·time, *a.* of the sea, navigation, shipping.

mar·jo·ram, *n.* sweet, savory herb.

mark, *n.* visible impression; symbol to show achievement, ownership, merit; distinctive trait; writing symbol; target. *v.* make marks on; set boundaries of; characterize; single out; notice. **marked,** *a.* **mark·ed·ly,** *adv.* **mark·er,** *n.*

mar·ket, *n.* traffic in goods, services; place of sale; the buying public; shop; public sale. *v.* deal in a market; purchase provisions. **mar·ket·a·ble,** *a.*

mark·ing, *n. often pl.* characteristic arrangement of natural coloring.

marks·man, *n. pl.,* **-men.** one who shoots well. **marks·man·ship,** *n.*

mar·lin, *n.* oceanic game fish.

mar·ma·lade, *n.* preserve with

pieces of fruit and rind.

ma·roon, v. leave abandoned and helpless.

mar·quee, n. rooflike projection for protection, advertising.

mar·quis, n. pl. **mar·quis·es, mar·quis.** British nobleman above an earl. **mar·quise,** n. fem., **mar·quis·es,** fem. pl.

mar·riage, n. wedlock; wedding; intimate union.

mar·row, n. tissue in bone cavities. fig. essence.

mar·ry, v., **-ried, -ry·ing.** join as husband or wife; take in marriage; unite intimately.

marsh, n. swamp.

mar·shal, n. high military officer; sheriff-like official; person in charge of arrangements. v., **-shaled, -shal·ing.** arrange; lead.

marsh·mal·low, n. soft confection.

mar·su·pi·al, a. of, like, or having a pouch; n. animal with a pouch.

mart, n. market.

mar·tial, a. military.

mar·tin, n. species of swallow.

mar·tyr, n. one who endures suffering for any principle or belief; one who exaggerates suffering to enlist sympathy. v. persecute.

mar·vel, n. a wonder. v., **-veled, -vel·ing.** to be struck with surprise. **mar·vel·ous,** a. astonishing; excellent.

mas·car·a, n. cosmetic for darkening eyelashes.

mas·cot, n. thing, animal thought to bring good luck.

mas·cu·line, a. of the male sex; virile. **mas·cu·lin·i·ty,** n.

mash, v., n. (reduce to) soft, pulpy mass.

mask, n. face covering worn for disguise, protection. v. cover with a mask; disguise; conceal.

mas·och·ism, n. tendency to derive pleasure from emotional, physical pain. **mas·och·ist,** n. **mas·och·is·tic,** a.

ma·son, n. builder, worker in stone.

ma·son·ry, n. work of a mason.

masque, n. mask, n. masquerade.

mas·quer·ade, n. festivity with costumed, masked guests; disguise. v. disguise oneself.

mass, n. body of coherent matter; large number or quantity;

main body; Cap. Communion service. a., v. gather into a mass.

mas·sa·cre, n. indiscriminate killing. inf. resounding defeat. v., **-cred, -cring.**

mas·sage, n. rubbing or kneading the body. v. treat by massage.

mas·seur, n. man who practices massage. **mas·seuse,** n. fem.

mas·sive, a. bulky and heavy; of great magnitude.

mass-pro·duce, v. produce in great number, usu. by machine. **mass pro·duc·tion,** n.

mast, n. large upright pole in a vessel.

mas·ter, n. one who rules, directs; skilled craftsman. v. overpower; become adept at. a. chief; controlling. **mas·ter·y,** n.

mas·ter·ful, a. authoritative; displaying great skill.

mas·ter·piece, n. highest achievement.

mas·ti·cate, v. chew.

mas·tiff, n. large, stoutly built dog.

mas·to·don, n. extinct mammal resembling elephant.

mas·toid, a., n. (of) the projection of the temporal bone behind the ear.

mas·tur·ba·tion, n. self-stimulation of genital organs. **mas·tur·bate,** v.

mat, n. woven or plaited fabric to lie on, cover a floor, table, etc. v. entangle.

mat, n. mat, matte, a. without luster.

mat·a·dor, n. bullfighter.

match, n. person, thing that closely resembles another; contest; marriage; stick ignited by friction. v. be equal to; correspond to; pair; place in opposition.

match·mak·er, n. one who makes matrimonial matches.

mate, n. one of a pair; companion; assisting officer in a ship; spouse. v. match; marry; pair for breeding.

ma·te·ri·al, n. substance of which a thing is made; textile fabric. a. physical; important.

ma·te·ri·al·ism, n. opinion, tendency based on purely material interests. **ma·te·ri·al·is·tic,** a.

ma·te·ri·al·ize, v. give, assume material form; become a reality.

ma·te·ri·el, *n.* things needed in any undertaking.

ma·ter·nal, *a.* motherly.

ma·ter·ni·ty, *n.* motherhood. *a.* pertaining to pregnancy.

math, *n. inf.* mathematics.

math·e·mat·ics, *n.* science of quantity, form, measurement, arrangement.

mat·i·nee, *n.* daytime performance.

ma·tri·arch, *n.* woman in a ruling position.

ma·tric·u·late, *v.* admit to membership; to be enrolled.

mat·ri·mo·ny, *n.* marriage ceremony; married state.

ma·trix, *n. pl.*, **ma·tri·ces**, **ma·trix·es**, that which originates, develops, encloses anything.

ma·tron, *n.* mature married woman; female superintendent.

mat·ter, *n.* substance of which physical objects are composed; thing of a specified kind; trouble. *v.* be of significance.

mat·ter-of-fact, *a.* treating of realities; not fanciful.

mat·ting, *n.* coarse, woven fabric to cover floors, etc.

mat·tress, *n.* case filled with resilient material, used as or on a bed.

ma·ture, *a.* ripe; completely developed physically or mentally. *v.* make, become mature. **ma·tu·ri·ty**, *n.*

maud·lin, *a.* excessively sentimental.

maul, mall, *n.* large hammer. *v.* batter; maltreat.

mau·so·le·um, *n.* magnificent tomb or burial monument.

mauve, *n.* light bluish-purple.

max·im, *n.* established principle.

max·i·mum, *n.*, *a.* greatest quantity, amount, degree.

may, *v. pt.* **might**. express permission, possibility, wish, contingency.

may·be, *adv.* perhaps.

may·hem, *n.* act of intentionally maiming a person; situation of violent behavior.

may·on·naise, *n.* salad dressing of egg yolks and oil.

may·or, *n.* chief executive of a city.

maze, *n.* confusing network of paths.

me, *pron.* objective case of **I**.

mead·ow, *n.* level, grassy land.

mea·ger, *a.* scanty; lacking in quality or quantity.

meal, *n.* food prepared, served, or taken; ground, unsifted.

mean, *v.*, **meant**, **mean·ing**. intend; design; signify; denote; to be significant. *a.* inferior, shabby; selfish, ill-tempered. midway between extremes. *n.* simple average. *pl.* what is used to accomplish an end; income. **by all means**, certainly. **by no means**, certainly not. **me·an·der**, *v.* to wind or turn; roam aimlessly.

mean·ing, *n.* intention; significance; import. **mean·ing·ful**, **mean·ing·less**, *a.* **mean·ing·ful·ly**, *adv.*

mean·time, *n.* interval between two periods. *adv.* during the interval.

mea·sles, *n.* infectious disease.

meas·ure, *n.* extent; capacity; standard or instrument of measurement; decree; purposeful act; section of notes in music, poetry. *v.* ascertain extent, capacity, import; proportion; compare; have a given measurement. **meas·ure·ment**, *n.* **meas·ur·a·ble**, *a.*

meat, *n.* animal flesh used as food; edible portion; essence. **meat·y**, *a.*

me·chan·ic, *n.* worker skilled in construction, operation, repair of machinery.

me·chan·i·cal, *a.* of tools, machinery; without spontaneity; of the material forces of nature.

me·chan·ics, *n.* study of motion and effect of forces on material bodies.

mech·an·ism, *n.* structure of a machine's working parts; piece of machinery.

mech·a·nize, *v.* make mechanical; introduce machinery into.

med·al, *n.* decorative piece of metal to award, honor a person.

me·dal·lion, *n.* large medal; circular or oval design.

med·dle, *v.* interfere.

me·di·an, *a.* situated in or referring to the middle.

me·di·ate, *v.* act as an agent between arguing parties. **me·di·a·tion**, **me·di·a·tor**, *n.*

med·ic, *n.* medical practitioner.

med·i·cal, *a.* of medicine.

med·i·cate, *v.* treat with medicine. **med·i·ca·tion,** *n.*

me·dic·i·nal, *a.* of medicine; curative.

med·i·cine, *n.* substance to treat disease, relieve pain. science of restoring, preserving health.

me·di·e·val, *a.* of the Middle Ages (8th–mid-15th centuries).

me·di·o·cre, *a.* average; barely adequate. **me·di·oc·ri·ty,** *n.*

med·i·tate, *v.* ponder; plan. **med·i·ta·tion,** *n.*

me·di·um, *n. pl.,* **me·di·a, me·di·ums.** thing placed, ranked between other things; that by which anything is accomplished; form, material used by an artist. *a.* middle.

med·ley, *n.* mixture; jumble.

meek, *a.* mild of temper; submissive.

meet, *v.,* met, **meet·ing.** come upon; go to the place of arrival of; come into contact, junction with; face directly; oppose; satisfy. *n.* sports gathering.

meet·ing, *n.* a coming together; assembly; junction.

meg·a·phone, *n.* funnel-shaped instrument for magnifying sound.

meg·a·ton, *n.* force equal to 1,000,000 tons of TNT.

mel·an·chol·y, *n., a.* state of despondency.

mel·low, *v., a.* (make or become) soft, rich, ripe, toned down.

mel·o·dra·ma, *n.* sentimental, emotional drama. **mel·o·dra·mat·ic,** *a.*

mel·o·dy, *n.* pleasant succession of tones. **me·lod·ic,** *a.*

mel·on, *n.* fruit of a gourd plant.

melt, *v.* reduce from a solid to a liquid or flowing state by heat; fuse or blend; soften.

mem·ber, *n.* constituent part; person in an organization.

mem·ber·ship, *n.* state of being a member; total number of members.

mem·brane, *n.* thin tissue that covers animal organs, lines cavities, joins parts.

me·men·to, *n. pl.,* -tos, -toes. souvenir.

mem·o, *n. inf.* memorandum.

mem·oir, *n.* record of something

noteworthy; biography.

mem·o·ra·ble, *a.* worthy of remembrance.

mem·o·ran·dum, *n. pl.,* -dums, -da. short note; brief record.

me·mo·ri·al, *n.* something to preserve the memory of a person, event. *a.* commemorative. **me·mo·ri·al·ize,** *v.*

mem·o·rize, *v.* commit to memory.

mem·o·ry, *n. pl.,* -ries. mental capacity to retain and revive impressions; totality of things retained; thing remembered; commemoration.

men·ace, *v.* threaten. *n.* a threat.

me·nag·er·ie, *n.* collection of animals.

mend, *v.* repair; reform; restore; improve.

me·ni·al, *a.* servile; low. *n.* domestic servant.

men·o·pause, *n.* permanent stopping of menstruation.

men·stru·a·tion, *n.* monthly discharge of blood and mucous from uterus. **men·stru·ate,** *v.* **men·stru·al,** *a.*

men·tal, *a.* of the mind or a disorder of the mind. **men·tal·ly,** *adv.*

men·tal·i·ty, *n.* mental capacity.

men·thol, *n.* derivative of peppermint.

men·tion, *n.* reference to. *v.* note briefly.

men·tor, *n.* wise adviser.

men·u, *n.* list of meals.

mer·can·tile, *a.* of merchants, trade, commerce.

mer·ce·nar·y, *a.* motivated by greed. *n.* soldier hired into foreign service.

mer·chan·dise, *v., n.* (buy and sell) goods, wares.

mer·chant, *n.* retail dealer; shopkeeper.

mer·cu·ri·al, *a.* lively; fickle.

mer·cu·ry, *n.* heavy, silver-white, liquid metallic element.

mer·cy, *n.* (act of) benevolence, clemency. **mer·ci·ful, mer·ci·less,** *a.*

mere, *a.* this or that and nothing else. **mere·ly,** *adv.*

merge, *v.* blend so individuality is obscured.

merg·er, *n.* combination (of businesses) into one whole.

me·rid·i·an, *n.* great circle of the earth passing through the poles; highest point.

me·ringue, *n.* light mixture of

mer·it, *n.* worth; *sometimes pl.* state of deserving. *v.* deserve. **mer·i·to·ri·ous**, *a.*

mer·maid, *n.* fabled marine creature, half woman, half fish.

mer·ry, *a.*, **-ri·er**, **-ri·est.** full of fun. **mer·ri·ly**, *adv.* **mer·ri·ment**, *n.*

mer·ry-go-round, *n.* revolving circular platform with hobby-horses and seats.

me·sa, *n.* small, high plateau with steep sides.

mesh, *n.* netted or netlike work; *pl.* threads that bind such network. *v.* entangle; interlock.

mes·mer·ize, *v.* hypnotize.

mes·quite, *n.* thorny tree or shrub.

mess, *n.* disorderly mixture; dirt and disorder; communal meal. *v.* make untidy; bungle; meddle. **mess·y**, *a.*, **-i·er**, **-i·est.**

mes·sage, *n.* communication; significance of a statement.

mes·sen·ger, *n.* one who delivers a message.

me·tab·o·lism, *n.* process of chemical change wherein food is broken down into simpler compounds and waste by energy.

met·al, *n.* shiny, opaque, ductile, solid elementary substance. **me·tal·lic**, *a.*

met·al·lur·gy, *n.* study of metals; refining and development of metals.

met·a·mor·pho·sis, *n. pl.*, **-ses**, change of form, structure, substance.

met·a·phor, *n.* phrase applied to something to which it is not literally applicable to suggest a resemblance.

met·a·phys·ics, *n.* branch of philosophy concerned with being, order, knowledge. **met·a·phys·i·cal**, *a.*

mete, *v.*, **met·ed**, **met·ing.** allot.

me·te·or, *n.* small, solid body entering earth's atmosphere at great speed. **me·te·or·ic**, *a.*

me·te·or·ite, *n.* meteor that reaches earth's crust still partially intact.

me·te·or·ol·o·gy, *n.* science of weather, climate. **me·te·or·ol·o·gist**, *n.*

me·ter, **me·tre**, *n.* arrangement of words in rhythmic lines or verses; unit of length equal to 39.37 inches; instrument that measures. **met·ric**, *a.*

meth·ane, *n.* colorless, odorless, flammable gas.

meth·od, *n.* manner of procedure; system. **me·thod·i·cal**, *a.*

me·tic·u·lous, *a.* exceedingly careful or fastidious.

met·ric sys·tem, *n.* decimal system of weights and measures.

met·ro·nome, *n.* instrument for marking exact time.

me·trop·o·lis, *n.* large city. **met·ro·pol·i·tan**, *a.*

mez·za·nine, *n.* story between two main ones; lower theater balcony or first rows of balcony seats.

mez·zo, *a.* middle; medium; half.

mi·ca, *n.* silicate of thin flexible scales with metallic luster.

mi·crobe, *n.* microscopic organism, esp. a disease-causing one.

mi·cro·cosm, *n.* little world; a world in miniature.

mi·cro·film, *n.* photographic copy of printed or graphic material, greatly reduced in size.

mi·crom·e·ter, *n.* device for measuring very small distances.

mi·cro·phone, *n.* instrument that converts sound waves into electrical waves.

mi·cro·scope, *n.* optical instrument that magnifies minute objects.

mi·cro·scop·ic, *a.* visible only by microscope; tiny.

mid, *a.*, *adv.* a point equal in distance from extremes; central position.

mid·day, *n.* noon.

mid·dle, *a.* equally distant from extremes; medium. *n.* point equidistant from extremes.

mid·dle·man, *n. pl.*, **-men.** person who intervenes between producer and consumer of goods.

midg·et, *n.* person, thing of unusually small size but with normal proportions. *a.* very small.

mid·night, *n.* twelve o'clock at night.

mid·riff, *n.* area of body between chest and waist.

mid·ship·man, *n. pl.*, **-men.** student naval officer.

midst, *n.* middle point, part, or stage. *prep.* amidst.

mid·way, *n.* amusement park

area where side shows, exhibitions are located. *adv., a.* halfway.

mid-wife, *n. pl.,* **-wives.** woman who assists a mother in childbirth.

mien, *n.* external manner.

might, *n.* ability; power. **mighty,** *a.,* **-i-er, -i-est.** *v.* pt. of may.

mi-graine, *n.* severe recurring headache.

mi-grate, *v.* move from one place to another. **mi-gra-tion,** *n.* **mi-gra-to-ry,** *a.*

mil, *n.* .001 of an inch.

mild, *a.* gentle in feeling or behavior; not sharp; pungent; moderate in intensity. **mild-ly,** *adv.*

mil-dew, *n.* parasitic fungi producing a whitish coating on plants, fabrics, etc.

mile, *n.* unit of linear measure, 5,280 feet.

mile-age, *n.* distance in miles traveled in a given time.

mile-stone, *n.* noteworthy event.

mi-lieu, *n. pl.,* **mi-lieus.** environment; setting.

mil-i-tant, *a.* combative; aggressive.

mil-i-ta-rism, *n.* military spirit. **mil-i-ta-rist,** *n.* **mil-i-ta-ris-tic,** *a.*

mil-i-tar-y, *a.* of soldiers, war. *n.* military personnel.

mi-li-tia, *n.* citizen's army.

milk, *n.* white liquid secreted by mammary glands of female mammals. *v.* extract milk from; exploit. **milk-y,** *a.*

milk-weed, *n.* plant with milky juice.

mill, *n.* place where grain is ground into flour; machine for cutting, grinding, etc.; ¹/₁₀th of a cent. *v.* grind in a mill; form grooves; move in a circular fashion.

mil-len-ni-um, *n. pl.,* **-ni-a, -ni-ums.** a thousand years; period of perfection, peace, happiness.

mil-let, *n.* small cereal grain.

mil-li-me-ter, *n.* .001 of a meter.

mil-li-ner, *n.* designer, seller of women's hats. **mil-li-ner-y,** *n.*

mil-lion, *n.* a thousand thousand. **mil-lionth,** *n., a.*

mil-lion-aire, *n.* person worth at least a million dollars.

mill-stone, *n.* stone for grinding grain; personal burden.

mime, *n.* (actor specializing in)

pantomime. *v.* mimic.

mim-e-o-graph, *n.* device for copying by using an inked stencil.

mim-ic, *v.,* **-icked, -ick-ing.** imitate, esp. in derision. *n.* one who imitates. **mim-ic-ry,** *n.*

mince, *v.* chop into very small pieces; diminish in speaking; affect delicacy.

mince-meat, *n.* chopped mixture of raisins, spices, suet, sometimes meat.

mind, *n.* sanity; state of thought and feeling; opinion; intelligence; memory. *v.* obey; take care of; concerning; object to; notice. **mind-ful,** *a.*

mine, *pron.* possessive of I: belonging to me. *n.* pit from which mineral substances are taken by digging; explosive device; rich source of something valued. *v.* dig a mine. **min-er, min-ing,** *n.*

min-er-al, *a., n.* inorganic substance, neither animal nor plant, obtained by mining.

min-gle, *v.* mix together to form one whole.

min-i-a-ture, *n., a.* (representation) on a very small scale.

min-i-mize, *v.* treat as of the least import or smallest part.

min-i-mum, *a., n.* (smallest or lowest) amount, degree.

min-ion, *n.* servile or fawning dependent.

min-is-ter, *n.* one who conducts religious services; government executive; lower-ranking diplomat. *v.* administer; perform service.

min-is-try, *n.* act of ministering; office of a minister; the clergy; government department headed by a minister.

mink, *n.* semi-aquatic weasel-like mammal, with valuable fur.

min-now, *n.* small bait fish.

mi-nor, *a.* lesser in size, importance; under legal age. *n.* one of inferior rank; course of study; subordinate; person under legal age.

mi-nor-i-ty, *n.* state of being under legal age; smaller part or number; group differing from the majority in race, religion, etc.

mint, *n.* place where currency is made; very great amount; aromatic plant. *v.* coin. *a.* in unused condition.

min·u·et, *n.* stately dance.

mi·nus, *prep.* less; lacking. *n.* minus sign; deficiency. *a.* less; negative.

min·ute, *n.* 1/60 of an hour, or si..; seconds; moment. *pl.* official record.

mi·nute, *a.*, **-nut·er**, **-nut·est.** extremely small; detailed.

mir·a·cle, *n.* a wonder; supernatural event. **mi·rac·u·lous,** *a.*

mi·rage, *n.* optical illusion by which reflected images of distant objects are seen.

mire, *v.*, *n.* mud (sink in); entangle.

mir·ror, *n.* polished surface that reflects images.

mirth, *n.* merriment. **mirth·ful,** *a.*

mis·ad·ven·ture, *n.* unfortunate event.

mis·an·thrope, *n.* hater of mankind.

mis·ap·pre·hend, *v.* misunderstand. **mis·ap·pre·hen·sion,** *n.*

mis·be·have, *v.* behave poorly. **mis·be·ha·vior,** *n.*

mis·cal·cu·late, *v.* judge erroneously. **mis·cal·cu·la·tion,** *n.*

mis·car·riage, *n.* premature delivery of a nonviable fetus; failure to achieve just, proper result. **mis·car·ry,** *v.*, **-ried,** **-ry·ing.**

mis·cel·la·ne·ous, *a.* mixed. **mis·cel·la·ny,** *n.*

mis·chance, *n.* bad luck.

mis·chief, *n.* playful behavior that annoys; trouble, harm. **mis·chie·vous,** *a.*

mis·con·ceive, *v.* misunderstand. **mis·con·cep·tion,** *n.*

mis·con·duct, *n.* bad, immoral conduct.

mis·cre·ant, *n.* scoundrel; *a.* wicked.

mis·deed, *n.* evil or immoral act.

mis·de·mean·or, *n.* offense not amounting to a felony.

mi·ser, *n.* hoarder of wealth.

mis·er·a·ble, *a.* in or causing misery; wretchedly poor, unhappy, sick. **mis·er·a·bly,** *adv.*

mis·er·y, *n.* distress caused by privation, poverty.

mis·fit, *n.* bad fit; one who cannot adjust to surroundings.

mis·for·tune, *n.* ill luck; calamity.

mis·giv·ing, *n.* often *pl.* feeling of doubt, apprehension.

mis·guide, *v.* mislead.

mis·hap, *n.* regrettable accident.

mis·judge, *v.* judge wrongly.

mis·lay, *v.*, **-laid,** **-lay·ing.** lay in a place not recollected; lay wrongly.

mis·lead, *v.*, **-led,** **-lead·ing.** lead astray; deceive. **mis·lead·ing,** *a.*

mis·no·mer, *n.* incorrect naming.

mi·sog·y·ny, *n.* hatred of women. **mi·sog·y·nist,** *n.*

mis·print, *n.* mistake in printing.

mis·rep·re·sent, *v.* represent falsely, badly.

miss, *v.* fail to hit, reach, meet, obtain, perceive; discover the absence of; omit; avoid. *n.* failure to hit, etc.; unmarried female. (*cap.* title of address for.)

mis·sal, *n.* Roman Catholic liturgical book for the mass.

mis·sile, *n.* weapon, projectile thrown or to be thrown.

miss·ing, *a.* absent; lost.

mis·sion, *n.* (group sent to perform) specific service; mission building.

mis·sion·ar·y, *n.* one who tries to convert others to a system or belief.

mis·sive, *n.* a letter.

mis·spell, *v.*, **-spelled** or **-spelt.** spell incorrectly. **mis·spell·ing,** *n.*

mist, *n.* visible watery vapor; thing which obscures vision. **mist·y,** *a.*

mis·take, *v.*, **-took,** **-tak·en,** **-tak·ing.** err in identifying; misjudge; misinterpret. *n.* error.

Mis·ter, *n.* title of respect for a man. Abbr. **Mr.**

mis·tle·toe, *n.* evergreen plant with white berries.

mis·treat, *v.* treat improperly. **mis·treat·ment,** *n.*

mis·tress, *n.* woman in charge; woman cohabiting unlawfully with a man.

mis·trust, *n.* lack of trust. *v.* suspect; doubt.

mis·un·der·stand, *v.*, **-stood,** **-stand·ing.** understand incorrectly.

mis·use, *v.* use improperly; abuse.

mite, *n.* small, minute animal, amount, particle.

mi·ter, mi·tre, *n.* bishop's headdress; angled joint.

mit·i·gate, *v.* become or make

less severe.

mitt, *n.* type of glove.

mit·ten, *n.* glove with a separate thumb cover and wide section for fingers.

mix, *v.* blend into one mass; confuse; join. *n.* combination of ingredients. **mixed,** *a.* **mixture,** *n.* **mixed up,** completely confused.

mne·mon·ic, *a.* assisting or training the memory.

moan, *v., n.* (utter) a low dull sound from grief, pain.

moat, *n.* deep trench surrounding a castle.

mob, *n.* disorderly crowd. *v.* overcrowd; attack by crowding.

mo·bile, *a.* easily moved. **mo·bil·i·ty,** *n.*

mo·bi·lize, *v.* put in a state of readiness.

moc·ca·sin, *n.* kind of soft shoe.

mock, *v.* imitate, esp. in derision. *a.* false. **mock·er·y,** *n.*

mode, *n.* manner of acting or doing; fashion.

mod·el, *n.* standard for imitation; representation in miniature; one who poses for artists, displays clothes. *v.* form; plan; wear for display.

mod·er·ate, *n., a.* (person) temperate in opinions, behavior. *v.* reduce in intensity, severity; preside over. **mod·er·ate·ly,** *adv.* **mod·er·a·tion,** *n.* **mod·er·a·tor,** *n.*

mod·ern, *n., a.* (person) of the current period. **mod·ern·ize,** *v.*

mod·est, *a.* holding a moderate estimation of oneself; not excessive. **mod·es·ty,** *n.*

mod·i·fy, *v.* alter in some respect. **mod·i·fi·ca·tion,** *n.*

mod·u·late, *v.* control, modify, as vocal tones. **mod·u·la·tion,** *n.*

mod·ule, *n.* unit of measurement. **mod·u·lar,** *a.*

mo·hair, *n.* cloth of goat hair.

moist, *a.* moderately wet.

mois·ten, *v.* make damp.

mois·ture, *n.* diffused wetness.

mo·lar, *n.* broad-surfaced tooth for grinding.

mo·las·ses, *n.* dark syrup left after refining of sugar.

mold, mould, *n.* rich, organic earth; form in which a thing is shaped; fungous growth. *v.* shape; fashion.

mold·ing, mould·ing, *n.* decorative edging.

mole, *n.* small, discolored spot on skin; small burrowing mammal.

mol·e·cule, *n.* smallest particle of a substance with all the properties of that substance.

mo·lest, *v.* annoy; attack sexually.

mol·lusk, mol·lusc, *n.* invertebrate animal with soft, unsegmented body and hard shell.

molt, moult, *v.* shed feathers, skin.

mol·ten, *a.* liquefied by heat.

mom, *n. inf.* mother.

mo·ment, *n.* the present or current brief space of time. **mo·men·tar·y,** *a.* **mo·men·tar·i·ly,** *adv.*

mo·men·tous, *a.* of great importance.

mo·men·tum, *n.* impetus of a moving body.

mon·arch, *n.* hereditary ruler.

mon·ar·chy, *n.* government ruled by a monarch.

mon·as·ter·y, *n.* residence for those living under religious vows.

mo·nas·tic, *a.* of, like monks.

Mon·day, *n.* 2nd day of week.

mon·e·tar·y, *a.* of money, currency.

mon·ey, *n.* coin, paper used as medium of exchange; wealth. **mon·eyed, mon·ied,** *a.* rich.

mon·goose, *n.* ferretlike animal.

mon·grel, *n., a.* (plant, animal) of mixed breed.

mon·i·tor, *n.* one who maintains discipline; receiver to check transmission of a broadcast. *v.* oversee; listen to, view.

monk, *n.* male inhabiting a monastery, vowed to celibacy, poverty, religious obedience.

mon·key, *n., pl.,* **-keys.** any member, except man, lemurs, apes, of the primates. *v.* mimic; play idly.

mon·o·cle, *n.* a single eyeglass.

mo·nog·a·my, *n.* practice of being married to only one person at a time.

mon·o·gram, *n.* initials of a person's name as a design.

mon·o·graph, *n.* scholarly book, article.

mon·o·lith, *n.* large single stone block. **mon·o·lith·ic,** *a.*

mon·o·logue, mon·o·log, *n.* speech by one person; series of short funny stories told by one comedian.

mo-nop-o-ly, n. (corporation having) exclusive control of a commodity, service. mo-nop-o-lize, v.

mon-o-rail, n. railway suspended from a single rail.

mon-o-syl-la-ble, n. word of one syllable.

mon-o-the-ism, n. belief in existence of one God only.

mon-o-tone, n. sameness in sound, color, style.

mo-not-o-ny, n. boring repetition. mo-not-o-nous, a.

mon-ox-ide, n. oxide with one oxygen atom to the molecule.

mon-sieur, n. pl., mes-sieurs, polite French title for a man.

mon-soon, n. seasonal wind; rainy season.

mon-ster, n. abnormal or huge person or thing. mon-stros-i-ty, n. mon-strous, a.

month, n. the twelfth part of a year.

month-ly, a., adv. done, happening, appearing every month.

mon-u-ment, n. memorial marker, building, etc.

mon-u-men-tal, a. massive.

moo, v. bellow, as a cow.

mood, n. temporary state of mind.

mood-y, a., -i-er, -i-est. subject to, showing melancholy.

moon, n. heavenly body which revolves around any planet. v. inf. wander, gaze idly. moon-light, n. moon-lit, a.

moon-stone, n. gem-quality feldspar.

moor, n. rolling waste land. v. confine or secure by cables, anchors, etc.

moor-ing, n. usu. pl. cables, place for securing a ship.

moose, n. pl., moose. large animal of deer family.

moot, a. debatable.

mop, n. bundle of absorbent material on a stick for cleaning floors. v. clean with a mop.

mope, v. act in a listless, dispirited way.

mor-al, a. of, concerned with right and wrong; virtuous; ethical; approved. n. ethical lesson. pl. principles; mode of life. mor-al-ly, adv.

mo-rale, n. mental attitude of courage, zeal, hope, confidence.

mo-ral-i-ty, n. moral quality; virtuous conduct.

mor-al-ize, v. explain in a moral sense; improve the morals of.

mo-rass, n. marsh; swamp.

mor-a-to-ri-um, n. pl., -ums, -a. temporary suspension of activity.

mor-bid, a. diseased; unwholesomely gloomy.

more, a. greater; additional. n. greater quantity, importance. adv. in, to a greater extent or degree.

more-o-ver, adv. besides.

mo-res, n. pl. customs; manners.

morgue, n. place where bodies of dead people are kept until burial.

mor-i-bund, a. dying; deathlike.

morn, n. morning.

morn-ing, n. day from midnight to noon.

mo-ron, n. mentally retarded adult. inf. stupid, foolish person. mo-ron-ic, a.

mo-rose, a. gloomy.

mor-phine, n. drug derived from opium.

mor-row, n. next day.

mor-sel, n. little piece of anything.

mor-tal, a. subject to death; fatal; pertaining to death; extreme. n. human being. mor-tal-ly, adv.

mor-tal-i-ty, n. state of being mortal; frequency of death; humanity.

mor-tar, n. bowl in which substances are reduced to powder; cannon; mixture for binding together stones, bricks.

mort-gage, n. (deed of) transfer of property to creditor as security for repayment of money. v. place under a mortgage.

mor-ti-cian, n. undertaker.

mor-ti-fy, v. humiliate; subdue by self-control.

mor-tu-ar-y, n. funeral home.

mo-sa-ic, n. inlaid design of bits of colored glass, stones.

mos-qui-to, n. pl., -toes, -tos. tiny, blood-sucking insect.

moss, n. small, flowerless plant that covers rocks, ground, etc.

most, a. greatest in any way; majority. adv. in the greatest, highest degree.

most-ly, adv. almost all; mainly.

mote, n. speck.

mo-tel, n. lodging place open

directly to parking.

moth, *n.* winged insect.

moth·er, *n.* female parent. *a.* of, like a mother. *v.* be the mother of; care for as a mother does. **moth·er·hood**, *n.* **moth·er·ly**, *a.*

moth·er-in-law, *n. pl.*, **mothers-in-law**. mother of one's spouse.

mo·tif, *n.* repeated theme, design.

mo·tion, *n.* process of moving; formal suggestion. *v.* gesture.

mo·tion pic·ture, *n.* photographs projected on a screen in rapid succession giving illusion of continuous movement.

mo·ti·vate, *v.* impel; induce. **mo·ti·va·tion**, *n.*

mo·tive, *n.* reason for a certain action.

mot·ley, *a.* of different colors; varied.

mo·tor, *n.* that which imparts motion; thing that receives and modifies natural energy to drive machinery; *a.* of or operated by a motor. *v.* travel by automobile. **mo·tor·ist**, *n.*

mo·tor·cy·cle, *n.* two-wheeled vehicle propelled by internal-combustion engine.

mot·tle, *v.* mark with spots, blotches. **mot·tled**, *a.*

mot·to, *n. pl.*, **-toes, -tos.** phrase, maxim expressing one's guiding idea or principle.

mound, *n.* pile or heap. *v.* pile up.

mount, *n.* hill, mountain; setting, support; animal used for riding. *v.* increase; place on high; ascend; get up on; put on a support; start.

moun·tain, *n.* very high mass of earth rising above adjacent land. **moun·tain·ous**, *a.*

moun·tain·eer, *n.* inhabitant, climber of mountains.

moun·te·bank, *n.* boastful pretender.

mourn, *v.* grieve for; deplore. **mourn·er**, *n.* **mourn·ful**, *a.*

mourn·ing, *n.* expression of grief; customary clothes of mourners.

mouse, *n. pl.*, **mice.** small rodent; *inf.* timid person.

mouth, *n.* facial opening for food; opening. *v.* speak without understanding or sincerity.

mouth or·gan, *n.* harmonica.

mouth·piece, *n.* part held

against, close to, or in the mouth; spokesman.

move, *v.* (cause to) change place, posture; set in motion; rouse the feelings of; change position of a game piece; change residence; take action; progress. *n.* action taken; player's turn. **mov·er**, *n.* **mov·ing**, *a.* **mov·a·ble** (*also* **move·a·ble**), *a.*

move·ment, *n.* act of moving; strategic relocation; group working toward some goal; moving parts; part of a musical piece.

mov·ie, *n.* motion picture.

mow, *v.*, **mowed; mowed** or **mown; mow·ing.** cut down; kill.

Mr., *n. pl.*, **Messrs.** Mister: man's title.

Mrs., *n. pl.*, **Mmes.** married woman's title.

Ms., *n.* married or unmarried woman's title.

much, *adv.*, *a.*, **more, most.** (to a) great amount or extent, nearly. *n.* great quantity; important thing.

mu·ci·lage, *n.* gummy adhesive substance.

muck, *n.* manure; filth; dirt.

mu·cous, *a.* of or secreting a slimy substance.

mu·cus, *n.* viscid fluid secreted by mucous membranes.

mud, *n.* wet, soft earth. **mud·dy**, *a.*

mud·dle, *v.* mix up, think in a confused or bungling way. *n.* mess; confusion.

muff, *n.* tubular cover to warm hands; failure; inept action.

muf·fin, *n.* bread baked in single cup-shaped molds.

muf·fle, *v.* enfold or wrap; deaden the sound of.

muf·fler, *n.* neck scarf; sound-deadening device.

mug, *n.* drinking vessel; *inf.* face. *v. inf.* assault; grimace.

mug·gy, *a.* warm and humid.

mul·ber·ry, *n.* (fruit of) tree used for silkworm culture.

mulch, *n.* loose organic covering on ground around plantings.

mule, *n.* offspring of ass and mare.

mul·ti·far·i·ous, *a.* diverse.

mul·ti·ple, *a.* having many parts. *n.* number that can be divided by another number without a remainder.

mul-ti-plic-i-ty, n. great number.

mul-ti-ply, v. increase; add to itself any given number of times. **mul-ti-pli-ca-tion,** n.

mul-ti-tude, n. a great number; a crowd.

mul-ti-tu-di-nous, a. many.

mum, a. silent; chrysanthemum.

mum-ble, v. speak indistinctly.

mum-my, n. embalmed, dried human body.

mumps, n. disease consisting of swelling salivary glands along the neck.

munch, v. chew audibly.

mun-dane, a. earthly; routine.

mu-nic-i-pal, a. of a town or city.

mu-nic-i-pal-i-ty, n. urban district with local self-government.

mu-ni-tion, n. usu. pl. war materials.

mu-ral, n., a. (painting) on a wall.

mur-der, n. unlawful killing of one human by another with premeditated malice. **mur-der-ous,** a.

murk, mirk, n. darkness; gloom. **murk-y,** a. **-i-er, -i-est.**

mur-mur, n. low, continuous, indistinct sound; muttered complaint. v. utter indistinctly.

mus-cle, n. contractive tissue that produces bodily motion; strength. **mus-cu-lar,** a.

muse, v. think in silence; spirit that inspire artistic effort.

mu-se-um, n. building for exhibiting interesting objects of art, history, etc.

mush, n. boiled cornmeal; maudlin sentiment.

mush-room, n. fleshy fungi with stalk and umbrella-like cap. v. develop quickly.

mu-sic, n. arrangement of sounds into meaningful patterns, with pitch, harmony, rhythm; (sound of) a musical piece. **mu-si-cal,** a.

mu-si-cian, n. person skilled in music.

musk, n. strong-smelling secretion of male musk deer.

mus-ket, n. large-caliber, smoothbore firearm.

musk-mel-on, n. edible melon.

musk-rat, n. pl. **-rat, -rats.** large, aquatic rodent.

mus-lin, n. cotton fabric.

muss, n. inf. mess.

mus-sel, n. edible marine mollusk.

must, v. obliged, bound, or compelled to; to be supposed, certain. n. an essential.

mus-tache, n. hair growing on upper lip.

mus-tard, n. spicy paste or powder from seeds of mustard plant.

mus-ter, v. collect; assemble; bring together.

mus-ty, a. tasting or smelling moldy.

mute, a. silent; incapable of speech. n., v. (device) to deaden sound.

mu-ti-late, v. cut off a part; damage.

mu-ti-ny, n. revolt against authority. v. engage in mutiny.

mut-ter, v. utter in a low indistinct manner.

mut-ton, n. edible flesh of mature sheep.

mu-tu-al, a. equally given and received; shared alike.

muz-zle, n. projecting mouth, nose of an animal; open end of a firearm; restrictive mouth harness. v. put a muzzle on.

my, pron. possessive case of I.

my-o-pi-a, n. nearsightedness. **my-op-ic,** a.

myr-i-ad, n. a multitude.

myrrh, n. fragrant gum resin.

myr-tle, n. evergreen shrub.

my-self, pron. pl. **our-selves.** intensive or reflexive form of I.

mys-ter-y, n. secret, unexplained, unknown thing; story of such a thing. **mys-te-ri-ous,** a.

mys-tic, a. mysterious; occult. n. believer in mysticism. **mys-ti-cal,** a.

mys-ti-cism, n. a seeking to solve mysteries of existence by internal illumination or special revelation.

mys-ti-fy, v. perplex; bewilder. **mys-ti-fi-ca-tion,** n.

myth, n. fable or legend; invented story. **myth-ic, myth-i-cal,** a.

my-thol-o-gy, n. study of myths; myths collectively. **myth-o-log-i-cal,** a.

N

nab, v., **nabbed, nab-bing.** inf. catch suddenly; arrest.

na-dir, n. fig. lowest point; time of greatest depression.

nag, v., **nagged, nag·ging.** harass; discomfort. n. act of nagging; worthless horse.

nail, n. piece of metal for driving into wood, etc., to hold pieces together; thin, horny plate on the end of a finger or toe. v. fix with a nail. **nail·er,** n.

na·ive, na·ïve, a. having a simple or trusting nature. **na·ive·te, na·ïve·te,** n.

na·ked, a. bare of clothing or covering. **na·ked·ness,** n.

name, n. title or appellation; reputation. v., **named, nam·ing.** give a name to; specify. a. famous.

name·ly, adv. that is to say.

name·sake, n. one named for someone in particular.

nap, v., **napped, nap·ping.** have a short sleep. n. short sleep; woolly substance on the surface of cloth. **napped,** a.

nape, n. back part of the neck.

naph·tha, n. petroleum distillate used as a solvent or fuel.

nap·kin, n. piece of cloth or paper used at meals.

nar·cis·sism, n. self-love.

nar·cis·sus, n. pl., **-cis·sus·es, -cis·si.** ornamental, bulbous plant.

nar·cot·ic, n. substance which relieves pain and induces sleep. a. of or relating to narcotics.

nar·rate, v., **-rat·ed, -rat·ing.** tell; relate. **nar·ra·tor,** n. **nar·ra·tion,** n. **nar·ra·tive,** n., a.

nar·row, a. of little width; limited. v. limit; decrease in breadth. **nar·row·ness,** n.

na·sal, a. of the nose. phon. nasal speech sound.

na·stur·tium, n. pungent garden herbs.

nas·ty, a., **-ti·er, -ti·est.** dirty; indecent; mean. **nas·ti·ly,** adv. **nas·ti·ness,** n.

na·tal, a. of one's birth.

na·tion, n. people of a certain territory united by common political institutions. **na·tion·al,** a., n.

na·tion·al·ism, n. devotion to the interests and independence of one's nation. **na·tion·al·ist,** n.

na·tion·al·i·ty, n. pl., **-ties.** fact of belonging to a nation, or origin with respect to a nation.

na·tive, a. of the place of one's birth; conferred by birth; indigenous. n. one born in a place or country.

na·tiv·i·ty, n. pl., **-ties.** birth; (cap.), birth of Christ.

nat·ty, a., **-ti·er, -ti·est.** neatly dressed. **nat·ti·ness,** n.

nat·u·ral, a. of nature; not artificial; normal. **nat·u·ral·ly,** adv. **nat·u·ral·ness,** n.

nat·u·ral·ize, v., **-ized, -iz·ing.** confer the rights and privileges of a citizen upon. **nat·u·ral·i·za·tion,** n.

na·ture, n. instincts or inherent tendencies; kind or sort: universe with all its phenomena.

naught, n. nothing; arith. zero.

naugh·ty, a., **-ti·er, -ti·est.** bad; ill-behaved; not proper. **naugh·ti·ness,** n.

nau·sea, n. stomach upset; loathing. **nau·seous,** a.

nau·se·ate, v., **-at·ed, -at·ing.** sicken; affect with disgust. **nau·se·at·ing,** a.

nau·ti·cal, a. of seamanship.

na·val, a. of ships or for ships of war; maritime.

nave, n. middle part, lengthwise, of a church.

na·vel, n. scar in the middle of the abdomen.

nav·i·ga·ble, a. affording passage to ships.

nav·i·gate, v., **-gat·ed, -gat·ing.** travel on water in ships; plan the course of. **nav·i·ga·tion,** n. **nav·i·ga·tion·al,** a. **nav·i·ga·tor,** n.

na·vy, n. pl., **-vies.** all of a nation's military vessels; dark blue color. Also **na·vy blue.**

nay, adv. no; indeed. n. denial.

near, a. not far; close. adv. almost; closely. prep. close to. v. approach. **near·ness,** n.

near·by, a., adv. close at hand; near.

near·sight·ed, a. short-sighted. **near·sight·ed·ness,** n.

neat, a. tidy; simple and precise. **neat·ly,** adv. **neat·ness,** n.

neb·u·la, n. pl., **-las, -lae.** vast cloudlike interstellar mass. **neb·u·lous,** a.

nec·es·sar·y, a. inevitable; essential. n. pl., **-ies.** requisite.

ne·ces·si·tate, v., **-tat·ed, -ta·ting.** make necessary; compel or force.

ne·ces·si·ty, n. pl., **-ties.** need; that which is requisite.

neck, n. part connecting the head and trunk; narrow connecting or projecting part.

nec·ro·man·cy, *n.* witchcraft; sorcery. **nec·ro·man·cer**, *n.*

nec·tar, *n.* beverage; sweet fluid in the flower.

need, *n.* lack of something required; necessity; poverty. *v.* want; be obliged to.

nee·dle, *n.* slender, pointed instrument. *v.*, **-dled, -dling.** *inf.* annoy; tease. **nee·dler**, *n.*

need·less, *a.* not needed.

need·y, *a.*, **-i·er, -i·est.** poverty-stricken.

ne·far·i·ous, *a.* wicked.

ne·gate, *v.*, **-gat·ed, -gat·ing.** deny; nullify. **ne·ga·tion**, *n.*

neg·a·tive, *a.* expressing denial; lacking positive attributes; denoting a quantity less than zero. *n.* negative reply; *photog.* negative picture. *v.*, **-tived, -tiv·ing.** deny; veto. **neg·a·tive·ness**, *n.*

ne·glect, *v.* disregard; fail to perform. *n.* act or fact of neglecting. **ne·glect·ful**, *a.*

neg·li·gee, *n.* woman's dressing gown.

neg·li·gent, *a.* guilty of neglect; casual. **neg·li·gence**, *n.*

neg·li·gi·ble, *a.* unimportant.

ne·go·ti·ate, *v.*, **-at·ed, -at·ing.** confer in order to reach an agreement; conduct; arrange for; transfer; sell. **ne·go·ti·a·ble**, *a.* **ne·go·ti·a·tion, ne·go·ti·a·tor,** *n.*

neigh, *v.* utter the cry of a horse. *n.* whinny.

neigh·bor, *n.* one who lives near another. *a.* adjoining. *v.* adjoin. **neigh·bor·ing, neigh·bor·ly,** *a.* **neigh·bor·hood,** *n.*

nei·ther, *a., conj.* not either. *pron.* not the one or the other.

ne·on, *n.* inert gaseous element. *a.* pertaining to neon.

neph·ew, *n.* son of one's brother, sister, sister-in-law or brother-in-law.

nerve, *n.* fiber which conveys sensation and originates motion through the body; courage; *inf.* impudence.

nerv·ous, *a.* of nerves; easily agitated; tense.

nerv·y, *a.*, **-i·er, -i·est.** *inf.* arrogant; bold. **nerv·i·ness**, *n.*

nest, *n.* place used by a bird, insects, etc., for its eggs and the rearing of its young. *v.* build or have a nest.

nes·tle, *v.*, **-tled, -tling.** lie close and snug. **nes·tler**, *n.*

net, *n.* meshed fabric; net income, profits, etc. *v.*, **net·ted**, **net·ting.** ensnare; screen; yield as clear profit. *a.* left after all deductions.

neth·er·most, *a.* lowest.

net·ting, *n.* piece of network.

net·tle, *n.* herb with stinging hairs. *v.*, **-tled, -tling.** *fig.* irritate; vex.

net·work, *n.* interlacement of threads, etc.; intermingling of lines, etc.; *TV, radio.* series of broadcasting stations working as a unit.

neu·ral·gia, *n.* pain along the course of a nerve. **neu·ral·gic**, *a.*

neu·ri·tis, *n.* inflammation of a nerve. **neu·rit·ic**, *a., n.*

neu·ro·sis, *n. pl.*, **-ses.** functional nervous or emotional disorder. **neu·rot·ic**, *a., n.*

neu·ter, *a.* neither masculine nor feminine.

neu·tral, *a.* on neither side; indefinite; of a color, without a decided hue. *n.* person or nation that remains neutral. **neu·tral·i·ty**, *n.*

neu·tral·ize, *v.*, **-ized, -iz·ing.** declare neutral; render ineffective or counteract. **neu·tral·i·za·tion**, *n.*

neu·tron, *n.* uncharged particle in the nucleus of an atom.

nev·er, *adv.* not ever; at no time; absolutely not.

nev·er·the·less, *adv.* however; in spite of.

new, *a.* recently made, invented, etc.; unfamiliar; never in existence or use before; novel; starting afresh. *adv.* newly. *n.* something new. **new·ness**, *n.*

new·fan·gled, *a.* new-fashioned; of the newest design.

new·ly, *adv.* lately; recently.

new·ly·wed, *n.* recently married person.

news, *n. pl.* current information; recent intelligence.

news·y, *a.*, **-i·er, -i·est.** *inf.* full of news.

newt, *n.* salamander.

next, *a.* nearest in place, time, etc.; directly following. *adv.* at the time nearest. *prep.* adjoining.

nib·ble, *v.*, **-bled, -bling.** bite a little at a time. *n.* little morsel. **nib·bler**, *n.*

nice, *a.*, **nic·er, nic·est.** pleasing; kind; refined. **nice·ness**, *n.*

nice·ty, *n. pl., -ties. usu. pl.* delicate point; fine distinction.

niche, *n.* recess or hollow, as in a wall.

nick, *n.* notch, chip, etc., in a surface. *v.* make a nick in.

nick·el, *n.* hard silver-white metallic element; five-cent coin.

nick·name, *n.* familiar form of a proper name; substitute name. *v., -named, -nam·ing.* give a nickname to.

nic·o·tine, *n.* poisonous alkaloid, derived from tobacco. Also **nic·o·tin.**

niece, *n.* daughter of a brother or sister or of a brother-in-law or sister-in-law.

nig·gard, *n.* miser. *a.* stingy.

nigh, *v., adv., prep., a., nigh·er, nigh·est.* near.

night, *n.* time from sunset to sunrise. *a.* of night.

night·in·gale, *n.* singing bird of the thrush family.

night·ly, *a.* occurring at night; or every night. *adv.* by night.

night·mare, *n.* terrifying dream. **night·mar·ish,** *a.*

night·time, *n.* time between evening and morning.

nil, *n.* nothing.

nim·ble, *a., -bler, -blest.* quick; agile; quick-witted.

nine, *n.* number between eight and ten. *a.* one more than eight. **ninth,** *a., n.*

nine·teen, *n.* number which follows 18. *a.* one more than 18. **nine·teenth,** *a., n.*

nine·ty, *n. pl., -ties.* number which follows 89. *a.* one more than 89. **nine·ti·eth,** *a., n.*

nin·ny, *n. pl., -nies.* fool.

nip, *v., nipped, nip·ping.* pinch; take off; sip. *n.* pinch; biting quality; sip. **nip·per,** *n.*

nip·ple, *n.* protuberance on the breast.

ni·trate, *n.* salt of nitric acid. *v., -trat·ed, -trat·ing.* convert into a nitrate.

ni·tric ac·id, *n.* highly corrosive liquid.

ni·tro·gen, *n.* gaseous element essential to life.

ni·tro·glyc·er·in, *n.* flammable, explosive liquid.

nit-wit, *n.* stupid person.

no, *adv.* nay; not at all. *n. pl.,* **noes, nos.** denial. *a.* not any.

no·bil·i·ty, *n. pl., -ties.* body of noblemen; noble birth or rank.

no·ble, *a., -bler, -blest.* illustri-

ous; distinguished by birth, rank, or title. *n.* nobleman.

no·ble·man, *n. pl., -men.* **no·ble·ness,** *n.* **no·bly,** *adv.*

no·bod·y, *pron.* no one. *n. pl., -ies.* person of no standing.

noc·tur·nal, *a.* pertaining to the night; done at night.

nod, *v., nod·ded, nod·ding.* let the head sink from sleep; incline, as the head. *n.* quick downward motion of the head.

node, *n.* little knot or lump. **nod·u·lar,** *a.*

nod·ule, *n.* little knot or lump.

noise, *n.* din; sound. *v.,* **noised, nois·ing.** make a noise.

nois·y, *a., -i·er, -i·est.* making much noise; abounding in noise. **nois·i·ly,** *adv.*

no·mad, *n.* wanderer. *a.* nomadic. **no·mad·ic,** *a.* **no·mad·ism,** *n.*

nom·i·nal, *a.* being something in name only; named as a mere matter of form.

nom·i·nate, *v., -nat·ted, -nat·ing.* designate for an office; propose the name of. **nom·i·na·tion,** *n.* **nom·i·na·tor,** *n.*

nom·i·nee, *n.* person nominated.

non·cha·lant, *a.* coolly unconcerned. **non·cha·lance,** *n.*

non·com·mit·tal, *a.* not indicating commitment.

non·con·form·ist, *n.* one who does not conform to the norms of thought. **non·con·form·i·ty,** *n.*

non·de·script, *a.* defying description.

none, *pron.* no one; not one; not any. *adv.* not at all.

non·en·ti·ty, *n. pl., -ties.* person or thing without consequence.

non·pa·reil, *n.* person or thing of peerless excellence. *a.* without equal.

non·par·ti·san, *a.* not bound to a regular political party.

non·plus, *v., -plused, -plus·ing.* utterly baffle.

non·prof·it, *a.* not for profit.

non·sense, *n.* absurd words or ideas; meaningless actions or behavior. **non·sen·si·cal,** *a.*

non·stop, *a., adv.* with no stops on the way.

noo·dle, *n.* dried flour dough, usu. shaped in flat strips.

nook, *n.* corner; recess; secluded retreat.

noon, *n.* midday; twelve o'clock. **noon·time,** *n.*

no one, *pron.* nobody. Also **no·one.**

noose, *n.* loop with a running knot.

nor, *conj.* and not.

norm, *n.* rule; model; authoritative standard.

nor·mal, *a.* usual; average. *n.* standard. **nor·mal·cy**, **nor·mal·i·ty**, *n.* **nor·mal·ly**, *adv.*

north, *a., adv.* in, toward, or from the north. *n.* point or area lying to the right of a person facing the setting sun. **north·ern**, *a.* **north·ward**, *a., adv.*

north·east, *n.* point or region midway between north and east. *a., adv.* from, toward, or in the northeast. **north·east·ern**, *a.*

north·ern lights, *n. pl.* Aurora borealis.

north·west, *n.* point or region midway between north and west. *a., adv.* toward or from the northwest. **north·west·ern**, *a.*

nose, *n.* facial feature which contains the nostrils; sense of smell. *v.*, nosed, nos·ing. pry.

nos·tal·gia, *n.* longing to return to a past time; homesickness. **nos·tal·gic**, *a.*

nos·tril, *n.* aperture of the nose.

nos·y, *a.*, -i·er, -i·est. *inf.* prying. **nos·i·ness**, *n.*

not, *adv.* in no way at all; to no extent.

no·ta·ble, *a.* remarkable; famous. *n.* person or thing of note. **no·ta·bly**, *adv.*

no·ta·rize, *v.*, -rized, -riz·ing. authenticate or certify. **no·ta·ry**, *n. pl.*, -ries. Also **no·ta·ry pub·lic**.

no·ta·tion, *n.* act of noting down; note; system of signs or symbols. **no·ta·tion·al**, *a.*

notch, *n.* cut; V-shaped nick. *v.* cut a notch in. **notched**, *a.*

note, *n. often pl.* memorandum; short statement; notice; *mus.* written character; tone. *v.*, not·ed, not·ing. heed; set down in writing. **not·er**, *n.*

not·ed, *a.* notable; celebrated.

note·wor·thy, *a.* significant.

noth·ing, *n.* not anything; naught; nonentity. *adv.* not at all.

no·tice, *n.* announcement; warning; attention; brief review. *v.*, -ticed, -tic·ing. become aware of. **no·tice·a·ble**, *a.*

no·ti·fy, *v.*, -fied, -fy·ing. give notice to. **no·ti·fi·ca·tion**, *n.*

no·tion, *n.* general concept; view; whim; *pl.* small useful articles.

no·to·ri·ous, *a.* widely known. **no·to·ri·e·ty**, *n.*

not·with·stand·ing, *prep.* in spite of. *adv.* nevertheless. *conj.* although.

nought, *n., a., adv.* naught.

noun, *n.* word that denotes a person, place, or thing.

nour·ish, *v.* feed and cause to grow. **nour·ish·ment**, *n.*

nov·el, *n.* long, fictitious prose narrative. *a.* of a new kind; unusual. **nov·el·ist**, *n.*

nov·el·ty, *n. pl.*, -ties. newness; something novel.

No·vem·ber, *n.* eleventh month.

nov·ice, *n.* beginner.

now, *adv.* at the present time or moment. *conj.* since.

no·where, *adv.* in, at, or to no place *n.* no place.

noz·zle, *n.* projecting spout of something.

nub, *n.* knob.

nu·cle·ar, *a.* of a nucleus.

nu·cle·us, *n. pl.*, -us·es, -i. central part, esp. of living cells, atoms, etc.

nude, *a.* naked. *n.* naked figure. **nu·di·ty**, *n.* **nud·ist**, *n.*

nudge, *n.* gentle poke. *v.*, nudged, nudg·ing. jog.

nug·get, *n.* lump, esp. of gold.

nui·sance, *n.* something or someone annoying; pest.

null, *a.* invalid.

nul·li·fy, *v.*, -fied, -fy·ing. make null.

numb, *a.* without physical sensation. *v.* make numb. **numb·ly**, *adv.* **numb·ness**, *n.* **numb·ing**, *a.*

num·ber, *n.* word or symbol used in counting or to denote a total; single performance; *pl.* numerical strength. *v.* enumerate. **num·ber·less**, *a.*

nu·mer·al, *n.* figure or word expressing a number.

nu·mer·a·tor, *n.* term above the line in a fraction.

nu·mer·i·cal, *a.* of a number or numbers.

nu·mer·ous, *a.* very many.

num·skull, *n.* dunce.

nun, *n.* woman devoted to a religious life.

nun·ner·y, *n. pl.*, -ies. convent in which nuns reside.

nup·tial, *a.* of marriage. *n. usu. pl.* wedding.

nurse, *n.* one who tends the sick, esp. one who has undergone training; *v.,* **nursed, nurs·ing.** suckle; try to cure.

nurs·er·y, *n. pl.,* **-ies.** area set apart for children; place where trees, plants, etc., are raised.

nur·ture, *n.* education; nourishes. *v.,* **-tured, -tur·ing.** nourish; train or bring up.

nut, *n.* edible kernel enclosed in a shell.

nut·meg, *n.* aromatic seed used as a spice.

nu·tri·ent, *a.* nourishing. *n.* substance which nourishes.

nu·tri·tion, *n.* act by which organisms absorb food into their systems.

nu·tri·tious, *a.* nourishing.

nut·ty, *a.,* **-ti·er, -ti·est.** producing nuts; tasting of nuts; *inf.* crazy. **nut·ti·ness,** *n.*

nuz·zle, *v.,* **-zled, -zling.** thrust the nose; nestle.

ny·lon, *n.* synthetic, thermoplastic substance; *pl.* sheer hosiery made of nylon.

nymph, *n.* inferior divinity, conceived as a beautiful maiden. **nym·phal,** *a.*

O

oaf, *n.* stupid dolt.

oak, *n.* tree with hard, durable wood. *a.* of oak. **oak·en,** *a.*

oar, *n.* shaft with a blade used to row a boat.

o·a·sis, *n. pl.,* **o·a·ses.** fertile area in the desert.

oat, *n. usu. pl.* cereal grass cultivated for its edible grain. **oat·en,** *a.*

oath, *n. pl.,* **oaths.** solemn appeal to of the truth of a statement; curse.

oat·meal, *n.* cooked cereal made from rolled oats.

ob·du·rate, *a.* indifferent to human feelings; stubborn.

o·be·di·ence, *n.* act or habit of obeying; compliance. **o·be·di·ent,** *a.*

o·bese, *a.* fat. **o·bes·i·ty,** *n.*

o·bey, *v.* comply with the commands of. **o·bey·er,** *n.*

o·bit·u·ar·y, *n. pl.,* **-ies.** death notice.

ob·ject, *n.* visible and tangible thing; that to which efforts are directed; aim; end. *v.* be adverse to; voice disapproval. **ob·jec·tion,** *n.*

ob·jec·tive, *a.* dealing with externals rather than thoughts or feelings. *n.* something aimed at. **ob·jec·tiv·i·ty,** *n.*

ob·li·gate, *v.,* **-gat·ed, -gat·ing.** bind morally or legally. *a.* bound. **ob·li·ga·tion,** *n.* **ob·li·ga·to·ry,** *a.*

o·blige, *v.,* **-bliged, -blig·ing.** constrain; compel; bind by some favor done. **o·blig·ing,** *a.*

o·blique, *a.* slanting; indirect. **ob·lique·ly,** *adv.*

ob·lit·er·ate, *v.,* **-at·ed, -at·ing.** erase; destroy any sign of. **ob·lit·er·a·tion,** *n.*

o·bliv·i·on, *n.* condition of forgetting or of being forgotten.

o·bliv·i·ous, *a.* forgetful; unaware. **ob·liv·i·ous·ness,** *n.*

ob·long, *a.* longer than. *n.* oblong figure.

ob·nox·ious, *a.* odious; offensive. **ob·nox·ious·ness,** *n.*

o·boe, *n.* double-reed wooden wind instrument. **o·bo·ist,** *n.*

ob·scene, *a.* indecent. **ob·scen·i·ty,** *n. pl.,* **-ties.**

ob·scure, *a.,* **-scur·er, -scur·est.** not clear; remote; unnoticed; dim. *v.,* **ob·scured, ob·scur·ing.** make dark or dim. **ob·scu·ri·ty,** *n. pl.,* **-ties.**

ob·ser·vance, *n.* action of observing, conforming to etc.; ceremony or rite.

ob·ser·va·to·ry, *n. pl.,* **-ries.** place used for making observations of natural phenomena.

ob·serve, *v.,* **-served, -serv·ing.** watch; keep or adhere to; remark. **ob·ser·vant,** *a.,* *n.* **ob·ser·va·tion,** *n.* **ob·serv·er,** *n.*

ob·sess, *v.* preoccupy the mind. **ob·ses·sive,** *a.* **ob·ses·sion,** *n.*

ob·so·les·cent, *a.* becoming obsolete. **ob·so·les·cence,** *n.*

ob·so·lete, *a.* fallen into disuse; out-of-date.

ob·sta·cle, *n.* obstruction or impediment.

ob·sti·nate, *a.* fixed firmly in resolution; stubborn. **ob·sti·na·cy,** *n. pl.,* **-cies.**

ob·struct, *v.* block; hinder; impede. **ob·struc·tion,** *n.*

ob·tain, *v.* get, acquire.

ob·tuse, *a.* not acute; blunt.

ob·vi·ate, *v.,* **-at·ed, -at·ing.** overcome.

ob·vi·ous, *a.* easily seen or understood; evident.

oc·ca·sion, *n.* time of an event, or the event itself; incidental cause, motive, etc. *v.* cause; bring about.

oc·ca·sion·al, *a.* occurring at times; intended for use as the need arises.

oc·cult, *a.* kept secret; of magic. **oc·cult·ism**, *n.*

oc·cu·pan·cy, *n. pl.*, **-cies.** act of occupying. **oc·cu·pant**, *n.*

oc·cu·pa·tion, *n.* one's principal employment; act of occupying. **oc·cu·pa·tion·al**, *a.*

oc·cu·py, *v.*, **-pied**, **-py·ing.** take and keep possession of; take up; employ; fill; inhabit.

oc·cur, *v.*, **-curred**, **-cur·ring.** suggest or come to the mind; befall; happen. **oc·cur·rence**, *n.*

o·cean, *n.* immense body of salt water. **o·ce·an·ic**, *a.*

o'clock, *adv.* of or by the clock.

oc·ta·gon, *n.* figure with eight sides and eight angles. **oc·tag·o·nal**, *a.*

oc·tave, *n. mus.* tone on the eighth degree from a given tone; stanza of eight lines.

Oc·to·ber, *n.* tenth month.

oc·to·pus, *n.* cephalopod having eight arms.

oc·u·lar, *a.* of the eye.

oc·u·list, *n.* ophthalmologist.

odd, *a.* singular; strange; remaining over; as a number, opposed to *even*; secluded. **odd·ly**, *adv.* **odd·ness**, *n.*

odd·i·ty, *n. pl.*, **-ties.** peculiarity.

odds, *n. pl.* probability ratio; difference in favor.

ode, *n.* poem. **o·dic**, *a.*

o·di·ous, *a.* arousing hatred or extreme dislike. **o·di·ous·ly**, *adv.* **o·di·ous·ness**, *n.*

o·dor, *n.* scent. **o·dored**, *a.* **o·dor·less**, *a.* **o·dor·ous**, *a.*

o'er, *adv.*, *prep.* over.

of, *prep.* at; by; on; due to; composed of; concerning.

off, *adv.* away; absent from. *a.* no longer operating; distant; odd. *prep.* away from; by means of. *int.* go away.

of·fal, *n.* entrails; refuse.

off·beat, *a. inf.* unusual; unexpected; mistaken.

of·fend, *v.* make angry; insult. **of·fend·er**, *n.*

of·fense, *n.* crime or sin; assault. **of·fen·sive**, *a.*, *n.*

of·fer, *v.* present for acceptance or rejection; volunteer; inflict;

bid. *n.* act of offering; that which is offered. **of·fer·ing**, *n.*

off·hand, *a.*, *adv.* extemporaneously; casual or curt. Also **off·hand·ed.**

of·fice, *n.* place where business is conducted; position in an organization; function entrusted to a person.

of·fic·er, *n.* person holding a title, office, or post of authority.

of·fi·cial, *a.* derived from the proper authority. *n.* one invested with an office. **of·fi·cial·ism**, *n.*

of·fi·cious, *a.* excessively forward in kindness; meddling.

off·set, *v.*, **-set**, **-set·ting.** equalize; compensate. *n.* start; offshoot.

off·shoot, *n.* anything proceeding from a main source.

off·spring, *n. pl.*, **-spring**, **-springs.** children; descendant.

off-the-cuff, *a. inf.* impromptu.

oft, *adv. poet.* often.

of·ten, *adv.* frequently; repeatedly.

of·ten·times, *adv.* frequently; often. Also **oft·times.**

o·gle, *v.*, **o·gled**, **o·gling.** eye; stare. **o·gler**, *n.*

o·gre, *n.* legendary monster who devoured human flesh; evil person.

oil, *n.* unctuous, combustible liquid; petroleum. *v.* anoint with oil; lubricate.

oil·cloth, *n.* cloth waterproofed with oil.

oil·skin, *n.* cotton fabric waterproofed with oil.

oil·y, *a.*, **-i·er**, **-i·est.** of or consisting of oil; greasy.

oint·ment, *n.* unguent; salve.

O.K., *a.*, *adv.* all right; correct. *v.*, **O.K.'d**, **O.K.'ing.** endorse; agree. *n.* approval. Also **OK**, **o·kay.**

old, *a.*, **old·er** or **eld·er**; **old·est** or **eld·est.** having lived, existed, etc., long ago; of great age. *n.* earlier time. **old·en**, *a.* **old·ness**, *n.*

old-fash·ioned, *a.* antiquated; out-of-date.

old·ster, *n. inf.* old person.

old-time, *a.* part of old times; long-lasting.

o·le·o, *n.* oleomargarine.

o·le·o·mar·ga·rine, *n.* substitute for butter.

ol·fac·tion, *n.* act of smelling; sense of smell. **ol·fac·to·ry**, *a.*, *n. pl.*, **-ries.**

ol·ive, *n.* evergreen tree; its fruit, valuable as a source of oil. *a.* of a dull, yellowish-green color.

om·buds·man, *n. pl.*, **-men.** official who investigates complaints of citizens against the government.

om·e·let, om·e·lette, *n.* beaten eggs fried until set.

o·men, *n.* sign or augury. *v.* foretell.

om·i·nous, *a.* betokening or threatening evil.

o·mis·sion, *n.* act of leaving out; something left out.

o·mit, *v.*, **o·mit·ted, o·mit·ting.** neglect; fail to do; leave out.

om·ni·bus, *n. pl.*, **-bus·es.** bus. *a.* referring to a number of objects at once.

om·nip·o·tence, *n.* unlimited or infinite power. **om·nip·o·tent,** *a.* **om·nip·o·tent·ly,** *adv.*

om·nis·cience, *n.* faculty of knowing everything. **om·nis·cient,** *a.*

om·niv·o·rous, *a.* eating both plant and animal foods. **om·ni·vore,** *n.*

on, *prep.* upon; based; at the time of; directed toward; with respect to. *adv.* forward; with continuous procedure. *a.* being in action; near.

once, *adv.* single time; at any time; formerly. *a.* former. *conj.* if ever. *n.* one time.

on·com·ing, *n.* approach. *a.* approaching.

one, *a.* being but a single object, unit, etc.; being in accord; undivided. *n.* first cardinal number; single person or thing. *pron.* single person or thing. **one·ness,** *n.*

on·er·ous, *a.* burdensome; oppressive. **on·er·ous·ness,** *n.*

one·self, *pron.* someone's own self. Also **one's self.**

one-sid·ed, *a.* having but one side; partial, unjust. **one-sid·ed·ness,** *n.*

one-time, *a., adv.* former.

on·ion, *n.* edible bulb with a strong pungent odor and taste. **on·ion·y,** *a.*

on·look·er, *n.* spectator.

on·ly, *adv.* for one purpose alone; merely; simply; just. *a.* single. *conj.* but.

on·set, *n.* attack; beginning; outset.

on·slaught, *n.* furious onset.

on·to, *prep.* to a place or position on; upon.

o·nus, *n.* burden.

on·ward, *a., adv.* forward. Also **on·wards.**

on·yx, *n.* agate with layers of chalcedony. *a.* black.

ooze, *n.* soft mud or slime; gentle flow. *v.*, **oozed, ooz·ing.** filter through pores; exude slowly. **oo·zi·ness,** *n.* **oo·zy,** *a.*, **-zi·er, -zi·est.**

o·pal, *n.* iridescent gem of hydrous silica.

o·paque, *a.* impermeable to light; dull; obscure. **o·pac·i·ty,** *n. pl.*, **-ties.**

o·pen, *a.* not closed; not enclosed; accessible; unfilled; candid; spread out. *v.* make accessible; clear of obstructions; set in action, begin, etc. *n.* outdoors. **o·pen·er,** *n.* **o·pen·ly,** *adv.* **o·pen·ness,** *n.*

o·pen-eyed, *a.* having the eyes open; aware.

o·pen-hand·ed, *a.* generous.

o·pen·ing, *n.* making or becoming open; aperture; start.

o·pen-mind·ed, *a.* unprejudiced.

o·pen·work, *n.* ornamental work, of wood, lace, etc., having openings.

op·er·a, *n.* drama set to music and sung, acted, etc. **op·er·at·ic,** *a.*

op·er·ate, *v.*, **-at·ed, -at·ing.** work, act, or function; perform an operation; control; effect. **op·er·a·tion,** *n.* **op·er·a·tive,** *a., n.* **op·er·a·tor,** *n.*

op·er·et·ta, *n.* short, often humorous opera.

o·pi·ate, *n.* medicine that contains opium; *inf.* narcotic. *a.* narcotic.

o·pine, *v.*, **opined,** **o·pin·ing.** think; state an opinion.

o·pin·ion, *n.* judgment or belief.

o·pin·ion·at·ed, *a.* obstinate in opinion; dogmatic.

o·pi·um, *n.* poisonous, narcotic, addictive alkaloid.

o·pos·sum, *n.* nocturnal mammal carrying its young in a pouch.

op·po·nent, *n.* adversary. *a.* opposing.

op·por·tune, *a.* suitable; well-timed; timely. **op·por·tune·ly,** *adv.*

op·por·tu·ni·ty, *n. pl.*, **-ties.** appropriate time; favorable position or chance.

op·pose, v., **-posed**, **-pos·ing**. act against; resist; combat. **op·pos·er**, n. **op·po·si·tion**, n.

op·po·site, a. situated on opposed sides of; contrary. n. one who or that which is contrary. adv. in an opposite direction. prep. facing. **op·po·site·ness**, n.

op·press, v. tyrannize; suppress; depress. **op·pres·sor**, n. **op·pres·sion**, n. **op·pres·sive**, a.

opt, v. choose.

op·tic, a. referring to sight or the eye.

op·ti·cal, a. of sight; visual; constructed to assist the sight. **op·ti·cal·ly**, adv.

op·ti·cian, n. one' who makes eyeglasses.

op·ti·mism, n. inclination to emphasize the happy aspect of anything. **op·ti·mist**, n.

op·tion, n. power of choice; thing chosen or elected. **op·tion·al**, a. **op·tion·al·ly**, adv.

op·tom·e·try, n. examination of the eyes and the prescribing of glasses. **op·to·met·ric**, a. **op·tom·e·trist**, n.

op·u·lent, a. yielding riches; richly or abundantly supplied. **op·u·lence**, n.

o·pus, n. pl., **o·pe·ra**, **o·pus·es**. literary work; musical composition.

or, conj. word used to connect alternative or equivalent terms.

or·a·cle, n. revelation, or the one who does such revealing. **o·rac·u·lar**, a.

o·ral, a. of the mouth; spoken. **o·ral·ly**, adv.

or·ange, n. round reddishyellow edible fruit. a. reddish-yellow.

or·ange·ade, n. drink of orange juice and sweetened water.

o·ra·tion, n. speech.

or·a·tor, n. public speaker. **or·a·tor·i·cal**, a.

or·a·to·ry, n. art of an orator.

orb, n. sphere or globe.

or·bit, n. path along which a planet moves. v. circle around. **or·bit·al**, a.

or·chard, n. land devoted to the raising of fruit trees.

or·ches·tra, n. company of performers on musical instruments; space reserved for them. **or·ches·tral**, a.

or·chid, n. plant with showy, colorful flowers. a. light purple.

or·dain, v. confer holy orders upon; decree.

or·deal, n. severe trial; strict test.

or·der, n. proper arrangement or state; rank; command; kind. v. arrange; regulate; direct to be made, supplied, etc.; issue orders. **or·dered**, a.

or·der·ly, a. arranged in order; not unruly. adv. in regular sequence. n. pl., **-lies**. attendant. **or·der·li·ness**, n.

or·di·nance, n. law; edict.

or·di·nar·i·ly, adv. usually.

or·di·nar·y, a. customary, usual, or normal.

ord·nance, n. artillery.

ore, n. metal-bearing mineral or rock, or a native metal.

or·gan, n. musical instrument of pipes, keyboards, etc.; part of organisms having some specific function.

or·gan·dy, **or·gan·die**, n. translucent, stiff muslin.

or·gan·ic, a. of the organs of an animal or plant; systematic; of carbon compounds. **or·gan·i·cal·ly**, adv.

or·gan·ism, n. life form.

or·gan·ize, v., **-ized**, **-iz·ing**. systematize; unionize; combine in an organized company, party, etc. **or·gan·i·za·tion**, n. **or·gan·iz·er**, n.

or·gy, n. pl., **or·gies**. drunken, licentious revelry.

o·ri·ent, n. east; (cap.) countries in the east. v. adjust with relation to surroundings, facts, etc.; find the bearings of. **O·ri·en·tal**, a.

o·ri·en·tate, v., **-tat·ed**, **-tat·ing**. orient. **o·ri·en·ta·tion**, n.

or·i·gin, n. beginning; source.

o·rig·i·nal, a. of the origin of something; created by one's own thought and imagination; inventive. n. original work. **o·rig·i·nal·i·ty**, n. **o·rig·i·nal·ly**, adv.

o·rig·i·nate, v., **-nat·ed**, **-nat·ing**. initiate; invent. **o·rig·i·na·tion**, n. **o·rig·i·na·tor**, n.

or·na·ment, n. adornment; decoration. v. furnish with ornaments. **or·na·men·ta·tion**, n.

or·nate, a. adorned; much embellished. **or·nate·ness**, n.

or·ni·thol·o·gy, n. study of birds.

or·ni·thol·o·gist, n.

or·phan, n. child who has lost through death his parents. v. reduce to the state of an orphan. **or·phan·age**, n.

or·tho·dox, a. sound or correct; conventional. **or·tho·dox·y**, n. pl., **-ies.**

os·cil·late, v., **-lat·ed**, **-lat·ing.** swing to and fro; vibrate. **os·cil·la·tion**, **os·cil·la·tor**, n. **os·cil·la·to·ry**, a.

os·cu·late, v., **-lat·ed**, **-lat·ing.** kiss. **os·cu·la·tion**, n.

os·mo·sis, n. tendency of a solution to pass through a membrane; gradual absorption. **os·mot·ic**, a.

os·si·fy, v., **-fied**, **-fy·ing.** form into bone or like bone.

os·ten·si·ble, a. professed or pretended; apparent. **os·ten·si·bly**, adv.

os·ten·ta·tion, n. pretentious display. **os·ten·ta·tious**, a.

os·tra·cize, v., **-cized**, **-ciz·ing.** banish; exclude. **os·tra·cism**, n.

os·trich, n. large flightless bird.

oth·er, a. being the remaining one; additional or further; different. pron. other one; another. adv. otherwise.

oth·er·wise, adv. differently; in other respects. a. other.

ot·ter, n. aquatic mammal.

ot·to·man, n. divan or sofa.

ouch, int. exclamation of sudden pain.

ought, aux. v. have a moral obligation; be correct or advisable; be assumed as likely.

ounce, n. one-sixteenth of a pound; fluid ounce.

our, pron. a. poss. case of **we**.

ours, pron. belonging to us; poss. form of **we**.

our·selves, pron. pl. reflexive or emphatic form of **we**.

oust, v. eject; forcibly remove.

out, adv. forth from; away from; into or in existence or activity. prep. outside of. int. begone. a. left exposed; lacking; senseless; removed from; extinguished. n. escape valve. v. go or come out.

out·bid, v., **-bid**, **-bid·den**, **-bid·ding.** bid more than.

out·brave, v., **-braved**, **-brav·ing.** surpass in bravery; confront.

out·break, n. sudden manifestation; riot.

out·burst, n. sudden, forceful breaking out; spurt.

out·cast, n. one who is cast out; exile. a. rejected.

out·come, n. issue; result.

out·cry, n. pl., **-cries.** loud cry; clamor.

out·dated, a. rendered obsolete.

out·do, v., **out·did**, **out·done**, **out·do·ing.** excel; surpass.

out·door, a. being or for the open air.

out·doors, adv. out of the house; in the open air.

out·er, a. external.

out·er·most, a. being the most distant.

out·face, v., **-faced**, **-fac·ing.** confront; defy; brave.

out·fit, n. assemblage of articles for equipping; ensemble of clothing; inf. body of persons associated as a unit. v., **-fit·ted**, **-fit·ting.** equip. **out·fit·ter**, n.

out·fox, v. outsmart.

out·go, v., **out·went**, **out·gone**, **out·go·ing.** excel; surpass. n. pl. **out·goes.** expenditure. **out·go·ing**, a., n.

out·grow, v., **-grew**, **-grown**, **-grow·ing.** surpass in growing; grow too large for; leave behind.

out·growth, n. offshoot; natural development or result.

out·ing, n. excursion; airing.

out·land·ish, a. bizarre; foreign.

out·law, n. criminal. v. prohibit. **out·law·ry**, n.

out·lay, n. disbursement. v., **-laid**, **-lay·ing.** spend, as money.

out·let, n. place or opening by which anything is let out.

out·line, n. contour; sometimes pl. sketch of a plan. v., **-lined**, **-lin·ing.** draw the outline of; give the main features of.

out·live, v., **-lived**, **-liv·ing.** survive longer than.

out·look, n. one's mental view; prospect.

out·mod·ed, a. obsolete.

out·num·ber, v. be greater in number.

out-of-date, a. obsolete.

out·put, n. production; yield.

out·rage, n. wanton transgression; enormous insult. v., **-raged**, **-rag·ing.** wantonly abuse; rape. **out·ra·geous**, a.

out·rank, v. rank above.

out·right, adv. completely; entirely; openly. a. complete; downright.

out·sell, v., **-sold**, **-sell·ing.** outdo

in selling.

out·set, *n.* setting out; beginning.

out·shine, *v.,* **-shone, -shin·ing.** shine more brightly than.

out·side, *n.* external parts; space immediately without. *a.* external; only remotely possible. *adv.* on or toward the outside. *prep.* to or on the external side of.

out·sid·er, *n.* one not of a set group.

out·skirts, *n. pl.* border district.

out·smart, *v.* outwit.

out·spo·ken, *a.* free or bold in speech.

out·stand·ing, *a.* prominent; eminent; unpaid.

out·ward, *a.* exterior; obvious; turned away from the inside. Also **out·wards.**

out·wear, *v.,* **-wore, -worn, -wear·ing.** last longer than.

out·wit, *v.,* **-wit·ted, -wit·ting.** prove too clever for; trick.

o·val, *a.* of the shape of an egg. *n.* elliptical figure.

o·va·ry, *n. pl.,* **-ries.** female reproductive gland.

o·va·tion, *n.* enthusiastic public reception of a person.

ov·en, *n.* chamber for baking, heating, or drying.

o·ver, *prep.* above; higher up than; in preference to; upon; across. *adv.* so as to bring the upper side under; remaining; from an upright to a prone position. *a.* upper; higher up; extra; completed or past.

o·ver·all, *a.* covering or including everything.

o·ver·awe, *v.,* **-awed, -aw·ing.** restrain by awe, fear, etc.

o·ver·bear·ing, *a.* domineering; arrogant.

o·ver·board, *adv.* over the side of a ship or boat.

o·ver·cast, *v.* darken; cover with gloom. *a.* cloudy; gloomy.

o·ver·charge, *v.,* **-charged, -charg·ing.** charge too high a sum; overload.

o·ver·coat, *n.* topcoat.

o·ver·come, *v.,* **-came, -come, -com·ing.** conquer; surmount; lay low. **o·ver·com·er,** *n.*

o·ver·do, *v.,* **-did, -done, -do·ing.** do to excess; overact.

o·ver·dose, *n.* too great a dose.

o·ver·due, *a.* past the time of payment; belated; delayed.

o·ver·es·ti·mate, *v.,* **-mat·ed,**

-mat·ing. overvalue. **o·ver·es·ti·ma·tion,** *n.*

o·ver·flow, *v.,* **-flowed, -flown, -flow·ing.** flow or spread over. *n.* inundation; superabundance.

o·ver·grow, *v.,* **-grew, -grown, -grow·ing.** cover with growth; grow beyond natural size. **o·ver·growth,** *n.*

o·ver·haul, *v.* repair or restore. *n.* examination and thorough repair.

o·ver·head, *a.* aloft; above one's head. *adv.* over; above. *n.* certain business expenses.

o·ver·hear, *v.,* **-heard, -hear·ing.** hear, thought not intended to hear.

o·ver·joy, *v.* give great joy to. **o·ver·joyed,** *a.*

o·ver·land, *a.* by land. *adv.* across, upon, or by means of land.

o·ver·lap, *v.,* **-lapped, -lap·ping.** extend over; lap over. *n.* overlapping.

o·ver·look, *v.* fail to notice; ignore; look over. *n.* land commanding a view.

o·ver·ly, *adv.* overmuch; too.

o·ver·night, *adv.* through or during the night; suddenly. *a.* made for nighttime use.

o·ver·pow·er, *v.* vanquish; subdue. **o·ver·pow·er·ing,** *a.*

o·ver·rate, *v.,* **-rat·ed, -rat·ing.** rate too favorably.

o·ver·ride, *v.,* **-rode, -rid·den, -rid·ing.** ride over; supersede; annul.

o·ver·rule, *v.,* **-ruled, -rul·ing.** exercise rule over; prevail over; rule against.

o·ver·run, *v.,* **-ran, -run, -run·ing.** swarm over; spread or grow rapidly over; exceed.

o·ver·seas, *adv.* abroad. *a.* beyond the sea. Also **over·sea.**

o·ver·see, *v.,* **-saw, -seen, -see·ing.** superintend. **o·ver·se·er,** *n.*

o·ver·shoe, *n.* outer waterproof shoe or boot.

o·ver·sight, *n.* mistake of omission; watchful care.

o·ver·sleep, *v.,* **-slept, -sleep·ing.** sleep beyond or through.

o·ver·spread, *v.,* **-spread, -spread·ing.** extend over; cover completely.

o·ver·state, *v.,* **-stat·ed, -stat·ing.** exaggerate. **o·ver·state·ment,** *n.*

o·ver·step, *v.,* **-stepped, -step·ping.** step over; exceed.

o·vert, *a.* open to view; public. **o·vert·ly,** *adv.*

o·ver·take, *v.,* **-took, -tak·en, -tak·ing.** come upon or catch up with.

o·ver·tax, *v.* oppress with taxes; make excessive demands on.

o·ver·throw, *v.,* **-threw, -thrown, -throw·ing.** cast down; upset. *n.* defeat.

o·ver·time, *n.* time one works beyond regular hours; payment for overtime. *a.,* *adv.* of, during, or for overtime.

o·ver·ture, *n.* introductory orchestral composition; proposal; offer.

o·ver·turn, *v.* turn over; overthrow; capsize.

o·ver·weight, *n.* extra weight. *a.* weighing more than normal.

o·ver·whelm, *v.* submerge; overcome

o·ver·work, *v.,* **-worked** or **-wrought, -work·ing.** use to excess; toil excessively. *n.* excessive work. **o·ver·wrought,** *a.*

o·vum, *n., pl.,* **o·va.** egg.

owe, *v.,* **owed, ow·ing.** be in debt or beholden for.

owl, *n.* large-headed, nocturnal bird of prey. **owl·ish,** *a.*

own, *a.* belonging to oneself. *v.* possess; admit. **own·er,** *n.*

ox, *n. pl.,* **ox·en.** animal of the bovine kind; castrated bull.

ox·ford, *n.* low shoe, usu. laced over the instep.

ox·ide, *n.* compound of oxygen with another element.

ox·i·dize, *v.,* **-diz·ed, -diz·ing.** convert into an oxide. **ox·i·da·tion,** *n.* **ox·i·dant,** *n.*

ox·y·gen, *n.* colorless, odorless, gaseous element.

oys·ter, *n.* edible marine bivalve mollusk.

o·zone, *n.* form of oxygen.

P

pa, *n. Inf.* father.

pab·u·lum, *n.* food.

pace, *n.* single step; tempo; gait. *v.,* **paced, pac·ing.** regulate; amble. **pac·er,** *n.*

pace·mak·er, *n.* one who sets the pace; instrument for regulating heartbeat.

pa·cif·ic, *a.* peaceable.

pa·cif·i·ca·tion, *n.* appeasement. **pa·cif·i·ca·tor,** *n.* **pa·cif·i·ca·to·ry,** *a.*

pac·i·fism, *n.* principle of peace without war. **pac·i·fist,** *n.*

pac·i·fy, *v.,* **-fied, -fy·ing.** make peaceful; calm.

pack, *n.* bundle; fixed quantity of something; a group of things or persons. *v.* fill; carry; send off.

pack·age, *n.* container. *v.* bundle. **pack·ag·er,** *n.*

pack·er, *n.* one who packs.

pack·et, *n.* small pack.

pact, *n.* contract.

pad, *n.* cushion. *v.,* **pad·ded, pad·ding.** stuff; walk softly.

pad·dle, *n.* short oar. *v.,* **-dled, -dling.** row gently; spank. **pad·dler,** *n.*

pad·dock, *n.* enclosed area for animals.

pad·dy, *n., pl.,* **-dies.** rice field.

pad·lock, *n.* portable lock.

pae·an, pe·an, *n.* song of triumph.

pa·gan, *n.* heathen. **pa·gan·ism,** *n.*

page, *n.* leaf of a book; youthful attendant. *v.,* **paged, pag·ing.** number the pages.

pag·eant, *n.* spectacular show.

pag·i·nate, *v.,* **-nat·ed, -nat·ing.** number the pages.

pa·go·da, *n.* temple.

pail, *n.* bucket. Also **pail·ful.**

pain, *n.* physical or emotional ache. *v.* cause distress; suffer. **pain·ful, pain·less,** *a.* **pain·less·ness,** *n.*

pain·kil·ler, *n. Inf.* pain reliever.

pains·tak·ing, *a.* careful labor. *a.* **pains·tak·ing·ly,** *adv.*

paint, *v.* makes pictures; cover with paint. *n.* pigment. **paint·er,** *n.* **paint·ing,** *n.*

pair, *n., pl.,* **pairs, pair.** two of a sort. *v.* match.

pa·jam·as, *n. pl.* garment worn for sleeping.

pal·ace, *n.* splendid residence.

pal·at·a·ble, *a.* savory. **pal·at·a·bil·i·ty,** *n.* **pal·at·a·bly,** *adv.*

pal·ate, *n.* roof of the mouth; taste.

pa·la·tial, *a.* like a palace. **pa·la·tial·ly,** *adv.*

pa·lav·er, *n.* idle talk. *v.* flatter. *v.i.* to talk.

pale, *a.* wan; feeble. *v.,* **paled, pal·ing.** turn pale. **pale·ly,** *adv.* **pale·ness,** *n.*

pa·le·on·tol·o·gy, *n.* science of ancient life. **pa·le·on·to·log·i·cal,** *a.* **pa·le·on·tol·o·gist,** *n.*

pal·ette, *n.* thin board to mix colors; selection of colors.

pal·in·drome, *n.* word, verse, or sentence that is the same read backward or forward.

pal·ing, *n.* fence formed of pickets.

pal·i·sade, *n.* fence for defense. *v.*, **-sad·ed**, **-sad·ing**. fortify.

pall, *v.* make uninteresting. *n.* large cloth over coffin; oppressive nature.

pal·la·di·um, *n.* metallic element.

pall·bear·er, *n.* coffin attendant at a funeral.

pal·let, *n.* straw bed.

pal·lid, *a.* pale.

pal·lor, *n.* paleness.

palm, *n.* tree with fan-shaped leaves; inside of hand. *v.*, pick up furtively. **palm off**, pass off. **pal·me·ceous**, *a.*

pal·mate, *a.* webbed.

palm·is·try, *n.* art of telling fortunes by lines of the hand. **palm·ist**, *n.*

palm·y, *a.*, **-i·er**, **-i·est**. prosperous.

pal·o·mi·no, *n. pl.*, **-nos**. golden-coated horse.

pal·pa·ble, *a.* tangible; obvious. **pal·pa·bil·i·ty**, *n.* **pal·pa·bly**, *adv.*

pal·pate, *v.*, **-pat·ed**, **-pat·ing**. examine by touch. **pal·pa·tion**, *n.*

pal·pi·tate, *v.*, **-tat·ed**, **-tat·ing**. throb; quiver. **pal·pi·ta·tion**, *n.*

pal·sy, *n.* paralysis. *v.*, **-sied**, **-sy·ing**. paralyze.

pal·ter, *v.* haggle.

pal·try, *a.*, **-tri·er**, **-tri·est**. trivial. **pal·tri·ness**, *n.*

pam·pa, *n. pl.* grassy plains.

pam·per, *v.* indulge.

pam·phlet, *n.* unbound publication.

pam·phlet·eer, *n.* writer of pamphlets.

pan, *n.* cooking vessel. *Inf.* face. *v.*, **panned**, **pan·ning**. separate by washing; move camera to follow object in motion. *Inf.* criticize severely.

pan·a·ce·a, *n.* cure-all. **pan·a·ce·an**, *a.*

pa·nache, *n.* flamboyance.

pan·cake, *n.* flat fried cake.

pan·cre·as, *n.* gland secreting digestive fluid.

pan·dem·ic, *a.* universal.

pan·de·mo·ni·um, *n.* chaos.

pan·der, *n.* pimp.

pane, *n.* single sheet of glass.

pan·el, *n.* distinct portion of any surface; body of persons; control board. **pan·el·ist**, *n. v.*, **-eled**, **-el·ing**. arrange with panels.

pan·el·ling, *n.* wall consisting of panels.

pang, *n.* spasm.

pan·han·dle, *n.* handle of a pan; narrow projection of land. *v.*, **-dled**, **-dling**. *Inf.* beg.

pan·ic, *n.* acute fear. *Inf.* humorous situation or person.

pan·o·ram·a, *n.* unobstructed view over a wide area. **pan·o·ram·ic**, *a.* **pan·o·ram·i·cal·ly**, *adv.*

pan·sy, *n. pl.*, **-sies**. perennial flower. *Inf.* male homosexual.

pant, *v.* gasp; long for. *n.* short breath.

pan·the·ism, *n.* worship of all aspects of the universe. **pan·the·ist**, *n.* **pan·the·is·tic**, *a.*

pan·ther, *n.* cougar. *Inf.* violent person.

pan·to·mime, *n.* communicating without speech.

pan·try, *n. pl.*, **-tries**. closet for provisions.

pap, *n.* nipple; soft food.

pa·pa, *n.* father.

pa·pa·cy, *n. pl.*, **-cies**. office of the pope.

pa·pal, *a.* belonging to the pope.

pa·per, *n.* chiefly fiber reduced to pulp used to write on or wrap in. *v.* cover with paper.

pa·per·back, *n.* book bound in paper.

pa·pier-mâ·ché, *n.* mass of pulp molded into shapes. *a.* unreal.

pa·pil·la, *n. pl.*, **-lae**. small protuberances of the tongue.

pa·poose, **pap·poose**, *n.* infant.

pa·pri·ka, *n.* condiment.

Pap smear, *n.* examination for uterine cancer. Also **Pap test.**

pa·py·rus, *n. pl.*, **-rus·es**, **-ri**. reedlike plant; ancient paper.

par, *n.* average. *a.* normal.

par·a·ble, *n.* allegorical story.

par·a·chute, *n.* umbrellalike device used to descend through air. *v.*, **-chut·ed**, **-chut·ing**. jump or drop. **par·a·chut·ist**, *n.*

pa·rade, *n.* organized march. *v.*, **-rad·ed**, **-rad·ing**. march. *a.*

par·a·dise, *n.* place of bliss. **par·a·di·si·a·cal**, *a.*

par·a·dox, *n.* self-contradictory statement.

par·af·fin, *n.* colorless waxy mixture.

par·a·gon, *n.* model of perfection.

par·a·graph, *n.* distinct portion of printed matter forming an undivided whole.

par·a·keet, *n.* small parrot.

par·al·lel, *a.* lines, planes, and curves which are equidistant at all corresponding points; analogous.

pa·ral·y·sis, *n. pl.*, **-ses.** inability to react or respond. **par·a·lyt·ic**, *a., n.* **par·a·lyze**, *v.*

par·a·me·ci·um, *n. pl.*, **-ci·a.** one-celled protozoan.

par·a·med·ic, *n.* trained medical assistant.

pa·ram·e·ter, *n.* fixed boundary or limit.

par·a·mount, *a.* superior.

par·a·mour, *n.* illicit lover.

par·a·noi·a, *n.* mental disorder. **par·a·noid**, *a., n.*

par·a·pet, *n.* protective wall.

par·a·pher·nal·ia, *n. pl., sing. or pl. in constr.* personal property; equipment.

par·a·phrase, *n.* restatement of words.

par·a·site, *n.* animal or plant lives on or in another.

par·a·troop·er, *n.* soldier parachutist.

par·boil, *v.* precook.

par·cel, *n.* package; collection.

parch, *v.* dry by exposure to heat or extreme cold.

parch·ment, *n.* skin of animals prepared for use as writing material.

par·don, *v.* forgive. *n.* forgiveness. **par·don·a·ble**, *a.* **par·don·a·bly**, *adv.*

pare, *v.*, **pared**, **par·ing.** cut; trim.

par·ent, *n.* father or mother. **pa·ren·tal**, *a.*

pa·ren·the·sis, *n. pl.*, **-ses.** explanatory comment set off by ( ).

par·fait, *n.* layered dessert.

pa·ri·ah, *n.* outcast.

par·ish, *n.* division of a diocese. **pa·rish·ion·er**, *n.*

par·i·ty, *n.* equality.

park, *n.* recreation or conservation area. *v.* leave temporarily. *Inf.* caress.

par·ka, *n.* hooded fur coat.

park·way, *n.* landscaped thoroughfare.

par·lance, *n.* idiom.

par·lay, *v.*, **-layed**, **-lay·ing.** exploit.

par·ley, *v.*, **-leyed**, **-ley·ing.** confer with an enemy. *n.* mutual conversation.

par·lia·ment, *n.* (*Usu. cap.*) legislature of the United Kingdom. **par·lia·men·tar·i·an**, *n.* **par·lia·men·ta·ry**, *a.*

par·lor, **par·lour**, *n.* living room.

pa·ro·chi·al, *a.* belonging to a parish; narrow.

par·o·dy, *n. pl.*, **-dies.** humorous imitation.

pa·role, *n.* early release of a prisoner. **pa·roled**, **pa·rol·ing**, *v.*

par·ox·ysm, *n.* sudden fit.

par·quet, *n.* mosaic wood flooring. **par·quet·ry**, *n.*

par·rot, *n.* birds which imitate speech. *v.* repeat without understanding.

par·ry, *v.*, **-ried**, **-ry·ing.** ward off. *n. pl.*, **-ries.** verbal evasion.

par·si·mo·ny, *n.* stinginess.

pars·ley, *n.* garden herb.

pars·nip, *n.* edible taproot.

par·son, *n.* clergyman.

part, *n.* section; divide; share; role. *v.* break; dissolve; participate. *adv.* partially. *a.* partial.

par·take, *v.*, **-took**, **-tak·en**, **-tak·ing.** take a part in.

par·the·no·gen·e·sis, *n.* development of an egg without fertilization.

par·tial, *a.* not complete; prejudiced. **par·tial·i·ty**, *n. pl.*, **-ties.** special fondness. **par·tial·ly**, *adv.*

par·tic·i·pant, *a.* sharing. *n.* take part in.

par·tic·i·pate, *v.*, **-pat·ed**, **-pat·ing.** take a part with others. **par·tic·i·pa·tion**, *n.* **par·tic·i·pa·tive**, *a.*

par·ti·ci·ple, *n.* verbal adjective.

par·ti·cle, *n.* minute portion; article.

par·tic·u·lar, *a.* referring to one category; unusual. *n.* distinct. *Usu. pl.* details. **in particular**, especially. **par·tic·u·lar·ly**, *adv.*

par·tic·u·lar·i·ty, *n. pl.*, **-ties.** detailed statement.

part·ing, *a.* leave-taking.

par·ti·san, *n.* biased. **par·ti·san·ship**, *n.*

par·ti·tion, *n.* division; distribute.

part·ly, *adv.* not wholly.

part·ner, *n.* associate. **part·ner·ship**, *n.*

part of speech, *n.* words classed by function in a sentence.

par·tridge, n. pl., -tridg·es, -tridge. game bird.

part-time, a. employed less than full-time.

par·tu·ri·ent, a. bringing forth something new.

par·ty, n. pl., -ties. group united in purpose or opinion; social gathering.

par·ve·nu, n. sudden wealth.

pas·chal, a. of Jewish Passover or Christian Easter.

pa·sha, n. title of courtesy.

pass, v. proceed; depart; elapse; happen; circulate; be accepted; excreted; give judgment. n. road; permission to move about; success in a test.

pass·a·ble, a. tolerable. **pass·a·bly**, adv.

pas·sage, n. passing; transition; lapse of time; route; portion of writing.

pas·sé, a. old-fashioned.

pas·sen·ger, n. traveler on a conveyance.

pass·ing, a. fleeting; transitory. **in pass·ing**, incidentally.

pas·sion, n. compelling emotion. **pas·sion·less**, a. **pas·sion·ate**, a.

pas·sive, a. not active.

pass-key, n. master key.

Pass·o·ver, n. Jewish festival.

pass·port, n. citizen's permission to travel.

pass·word, n. watchword.

past, a. ended; over; bygone. prep. after. n. earlier time. adv. beyond.

pas·ta, n. unleavened dough.

paste, n. adhesive; dough. v., **pas·ted, pas·ting**. adhere.

paste·board, n. cardboard.

pas·tel, n. soft color; drawing.

pas·teur·ize, v., -ized, -iz·ing. bacteria killing process. **pas·teur·i·za·tion**, n.

pas·till, n. lozenge.

pas·time, n. diversion.

pas·tor, n. minister.

pas·to·ral, a. rustic or rural.

pas·tra·mi, n. pickled beef.

pas·try, n. pl., -tries. sweet bakery.

pas·ture, n. grazing ground. v., -tured, -tur·ing. graze. **pas·tur·age**, n.

past·y, a., -i·er, -i·est. like paste; pale.

pat, n. gentle stroke; small mass. v., -pat·ted, pat·ting. strike lightly. a. glib. adv. promptly. **stand pat**, unyielding.

patch, n. piece of cloth used to mend. v. mend. **patch·y**, a., -i·er, -i·est.

pate, n. top of the head.

pat·ent, a. open; exclusive rights. n. by document conferring privilege. **pa·ten·cy**, n. **pat·ent·ly**, adv.

pa·ter·nal, a. fatherly. **pa·ter·nal·ly**, adv. **pa·ter·nal·ism**, n.

pa·ter·ni·ty, n. fatherhood; origin.

path, n. footway; procedure.

pa·thet·ic, a. arousing pity.

pa·thol·o·gy, n. pl., -gies. study of the nature of diseases. **path·o·log·i·cal**, a. **path·o·log·i·cal·ly**, adv. **pa·thol·o·gist**, n.

pa·thos, n. quality that arouses deep feeling.

path·way, n. path.

pa·tience, n. act of being patient.

pa·tient, a. uncomplaining. n. person under medical care. **pa·tient·ly**, adv.

pa·ti·o, n. pl., -os. inner court; paved area.

pat·ois, n. pl., **pat·ois**. dialect.

pa·tri·ar·chy, n. pl., -chies. organization led by a male. **pa·tri·cian**, n. aristocrat.

pat·ri·mo·ny, n. pl., -nies. heritage.

pa·tri·ot, n. person who loves his country. **pa·tri·ot·ic**, a.

pa·trol, v., **pa·trolled, pa·trol·ling**. walk around to guard. n. person(s) guarding.

pa·tron, n. regular client; one who supports.

pat·ron·ize, v. move quickly; repeat glibly. n. rapid talk.

pat·tern, n. model. v. make.

pat·ty, n. pl., -ties. small flat cake.

pau·ci·ty, n. scarcity.

paunch, n. potbelly.

pau·per, n. extremely poor person.

pause, n. short stop; delay. v. wait.

pave, v., paved, **pav·ing**. cover surface of road.

pave·ment, n. paved surface.

pa·vil·ion, n. open exhibition building.

paw, n. foot of animals having claws. v. scrape with the forefoot. Inf. handle roughly.

pawn, n. security for a loan; hostage. v. stake.

pawn bro·ker, n. lends money

on personal property.

pay, *v.,* **paid,** **pay·ing.** discharge a debt; compensate. *n.* payment.

pay·a·ble, *a.* due.

pay·check, *n.* salary.

pay·roll, *n.* list to be paid.

pea, *n. pl.,* **peas, pease.** round nutritious seed.

peace, *n.* tranquility; freedom from war. **peace·a·ble,** *a.* **peace·a·bly,** *adv.*

peace·ful, *a.* tranquil. **peace·ful·ly,** *adv.* **peace·ful·ness,** *n.*

peach, *n.* fruit. *Inf.* greatly admired person.

pea·cock, *n. pl.,* **-cocks, -cock.** male bird with long colored tail.

peak, *n.* pointed top; highest degree.

peak·ed, *a.* sickly.

peal, *n.* loud, prolonged sound. *v.* ring.

pea·nut, *n.* legume with edible oily seeds. *Inf.* unimportant; *pl.* small sum.

pear, *n.* edible fruit.

pearl, *n.* gem produced by oysters. *v.* hunt for pearls. **pearl·y,** *a.*

peas·ant, *n.* farm laborer; rustic. *Inf.* simpleminded. *a.* rural. **peas·ant·ry,** *n.*

peat, *n.* decayed plant material. **peat·y,** *a.*

peb·ble, *n.* small stone. **peb·bly,** *a.*

pe·can, *n.* nut tree.

pec·ca·dil·lo, *n. pl.,* **-loes, -los.** slight offense.

peck, *n.* eight quarts. *Inf.* great amount. *v.* strike with a pointed object; nibble; nag. *Inf.* perfunctory kiss.

pec·tin, *n.* carbohydrate.

pec·to·ral, *a.* of or pertaining to the breast or chest.

pe·cu·liar, *a.* unusual. **pe·cu·liar·ly,** *adv.* **pe·cu·li·ar·i·ty,** *n. pl.,* **-ties.**

pe·cu·ni·ar·y, *a.* money related.

ped·a·gogue, **ped·a·gog,** *n.* teacher.

ped·al, *n.* lever pressed by foot; treadle.

ped·ant, *n.* lays undue stress on details. **pe·dan·tic,** *a.* **pe·dan·ti·cal·ly,** *adv.* **ped·ant·ry,** *n.*

ped·dle, *v.,* **-dled, -dling.** small traveling business. **ped·dler,** **ped·ler, ped·lar,** *n.*

ped·es·tal, *n.* base.

pe·des·tri·an, *n.* walker. *a.* commonplace. **pe·des·tri·an·ism,** *n.*

pe·di·at·rics, *n.* medical care of children. **pe·di·at·ric,** *a.* **pe·di·a·tri·cian,** *n.*

ped·i·gree, *n.* genealogy. **ped·i·greed,** *a.*

peek, *v.* look quickly. *n.* peep.

peel, *v.* strip. *n.* rind.

peep, *v.* squeak; look slyly. *n.* cry of bird; brief look.

peer, *n.* equal. **peer·age,** *n.* **peer·ess,** *n.* **peer·less,** *a.* unequaled. **peer·less·ly,** *adv.*

peeve, *v.,* **peeved, peev·ing.** irritate. *n.* annoyance.

peev·ish, *a.* querulous.

peg, *n.* wooden bolt; mark. *Inf.* throw.

pe·koe, *n.* fine black tea.

pel·i·can, *n.* water bird with pouched bill.

pel·let, *n.* small round body; bullet.

pell-mell, pell·mell, *adv.* disordered manner. *a. n.*

pelt, *n.* untanned hide. *v.* hurl; assail verbally.

pel·vis, *n. pl.,* **-vis·es, -ves.** cavity in the lower trunk of many vertebrates. **pel·vic,** *a.*

pen, *n.* instrument for writing with ink; enclosure for animals. *n. Inf.* penitentiary. *v.,* **penned, pen·ning.** compose.

pe·nal, *a.* of penalties. **pe·nal·ize,** *v.,* **-ized, -iz·ing.** declare liable.

pen·al·ty, *n. pl.,* **-ties.** punishment.

pen·ance, *n.* voluntary suffering for repentance.

pen·chant, *n.* bias.

pen·cil, *n.* writing instrument with chalk or graphite core.

pend·ant, pend·ent, *n.* hanging ornamentation.

pend·ing, *a.* undecided; imminent. *prep.* during.

pen·du·lum, *n.* body suspended to swing freely.

pen·e·trate, *v.,* **-trat·ed, -trat·ing.** enter; affect deeply; comprehend. **pen·e·tra·tive,** *a.*

pen·e·trat·ing, *a.* piercing.

pen·i·cil·lin, *n.* antibiotic grown from molds.

pen·in·su·la, *n.* land almost surrounded by water. **pen·in·su·lar,** *a.*

pen·i·tent, *a.* contrite. *n.* one who is penitent.

pen·i·ten·tia·ry, *n. pl.,* **-ries.** reformatory; prison.

pen name, *n.* pseudonym.

pen·nant, *n.* banner.

pen·ni·less, *a.* destitute.

pen·non, *n.* flag; pennant.

pen·ny, *n. pl.*, **-nies.** cent.

pe·nol·o·gy, *n.* study of crime prevention. **pe·no·log·i·cal**, *a.* **pe·nol·o·gist**, *n.*

pen·sion, *n.* retirement allowance. *v.* grant a pension.

pen·sive, *a.* thoughtful. **pen·sive·ly**, *adv.* **pen·sive·ness**, *n.*

pent, *a.* kept in.

pen·ta·gon, *n.* five sided figure.

pen·tag·o·nal, *a.* **pen·tag·o·nal·ly**, *adv.*

pen·tath·lon, *n.* athletic contest of five events.

pent·house, *n.* dwelling on the roof of a building.

pent-up, *a.* shut in.

pe·nuit, *n.* one next to the last.

pe·num·bra, *n. pl.*, **-bras, -brae.** area of partial shadow during an eclipse.

pe·nu·ri·ous, *a.* stingy.

pen·u·ry, *n.* extreme poverty.

pe·on, *n.* day laborer.

pe·o·ny, *n. pl.*, **-nies.** subshrub with large colored flowers.

peo·ple, *n. pl.*, **-ple, -ples.** a community; human beings. *v.*, **-pled, -pling.** populate.

pep, *n. Inf.* energy.

pep·per, *n.* pungent spice. *v.* sprinkle; pelt.

pep·per·mint, *n.* pungent herb of the mint family.

per, *prep.* through; by means of.

per·am·bu·late, *v.*, **-lat·ed, -lat·ing.** walk, **per·am·bu·la·tor**, *n.* baby carriage.

per an·num, *adv.* annually.

per·cale, *n.* cotton fabric.

per cap·i·ta, *adv.*, *a.* for each person.

per·ceive, *v.*, **-ceived, -ceiv·ing.** discern; understand.

per·cent, per cent, *n. pl.*, **per·cent, per·cents.** proportion of every hundred. **per·cent·age**, *a.* **per·cent·age**, *n.* discount.

per·cep·ti·ble, *a.* discernible.

per·cep·tion, *n.* intuitive recognition.

perch, *n.* roost; elevated station; edible fish; linear measure. *v.* alight.

per·chance, *adv.* maybe.

per·co·late, *v.*, **-lat·ed, -lat·ing.** filter.

per·co·la·tor, *n.* coffeepot.

per·cus·sion, *n.* impact.

per·di·tion, *n.* hell.

per·emp·to·ry, *a.* dogmatic.

per·en·ni·al, *a.* continuing more than two years. *n.* **per·en·ni·al·ly**, *adv.*

per·fect, *a.* faultless; exact. *v.* improve. **per·fec·tion**, *n.* flawlessness. **per·fect·ly**, *adv.*

per·fi·dy, *n.* treachery.

per·fo·rate, *v.*, **-rat·ed, -rat·ing.** make a hole by boring.

per·force, *adv.* of necessity.

per·form, *v.* do; act.

per·for·mance, *n.* entertainment.

per·fume, *n.* scent. *v.*, **-fumed, -fum·ing.** fill with a pleasing odor.

per·func·to·ry, *a.* careless.

per·i·gee, *n.* point nearest the earth.

per·i·he·li·on, *n. pl.*, **-a.** point nearest the sun.

per·il, *n.* danger. *v.*, **-riled**, or **-rilled, -il·ing** or **-il·ling.** expose to danger.

pe·rim·e·ter, *n.* boundary of a two dimensional figure.

pe·ri·od, *n.* portion of time; punctuation mark (.).

pe·ri·od·ic, *a.* recurring.

pe·ri·od·i·cal, *n.* publication appearing at regular intervals.

per·i·pa·tet·ic, *a.* itinerant.

pe·riph·er·y, *n. pl.*, **-ies.** external boundary.

per·i·phrase, *n.* roundabout statement.

per·i·scope, *n.* tube used to view objects out of direct vision.

per·ish, *v.* die.

per·ish·a·ble, *a.* liable to spoil. *n.*

per·i·style, *n.* open space enclosed by columns.

per·i·to·ne·um, *n. pl.*, **-ums, -a.** membrane of the abdomen.

per·i·wig, *n.* small wig.

per·i·win·kle, *n.* ground cover; sea snail.

per·jure, *v.*, **-jured, -jur·ing.** lie under oath.

per·ju·ry, *n. pl.*, **-ries.** false oath.

perk, *v.* regain liveliness.

perk·y, *a.*, **-i·er, -i·est.** jaunty.

per·ma·nent, *a.* durable.

per·me·a·ble, *a.* open to penetration.

per·me·ate, *v.*, **-at·ed, -at·ing.** pass through; saturate.

per·mis·si·ble, *a.* allowable.

per·mis·sion, *n.* formal consent.

per·mit, *v.*, **-mit·ted, -mit·ting.** allow; tolerate; grant leave. *n.* license.

per·ni·cious, *a.* injurious.

per·o·ra·tion, *n.* conclusion of a

speech.

per·pen·dic·u·lar, *a.* at right angles with a plane.

per·pe·trate, *v.,* **-trat·ed, -trat·ing.** commit.

per·pet·u·al, *a.* continuous. **per·pet·u·al·ly,** *adv.*

per·pet·u·ate, *v.,* **-at·ed, -at·ing.** cause to endure.

per·plex, *v.* confuse.

per se, *adv.* by itself.

per·se·cute, *v.,* **-cut·ed, -cut·ing.** harass. **per·se·cu·tion,** *n.*

per·se·vere, *v.,* **-vered, -ver·ing.** continue despite difficulties.

per·sim·mon, *n.* tree with plumlike fruit.

per·sist, *v.* be insistent.

per·sist·ent, *a.* persevering.

per·snick·et·y, *a.* Inf. finicky.

per·son, *n.* human being; self.

per·son·a·ble, *a.* having a pleasant disposition.

per·son·al, *a.* private.

per·son·al·i·ty, *n. pl.,* **-ties.** characteristics of an individual; famous person.

per·son·al·ly, *adv.* in person.

per·son·i·fy, *v.,* **-fied, -fy·ing.** represent; typify. **per·son·i·fi·ca·tion,** *n.*

per·son·nel, *n.* persons engaged in any work. *a.*

per·spec·tive, *n.* appearance; ability to evaluate.

per·spi·ra·tion, *n.* sweat.

per·spire, *v.,* **-spired, -spir·ing.** sweat.

per·suade, *v.,* **-suad·ed, -suad·ing.** convince. **per·sua·sion,** *n.*

pert, *a.* lively.

per·tain, *v.* relate; be appropriate.

per·ti·nent, *a.* relevant.

per·turb, *v.* agitate.

pe·ruse, *v.,* **-rused, -rus·ing.** read.

per·vade, *v.,* **-vad·ed, -vad·ing.** extend activity. **per·va·sion,** *n.* **per·va·sive,** *a.*

per·verse, *a.* contrary. **per·verse·ly,** *adv.*

per·ver·sion, *n.* abnormal activity.

per·vert, *v.* corrupt.

pes·ky, *a.,* **-ki·er, -ki·est.** Inf. annoying.

pes·si·mism, *n.* tendency to take unfavorable view. **pes·si·mist,** *n.*

pest, *n.* anything noxious.

pes·ter, *v.* annoy.

pes·ti·cide, *n.* substance used to kill weeds.

pes·ti·lence, *n.* contagious disease; evil.

pes·tle, *n.* tool for grinding substances.

pet, *n.* tamed animal; favorite individual. *a.* particular. *v.,* **-ted, -ting.** fondle.

pet·al, *n.* leaflike part of a blossom.

pet·cock, *n.* small faucet.

pe·tite, *a.* tiny.

pe·ti·tion, *n.* written request; entreaty. *v.* solicit.

pet·ri·fy, *v.,* **-fied, -fy·ing.** convert to stone; stupefy.

pe·tro·le·um, *n.* oily, flammable liquid.

pet·ti·coat, *n.* underskirt.

pet·ty, *a.,* **-ti·er, -ti·est.** small-minded.

pet·u·lance, pet·u·lan·cy, *n.*

pet·u·lant, *a.* showing irritation.

pe·tu·ni·a, *n.* plant with funnel-form flowers.

pew, *n.* benchlike seat.

pew·ter, *n.* alloy of tin and lead. *a.*

pe·yo·te, *n. pl.,* **-tes.** cactus used for drug.

phal·lus, *n. pl.,* **phal·li, phal·lus·es.** penis or clitoris. **phal·lic,** *a.*

phan·tasm, *n.* apparition.

phan·tom, *n.* apparition. *a.* spectral.

phar·aoh, *n.* Egyptian king.

phar·ma·ceu·ti·cal, *a.* knowledge of pharmacy. *n.* drug product.

phar·ma·cist, *n.* druggist.

phar·ma·cy, *n. pl.,* **-cies.** drugstore.

phase, *n.* aspect; stage. *v.,* **phased, phas·ing.** synchronize.

pheas·ant, *n. pl.,* **-ant, -ants.** long-tailed game bird.

phe·no·bar·bi·tal, *n.* barbiturate.

phe·nom·e·non, *n. pl.,* **-na, -nons.** something extraordinary. **phe·nom·e·nal, phe·nom·e·nal·ly,** *adv.*

phi·lan·thro·phy, *n. pl.,* **-pies.** love of mankind; benevolent activity. **phil·an·throp·ic,** *a.* **phil·an·throp·i·cal·ly,** *adv.* **phi·lan·thro·pist,** *n.*

phil·har·mon·ic, *a.* fond of music.

phi·lo·den·dron, *n. pl.,* **-drons, -dra.** climbing vine.

phi·los·o·pher, *n.* person who studies philosophy. **phil·o·soph·i·cal,** *a.* **phi·los·o·phize,** *v.*

phi·los·o·phy, *n. pl.,* **-phies.** study of principles underlying all knowledge; principles for guidance.

phlegm, n. thick mucus; indifference.

phleg·mat·ic, a. apathetic. **phleg·mat·i·cal**.

phlox, n. plant with showy flowers.

pho·bi·a, n. illogical fear or dread. **pho·bic**, a.

phoe·nix, phe·nix, n. emblem of immortality.

phone, n. Inf. telephone.

pho·no·graph, n. record player. **pho·no·graph·ic**, a. **pho·no·graph·i·cal·ly**, adv.

pho·ny, pho·ney, a., -ni·er, -ni·est, -ney·er, -ney·est. Inf. bogus. n. pl., -nies, -neys. **pho·ni·ness**, n.

phos·phate, n. salt of phosphoric acid.

phos·pho·res·cence, n. luminous without heat. **phos·pho·resce**, v., -resced, -resc·ing. **phos·pho·res·cent**, a. **phos·pho·res·cent·ly**, adv.

phos·pho·rus, n. solid nonmetallic element.

pho·to·cop·y, n. photographic reproduction.

pho·to·e·lec·tric, a. pertaining to the electricity produced by light.

pho·to·en·grav·ing, n. process to obtain a picture upon a plate or block.

pho·to fin·ish, n. close finish of a horse race.

pho·to·gen·ic, a. favorable subject for photography.

pho·to·graph, n. picture made by photography. v. take a photograph of.

pho·tog·ra·phy, n. producing images on a surface.

pho·to·stat, n. device for making facsimile copies of printed matter.

pho·to·syn·the·sis, n. making of carbohydrates in plants by the action of the sun.

phrase, n. words not including a verb and subject.

phra·se·ol·o·gy, n. wording.

phy·lum, n. classification of animals and plants.

phys·ic, n. cathartic.

phys·i·cal, a. body.

phy·si·cian, n. doctor of medicine.

phys·ics, n. science which deals with matter and energy.

phys·i·og·no·my, n. face.

phys·i·ol·o·gy, n. science of living plant and animal organisms.

phys·i·o·ther·a·py, n. treatment of disease by physical remedies.

phy·sique, n. body structure.

pi, n. Greek letter Π, π.

pi·a·nis·si·mo, a. soft.

pi·an·ist, n. piano player.

pi·an·o, n. musical instrument with a keyboard.

pi·az·za, n. open square in a city, esp. in Italy.

pi·ca, n. size of printing type.

pic·a·dor, n. horseman in a bull-fight who prods the bull.

pic·a·resque, a. fiction story describing the adventures of a vagabond hero.

pic·a·yune, a. petty.

pic·ca·lil·li, n. relish of vegetables and spices.

pic·co·lo, n. small flute.

pick, v. choose; pluck. n. choice or selection; pointed tool for picking.

pick·ax, n. pick with a sharp point at one end and a broad blade at the other.

pick·er·el, n. smaller species of pike.

pick·et, n. stake that is pointed; demonstrator.

pick·ing, n. profits not honestly obtained.

pick·le, n. cucumber preserved in a brine.

pick·pock·et, n. one who steals from pockets.

pick·up, n. acceleration; small truck.

pick·y, a. fussy.

pic·nic, n. outdoor meal.

pic·to·ri·al, a. expressed in a picture.

pic·ture, n. painting, drawing, or other visual representation.

pic·tur·esque, a. charming.

pid·dle, v. deal in trifles.

pidg·in, n. composite language of different languages.

pie, n. crust filled with fruit or meat.

pie·bald, a. having spots of different colors.

piece, n. part of anything separated from the whole.

piece·meal, adv. bit by bit.

piece·work, n. work paid for by the unit.

pied, a. variegated.

pier, n. wharf built over water serves as a dock for ships.

pierce, v. penetrate; make a hole.

pi·e·tism, n. religiosity.

pi·e·ty, n. regard for religious obligations.

pig, n. swine.

pi·geon, n. bird with a compact body and short legs.

pi·geon·hole, n. small compartment in a desk.

pi·geon-toed, a. toes or feet turning inward.

pig·gy·back, adv. on the back or shoulders.

pig·head·ed, a. stubborn.

pig i·ron, n. crude iron.

pig·ment, n. coloring matter.

pig·men·ta·tion, n. coloration of skin.

pig·skin, n. skin of a pig.

pig·tail, n. hair in a braid.

pike, n. freshwater fish; turnpike; spear.

pi·las·ter, n. column projecting from a wall.

pile, n. heavy stake driven into the ground for support; heap; nap.

pil·fer, v. to steal.

pil·grim, n. traveler to sacred place.

pill, n. medicine to be swallowed whole.

pil·lage, v. plunder.

pil·lar, n. upright support.

pil·lion, n. place on a horse for another rider.

pil·lo·ry, n. frame with holes for head and hands, used to punish an offender.

pil·low, n. support for the head during sleep.

pil·low·case, n. removable case for a pillow.

pi·lot, n. operator of aircraft or ships.

pi·men·to, n. sweet pepper.

pimp, n. solicitor for prostitutes.

pim·ple, n. small swelling of the skin.

pin, n. piece of metal, used for fastening articles together.

pin·a·fore, n. sleeveless garment.

pin·cers, n. tool with two handles and jaws for gripping.

pinch, v. squeeze between the fingers.

pinch hit·ter, n. one who substitutes for another person.

pin·cush·ion, n. small cushion to stick pins in.

pine, n. tree. v. long intensely.

pine·ap·ple, n. tropical plant.

pine tar, n. thick tar derived from pine wood.

pin-feath·er, n. undeveloped feather.

pin·fold, n. pound or pen.

ping, n. ringing sound.

Ping-Pong, n. Trademark. table tennis.

pin·hole, n. small hole.

pin·ion, n. wing of a bird; cogwheel. v. bind.

pink, v. pierce. n. pale reddish color.

pink·eye, n. inflammation of the eyelids.

pink·ing shears, n. scissors having serrated blades.

pin mon·ey, n. small amount of money.

pin·na·cle, n. high peak.

pi·noch·le, n. card game.

pin·point, n. insignificant object. v. locate precisely.

pin·prick, n. minor irritation.

pin stripe, n. narrow stripe used as a fabric design.

pint, n. one half quart.

pin·to, a. spotted.

pin-up, n. wall accessory.

pin·wheel, n. spokes fastened by a pin to a stick so as to revolve in the wind.

pin·worm, n. worm infesting intestine and rectum.

pi·o·neer, n. one who first enters a region. v. go before.

pi·ous, a. religious.

pip, n. seed of a fruit.

pip, v. chirp.

pipe, n. tube; wind instrument; used for smoking tobacco. v. make shrill sound.

pipe dream, n. fantastic idea.

pipe·line, n. pipe used to transmit oil, water, etc.

pip·er, n. player of a pipe.

pip·ing, n. act of one who pipes; fabric used for trimming garments.

pip·it, n. bird that wags its tail and walks.

pip·pin, n. variety of apple.

pi·quant, a. agreeably pungent.

pique, n. offense taken. v. irritate.

pi·qué, n. fabric woven with a quilted effect.

pi·rate, n. robber on the high seas.

pi·rogue, n. canoe made from a single trunk of a tree.

pir·ou·ette, n. whirling on the toes.

Pis·ces, *n.* fishes; a zodiacal constellation.

pis·ta·chi·o, *n.* light green nut.

pis·til, *n.* female reproductive organ in a plant.

pis·tol, *n.* firearm fired with one hand.

pis·ton, *n.* disk that moves back and forth under pressure of a fluid.

pit, *n.* hole in the ground; stone of a fruit.

pitch, *n.* sticky substance left after the distillation of coal tar or wood tar; variation in flight. *v.* set up; toss.

pitch·blende, *n.* mineral consisting of uranium oxide.

pitch·er, *n.* container with a handle and a lip; player who throws the ball.

pitch·fork, *n.* fork used in lifting hay.

pit·e·ous, *a.* deserving sympathy.

pit·fall, *n.* hidden trap.

pith, *n.* soft cellular tissue in the center of the stems of many plants.

pith·y, *a.* forceful.

pit·i·a·ble, *a.* arousing pity.

pit·i·ful, *a.* arousing compassion.

pit·i·less, *a.* merciless.

pit·tance, *n.* small amount.

pi·tu·i·tar·y, *a.* pertaining to the pituitary gland.

pi·tu·i·tar·y gland, *n.* small gland at the base of brain.

pit·y, *n.* compassion.

piv·ot, *n.* thing upon which a related part rotates.

pix·i·lat·ed, *a.* eccentric.

pix·y, *n.* fairy.

piz·za, *n.* spicy Italian dish.

piz·zi·ca·to, *a.* played by plucking the strings with the finger.

plac·a·ble, *a.* easily appeased.

plac·ard, *n.* notice posted in a public place.

pla·cate, *v.* appease.

place, *n.* portion of space marked off; original position of something.

pla·ce·bo, *n.* anything intended to gratify.

place·ment, *n.* act of placing.

pla·cen·ta, *n.* organ through which the fetus receives nourishment.

plac·er, *n.* glacial deposit containing particles of gold or other minerals.

place set·ting, *n.* dishes and utensils needed for a meal.

plac·id, *a.* quiet.

plack·et, *n.* slit in a skirt.

pla·gia·rism, *n.* offering of another's ideas as one's own.

pla·gia·rize, *v.* appropriate by plagiarism.

plague, *n.* disease with a high mortality rate.

pla·guy, *a.* annoying.

plaid, *n.* a fabric woven in a tartan pattern.

plain, *a.* flat; no embellishment.

plaint, *n.* lamentation.

plain·tiff, *n.* person who brings a lawsuit.

plain·tive, *a.* voicing melancholy.

plait, *n.* fold.

plan, *n.* scheme.

plane, *n.* carpenter's tool with an oblique cutting blade; level surface.

plan·et, *n.* one of the heavenly bodies revolving about the sun.

plan·e·tar·i·um, *n.* mechanism which represents the motions and orbits of the planets.

plan·e·tar·y, *a.* pertaining to a planet.

plank, *n.* flat piece of timber thicker than a board.

plank·ton, *n.* organisms floating in a body of water.

plant, *n.* organism of the vegetable kingdom, having cellulose cell walls.

plan·tain, *n.* weed; tropical plant in the banana family.

plan·ta·tion, *n.* large estate.

plant·er, *n.* one who plants.

plaque, *n.* plate intended for ornament.

plas·ma, *n.* fluid in which the corpuscles of the blood are suspended.

plas·ter, *n.* composition used for covering walls and ceilings.

plas·ter·board, *n.* large boardlike sheets used for forming walls.

plas·ter of Par·is, *n.* calcined gypsum.

plas·tic, *a.* having the power of molding or shaping formless material.

plat, *v.* interweave.

plate, *n.* vessel from which food is eaten.

pla·teau, *n.* broad, flat area of elevated land.

plate glass, *n.* glass used for

mirrors and large window-panes.

plat·form, *n.* flat structure raised above an adjoining level.

plat·ing, *n.* an external layer of metal.

plat·i·num, *n.* grayish-white metallic element.

plat·i·tude, *n.* trite remark.

plat·i·tu·di·nize, *v.* utter platitudes.

Pla·ton·ic, *a.* pertaining to the Greek philosopher Plato or his doctrines.

pla·toon, *n.* unit of a company or troop.

plat·ter, *n.* serving dish.

plat·y·pus, *n.* primitive mammal.

plau·dit, *n.* praise bestowed.

plau·si·ble, *a.* apparently right.

play, *n.* dramatic performance; fun; game or pastime.

play·act, *v.* pretend.

play·bill, *n.* notice of a play.

play·boy, *n.* man whose time is spent in pleasure.

play·er, *n.* one who plays.

play·er pi·an·o, *n.* piano which plays automatically.

play·ful, *a.* full of humor.

play·go·er, *n.* frequenter of the theater.

play·ground, *n.* piece of ground set apart for recreation.

play·house, *n.* a toy house.

play·ing card, *n.* one of pack of cards for use in playing games.

play·let, *n.* short play.

play·mate, *n.* companion.

play·off, *n.* succession of games to determine a championship.

play·pen, *n.* movable enclosure for child to play in.

play·thing, *n.* toy.

play·wright, *n.* author of plays.

pla·za, *n.* public square.

plea, *n.* appeal.

plead, *v.* argue in support of a claim.

pleas·ant, *a.* agreeable.

pleas·ant·ry, *n.* banter.

please, *v.* satisfy.

pleas·ing, *a.* giving satisfaction.

pleas·ur·a·ble, *a.* pleasing.

pleas·ure, *n.* delight.

pleat, *n.* fold of cloth.

ple·be·ian, *a.* common.

pleb·i·scite, *n.* vote to determine the popular will on an issue.

pledge, *n.* promise.

ple·na·ry, *a.* complete.

plen·i·po·ten·ti·ar·y, *n.* person invested with full power to transact business.

plen·i·tude, *n.* state of being full.

plen·te·ous, *a.* abundant.

plen·ti·ful, *a.* ample.

plen·ty, *n.* abundance.

pleth·o·ra, *n.* superabundance.

pleu·ri·sy, *n.* inflammation of the pleura.

pli·a·ble, *a.* flexible.

pli·ant, *a.* flexible.

pli·ca·tion, *n.* folding.

pli·ers, *n.* pair of pincers.

plight, *n.* situation. *v.* pledge.

plod, *v.* walk heavily.

plop, *v.* make small a sound.

plot, *n.* small piece of land; a plan.

plow, *n.* implement for cutting furrows in the soil.

plow·share, *n.* cutting edge of a plow.

ploy, *n.* tactic.

pluck, *v.* pick.

pluck·y, *a.* spirited.

plug, *n.* wood used to stop a hole.

plum, *n.* fleshy fruit.

plum·age, *n.* feathers.

plumb, *n.* small weight of lead used in testing the perpendicularity of walls.

plumb·er, *n.* one who fits and repairs water pipes.

plumb·ing, *n.* pipes and fixtures used to convey water and waste.

plume, *n.* feather of a bird.

plum·met, *n.*, *v.* drop straight down.

plump, *v.* fall heavily. *a.* chubby.

plun·der, *v.* rob. *n.* that which is taken by theft.

plunge, *v.* immerse.

plung·er, *n.* device used in unclogging drains.

plunk, *v.* strum.

plu·ral, *a.* two or more.

plu·ral·ism, *n.* diverseness.

plu·ral·i·ty, *n.* majority.

plus, *a.* denoting addition.

plush, *n.* fabric with a nap.

plus sign, *n.* symbol used in math.

plu·toc·ra·cy, *n.* government by the wealthy.

plu·to·ni·um, *n.* radioactive element.

ply, *n.* individual layer. *v.* employ with diligence.

ply·wood, *n.* building material.

p.m., afternoon.

pneu·mat·ic, *a.* pertaining to air, gas, or wind.

pneu·mo·nia, *n.* inflammation of the lungs.

poach, *v.* cook in simmering water; trespass to steal game or fish.

pock, *n.* pustule of the body.

pock·et, *n.* any pouchlike receptacle.

pock·et·book, *n.* handbag.

pock·et·knife, *n. pl.*, **-knives**. small knife with folding blades.

pock·mark, *n.* scar.

pod, *n.* elongated, two-valved fruit.

po·di·a·trist, *n.* one who treats disorders of the foot. Also **chiropodist. po·di·a·try**, *n.*

po·di·um, *n. pl.*, **-a**, **-ums**. dais.

po·em, *n.* verse composition.

po·et·ic, **po·et·i·cal**, *a.* **po·et·i·cal·ly**, *adv.*

po·et, *n.* person who writes poetry. *n.*

po·et·ry, *n.* art of writing poems; poems.

poign·ant, *a.* keen; moving the emotions. **poign·an·cy**, *n.* **poign·ant·ly**, *adv.*

poin·set·ti·a, *n.* small flowering winter shrub.

point, *n.* end of; tip; sharp end; tool which pricks; period; place; limit reached; moment; critical idea; suggestion; unit of scoring. *v.* direct; aim; punctuate; face.

point-blank, *a.* direct. *adv.*

point·er, *n.* indicator. *Inf.* tip.

poise, *n.* equilibrium; composure. *v.*, **poised**, **pois·ing**. hover.

poi·son, *n.* agent that chemically destroys an organism. *v.* harm with poison; corrupt. **poi·son·ous**, *a.* **poi·son·ing**, **poi·son·er**, *n.*

poke, *n.* sack; dawdler; punch. *v.*, **poked**, **pok·ing**. thrust; jab; push out.

pok·er, *n.* card game; iron or steel bar.

pok·y, **pok·ey**, *n.* jail.

po·lar, *a.* having direct opposites.

po·lar·i·ty, *n. pl.*, **-ties**. quality of possessing magnetic poles.

po·lar·i·za·tion, *n.* acquisition of polarity.

po·lar·oid, *n. Trademark.* lens which polarizes light.

pole, *n.* long slender piece of wood; unit of measurement; end of the axis.

po·lem·ic, *n.* controversial argument.

po·lice, *n.* civil force for maintaining order. *Pl. in constr.* members of such a force. *v.*, **-liced**, **-lic·ing**. control.

pol·i·cy, *n. pl.*, **-cies**. governing principle; insurance contract.

po·li·o·my·e·li·tis, *n.* disease causing paralysis.

pol·ish, *v.* make smooth; make elegant. *n.* gloss; act of polishing; refinement.

po·lite, *a.* showing regard; cultured. **po·lite·ly**, *adv.* **po·lite·ness**, *n.*

pol·i·tic, *a.* artful.

po·lit·i·cal, *a.* of the government. **po·lit·i·cal·ly**, *adv.*

pol·i·ti·cian, *n.* one skilled in politics.

pol·i·tics, *n. pl., sing. or pl. in constr.* science of government; political affairs.

pol·ka, *n.* lively dance. *v.*, **-kaed**, **-ka·ing**. dance the polka.

poll, *n.* list of individuals; survey; voting at an election. *Usu. pl.* voting place. *v.* crop; enroll; register votes; cast a vote; canvass.

pol·len, *n.* male element in flowering plants.

pol·li·nate, *v.*, **-nat·ed**, **-nat·ing**. fertilize with pollen. **pol·li·na·tion**, **pol·li·na·tor**, *n.*

pol·lute, *v.*, **-lut·ed**, **-lut·ing**. make foul; corrupt. **pol·lut·er**, *n.* **pol·lu·tion**, *n.*

po·lo, *n.* game played on horseback. **po·lo·ist**, *n.*

po·lo·ni·um, *n.* radioactive element.

pol·ter·geist, *n.* ghost.

pol·y·chrome, *a.* having many colors.

pol·y·es·ter, *n.* man-made fiber.

pol·y·eth·yl·ene, *n.* polymer of ethylene.

po·lyg·a·my, *n.* practice of plural marriage. **po·lyg·a·mist**, *n.* **po·lyg·a·mous**, *a.*

pol·y·gon, *n.* closed plane figure with three or more straight sides.

pol·y·graph, *n.* duplicating machine; instrument employed in lie detection.

pol·y·he·dron, *n. pl.*, **-drons**, **-dra**. solid bounded by many plane faces.

pol·y·no·mi·al, *a.* consisting of

several terms. n.

pol·yp, n. sedentary coelenterate animal; malformation.

pol·y·syl·lab·ic, a. of many syllables.

pol·y·tech·nic, n. school of applied sciences.

pol·y·the·ism, n. worship of many gods.

pol·y·un·sat·u·rat·ed, a. of fats having two or more double bonds per molecule.

pom·ace, n. pulpy matter.

po·made, n. perfumed ointment. v., **-mad·ed,** **-mad·ing.** groom.

pome·gran·ate, n. edible fruit with many seeds.

pom·mel, n. knob. v., **-meled,** **-mel·ing.** beat with fists. Also pum·mel.

pomp, n. pretentious display.

pom·pa·dour, n. hair style.

pom·pon, n. ball-shaped ornament.

pomp·ous, a. ostentatious. **pom·pos·i·ty,** n. **pomp·ous·ly,** adv. **pomp·ous·ness,** n.

pon·cho, n. pl., **-chos.** blanket-like garment.

pond, n. body of still water.

pon·der, v. reflect; think. **pon·der·a·ble,** a.

pon·der·ous, a. very heavy; dull.

pon·tiff, n. pope; bishop.

pon·tif·i·cal, a. papal.

pon·toon, n. float used to support.

po·ny, n. pl., **po·nies.** small horse. Inf. illicit aid.

pooch, n. dog.

poo·dle, n. dog with long, curly or silky hair.

pooh, interj. expression of scorn.

pool, n. small pond; group with common interest; stakes; billiards. v. put into common fund.

poop, n. stern of a ship. n. Inf. information. v. Inf. exhaust.

poor, a. having little; deficient; humble.

pop, n. short, explosive sound; effervescent beverage. v., **popped,** **pop·ping.** make a quick sound; come or go quickly; protrude.

pop·corn, n. corn whose kernels open when heated.

pope, n. (Often cap.) head of the Roman Catholic Church.

pop·lar, n. tree yielding a light, soft wood.

pop·lin, n. corded fabric.

pop·py, n. pl., **-pies.** colorful flower.

pop·u·lace, n. common people.

pop·u·lar, a. well-liked. **pop·u·lar·ly,** adv. **pop·u·lar·i·ty,** n.

pop·u·late, v., **-lat·ed** **-lat·ing.** to inhabit.

pop·u·la·tion, n. the total number of inhabitants.

pop·u·lous, a. full of people.

por·ce·lain, n. strong glazed ceramic.

porch, n. vestibule; veranda.

por·cu·pine, n. rodent with quilled coat.

pore, v., pored, **por·ing.** examine. n. minute opening.

pork, n. flesh of swine. Inf. political favors.

por·nog·ra·phy, n. obscene literature or art. **por·no·graph·ic,** a.

po·rous, a. permeable by liquids, light, or air.

por·poise, n. pl., **-pois·es,** **-poise.** sea mammal.

por·ridge, n. thick boiled meal.

port, n. harbor; opening; left side as one faces forward; sweet red wine; refuge. Inf. airport. v. turn to the left; carry.

port·a·ble, a. easily carried. n. something portable.

por·tage, n. act of carrying. v., **-taged,** **-tag·ing.**

por·tal, n. entranceway.

por·tend, v. forebode.

por·tent, n. omen. **por·ten·tious,** a.

por·ter, n. doorkeeper; carrier; attendant.

por·ter·house, n. beefsteak.

port·fo·li·o, n. pl., **-os.** portable case; list of investments.

port·hole, n. window in a ship.

por·ti·co, n. pl., **-coes,** **-cos.** open porch with columns.

por·tion, n. allotment; share. v. divide.

port·ly, a., **-li·er,** **-li·est.** stout. **port·li·ness,** n.

por·trait, n. picture of a person. **por·trait·ist,** n.

por·tray, v. draw the likeness; act the part. **por·tray·al,** n.

pose, v., posed, **pos·ing.** assume a position; ask; falsely represent oneself. n. attitude.

posh, a. elegant.

po·si·tion, n. situation; status; point of view. v. place.

pos·i·tive, a. explicit; definite; dogmatic; affirmative; greater than zero. **pos·i·tive·ly,** adv.

pos·se, *n.* body armed with legal authority.

pos·sess, *v.* own; have as a quality; control. **pos·ses·sor,** *n.*

pos·sessed, *a.* dominated.

pos·ses·sion, *n.* ownership. **pos·ses·sive,** *a.*

pos·si·bil·i·ty, *n. pl.,* **-ties.** something that can happen.

pos·si·ble, *a.* may be; may happen.

pos·si·bly, *adv.* perhaps.

post, *n.* stout piece of timber set to support; position; mail. *v.* put up; appoint; mail; travel with speed. *adv.* **pos·tal,** *a.*

post·age, *n.* mailing charge.

post card, *n.* card transmitted through the mail.

post·er, *n.* large printed placard.

pos·te·ri·or, *a.* situated behind.

pos·ter·i·ty, *n.* all future generations.

post·haste, *adv.* promptly.

post·hu·mous, *a.* after one's death.

post·man, *n. pl.,* **-men.** mail carrier.

post·mark, *n.* official mark stamped on mail.

post·mas·ter, *n.* official in charge of a post office.

post me·rid·i·em, *a.* after noon. *Abbr.* p.m., P.M.

post·mor·tem, *n.* autopsy.

post·na·tal, *a.* subsequent to birth.

post·par·tum, *a.* after childbirth.

post·pone, *v.,* **-poned, -pon·ing.** put off; defer. *n.*

post·script, *n.* something appended.

pos·tu·lant, *n.* candidate.

pos·tu·late, *v.,* **-lat·ed, -lat·ing.** ask; assume without proof. *n.* axiom.

pos·ture, *n.* an unnatural attitude; pose.

post·war, *a.* period after a war.

po·sy, *n. pl.,* **po·sies.** single flower.

pot, *n.* deep, round vessel; liquor; gradual ruination. *Inf.* sum of money; marijuana.

po·tas·si·um, *n.* metallic element. *Sym.* K.

po·ta·to, *n. pl.,* **-toes.** edible tuber.

pot·bel·ly, *n.* protuberant belly.

pot·boil·er, *n. Inf.* inferior literature, produced for profit.

po·tent, *a.* powerful; capable.

po·ten·cy, *n.* **po·tent·ly,** *adv.*

po·ten·tate, *n.* sovereign.

po·ten·tial, *a.* possibility. *n.* anything possible.

po·tion, *n.* drink.

pot·luck, *n.* informal meal.

pot·pour·ri, *n.* dried petals and spices; medley; mixed collection.

pot·tage, *n.* thick vegetable soup.

pot·ter, *n.* one who makes crockery.

pot·ter·y, *n. pl.,* **-ies.** moist clay shaped and heated.

pouch, *n.* bag. *v.* put into; pocket.

poul·tice, *n.* soft dressing for sores.

poul·try, *n.* domestic fowls.

pounce, *n.* talon; sudden swoop. *v.,* **pounced, pounc·ing.** seize; swoop down.

pound, *n.* unit of measurement; enclosed place; heavy blow; shelter. *v.* crush; pulverize; impound.

pour, *v.* express freely; flow continuously. *n.* down pour.

pout, *v.* sulk. *n.* a fit of sullenness.

pov·er·ty, *n.* being poor; deficiency.

POW, *n.* prisoner of war. Also **P.O.W.**

pow·der, *n.* dust. *v.* cover with powder; pulverize. **pow·der·y,** *a.*

pow·er, *n.* capability; might; authority. *Inf.* large number.

pow·er·ful, *a.* potent; mighty. **pow·er·ful·ly,** *adv.*

pow·er·less, *a.* helpless.

pow·wow, *n.* council.

pox, *n.* disease marked by watery blisters.

prac·ti·ca·ble, *a.* feasible; usable. **prac·ti·ca·bil·i·ty, prac·ti·ca·ble·ness,** *n.* **prac·ti·ca·bly,** *adv.*

prac·ti·cal, *a.* suitable; useful.

prac·ti·cal·i·ty, *n.* **prac·ti·cal·ly,** *adv.*

prac·tice, *v.* carry out; pursue; do something habitually. *n.* habit; exercise. **prac·ti·tion·er,** *n.*

prac·ticed, *a.* skilled.

prag·mat·ic, *a.* practical; meddlesome; dogmatic. *n.* busybody.

prag·ma·tism, *n.* practical philosophy.

prai·rie, *n.* grassland.

praise, *n.* commendation; homage. *v.,* **praised, prais·ing.**

pra·line, *n.* sweets made of nuts and syrup.

prance, *v.*, **pranced, pranc·ing.** ride spiritedly; strut about.

prank, *n.* mischievous trick. **prank·ster**, *n.*

prate, *v.*, **prat·ed, prat·ing.** babble.

prat·tle, *v.*, **-tled, -tling.** talk idly. *n.* babble.

prawn, *n.* shrimplike shellfish.

pray, *v.* beg; entreat.

prayer, *n.* petition; supplication to God.

preach, *v.* deliver a sermon. **preach·er**, *n.*

pre·ad·o·les·cence, *n.* ages 9 to 12.

pre·am·ble, *n.* preface.

pre·car·i·ous, *a.* risky. **pre·car·i·ous·ly**, *adv.*

pre·cau·tion, *n.* care taken beforehand. **pre·cau·tion·ar·y**, *a.*

pre·cede, *v.*, **-ced·ed, -ced·ing.** go before; preface.

prec·e·dence, *n.* order; adjustment of place.

prec·e·dent, *n.* an example. *a.* antecedent.

pre·cept, *n.* commandment; maxim.

pre·cinct, *n.* divisions within a city.

pre·cious, *a.* of high value. *adv.* very. *n.* loved one.

prec·i·pice, *n.* steep cliff.

pre·cip·i·tant, *a.* rushing headlong.

pre·cip·i·tate, *v.*, **-tat·ed, -tat·ing.** bring about; separate out. *n.* substance precipitated.

pre·cip·i·ta·tion, *n.* snow, dew, fog, or rain.

pre·cip·i·tous, *a.* very steep; headlong.

pre·cise, *a.* sharply defined; exact. **pre·cise·ness**, *n.*

pre·ci·sion, *n.* accuracy.

pre·clude, *v.*, **-clud·ed, -clud·ing.** impede; hinder. **pre·clu·sion**, *n.* **pre·clu·sive**, *a.*

pre·co·cious, *a.* prematurely developed. **pre·coc·i·ty**, *n.*

pre·cog·ni·tion, *n.* foreknowledge.

pre·con·ceive, *v.*, **-ceived, -ceiv·ing.** form a notion in advance.

pre·cur·sor, *n.* forerunner.

pred·a·to·ry, *a.* a plundering; pillaging. **pred·a·tor**, *n.*

pred·e·ces·sor, *n.* one who goes before.

pre·des·ti·nate, *v.*, **-nat·ed, -nat·ing.** foreordain.

pre·des·ti·na·tion, *n.* fate.

pre·dic·a·ment, *n.* unpleasant situation.

pred·i·cate, *v.*, **-cat·ed, -cat·ing.** declare; imply.

pre·dict, *v.* foretell. **pre·dict·a·ble**, *a.*

pre·dic·tion, *n.* prophecy.

pre·di·lec·tion, *n.* partiality.

pre·dis·po·si·tion, *n.* tendency. **pre·dis·pose**, **-posed, -pos·ing,** *v.*

pre·dom·i·nant, *a.* superior.

pre·dom·i·nate, *v.*, **-nat·ed, -nat·ing.** surpass; rule over.

pre·em·i·nent, *a.* surpassing others. **pre·em·i·nence**, *n.*

pre·empt, *v.* take before others. *n.* **pre·emp·tion**, *n.*

preen, *v.* groom; primp.

pre·fab·ri·cate, *v.*, **-cat·ed, -cat·ing.** construct beforehand. **pre·fab·ri·ca·tion**, *n.*

pref·ace, *n.* introduction.

pre·fer, *v.*, **-ferred, -fer·ring.** choose rather than.

pref·er·a·ble, *a.* more desirable.

pref·er·ence, *n.* preferring; special advantage.

pref·er·en·tial, *a.* showing partiality.

pre·fix, *v.* put before. *n.* syllable put to the beginning of a base.

preg·na·ble, *a.* vulnerable.

preg·nant, *a.* carrying a fetus; replete. **preg·nan·cy**, *n.* *pl.*, **-cies.**

pre·hen·sile, *a.* capable of grasping.

pre·his·tor·ic, *a.* period before written history.

prej·u·dice, *n.* strong opinion; bias. *v.*, **-diced, -dic·ing.** implant a prejudice. **prej·u·di·cial**, *a.*

prel·ate, *n.* dignitary of the church.

pre·lim·i·nar·y, *a.* introductory. *n. pl.*, **-ies.**

prel·ude, *n.* leading up to what follows.

pre·ma·ture, *a.* before the proper time; untimely.

pre·med·i·tate, *v.*, **-tat·ed, -tat·ing.** plan beforehand.

pre·men·stru·al, *a.* period prior to menstruation.

pre·mier, *a.* chief; principal. *n.* chief minister.

pre·miere, *n.* initial performance.

prem·ise, *v.*, **-ised, -is·ing.** set forth. *n.* proposition. *Pl.* land.

pre·mi·um, *n.* reward; bonus;

pre·mo·ni·tion, n. foreboding.

pre·na·tal, a. previous to birth.

pre·oc·cu·py, v., **-pied, -py·ing.** engross. **pre·oc·cu·pa·tion,** n. **pre·oc·cu·pied,** a.

prep·a·ra·tion, n. being prepared.

pre·par·a·to·ry, a. introductory.

pre·pare, v., **-pared, -par·ing.** make ready; equip.

pre·pay, v., **-paid, -pay·ing.** pay in advance. **pre·pay·ment,** n.

pre·pon·der·ate, v., **-at·ed, -at·ing.** predominate. **pre·pon·der·ance,** n.

prep·o·si·tion, n. word showing noun's relation to other words.

pre·pos·sess, v. favorable bias.

pre·pos·ter·ous, a. absurd.

pre·puce, n. foreskin.

pre·req·ui·site, a. required before. n.

pre·rog·a·tive, n. hereditary right. a.

pres·age, n. prognostic.

pres·by·ter·y, n. pl., **pres·by·ter·ies.** elders; part of a church for clergy.

pre·scribe, v., **-scribed, -scrib·ing.** ordain; order for use; direct.

pre·scrip·tion, n. medicine prescribed.

pres·ence, n. attendance; close proximity.

pre·sent, v. introduce; in or at a place; show; turn to; give. n. gift. n. now. a. being with one or others; existing.

pre·sent·a·ble, a. suitable.

pres·en·ta·tion, n. introduction; that which is given.

pres·ent·ly, adv. soon.

pre·serv·a·tive, n. tending to preserve. n. that which preserves.

pre·serve, v., **-served, -serv·ing.** keep from harm; sustain. n. usu. pl. cooked and canned fruit; game shelter.

pre·side, v., **-sid·ed, -sid·ing.** direct.

pres·i·dent, n. (Often cap.) chief executive.

press, n. compacting machine; printing press; newspapers; publishing house; crowd; wine vat; urgency. v. squeeze; iron; compel; solicit.

press·ing, a. urgent.

pres·sure, n. constraining force;

severity; urgency. v., **-sured, -sur·ing.** compel.

pres·su·rize, v., **-rized, -riz·ing.** fill with compressed gas.

pres·ti·dig·i·ta·tion, n. sleight of hand.

pres·tige, n. renown.

pres·ti·gious, a. having an excellent reputation.

pres·to, n. quick passage.

pre·sum·a·ble, a. probable. **pre·sum·a·bly,** adv.

pre·sume, v., **-sumed, -sum·ing.** take for granted; suppose; dare.

pre·sum·ing, a. presumptuous.

pre·sump·tion, n. supposition.

pre·sump·tu·ous, a. arrogant.

pre·tend, v. feign; make believe.

pre·tense, n. excuse.

pre·ten·sion, n. claim to privilege.

pre·ten·tious, a. showy.

pre·text, n. false motive.

pret·ty, a. pleasing; nice. adv. in some degree. n. pl., **-ties.**

pret·zel, n. salted knot-shaped cracker.

pre·vail, v. overcome; influence; succeed.

pre·vail·ing, a. predominant.

prev·a·lent, a. widely existing.

pre·vent, v. thwart. **pre·vent·a·bil·i·ty, pre·ven·tion,** n. **pre·vent·a·ble, pre·vent·i·ble,** a.

pre·ven·tive, a. hinder. n. precautionary agent.

pre·view, n. view in advance.

pre·vi·ous, a. prior.

prey, n. animal hunted as food; victim. v. victimize; plunder.

price, n. cost; value. v., **priced, pric·ing.**

price·less, a. invaluable. Inf. amusing.

prick, n. puncture; any pointed instrument. v. pierce; sting; incite; point upward.

prick·le, n. sharp small point.

prick·ly, a. tingling.

pride, n. vanity; group of lions.

priest, n. clergyman.

prig, n. one who is pedantic.

prim, a., **prim·mer, prim·mest.** stiffly formal.

pri·ma·cy, n. pl., **-cies.** first in rank.

pri·mal, a. original.

pri·ma·ri·ly, adv. chiefly.

pri·ma·ry, a. earliest; first in order; principal. n. pl., **-ries.** political caucus.

pri·mate, n. archbishop; mammal of the highest order.

prime, *a.* first; principal. *n.* best part. *v.*, **primed, prim·ing.** prepare; pour liquid into.

prime me·rid·i·an, *n.* longitudinal reckoning point.

prim·er, *n.* first reader.

pri·me·val, *a.* original.

prim·i·tive, *a.* earliest of the kind; unaffected; rude. *n.* something primitive.

pri·mo·gen·i·ture, *n.* right of the first-born son.

pri·mor·di·al, *a.* first in order.

primp, *v.* adorn.

prim·rose, *n.* perennial herb with yellow flowers.

prince, *n.* king's son. **prin·cess**, *n.* **prince·ly**, *a.* noble.

prin·ci·pal, *a.* authority. *n.* chief; sum owed.

prin·ci·pal·i·ty, *n. pl.*, **-ties.** territory of a prince.

prin·ci·ple, *n.* general truth; law; precept.

print, *n.* mark; impression; die; design; photographic picture. *v.* indent; impress; produce; write. **print·a·ble**, *a.*

print·ing, *n.* typography; printed matter.

print-out, *n.* processed data.

pri·or, *a.* earlier; religious man.

pri·or·i·ty, *n. pl.*, **-ties.** precedence.

pri·or·y, *n. pl.*, **-ries.** religious house.

prism, *n.* that which refracts light.

pris·on, *n.* jail.

pris·sy, *a.*, **-si·er, -si·est.** prim.

pris·tine, *a.* pure.

pri·va·cy, *n.* solitude.

pri·vate, *a.* personal; confidential. *n.* enlisted man below corporal.

pri·va·tion, *n.* destitution.

priv·et, *n.* ornamental shrub.

priv·i·lege, *n.* favor enjoyed by some.

priv·y, *a.* confidential. *n. pl.*, **-ies.** outdoor toilet.

prize, *n.* reward; something won; of value. *v.* esteem.

pro, *adv.* opposed to **con.** *a.* professional.

prob·a·bil·i·ty, *n. pl.*, **-ties.** likelihood.

prob·a·ble, *a.* likely. **prob·a·bly**, *adv.*

pro·bate, *n.* validation of a will.

pro·ba·tion, *n.* proof; preliminary trial; suspension.

probe, *n.* instrument used to explore a wound; search. *v.*,

probed, prob·ing. inquire.

prob·lem, *n.* unsolved question. *a.* maladjusted.

prob·lem·at·ic, *a.* doubtful. **prob·lem·at·i·cal**, *a.*

pro·bos·cis, *n. pl.*, **-cis·es, -ci·des.** snout.

pro·ce·dure, *n.* process; course.

pro·ceed, *v.* continue; renew; advance.

pro·ceed·ing, *n.* action; legal step.

pro·ceeds, *n. pl.* financial return.

proc·ess, *n.* series of changes; writ; proceedings. *v.* prepare by some process.

pro·ces·sion, *n.* parade.

pro·claim, *v.* announce.

proc·la·ma·tion, *n.* official announcement.

pro·cliv·i·ty, *n. pl.*, **-ties.** tendency.

pro·cras·ti·nate, *v.*, **-nat·ed, -nat·ing.** delay.

pro·cre·ate, *v.*, **-at·ed, -at·ing.** reproduce. **pro·cre·a·tion**, *n.*

proc·tor, *n.* supervisor.

pro·cure, *v.*, **-cured, -cur·ing.** obtain; gain; pimp.

prod, *v.*, **prod·ded, prod·ding.** poke; rouse.

prod·i·gal, *a.* wasteful. *n.* waster.

pro·di·gious, *a.* extraordinary.

prod·i·gy, *n. pl.*, **-gies.** marvel.

pro·duce, *v.*, **-duced, -duc·ing.** bring about; bear; extend. *n.* yield; product.

prod·uct, *n.* thing produced; result.

pro·duc·tive, *a.* fertile.

pro·fane, *a.* irreverent; secular. *v.*, **-faned, -fan·ing.** desecrate.

pro·fan·i·ty, *n. pl.*, **-ties.** swearing.

pro·fess, *v.* acknowledge.

pro·fes·sion, *n.* vocation.

pro·fes·sion·al, *a.* engaged in a profession.

pro·fes·sor, *n.* highest ranking teacher. **pro·fes·so·ri·al**, *a.*

prof·fer, *v.* offer. *n.* offer made.

pro·fi·cien·cy, *n.* skill.

pro·fi·cient, *a.* skilled. *n.* expert.

pro·file, *n.* outline.

prof·it, *n.* benefit; gain. *v.* advance.

prof·it·a·ble, *a.* useful.

prof·li·gate, *a.* very immoral. *n.* spend thrift.

pro·found, *a.* intellectually deep.

pro·fuse, *a.* extravagant.

pro·fu·sion, *n.* great amount.

pro·gen·i·tor, *n.* forefather.

prog·e·ny, *n. pl.,* **-nies.** children.

pro·ges·ter·one, *n.* female sex hormone.

prog·no·sis, *n. pl.,* **-ses.** forecast.

pro·gram, *n.* schedule; entertainment. *v.,* **-grammed, -gram·ming,** or **-gramed, -gram·ing.** arrange.

prog·ress, *n.* going forward. *v.* proceed.

pro·gres·sive, *a.* liberal move forward.

pro·gres·sive jazz, *n.* modern jazz.

pro·hib·it, *v.* forbid. **pro·hib·i·tive,** *a.*

pro·hi·bi·tion, *n.* decree forbidding.

pro·ject, *v.* propose; plan; use. *n.* scheme.

pro·jec·tile, *n.* missile.

pro·jec·tion, *n.* image produced.

pro·jec·tive, *a.* produced.

pro·jec·tor, *n.* device for projecting.

pro·le·tar·i·at, *n.* laboring class.

pro·lif·er·ate, *v.,* **-at·ed, -at·ing.** grow by multiplication.

pro·lif·ic, *a.* fruitful.

pro·logue, *n.* preface. *v.,* **-logued, -log·uing.**

pro·long, *v.* lengthen.

prom·e·nade, *n.* walk; grand march.

prom·i·nent, *a.* conspicuous; important. **prom·i·nence,** *n.*

pro·mis·cu·ous, *a.* indiscriminate. **pro·mis·cu·i·ty,** *n. pl.,* **-ties.**

prom·ise, *n.* pledge; expectation of hope.

Prom·ised Land, *n.* heaven.

prom·is·so·ry, *a.* containing a promise.

prom·on·to·ry, *n. pl.,* **-ries.** high point of land.

pro·mote, *v.,* **-mot·ed, -mot·ing.** advance; help organize. *Inf.* wangle.

pro·mo·tion, *n.* advancement.

prompt, *a.* punctual. *v.* move.

pro·mul·gate, *v.,* **-gat·ed, -gat·ing.** announce.

prone, *a.* inclined.

prong, *n.* pointed projection.

pro·noun, *n.* word used instead of a noun.

pro·nounce, *v.,* **-nounced, -nounc·ing.** declare; articulate.

pro·nounced, *a.* strongly defined.

pro·nounce·ment, *n.* announce-ment.

pro·nun·ci·a·tion, *n.* articulation.

proof, *n.* evidence. *a.* impenetrable. *v.* examine for errors.

proof·read, *v.,* **-read, -red, -read·ing.** detect and mark errors.

prop, *n.* support. *Inf.* theatrical property; airplane propeller.

prop·a·gan·da, *n.* biased information.

prop·a·gate, *v.,* **-gat·ed, -gat·ing.** breed; originate. **prop·a·ga·tion,** *n.*

pro·pel, *v.,* **-pelled, -pel·ling.** drive forward.

pro·pel·lant, *n.* something that propels.

pro·pel·ler, *n.* rotating shaft fitted with blades.

pro·pen·si·ty, *n. pl.,* **-ties.** tendency.

prop·er, *a.* applicable; appropriate; decent.

prop·er·ty, *n. pl.,* **-ties.** something owned.

proph·e·cy, *n. pl.,* **-cies.** foretelling.

proph·e·sy, *v.,* **-sied, -sy·ing.** predict.

proph·et, *n.* predictor.

pro·phy·lac·tic, *a.* preventive.

pro·phy·lax·is, *n.* protective treatment.

pro·pi·ti·ate, *v.,* **-at·ed, -at·ing.** conciliate.

pro·pi·tious, *a.* favorably disposed.

pro·po·nent, *n.* one in favor.

pro·por·tion, *n.* comparative relation; ratio.

pro·por·tion·al, *a.* corresponding.

pro·por·tion·ate, *a.* proportioned.

pro·pose, *v.,* **-posed, -pos·ing.** state; present; offer.

prop·o·si·tion, *n.* plan.

pro·pound, *v.* propose.

pro·pri·e·tar·y, *a.* denoting exclusive control.

pro·pri·e·tor, *n.* owner.

pro·pri·e·ty, *n. pl.,* **-ties.** conformity.

pro·pul·sion, *n.* propelling force.

pro·sa·ic, *a.* commonplace; dull.

pro·scribe, *v.,* **-scribed, -scrib·ing.** prohibit.

prose, *n.* opposed to *verse.*

pros·e·cute, *v.* follow up; pursue; enforce legally. **pros·e·cu·tor,** *n.*

pros·pect, *n.* outlook. *v.* explore.

pro·spec·tive, *a.* potential.

pro·spec·tus, *n.* brief report.

pros·per, *v.* thrive.

pros·per·i·ty, *n.* good fortune.

pros·per·ous, *a.* successful.

pros·tate gland, *n.* organ near the base of the bladder.

pros·the·sis, *n. pl., -ses.* artificial part.

pros·thet·ics, *n. pl., sing. or pl. in constr.* medical branch dealing in artificial replacements.

pros·ti·tute, *n.* harlot.

pros·trate, *v., -trat·ed, -trat·ing.* lay flat; cast down; overthrow.

pros·y, *a., -i·er, -i·est.* tedious.

pro·tag·o·nist, *n.* hero.

pro·tect, *v.* shield; defend.

pro·tec·tor·ate, *n.* dependent state.

pro·té·gé, *n.* one under the protection of another.

pro·tein, *n.* chemical compound.

pro·test, *v.* object. *n.* declaration against.

prot·es·ta·tion, *n.* protest.

pro·tist, *n.* group of organisms.

pro·to·col, *n.* diplomatic etiquette.

pro·ton, *n.* positive particle.

pro·to·plasm, *n.* living matter of all cells.

pro·to·type, *n.* model.

pro·to·zo·an, *n.* single-celled organisms.

pro·tract, *v.* prolong.

pro·trac·tor, *n.* instrument for measuring angles.

pro·trude, *v., -trud·ed, -trud·ing.* stand out. **pro·tru·sion**, *n.*

pro·tu·ber·ant, *a.* sticking out. **pro·tu·ber·ance**, *n.*

proud, *a.* arrogant.

prove, *v., proved, proved or prov·en, prov·ing.* test; establish the truth.

prov·erb, *n.* adage; wise saying.

pro·vide, *v., -vid·ed, -vid·ing.* arrange for; supply.

pro·vid·ed, *conj.* understood.

prov·i·dence, *n.* prudence; God's guidance.

prov·ince, *n.* unit of a country. *Pl.* territory at some distance from the city.

pro·vin·cial, *a.* simple; of narrow interests. *n.* naive person.

pro·vi·sion, *n.* accumulation of materials. *Pl.* stock.

pro·vi·sion·al, *a.* temporary.

pro·voc·a·tive, *a.* stimulating.

prov·o·ca·tion, *n.*

pro·voke, *v., -voked, -vok·ing.* irritate; arouse.

prow, *n.* forepart of a ship.

prow·ess, *n.* bravery; ability.

prowl, *v.* wander stealthily. **prowl·er**, *n.*

prox·i·mate, *a.* nearest.

prox·im·i·ty, *n.* state of being proximate.

prox·y, *n. pl., -ies.* substitute; deputy.

prude, *n.* one who is very modest.

pru·dence, *n.* cautious.

prune, *n.* dried plum. *v.,* **pruned, prun·ing.** cut off; trim with a knife.

pru·ri·ent, *a.* inclined to erotic thoughts.

pry, *v., pried, pry·ing.* peep; search; raise; open. *n. pl.,* **pries.** leverage.

psalm, *n.* sacred song.

psalm·book, *n.* book of psalms.

pseu·do, *a.* false.

pseu·do·nym, *n.* false name.

pseu·do·preg·nan·cy, *n.* false pregnancy.

pshaw, *interj.* exclamation of contempt.

Psy·che, *n.* spirit personified.

psych·e·del·ic, *a.* hallucination.

psy·chi·a·try, *n.* branch of medicine which deals with mental disorders. **psy·chi·a·trist**, *n.*

psy·chic, *a.* mental; clairvoyance. *n.* medium.

psy·cho·a·nal·y·sis, *n.* treatment of mental conflicts. **psy·cho·a·lyst**, *n.* **psy·cho·an·a·lyze**, *v.*

psy·cho·bi·ol·o·gy, *n.* biological aspects of psychology.

psy·cho·gen·e·sis, *n.* origin and development of the mind.

psy·cho·gen·ic, *a.* of mental origin.

psy·cho·log·i·cal, *a.* mental; subjective.

psy·chol·o·gy, *n.* knowledge dealing with the human mind and behavior.

psy·chop·a·thy, *n.* abnormal mental condition.

psy·cho·sis, *n. pl., -ses.* mental disorder.

psy·cho·ther·a·py, *n.* treatment to correct mental disorders.

pto·maine, **pto·main**, *n.* poisonous organic compounds.

pub, *n. Inf.* tavern.

pu·ber·ty, *n.* period of sexual maturity.

pu·bes·cence, *n.* state of puberty.

pub·lic, *a.* not private; affecting a community; widely known. *n.* people.

pub·li·ca·tion, *n.* something printed and published.

pub·li·cist, *n.* press agent.

pub·lic·i·ty, *n.* spreading of information.

pub·li·cize, *v.*, **-cized**, **-ciz·ing**. advertise.

pub·lic school, *n.* free school maintained by taxes.

pub·lic serv·ant, *n.* employee of the government.

pub·lic serv·ice, *n.* service furnished free to the public.

pub·lish, *v.* print for sale.

pub·lish·er, *n.* one who publishes.

puck, *n.* rubber disk.

puck·er, *v.* gather into wrinkles.

pud·ding, *n.* baked dish made of starch, milk and eggs.

pud·dle, *n.* small pool of liquid.

pudg·y, *a.*, **-i·er**, **-i·est**. fat and short.

pueb·lo, *n. pl.*, **-los**. village built of adobe.

pu·er·ile, *a.* juvenile.

puff, *v.* breathe quick and hard; smoke; become inflated. *n.* short, quick blast; swelling; light pastry.

puff ad·der, *n.* venomous viper.

pug, *n.* small bulldog. *Inf.* prizefighter.

pu·gil·ism, *n.* boxing with the fists.

pug·na·cious, *a.* belligerent.

puke, *v.*, **puked**, **puk·ing**. vomit.

pull, *v.* tug at; draw toward; tear. *n.* tug; force. *Inf.* influence.

pull·back, *n.* withdrawal.

pul·let, *n.* young chicken.

pul·ley, *n.* wheel and cord which lifts or turns.

pull·out, *n.* leaving.

pul·mo·nar·y, *a.* of the lungs.

pulp, *n.* soft organic matter; succulent part of fruit; lurid magazine.

pul·pit, *n.* platform from which the clergyman preaches.

pulp·wood, *n.* wood used to make paper.

pul·sate, *v.*, **-sat·ed**, **-sat·ing**. vibrate; throb.

pulse, *n.* rhythmic throbbing.

pul·ver·ize, *v.*, **-ized**, **-iz·ing**. reduce to fine powder; crush.

pu·ma, *n. pl.*, **-mas**, **-ma**. large, wild cat.

pum·ice, *n.* porous stone.

pump, *n.* machine for raising liquid; low-cut shoe. *v.* inflate; drive; force.

pum·per·nick·el, *n.* dark bread.

pump·kin, *n.* edible orange gourd.

pun, *n.* play on words.

punch, *v.* pierce; poke. *n.* tool for piercing; blow; cold beverage; vitality.

punch-drunk, *a. Inf.* confused; groggy.

punc·tu·al, *a.* exact to the time.

punc·tu·ate, *v.*, **-at·ed**, **-at·ing**. mark with punctuation; give emphasis. **punc·tu·a·tion**, *n.*

punc·ture, *n.* hole. *v.*, **-tured**, **-tur·ing**. prick; perforate.

pun·gent, *a.* biting; caustic.

pun·ish, *v.* inflict a penalty.

punk, *n. Inf.* naive hoodlum.

punt, *v.* kick a football before it touches the ground.

pu·ny, *a.*, **-ni·er**, **-ni·est**. underdeveloped.

pup, *n.* young dog, seal.

pu·pa, *n. pl.*, **pu·pae**, **-pas**. intermediate form of an insect.

pu·pil, *n.* student; round opening in the eye's iris.

pup·pet, *n.* doll moved by hand or cords.

pur·chase, *v.*, **-chased**, **-chas·ing**. gain; buy. *n.* acquisition.

pure, *a.* innocent; unpolluted.

pu·ree, *n.* strained food.

pur·ga·tive, *n.* a cleansing.

pur·ga·to·ry, *n. pl.*, **-ries**. *Inf.* state of temporary suffering.

purge, *v.*, **purged**, **purg·ing**. purify; become clean.

pu·ri·fy, *v.*, **-fied**, **-fy·ing**. make pure; free.

pur·ism, *n.* insistence on rigid purity.

pu·ri·tan, *n.* one who affects strictness of life.

pu·ri·ty, *n.* chastity.

purl, *v.* invert a stitch.

pur·loin, *v.* steal.

pur·ple, *a.* color that is a blend of red and blue.

pur·port, *n.* meaning.

pur·pose, *n.* objective; resolution.

pur·pose·ly, *adv.* intentionally.

pur·pos·ive, *a.* firm.

purr, **pur**, *n.* soft murmuring.

purse, *n.* handbag; prize money. *v.*, **pursed**, **purs·ing**. pucker.

purs·er, *n.* ship's officer.

pur·su·ant, *a.* agreeable with.

pur·sue, *v.*, **-sued**, **-su·ing**. follow; chase.

pur·suit, *n.* regular pastime.

pur·vey, *v.* furnish.

pur·vey·ance, *n.* provisions.

pus, *n.* yellowish substance found in sores.

push, *v.* press against; shove. *n.* impetus.

push·y, *a.*, **push·i·er**, **push·i·est**. aggressive.

push·o·ver, *n. Inf.* anyone easily deceived.

pu·sil·lan·i·mous, *a.* cowardly.

puss, *n.* cat. *Inf.* face; mouth.

puss·y, *n. pl.*, **-ies**. kitten.

puss·y·foot, *v.* act cautiously.

pus·tule, *n.* blister.

put, *v.*, **put**, **put·ting**. move; place; lay.

pu·ta·tive, *a.* supposed.

put-on, *a.* pretended. *n. Inf.* hoax.

pu·tre·fac·tion, *n.* that which is putrefied.

pu·tre·fy, *v.*, **-fied**, **-fy·ing**. rot.

pu·trid, *a.* offensive; vile.

putt, *n.* gentle golf stroke.

put·ter, *v.* dawdle.

put·ting green, *n.* smooth turf for golf.

put·ty, *n.* paste made of lime and linseed oil; one who is easily influenced.

puz·zle, *v.*, **-zled**, **-zling**. perplex; ponder. *n.* toy which tries the ingenuity.

puz·zle·ment, *n.* bewilderment.

Pyg·my, Pig·my, *n. pl.*, **Pyg·mies**, **Pig·mies**. dwarfish person. *a.* (*Often l.c.*) of very small size.

py·lon, *n.* metal tower.

pyr·a·mid, *n.* solid structure whose base is square and whose sides are triangular and meet at a point. *v.* increase by gradual additions.

pyre, *n.* funeral pile.

Py·rex, *n. Trademark.* heat-resistant glass.

py·ric, *a.* caused by burning.

py·ro·ma·ni·a, *n.* uncontrollable impulse to set things on fire.

py·rom·e·ter, *n.* instrument which measures extremely high temperatures.

py·ro·tech·nics, *n. pl.*, *sing. or pl. in constr.* display of fireworks.

py·thon, *n.* non-poisonous snakes.

Q

quack, *n.* duck sound; a pretender. **quack·ish**, *a.* **quackery** *n.*

quad·ran·gle, *n.* figure with four sides and angles. **quad·ran·gu·lar**, *a.*

quad·rant, *n.* quarter of a circle. **quad·ran·tal**, *a.*

quad·ri·lat·er·al, *a.* four sided.

quad·ru·ped, *n.* four-footed animal.

quad·ru·ple, *v.*, **-pled**, **-pling**. multiply by four.

quad·ru·plet, *n.* one of four children born at one birth.

quaff, *v.* drink with gusto.

quag·mire, *n.* bog. **quag·mired**, **quag·mir·y**, *a.*

quail, *n.* small bird. *v.* cower.

quaint, *a.* antique.

quake, *v.*, **quaked**, **quak·ing**. shake. *n.* earthquake.

qual·i·fy, *v.*, **-fied**, **-fy·ing**. make fit; restrict; modify. **qual·i·fi·a·ble**, *a.*, **qual·i·fi·er**, *n.*

qual·i·ty, *n. pl.*, **-ties**. characteristic; excellence.

qualm, *n.* sick feeling.

quan·da·ry, *n. pl.*, **-ries**. difficulty.

quan·ti·ty, *n. pl.*, **-ties**. amount.

quar·an·tine, *n.* isolation to prevent spread of disease. *v.*, **-tined**, **-tin·ing**. isolate.

quar·rel, *n.* angry dispute. *v.*, **-reled**, **-rel·ing**, **-relled**, **-rel·ling**.

quar·ry, *n. pl.*, **-ries**. prey; open pit where stones are dug.

quart, *n.* two liquid pints.

quar·ter, *n.* one-fourth of anything; *pl.* shelter.

quar·ter·back, *n.* football signal caller.

quar·ter·ly, *a.* done every quarter year. *n. pl.*, **-lies**.

quar·tet, *n.* any set of four.

quartz, *n.* crystallized mineral.

quash, *v.* put down.

qua·si, *a.* resembling.

qua·ver, *v.* shake, **qua·ver·y**, *a.*

quay, *n.* landing place; wharf.

queen, *n.* female ruler. **queen·ly**, *adv.*, *a.*

queer, *a.* strange.

quell, *v.* crush; quiet.

quench, *v.* put out; satisfy; check.

quer·u·lous, *a.* complaining.

que·ry, *n. pl.*, **-ries**. question. *v.*, **-ried**, **-ry·ing**.

quest, *n.* search.

ques·tion, *n.* inquiry; point of doubt.

ques·tion·a·ble, *a.* doubtful. **ques·tion·a·bly**, *adv.*

ques·tion mark, *n.* symbol (?) used to indicate a question.

ques·tion·naire, *n.* series of questions to gather information.

queue, *n.* braided hair; line of people.

quib·ble, *n.* argument over trivialities. *v.*, **-bled, -bling.**

quick, *a.* rapid.

quick·en, *v.* make quicker. **quick·en·er**, *n.*

quick·sand, *n.* deep wet sand area.

quick·sil·ver, *n.* mercury.

quick·tem·pered, *a.* easily angered.

quick·wit·ted, *a.* mentally alert.

qui·es·cent, *a.* still; quiet. **qui·es·cence**, *n.*

qui·et, *a.* silent; still. *n.* rest. **qui·et·ly**, *adv.*, **qui·et·ness**, **qui·et·er**, *n.*

quill, *n.* large bird feather used as a pen.

quilt, *n.* thick, warm coverlet. **quilt·er**, *n.*

quince, *n.* acid fruit used in making jellies.

qui·nine, *n.* bitter alkaloid used as a malaria remedy.

quin·tes·sence, *n.* perfect example.

quin·tu·ple, *a.* five times as many. *v.*, **-pled, -pling.**

quin·tu·plet, *n.* five of a kind.

quip, *n.* clever remark. *v.*, **quipped, quip·ping. quip·ster,** *n.*

quirk, *n.* peculiar characteristic. **quirk·y**, *a.*, **-i·er, -i·est.**

quit, *v.*, **quit** or **quit·ted, quit·ting.** leave; stop; resign.

quite, *adv.* totally; very.

quiv·er, *n.* arrow case; tremor. *v.* shake.

quix·ot·ic, *a.* impractical.

quiz, *n. pl.*, **quiz·zes.** brief test. *v.*, **quizzed, quiz·zing. quiz·zi·cal**, *a.* comical.

quo·rum, *n.* number of group members necessary to legally act.

quo·ta, *n.* share assigned to each.

quo·ta·tion, *n.* passage quoted; current price.

quo·ta·tion mark, *n.* symbol (" ") used to indicate a quotation.

quote, *v.*, **quot·ed, quot·ing.** repeat the words of exactly.

quo·tient, *n.* result of dividing one number by another.

R

rab·bi, *n. pl.*, **-bis.** ordained leader of a synagogue.

rab·bit, *n.* hare.

rab·ble, *n.* disorderly crowd. *v.*, **-bled, -bling.** mob.

rab·id, *a.* raging; mad.

ra·bies, *n.* infectious viral disease.

race, *n.* contest of speed; division of mankind; rapid current. *v.*, **raced, rac·ing.** run swiftly.

ra·ceme, *n.* flower cluster.

ra·chis, *n. pl.*, **ra·chis·es, rach·i·des.** axial structure.

ra·cial, *a.* characteristic of race.

rac·ism, *n.* belief that one race is inherently superior.

rack, *n.* framework; instrument of torture. *v.* torture; torment.

rack·et, *n.* nettled paddle; loud noise. *Inf.* scheme.

rack·et·eer, *n. Inf.* one engaged in something dishonest.

rac·on·teur, *n.* teller of stories.

rac·y, *a.*, **-i·er, -i·est.** spirited; slightly risqué.

ra·dar, *n.* electronic system for determining the location of an object by radio signals.

ra·di·al, *a.* grouped like radii.

ra·di·ance, *n.* sparkling luster.

ra·di·ant, *a.* shining.

ra·di·ate, *v.* emit rays; give an aura of.

ra·di·a·tion, *n.* radiant energy.

ra·di·a·tor, *n.* appliance for heating.

rad·i·cal, *a.* of a root; thorough; extreme. *Math.* forming a root. *n.* extremist. *Math.* quantity expressed as a root.

rad·i·cal sign, *n.* mathematical symbol $(\sqrt{})$

ra·di·o, *n. pl.*, **-os.** wireless telegraphy; broadcast. *a.* wireless. *v.*, **-oed, -o·ing.** transmit by radio.

ra·di·o·ac·tiv·i·ty, *n.* emission of alpha, beta, or gamma rays.

ra·di·ol·o·gy, *n.* science dealing with rays.

rad·ish, *n.* pungent, edible root.

ra·di·um, *n.* radioactive metallic element. Sym. Ra.

ra·di·us, *n. pl.*, **-i, -us·es.** straight line from the center to the circumference of a circle.

ra·don, *n.* radioactive gaseous element. Sym. Rn.

raf·fle, *n.* lottery.

raft, *n.* float of timber fastened together. *Inf.* great quantity.

raft·er, *n.* support timbers of a roof.

rag, *n.* discarded cloth. *v.,* **rag·ged, rag·ging.** *Inf.* tease.

rage, *n.* violent anger; passion. *v.,* **raged, rag·ing.** act furiously.

rag·ged, *a.* torn; shaggy; rough.

rag·weed, *n.* herb which causes hay fever.

raid, *n.* sudden attack. *v.* take part in a raid.

rail, *n.* bar extending from one post to another; railroad; marsh bird. *v.* reproach.

rail·ing, *n.* barrier; balustrade.

rail·road, *n.* tracks on which train run. *Inf.* rush through.

rai·ment, *n.* garments.

rain, *n.* water which is condensed and falls from the atmosphere. *v.*

rain·bow, *n.* arc of prismatic colors.

rain·coat, *n.* waterproof coat.

rain·fall, *n.* shower of rain.

raise, *v.,* **raised, rais·ing.** set upright; elevate; rouse; breed; rear; increase in amount; bet. *n.* increase.

rai·sin, *n.* dried grape.

rake, *n.* farm tool with tines; libertine. *v.,* **raked, rak·ing.** gather together; search through.

rak·ish, *a.* jaunty.

ral·ly, *v.,* **-lied, -ly·ing.** bring to order; call together; tease; revive. *n. pl.,* **-lies.** recovery; drawing together.

ram, *n.* male sheep; device for battering.

ram·ble, *v.,* **-bled, -bling.** wander. *n.* carefree; aimless.

ram·bler, *n.* that which rambles; climbing rose.

ram·bunc·tious, *a.* unruly.

ram·i·fi·ca·tion, *n.* result; branch.

ram·i·fy, *v.,* **-fied, -fy·ing.** divide into parts.

ramp, *n.* sloping surface.

ram·page, *v.,* **-paged, -pag·ing.** storm about. *n.* violent conduct.

ram·pant, *a.* unchecked.

ram·part, *n.* bulwark.

ram·rod, *n.* rod to clean firearms.

ram·shack·le, *a.* tumble-down.

ranch, *n.* extensive farm.

ranch·er, *n.* one who owns ranch.

ran·cid, *a.* sour-smelling.

ran·cor, *n.* bitterness.

ran·dom, *n.* lack of direction. *a.* left to chance.

range, *v.,* **ranged, rang·ing.** set in rows; classify; rank; place. *n.* row; open country; distance; stove.

rang·er, *n.* mounted policeman.

rang·y, *a.,* **-i·er, -i·est.** slender and long-limbed.

rank, *n.* line of things; position; standing. *a.* vigorous growth; total; utter.

ran·kle, *v.,* **-kled, -kling.** irritate; inflame.

ran·sack, *v.* plunder.

ran·som, *n.* payment for the release of a captive.

rant, *v.* rave. *n.* agitated speech.

rap, *v.,* **rapped, rap·ping.** quick blow; knock. *Inf.* discuss. *n.* knock. *Inf.* blame.

ra·pa·cious, *a.* avaricious.

rape, *n.* sexual intercourse against an individual's will; annual herb. *v.* ravish.

rap·id, *a.* quick; showing speed.

ra·pi·er, *n.* sword.

rap·port, *n.* harmony.

rap·proche·ment, *n.* reconciling.

ras·cal·lion, *n.* rascal.

rapt, *a.* absorbed.

rap·ture, *n.* state of ecstasy.

rare, *a.,* **rar·er, rar·est.** seldom seen; unusual; underdone.

rar·e·fy, *v.,* **-fied, -fy·ing.** refine; become thin.

rare·ly, *adv.* seldom.

rar·i·ty, *n. pl.,* **-ties.** something that is rare.

ras·cal, *n.* dishonest person; rogue.

rash, *a.* acting hastily. *n.* eruption.

rasp, *v.* scrape; irritate. *n.* coarse file; grating sound.

rasp·ber·ry, *n. pl.,* **-ries.** small juicy fruit.

rat, *n.* long-tailed rodent. *Inf.* informer.

ratch·et, *n.* toothed bar.

rate, *n.* value related to a standard; price; degree. *v.,* **rat·ed, rat·ing.** fix the value; scold. *Inf.* be entitled to.

rath·er, *adv.* more readily; somewhat.

rat·i·fy, *v.,* **-fied, -fy·ing.** confirm.

rat·ing, *n.* grading.

ra·tio, *n. pl.,* **-tios.** relation between two similar values.

ra·tion, *n.* fixed amount; portion.

ra·tion·al, *a.* endowed with reason; sane.

ra·tion·ale, *n.* statement of reasons.

ra·tion·al·ize, *v.,* -ized, -iz·ing. justify.

rat·tan, ra·tan, *n.* palm used for wickerwork.

rat·tle, *v.,* -tled, -tling. chatter; make quick, clicking sounds. *Inf.* confuse. *n.* clattering sound; infant's toy.

rat·tle·brain, *n.* flighty person.

rat·tle·snake, *n.* venomous snakes with rattles on the tail.

rau·cous, *a.* unruly.

raun·chy, *a.,* -i·er, -i·est. *Inf.* lewd.

rav·age, *n.* ruin. *v.,* -aged, -ag·ing. devastate.

rave, *v.,* raved, rav·ing. speak irrationally. *n.* frenzy.

rav·el, *v.,* -eled, -el·ing. unwind; involve.

ra·ven, *n.* black bird of the crow family.

rav·en·ous, *a.* starved.

ra·vine, *n.* gorge.

rav·ish, *v.* rape; violate; give joy.

rav·ish·ing, *a.* entrancing.

raw, *a.* not cooked; harsh; unrefined; chilly. *Inf.* naked.

ray, *n.* narrow beam; gleam; material particles; flat fish. *v.* radiate.

ray·on, *n.* synthetic fiber.

raze, rase, *v.,* razed, raz·ing, rased, ras·ing. demolish.

ra·zor, *n.* sharp-edged instrument used for shaving.

razz, *v.* *Inf.* tease.

raz·zle-daz·zle, *n.* *Inf.* gaudy, activity.

re, *n.* *Mus.* second tone of a major scale. *prep.* about.

reach, *v.* touch by stretching; penetrate to. *n.* act of stretching; range.

re·act, *v.* act in response to.

re·ac·tion, *n.* action in response to.

re·ac·tion·ar·y, *n.* ultraconservative.

re·ac·ti·vate, *v.,* -vat·ed, -vat·ing. to become operative again.

re·ac·tor, *n.* apparatus that produces atomic energy.

read, *v.,* read, read·ing. apprehend the meaning of something written; utter aloud; explain the meaning of; indicate.

a. well-informed.

read·a·ble, *a.* easy to read.

read·er, *n.* one who reads; schoolbook.

read·ing, *n.* action of one who reads; literary knowledge; a given passage.

re·ad·just, *v.* settle again.

read·y, *a.,* -i·er, -i·est. inclined; at hand. *v.,* -ied, -y·ing. prepare.

read·y-made, *a.* made beforehand.

re·al, *a.* true; genuine; sincere.

re·al es·tate, *n.* land and whatever is a part of it.

re·al·ism, *n.* attention to what is real.

re·al·i·ty, *n. pl.,* -ties. real thing or fact.

re·al·ize, *v.,* -ized, -iz·ing. understand clearly; convert into cash.

re·al·ly, *adv.* actually.

realm, *n.* domain.

Re·al·tor, *n. Trademark.* broker of real estate.

re·al·ty, *n.* real estate.

ream, *n.* bundle of paper of 480, 500, or 516 sheets. *v.* enlarge (a hole).

re·an·i·mate, *v.,* -mat·ed, -mat·ing. resuscitate.

reap, *v.* harvest.

re·ap·por·tion·ment, *n.* redistribution of representatives.

rear, *v.* bring up; breed; grow; erect. *n.* backside.

re·ar·range, *v.,* -ranged, -rang·ing. put in proper order again.

rear·ward, *a.* backward.

rea·son, *n.* justification; intellectual faculty; sanity. *v.* discuss; think logically.

rea·son·a·ble, *a.* rational; moderate.

rea·son·ing, *n.* process of thinking logically.

re·as·sume, *v.* take up again.

re·as·sure, *v.,* -sured, -sur·ing. hearten.

re·bate, *v.,* -bat·ed, -bat·ing. return; deduct. *n.* refund.

reb·el, *n.* one who revolts. *a.* defiant.

re·bel·lion, *n.* armed rising.

re·bel·lious, *a.* mutinous.

re·bound, *v.* spring back. *n.* recoil.

re·buff, *n.* refusal. *v.* beat back; snub.

re·buke, *v.,* -buked, -buk·ing. reprimand. *n.* reproof.

re·but, *v.,* -but·ted, -but·ting. refute.

re·but·tal, *n.* refutation.

re·call, *v.* order to return; revoke. *n.* revocation.

re·cant, *v.* retract.

re·ca·pit·u·late, *v.*, **-lat·ed, -lat·ing.** summarize.

re·cap·ture, *v.*, **-tured, -tur·ing.** capture again. *n.* recovery.

re·cede, *v.*, **-ced·ed, -ced·ing.** retreat.

re·ceipt, *n. usu. pl.* paper showing something received.

re·ceive, *v.*, **-ceived, -ceiv·ing.** obtain; take; welcome.

re·ceiv·er, *n.* one who receives.

re·ceiv·er·ship, *n.* legal status of an enterprise under control of a receiver.

re·cent, *a.* of late origin.

re·cep·ta·cle, *n.* repository.

re·cep·tion, *n.* receiving; formal ceremony.

re·cess, *n.* work break; cavity in a wall.

re·ces·sion, *n.* withdrawal; temporary business slump.

rec·i·pe, *n.* instructions for preparing a particular dish.

re·cip·i·ent, *n.* receiver.

re·cip·ro·cal, *a.* moving alternately backward and forward.

re·cip·ro·cate, *v.*, **-cat·ed, -cat·ing.** give in return; interchange.

rec·i·proc·i·ty, *n.* equal trade rights.

re·cit·al, *n.* entertainment usu. given by a soloist.

rec·i·ta·tion, *n.* anything recited. *n.*

re·cite, *v.*, **-cit·ed, -cit·ing.** enumerate; repeat from memory.

reck·less, *a.* careless.

reck·on, *v.* compute; consider. *Inf.* suppose.

reck·on·ing, *n.* computation; bill; accounting.

re·claim, *v.* recover in a usable form.

re·cline, *v.*, **-clined, -clin·ing.** lean or lie back.

re·cluse, *n.* one who lives in seclusion. *a.* sequestered.

rec·og·ni·tion, *n.* acknowledgment.

rec·og·nize, *v.*, **-nized, -niz·ing.** know again; acknowledge.

re·coil, *v.* fall back; shrink back. *n.* rebound.

re·col·lect, *v.* compose; recover; remember.

rec·om·mend, *v.* commend; entrust; advise.

rec·om·men·da·tion, *n.* favorable representation.

rec·om·pense, *v.*, **-pensed, -pens·ing.** reward; compensate. *n.* reward.

rec·on·cile, *v.*, **-ciled, -cil·ing.** adjust; settle. **rec·on·cil·a·ble**, *a.* **rec·on·cil·a·bly**, *adv.* **rec·on·cil·i·a·tion**, *n.*

re·con·dite, *a.* obscure.

re·con·di·tion, *v.* restore.

re·con·firm, *v.* confirm again.

re·con·nais·sance, *n.* observation of territory.

re·con·noi·ter, *v.*, **-tered, -ter·ing.** make a survey of.

re·con·struct, *v.* rebuild.

re·con·struc·tion, *n.* something reconstructed.

re·cord, *v.* chart; set down; make a record. *n.* account; phonograph disc.

re·count, *v.* count again; enumerate. *n.* second count.

re·coup, *v.* regain; repay.

re·course, *n.* a going to for help or protection.

re·cov·er, *v.* regain after losing; restore; retrieve.

re·cov·er·y, *n. pl.*, **-ies.** regain health.

rec·re·ant, *a.* cowardly; unfaithful. *n.* deserter.

re·cre·ate, *v.*, **-at·ed, -at·ing.** to create anew.

rec·re·a·tion, *n.* diversion; relaxation.

re·crim·i·nate, *v.*, **-nat·ed, -nat·ing.** accuse in return.

re·cruit, *n.* new member of a group. *v.* enlist new soldiers.

rec·tal, *a.* involving the rectum.

rec·tan·gle, *n.* right-angled parallelogram.

rec·tan·gu·lar, *a.* right-angled.

rec·ti·fy, *v.*, **-fied, -fy·ing.** put right; refine. **rec·ti·fi·a·ble**, *a.*

rec·ti·tude, *n.* integrity.

rec·tor, *n.* clergyman in charge of a parish.

rec·tum, *n. pl.*, **-tums, -ta.** lower part of the large intestine.

re·cum·bent, *a.* reclining.

re·cu·per·ate, *v.*, **-at·ed, -at·ing.** regain what was lost. **re·cu·per·a·tion**, *n.*

re·cur, *v.*, **-curred, -cur·ring.** occur again. **re·cur·rence**, *n.*

red, *a.*, **redder, red·dest.** color of blood; communistic. *n.* color like blood; Communist.

red·bird, *n.* cardinal.

red-blood·ed, *a.* vigorous.

red·den, *v.* blush.

red·dish, *a.* somewhat red.

re·deem, *v.* pay off; buy back; make amends.

re·demp·tion, *n.* repurchase; recovery; salvation.

red her·ring, *n.* subterfuge.

red-hot, *a.* very hot; greatly excited.

red-let·ter, *a.* memorable.

re·do, *v.,* **-did, -done, -do·ing.** do over.

red·o·lent, *a.* reminiscent.

re·doubt·a·ble, *a.* formidable.

re·dress, *v.* remedy. *n.* relief from oppression.

re·duce, *v.,* **-duced, -duc·ing.** diminish in quantity; make less; subdue.

re·duc·tion, *n.* subjugation; small copy.

re·dun·dant, *a.* superfluous; verbose. **re·dun·dance, re·dun·dan·cy,** *n.*

red·wood, *n.* huge pine-like tree.

re·ech·o, *v.,* **-oed, -o·ing.** reverberate.

reed, *n.* tall marsh grass; musical pipe; mouthpiece of wind instruments.

reef, *n.* ledge of rocks or coral in water; part of a sail.

reef·er, *n.* close-fitting jacket.

reek, *v.* emit a strong odor. *n.* unpleasant smell.

reel, *n.* spool; lively dance. *v.* sway; stagger.

re·fec·to·ry, *n. pl.,* **-ries.** dining hall.

re·fer, *v.,* **-ferred, -fer·ring.** hand over; assign; consult. *n.*

ref·er·ee, *n.* one who settles a dispute. *v.,* **-eed, -ee·ing.**

ref·er·ence, *n.* direct allusion; regard.

ref·er·en·dum, *n. pl.,* **-dums, -da.** referral to public vote.

ref·er·ent, *n.* something referred to.

re·fill, *v.* fill again. *n.* second serving.

re·fine, *v.,* **-fined, -fin·ing.** make pure; cultivate.

re·fined, *a.* polished.

re·fine·ment, *n.* elegance of manners.

re·fin·er·y, *n. pl.,* **-ies.** place for refining.

re·fit, *v.,* **-fit·ted, -fit·ting.** repair.

re·flect, *v.* to mirror; reveal; consider seriously.

re·flec·tion, *n.* image given back; meditation.

re·flex, *n.* image; movement. *a.* pertaining to an involuntary action.

re·flex·ive, *a.* a verb, having a pronoun object which is the same as its subject.

re·for·est, *v.* replant with trees.

re·form, *v.* amend one's behavior. *n.* improvement.

re·form·a·to·ry, *n. pl.,* **-ies.** corrective institution for juveniles.

re·fract, *v.* deflect light.

re·frac·to·ry, *a.* unmanageable.

re·frain, *v.* abstain. *n.* phrase repeated at intervals in a verse.

re·fresh, *v.* give new energy to.

re·fresh·ment, *n. pl.* light meal.

re·frig·er·ant, *n.* cooling agent.

re·frig·er·ate, *v.,* **-at·ed, -at·ing.** keep cool.

ref·uge, *n.* shelter.

ref·u·gee, *n.* one who flees for safety.

re·ful·gent, *a.* radiant.

re·fund, *v.* reimburse. *n.* repayment.

re·fur·bish, *v.* renovate.

re·fus·al, *n.* denial. *v.,* **-fused, -fus·ing.** deny; decline to do.

re·fuse, *n.* rubbish. *a.* discarded.

re·fute, *v.,* **-fut·ed, -fut·ing.** disprove.

re·gain, *v.* recover.

re·gal, *a.* royal.

re·gale, *v.,* **-galed, -gal·ing.** entertain lavishly.

re·gard, *v.* look upon; consider; esteem. *n.* reference; notice; esteem.

re·gard·ing, *prep.* concerning.

re·gard·less, *a.* showing no regard. *adv.* despite.

re·gat·ta, *n.* boat race.

re·gen·er·ate, *v.,* **-at·ed, -at·ing.** recreate; reform. **re·gen·er·a·tion,** *n.*

re·gent, *n.* ruling power during disability of the sovereign.

re·gime, *n.* administration.

reg·i·men, *n.* regulated course of living.

reg·i·ment, *n.* unit of organization. *v.* systematize; organize.

re·gion, *n.* locality; a part of a space.

reg·is·ter, *n.* list; machine which records data; contrivance which regulates the passage of air; tonal quality. *v.* enroll; indicate.

reg·is·tered nurse, *n.* licensed nurse.

reg·is·trar, *n.* record keeper.

reg·is·tra·tion, *n.* enrollment.

re·gress, v. go back. n. retrogression. **re·gres·sion**, n.

re·gret, v., **-gret·ted**, **-gret·ting**. feel sorrow. n. disappointment.

reg·u·lar, a. common; habitual. n. one who is loyal.

reg·u·late, v., **-lat·ed**, **-lat·ing**. adjust; control.

reg·u·la·tion, n. rule; precept. a. ordinary.

re·ha·bil·i·tate, v., **-tat·ed**, **-tat·ing**. reinstate. **re·ha·bil·i·ta·tion**, n.

re·hash, v. discuss again.

re·hearse, v., **-hearsed**, **-hears·ing**. practice repeatedly.

reign, n. sovereignty; influence. v. rule.

re·im·burse, v., **-bursed**, **-burs·ing**. pay back; refund. **re·im·burse·ment**, n.

rein, n. usu. pl. strap which restrains a horse. v. guide.

re·in·car·na·tion, n. new embodiment.

re·in·force, v., **-forced**, **-forc·ing**. strengthen.

re·in·state, v., **-stat·ed**, **-stat·ing**. restore to a former state. **re·in·state·ment**, n.

re·it·er·ate, v., **-at·ed**, **-at·ing**. repeat again and again. **re·it·er·a·tion**, n.

re·ject, v. cast off; discard. **re·jec·tion**, n.

re·joice, v., **-joiced**, **-joic·ing**. exult.

re·join, v. reunite; answer.

re·join·der, n. retort.

re·ju·ve·nate, v., **-nat·ed**, **-nat·ing**. restore to youthful vigor. **re·ju·ve·na·tion**, n.

re·lapse, v., **-lapsed**, **-laps·ing**. backslide. n. recurrence of illness.

re·late, v., **-lat·ed**, **-lat·ing**. narrate; show a connection.

re·lat·ed, a. allied.

re·la·tion, n. connection between things; kinship; narrative.

rel·a·tive, a. relevant. n. related person.

rel·a·tiv·i·ty, n. interdependence of space and time.

re·lax, v. slacken; make less tense.

re·lay, v., **-laid**, **-lay·ing**. **-layed**, **-lay·ing**. transmit by a relay; lay anew. n. race; fresh supply; device to send messages.

re·lease, v., **-leased**, **-leas·ing**. set free; let go. n. liberation; relief; waiver.

rel·e·gate, v., **-gat·ed**, **-gat·ing**. banish.

re·lent, v. yield.

rel·e·vant, a. pertinent. **rel·e·vance**, **rel·e·van·cy**, n.

re·li·a·ble, a. dependable.

re·li·ance, n. confidence; trust.

rel·ic, n. something outmoded.

re·lief, n. ease from pain; a relieving.

re·lieve, v., **-lieved**, **-liev·ing**. lessen; free from something.

re·li·gion, n. worship of a god or gods.

re·li·gious, a. devout; faithful.

re·lin·quish, v. give up.

rel·ish, v. be pleased with. n. liking; pickled seasoning.

re·luc·tance, n. unwillingness.

re·luc·tant, a. unwilling.

re·ly, v., **-lied**, **-ly·ing**. depend on.

re·main, v. endure; to last.

re·mand, v. send back.

re·mark, n. brief statement. v. comment.

re·mark·a·ble, a. unusual.

rem·e·dy, n. pl., **-dies**. something that corrects. v., **-died**, **-dy·ing**. cure.

re·mem·ber, v. recall; have in mind. v. recollect.

re·mem·brance, n. keepsake. often pl. warm greetings.

re·mind, v. cause to remember.

rem·i·nisce, v., **-nisced**, **-nisc·ing**. recall the past.

rem·i·nis·cence, n. recollection.

re·miss, a. careless.

re·mis·sion, n. forgiveness.

re·mit, v., **-mit·ted**, **-mit·ting**. send in payment; pardon.

re·mit·tance, n. payment.

rem·nant, n. fragment.

re·mod·el, v. reconstruct.

re·mon·strate, v., **-strat·ed**, **-strat·ing**. present strong reasons against. **re·mon·strance**, n.

re·morse, n. guilty anguish. **re·morse·ful**, a.

re·mote, a., **-mot·er**, **-mot·est**. distant.

re·mount, v. mount again. n. fresh horse.

re·mov·al, n. change of place or site; dismissal. **re·mov·a·ble**, a.

re·move, v., **-moved**, **-mov·ing**. displace; cause to leave.

re·mu·ner·ate, v., **-at·ed**, **-at·ing**. pay. **re·mu·ner·a·tion**, n.

ren·ais·sance, n. revival.

re·nas·cence, n. rebirth.

rend, v., **rent** or **rend·ed**, **rend·ing**. tear; split.

ren·der, v. pay back; furnish; boil down.

ren·dez·vous, n. pl., **-vous**. special meeting. v., **-voused**, **-vous·ing**, assemble.

ren·di·tion, n. interpretation.

ren·e·gade, n. deserter.

re·nege, v., **-neged**, **-neg·ing**. Inf. fail to keep one's word.

re·new, v. restore; resume.

re·new·al, n. renewing.

re·nounce, v., **-nounced**, **-nounc·ing**. repudiate.

ren·o·vate, v., **-vat·ed**, **-vat·ing**. restore. **ren·o·va·tion**, n.

re·nown, n. fame.

rent, n. compensation to the owner of a property; breach. v. lease.

rent·al, n. sum paid for rent.

re·pair, v. restore; to go.

rep·a·ra·tion, n. repair. Pl. amends.

rep·ar·tee, n. witty reply.

re·past, n. meal.

re·pay, v., **-paid**, **-pay·ing**. pay back; make return.

re·peal, v. rescind. n. revocation.

re·peat, v. say again; execute again. n. repetition.

re·pel, v., **-pelled**, **-pel·ling**. reject; repulse.

re·pent, v. feel remorse. **re·pent·ance**, n.

re·per·cus·sion, n. reverberation.

rep·er·toire, n. collective works.

rep·e·ti·tion, n. something done a second time. **rep·e·ti·tious**, a.

re·place, v., **-placed**, **-plac·ing**. restore. **re·place·a·ble**, a.

re·plen·ish, v. restock.

rep·li·ca, n. reproduction.

re·ply, v., **-plied**, **-ply·ing**. answer; respond.

re·port, v. bring back; relate; present oneself. n. statement.

re·port·er, n. one who reports.

re·pose, v., **-posed**, **-pos·ing**. put trust (in a person or thing); rest. n. peace.

rep·re·hen·si·ble, a. censurable.

re·press, v. subdue; restrain. **re·pres·sion**, n.

re·prieve, v., **-prieved**, **-priev·ing**. delay. n. temporary ease. v., **-prieved**, **-priev·ing**. delay.

rep·ri·mand, n. sharp rebuke. v. reprove severely.

re·pris·al, n. retaliatory act.

re·proach, v. censure. n. blame; disgrace.

rep·ro·bate, a. unprincipled. n. wicked person.

re·pro·duce, v., **-duced**, **-duc·ing**. produce again.

re·proof, n. censure.

re·prove, v., **-proved**, **-prov·ing**. charge with a fault.

rep·tile, n. cold-blooded vertebrate.

re·pub·lic, n. political unit in which power is vested in whole community.

re·pu·di·ate, v., **-at·ed**, **-at·ing**. reject. **re·pu·di·a·tion**, n.

re·pug·nant, a. objectionable.

re·pulse, v., **-pulsed**, **-puls·ing**. repel; rebuff. n. rejection.

re·pul·sive, a. causing aversion.

rep·u·ta·ble, a. honorable. **rep·u·ta·bly**, adv.

rep·u·ta·tion, n. opinion of character.

re·pute, v., **-put·ed**, **-put·ing**. regard. n. reputation. **re·put·ed·ly**, adv.

re·quest, n. petition. v. solicit.

re·quire, v., **-quired**, **-quir·ing**. demand; insist on.

req·ui·site, a. necessary. n. something indispensable.

req·ui·si·tion, n. written application. v. demand upon.

re·run, n. a reshowing. v., **-ran**, **-run**, **-run·ning**. run again.

re·scind, v. revoke.

res·cue, v., **-cued**, **-cu·ing**. free from danger; save. n. act of rescuing.

re·search, n. diligent examination of something. v. investigate.

re·sem·ble, v., **-bled**, **-bling**. be or look like.

re·sent, v. be indignant.

res·er·va·tion, n. concealment; qualification; public land set aside.

re·serve, v., **-served**, **-serv·ing**. keep back. n. land set aside; something withheld; reticence.

res·er·voir, n. receptacle for storing.

re·side, v., **-sid·ed**, **-sid·ing**. dwell permanently; exist. **res·i·dence**, n.

res·i·dent, a. inherent. n. doctor during training period.

re·sid·u·al, a. left over.

res·i·due, *n.* remainder.

re·sign, *v.* give up. **res·ig·na·tion,** *n.* **re·signed,** *a.*

re·sil·ient, *a.* springing back; buoyant. **re·sil·ien·cy,** *n.*

res·in, *n.* substance from plants used in making plastics.

re·sist, *v.* withstand; oppose. **re·sist·er,** *n.*

re·sist·ance, *n.* act of resisting. (*Often cap.*) guerrilla force.

re·sis·tor, *n.* conducting body.

res·o·lute, *a.* determined.

res·o·lu·tion, *n.* determination; formal decision.

re·solve, *v.,* **-solved, -solv·ing.** analyze; explain; form an opinion. *n.* resolution.

res·o·nance, *n.* sympathetic vibrations.

res·o·nant, *a.* echoing back.

re·sort, *v.* have recourse; refuge oneself. *n.* recourse; refuge.

re·sound, *v.* echo; extol.

re·source, *n.* source of support. *pl.* funds. **re·source·ful·ness,** *n.*

re·spect, *v.* regard; honor; courtesy; reference.

re·spect·a·ble, *a.* decent; average. **re·spect·a·bil·i·ty,** *n.*

res·pi·ra·tion, *n.* breathing. **res·pi·ra·to·ry,** *a.*

res·pi·ra·tor, *n.* machine which provides artificial respiration.

res·pite, *n.* reprieve.

re·splend·ent, *a.* magnificent.

re·spond, *v.* answer; react.

re·sponse, *n.* reply; reaction.

re·spon·si·bil·i·ty, *n. pl.,* **-ties.** obligation; duty.

re·spon·si·ble, *a.* accountable; reliable.

re·spon·sive, *a.* sensitive.

rest, *n.* sleep; relief; absence of motion; remainder. *v.* relax; be at ease; cease motion.

res·tau·rant, *n.* commercial business serving meals.

rest·ful, *a.* peaceful.

res·ti·tu·tion, *n.* restoration to the former state.

res·tive, *a.* unruly.

rest·less, *a.* unsettled; discontented.

re·store, *v.,* **-stored, -stor·ing.** re-establish; renew. **res·to·ra·tion,** *n.*

re·strain, *v.* check.

re·straint, *n.* a holding back; reserve.

re·strict, *v.* limit; confine.

re·stric·tion, *n.* restraint; limitation.

re·stric·tive, *a.* limiting.

re·sult, *v.* to rise as a consequence. *n.* outcome; effect.

re·sume, *v.,* **-sumed, -sum·ing.** take up again.

re·su·me, re·su·me, *n.* summary.

re·sur·gent, *a.* rising again. **re·sur·gence,** *n.*

res·ur·rect, *v.* restore to life; to bring back into use.

re·sus·ci·tate, *v.,* **-tat·ed, -tat·ing.** revive; regain consciousness. **re·sus·ci·ta·tion,** *n.*

re·tail, *n.* small sales directly to a consumer. *v.* sell in small quantities.

re·tain, *v.* keep possession of.

re·tain·er, *n.* fee paid to secure services.

re·take, *v.,* **-took, -taken, -taking.** recapture. *n.* a retaking.

re·tal·i·ate, *v.,* **-at·ed, -at·ing.** re-pay; return like for like. **re·tal·i·a·tion,** *n.*

re·tard, *v.* cause to hinder. *n.* delay.

re·ten·tion, *n.* power of memory.

ret·i·cent, *a.* reserved. **ret·i·cence,** *n.*

ret·i·na, *n. pl.,* **-nas, -nae.** part of the eyeball.

ret·i·nue, *n.* attendants.

re·tire, *v.,* **-tired, -tir·ing.** withdraw; retreat from action.

re·tir·ing, *a.* reserved.

re·tort, *v.* reply quickly. *n.* incisive reply.

re·trace, *v.,* **-traced, -trac·ing.** track back.

re·tract, *v.* withdraw or disavow.

re·treat, *n.* withdrawal; place of retirement.

re·trench, *v.* economize. **re·trench·ment,** *n.*

ret·ri·bu·tion, *n.* requital.

re·trieve, *v.,* **-trieved, -triev·ing.** recover; rescue or save; repair.

ret·ro·ac·tive, *a.* retrospective.

ret·ro·rock·et, *n.* decelerating rocket.

ret·ro·spect, *n.* survey of past time.

re·turn, *v.* give back; restore; repay. *n.* that which is returned.

re·un·ion, *n.* meeting after separation.

rev, *n. Inf.* revolution. *v.,* revved, rev·ving. *Inf.* increase the speed of.

re·veal, *v.* make known.

rev·eil·le, *n.* signal given about daybreak.

rev·el, *v.* take great pleasure.

rev·e·la·tion, *n.* disclosure.

re·venge, *v.*, **-venged**, **-veng·ing**. avenge; to inflict injury for. *n.* retaliation.

rev·e·nue, *n.* income.

re·ver·ber·ate, *v.*, **-at·ed**, **-at·ing**. reecho; reflect. **re·ver·ber·a·tion**, *n.*

re·vere, *v.*, **-vered**, **-ver·ing**. regard with respect; venerate. **rev·er·ence**, *n.*

rev·er·end, *n. Inf.* clergyman.

rev·er·ie, **rev·er·y**, *n. pl.*, **-ies**. irregular train of thought.

re·verse, *v.*, **-versed**, **-vers·ing**. turn in an opposite direction. *a.* of an opposite condition. *n.* opposite side; unfavorable turn of events. **re·ver·sal**, *n.*

re·vers·i·ble, *a.* having two usable sides.

re·vert, *v.* return or come back.

re·view, *v.* examine again; study critically; inspect; write reviews. *n.* revision; general survey; critique.

re·vile, *v.*, **-viled**, **-vil·ing**. speak evil of.

re·vise, *v.*, **-vised**, **-vis·ing**. change and amend. *n.* a change. **re·vi·sion**, *n.*

re·viv·al, *n.* restoration; religious awakening.

re·vive, *v.*, **-vived**, **-viv·ing**. activate again; present again; gain vigor.

re·voke, *v.*, **-voked**, **-vok·ing**. make void; cancel.

re·volt, *v.* rebel against; disgust. *n.* rebellion.

rev·o·lu·tion, *n.* overthrow of a government; radical change; circular motion.

rev·o·lu·tion·ar·y, *a.* suggesting drastic change.

rev·o·lu·tion·ize, *v.*, **-ized**, **-iz·ing**. effect a complete change in.

re·volve, *v.*, **-volved**, **-volv·ing**. travel in an orbit; rotate; ponder.

re·volv·er, *n.* pistol.

re·vue, *n.* satirical theatrical exhibition.

re·vul·sion, *n.* repulsion; strong recoil.

re·ward, *v.* bestow a remuneration; recompense.

rhap·sod·ic, *a.* excessively enthusiastic. Also **rhap·sod·i·cal**.

rhap·so·dy, *n. pl.*, **-dies**. emotional writing; musical composition.

rhe·ni·um, *n.* metallic element. *Sym.* Re.

rhet·o·ric, *n.* persuasive oratory. **rhe·tor·i·cal**, *a.*

rheum, *n.* watery matter.

rheu·mat·ic, *a.* affected with rheumatism.

rheu·mat·ic fe·ver, *n.* severe infectious disease.

rheu·ma·tism, *n.* painful inflammation of the muscles and joints.

rhine·stone, *n.* artificial gem of glass.

rhi·noc·er·os, *n. pl.*, **-os·es**, **-os**. large mammal with horns on the snout.

rho·di·um, *n.* silver-white metallic element. *Sym.* Rh.

rho·do·den·dron, *n.* evergreen shrubs with showy flowers.

rhu·barb, *n.* garden plant having edible stalks. *Inf.* noisy dispute.

rhyme, *n.* word having a sound similar to another; meter. **rhymed**, **rhym·ing**, *v.*

rhythm, *n.* movement with a beat.

rib, *n.* curved bones around the chest; a cut of meat; something riblike.

rib·ald, *a.* vulgar.

rib·bon, *n.* narrow band.

rice, *n.* starchy grain.

rich, *a.* wealthy; productive; sweet.

rich·es, *n. pl.* wealth.

rick, *n.* stack corn or hay.

rick·ets, *n.* bone softening disease.

rick·et·y, *a.*, **-i·er**, **-i·est**. shaky; irregular.

ric·o·chet, *n.* glancing rebound.

rid, *v.*, **rid** or **rid·ded**, **rid·ding**. free; deliver.

rid·dle, *n.* large sieve; puzzling question. *v.*, **-dled**, **-dling**. speak ambiguously; screen.

ride, *v.*, **rode**, **rid·den**, **rid·ing**. sit on and manage; be borne along; control. *Inf.* harass. *n.* journey.

rid·er, *n.* passenger; clause added to bill.

ridge, *n.* crest of something; chain of hills. *v.*, **ridged**, **ridg·ing**. form ridges.

rid·i·cule, *n.* derision. *v.*, **-culed**, **-cul·ing**. make fun of.

ri·dic·u·lous, *a.* absurd.

rife, *a.* prevalent.

riff·raff, *n.* rabble.

ri·fle, n. shoulder gun. v., **-fled, -fling.** ransack and rob.

rift, n. fissure; geological fault; estrangement.

rig, v., **rigged, rig·ging.** fit; equip. Inf. dress; manipulate. n. equipment on a ship.

right, a. just or good; correct; sound or normal; most fitting; side which is turned toward the east when the face is turned toward the north. n. that which is moral. adv. directly. v. redress.

right·eous, a. virtuous.

right·ful, a. legitimate.

right·ism, n. (Sometimes cap.) advocacy of political conservatism.

rig·id, a. not pliant; rigorous. **ri·gid·i·ty**, n.

rig·ma·role, n. nonsense.

rig·or, n. austerity; strictness. **rig·or·ous**, a.

rile, v., **riled, ril·ing.** Inf. anger; irritate.

rill, n. small brook.

rim, n. edge esp. of an object that is circular. **rimmed, rim·ming,** v.

rime, n. hoarfrost.

rime, n. rhyme.

rind, n. firm outward coat or covering.

ring, n. circular band of material; circle; sound of a bell; group of persons. v., **rang, rung, ring·ing.** form a ring. resound or reverberate; summon.

ring·lead·er, n. leader of a group, esp. in violation of law.

ring·let, n. curl.

ring·mas·ter, n. leader of circus performance.

ring·side, n. place which offers a very close view.

ring·worm, n. disease caused by fungi.

rink, n. smooth area for skating.

rinse, v., **rinsed, rins·ing.** wash lightly. n. product used for rinsing.

ri·ot, n. public disturbance of a violent nature; vivid display; revelry. v. participate in a public disorder. **ri·ot·ous**, a.

rip, v., **ripped, rip·ping.** tear; cut open. n. rent; tear; stretch of choppy water.

ripe, a. ready for reaping; matured. **rip·en**, v.

rip·ple, v., **-pled, -pling.** form small waves; agitate lightly. n.

small wave; light movement.

rise, v., **rose, ris·en, ris·ing.** get up; become active; appear; ascend; prove equal. n. increase; extension upward; upward slope.

risk, n. hazard. v. expose to the chance of injury.

ris·que, a. off-color.

rite, n. formal ceremonial practice. **rit·u·al**, a.

rit·u·al·ism, n. study of rituals. **rit·u·al·ist**, n. **rit·u·al·is·tic**, a.

ritz·y, a., **-i·er, -i·est.** Inf. ostentatiously elegant.

ri·val, n. competitor. a. having the same claims. v. strive to equal or excel.

ri·val·ry, n. pl., **-ries.** competition.

riv·er, n. natural stream of flowing water.

riv·et, n. short metallic bolt with a head. v. fasten firmly; engross.

riv·i·er·a, n. coastal resort area.

riv·u·let, n. small stream.

roach, n. pl., **roach, roach·es.** freshwater fish; cockroach.

road, n. highway; route. Inf. on tour.

road·ster, n. open automobile with a rumble seat.

roam, v. wander. n. a wandering.

roar, v. howl. n. full loud sound.

roast, v. cook by exposure to heat; dry and parch. Inf. ridicule. n. piece of beef.

roast·er, n. pan for roasting.

rob, v., **robbed, rob·bing.** deprive of something illegally.

robe, n. flowing gown. v., **robed, rob·ing.** dress.

rob·in, n. common thrush.

ro·bot, n. automaton.

ro·bust, a. vigorous; strong.

rock, n. stone; firm foundation. Inf. any gem. v. move to and fro; shake or sway.

rock·er, n. rocking chair.

rock·et, n. missile.

rock·et·ry, n. science of rocket flight.

rock·y, a., **-i·er, -i·est.** tottering; unsteady; resolute.

ro·co·co, a. gaudy.

rod, n. bar; linear measurement equal to $5^{1}/_{2}$ yards.

ro·dent, n. mammal characterized by incisors adapted for nibbling or gnawing.

ro·de·o, n. pl., **-os.** performance of cowboy skills.

roe, *n.* fish eggs; small deer.

roent-gen, *n.* unit used as a measure of radiation.

rogue, *n.* rascal. **ro-guish**, *a.*

roil, *v.* annoy or anger.

roist-er, *v.* bluster; swagger.

role, *n.* character portrayed by an actor; customary function.

roll, *v.* move by turning; flow; take the shape of a ball; pass; make level by pressing with a roller; trill. *Inf.* rob. *n.* list of names; anything rolled up; small lump of bread.

rol-lick, *v.* be jovial; frolic. **rol-lick-ing**, *a.*

roll-ing pin, *n.* cylinder for rolling out dough.

ro-ly-po-ly, *a.* rotund; plump.

ro-maine, *n.* variety of lettuce.

Ro-man Cath-o-lic, *a.* pertaining to the Roman Catholic Church. *n.*

ro-mance, *n.* tale of chivalric love or unusual adventures; love affair. *v. Inf.* seek a romance with.

Ro-man-esque, *a.* massive, weighty decorative effects.

Ro-man nu-mer-als, *n.* letters of ancient Rome used as numerals.

ro-man-tic, *a.* amorous; fanciful. *n.* romanticist.

ro-man-ti-cism, *n.* artistic movement of the 19th century. **ro-man-ti-cist**, *n.*

romp, *v.* play boisterously. *n.* frolic.

rood, *n.* crucifix.

roof, *n.* cover of a building. *v.* cover with a roof.

roof-ing, *n.* material suitable for a roof.

rook, *n.* chess piece; crow; cheat. *v.* defraud.

rook-ie, *n. Inf.* beginner; new recruit.

room, *n.* place of lodging; amount of space. *v.* have lodgings.

room-mate, *n.* one who shares a room or rooms with another.

room-y, *a.*, **-i-er, -i-est.** spacious. **room-i-ly**, *adv.* **room-i-ness**, *n.*

roost, *n.* place for resting. *v.* lodge.

roost-er, *n.* male chicken.

root, *n.* that part of a plant which fixes itself in the earth; foundation; essence; cause of; elemental form of a word. *v.* send forth roots; be firmly fixed; have a beginning; un-

earth.

root-stock, *n.* origin or source.

rope, *n.* cord of twisted fibers. *v.*, roped, rop-ing. tie with a rope.

ro-sa-ry, *n. pl.*, **-ries.** sequence of prayers; rose garden.

rose, *n.* attractive flower; pinkish color. *a.* like the rose flower in color or scent.

ro-se-ate, *a.* rosecolored; optimistic.

ro-sette, *n.* formation which resembles a rose.

Rosh Ha-sha-nah, *n.* Jewish New Year.

ros-in, *n.* resin used in making varnish.

ros-ter, *n.* list of persons.

ros-trum, *n. pl.*, **-tra, -trums.** speaker's platform.

ros-y, *a.*, **-i-er, -i-est.** pinkish-red; promising.

rot, *v.*, rot-ted, rot-ting. decompose; become corrupt morally; weaken. *n.* decay.

ro-ta-ry en-gine, *n.* radial internal-combustion engine.

ro-tate, *v.*, -tat-ed, -tat-ing. revolve around a center; succeed. **ro-ta-tion**, *n.*

rote, *n.* repetition. **by rote**, merely by memory.

rot-ten, *a.* decaying; corrupt.

ro-tund, *a.* spherical; plump; sonorous. **ro-tun-di-ty**, *n. pl.*, **-ties.**

ro-tun-da, *n.* round domed building.

rouge, *n.* cosmetic; powder used for polishing glass.

rough, *a.* not smooth; uneven; unruly; stormy; rebellious; crude; not perfected. *n.* something coarse. *v.* treat violently. *adv.*

rough-age, *n.* coarse material; foods high in cellulose, such as celery.

rough-house, *n. Inf.* rowdy conduct.

rough-neck, *n. Inf.* rough, coarse fellow.

rou-lette, *n.* game of chance.

round, *a.* spherical; having a curved form; plump; returning; closest multiple of ten. *adv.* circularly; through a series; recurring. *prep.* around; about. *n.* that which is round; series; interval of play; discharge of firearms in a series. *v.* make full; grow round.

round-a-bout, *n.* circuitous

road. *a.* indirect.

round·up, *n.* driving or bringing together.

rouse, *v.*, **roused, rous·ing.** wake from sleep; excite; agitate.

rous·ing, *a.* stirring; vigorous.

roust, *v. Inf.* arouse.

roust·a·bout, *n.* transient laborer.

rout, *n.* uproar; disorder of troops; rabble. *v.* dig up; rummage; put to flight in disorder.

route, *n.* course taken; regular line of travel. *v.*, **rout·ed, rout·ing.** fix the route of.

rout·er, *n.* tool for hollowing out.

rou·tine, *n.* actions done regularly; habit. *a.* commonplace.

rove, *v.*, **roved, rov·ing.** wander.

row, *v.* propel with oars; place in a row; quarrel. *n.* excursion in a rowboat; line; commotion.

row·dy, *n. pl.*, **-dies.** rough, disorderly person. **row·di·er, -di·est**, *a.*

roy·al, *a.* sovereign; majestic; noble. **roy·al·ly**, *adv.*

roy·al·ty, *n. pl.*, **-ties.** sovereignty; nobility; generosity; portion of proceeds paid to the owner of a right.

rub, *v.*, **rubbed, rub·bing.** apply friction to; scour; smear all over; chafe. *n.* a rubbing difficulty; gibe.

rub·ber, *n.* series of games; elastic solid.

rub·ber·neck, *n. Inf.* sightseer.

rub·bish, *n.* debris; nonsense. **rub·bish·y**, *a.*

rub·ble, *n.* pieces of solid material.

rube, *n. Inf.* hick.

ru·bel·la, *n.* German measles.

ru·be·o·la, *n.* measles.

ru·bi·cund, *a.* ruddy.

ru·bid·i·um, *n.* metallic element. Sym. Rb.

ru·bric, *n.* title of a statute; distinctive mark.

ru·by, *n. pl.*, **ru·bies.** deep red gem.

ruck·sack, *n.* knapsack.

ruck·us, *n. Inf.* uproar.

rud·der, *n.* instrument used in steering a ship.

rud·dy, *a.*, **-di·er, -di·est.** having a red color.

rude, *a.*, **rud·er, rud·est.** having coarse manners; discourteous.

ru·di·ment, *n.* unformed beginning. *usu. pl.* first principles.

ru·di·men·ta·ry, *a.*

rue, *v.*, **rued, ru·ing.** regret.

rue, *n.* perennial herb.

rue·ful, *a.* sorrowful.

ruf·fi·an, *n.* brutal fellow.

ruf·fle, *v.*, **-fled, -fling.** disturb; rumple; adorn with ruffles; shuffle. *n.* disturbance; frill.

rug, *n.* floor covering.

rug·ged, *a.* rough; rocky; severe; stern.

ru·in, *n.* destruction; downfall; dilapidation. *v.* defeat; fall into ruins.

ru·in·a·tion, *n.* destruction.

rule, *n.* control; maxim; custom; point of law. *v.*, **ruled, rul·ing.** govern; control.

rul·er, *n.* one that rules; instrument used for measuring length.

rul·ing, *a.* predominant. *n.* decision.

rum, *n.* type of liquor.

rum·ble, *v.*, **-bled, -bling.** make muffled sound. *n.* heavy sound; seat in a roadster. *Inf.* street fight.

ru·mi·nant, *a.* chewing again; contemplative. *n.* cud chewing mammal.

ru·mi·nate, *v.*, **-nated, -nating.** ponder; muse. **ru·mi·na·tion**, *n.*

rum·mage, *v.*, **-maged, -mag·ing.** ransack; search actively. *n.* odds and ends.

rum·my, *n.* card game. *Inf.* habitual drunk.

ru·mor, *n.* hearsay; gossip. *v.* circulate gossip.

ru·mor·mon·ger, *n.* one who spreads malicious rumors.

rump, *n.* buttocks.

rum·ple, *v.*, **-pled, -pling.** wrinkle; crease.

rum·pus, *n.* riot. *Inf.* fracas.

run, *v.*, **ran, run, run·ning.** move more quickly than in walking; flee; make a hasty trip; contend in a race; campaign; flow; operate. *n.* act of running; trip; period of continuous operation; undone stitches; tendency; path. *a.* melted.

run·a·round, *n. Inf.* evasive action.

run·a·way, *n.* someone (or something) that runs away. *a.* escaped; uncontrolled.

run·down, *n.* summing-up. *a.* tired; dilapidated.

rung, *n.* step of a ladder; piece

run-in, *n.* altercation.

run-ner, *n.* racer; messenger; that on which something runs or slides; narrow piece of cloth.

run-ning, *a.* moving rapidly; functioning; current; succession. *n.* quantity run.

run-ny, *a.,* **-ni-er, -ni-est.** tending to drip.

run-of-the-mill, *a.* average.

runt, *n.* smallest in a litter.

run-through, *n.* cursory review.

run-way, *n.* clear pathway.

rup-ture, *n.* hernia; a breach.

ru-ral, *a.* pertaining to the country.

ruse, *n.* artifice; trick.

rush, *v.* act with speed; attack suddenly. *n.* grasslike herb; unexpected sudden surge; busy haste. *a.* requiring haste.

rus-set, *n.* yellowish-brown.

rust, *n.* coating which forms on iron when exposed to air and moisture. *v.* contract rust; deteriorate.

rus-tic, *a.* simple; rural.

rus-tle, *v.,* **-tled, -tling.** make slight, soft sounds. *Inf.* get by energetic action; steal.

rust-y, *a.,* **-i-er, -i-est.** covered with rust; impaired through disuse.

rut, *n.* furrow; stereotyped behavior.

ru-ta-ba-ga, *n.* edible tuber of the mustard family.

ru-the-ni-um, *n.* metallic element. *Sym.* Ru.

ruth-less, *a.* cruel.

rye, *n.* hardy cereal plant allied to wheat.

S

Sab-bath, *n.* day of rest and religious observances. *a.* of the Sabbath.

sa-ber, *n.* cavalry sword.

sa-ble, *n.* carnivorous mammal having dark, lustrous fur. *a.* black; of sable fur.

sab-o-tage, *n.* malicious injury or destruction. *v.,* **-taged, -tag-ing.** destroy by sabotage. **sab-o-teur,** *n.*

sac, *n.* bag or cyst.

sac-cha-rin, *n.* synthetic sugar substitute. **sac-cha-rine,** *a., n.*

sack, *n.* large, strong bag. *v.* put into a sack; pillage.

sack-ful, *n. pl.,* **-fuls.** amount a sack will hold.

sac-ra-ment, *n.* solemn religious ceremony; (*often cap.*) Eucharist. **sac-ra-men-tal,** *a.*

sa-cred, *a.* consecrated; holy.

sac-ri-fice, *n.* offering to a deity; giving up of something valued. *v.* **-ficed, -fic-ing.** make a sacrifice of; offer. **sac-ri-fi-cial,** *a.*

sac-ri-lege, *n.* violation of anything sacred. **sac-ri-le-gious,** *a.*

sad, *a.,* **sad-der, sad-dest.** full of sorrow; grieving. **sad-ly,** *adv.* **sad-ness,** *n.*

sad-den, *v.* make or become sad.

sad-dle, *n.* seat for a rider. *v.,* **-dled, -dling.** put a saddle upon; impose as a burden.

sad-ism, *n.* tendency to take pleasure in cruelty. **sad-ist,** *n.,* *a.* **sa-dis-tic,** *a.*

sa-fa-ri, *n. pl.,* **-ris.** expedition, esp. in eastern Africa, as for hunting.

safe, *a.,* **saf-er, saf-est.** free from danger; having escaped hurt, injury, etc.; involving no danger or risk. *n.* metal box for keeping valuables.

safe-guard, *n.* defense; protection. *v.* guard; defend.

safe-keep-ing, *n.* act of keeping in safety.

safe-ty, *n. pl.,* **-ties.** freedom from danger or injury

safe-ty belt, *n.* life or seat belt.

sag, *v.,* **sagged, sag-ging.** sink in the middle; lose vigor or firmness. *n.* sagging area.

sa-ga, *n.* story of heroic exploits.

sa-ga-cious, *a.* wise; shrewd. **sa-gac-i-ty,** *n.*

sage, *a.,* **sag-er, sag-est.** wise. *n.* extremely wise person; shrubby perennial used for seasoning. **sage-ness,** *n.*

sail, *n.* cloth, usu. canvas, spread to the wind to cause a boat to move. *v.* be conveyed in a vessel on water; glide; navigate. **sail-or,** *n.*

sail-boat, *n.* boat propelled by a sail or sails.

saint, *n.* canonized, holy person. *a.* holy. **saint-hood,** *n.* **saint-ly,** *a.,* **-li-er, -li-est.**

sake, *n.* purpose; benefit.

sal-a-ble, sale-a-ble, *a.* capable of being sold.

sa-la-cious, *a.* lustful; lewd.

sal-ad, *n.* cut vegetables or fruits with dressing.

sal-a-man-der, *n.* lizardlike,

scaleless amphibian.

sa·la·mi, *n.* spicy beef, or beef and pork sausage.

sal·a·ry, *n. pl.,* **-ies.** recompense paid for regular work. **sal·a·ried,** *a.*

sale, *n.* act of selling; amount sold; offering of goods at reduced prices. **sales,** *a.,* **sales·clerk,** *n.*

sa·li·ent, *a.* conspicuous.

sa·line, *a.* consisting of salt; salty. **sa·lin·i·ty,** *n.*

sa·li·va, *n.* watery, viscid fluid of the mouth. **sal·i·var·y,** *a,*

sal·low, *a.* of a pale, sickly, grayish-yellow color.

sal·ly, *n. pl.,* **-lies.** offensive sortie; brief outburst; clever remark. *v.,* **-lied, -ly·ing.** make a sally.

salm·on, *n. pl.,* **-ons, -on.** marine and freshwater food fish.

sa·lon, *n.* drawing room; stylish shop.

sa·loon, *n.* bar; large public room or place.

salt, *n.* sodium chloride. *a.* preserved with salt; tasting of salt. *v.* season or preserve with salt. **salt·ed,** *a.* **salt·y,** *a.,* **-i·er, -i·est.**

sa·lu·bri·ous, *a.* healthful.

sai·u·tar·y, *a.* promoting health; beneficial.

sal·u·ta·tion, *n.* greeting.

sa·lute, *v.,* **-lut·ed, -lut·ing.** greet with words or a gesture of welcome, homage, respect, etc. *n.* act of saluting.

sal·vage, *n.* act of saving a ship or its cargo from wreck or capture; property so saved. *v.,* **-vaged, -vag·ing.** make salvage of. **sal·vag·er,** *n.*

sal·va·tion, *n.* act of saving; means of saving; redemption.

salve, *n.* soothing ointment; balm. *v.,* **salved, salv·ing.** ease or soothe.

sal·vo, *n. pl.,* **-vos, -voes.** volley.

same, *a.* identical; not different or another. *pron.* same thing or person. *adv.* similarly. **same·ness,** *n.*

sam·o·var, *n.* tea urn.

sam·ple, *n.* small part representative of the whole. *v.,* **-pled, -pling.** take a sample of. **sam·pler,** *n.* **sam·pling,** *n.*

san·a·to·ri·um, *n. pl.,* **-ums, -a.** establishment for the treatment of diseases, or for invalids. Also **san·i·tar·i·um.**

sanc·ti·fy, *v.,* **-fied, -fy·ing.** make holy; purify from sin. **sanc·ti·fi·ca·tion,** *n.*

sanc·ti·mo·ny, *n.* external appearance of sanctity. **sanc·ti·mo·ni·ous,** *a.*

sanc·tion, *n.* authoritative permission. *v.* ratify or confirm; approve.

sanc·ti·ty, *n. pl.,* **-ties.** holiness.

sanc·tu·ar·y, *n. pl.,* **-ies.** sacred place; asylum; refuge.

sand, *n.* fine debris of rocks, consisting of small, loose grains. *v.* abrade or polish. **sand·er,** *n.*

san·dal, *n.* shoe, consisting of a sole fastened to the foot by means of straps.

sand·blast, *n. v.* cleanse or engrave by a blast of sand.

sand·stone, *n.* stone of agglutinated grains of sand.

sand·wich, *n.* two slices of bread between which is meat, cheese, etc.

sand·y, *a.,* **-i·er, -i·est.** of, like, or abounding with sand.

sane, *a.,* **san·er, san·est.** mentally sound. **sane·ness,** *n.*

san·gui·nar·y, *a.* attended by bloodshed; bloodthirsty.

san·guine, *a.* having the color of blood; confident; cheerful.

san·i·tar·y, *a.* hygienic.

san·i·ta·tion, *n.* adoption of sanitary measures to eliminate unhealthy elements.

san·i·ty, *n.* state of being sane or of sound mind.

sans, *prep.* without.

sap, *n.* juice of a plant; vitality. *v.,* **sapped, sap·ping.** enervate; undermine.

sa·pi·ent, *a.* wise.

sap·ling, *n.* young tree.

sap·phire, *n.* blue gem.

sap·py, *a.,* **-pi·er, -pi·est.** juicy; energetic.

sar·casm, *n.* caustic remark; taunt. **sar·cas·tic,** *a.*

sar·coph·a·gus, *n. pl.,* **-gi, -gus·es.** stone coffin.

sar·dine, *n. pl.,* **-dines, -dine.** small edible fish.

sar·don·ic, *a.* bitterly ironical; sarcastic.

sa·ri, sa·ree, *n. pl.,* **sa·ris, sa·rees.** chief garment of a Hindu woman.

sash, *n.* band worn over the shoulder or around the waist;

framed part of a window.

sass, *n. inf.* pert retort. *v.* talk back.

sas·sy, *a.,* **-si·er, -si·est.** saucy; pert; impudent.

Sa·tan, *n.* devil. **sa·tan·ic,** *a.* Also **sa·tan·i·cal.**

satch·el, *n.* small suitcase or bag.

sate, *v.,* **sat·ed, sat·ing.** satisfy completely; glut.

sat·el·lite, *n.* secondary planet or moon; subservient follower; man-made object orbiting a planet.

sa·ti·ate, *v.,* **-at·ed, -at·ing.** fill or gratify to excess. **sa·ti·a·tion,** *n.* **sa·ti·e·ty,** *n.*

sat·in, *n.* silk fabric having a smoothness and gloss on one surface. *a.* of or like satin. **sat·in·y,** *a.*

sat·ire, *n.* use of irony or ridicule in exposing vice, folly, etc.; literary composition of this. **sa·tir·i·cal,** *a.*

sat·i·rize, *v.,* **-rized, -riz·ing.** assail with satire. **sat·i·rist,** *n.*

sat·is·fy, *v.,* **-fied, -fy·ing.** fulfill the desires, demands or needs of; make reparation. **sat·is·fac·tion,** *n.* **sat·is·fac·to·ry,** *a.*

sat·u·rate, *v.,* **-rat·ed, -rat·ing.** cause to become completely penetrated or soaked. **sat·u·ra·tion,** *n.*

Sat·ur·day, *n.* seventh day of the week.

sat·ur·nine, *a.* gloomy; grave.

sa·tyr, *n.* deity, half man and half goat. **sa·tyr·ic,** *a.*

sauce, *n.* relish, dressing, or gravy; stewed fruit.

sau·cer, *n.* shallow dish in which a cup is set.

sau·cy, *a.,* **-ci·er, -ci·est.** flippant; pert. **sau·ci·ness,** *n.*

sauer·kraut, *n.* fermented, cut cabbage.

sau·na, *n.* steam bath taken in the Finnish manner.

saun·ter, *v.* walk along leisurely. *n.* stroll.

sau·sage, *n.* minced, spiced meats stuffed into a casing or formed into patties.

sau·té, *v.,* **-téed, -tée·ing.** pan-fry quickly using a little fat.

sav·age, *a.* untamed; fierce. *n.* uncivilized person; barbarian. **sav·age·ness,** *n.* **sav·age·ry,** *n.,* *pl.,* **-ries.**

save, *v.,* **saved, sav·ing.** rescue; lay by; avoid the spending or waste of. *n.* act of saving.

sav·ing, *a.* that which saves; redeeming. *n.* economy; *pl.* money saved. *prep.* except or save. *conj.* except; but.

sav·ior, *n.* one who saves; (*cap.*) title of God and esp. of Christ.

sa·vor, *n.* specific flavor or smell. *v.* have a particular taste, flavor, quality, etc.; take delight in. **sa·vor·er,** *n.*

sa·vor·y, *a.,* **-i·er, -i·est.** having a pleasant flavor and smell. **sa·vor·i·ness,** *n.*

saw, *n.* toothed cutting instrument. *v.,* **sawed, sawed** or **sawn, saw·ing.** cut with a saw. **saw·er,** *n.* **saw·like,** *a.*

saw, *v.* past tense of **see.**

saw-toothed, *a.* serrated.

sax·o·phone, *n.* tubular brass or silver wind instrument.

say, *v.,* **said, say·ing.** speak; declare; state an opinion. *n.* turn to speak; authority. *adv.* about. **say·a·ble,** *a.*

say·ing, *n.* proverb; maxim.

scab, *n.* crust formed over a sore in healing. *v.,* **scabbed, scab·bing.** form scabs. **scab·by,** *a.,* **-bi·er, -bi·est.**

scab·bard, *n.* sheath of a sword.

scaf·fold, *n.* structure for holding workers and materials. **scaf·fold·ing,** *n.*

scald, *v.* burn with hot liquid or steam. *n.* burn caused by this. **scald·ing,** *a.*

scale, *n.* device for weighing; thin plate, as on fish; graduated series; relative size; *mus.* series of tones. *v.,* **scaled, scal·ing.** remove the scales from; climb; measure by a scale; make according to scale. **scal·i·ness,** *n.*

scal·lop, *n.* bivalve mollusk; wavy outer edge. *v.* ornament with scallops. **scal·lop·er,** *n.*

scalp, *n.* skin and hair of the top of the head. *v.* cut the scalp from.

scal·pel, *n.* small, sharp-bladed knife.

scal·y, *a.,* **-i·er, -i·est.** covered with scales.

scamp, *n.* rascal. *v.* act in a careless manner.

scamp·er, *v.* run hastily or in a frolicking manner.

scan, *v.,* **scanned, scan·ning.** examine; pass over quickly, as with the eyes. **scan·ner,** *n.*

scan·dal, *n.* discreditable event, action, etc.; disgrace; defamatory talk. **scan·dal·ous,** *a.*

scan·dal·ize, *v.,* **-ized, -iz·ing.** offend; shock. **scan·dal·i·za·tion,** *n.*

scant, *a.* scarcely sufficient.

scant·y, *a.,* **-i·er, -i·est.** barely adequate. **scant·i·ness,** *n.*

scape·goat, *n.* one who bears the blame for the misdeeds of others.

scar, *n.* mark of a wound remaining after healing. *v.,* **scarred, scar·ring.** mark with a scar.

scarce, *a.* not plentiful; rare. **scar·ci·ty,** *n.*

scare, *v.,* **scared, scar·ing.** frighten. *n.* sudden fright.

scare·crow, *n.* usu. a figure of a man set up to frighten away birds.

scarf, *n. pl.,* **scarfs, scarves.** necktie, kerchief, or muffler.

scar·let, *n.* bright red color. *a.* of the color scarlet.

scar·y, *a.,* **-i·er, -i·est.** causing fright or alarm.

scath·ing, *a.* bitterly severe.

scat·ter, *v.* throw loosely about; disperse.

scav·enge, *v.,* **-enged, -eng·ing.** search out, as useful material, from amid refuse. **scav·en·ger,** *n.*

scene, *n.* surroundings; locale; view; part of a play; display of strong emotion.

scen·er·y, *n. pl.,* **-ies.** natural features of a place; backdrops representing the setting of a stage.

sce·nic, *a.* of natural scenery.

scent, *n.* smell; perfume. *v.* recognize by smelling; be suspicious of. **scent·ed,** *a.*

scep·ter, *n.* rod; emblem of regal power.

sched·ule, *n.* list, esp. a timetable; statement of details. *v.,* **-uled, -ul·ing.** plan for a specified date.

scheme, *n.* plan; plot. *v.* plot; lay plans. **schem·er,** *n.*

schism, *n.* division; separation. **schis·mat·ic,** *a.*

schiz·o·phre·ni·a, *n.* psychosis characterized by withdrawal from reality, delusions, etc. **schiz·o·phren·ic,** *a.*

schol·ar, *n.* person of great learning; student. **schol·ar·ly,** *a.*

schol·ar·ship, *n.* learning and knowledge; aid or award given to a student.

scho·las·tic, *a.* of schools, scholars, or education.

school, *n.* place where instruction is given; body of students. *v.* teach or educate.

school·ing, *n.* education.

school·mate, *n.* companion at school.

schoon·er, *n.* sailing vessel having at least two masts.

sci·ence, *n.* knowledge gained by systematic study; particular branch of knowledge. **sci·en·tif·ic,** *a.*

sci·en·tist, *n.* person versed in science.

scim·i·tar, sim·i·tar, *n.* sword having a curved, single-edged blade. Also **scim·i·ter.**

scin·til·late, *v.,* **-lat·ed, -lat·ing.** emit sparks; sparkle. **scin·til·la·tion,** *n.*

sci·on, *n.* descendant; cutting from a plant.

scis·sors, *n. pl.* cutting instrument of two blades with handles movable on a pivot.

scoff, *n.* jeer. *v.* mock.

scold, *v.* chide; find fault. *n.* one who scolds. **scold·ing,** *n.*

scoop, *n.* ladlelike utensil; shovellike bucket attached to construction equipment; amount taken up. *v.* take up or out with a scoop. **scoop·er,** *n.*

scoot, *v. inf.* dart; go swiftly.

scoot·er, *n.* child's vehicle with a board set between tandem wheels; motor scooter.

scope, *n.* extent or range.

scorch, *v.* burn superficially or slightly. *n.* superficial burn. **scorch·er,** *n.*

score, *n.* record of points made in a game; grade; twenty; *pl.* indeterminately large number. *v.,* **scored, scor·ing.** make a score of; grade; orchestrate; keep score. **score·less,** *a.* **scor·er,** *n.*

scorn, *n.* contempt. *v.* act or feel toward with disdain. **scorn·er,** *n.* **scorn·ful,** *a.*

scor·pi·on, *n.* arachnid.

scotch, *v.* cut; stamp out.

scot-free, *a.* unhurt or unpunished.

scoun·drel, *n.* base person; rascal. **scoun·drel·ly,** *a.*

scour, *v.* cleanse by hard rubbing; clear out; move rapidly;

range over. **scour·er,** *n.*

scourge, *n.* lash; punishment; affliction; *v.,* **scourged, scourg·ing.** whip; afflict.

scout, *n.* one sent out to gain and bring in information. *v.* act as a scout.

scow, *n.* flat-bottomed boat.

scowl, *v.* look sullen, angry, or threatening. *n.* deep angry frown. **scowl·er,** *n.*

scrag·gly, *a.,* **-gli·er, -gli·est.** rough; ragged; unkempt.

scrag·gy, *a.,* **-gi·er, -gi·est.** rough; lean; scrawny.

scram, *v.,* **scrammed, scram·ming.** *inf.* go away at once.

scram·ble, *v.,* **-bled, -bling.** climb quickly on all fours; struggle to get; mix together; disorder. **scram·bler,** *n.*

scrap, *n.* fragment; portion of leftover food; fragmental excess. *v.,* **scrapped, scrap·ping.** discard. *a.* discarded.

scrape, *v.,* **scraped, scrap·ing.** rub so as to smooth, roughen, or remove; grate or scratch. *n.* act, noise, or result of scraping; predicament. **scrap·able,** *a.* **scrap·er,** *n.*

scratch, *v.* mark the surface of; gouge; ease an itch; strike out; scrape. *n.* mark. **scratch·y,** *a.,* **-i·er, -i·est.**

scrawl, *v.* write hastily, or illegibly. *n.* illegible writing. **scrawl·y,** *a.,* **-i·er, -i·est.**

scrawn·y, *a.,* **-i·er, -i·est.** thin. **scrawn·i·ness,** *n.*

scream, *v.* cry out with a loud, shrill voice. *n.* shriek. **scream·er,** *n.*

screech, *v.* shriek. *n.* shrill noise. **screech·er,** *n.*

screen, *n.* anything which shelters or conceals; surface on which a picture is projected; frame containing mesh. *v.* protect; conceal; sift. **screen·er,** *n.* **screen·ing,** *n.*

screw, *n.* pointed metal cylinder driven into a surface by turning. *v.* twist; contort. **screw·er,** *n.* **screw·driv·er,** *n.*

screw·y, *a.,* **-i·er, -i·est.** *inf.* crazy.

scrib·ble, *v.,* *n.* scrawl.

scribe, *n.* one who writes; copyist. **scrib·al,** *a.*

scrim·mage, *n.* skirmish. *v.,* **-maged, -mag·ing.** struggle.

scrimp, *v.* use severe economy. **scrimp·y,** *a.,* **-i·er, -i·est.** scanty;

meager.

script, *n.* handwriting; manuscript of a play or movie.

scrip·ture, *n.* (*cap.*) Bible; passage from the Bible. **scrip·tur·al,** *a.*

scroll, *n.* writing formed into a roll.

scrooge, *n.* (*often cap.*) stingy, miserly person.

scrounge, *v.* forage; pilfer.

scrub, *v.,* **scrubbed, scrub·bing.** cleanse things by hard rubbing. *n.* scrubbing; low tree.

scrub·by, *a.,* **-bi·er, -bi·est.** low or stunted; undersized.

scruff, *n.* back of the neck.

scruff·y, *a.,* **-i·er, -i·est.** slovenly; threadbare.

scrump·tious, *a.* *inf.* splendid.

scru·ple, *n.* feeling of uneasiness affecting the conscience. *v.,* **-pled, -pling.** hesitate at. **scru·pu·lous,** *a.*

scru·ti·nize, *v.,* **-nized, -niz·ing.** conduct a careful investigation. **scru·ti·niz·er,** *n.* **scru·ti·ny,** *n. pl.,* **-nies.**

scu·ba, *n.* underwater breathing device.

scud, *v.,* **scud·ded, scud·ding.** dart.

scuff, *v.* shuffle; mar by scraping. *n.* scuffing.

scuf·fle, *v.,* **-fled, -fling.** grapple closely. *n.* fight.

sculp·ture, *n.* art form of a three-dimensional work. *v.,* **-tured, -tur·ing.** fashion and produce a sculpture. **sculp·tor,** *n.* **sculp·tress,** *n. fem.*

scum, *n.* impure matter on the surface of liquids; rabble. **scum·my,** *a.,* **-mi·er, -mi·est.**

scur·ri·lous, *a.* obscenely jocular; abusive. **scur·ril·i·ty,** *n. pl.,* **-ties.**

scur·ry, *v.,* **-ried, -ry·ing.** scamper; hurry.

scur·vy, *n.* disease affecting persons deprived of vitamin C. *a.,* **-vi·er, -vi·est.** vile; low.

scut·tle, *n.* hatchway. *v.,* **-tled, -tling.** sink (a ship) by making holes in the bottom; run hastily.

scythe, *n.* long curving blade used in mowing.

sea, *n.* mass of salt water; ocean.

sea·far·ing, *a.* traveling by sea. *n.* sailor's calling. **sea·far·er,** *n.*

seal, *n. pl.,* **seals, seal.** large marine mammal, having webbed flippers. **seal·like**, *a.*

seal, *n.* that which fastens or secures; mark which authenticates, confirms, etc. *v.* fasten securely. **seal·er**, *n.*

seam, *n.* line formed by the joining of any two edges.

sea·maid, *n.* mermaid.

sea·man, *n. pl.*, **-men.** sailor.

seam·stress, *n.* woman whose occupation is sewing.

seam·y, *a.*, **-i·er**, **-i·est.** lowly; sordid. **seam·i·ness**, *n.*

se·ance, *n.* spiritualist meeting.

sea·port, *n.* port on or near the sea.

sear, *v.* wither; scorch. *a.* dry.

search, *v.* explore thoroughly; probe. *n.* searching. **search·a·ble**, *a.* **search·er**, *n.*

sea·shore, *n.* place where land meets the sea.

sea·sick·ness, *n.* nausea and vomiting. **sea·sick**, *a.*

sea·son, *n.* one of the four divisions of the year. *v.* enhance the flavor of. **sea·son·al**, *a.* **sea·son·ing**, *n.*

sea·son·a·ble, *a.* suitable to the time; opportune.

seat, *n.* something made or used for sitting on; site. *v.* accommodate with seats; install in a position of authority. **seat·er**, *n.* **seat·ing**, *n.*

sea·way, *n.* ocean traffic lane; inland waterway.

sea·weed, *n.* marine alga.

se·cede, *v.*, **-ced·ed**, **-ced·ing.** withdraw formally from an association. **se·ces·sion**, *n.*

se·clude, *v.*, **-clud·ed**, **-clud·ing.** isolate; separate. **se·clud·ed**, *a.* **se·clu·sion**, *n.*

sec·ond, *a.* next after the first; inferior to a first; other or another. *n.* that which follows the first; sixtieth part of a minute. *adv.* in the second place; rank, etc. *v.* support; advance. **sec·ond·ar·y**, *a.* subordinate; derivative.

sec·ond·hand, *a.* not original; not new; having been used or worn. **second hand**, *n.*

sec·ond·rate, *a.* inferior; mediocre. **sec·ond·rat·er**, *n.*

se·cret, *a.* not made public; hidden. *n.* something concealed; mystery. **se·cre·tive**, *a.* **se·cre·cy**, *n. pl.*, **-cies.**

sec·re·tar·y, *n. pl.*, **-ies.** one who carries on another's correspondence; (*cap.*) officer of a

department of government. **sec·re·tar·i·al**, *a.*

se·crete, *v.*, **-cret·ed**, **-cret·ing.** release, or discharge; conceal. **se·cre·tion**, *n.* **se·cre·tive**, *a.*

sect, *n.* body of persons united by philosophical or religious tenets. **sec·tar·i·an**, *a.*, *n.* **sec·tar·i·an·ism**, *n.*

sec·tion, *n.* portion or division. *v.* separate or divide into sections. **sec·tion·al**, *a.*, *n.*

sec·tor, *n.* separate part; distinguishable subdivision. **sec·to·ri·al**, *a.*

sec·u·lar, *a.* worldly. *n.* layman. **sec·u·lar·ize**, *v.*, **-ized**, **-iz·ing.** make secular. **sec·u·lar·i·za·tion**, *n.*

se·cure, *a.* safe; stable; sure. *v.*, **-cured**, **-cur·ing.** make secure; make fast; get possession of. **se·cure·ment**, *n.*

se·cu·ri·ty, *n. pl.*, **-ties.** state of being secure; surety; *pl.* certificate of stocks, bonds, or notes.

se·dan, *n.* enclosed car.

se·date, *a.* calm; staid; dignified. **se·date·ness**, *n.*

sed·a·tive, *a.* tending to calm; allaying pain. *n.* medicine which sedates.

sed·en·tar·y, *a.* accustomed to sit; inactive.

sed·i·ment, *n.* settlings; dregs. **sed·i·men·ta·ry**, *a.* **sed·i·men·ta·tion**, *n.*

se·di·tion, *n.* incitement of rebellion against authority. **se·di·tious**, *a.*

se·duce, *v.*, **-duced**, **-duc·ing.** lead astray; tempt. **se·duc·er**, *n.* **se·duc·tion**, **se·duce·ment**, *n.* **se·duc·tive**, *a.*

sed·u·lous, *a.* assiduous; diligent. **se·du·li·ty**, *n.*

see, *v.*, **saw**, **seen**, **see·ing.** perceive by the eye; visualize; visit; attend; discern. *n.* office of a bishop. **see·a·ble**, *a.*

seed, *n. pl.*, **seeds**, **seed.** ovule of a plant; semen; that from which anything springs. *v.* sow; take the seeds out of.

seed·ling, *n.* very small or young plant.

seed·y, *a.*, **-i·er**, **-i·est.** abounding with seeds. *Inf.* worn-out; shabby. **seed·i·ness**, *n.*

see·ing, *conj.* since.

seek, *v.*, **sought**, **seek·ing.** go in search of; ask for; try. **seek·er**, *n.*

seem, v. appear; feel as if. **seem·er,** n.

seem·ing, a. appearing.

seem·ly, a., **-li·er, -li·est.** becoming; fitting. adv. fittingly. **seem·li·ness,** n.

seep, v. pass gradually through; ooze. **seep·age,** n.

se·er, n. prophet. **seer·ess,** n. fem.

seethe, v., **seethed, seeth·ing.** boil; steep. **seeth·ing,** a.

seg·ment, n. division or section. **seg·men·tar·y,** a.

seg·re·gate, v., **-gat·ed, -gat·ing.** separate or set apart. **seg·re·gat·ed,** a. **seg·re·ga·tion,** n.

seine, n. fishing net. v., **seined, sein·ing.** fish with a seine.

seis·mo·graph, n. instrument for recording the intensity of an earthquake. **seis·mog·ra·pher,** n.

seize, v., **seized, seiz·ing.** lay hold of suddenly or forcibly; grasp; capture. **seiz·er,** n. **sei·zure,** n.

sel·dom, adv. rarely. a. infrequent.

se·lect, v. choose; pick out. a. choice; exclusive. **se·lect·ed,** a. **se·lec·tor,** n. **se·lec·tion,** n. **se·lec·tive,** a.

self, n. pl., **selves.** person or thing, with respect to person or identity.

self-as·sur·ance, n. self-confidence. **self-as·sured,** a.

self-cen·tered, a. centered in oneself.

self-com·mand, n. self-control.

self-con·fi·dence, n. quality of being confident of oneself. **self-con·fi·dent,** a.

self-con·scious, a. excessively conscious of oneself. **self-con·scious·ness,** n.

self-con·trol, n. self-restraint. **self-con·trolled,** a.

self-de·ter·mi·na·tion, n. free will. **self-de·ter·min·ing,** a., n.

self-ef·fac·ing, a. retiring.

self-ev·i·dent, a. evident without proof. **self-ev·i·dence,** n.

self-ex·plan·a·to·ry, a. obvious.

self-gov·ern·ment, n. autonomy. **self-gov·ern·ing,** a.

self-im·por·tance, n. conceit. **self-im·por·tant,** a.

self-in·dul·gence, n. free indulgence of one's desires. **self-in·dul·gent,** a.

self·ish, a. caring only for oneself. **self·ish·ness,** n.

self·less, a. unselfish.

self-made, a. having achieved success by one's personal efforts.

self-pit·y, n. pity for oneself. **self-pit·y·ing,** a.

self-pos·sessed, a. composed; cool. **self-pos·ses·sion,** n.

self-re·li·ance, n. dependence on one's own powers. **self-re·li·ant,** a.

self-re·straint, n. restraint imposed on oneself. **self-re·strain·ing,** a.

self-right·eous, a. assured of one's own virtue, esp. when intolerant of others. **self-right·eous·ness,** n.

self-same, a. identical.

self-serv·ice, n. serving of oneself in a restaurant, shop, etc.

self-styled, a. called or styled by oneself.

self-suf·fi·cient, a. independent of the aid of others. **self-suf·fi·cien·cy,** n.

self-will, n. willfulness; obstinacy. **self-willed,** a.

sell, v., **sold, sell·ing.** give possession of for payment; invite purchase of; be on sale at a particular price. **sell·er,** n.

se·man·tics, n. pl. study of word meanings. **se·man·tic,** a.

sem·blance, n. similarity; mere external show.

se·men, n. substance carrying spermatozoa secreted by the male reproductive organs.

sem·i·nal, a.

se·mes·ter, n. half an academic year.

sem·i·au·to·mat·ic, a. partly self-operating.

sem·i·cir·cle, n. half of a circle. **sem·i·cir·cu·lar,** a.

sem·i·co·lon, n. punctuation sign (;).

sem·i·con·scious, a. half conscious. **sem·i·con·scious·ness,** n.

sem·i·fi·nal, a. of a contest or match which immediately precedes the final one. n. often pl. semifinal contest, etc. **sem·i·fi·nal·ist,** n.

sem·i·for·mal, a. moderately formal, esp. in dress.

sem·i·nar, n. group of students engaged in advanced study.

sem·i·nar·y, n. pl., **-nar·ies.** school for the instruction of priests, ministers, etc. **sem·i·nar·i·an,** n.

sem·i·of·fi·cial, a. partly official.

sem·i·pre·cious, a. of gems

ranked below precious gems.

sem·i·pri·vate, *a.* not completely private.

sem·i·skilled, *a.* having some degree of skill.

sem·i·trop·ics, *n. pl.* subtropics. **sem·i·trop·i·cal,** *a.*

sem·i·week·ly, *a.* occurring every half week. *n. pl.,* **-ies.** semi-weekly publication.

sen·ate, *n.* assembly having legislative powers; (*cap.*) upper of the two houses in various legislatures. **sen·a·tor,** *n.* **sen·a·to·ri·al,** *a.*

send, *v.,* **sent, send·ing.** cause or enable to go; cause to be conveyed; direct to go; drive; impel; emit. **send·er,** *n.*

se·nile, *a.* of old age; weakened by old age, esp. in mental faculties. **se·nil·i·ty,** *n.*

sen·ior, *a.* older or elder, abbr. *Sr.;* of higher rank or standing. *n.* aged person; member of the highest class in a college or high school.

sen·ior·i·ty, *n.* state of being senior; priority due to length of service.

se·ñor, *n. pl.,* **se·ñors.** gentleman; (*cap.*) Mr.

se·ño·ra, *n.* lady; (*cap.*) Mrs.

se·ño·ri·ta, *n.* young lady; (*cap.*) Miss.

sen·sa·tion, *n.* impression made through sensory stimulation; something that produces excited interest.

sen·sa·tion·al, *a.* relating to sensation; startling; exciting. **sen·sa·tion·al·ism,** *n.*

sense, *n.* sight, hearing, etc.; feeling or perception; sound practical intelligence; meaning. *v.,* **sensed, sens·ing.** perceive; become aware of.

sense·less, *a.* lacking sensation; unconscious; stupid. **sense·less·ness,** *n.*

sen·si·bil·i·ty, *n. pl.,* **-ties.** capacity to experience emotion; delicacy of feeling.

sen·si·ble, *a.* possessing sense, judgment, etc.; reasonable; aware. **sen·si·bly,** *adv.*

sen·si·tive, *a.* able to receive impressions; of keen sensibility; easily affected. **sen·si·tiv·i·ty,** *n. pl.,* **-ties.**

sen·si·tize, *v.,* **-tized, -tiz·ing.** render sensitive.

sen·so·ry, *a.* conveying sense impulses. Also **sen·so·ri·al.**

sen·su·al, *a.* referring to the physical senses; indulging in lust. **sen·su·al·i·ty,** *n.* **sen·su·al·ly,** *adv.*

sen·su·al·ize, *v.,* **-ized, -iz·ing.** make sensual.

sen·su·ous, *a.* referring or appealing to the senses.

sen·tence, *n.* group of words which conveys a complete thought; court judgment. *v.,* **-tenced, -tenc·ing.** pronounce sentence on.

sen·ti·ment, *n.* thought prompted by feeling; emotion. **sen·ti·men·tal,** *a.*

sen·ti·men·tal·ize, *v.,* **-ized, -iz·ing.** indulge in sentiment.

sen·ti·nel, *n.* sentry. *v.,* **-neled, -nel·ing.** watch over.

sen·try, *n. pl.,* **-tries.** guard or watch.

se·pal, *n.* part of the calyx of a flower. **se·paled,** *a.*

sep·a·rate, *v.,* **-rat·ed, -rat·ing.** divide; keep apart; sever; split. *a.* disjoined; distinct.

sep·a·ra·tion, *n.* **sep·a·ra·tist,** *n., a.* **sep·a·ra·tism,** *n.*

Sep·tem·ber, *n.* ninth month.

sep·tic, *a.* infective.

sep·tu·a·ge·nar·i·an, *n.* person seventy years of age.

sep·ul·cher, *n.* tomb. *v.,* **-chered, -cher·ing.** bury in a sepulcher. **se·pul·chral,** *a.*

se·quel, *n.* succeeding part; result.

se·quence, *n.* arrangement of succession; series; consequence.

se·quen·tial, *a.* following in sequence.

se·ques·ter, *v.* set apart; seclude; withdraw. **se·ques·tered,** *a.* **se·ques·tra·ble,** *a.*

se·quin, *n.* small glittering disk. **se·quined, se·quinned,** *a.*

se·quoi·a, *n.* gigantic coniferous tree.

ser·aph, *n. pl.,* **-aphs, -a·phim.** angel of the highest order. **se·raph·ic,** *a.*

ser·e·nade, *n.* music performed at night in the open air. *v.,* **-nad·ed, -nad·ing.** entertain with a serenade. **ser·e·nad·er,** *n.*

se·rene, *a.* calm; (*usu. cap.*) exalted. **se·rene·ness,** *n.* **se·ren·i·ty,** *n. pl.,* **-ties.**

serf, *n.* person bound in the service of a landowner.

serge, *n.* twilled fabric.

ser·geant, n. non-commissioned officer; police officer.

se·ri·al, a. of a series. n. story running through a series. **se·ri·al·ist,** n. **se·ri·al·ize,** v., **-ized, -iz·ing.**

se·ries, n. succession of like items or events.

se·ri·ous, a. grave; being in earnest; important; weighty. **se·ri·ous·ness,** n.

ser·mon, n. discourse delivered by a clergyman; homily. **ser·mon·ize,** v., **-ized, -iz·ing.** preach. **ser·mon·iz·er,** n.

ser·pent, n. snake. **ser·pen·tine,** a.

ser·rate, a. toothed. Also **ser·rat·ed.** v., **-rat·ed, -rat·ing.** render serrate. **ser·ra·tion,** n.

se·rum, n. pl., **se·rums, se·ra.** pale-yellow liquid in the blood; fluid from the serum of an immunized animal.

serv·ant, n. person who is employed by another for domestic duties; slave.

serve, v., **served, serv·ing.** wait at table; go through a term of service; perform official duty; be a servant to; promote. **serv·er,** n. **serv·ing,** n. serving, as in tennis.

serv·ice, n. performance of duties for others; duty or work of public servants; armed forces; religious worship or ritual. a. of services. v., **-iced, -ic·ing.** make fit for service.

serv·ice·a·ble, a. useful; durable. **serv·ice·a·bil·i·ty,** **serv·ice·a·ble·ness,** n.

serv·ice·man, n. pl., **-men.** member of the armed forces; repairman.

ser·vile, a. characteristic of a slave; submissive. **ser·vil·i·ty,** **ser·vile·ness,** n.

ser·vi·tude, n. slavery; bondage.

ses·sion, n. sitting together of a court, legislature, conference, etc.; continuous series of meetings.

set, v., **set, set·ting.** put; fix or appoint; mount in a setting; curl, as hair; arrange; pass below the horizon; become firm or solid. n. number of things having in common their nature or function. a. fixed; rigid; ready. **set a·bout,** start work upon. **set back,** hold up. **set forth,** declare. **set on,** attack. **set out,** begin; try; place on display.

set·back, n. halt.

set·tee, n. long seat with a back to it.

set·ter, n. long-haired hunting dog.

set·ting, n. that in which something is set; surroundings of anything.

set·tle, v., **-tled, -tling.** resolve; pay, satisfy, or close; establish residence in; quiet; clear, as liquid, of dregs; sink to the bottom; bring to a conclusion. **set·tler,** n.

set·tle·ment, n. settling; colonization; adjustment of a claim.

set-to, n. brief fight.

sev·en, a., n. one more than six. **sev·enth,** a., n.

sev·en·teen, n., a. one more than sixteen. **sev·en·teenth,** a., n.

sev·en·ty, n., a. seven times ten. **sev·en·ti·eth,** a., n.

sev·er, v. part; separate; disunite. **sev·er·ance,** n.

sev·er·al, a. more than two but not very many; divers. **sev·er·al·ly,** adv.

se·vere, v., **se·ver·er, se·ver·est.** very strict or harsh; critical; plain; rigorous. **se·ver·i·ty,** n. pl., **-ties.**

sew, v., **sewed, sewn** or **sewed, sew·ing.** unite with stitches. **sew·er,** n. **sew·ing,** n.

sew·age, n. waste matter carried away by sewers.

sew·er, n. underground canal which carries off water and waste materials.

sex, n. male and female characteristics; either of the two groups into which organisms are divided. **sex·u·al,** a. **sex·u·al·i·ty,** n.

sex·tant, n. device for determining angular distances.

sex·tet, n. group of six.

sex·tu·plet, n. one of six born at the same birth.

sex·y, a., **sex·i·er, sex·i·est.** sexually exciting. **sex·i·ness,** n.

shab·by, a., **-bi·er, -bi·est.** threadbare; much worn; despicable. **shab·bi·ness,** n.

shack, n. shanty.

shack·le, n. handcuff, or the like, for either set of limbs. v., **-led, -ling.** confine; inhibit. **shack·ler,** n.

shade, n. dimness; anything used to intercept light; degree of brightness of color. v.,

shad·ed, shad·ing. produce a darkening effect. **shad·ing,** n.
shade·less, a.

shad·ow, n. figure projected in silhouette by means of interception of light; merest hint; pl. semidarkness. v. shade; darken; follow closely. **shadow·like,** a. **shad·ow·y,** a.

shad·y, a., **-i·er, -i·est.** abounding with shade; inf. disreputable. **shad·i·ness,** n.

shaft, n. spear or arrow; pointed remark; columnar part of anything; narrow passageway. **shaft·ing,** n.

shag·gy, a., **-gi·er, -gi·est.** covered with long, rough growth; having a rough nap; untrimmed. **shag·gi·ness,** n.

shake, v., **shook, shak·en, shak·ing.** quiver, tremble, or vibrate; totter; clasp each other's hand; grab and jostle; disturb. n. shaking. **shake a leg,** inf. hurry. **shake up,** stir; upset. **shak·er,** n.

shake-up, n. upsetting change or reorganization.

shak·y, a., **-i·er, -i·est.** shaking; trembling; weak; unreliable. **shak·i·ness,** n.

shale, n. rock of claylike, fine-grained sediments.

shall, aux. v., **should.** used to indicate futurity, determination, resolve, obligation, etc.

shal·low, a. not deep. n. often pl. shoal. **shal·low·ness,** n.

sham, n. pretender. a. counterfeit. v., **shammed, sham·ming.** pretend falsely to be. **sham·mer,** n.

sha·man, n. tribal priest; medicine man. **sha·man·ism,** n.

sham·bles, n. pl. slaughterhouse; state or scene of disorder or destruction.

shame, n. painful feeling arising from dishonorable acts, or offensive situations; disgrace. v., **shamed, sham·ing.** cause to feel shame; dishonor. **shame·ful,** a.

shame·less, a. having no shame or modesty.

sham·poo, v., **-pooed, -poo·ing.** wash, as the hair; clean, as a carpet. n. cleansing compound. **sham·poo·er,** n.

shang·hai, v., **-haied, -hai·ing.** bring about by deception or force.

shank, n. part of the leg between the knee and ankle; cut of meat.

shan·ty, n. pl., **-ties.** roughly built hut. **shan·ty·town,** n.

shape, n. form, outline, or contour of a thing. v., **shaped, shap·ing.** create or give a definite form to. **shaped,** a. **shap·er,** n. **shape·less,** a.

shape·ly, a., **-li·er, -li·est.** well-formed. **shape·li·ness,** n.

share, n. one's just or full portion; capital stock division. v., **shared, shar·ing.** distribute in shares; use jointly. **shar·er,** n.

shark, n. large, ferocious fish; swindler.

sharp, a. having a thin cutting edge or a fine point; clear or distinct; severe; mentally acute. adv. in a sharp manner. n. mus. tone one half step above a given tone. **sharp·ness,** n.

sharp·en, v. make sharp or sharper. **sharp·en·er,** n.

sharp-eyed, a. observant.

sharp-shoot·er, n. excellent marksman. **sharp·shoot·ing,** n.

shat·ter, v. reduce to scattered fragments; break in pieces. **shat·ter·proof,** a.

shave, v., **shaved, shaved** or **shav·en, shav·ing.** remove hair by means of a razor; reduce to the form of thin slices; scrape. n. shaving. **shav·er,** n. **shav·ing,** n.

shawl, n. loose covering for the shoulders or head.

she, pron. pronoun referring to the female in question or last mentioned.

sheaf, n. pl., **sheaves.** grain stalks bound together; bundle. **sheaf·like,** a.

shear, v., **sheared, sheared** or **shorn, shear·ing.** cut off with a sharp instrument. **shears,** n. pl. **shear·er,** n.

sheath, n. pl., **sheaths.** case for the blade of a sword, or the like. **sheath·less,** a.

sheathe, v., **sheathed, sheath·ing.** put into or supply with a sheath. **sheath·er,** n.

shed, v., **shed, shed·ding.** let flow; throw off; drop; repel. n. crude structure.

sheen, n. radiance; luster. v. shine. **sheen·y,** a.

sheep, n. pl., **sheep.** ruminant mammal valuable for its wool.

sheep·ish, a. foolishly bashful;

meek.

sheer, *a.* being nearly transparent; total or complete; of steepness that is extreme. *adv.* vertically. **sheer·ness,** *n.*

sheet, *n.* large piece of cloth bedding; piece of paper; thin layer. **sheet·ing,** *n.*

sheik, sheikh, *n.* chief of an Arabic tribe; title of respect.

shelf, *n. pl.,* **shelves.** board fixed horizontally for holding articles; ledge shoal. **shelv·ing,** *n.*

shell, *n.* hard outside covering; projectile containing a bursting charge. *v.* remove from a natural casing; bombard. **shelled,** *a.* **shel·ler,** *n.*

shel·lac, shel·lack, *n.* lac used for making varnish. *v.,* **-lacked, -lack·ing.** coat with shellac.

shell·fish, *n. pl.,* **-fish, -fish·es.** crustacean or a mollusk.

shell shock, *n.* combat fatigue.

shel·ter, *n.* that which provides a cover or protection; refuge. *v.* provide shelter for. **shel·ter·er,** *n.*

shelve, *v.,* **shelved, shelv·ing.** place on a shelf; dismiss.

shep·herd, *n.* person employed in tending sheep. *v.* guard like a shepherd.

sher·bet, *n.* fruit-flavored water ice.

sher·iff, *n.* chief law enforcement officer of a county.

sher·ry, *n. pl.,* **-ries.** fortified wine.

shield, *n.* defensive armor carried on the arm; protection. *v.* protect from danger.

shift, *v.* remove and exchange for another; undergo a change; get along. *n.* shifting; specified period of working time. **shift·er,** *n.*

shift·less, *a.* lazy.

shift·y, *a.,* **-i·er, -i·est.** changing; tricky. **shift·i·ly,** *adv.* **shift·i·ness,** *n.*

shil·ly-shal·ly, *v.,* **-lied, -ly·ing.** hesitate.

shim·mer, *v.* shine with a tremulous light; glimmer. *n.* subdued gleam. **shim·mer·y,** *a.*

shin, *n.* forepart of the leg between the ankle and knee.

shine, *v.,* **shone** or **shined, shin·ing.** emit light; exhibit brightness; polish. *n.* brightness; luster. **shin·ing,** *n.*

shin·gle, *n.* thin piece of wood

or other material used as a roof covering. *v.,* **-gled, ·gling.** cover with shingles.

shin·ny, *v.,* **-nied, -ny·ing.** *inf.* climb, as a pole, using shins and arms.

shin·y, *a.,* **-i·er, -i·est.** bright; glossy. **shin·i·ness,** *n.*

ship, *n.* large seagoing vessel. *v.,* **shipped, ship·ping.** transport by ship, rail, or other means. **ship·per,** *n.*

ship·mate, *n.* fellow sailor.

ship·ment, *n.* act of transporting goods; cargo.

ship·shape, *a.* neat and trim.

ship·wreck, *n.* wreck of a ship. *v.* suffer shipwreck.

ship·yard, *n.* place in which ships are constructed or repaired.

shirk, *v.* avoid or get out of. *n.* one who seeks to avoid duty. **shirk·er,** *n.*

shirt, *n.* loose garment worn on the upper part of the body. **shirt·less,** *a.*

shiv·er, *v.* shake; tremble. *n.* shivering. **shiv·er·y,** *a.*

shoal, *n.* place where water is shallow; school of fish. *v.* throng.

shock, *n.* sudden blow; sudden disturbance to the mind or body. *v.* experience a shock; give an electric shock to; outrage. **shock·er,** *n.* **shock·ing,** *a.*

shod·dy, *a.,* **-di·er, -di·est.** inferior or but pretentious. **shod·di·ness,** *n.*

shoe, *n. pl.,* **shoes.** external covering for the foot; horseshoe. *v.,* **shod, shod, shoe·ing.** fit with a shoe, metal plate, etc. **sho·er,** *n.*

shoe·horn, *n.* curved device used to aid in putting on shoes.

shoe·lace, *n.* shoestring.

shoot, *v.,* **shot, shoot·ing.** fire or hit with a discharge; put forth; dart; take a picture of; project or jut. *n.* offshoot; rapid. **shoot at, shoot for,** aim at or aspire to. **shoot up,** grow rapidly. **shoot·er,** *n.*

shoot·ing i·ron, *n. inf.* firearm.

shoot·ing star, *n.* meteor.

shop, *n.* store; workshop. *v.,* **shopped, shop·ping.** visit shops to purchase or examine goods. **shop·per,** *n.*

shop·keep·er, *n.* tradesman.

shop·lift·er, *n.* one who steals

goods from a shop. **shop·lift·ing**, *n.*

shore, *n.* land adjacent to water. *a.* of land. **shore·line**, *n.*

short, *a.* not having great length; curt; brief; deficient. *adv.* abruptly. *n.* deficiency; *pl.* short pants. *v.* cheat; short circuit. **in short**, in summary. **short·ness**, *n.*

short·age, *n.* deficiency.

short-change, *v.*, **-changed**, **-chang·ing.** cheat.

short cir·cuit, *n.* side circuit. **short-cir·cuit**, *v.*

short·com·ing, *n.* deficiency; defect.

short-cut, *v.*, **-cut**, **-cut·ting.** use a shorter way or method. **short-cut**, *n.*

short·en, *v.* make or become short or shorter.

short·en·ing, *n.* butter, lard, or other edible fat.

short·hand, *n.* stenography.

short-lived, *a.* not living or lasting long.

short·sight·ed, *a.* near-sighted; lacking in foresight. **short·sight·ed·ness**, *n.*

short-tem·pered, *a.* quick-tempered.

short-wind·ed, *a.* affected with shortness of breath after physical effort.

shot, *n.* discharge of a firearm; shooting; one who shoots; try; *inf.* injection; jigger of liquor; snapshot. **like a shot**, quickly. **not by a long shot**, *inf.* never. **shot in the dark**, *inf.* random guess.

shot·gun, *n.* double-barreled gun. *v.*, **-gunned**, **-gun·ning.** coerce.

should, *aux. v.* past form of **shall**, used to show obligation, duty, probability, etc.

shoul·der, *n.* joint connecting the arm with the body; projecting part; space bordering a roadway. *v.* shove.

shout, *n.* loud cry. *v.* utter with a shout. **shout·er**, *n.*

shove, *v.*, **shoved**, **shov·ing.** force or push; jostle; drive forward. *n.* push. **shov·er**, *n.*

shov·el, *n.* implement having a broad, shallow scoop. *v.*, **-eled**, **-el·ing.** take up and throw with a shovel.

show, *v.*, **showed**, **shown** or **showed**, **show·ing.** expose to view; display; guide; appear.

n. display or performance; trace. **show·ing**, *n.*

show·case, *n.* display case. *v.*, **-cased**, **-cas·ing.** exhibit.

show·down, *n.* confrontation.

show·er, *n.* brief fall of rain; similar fall, as of tears, bullets, etc.; bath in which water is showered upon the body. *v.* pour down; bestow lavishly. **show·er·y**, *a.*

show·man, *n. pl.*, **-men.** one who skillfully produces a show. **show·man·ship**, *n.*

show-off, *n.* person who shows off. **show off**, *v.* display arrogantly.

show·y, *a.*, **-i·er**, **-i·est.** gaudy. **show·i·ness**, *n.*

shrap·nel, *n.* shell fragments.

shred, *n.* tatter; fragment. *v.*, **shred·ded** or **shred**, **shred·ding.** tear or cut into small pieces. **shred·der**, *n.*

shrew, *n.* small insect-eating mammal; ill-tempered scold. **shrew·ish**, *a.* **shrew-like**, *a.*

shrewd, *a.* astute; sharp. **shrewd·ness**, *n.*

shriek, *n.* loud, shrill cry. *v.* cry in a shriek.

shrill, *a.* high-pitched and piercing. **shrill·ness**, *n.*

shrimp, *n. pl.*, **shrimps**, **shrimp.** small, long-tailed shellfish.

shrine, *n.* place hallowed because of significant associations.

shrink, *v.*, **shrank** or **shrunk**, **shrunk·en**, **shrink·ing.** draw back; recoil; contract; diminish. **shrink·age**, *n.*

shriv·el, *v.*, **-eled**, **-el·ing.** shrink; wither.

shroud, *n.* garment of the dead. *v.* enshroud for burial; cover or veil.

shrub, *n.* low, woody plant. **shrub·ber·y**, *n. pl.*, **-ies.** shrubby, *a.*, **-bi·er**, **-bi·est.**

shrug, *v.*, **shrugged**, **shrug·ging.** raise the shoulders, as in expressing uncertainty. *n.* shrugging.

shuck, *n.* husk or pod; shell.

shud·der, *n.* tremble. *v.* convulsive shaking of the body.

shuf·fle, *v.*, **-fled**, **-fling.** move the feet without lifting them; mix; jumble together. *n.* scraping movement; evasive trick. **shuf·fler**, *n.*

shun, *v.*, **shunned**, **shun·ning.** avoid. **shun·ner**, *n.*

shunt, *v.* shove; shift; switch; sidetrack.

shush, *int.* be quiet. *v.* hush.

shut, *v.,* **shut, shut·ting.** close; enclose; bar. *a.* closed. **shut down,** close for a time. **shut out,** bar. **shut up,** close tightly; confine; *inf.* stop talking.

shut·ter, *n.* cover for a window; movable cover for closing an opening.

shut·tle, *n.* device in a loom, for passing thread from one side to the other. *v.* move to and fro. **shut·tle·like,** *a.*

shy, *a.,* **shi·er, shi·est, shy·er, shy·est.** reserved; timid; wanting. *v.,* **shied, shy·ing.** rear in fright. **shy·ness,** *n.*

shy·ster, *n. inf.* dishonest lawyer.

sic, *v.,* **sicked, sick·ing.** pursue; attack.

sick, *a.* not healthy; ill; affected with nausea. *n.* those who are sick. **sick·ness,** *n.*

sick·en, *v.* disgust; become sick. **sick·en·ing,** *a.*

sick·le, *n.* blade for use in cutting grain or grass.

sick·ly, *a.,* **-li·er, -li·est.** habitually ailing; mawkish. **sick·li·ness,** *n.*

side, *n.* surface or line bounding a thing, usu. specified as right or left; aspect; party. *a.* being at or on one side; incidental.

side·board, *n.* piece of furniture in which silver and linens are kept.

side·burns, *n. pl.* whiskers on the sides of the face.

side·kick, *n. inf.* pal.

side·long, *a.,* *adv.* inclined, slanting, subtle.

side·split·ting, *a.* extremely hearty or uproarious.

side·step, *v.,* **-stepped, -step·ping.** avoid by stepping to one side.

side·track, *v.* shift to a side track; divert. *n.* railroad siding.

side·walk, *n.* walk, usu. paved, by the side of a street.

side·ward, *adv., a.* toward one side. **side·wards,** *adv.*

side·way, *n.* byway. *adv., a.* sideways.

side·ways, *adv.* toward or from one side; facing to the side. *a.* oblique.

sid·ing, *n.* material that covers the outer wall of buildings.

si·dle, *v.,* **-dled, -dling.** approach by moving side foremost. *n.* sideways movement.

siege, *n.* encampment of an army about a fortified place; prolonged endeavor to overcome resistance.

si·es·ta, *n.* midday rest.

sieve, *n.* instrument with a meshed bottom. *v.,* **sieved, siev·ing.** sift.

sift, *v.* separate by or as by a sieve; examine with close scrutiny. **sift·er,** *n.*

sigh, *v.* emit a prolonged and audible breath; yearn. *n.* sighing. **sigh·er,** *n.*

sight, *n.* power of seeing; vision; view or glimpse; spectacle. *v.* see; aim. **catch sight of,** glimpse. **on sight,** as soon as seen. **sight·ed,** *a.*

sight·less, *a.* blind.

sight·ly, *a.* pleasing to the eye.

sight-see·ing, *n.* act of visiting points of general interest. **sight-se·er,** *n.*

sign, *v.* affix a signature; engage by written agreement. *n.* indication; symbol; signal; inscribed board, space, etc.; providing information; omen. **sign·er,** *n.*

sig·nal, *n.* gesture, sound, or object giving warning, information, etc. *a.* outstanding. *v.,* **-naled, -nal·ing.** make a signal to. **sig·nal·er,** *n.*

sig·na·ture, *n.* person's name as signed by that person.

sign·board, *n.* board displaying information or advertising.

sig·net, *n.* small seal; stamp made by a signet.

sig·nif·i·cance, *n.* meaning; importance. **sig·nif·i·cant,** *a.*

sig·ni·fi·ca·tion, *n.* meaning.

sig·ni·fy, *v.,* **-fied, -fy·ing.** be a sign or indication of; represent. **sig·ni·fi·er,** *n.*

si·lence, *n.* absence of any sound. *v.,* **-lenced, -lenc·ing.** put or bring to silence; still. **si·lent,** *a.*

sil·hou·ette, *n.* dark solid outline of a thing against a light background. *v.,* **-et·ted, -et·ting.** show in or as in a silhouette.

sil·i·ca, *n.* silicon dioxide, used in glass manufacture.

sil·i·con, *n.* nonmetallic element.

sil·i·cone, *n.* compound made by substituting silicon for carbon in substances, as oils, resins, etc.

silk, *n.* soft, lustrous fiber from the silkworm; material made of this. **silk·en,** *a.* **silk·like,** *a.*

silk·worm, *n.* caterpillar which produces a cocoon of silk.

silk·y, *a.,* **-i·er, -i·est.** of silk; soft and smooth; glossy. **silk·i·ness,** *n.*

sill, *n.* piece at the bottom of the door, window, etc.

sil·ly, *a.,* **-li·er, -li·est.** foolish; senseless; absurd. **sil·li·ly,** *adv.* **sil·li·ness,** *n.*

si·lo, *n. pl.,* **si·los,** pit or chamber for storing grain.

silt, *n.* fine earthy sediment. **silt·y,** *a.,* **-i·er, -i·est.**

sil·ver, *n.* white metallic element; money, esp. coin; flatware; shade of gray. *a.* of this metal. **sil·ver·y,** *a.*

sil·ver·smith, *n.* person who works with silver.

sil·ver-tongued, *a.* eloquent.

sil·ver·ware, *n.* eating utensils of silver, silverplate, or other metals.

sim·i·an, *a.* of or like apes and monkeys. *n.* ape or monkey.

sim·i·lar, *a.* like; resembling. **sim·i·lar·i·ty,** *n. pl.,* **-ties.**

si·mil·i·tude, *n.* likeness; counterpart.

sim·mer, *v.* continue in a state approaching boiling. *n.* simmering.

si·mon·ize, *v.,* **-ized, -iz·ing.** polish, esp. with wax.

sim·per, *v.* smirk. *n.* silly or affected smile. **sim·per·er,** *n.*

sim·ple, *a.,* **-pler, -plest.** not complicated; not difficult; plain; weak in intellect. **sim·plic·i·ty,** *n. pl.,* **-ties.**

sim·ple·ton, *n.* silly or foolish person.

sim·pli·fy, *v.,* **-fied, -fy·ing.** make simple, or easier. **sim·pli·fi·ca·tion,** *n.*

sim·ply, *adv.* in a simple manner; merely.

sim·u·late, *v.,* **-lat·ed, -lat·ing.** feign; imitate. **sim·u·la·tion,** *n.* **sim·u·la·tor,** *n.*

si·mul·cast, *v.,* **-cast or -cast·ed, -cast·ing.** broadcast by radio and television simultaneously.

si·mul·ta·ne·ous, *a.* happening or done at the same time. **si·mul·ta·ne·i·ty,** *n.*

sin, *n.* wickedness; transgression. *v.,* **sinned, sin·ning.** com-

mit a sin. **sin·ner,** *n.*

since, *adv.* from then till now. *prep.* after. *conj.* after the time when; because; seeing that.

sin·cere, *a.* without guile; honest; real; genuine. **sin·cer·i·ty,** *n.*

si·ne·cure, *n.* very easy job.

sin·ew, *n.* tendon. *v.* strengthen. **sin·ew·y,** *a.*

sin·ful, *a.* wicked. **sin·ful·ly,** *adv.* **sin·ful·ness,** *n.*

sing, *v.,* **sang or sung, sung, sing·ing.** utter with musical modulations of the voice. *n.* singing. **sing·er,** *n.*

singe, *v.,* **singed, singe·ing.** scorch. *n.* slight burn.

sin·gle, *a.* unmarried; unique; suitable for one person. *n.* one individual person or thing. *v.,* **-gled, -gling.** *baseball.* make a one-base hit.

sin·gle-hand·ed, *a.* unassisted. **sin·gle-hand·ed·ness,** *n.*

sin·gly, *adv.* individually; one at a time.

sing·song, *n.* regular, rhythmical sounds. *a.* monotonous.

sin·gu·lar, *a.* remarkable; unique. *n.* singular number; word form in this number. **sin·gu·lar·i·ty,** *n. pl.,* **-ties.**

sin·is·ter, *a.* ominous; evil.

sink, *v.,* **sank or sunk, sunk or sunk·en, sink·ing.** go under or to the bottom, as in water; fall gently downward; pass into some lower state. *n.* basin or receptacle; sinkhole. **sink·a·ble,** *a.* **sink·er,** *n.*

sin·u·ous, *a.* winding; indirect. **sin·u·os·i·ty,** *n.*

si·nus, *n.* cranial hollow, containing air.

sip, *v.,* **sipped, sip·ping.** drink in small quantities. *n.* small draft. **sip·per,** *n.*

si·phon, sy·phon, *n.* tube used to convey a liquid up over a side to a lower level. *v.* convey by means of a siphon.

sir, *n.* respectful term of address used to a man.

sire, *n.* male parent of a mammal; term of address used to a sovereign. *v.,* **sired, sir·ing.** beget.

si·ren, *n.* dangerously enticing woman; instrument producing a loud, piercing sound.

sir·loin, *n.* upper part of a loin cut of beef.

sis·sy, *n. pl.,* **-sies.** *inf.* effeminate boy or man; coward.

sis-ter, *n.* female born of the same parents with respect to other offspring; nun. **sis-ter-ly,** *a.*

sis-ter-in-law, *n. pl.,* **sis-ters-in-law.** husband's or wife's sister; brother's wife.

sit, *v.,* **sat, sit-ting.** rest upon the haunches; repose on a seat; be situated; perch; contain seats for. **sit-ting,** *a., n.*

site, *n.* place; scene of an event.

sit-u-ate, *v.,* **-at-ed, -at-ing.** give a place to; locate; position. **sit-u-at-ed,** *a.* **sit-u-a-tion,** *n.*

six, *n.* number between five and seven. *a.* twice three. **sixth,** *a., n.*

six-teen, *n.* number between 15 and 17. *a.* one more than 15. **six-teenth,** *a., n.*

sixth sense, *n.* intuition.

six-ty, *n.* number between 59 and 61. *a.* six times ten. **six-ti-eth,** *a., n.*

siz-a-ble, size-a-ble, *a.* quite large. **siz-a-ble-ness,** *n.*

size, *n.* dimensions of anything; relative measure of dimension, as of shoes, etc.; degree, or amount. *v.,* **sized, siz-ing.** make or arrange according to size. **sized,** *a.*

siz-zle, *v.,* **-zled, -zling.** make a hissing sound, as in frying; *inf.* be very hot. *n.* sizzling sound. **siz-zler,** *n.*

skate, *n.* steel runner on a shoe for gliding over ice. *v.,* **skat-ed, skat-ing.** move on skates. **skat-er,** *n.*

ske-dad-dle, *v.,* **-dled, -dling.** *inf.* run away. *n.* hurried departure.

skein, *n.* coil of thread or yarn of uniform size.

skel-e-ton, *n.* bony framework of the body; supporting framework. *a.* barest minimum. **skel-e-tal,** *a.*

skep-tic, scep-tic, *n.* doubter; disbeliever. **skep-ti-cal, scep-ti-cal,** *a.* **skep-ti-cism, scep-ti-cism,** *n.*

sketch, *n.* drawing giving only general features; rough draft; outline. *v.* delineate.

sketch-y, *a.,* **-i-er, -i-est.** giving rough outlines. **sketch-i-ly,** *adv.* **sketch-i-ness,** *n.*

skew-er, *n.* pin of wood or metal for holding meat while cooking. *v.* pierce.

ski, *n. pl.,* **skis, ski.** long, narrow runner fastened to the foot for gliding over snow. *v.,* **skied, ski-ing.** travel on skis. **ski-er,** *n.* **ski-ing,** *n.*

skid, *n.* sideslip; skidway; low, small platform. *v.,* **skid-ded, skid-ding.** slip sidewards while in motion. **skid-der,** *n.*

skiff, *n.* small, light boat.

skill, *n.* developed proficiency; trade or craft. **skilled,** *a.* **skill-ful,** *a.*

skil-let, *n.* frying pan.

skim, *v.,* **skimmed, skim-ming.** lift, as floating substance, from liquid; glance over. *n.* something skimmed off. *a.* skimmed. **skim-mer,** *n.*

skimp, *v.* scrimp. **skimp-i-ly,** *adv.* **skimp-i-ness,** *n.*

skimp-y, *a.,* **-i-er, -i-est.** scanty; meager.

skin, *n.* external covering of the body; hide or pelt; outer coating. *v.,* **skinned, skin-ning.** strip of skin; peel. **skinned,** *a.* **skin-ner,** *n.*

skin-flint, *n.* stingy person.

skin-ny, *a.,* **-ni-er, -ni-est.** very thin; emaciated.

skip, *v.* jump, or leap lightly; miss, or disregard. *n.* skipping movement.

skip-per, *n.* captain of a ship.

skir-mish, *n.* brief fight in war. **skir-mish-er,** *n.*

skirt, *n.* garment resembling a petticoat. *v.* evade.

skit, *n.* short comic theatrical scene.

skit-tish, *a.* easily frightened; shy; lively.

skulk, *v.* lurk. **skulk-er,** *n.*

skull, *n.* cranium.

skunk, *n.* small, black-and-white mammal.

sky, *n. pl.,* **skies.** region of clouds.

sky-light, *n.* window in the roof of a house.

sky-line, *n.* horizon; silhouette, as of buildings, against the sky.

sky-rock-et, *n.* rocket exploding with fireworks. *v.* shoot up rapidly, as prices.

sky-scrap-er, *n.* very high building.

slab, *n.* broad, flat, thick piece of anything.

slack, *a.* loose; remiss; not brisk. *n.* slack condition. *v.* neglect. **slack-ness,** *n.*

slack·en, v. make less active; loosen.

slacks, n. pl. trousers.

slag, n. vitrified mineral waste; cinder.

slake, v., **slaked, slak·ing.** quench; satisfy; lessen.

slam, v., **slammed, slam·ming.** shut with a bang; strike or hit violently. n. slamming.

slan·der, n. false report uttered of another. v. defame by slander. **slan·der·er,** n.

slang, n. colloquial words and phrases; jargon. **slang·y,** a., **-i·er, -i·est.**

slant, v. slope; have bias. n. slope; bias. a. oblique. **slant·ways,** adv. **slant·wise,** a., adv.

slap, n. smart blow; smack. v., **slapped, slap·ping.** strike, esp. with the open hand.

slap·hap·py, a., **-pi·er, -pi·est.** inf. punch-drunk.

slash, v. gash; make slits in. n. sweeping stroke.

slat, n. long, narrow strip; lath. v., **-ted, -ting.** furnish with slats. **slat·ted,** a.

slate, n. dark rock; plate of this used esp. for roofing; list of candidates. v., **slat·ed, slat·ing.** cover with slates; set down for nomination. **slat·y,** a.

slaugh·ter, n. butchering; carnage. v. kill or butcher. **slaugh·ter·er,** n.

slave, n. bond servant; drudge. v., **slaved, slav·ing.** work like a slave. **slav·er·y,** n.

slaw, n. coleslaw.

slay, v., **slew, slain, slay·ing.** kill in a violent manner. **slay·er,** n.

slea·zy, a., **-zi·er, -zi·est.** lacking firmness of texture; cheap. **slea·zi·ness,** n.

sled, n. vehicle on runners for conveying over snow. v., **sled·ded, sled·ding.** ride on a sled. **sled·der,** n.

sledge, n. heavy hammer; sled.

sleek, a. smooth or glossy; suave. **sleek·ness,** n.

sleep, v., **slept, sleep·ing.** take rest afforded by a natural suspended state. n. state of sleep. **sleep·er,** n.

sleep·y, a., **-i·er, -i·est.** drowsy. **sleep·i·ness,** n.

sleet, n. half-frozen rain. v. fall as sleet. **sleet·y,** a.

sleeve, n. part of a garment fitted to cover the arm. **sleeved,** a. **sleeve·less,** a.

sleigh, n. open vehicle on runners drawn by horses over snow. **sleigh·er,** n.

sleight, n. skill. **sleight of hand,** legerdemain.

slen·der, a. slim; thin. **slen·der·ness,** n.

sleuth, n. inf. detective.

slice, n. thin, flat piece cut from something. v., **sliced, slic·ing.** cut into slices; divide into parts. **slic·er,** n.

slick, a. sleek; sly; slippery. n. greasily smooth place. v. make sleek. **slick·ness,** n.

slick·er, n. raincoat.

slide, v., **slid, slid or slid·den, slid·ing.** glide over a smooth surface; slip. n. sliding; chute; landslide; photographic plate for projection on a screen. **slid·er,** n.

slight, a. small; of little importance; slim. v. disregard. n. slighting treatment. **slight·er,** n. **slight·ing,** a.

slim, a., **slim·mer, slim·mest.** slender; small. v., **slimmed, slim·ming.** make or become slender. **slim·ness,** n.

slime, n. viscous liquid matter. **slim·y,** a., **-i·er, -i·est.**

sling, n. slingshot; bandage for holding an injured limb; shoulder strap. v., **slung, sling·ing.** cast; hurl; suspend.

slink, v., **slunk, slink·ing.** creep stealthily. **slink·y,** a., **-i·er, -i·est.**

slip, v., **slipped, slip·ping.** pass smoothly; glide; lose one's foothold; get away, escape; make an error. n. slipping; mistake; woman's undergarment; strip of paper.

slip·knot, n. knot easily slipped or undone.

slip·page, n. slipping.

slip·per, n. low-cut, lightweight shoe.

slip·per·y, a., **-i·er, -i·est.** allowing or causing anything to slip readily; tricky. **slip·per·i·ness,** n.

slip·shod, a. slovenly.

slip-up, n. inf. mistake, or oversight. **slip up,** v.

slit, v., **slit, slit·ting.** cut lengthwise. n. slash.

slith·er, v. slide along a surface. **slith·er·y,** a.

sliv·er, n. slender fragment; splinter.

slob, n. inf. untidy person.

slob·ber, v. drool.

slo·gan, n. catchword or phrase. **slo·gan·eer,** n.

sloop, n. vessel with one mast.

slop, n. liquid refuse. v., **slopped, slop·ping.** splash.

slope, n. slant; inclined surface. v., **sloped, slop·ing.** slant. **slop·er,** n.

slop·py, a., **-pi·er, -pi·est.** slushy; soiled with liquid; inf. careless. **slop·pi·ness,** n.

slosh·y, a., **-i·er, -i·est.** slushy.

slot, n. slit, or groove; place in a series. v., **slot·ted, slot·ting.** make a slot in.

sloth, n. laziness; mammal which lives in a tree.

slouch, v. sit, stand, etc., in a drooping manner. n. drooping. **slouch·y,** a., **-i·er, -i·est.**

slough, n. marsh; swamp; any part shed or molted. v. shed or cast off. **slough·y,** a.

slov·en·ly, a., **-li·er, -li·est.** careless; slipshod.

slow, a. sluggish; dull; not fast. v. make or become slow or slower. **slow·ness,** n.

slug, n. slimy animal related to the land snail; bullet; metal formed like a coin. v., **slugged, slug·ging.** hit hard.

slug·gish, a. lazy; slow.

slum, n. often pl. squalid part of a city. v., **slummed, slum·ming.** visit, esp. out of curiosity; slums. **slum·mer,** n.

slum·ber, v. drowse or doze. n. light sleep. **slum·ber·er,** n.

slump, v. drop heavily; fall suddenly; assume a slouching posture. n. drop; decline.

slur, v., **slurred, slur·ring.** pronounce indistinctly; slander; belittle. n. slurred utterance or sound; slight.

slush, n. partly melted, watery snow. **slush·i·ness,** n. **slush·y,** a., **-i·er, -i·est.**

slut, n. slattern; female dog.

sly, a., **sli·er** or **sly·er, sli·est** or **sly·est.** cunning; wily; underhand. **sly·ness,** n.

smack, v. produce a sharp sound; strike smartly; inf. kiss loudly. n. smacking of the lips; blow.

small, a. little; trivial; ungenerous. **small·ish,** a.

small-mind·ed, a. petty; narrowminded.

small·pox, n. acute virus disease, marked by fever and pustular eruptions.

small-time, a. unimportant.

smart, v. suffer from wounded feelings; cause a sharp pain. a. keen; stinging; having quick intelligence; chic; saucy. **smart·ness,** n. **smart·en,** v.

smash, v. break in pieces; strike violently. n. shattering blow; crash. **smash·ing,** a.

smat·ter·ing, n. superficial or slight knowledge.

smear, v. soil; defame; overspread. n. substance that smears. **smear·er,** n. **smear·y,** a., **-i·er, -i·est.**

smell, v., **smelled** or **smelt, smel·ling.** detect the odor of; have a scent or odor. n. sense of perceiving with the nose; odor. **smell·er,** n. **smell·y,** a., **-i·er, -i·est.**

smelt, n. small food fish. v. melt, as ore, separate the metal from extraneous substances.

smile, v. express pleasure, etc., by an upward turning of the corners of the mouth. n. act of smiling. **smil·er,** n.

smirch, v. stain; smudge; disgrace. Also **besmirch.**

smirk, v. smile in an affected way. n. smirking. **smirk·er,** n.

smite, v., **smote, smit·ten** or **smit, smit·ing.** strike forcibly; kill. **smit·er,** n.

smith, n. one who works in metals. Also **smith·y.**

smock, n. loose outer garment.

smog, n. mixture of smoke and fog. **smog·gy,** a., **-gi·er, -gi·est.**

smoke, n. cloudlike mixture resulting from combustion. v., **smoked, smok·ing.** give off smoke; puff on a pipe, cigar, etc.; cure, as meat. **smok·er,** n.

smoke·stack, n. chimney.

smok·y, a., **-i·er, -i·est.** emitting much smoke; hazy. **smok·i·ly,** adv. **smok·i·ness,** n.

smol·der, smoul·der, v. burn without flame; exist in a suppressed state.

smooch, v., n. inf. kiss.

smooth, a. even; flat; free from roughness; pleasant; suave. v. make smooth; calm. adv. evenly. **smooth·ness,** n.

smor·gas·bord, n. buffet of a variety of foods.

smoth·er, v. stifle; suffocate; cover closely or thickly; quell. **smoth·er·y,** a.

smudge, n. spot; blur. v.,

smudged, smudg·ing. smear; protect by a smoldering fire. **smudg·y,** *a.,* **-i·er, -i·est.**

smug, *a.,* **smug·ger, smug·gest.** self-important or self-satisfied. **smug·ness,** *n.*

smug·gle, *v.,* **-gled, -gling.** import or export secretly. **smug·gler,** *n.*

smut, *n.* sooty matter; obscenity. **smut·ty,** *a.,* **-ti·er, -ti·est. smut·ti·ness,** *n.*

snack, *n.* light portion of food. *v.* eat between meals.

snag, *n.* sharp protection; jagged hole or tear; obstacle. *v.* **snagged, snag·ging.** damage by a snag; impede.

snail, *n.* mollusk having a spiral shell. **snail·like,** *a.*

snake, *n.* scaly, limbless reptile. *v.,* **snaked, snak·ing.** move in the manner of a snake. **snake·like,** *a.* **snak·i·ly,** *adv.*

snap, *v.,* **snapped, snap·ping.** crackle; break suddenly; make a quick bite; take a photograph of. *n.* sharp cracking sound; fastener operating with such a sound. *a.* without thought. *adv.* briskly. **snap·per,** *n.* **snap·pish,** *a.*

snap·py, *a.,* **-pi·er, -pi·est.** snappish; quick; *inf.* lively. **snap·pi·ness,** *n.*

snap·shot, *n.* photograph.

snare, *n.* trap; lure. *v.,* **snared, snar·ing.** trap. **snar·er,** *n.*

snarl, *v.* entangle; growl exposing the teeth; speak in surly tones. *n.* knot; menacing growl. **snarl·er,** *n.* **snarl·y,** *a.*

snatch, *v.* catch or grasp; take suddenly. *n. pl.,* **snatch·es.** snatching; bit or scrap. **snatch·er,** *n.*

snatch·y, *a.,* **-i·er, -i·est.** spasmodic.

snaz·zy, *a.,* **-zi·er, -zi·est.** *inf.* stylish; fancy.

sneak, *v.* act in a furtive way; move, put or pass in a stealthy manner. *n.* one who sneaks. **sneak·er,** *n.*

sneak·y, *a.,* **-i·er, -i·est.** of a sneak. **sneak·i·ness,** *n.*

sneer, *v.* show contempt. *n.* look or expression of contempt. **sneer·er,** *n.*

sneeze, *v.,* **sneezed, sneez·ing.** emit breath suddenly through the nose by spasmodic action. *n.* act or sound of sneezing. **sneez·er,** *n.*

snick·er, *v.* titter. *n.* half-smothered derisive laugh.

snide, *a.* malicious.

sniff, *v.* draw air audibly through the nose; sense. *n.* act of sniffing.

snif·fle, *v.,* **-fled, -fling.** sniff repeatedly, as from a cold. *n.* sniffling.

snip, *v.,* **snipped, snip·ping.** cut with a small, quick stroke. *n.* snipping.

snipe, *n.* game bird. *v.,* **sniped, snip·ing.** from undercover. **snip·er,** *n.*

snitch, *v. inf.* steal; tattle.

snob, *n.* one who snubs those he considers his inferiors. **snob·ber·y,** *n.* **snob·bish,** *a.*

snoop, *v. inf.* pry. *n.* one who snoops. **snoop·y,** *a.*

snoot·y, *a.,* **-i·er, -i·est.** snobbish. **snoot·i·ness,** *n.*

snooze, *v.,* **snoozed, snooz·ing.** *inf.* sleep. *n.* nap. **snooz·er,** *n.*

snore, *v.,* **snored, snor·ing.** breathe hoarsely during sleep. *n.* snoring. **snor·er,** *n.*

snort, *v.* force the breath violently through the nostrils. *n.* snorting.

snout, *n.* muzzle.

snow, *n.* water vapor in frozen, white flakes. *v.* send down snow. **snow·flake,** *n.*

snow·ball, *n.* round mass of snow. *v.* throw snowballs at; increase quickly.

snow·bound, *a.* shut in by snow.

snow·man, *n. pl.,* **-men.** figure made of snow.

snow·mo·bile, *n.* automotive vehicle for travel on snow.

snow·y, *a.,* **-i·er, -i·est.** covered with snow; pure.

snub, *v.,* **snubbed, snub·bing.** treat with contempt. *n.* rebuke; rebuff. *a.* turned up.

snuff, *v.* extinguish; snort or sniff. *n.* powdered tobacco.

snug, *a.,* **snug·ger, snug·gest.** cozy; trim; fitting closely; secret. *v.,* **snugged, snug·ging.** nestle; make snug. **snug·ness,** *n.*

snug·gle, *v.,* **-gled, -gling.** nestle; cuddle. *n.* snuggling.

so, *adv.* likewise; in this manner; indeed; thereupon. *a.* very well. *conj.* therefore. **so as,** in order to. **so that,** in order that. **so to speak,** in a manner of speaking.

soak, *v.* become saturated; place and keep in liquid; drench; take up. **soak·age,** *n.*

soap, *n.* compound used for detergent or cleansing purposes. *v.* rub with soap. **soap·y,** *a.,* **-i·er, -i·est**

soar, *v.* fly aloft; rise to a height. **soar·er,** *n.*

sob, *v.,* **sobbed, sob·bing.** weep with convulsive catching of the breath. *n.* sound like a sob.

so·ber, *a.* not drunk; serious, grave, or solemn; sane. *v.* make or become sober. **so·ber·ness,** *n.* **so·bri·e·ty,** *n.*

so·bri·quet, sou·bri·quet, *n.* nickname.

so-called, *a.* commonly or falsely called thus.

soc·cer, *n.* variation of football in which the hands and arms are not used.

so·cia·ble, *a.* companionable. **so·cia·bil·i·ty,** *n.*

so·cial, *a.* of society; relating to humans living in society; gregarious. *n.* gathering. **so·cial·i·ty,** *n.*

so·cial·ism, *n.* organization whereby the citizenry owns the means of production, and administrative control is vested in the state. **so·cial·ist,** *n.*

so·cial·ite, *n.* person of socially elite circles.

so·cial·ize, *v.,* **-ized, -iz·ing.** render social, as to suit something to the needs of society; participate in friendly interchange. **so·cial·i·za·tion,** *n.*

so·ci·e·ty, *n. pl.,* **-ties.** organization; persons from any region or period; human beings collectively; companionship. **so·ci·e·tal,** *a.*

so·ci·ol·o·gy, *n.* study of human society. **so·ci·o·log·i·cal,** *a.* **so·ci·ol·o·gist,** *n.*

sock, *n. pl.,* **socks, sox.** short stocking. *v. inf.* hit hard. *n.* hard blow.

sock·et, *n.* hollow part for receiving and holding some part or thing.

sod, *n.* turf; sward. *v.,* **sod·ded, sod·ding.** cover with sod.

so·da, *n.* compound of sodium; soft drink.

so·dal·i·ty, *n. pl.,* **-ties.** fellowship; society.

so·da wa·ter, *n.* water charged with carbon dioxide.

sod·den, *a.* soaked; soggy;

bloated.

so·di·um, *n.* soft, silver-white metallic element.

so·di·um bi·car·bo·nate, *n.* baking soda.

so·di·um chlo·ride, *n.* salt.

sod·om·y, *n.* unnatural sexual intercourse.

so·fa, *n.* couch.

soft, *a.* not hard or stiff; not glaring; gentle; mild. **soft·ness,** *n.*

soft·en, *v.* make soft or more soft; alleviate; become less hard. **soft·en·er,** *n.*

soft-head·ed, *a.* silly.

soft-heart·ed, *a.* sympathetic.

soft-shoe, *a.* of a type of tap dancing.

soft-spo·ken, *a.* speaking softly; suave.

sog·gy, *a.,* **-gi·er, -gi·est.** soaked; damp and heavy. **sog·gi·ness,** *n.*

soil, *n.* earth; ground; country or region; soiling. *v.* make dirty; tarnish.

soi·ree, soi·rée, *n.* evening party; social gathering.

so·journ, *v.* make a temporary stay. *n.* temporary stay. **so·journ·er,** *n.*

Sol, *n.* sun.

sol·ace, *n.* comfort. *v.,* **-aced, -ac·ing.** comfort; relieve. **sol·ac·er,** *n.*

so·lar, *a.* of, by, or from the sun.

so·lar·i·um, *n. pl.,* **-ums, -a.** glass-enclosed porch; area having overhead sun lamps.

so·lar·ize, *v.,* **-ized, -iz·ing.** affect or harm by sunlight. **so·lar·i·za·tion,** *n.*

sol·der, *n.* fusible alloy applied to metal surfaces to unite them. *v.* unite with solder. **sol·der·er,** *n.*

sol·dier, *n.* one who serves in an army for pay. *v.* serve as a soldier. **sol·dier·y,** *n.*

sole, *n.* bottom of the foot, shoe, etc.; flatfish. *v.,* **soled, sol·ing.** furnish with a sole. *a.* being the only one or ones; solitary. **soled,** *a.*

sol·e·cism, *n.* mistake in using language; breach of etiquette.

sole·ly, *adv.* as the only one or ones; wholly; merely.

sol·emn, *a.* grave; serious.

so·lem·ni·ty, *n. pl.,* **-ties.** solemnness; *usu. pl.* solemn observance.

so·lic·it, *v.* request; urge or importune. **so·lic·i·ta·tion**, n. **so-lic·i·tor**, n.

so·lic·i·tous, a. anxious; careful. **so·lic·i·tude**, n.

sol·id, a. not hollow; neither liquid nor gaseous; not flimsy; sound. n. matter exhibiting relative firmness and volume. **so·lid·i·ty**, n.

sol·i·dar·i·ty, n. pl., -ties. union or fellowship.

so·lil·o·quize, v., -quized, -quizing. talk to oneself. **so·lil·o·quy**, n. pl., -quies.

sol·i·tar·y, a. alone; being the only one or ones; lonely.

sol·i·tude, n. state of being alone; deserted place.

so·lo, n. pl., solos, so·li. musical composition for one person; performance by one person. a. alone. adv. unaccompanied. v., -loed, -lo·ing. perform a solo. **so·lo·ist**, n.

sol·u·ble, a. dissolvable; capable of being solved. **sol·u·bil·i·ty**, n.

so·lu·tion, n. explanation; answer; combination of dissolved substances.

solve, v., solved, solv·ing. find an answer for; explain.

sol·vent, a. able to pay all debts. n. substance that dissolves other substances. **sol·ven·cy**, n.

som·ber, a. dark; gloomy; depressing. **som·ber·ness**, n.

some, a. of indeterminate quantity; certain. pron. unspecified. adv. approximately.

some·bod·y, pron. person unknown. n. pl., -ies. person of consequence.

some·day, adv. at some unspecified time.

some·how, adv. in some way.

some·one, pron. somebody.

som·er·sault, n. head-over-heels revolution of the body. v. execute a somersault.

some·thing, n. indeterminate or unknown event or thing.

some·time, adv. at some time. a. former.

some·times, adv. at times.

some·way, adv. somehow.

some·what, adv. rather; slightly.

some·where, adv. in, at, or to some place unspecified.

som·nam·bu·late, v., -lat·ed, -lat·ing. walk in one's sleep. **som·nam·bu·list**, n.

som·no·lent, a. sleepy.

son, n. male descendant.

song, n. vocal music; ballad. **for a song**, for a low price.

son·ic, a. of sound waves; of speeds approximating that of sound. **son·i·cal·ly**, adv.

son-in-law, n. pl., sons-in-law. man married to one's daughter.

son·net, n. poem of 14 lines.

so·no·rous, a. giving out sound; resonant.

soon, adv. before long; promptly; readily.

soot, n. fine, black substance formed in combustion. **soot·y**, a., -i·er, -i·est.

soothe, v., soothed, sooth·ing. calm; ease; comfort. **sooth·er**, n. **sooth·ing**, a.

sooth·say·er, n. person who claims to foretell the future. **sooth·say·ing**, n.

sop, n. wet mass. v., sopped, sop·ping. soak; absorb. **sop·ping**, a.

so·phis·ti·cate, v., -cat·ed, -cating. make less natural or simple; refine. n. one who is sophisticated. **so·phis·ti·ca·tion**, n.

soph·is·try, n. pl., -ries. specious reasoning.

soph·o·more, n. student in the second year of a four-year course.

so·pran·o, n. pl., so·pran·os, so·pran·i. highest female voice; one who sings soprano.

sor·cer·er, n. conjuror. **sor·cer·ess**, n. fem.

sor·cer·y, n. pl., -ies. black magic; witchcraft.

sor·did, a. filthy; squalid; mean. **sor·did·ness**, n.

sore, a., sor·er, sor·est. painful or tender; inf. angered. n. bruised flesh. **sore·ness**, n.

sor·row, n. grief; sadness. v. grieve. **sor·row·ful**, a.

sor·ry, a., -ri·er, -ri·est. feeling regret; sorrowful; mean; pitiful.

sort, n. kind; variety; class. v. classify. **af·ter a sort**, after a fashion. **out of sorts**, not in high spirits. **sort·a·ble**, a. **sort·er**, n.

so-so, a. indifferent; mediocre. adv. tolerably.

sot, n. drunkard.

soul, n. spiritual part of humans; seat of the feelings; human being; essential element. **souled**, a. **soul·ful**, a.

soul·less, *a.* heartless.

sound, *n.* audibly perceptible vibrations; passage or channel of water. *v.* make or cause to make a sound; impart a certain effect; seek to elicit the views of. *a.* in good condition; solid; sensible; deep. *adv.* deeply. **sound·ly**, *adv.* **sound·ness**, *n.*

sound·ing, *n. often pl.* act or process of measuring depth. **sound·er**, *n.*

sound·less, *a.* noiseless; silent. **sound·less·ness**, *n.*

sound·proof, *a.* impervious to sound. *v.* insulate against sound.

soup, *n.* liquid food with meat, fish, or vegetables added. **soup·y**, *a.*, **-i·er**, **-i·est.**

sour, *a.* having an acid taste; tart. *v.* turn sour; make sour or acid; embitter. **sour·ish**, *a.* **sour·ness**, *n.*

source, *n.* origin.

souse, *v.*, **soused**, **sous·ing.** plunge into water or other liquid; drench. *n.* sousing; *inf.* drunkard.

south, *n.* point and region opposite to the north. *a.* of, in, to, or from the south. *adv.* toward, from, or in the south. **south·er·ly**, *a.*, *adv.* **south·ern**, *a.* **south·ward**, *a.*, *adv.*

south·bound, *a.* going or traveling south.

south·east, *n.* direction midway between south and east; region in this direction. *a.* in, to, or from the southeast. *adv.* in or toward the southeast. **south·east·er·ly**, *a.*, *adv.* **south·east·ern**, *a.* **south·east·ward**, *a.*, *adv.*

south·ern·er, *n.* native or inhabitant of the south.

south·ern lights, *n. pl.* aurora australis.

south·west, *n.* direction midway between south and west; region in this direction. *a.* in, to, or from the southwest. *adv.* from, toward, or in the southwest. **south·west·er·ly**, *a.*, *adv.* **south·west·ern**, *a.* **south·west·ward**, *a.*, *adv.*

sou·ve·nir, *n.* memento; keepsake.

sov·er·eign, *a.* supreme in power; independent. *n.* supreme ruler; monarch. **sov·er·eign·ty**, *pl.*, **-ties.**

sow, *v.*, **sowed**, **sown** or **sowed**, **sow·ing.** propagate; scatter seed for growth. **sow·er**, *n.*

sow, *n.* female of the swine.

soy·bean, *n.* protein-rich leguminous plant.

spa, *n.* mineral spring; resort.

space, *n.* unlimited expanse of three dimensions; portion of this; reserved seat or room. *v.*, **spaced**, **spac·ing.** set some distance apart. **space·less**, *a.* **spac·ing**, *n.*

space·man, *n. pl.*, **-men.** astronaut.

space·ship, *n.* vehicle for travel outside of the earth's atmosphere. Also **spacecraft.**

spa·cious, *a.* amply large; vast. **spa·cious·ness**, *n.*

spade, *n.* figure like a heart with the point upward; card of this suit; instrument for digging. *v.*, **spad·ed**, **spad·ing.** dig with a spade. **spad·er**, *n.*

spa·ghet·ti, *n.* flour paste cut in long pieces.

span, *n.* short space of time; extent, or reach of anything. *v.*, **spanned**, **span·ning.** measure or extend across.

span·gle, *n.* small circular ornament. *v.*, **-gled**, **-gling.** adorn with spangles.

span·iel, *n.* dog with a long, silky coat.

spank, *v.* slap against the buttocks. **spank·er**, *n.* **spank·ing**, *n.*

spar, *n.* large piece of timber. *v.*, **sparred**, **spar·ring.** box; argue.

spare, *v.*, **spared**, **spar·ing.** refrain from harming; save; part with; refrain from using. *a.*, **spar·er**, **spar·est.** kept in reserve; lean. *n.* spare thing. **spare·a·ble**, *a.*

spare·rib, *n.* cut of pork containing ribs.

spar·ing, *a.* saving; frugal; meager.

spark, *n.* ignited or fiery particle; small arc; trace; flash. *v.* emit sparks.

spar·kle, *n.*, **-kled**, **-kling.** emit little sparks; glitter; be lively. *n.* luster. **spar·kler**, *n.*

spar·row, *n.* small, hardy bird.

sparse, *a.*, **spars·er**, **spars·est.** thinly scattered; scanty. **sparse·ness**, *n.*

spasm, *n.* involuntary muscular contraction. **spas·mod·ic**, *a.*

spas·tic, *a.* of, or characterized

by spasm. *n.* person given to spasms.

spat, *v.,* petty quarrel; slap. *v.,* **spat·ted, spat·ting.** engage in a petty quarrel; splash.

spa·tial, *a.* of space; occurring in space. Also **spa·cial. spa·ti·al·i·ty,** *n.*

spat·ter, *v., n.* splash; spot.

spat·u·la, *n.* implement with a thin, flexible blade.

spawn, *n.* eggs of fishes, mollusks, etc.; swarming blood. *v.* produce spawn; give rise to, as rumors.

speak, *v.,* **spoke, spok·en, speak·ing.** utter words; talk; deliver an address; use in oral utterance, as a language. **speak·a·ble,** *a.* **speak·er,** *n.* **speak·ing,** *n.*

spear, *n.* long-staffed weapon; spearing. *v.* pierce with or as with a spear. **spear·er,** *n.*

spear·mint, *n.* common mint.

spe·cial, *a.* unique; having a particular function; exceptional. *n.* special person or thing. **spe·cial·ly,** *adv.*

spe·cial·ize, *v.,* **-ized, -iz·ing.** pursue a particular line of study, work, etc. **spe·cial·i·za·tion,** *n.* **spe·cial·ist,** *n.*

spe·cial·ty, *n. pl.,* **-ties.** special study, line of work, article of trade, etc.

spe·cies, *n. pl.,* **spe·cies.** distinct kind; classification of animals or plants.

spe·cif·ic, *a.* explicit; definite; of a special or particular kind. *n.* something specific. **spec·i·fic·i·ty,** *n.*

spec·i·fy, *v.,* **-fied, -fy·ing.** state explicitly; designate. **spec·i·fi·ca·tion,** *n.*

spec·i·men, *n.* example; sample.

spe·cious, *a.* apparently good or right but without real merit. **spe·cious·ness,** *n.*

speck, *n.* tiny spot; particle; fleck. *v.* spot; mark.

speck·le, *n.* speck. *v.,* **-led, -ling.** mark with specks.

specs, *n. pl.* eyeglasses; abbr. for *specifications.*

spec·ta·cle, *n.* striking sight or view; public show or display; *pl.* eyeglasses. **spec·ta·cled,** *a.*

spec·tac·u·lar, *a.* marked by a strikingly unusual display. **spec·tac·u·lar·ly,** *adv.*

spec·ta·tor, *n.* one who looks on. **spec·ter,** *n.* ghost.

spec·trum, *n. pl.,* **-tra, -trums.** broad range; series of colors.

spec·u·late, *v.,* **-lat·ed, -lat·ing.** reflect; theorize; take business risks. **spec·u·la·tion,** *n.* **spec·u·la·tor,** *n.*

speech, *n.* power or act of speaking; public address; language or dialect. **speech·less,** *a.*

speed, *n.* rapidity of movement. *v.,* **sped** or **speed·ed, speed·ing.** accelerate the rate of; make haste. **speed·er,** *n.*

speed·om·e·ter, *n.* instrument for indicating speed.

speed·up, *n.* increase in the rate of speed.

speed·way, *n.* course for racing.

speed·y, *a.,* **-i·er, -i·est.** swift; fast. **speed·i·ness,** *n.*

spell, *v.,* **spelled** or **spelt, spell·ing.** form by letters. *n.* charm; period of time, illness, etc. **spell·er,** *n.*

spell·bind, *v.,* **-bound, -bind·ing.** entrance. **spell·bind·er,** *n.* spell-bound. *a.*

spell·ing, *n.* orthography.

spend, *v.,* **spent, spend·ing.** expend or pay out; exhaust; waste; pass. **spend·er,** *n.*

spend·thrift, *n.* one who spends his means lavishly.

spent, *a.* expended.

sperm, *n. pl.,* **sperm, sperms.** semen.

sperm whale, *n.* enormous, toothed whale.

spew, *v.* vomit; eject. Also **spue.** **spew·er,** *n.*

sphere, *n.* globe; heavenly body; field of activity. **spher·ic,** *a.* **sphe·ric·i·ty,** *n.*

spher·i·cal, *a.* globular.

spice, *n.* aromatic substance used as seasoning; something that gives zest. *v.,* **spiced, spic·ing.** season. **spic·y,** *a.,* **-i·er, -i·est.**

spi·der, *n.* eight-legged, wingless arachnid. **spi·der·y,** *a.*

spiel, *n. inf.* pitch.

spiff·y, *a.,* **-i·er, -i·est.** *inf.* spruce; smart.

spig·ot, *n.* faucet; plug.

spike, *n.* large nail or pin; sharp-pointed piece or part; ear, as of wheat. *v.,* **-spiked, spik·ing.** fasten with a spike; impale. **spiked,** *a.*

spik·y, *a.,* **-i·er, -i·est.** in the shape of a spike.

spill, *v.,* **spilled** or **split, spill·ing.** shed, esp. blood; cause to fall;

run or escape from a container. n. spilling. **spil·lage,** n.

spin, v., **spun, spun, spin·ning.** twist fiber into thread or yarn; produce, as a cobweb; whirl. n. spinning; rapid run, ride, etc.

spin·ach, n. plant with edible, fleshy leaves.

spi·nal, a. of the spine. n. anesthetic injected into the spinal cord.

spin·dle, n. rod on a spinning wheel; rod on which something turns. v., **-dled, -dling.** grow long and slender.

spin·dle·legs, n. pl. long, slender legs.

spin·dling, a. long.

spin·dly, a., **-dli·er, -dli·est.** of a slender weak form.

spine, n. backbone; quill; inner quality of strength.

spine·less, a. having no spine; without courage.

spin·et, n. small, compact, upright piano.

spin·na·ker, n. triangular racing sail.

spin·ning wheel, n. device for spinning wool, flax, etc., into thread. **spin·ner,** n.

spi·nose, a. spiny.

spi·nous, a. thorny.

spin·ster, n. old maid.

spin·y, a. having spines. **spin·i·ness,** n.

spi·ral, n. helix. a. winding about an axis in continually advancing planes. v., **-raled, -ral·ing.** move in a spiral. **spi·ral·ly,** adv.

spire, n. slender, tapering formation; upper part of a steeple. v., **spired, spir·ing.** taper upwards. **spired,** a.

spir·it, n. soul; supernatural being; mettle or courage; vigor; attitude; pl. feelings; dominant tendency; often pl. alcoholic liquor. v. carry off; encourage. **spir·it·less,** a.

spir·it·ed, a. animated; lively.

spir·it·u·al, a. of the spirits of the dead; of the soul; religious; sacred. n. religious song. **spir·it·u·al·ly,** adv.

spir·it·u·al·ism, n. belief that the spirits of the dead communicate with the living. **spir·it·u·al·ist,** n.

spir·it·u·al·ize, v., **-ized, -iz·ing.** make spiritual. **spir·it·u·al·i·za·tion,** n.

spir·it·u·ous, a. alcoholic. **spir·it·u·os·i·ty,** n.

spit, v.i., **spit** or **spat, spit·ting.** eject saliva from the mouth; sputter; utter angrily. v.t. **spit·ted, spit·ting.** stab, as with a spit. n. saliva; pointed rod for holding meat. **spit·ter,** n.

spite, n. malicious ill will. v., **spit·ed, spit·ing.** show malice toward; thwart. **in spite of,** despite. **spite·ful,** a.

spit·fire, n. person of fiery disposition.

spit·tle, n. spit.

spit·toon, n. cuspidor.

splash, v. wet or soil by dashing water, mud, etc.; fall, move, or go with a splash or splashes. n. splashing. **splash·y,** a., **-i·er, -i·est.**

splash·down, n. landing at sea of a spacecraft. **splash down,** v.

splat·ter, v. splash; spatter.

splay, v. spread out; bevel. a. spread out.

spleen, n. ductless, glandular organ; ill humor. **spleen·ful,** a.

splen·did, a. magnificent; grand; brilliant. **splen·dor,** n.

splice, v., **spliced, splic·ing.** overlap and fasten; butt and bind; graft. n. splicing. **splic·er,** n.

splint, n. stiff material used to hold a fractured bone in position.

splin·ter, n. silver. v. split or break into splinters. **splin·ter·y,** a.

split, v., **split, split·ting.** separate; break apart; divide. n. crack; rupture. a. divided.

split-second, a. accurate.

splurge, n. inf. showing off; exorbitant expenditure. v., **splurged, splurg·ing.** show off with spending a lot.

spoil, v., **spoiled** or **spoilt, spoil·ing.** damage; impair; pillage; become unfit for use. n. often pl. booty. **spoil·age,** n. **spoil·er,** n.

spoke, n. rod supporting a wheel rim.

spo·ken, a. oral; equivalent to speaking.

spokes·man, n. pl., **-men.** one who speaks for another. **spokes·wom·an,** n. fem. pl., **-wom·en.**

sponge, n. water-dwelling animal having an absorbant skeleton; inf. parasite. v., **sponged,**

spong·ing. cleanse with a sponge. **spong·er,** n.

spon·gy, a., **-gi·er, -gi·est.** resembling a sponge; soft and full of cavities. **spon·gi·ness,** n.

spon·sor, n. one who answers for another; firm financing, and advertising on, a TV or radio program. v. be or act as sponsor for. **spon·sor·ship,** n.

spon·ta·ne·ous, a. without forethought; caused by inborn qualities. **spon·ta·ne·i·ty,** n. pl., **-ties.**

spoof, n. inf. playful hoax; deception. v. hoax; tease.

spook, n. inf. ghost. v. haunt; startle. **spook·y,** a., **-i·er, -i·est. spook·i·ness,** n.

spool, n. cylindrical piece on which something is wound.

spoon, n. utensil having a small, shallow bowl and handle. v. take up in a spoon. **spoon·ful,** n. pl., **-fuls.**

spoon-fed, a. fed with a spoon; coddled.

spo·rad·ic, a. irregular; occasional.

spore, n. asexual reproductive cell of algae, fungi, etc. v., **spored, spor·ing.** develop spores.

sport, n. diversion; athletic pastime; mere jest. a. of sport. v. pass, as time, in amusement; trifle. **sport·er,** n. **sport·ful,** a. **sport·ive,** a.

sport·ing, a. of athletic sports; sportsmanlike; inf. involving risk. **sport·ing·ly,** adv.

sports·man, n. pl., **-men.** one who engages in sports; one who exhibits such qualities as fairness, courtesy, etc. **sports·man·like,** a. **sports·man·ship,** n.

sports·writ·er, n. one writing about sporting events.

sport·y, a., **-i·er, -i·est.** inf. flashy; stylish; sporting. **sport·i·ness,** n.

spot, n. mark; stain; place or locality. v., **spot·ted, spot·ting.** stain. a. made at random. **in a spot,** in a difficult situation. **on the spot,** inf. at the very place; at once. **spot·less,** a.

spot·light, n. strong light beam. v. focus attention on.

spot·ted, a. marked with or characterized by spots.

spot·ty, a., **-ti·er, -ti·est.** spotted; lacking in uniformity. **spot·ti-**

ness, n.

spouse, n. husband or wife.

spout, n. nozzle etc., for pouring out a liquid; pipe. v. issue in a strong jet.

sprain, v. overstrain or wrench. n. spraining.

sprawl, v. straggle or spread out. n. awkward, sprawling position.

spray, n. mist; jet of fine particles of a squirted liquid. v. apply as a spray; issue forth as spray. **spray·er,** n.

spread, v., **spread, spread·ing.** extend; distribute in a sheet or layer; disseminate; be forced apart. n. spreading; covering for a bed, etc.; food spread, etc. on bread; ranch. **spread·er,** n.

spread-ea·gled, a. stretched out.

spree, n. merry frolic.

sprig, n. twig; spray of some plant. v., **sprigged, sprig·ging.** decorate with a design of sprigs.

spright·ly, a., **-li·er, -li·est.** vivacious; spirited. adv. lively. **spright·li·ness,** n.

spring, v., **sprang** or **sprung, sprung, spring·ing.** leap; fly back or away; issue suddenly; originate. n. leap; elasticity; elastic device or body; issue of water from the earth; season following winter. a. of or for the season of spring.

spring·time, n. spring season.

spring·y, a., **-i·er, -i·est.** having elasticity; light and lively.

sprin·kle, v., **-kled, -kling.** scatter in drops or particles; rain slightly. n. sprinkling. **sprink·ler,** n.

sprint, v. race. n. short run or race at high speed. **sprint·er,** n.

sprite, n. kind of elf or goblin.

sprout, v. begin growth; bud. n. shoot or bud.

spruce, n. cone-bearing evergreen tree. a., **spruc·er, spruc·est.** smart; trim. v., **spruced, spruc·ing.** dress in a spruce manner.

spry, a., **spry·er, spry·est** or **spri·er, spri·est.** nimble; active. **spry·ness,** n.

spue, n., **spued, spu·ing.** spew.

spume, n. froth; foam. v., **spumed, spum·ing.** froth; eject. **spum·ous, spum·y,** a. covered with spume.

spunk, n. inf. mettle.

spunk·y, *a.*, **-i·er**, **-i·est**. *inf.* full of pluck.

spur, *n.* sharp instrument worn on a horse rider's heel; stimulus. *v.*, **spurred**, **spur·ring**. prick with spurs; urge; hurry.

spu·ri·ous, *a.* not legitimate or genuine.

spurn, *v.* reject with disdain. *n.* rejection. **spurn·er**, *n.*

spurt, *v.* gush; squirt. *n.* spurting; marked increase of effort. **spurt·er**, *n.* **spur·tive**, *a.*

sput·nik, *n.* Russian artificial earth satellite.

sput·ter, *v.* give off particles explosively; jabber. *n.* sputtering. **sput·ter·er**, *n.*

spu·tum, *n. pl.*, **spu·ta**. spittle.

spy, *n. pl.*, **spies**. secret observer; one who obtains secret information. *v.*, **spied**, **spy·ing**. act as a spy; see.

spy·glass, *n.* telescope.

squab·ble, *v.*, **-bled**, **-bling**. quarrel. *n.* petty dispute. **squab·bler**, *n.*

squad, *n.* small unit of soldiers; small group.

squad·ron, *n.* flight formation of airplanes; basic tactical unit.

squal·id, *a.* filthy; wretched; sordid. **squal·id·ness**, *n.*

squall, *v.* cry out loudly. *n.* loud, discordant cry; violent gust of wind. **squall·er**, *n.*

squal·or, *n.* wretchedness and filth.

squan·der, *v.* spend wastefully. **squan·der·er**, *n.*

square, *n.* four-sided plane figure having all its sides equal. *a.* of or like a square; just; *inf.* old-fashioned. *adv.* at right angles. *v.*, **squared**, **squar·ing**. make cubical; multiply, as a number, by itself. **square·ly**, *adv.* **square·ness**, *n.*

squar·ish, *a.* approximately square.

squash, *v.* crush; suppress; splash. *n. pl.*, **squash·es**, **squash**. pulpy food plant.

squash·y, *a.*, **-i·er**, **-i·est**. soft or pulpy; muddy.

squat, *v.*, **squat·ted** or **squat**, **squat·ting**. crouch down; settle on land. *a.* short and thickset. **squat·ter**, *n.*

squaw, *n.* N. American Indian woman, esp. a wife.

squawk, *v.* utter a loud, harsh cry; *inf.* complain. *n.* harsh cry. **squawk·er**, *n.*

squeak, *v.* utter shrill cry; make a sharp noise. *n.* shrill cry or noise. **squeak·er**, *n.*

squeal, *v.* prolonged, shrill cry or sound. *v.* emit a shrill sound; *inf.* turn informer. **squeal·er**, *n.*

squeam·ish, *a.* prudish; easily nauseated.

squeeze, *v.*, **squeezed**, **squeez·ing**. compress; hug; force a way through. *n.* squeezing.

squelch, *v.* squash; *inf.* suppress. *v. n.* crushed mass; crushing retort. **squelch·er**, *n.*

squid, *n. pl.*, **squids**, **squid**. ten-armed marine animal.

squint, *v.* look with partially closed eyes. *n.* cross-eye; side glance. **squint·er**, *n.*

squirm, *v.* wriggle. **squirm·y**, *a.*

squir·rel, *n.* bushy-tailed rodent.

squirt, *v.* eject liquid in a jet; wet. *n.* jet, as of water.

squish, *v.* squash; squeeze.

stab, *v.*, **stabbed**, **stab·bing**. pierce; wound with a pointed weapon. *n.* thrust.

sta·bil·i·ty, *n. pl.*, **-ties**. firmness; continuance.

sta·bi·lize, *v.*, **-lized**, **-liz·ing**. make or keep firm or stable. **sta·bi·li·za·tion**, *n.*

sta·ble, *n.* building fitted for horses and cattle. *v.*, **-bled**, **-bling**. lodge in a stable. *a.* firm; steady; enduring.

stac·ca·to, *a.* in a crisp manner.

stack, *n.* pile; smokestack. *v.* pile; arrange one above another. **stack·er**, *n.*

sta·di·um, *n. pl.*, **-di·ums**, **-di·a**. structure for athletic games having tiers of seats.

staff, *n. pl.*, **staves**, **staffs**. stick for support or combat; supporting pole; group assisting a supervisor. *v.* provide with personnel.

stag, *n.* male deer, hart, etc. *a.* for men only.

stage, *n.* single step or degree in a process; raised platform; theater. *v.*, **staged**, **stag·ing**. present on the theatrical stage; go by stages. **stag·ing**, *n.*

stage·coach, *n.* coach drawn by horses.

stage-struck, *a.* having a great desire to become an actor.

stag·ger, *v.* reel; waver; amaze. *n.* sudden reel of the body. **stag·ger·er**, *n.*

stag·nant, *a.* not flowing; impure. **stag·nan·cy**, *n.*

stag·nate, *v.*, **-nat·ed**, **-nat·ing**. become impure from lack of current; become dull. **stag·na·tion**, *n.*

staid, *a.* sober. **staid·ness**, *n.*

stain, *v.* spot; bring shame upon; blemish; color. *n.* blemish; dye. **stained**, *a.*

stair, *n.* succession of steps; *pl.* stairway.

stair·case, *n.* structure of stairs. **stair·way**, *n.*

stake, *n.* sharpened piece of wood; something hazarded. *v.*, **staked**, **stak·ing**. mark the limits of; pledge.

sta·lac·tite, *n.* stony matter originating from the roof of a cavern.

sta·lag·mite, *n.* stony matter on the floor of a cavern.

stale, *a.*, **stal·er**, **stal·est**. tasteless from age; trite. *v.*, **staled**, **stal·ing**. make or be stale. **stale·ness**, *n.*

stale·mate, *n.* deadlock. *v.*, **-mat·ed**, **-mat·ing**. bring to a stalemate.

stalk, *n.* stem of a plant. *v.* pursue stealthily; walk with stiff, or haughty strides. **stalk·er**, *n.*

stall, *n.* compartment for one animal; booth. *v.* come to a standstill. **stalled**, *a.*

stal·lion, *n.* uncastrated male horse.

stal·wart, *a.* muscular; sturdy; brave. *n.* partisan.

sta·men, *n.*, *pl.*, **sta·mens**, **stam·i·na**. pollen-bearing organ of a flower.

stam·i·na, *n.* strength; endurance.

stam·mer, *v.* pause or falter while speaking.

stamp, *v.* imprint; affix a stamp to; strike the foot forcibly downward. *n.* mark imprinted; postage stamp.

stam·pede, *n.* sudden rush or headlong flight. *v.*, **-ped·ed**, **-ped·ing**. scatter.

stance, *n.* style of standing; particular attitude.

stanch, *v.* stop the flow of. Also **staunch**. **stanch·er**, *n.*

stand, *v.*, **stood**, **stand·ing**. take or be in an upright position; be located; set upright; endure; tolerate. *n.* halt; determined effort; position; *usu. pl.* raised platform; small table; stall. **stand·er**, *n.*

stand·ard, *n.* basis of comparison; established criterion; flag. *a.* serving as a standard.

stand·ard·ize, *v.*, **-dized**, **-diz·ing**. conform to or regulate by a standard. **stand·ard·i·za·tion**, *n.*

stand·by, *n.* *pl.*, **-bys.** supporter; substitute.

stand·in, *n.* substitute.

stand·ing, *n.* position or status; continuance. *a.* in an upright position; lasting.

stand·off·ish, *a.* somewhat reserved.

stand·point, *n.* view point.

stand·still, *n.* halt; stop.

stan·za, *n.* group of lines; division of a poem. **stan·za·ic**, *a.*

sta·pes, *n.*, *pl.*, **sta·pes**, **sta·ped·es**. innermost small bone in the middle ear.

sta·ple, *n.* wire fastener; *usu. pl.* necessary article; principal commodity. *a.* chief. *v.*, **-pled**, **-pling**. sort; fasten with a staple. **sta·pler**, *n.*

star, *n.* luminous celestial body; figure with five or six points; brilliant performer. *v.*, **starred**, **star·ring**. feature as the leading performer. **star·less**, *a.*

star·board, *n.* right-hand side of a ship looking toward the prow. *a.* referring to starboard.

starch, *n.* white tasteless carbohydrate; preparation used to stiffen fabrics.

stare, *v.*, **stared**, **star·ing**. gaze intently. *n.* fixed, wide-eyed look. **star·er**, *n.*

star·fish, *n.* *pl.*, **-fish**, **-fish·es**. star-shaped marine animal.

star·gaze, *v.*, **-gazed**, **-gaz·ing**. *fig.* daydream.

stark, *a.* downright; desolate; stiff. *adv.* wholly.

star·let, *n.* young actress.

star·ry, *a.*, **-ri·er**, **-ri·est**. of or resembling a star.

star·ry-eyed, *a.* idealistic.

start, *v.* set out; commence; originate. *n.* twitch; beginning. **start·er**, *n.*

star·tle, *v.*, **-tled**, **-tling**. shock; alarm. *n.* shock. **star·tling**, *a.*

starve, *v.*, **starved**, **starv·ing**. perish or suffer from want of food; kill with hunger. **star·va·tion**, *n.*, *a.*

stash, *v.* *inf.* hide in a secret

place.

state, *n.* condition; nation; one of the commonwealths of a federal union. *a.* of a state. *v.,* **stated, stat·ing.** aver; declare.

stat·a·ble, *a.*

state·craft, *n.* statesmanship.

stat·ed, *a.* determined or fixed.

state·ly, *a.,* **-li·er, -li·est.** dignified; majestic.

state·ment, *n.* something stated; *com.* abstract of an account.

states·man, *n. pl.,* **-men.** man versed in government. **statesman·ship,** *n.*

stat·ic, *a.* fixed; at rest. *n.* electrical interference.

sta·tion, *n.* position; place for particular work; standing. *v.* assign; post.

sta·tion·ar·y, *a.* not moving; fixed.

sta·tion·er·y, *n.* materials employed in writing.

sta·tis·tic, *n.* datum; statistical fact.

sta·tis·tics, *n. pl.* study of data; numerical data. **stat·is·ti·cian,** *n.*

stat·ue, *n.* representation carved, molded, etc.

stat·ure, *n.* natural height of an animal body; growth.

sta·tus, *n.* standing; postion; prestige.

stat·ute, *n.* law.

staunch, *a.* watertight; firm; steadfast.

stave, *n.* piece of wood forming the side of a cask; rod; stanza. *v.,* **staved** or **stove, stav·ing.** break or crush.

stay, *v.,* **stayed** or **staid, stay·ing.** remain; support; stop; restrain. *n.* continuance in a place; support. **stay·er,** *n.*

stead, *n.* place for which someone is substituted.

stead·fast, sted·fast, *a.* firm; constant. **stead·fast·ness,** *n.*

stead·y, *a.,* **-i·er, -i·est.** firm; stable; uniform. *v.,* **-ied, -y·ing.** make or become steady. **stead·i·ness,** *n.*

steak, *n.* cut of beef, fish, etc.

steal, *v.,* **stole, stol·en, steal·ing.** take dishonestly or wrongfully; move or go secretly. *n. inf.* theft; bargain.

stealth, *n.* secret method of procedure. **stealth·i·ly,** *adv.*

steam, *n.* heated water. *v.* give out or be covered by steam. **steam·er,** *n.*

steam·boat, *n.* ship powered by a steam engine.

steam-roll·er, *n.* heavy machine for crushing materials.

steam·ship, *n.* ship propelled by steam.

steam·y, *a.,* **-i·er, -i·est.** vaporous; misty.

steed, *n.* horse.

steel, *n.* alloy of iron and carbon. *a.* of steel; strong. *v.* make hard.

steel·y, *a.,* **-i·er, -i·est.** of or resembling steel.

steep, *a.* sloping sharply; *inf.* high in price. *v.* soak. **steepness,** *n.* **steep·en,** *v.*

stee·ple, *n.* tall, tapering structure.

steer, *v.* guide; pilot; direct. *n. inf.* tip; castrated bovine. **steer·a·ble,** *a.* **steer·er,** *n.*

steer·age, *n.* part of a ship for passengers traveling at the cheapest rate.

stein, *n.* mug, esp. for beer.

stel·lar, *a.* of or resembling stars.

stem, *n.* stalk; slender part; base of a word. *v.,* **stemmed, stem·ming.** remove the stem from; be derived; stop. **stem·less,** *a.* **stemmed,** *a.*

stench, *n.* stink. **stench·y,** *a.*

sten·cil, *n.* pierced sheet of metal, etc., for reproducing letters etc. *v.,* **-ciled, -cil·ing.** mark by means of a stencil.

ste·nog·ra·phy, *n.* shorthand writing. **ste·nog·ra·pher,** *n.*

sten·to·ri·an, *a.* very loud.

step, *n.* one movement of the foot; gait; stage; support for the foot, as on a stair. *v.,* **stepped, step·ping.** go briskly; tread.

step-broth·er, *n.* one's stepparent's son.

step-child, *n. pl.,* **-child·ren.** child of one's spouse by a former marriage.

step-daugh·ter, *n.* daughter of one's spouse by a former marriage.

step-fa·ther, *n.* husband of one's remarried mother.

step-lad·der, *n.* ladder having four legs and flat steps.

step-moth·er, *n.* wife of one's remarried father.

step-par·ent, *n.* stepfather or stepmother.

steppe, *n.* vast plain.

stepped-up, *a. inf.* increased.

step·sis·ter, *n.* one's stepparent's daughter.

step·son, *n.* son of one's spouse by a former marriage.

ster·e·o·phon·ic, *a.* of a sound system reproducing the spatial distribution of a sound.

ster·e·o·typed, *a.* fixed, typified; conventional.

ster·ile, *a.* free from living germs; barren; infertile. **ste·ril·i·ty,** *n.*

ster·i·lize, *v.,* **-ized, -iz·ing.** render sterile. **ster·i·li·za·tion, ster·i·li·zer,** *n.*

ster·ling, *a.* of English money; of silver.

stern, *a.* severe; harsh. *n.* hinder part of a ship. **stern·ly,** *adv.* **stern·ness,** *n.*

ster·num, *n. pl.,* **ster·na, ster·nums.** breastbone.

steth·o·scope, *n.* instrument used to convey body sounds to the ear.

ste·ve·dore, *n.* one who loads or unloads vessels. *v.,* **-dored, -dor·ing.** load or unload freight.

stew, *n.* food preparation cooked by stewing. *v.* simmer.

stew·ard, *n.* manager; ship attendant. **stew·ard·ess,** *n. fem.*

stick, *n.* long, slender piece of wood; rod. *v.,* **stuck, stick·ing.** pierce; attach; set; cling; stay close; protrude.

stick·er, *n.* adhesive label.

stick·ler, *n.* one who insists on perfection.

stick·up, stick·up, *n. inf.* holdup.

stick·y, *a.,* **-i·er, -i·est.** viscous; humid. **stick·i·ness,** *n.*

stiff, *a.* rigid; not supple; constrained; potent. *n. inf.* corpse. **stiff·ly,** *adv.* **stiff·ness,** *n.* **stiff·en,** *v.*

sti·fle, *v.,* **-fled, -fling.** smother; suppress; conceal. **sti·fler,** *n.* **sti·fling,** *a.*

stig·ma, *n. pl.,* **-mas, -ma·ta.** mark of infamy; stain; upper extremity of the style.

sti·let·to, *n. pl.,* **-tos, -toes.** small, slender dagger.

still, *a.* motionless; silent. *v.* quiet; allay. *n.* distilling apparatus. *adv.* continuously; nonetheless. **still·ness,** *n.*

stilt, *n.* pillar used to support a structure.

stilt·ed, *a.* pompous; stiff.

stim·u·lant, *n.* that which stimulates.

stim·u·late, *v.,* **-lat·ed, -lat·ing.** excite or arouse; spur on.

stim·u·la·tion, *n.*

stim·u·lus, *n. pl.,* **-li.** incitement; stimulant.

sting, *v.,* **stung, sting·ing.** prick; pain sharply; use a sting, as bees. *n.* stinging; sharp-pointed organ of insects. **sting·er,** *n.*

stin·gy, *a.,* **-i·er, -i·est.** miserly; niggardly

stink, *v.,* **stank** or **stunk, stunk, stink·ing.** emit or have an offensive smell. *n.* stench. **stink·y,** *a.,* **-i·er, -i·est.**

stint, *v.* limit; restrict. *n.* specific amount of work assigned. **stint·er,** *n.*

sti·pend, *n.* periodical payment.

stip·u·late, *v.,* **-lat·ed, -lat·ing.** specify as a condition. **stip·u·la·tion,** *n.*

stir, *v.,* **stirred, stir·ring.** mix; agitate; excite. *n.* stirring; hustle.

stir·ring, *a.* busy; rousing.

stir·rup, *n.* strap hanging from a saddle for the foot.

stitch, *v.* sew. *n.* single pass of the needle in sewing, etc. **stitch·er,** *n.*

stock, *n.* transferable share of a company; goods kept on hand; horses, cattle, etc.; broth; lineage; race. *v.* furnish with; accumulate. *a.* standard; in common use. **stock·brok·er,** *n.*

stock·ade, *n.* barrier; pen made with posts and stakes. *v.,* **-ad·ed, -ad·ing.** protect with a stockade.

stock·hold·er, *n.* owner of shares of stock.

stock·ing, *n.* covering for the foot and leg.

stock mar·ket, *n.* market where stocks are bought and sold.

stock·pile, *n.* accumulation of supplies. *v.,* **-piled, -pil·ing.** store; hoard.

stock·y, *a.,* **-i·er, -i·est.** thickset.

stodg·y, *a.,* **-i·er, -i·est.** heavy; dull; dowdy.

sto·ic, *n.* person unmoved by joy or grief.

sto·i·cal, *a.* impassive.

stoke, *v.,* **stoked, stok·ing.** poke, stir up, and feed, as a fire. **stok·er,** *n.*

stol·id, *a.* dull; unexcitable. **sto·lid·i·ty,** *n.*

stom·ach, *n.* main organ of digestion. *v.* bear.

stomp, *v. inf.* stamp.

stone, *n.* hard concretion of mineral matter. *v.*, **stoned**, **ston·ing**. throw stones at; remove the seed from.

stone-deaf, *a.* totally deaf.

stone-wall, *v.* filibuster.

ston·y, **ston·ey** *a.*, **-i·er**, **-i·est**. of stone; pitiless; rigid. **ston·i·ness**, *n.*

stool, *n.* seat without arms or back for one person; discharge from the bowels.

stoop, *v.* bend from an erect position; deign; lower oneself. *n.* stooping; small porch.

stop, *v.*, **stopped**, **stop·ping**. halt; restrain; cease; stanch; sojourn. *n.* standstill; check; stay; plug. **stop·page**, *n.* **stop·per**, *n.*

stop·gap, *n.* temporary expedient or substitute.

stop-light, *n.* traffic signal.

stor·age, *n.* storing; place to keep something.

store, *n.* shop; supply or stock. *v.*, **stored**, **stor·ing**. supply or stock with something. **store·house**, *n.*

sto·ried, **sto·reyed**, *a.* having stories or floors.

stork, *n.* tall wading bird.

storm, *n.* tempest; heavy fall of rain, snow, etc.; violent disturbance. *v.* blow, rain, etc., with violence; rage; rush to an assault.

storm·y *a.*, **-i·er**, **-i·est**. tempestuous. **storm·i·ness**, *n.*

sto·ry, *n. pl.*, **-ries**. narrative; fictitious tale; plot; floor of a building; *inf.* lie. **sto·ried**, *a.*

sto·ry·tell·er, *n.* one who tells stories; *inf.* fibber. **sto·ry·tell·ing**, *a.*, *n.*

stout, *a.* thickset; dauntless; firm. **stout·ness**, *n.*

stout-heart·ed, *a.* courageous.

stove, *n.* cooking or heating apparatus.

stow, *v.* place, as cargo, in a ship; pack. **stow·age**, *n.*

stow·a·way, *n.* one who conceals himself aboard a ship.

strad·dle, *v.*, **-dled**, **-dling**. stand or sit with one leg on each side of. **strad·dler**, *n.*

strafe, *v.*, **strafed**, **straf·ing**. bombard heavily.

strag·gle, *v.*, **-gled**, **-gling**. wander about. **strag·gler**, *n.*

strag·gly, *a.*, **-gli·er**, **-gli·est**. disorganized; rambling.

straight, *a.* without crooks, bends, etc.; direct; honest; unmodified. *n.* straight section. *adv.* in a straight line; directly; without delay. **straight·ness**, *n.*

straight·en, *v.* make or become straight. **straight·en·er**, *n.*

straight-for·ward, *a.* honest; open.

straight·way, *adv.* immediately.

strain, *n.* ancestry; trace; kind; stress; wrench. *v.* draw tight; stretch to the upmost; filter; overtax. **strain·er**, *n.*

strait, *n.* narrow passage of water; *often pl.* distress; need.

strait-laced, *a.* constrained; strict.

strand, *n.* shore; threads twisted together forming cord, etc. *v.* leave helpless or isolated.

strange, *a.*, **stra·ger**, **strang·est**. unfamiliar; unknown; odd. **strangeness**, *n.*

stran·ger, *n.* foreigner; newcomer; outsider.

stran·gle, *v.*, **-gled**, **-gling**. kill by, or die from, choking. **stran·gler**, *n.* **stran·gu·la·tion**, *n.*

strap, *n.* narrow strip of leather, etc., for binding or holding. *v.*, **strapped**, **strap·ping**. beat with a strap; bind. **strap·less**, *a.*

strap·ping, *a. inf.* of imposing build.

strat·a·gem, *n.* clever plan to gain an advantage.

strat·e·gy, *n. pl.*, **-gies**. science of military operations; use of artifice in planning. **strat·e·gist**, *n.* **stra·te·gic**, *a.*

strat·i·fy, *v.*, **-fied**, **-fy·ing**. form, put, or divide in layers. **strat·i·fi·ca·tion**, *n.*

strat·o·sphere, *n.* atmosphere about seven miles above the earth.

stra·tum, *n. pl.*, **stra·ta**, **stra·tums**. layer; level.

straw, *n.* stalk of grain after being thrashed; tube used to draw up a beverage. *a.* of straw.

straw·ber·ry, *n. pl.*, **-ries**. succulent fruit.

stray, *v.* wander; err. *n.* one that wanders.

streak, *n.* long, narrow mark, stripe, etc. **streak·y**, *a.*

stream, *n.* brook; steady current. *v.* flow in a stream.

stream·er, *n.* banner.

stream·line, *v.*, **-lined**, **-lin·ing.** shape in a way that decreases resistance; simplify. **stream·lined**, *a.*

street, *n.* thoroughfare in a city.

street·car, *n.* passenger car running on rails set in the street.

strength, *n.* state or inherent capacity of being strong; potency. **strength·en**, *v.* **strength·en·er**, *n.*

stren·u·ous, *a.* requiring great exertion.

stress, *n.* force; strain; tension; emphasis. *v.* emphasize. **stress·ful**, *a.* **stress·less**, *a.*

stretch, *v.* extend; draw tight. *n.* stretching; elasticity. **stretch·a·ble**, *a.*

stretch·er, *n.* litter.

strew, *v.*, **strewed**, **strewed** or **strewn**, **strew·ing.** scatter.

stri·ate, *v.*, **-at·ed**, **-at·ing.** furrow; stripe.

strick·en, *a.* afflicted.

strict, *a.* exact or precise; austere; rigorously enforced. **strict·ness**, *n.*

stric·ture, *n.* sharp criticism; censure.

stride, *v.*, **strode**, **strid·den**, **strid·ing.** walk with long steps. *n.* gait; long step; rapid progress.

stri·dent, *a.* shrill.

strife, *n.* contention. **strife·less**, *a.* **strife·ful**, *a.*

strike, *v.*, **struck**, **struck** or **strick·en**, **strik·ing.** hit; attack; sound a percussion set; ignite, as a match; come upon; assume, as an attitude; quit in a body, as work. *n.* act of striking. **strike·less**, *a.*

strik·ing, *a.* remarkable; impressive. **strik·ing·ly**, *adv.*

string, *n.* slender cord or thick thread; series of objects, events, etc., in a row; set of. *v.*, **strung**, **strung** or **stringed**, **string·ing.** thread on or as on a line; extend.

strin·gent, *a.* compelling; strict. **strin·gen·cy**, *n.*

string·y, *a.*, **-i·er**, **-i·est.** fibrous; ropy; wiry. **string·i·ness**, *n.*

strip, *v.*, **stripped**, **strip·ping.** plunder; divest; undress. *n.* long, narrow piece or tract.

stripe, *n.* narrow band of a different nature within a substance. *v.*, **striped**, **strip·ing.** mark with a stripe. **striped**, *a.*

strip·ling, *n.* boy.

strive, *v.*, **strove**, **striv·en**, **striv·ing.** make efforts; endeavor; vie.

stroke, *n.* blow; striking; attack of apoplexy; single movement. *v.*, **stroked**, **strok·ing.** caress.

stroll, *v.* walk leisurely; wander. *n.* leisurely walk. **stroll·er**, *n.*

strong, *a.* having physical power; healthy; firm. *adv.* in a strong manner.

strong·hold, *n.* fortified place; place of security.

strong-mind·ed, *a.* showing independent thinking.

stron·ti·um, *n.* yellow metallic element. **stron·tic**, *a.*

strop, *n.* razorstrop. *v.*, **stropped**, **strop·ping.** sharpen with a strop.

struc·ture, *n.* arrangement of parts, etc.; something built. *v.*, **-tured**, **-tur·ing.** construct. **struc·tur·al**, *a.* **struc·tured**, *a.*

strug·gle, *v.*, **-gled**, **-gling.** fight; do something that is difficult. *n.* strong effort. **strug·gler**, *n.* **strug·gling**, *a.*

strum, *v.* brush the fingers across the strings of, as a guitar. **strum·mer**, *n.*

strum·pet, *n.* prostitute.

strut, *v.*, **strut·ted**, **strut·ting.** walk with affected dignity. *n.* proud walk; brace.

strych·nine, *n.* poisonous alkaloid. **strych·nic**, *a.*

stub, *n.* remaining part after use or wear. *v.*, **stubbed**, **stub·bing.** strike, as one's foot, against. **stub·by**, *a.*

stub·ble, *n.* stumps of grain; rough growth. **stub·bly**, *a.*

stub·born, *a.* obstinate; inflexible. **stub·born·ness**, *n.*

stuc·co, *n. pl.*, **-coes**, **-cos.** stonelike cement; plaster.

stud, *n.* stallion kept for breeding; upright prop; ornamental fastener.

stu·dent, *n.* one studying anything. **stu·dent·ship**, *n.*

stud·ied, *a.* deliberate.

stu·di·o, *n. pl.*, **-os.** working room of a creative person.

stu·di·ous, *a.* given to study; diligent.

stud·y, *n. pl.*, **-ies.** application for the purpose of learning; place devoted to study. *v.*, **-ied**, **-y·ing.** apply one's mind to learning.

stuff, *n.* substance; refuse. *v.* cram; fill; feed gluttonously. **stuff·er**, *n.* **stuff·ing**, *n.*

stuff·y, *a.*, **-i·er**, **-i·est.** difficult to breathe in; *inf.* stodgy. **stuff·i·ness**, *n.*

stum·ble, *v.*, **-bled**, **-bling.** trip in walking; discover by chance. *n.* blunder.

stum·bling·block, *n.* obstacle.

stump, *n.* basal portion remaining. *inf.* nonplus; walk heavily. **stump·y**, *a.*

stun, *v.*, stunned, stun·ning. render insensible; surprise completely. *n.* stunning.

stun·ning, *a.* striking.

stunt, *v.* check in growth. *n.* unusual or daring feat.

stu·pe·fy, *v.*, **-fied**, **-fy·ing.** make stupid; stun. **stu·pe·fac·tion**, *n.*

stu·pen·dous, *a.* great and wonderful.

stu·pid, *a.* mentally slow; senseless. **stu·pid·i·ty**, *n.*

stu·por, *n.* state of suspended sensibility.

stur·dy, *a.*, **-di·er**, **-di·est.** strong; firm; stout. **stur·di·ness**, *n.*

stur·geon, *n. pl.*, **stur·geon**, **stur·geons.** fish valued as a source of caviar.

stut·ter, *v.*, *n.* stammer. **stut·ter·er**, *n.*

sty, *n. pl.*, **sties.** pen for swine; small inflamed bump on the eyelid.

style, *n.* manner of writing; way; fashion. *v.*, styled, styl·ing. name; give a particular form to. **styl·er**, *n.*

styl·ish, *a.* chic.

sty·mie, *v.*, **-mied**, **-mie·ing.** hinder; obstruct.

styp·tic, *a.* astringent. *n.*

suave, *a.* gracious; polished. **suave·ness**, *n.* **suav·i·ty**, *n.*

sub, *n. inf.* submarine.

sub-chas·er, *n.* submarine chaser.

sub·class, *n.* subgroup of a class.

sub·con·scious, *a.* not wholly conscious. *n.* unconscious mental process.

sub·con·ti·nent, *n.* independent subdivision of a continent; large landform. **sub·con·ti·nen·tal**, *a.*

sub·cu·ta·ne·ous, *a.* immediately under the skin.

sub·di·vide, *v.*, **-vid·ed**, **-vid·ing.** divide parts into more parts; divide into lots. **sub·di·vi·sion**, *n.*

sub·due, *v.*, **-dued**, **-du·ing.** conquer and bring into subjection; tone down. **sub·du·er**, *n.*

sub·en·try, *n. pl.*, **-tries.** entry under a main entry.

sub·group, *n.* secondary grouping or division.

sub·head, *n.* subordinate head or title.

sub·hu·man, *a.* almost human.

sub·ject, *n.* one under control; theme. *a.* being under domination; liable. *v.* bring under control; cause to undergo; lay open. **sub·jec·tion**, *n.*

sub·jec·tive, *a.* personal. **sub·jec·tiv·i·ty**, *n.*

sub·join, *v.* add at the end.

sub·ju·gate, *v.*, **-gat·ed**, **-gat·ing.** conquer; enslave. **sub·ju·ga·tion**, *n.* **sub·ju·ga·tor**, *n.*

sub·lease, *v.*, **-leased**, **-leas·ing.** sublet.

sub·let, *v.*, **-let**, **-let·ting.** let under a subcontract.

sub·li·mate, *v.*, **-mat·ed**, **-mat·ing.** transfer the energy of into a higher goal. **sub·li·ma·tion**, *n.*

sub·lime, *a.*, **-lim·er**, **-lim·est.** elevated or lofty. **sub·lim·i·ty**, *n. pl.*, **-ties.**

sub·lim·i·nal, *a.* beneath the conscious level.

sub·ma·rine, *n.* vessel navigated under water.

sub·merge, *v.*, **-merged**, **-merg·ing.** put or sink below the surface of. **sub·mer·gence**, *n.*

sub·merse, *v.*, **-mersed**, **-mers·ing.** submerge. **sub·mer·sion**, *n.*

sub·mis·sion, *n.* submitting.

sub·mis·sive, *a.*

sub·mit, *v.*, **-mit·ted**, **-mit·ting.** yield; surrender; refer or present for approval.

sub·nor·mal, *a.* below the normal. **sub·nor·mal·i·ty**, *n.*

sub·or·di·nate, *a.* of a lower order or rank; dependent. *n.* subordinate person. *v.*, **-nat·ed**, **-nat·ing.** place in a lower rank. **sub·or·di·na·tion**, *n.*

sub·poe·na, **sub·pe·na**, *n.* judicial writ commanding attendance in court. *v.*, **-naed**, **-na·ing.** serve with a writ of subpoena.

sub·scribe, *v.*, **-scribed**, **-scrib·ing.** contribute; agree to pay for the future delivery of; sign. **sub·scrib·er**, *n.* **sub·scrip·tion**, *n.*

sub·se·quent, *a.* following.

sub·ser·vi·ent, *a.* servile; submissive.

sub·side, *v.,* **-sid·ed, -sid·ing.** sink to a lower level; abate. *n.*

sub·sid·i·ar·y, *a.* lending some aid; subordinate. *n. pl.,* **-ar·ies.** company controlled by another company.

sub·si·dize, *v.,* **-dized, -diz·ing.** furnish with a subsidy. **sub·si·diz·er,** *n.*

sub·si·dy, *n. pl.,* **-dies.** gift of money; grant.

sub·sist, *v.* exist.

sub·sist·ence, *n.* existence; means of support.

sub·stance, *n.* matter; body; essential part; firmness; material means.

sub·stan·tial, *a.* of considerable size, value, etc.; real.

sub·stan·ti·ate, *v.,* **-at·ed, -at·ing.** establish by proof. **sub·stan·ti·a·tion,** *n.*

sub·stan·tive, *n.* noun.

sub·sti·tute, *v.,* **-tut·ed, -tut·ing.** put or act in the place of another. *n.* person or thing acting for another. **sub·sti·tu·tion,** *n.*

sub·stra·tum, *n. pl.,* **-tas, -tums.** foundation.

sub·ter·fuge, *n.* deception to conceal or to escape difficulty.

sub·ter·ra·ne·an, *a.* underground; hidden.

sub·ti·tle, *n.* secondary title; written translation of foreign dialogue.

sub·tle, *a.* sly; ingenious; delicate; acute. **sub·tle·ty,** *n.*

sub·tract, *v.* take away. **sub·trac·tion,** *n.*

sub·urb, *n. often pl.* district lying immediately outside a city. **sub·ur·ban,** *a., n.*

sub·vert, *v.* overthrow. **sub·ver·sion,** *n.* **sub·ver·sive,** *a., n.*

sub·way, *n.* underground electric railway.

suc·ceed, *v.* accomplish what is attempted; come after.

suc·cess, *n.* favorable termination; attainment of wealth, etc.; person that is successful. **suc·cess·ful,** *a.*

suc·ces·sion, *n.* coming of one after another in order, course, etc. **suc·ces·sive,** *a.*

suc·ces·sor, *n.* person that succeeds or follows.

suc·cinct, *a.* concise.

suc·cor, *n., v.* aid; help.

suc·cu·lent, *a.* juicy.

suc·cumb, *v.* yield; die.

such, *a.* of the kind of that or those indicated. *pron.* such a person or thing. *adv.* so; very.

suck, *v.* draw in or imbibe by suction. *n.* act of drawing with the mouth. **suck·er,** *n.*

suck·le, *v.,* **-led, -ling.** nurse at the breast.

suc·tion, *n.* sucking; sucking force.

sud·den, *a.* coming unexpectedly; quick. **sud·den·ly,** *adv.*

suds, *n. pl.* soapy water. **suds·y,** *a.,* **-i·er, -i·est.**

sue, *v.,* **sued, su·ing.** seek justice by legal process; make legal claim. **su·er,** *n.*

suede, *n.* kid or leather finished with a soft nap.

su·et, *n.* fatty animal tissue yielding tallow. **su·et·y,** *a.*

suf·fer, *v.* feel or undergo pain of body or mind; allow. **suf·fer·ance,** *n.*

suf·fice, *v.,* **-ficed, -fic·ing.** be enough; satisfy.

suf·fi·cient, *a.* adequate to wants; enough. **suf·fi·cien·cy,** *n. pl.,* **-cies.**

suf·fix, *n.* syllable affixed to the end of a word.

suf·fo·cate, *v.,* **-cat·ed, -cat·ing.** choke or kill by stopping respiration. **suf·fo·ca·tion,** *n.*

suf·frage, *n.* right to vote.

suf·fuse, *v.,* **-fused, -fus·ing.** overspread. **suf·fu·sion,** *n.*

sug·ar, *n.* sweet, white crystalline substance; sucrose. *v.* sweeten. **sug·ar·y,** *a.*

sug·gest, *v.* propose; call up in the mind. **sug·ges·tion,** *n.*

sug·ges·tive, *a.* that suggests; giving a seeming indication of, as something indecent.

su·i·cide, *n.* one who intentionally takes one's own life; this act. *v.,* **-cid·ed, -cid·ing.** commit suicide.

suit, *n.* set of garments worn together; law process; one of the four sets of playing cards. *v.* adapt; suitable.

suit·a·ble, *a.* fitting; proper.

suit·case, *n.* valise.

suite, *n.* connected series of rooms.

suit·or, *n.* wooer; petitioner.

sul·fa, sul·pha, *a.* of a family of drugs chemically related to sulfanilamide.

sul·fur, sul·phur, *n.* yellow nonmetallic element.

sul·fu·ric ac·id, *n.* oily, corrosive compound.

sulk, *v.* be sulky. *n.* state or fit of sulking.

sulk·y, *a.,* **-i·er, -i·est.** sullenly ill-humored.

sul·len, *a.* showing ill humor by a gloomy silence; morose. **sul·len·ness,** *n.*

sul·ly, *v.,* **-lied, -ly·ing.** soil; defile.

sul·tan, *n.* sovereign of a Mohammedan country. **sul·tan·ate,** *n.*

sul·try, *a.,* **-tri·er, -tri·est.** hot, close, and heavy.

sum, *n.* total; indefinite quantity, esp. of money; essence of a matter. *v.,* **summed, sum·ming.** summarize.

su·mac, su·mach, *n.* shrub or tree.

sum·ma·rize, *v.,* **-rized, -riz·ing.** make a summary of.

sum·ma·ry, *a.* concise; quickly executed. *n. pl.,* **-ries.** condensed statement.

sum·mer, *n.* season between spring and autumn. *a.* of summer. **sum·mer·y,** *a.*

sum·mit, *n.* highest point; top or apex. **sum·mit·al,** *a.*

sum·mon, *v.* call to appear; order together; muster.

sum·mons, *n. pl.,* **sum·mons·es.** call by authority to appear in court.

sump·tu·ous, *a.* costly; luxurious.

sun, *n.* star around which the earth and other planets revolve; sunlight. *v.,* **sunned, sun·ning.** expose to the light of the sun.

sun·bathe, *v.,* **-bathed, -bath·ing.** lie exposed to the sun. **sun·bath·er,** *n.*

sun·dae, *n.* ice cream with fruit, syrup, nuts, etc.

Sun·day, *n.* first day of the week.

sun·der, *v.* part; divide.

sun·down, *n.* sunset.

sun·dries, *n. pl.* various small things.

sun·dry, *a.* several; various.

sun·flow·er, *n.* tall herb with yellow-rayed flowers.

sun·glass·es, *n. pl.* eyeglasses having tinted lenses.

sunk·en, *a.* submerged; hollow; recessed.

sun·light, *n.* light of the sun.

sun·lit, *a.* lighted by the sun.

sun·ny, *a.,* **-ni·er, -ni·est.** lighted by sunshine; cheery.

sun·rise, *n.* appearance of the sun above the horizon.

sun·set, *n.* time when the sun sets.

sun·shine, *n.* light of the sun. **sun·shin·y,** *a.*

sun·stroke, *n.* type of heatstroke resulting from exposure to the sun.

sup, *v.,* **supped, sup·ping.** take supper.

su·per·an·nu·ate, *v.,* **-at·ed, -at·ing.** discard as too old; become retired.

su·perb, *a.* grand; august; first-rate. **su·perb·ness,** *n.*

su·per·charge, *v.,* **-charged, -charg·ing.** overload; increase the power of an engine.

su·per·cil·i·ous, *a.* disdainful; haughty; arrogant.

su·per·fi·cial, *a.* lying on the surface; not deep.

su·per·fine, *a.* very fine; faultily subtle.

su·per·flu·ous, *a.* being more than is wanted. **su·per·flu·i·ty,** *n. pl.,* **-ties.**

su·per·high·way, *n.* multilane highway.

su·per·hu·man, *a.* above what is human; divine.

su·per·im·pose, *v.,* **-posed, -pos·ing.** add over something else.

su·per·in·tend, *v.* have the charge and oversight of. **su·per·in·tend·ent,** *n.*

su·pe·ri·or, *a.* higher in rank, office, etc.; excellent. *n.* one who is superior. **su·pe·ri·or·i·ty,** *n.*

su·per·la·tive, *a.* of the highest rank or degree. *n.* that which is superlative.

su·per·mar·ket, *n.* large retail store.

su·per·nat·u·ral, *a.* of happenings or forces above the natural; eerie.

su·per·nu·mer·ar·y, *n. pl.,* **-ies.** extra person or thing. *a.* extra; superfluous.

su·per·scribe, *v.,* **-scribed, -scrib·ing.** write on the top of.

su·per·scrip·tion, *n.*

su·per·sede, *v.,* **-sed·ed, -sed·ing.** supplant.

su·per·son·ic, *a.* attaining speeds greater than sound; of sounds above those that can be heard.

su·per·sti·tion, *n.* belief of the ominous significance of a thing, occurrence, etc. **su·per·sti·tious,** *a.*

su·per·vise, *v.,* **-vised, -vis·ing.** oversee; superintend. **su·per·vi·sion,** *n.* **su·per·vi·sor,** *n.*

su·pine, *a.* lying on the back; inactive.

sup·per, *n.* evening meal.

sup·plant, *v.* displace; take the place of. **sup·plant·er,** *n.*

sup·ple, *a.,* **-pler, -plest.** bending readily; flexible.

sup·ple·ment, *n.* addition. *v.* furnish what is lacking. **sup·ple·men·ta·ry,** *a.*

sup·pli·cate, *v.,* **-cat·ed, -cat·ing.** entreat; implore. **sup·pli·cant,** *n., a.* **sup·pli·ca·tion,** *n.*

sup·ply, *v.,* **-plied, -ply·ing.** furnish or provide. *n. pl.,* **-plies.** stock or store. **sup·pli·er,** *n.*

sup·port, *v.* bear; hold up; tolerate; maintain; provide for. *n.* maintenance. **sup·port·er,** *n.* **sup·port·ive,** *a.*

sup·pose, *v.,* **-posed, -pos·ing.** assume; imagine; expect; imply; think. **sup·posed,** *a.* **sup·po·si·tion,** *n.*

sup·pos·ing, *conj.* in the event that.

sup·press, *v.* overpower and crush; quell; conceal. **sup·pres·sion,** *n.*

sup·pu·rate, *v.,* **-rat·ed, -rat·ing.** fester. **sup·pu·ra·tion,** *n.*

su·preme, *a.* highest; final. **su·prem·a·cy,** *n. pl.,* **-cies.**

sur·charge, *n.* extra tax; overcharge. *v.,* **-charged, -charg·ing.** add on an extra charge.

sure, *a.,* **sur·er, sur·est.** certain; fully persuaded; infallible. *adv.* certainly. **sure·ly,** *adv.* **sure·ness,** *n.*

sure·ty, *n. pl.,* **-ties.** security; certainty; guarantee.

surf, *n.* swell of the sea which breaks upon a shore.

sur·face, *n.* exterior boundary; face of an object. *a.* external; superficial. *v.,* **-faced, -fac·ing.** come to the surface. **sur·face·less,** *a.*

sur·feit, *n.* excessive amount; overindulgence. *v.* do anything excessively.

surge, *n.* billow. *v.,* **surged, surg·ing.** swell; flow suddenly or powerfully.

sur·geon, *n.* medical man who specializes in surgery.

sur·ger·y, *n. pl.,* **-ies.** performance or place of medical ope-

rations. **sur·gi·cal,** *a.*

sur·ly, *a.,* **-li·er, -li·est.** cross and rude.

sur·mise, *n.* guess. *v.,* **-mised, -mis·ing.** guess; conjecture.

sur·mount, *v.* rise above; overcome.

sur·name, *n.* last name.

sur·pass, *v.* exceed; excel; go beyond. **sur·pass·ing,** *a.*

sur·plus, *n., a.* that which remains.

sur·prise, *n.* surprising. *v.,* **-prised, -pris·ing.** fall upon unexpectedly; take unawares; astonish. **sur·pris·ing,** *a.*

sur·ren·der, *v.* yield to the power of another; abandon. *n.* yielding or giving up.

sur·ro·gate, *n.* substitute. *v.,* **-gat·ed, -gat·ing.** put in the place of another.

sur·round, *v.* encompass; enclose. **sur·round·ing,** *n., a.*

sur·veil·lance, *n.* watch kept over some person. **sur·veil·lant,** *a., n.*

sur·vey, *v.* view closely; determine the boundaries, etc., of. *n.* inspection; random sampling; surveying of land. **sur·vey·or,** *n.*

sur·vive, *v.,* **-vived, -viv·ing.** outlive; remain alive. **sur·viv·al,** *n.* **sur·vi·vor,** *n.*

sus·cep·ti·ble, *a.* capable of being affected. **sus·cep·ti·bil·i·ty,** *n.*

sus·pect, *v.* mistrust; imagine to be guilty. *n.* one suspected, esp. of a crime. *a.* open to suspicion.

sus·pend, *v.* hang; debar for a time; cease for a while. **sus·pen·sion,** *a.*

sus·pense, *n.* state of uncertainty; sense of insecurity. **sus·pense·ful,** *a.*

sus·pi·cion, *n.* suspecting; feeling of one who suspects; slight trace. **sus·pi·cious,** *a.*

sus·tain, *v.* support or bear up; suffer; endure; nourish.

sus·te·nance, *n.* that which supports life, as food.

svelte, *a.* slender.

swab, *n.* mop; bit of cotton, etc., attached to a stick. *v.,* **swabbed, swab·bing.** clean with a swab or mop.

swad·dle, *v.,* **-dled, -dling.** wrap with strips of cloth, as an infant.

swag·ger, *v.* strut; brag. *n.* arrogant strut. **swag·ger·er,** *n.*

swal·low, *n.* migratory bird; amount swallowed. *v.* receive, as food, through the throat; draw into; forbear.

swamp, *n.* spongy land; bog. *v.* overwhelm; sink or cause to become filled. **swamp·y,** *a.,* **-i·er, -i·est. swamp·i·ness,** *n.*

swan, *n.* long-necked bird.

swank, *a.* ostentatious. **swank·y,** *a.,* **-i·er, -i·est.**

swap, *n., v.* **swapped, swap·ping.** *inf.* barter; trade.

swarm, *n.* body of honeybees; great number of things or persons, esp. in motion. *v.* abound or teem; swarm about.

swarth·y, *a.,* **-i·er, -i·est.** dark-colored.

swash·buck·ler, *n.* swaggering fellow. **swash·buck·ling,** *a.*

swat, *v.* **swat·ted, swat·ting.** hit with a smart blow. *n.* smart blow. **swat·ter,** *n.*

swatch, *n.* sample of cloth or other material.

swathe, *v.* **swathed, swath·ing.** wrap with a band or bandage. *n.* wrapping.

sway, *v.* swing backward and forward; incline; bias; rule. *n.* influence. **sway·er,** *n.*

swear, *v.,* **swore, sworn, swear·ing.** utter a solemn declaration; vow; use profane language. **swear·er,** *n.*

swear-word, *n.* oath.

sweat, *v.* sweat or **sweat·ed, sweat·ing.** perspire, esp. profusely; gather moisture on the surface; *inf.* toil. *n.* perspiration; condensation. **sweat·y,** *a.,* **-i·er, -i·est.**

sweat·er, *n.* knitted or crocheted blouselike garment.

sweep, *v.,* **swept, sweep·ing.** clean, as a floor, by a broom; clear. *n.* swift onward course; range or compass. **sweep·er,** *n.* **sweep·ing,** *a.*

sweet, *a.* pleasant tasting, as of sugar; kind; fresh. *n. pl.* candy. **sweet·ness,** *n.* **sweet·en,** *v.*

sweet·heart, *n.* beloved person; lover.

sweet·meat, *n.* confection, candy, etc. often *pl.*

sweet potato, *n.* plant having edible tuberous roots.

sweet-talk, *v. inf.* cajole; coax.

swell, *v.,* **swelled, swelled** or **swoll·en, swell·ing.** increase in size or extent; inflate. *n.*

gradual increase; surge. **swell·ing,** *n.*

swel·ter, *v.* be overcome and faint with heat. *n.* intense heat. **swel·ter·ing,** *a.*

swerve, *v.,* **swerved, swerv·ing.** turn; deviate; turn to one side. *n.* swerving.

swift, *a.* moving with great speed. *n.* bird resembling the swallow. **swift·ness,** *n.*

swig, *n. inf.* large draft. *v.,* **swigged, swig·ging.** drink rapidly.

swill, *n.* liquid food, esp. kitchen refuse given to swine. *v.* guzzle.

swim, *v.,* **swam, swum, swim·ming.** move through water by moving the hands, feet, or fins; be dizzy. *n.* act of swimming. **swim·mer,** *n.*

swin·dle, *v.,* **-dled, -dling.** cheat and defraud. *n.* fraudulent scheme. **swin·dler,** *n.*

swine, *n. pl.,* **swine.** hog or pig. **swin·ish,** *a.*

swing, *v.,* **swung, swing·ing.** move to and fro; sway. *n.* curving movement; marked rhythm; seat suspended from above. **swing·ing,** *a.* **swing·er,** *n.*

swing shift, *n.* evening work shift.

swipe, *v.,* **swiped, swip·ing.** strike with a sweeping blow; *inf.* steal. *n.* glancing blow.

swirl, *v.* whirl in eddies. *n.* whirling motion; twist. **swirl·y,** *a.*

swish, *v.* move with or make a sibilant sound; rustle. *n.* swishing. **swish·y,** *a.,* **-i·er, -i·est.**

switch, *n.* flexible rod, esp. for whipping; sudden shift; device for connecting or breaking an electric circuit. *v.* whip; divert; shift; *elect.* turn on or off by means of a switch. **switch·er,** *n.*

switch·board, *n.* control panel with switches for making electric circuit connections.

swiv·el, *n.* fastening allowing the thing fastened to turn freely. *v.,* **-eled, -el·ing.** turn on or as on a swivel.

swiz·zle stick, *n.* small slender rod for mixing drinks.

swob, *n., v.* swab.

swoon, *v.* faint. *n.* fainting fit. **swoon·er,** *n.*

swoop, v. descend upon suddenly; seize. n. swooping. **swoop·er,** n.

swop, v., **swopped, swop·ping.** swap. n. swap.

sword, n. weapon having a long blade fixed in a hilt. **sword·like,** a.

sword·play, n. action or skill involved in handling a sword. **sword·play·er,** n.

swords·man, n. pl., -men. man skillfully using a sword. **swords·man·ship,** n.

syc·a·more, n. plane tree; shade tree.

syc·o·phant, n. servile parasite. **syc·o·phan·cy,** n.

syl·lab·i·cate, v., -cat·ed, -cat·ing. syllabify. **syl·lab·i·ca·tion,** n.

syl·lab·i·fy, v., -fied, -fy·ing. form into syllables. **syl·lab·i·fi·ca·tion,** n.

syl·la·ble, n. single sound uttered constituting a part of a word. v., -bled, -bling. articulate. **syl·lab·ic,** a.

syl·la·bus, n. pl., -bus·es, -bi. summary of principal points.

syl·van, sil·van, a. of or inhabiting the woods; wooded.

sym·bol, n. object which stands for an intangible object or idea. **sym·bol·ic,** a. **sym·bol·ism,** n. **sym·bol·ize,** v.

sym·me·try, n. pl., -tries. correspondence of parts on opposite sides; excellence of proportion. **sym·met·ric,** a.

sym·pa·thet·ic, a. of, or exhibiting sympathy.

sym·pa·thy, n. pl., -thies. agreement; compassion; commiseration. **sym·pa·thize,** v.

sym·pho·ny, n. pl., -nies. composition for a full orchestra; concert. **sym·phon·ic,** a.

symp·tom, n. circumstance or condition as of disease. **symp·to·mat·ic,** a.

syn·a·gogue, syn·a·gog, n. Jewish place of worship.

syn·chro·nize, v., -nized, -niz·ing. concur or make to agree in time.

syn·di·cate, n. combination of persons, companies, etc. v., -cat·ed, -cat·ing. combine into a syndicate; publish simultaneously. **syn·di·ca·tion,** n.

syn·od, n. assembly of ecclesiastics.

syn·o·nym, n. word that has the same meaning as another.

syn·on·y·mous, a.

syn·op·sis, n. pl., -ses. summary.

syn·the·sis, n. pl., -ses. combination of parts into a complex whole.

syn·thet·ic, a. of, or involving synthesis; man-made. n. product of synthesis.

syph·i·lis, n. venereal disease. **syph·i·lit·ic,** a.

sy·ringe, n. tube fitted with a piston for ejecting fluids.

syr·up, sir·up, n. sweet usu. viscous liquid. **syr·up·y, sir·up·y,** a.

sys·tem, n. ordered assemblage, as of facts, phenomena, etc.; coordinated body of methods. **sys·tem·at·ic,** a.

sys·tem·a·tize, v., -tized, -tiz·ing. arrange in or according to a system. **sys·tem·a·ti·za·tion,** n.

T

tab, n. small flap; tag.

tab·er·na·cle, n. place or house of worship.

ta·ble, n. flat top on legs or a pillar; arrangement or list of items or particulars. v. postpone.

ta·ble·spoon, n. spoon equivalent to 3 teaspoons, or ½ fluid ounce. **ta·ble·spoon·ful,** n. pl., -fuls.

tab·let, n. pad of paper; flat piece or sheet for writing or drawing; small medicine disk.

ta·ble·ware, n. dishes, utensils used at meals.

ta·boo, ta·bu, a. forbidden, as by social usage. n. a prohibition.

tab·u·lar, a. in a table or tabulated arrangement.

tab·u·late, v. put or form into a table, scheme, list, synopsis.

tac·it, a. unspoken.

tac·i·turn, a. habitually silent.

tack, n. stubby, broad-headed nail; loosely sewed stitch; course of action; course of a sailing ship relative to position of sails. v. attach with tacks; add on; change abruptly.

tack·le, n. equipment; act of grabbing and grounding. v. try to do, master, resolve; throw to the ground.

tact, n. skill in doing, saying what is required. **tact·ful,** a.

tac·tics, n. pl. maneuvering of battle forces.

tad·pole, *n.* young frog.

taf·fe·ta, *n.* stiff silk or synthetic fabric.

taf·fy, *n.* chewy candy.

tag, *n.* piece or strip, used as a mark, label; a loose end; children's chase game. *v.* furnish with a tag; touch.

tail, *n.* extreme rear part of animal, usu. a flexible appendage; bottom, concluding part. **tails,** *inf.* reverse of a coin; men's formal attire. *v. inf.* follow closely. *a.* coming from, being in, the rear.

tai·lor, *n.* one who makes, alters clothes.

taint, *v.* infect; corrupt; disgrace. *n.* trace of that which is bad.

take, *v.* **took, tak·en, tak·ing.** grasp; obtain; lay hold of and remove; entrap; choose and make one's own; receive; submit to; understand; experience or feel; subtract; travel by; conduct or lead; avail oneself of; have recourse to; use; occupy; consume; require; photograph. *n.* quantity of anything taken. **take after,** imitate; resemble. **take back,** retract. **take in,** admit; comprehend. **take over,** assume control of. **take up,** shorten; adopt.

take·off, *n.* leaving ground in leaping or flight.

tal·cum pow·der, *n.* soft mineral in a refined, powdered form.

tale, *n.* short story, true or fictitious.

tal·ent, *n.* special natural ability. **tal·ent·ed,** *a.*

tal·is·man, *n.* object thought to protect bearer and bring good luck.

talk, *v.* utter words; speak; gossip; confer. *n.* act of talking; conversation; report; discussion.

talk·a·tive, *a.* tending to talk excessively.

tall, *a.* high in stature.

tal·low, *n.* harder animal fat.

tal·ly, *n. pl.,* **-lies.** record of debit and credit; score of a game. *v.* **-lied, -ly·ing.** mark on a tally; count up; agree.

tal·on, *n.* claw, esp. of a bird.

ta·ma·le, *n.* Mexican dish of ground meat and peppers rolled in cornmeal dough.

tam·bou·rine, *n.* musical instru-

ment of stretched parchment over a hoop with metal jingles in rim.

tame, *a.* domesticated; submissive; dull. *v.* render obedient or spiritless.

tamp, *v.* force down by light blows.

tam·per, *v.* interfere (with).

tan, *v.* convert animal skins into leather; brown in the sun. *n.* yellowish-brown color; brown skin color.

tan·dem, *adv., a.* one before the other.

tang, *n.* strong taste. **tang·y,** *a.,* **-i·er, i·est.**

tan·gent, *a.* touching; touching at one point only and not intersecting.

tan·ge·rine, *n.* small shiny orange.

tan·gi·ble, *a.* perceptible by touch; real.

tan·gle, *v., n.* (make, become) a confused, interwoven mass.

tan·go, *n. pl.,* **-gos.** Argentinian ballroom dance. *v.* perform the tango.

tank, *n.* large receptacle; armored vehicle.

tank·er, *n.* vehicle for transporting liquids.

tan·ta·lize, *v.* excite by unrealized expectations. **tan·ta·liz·ing,** *a.*

tan·ta·mount, *a.* equivalent.

tan·trum, *n.* angry outburst.

tap, *n.* faucet; gentle blow. *v.* pierce to let out fluid from; penetrate; strike lightly.

tape, *n.* narrow band for tying, fastening; long strip. *v.* tie with tape; record on magnetic tape.

ta·per, *v.* become gradually slenderer; diminish. *n.* small, slender candle.

tap·es·try, *n.* colorful, handwoven, patterned or pictorial cloth.

tape·worm, *n.* flat, parasitic intestinal worm.

tap·i·o·ca, *n.* substance from dried cassava starch.

ta·pir, *n.* nocturnal, hoglike mammal with flexible snout.

tap·root, *n.* main root.

tar, *v., n.* (smear with) a thick, dark, viscid product of wood and coal.

ta·ran·tu·la, *n.* large, hairy spider.

tar·dy, *a.* late; slow-paced.

tare, n. weed.

tar·get, n. object aimed at in shooting.

tar·iff, n. tax on imports, exports.

tar·nish, v. lose luster; become discolored, sullied. n. discoloration; blot.

tar·pau·lin, n. waterproofed covering.

tar·ry, v., -ried, -ry·ing. delay; linger.

tart, a. sour; cutting. n. small, filled pastry shell.

tar·tar, n. yellowish, hard deposit on teeth.

task, n. work to be done; burdensome chore.

task·mas·ter, n. one who assigns, oversees tasks.

tas·sel, n. bunch of threads hanging from a knob.

taste, v. try flavor by taking into mouth; eat; drink a little of; have a particular taste. n. sense for perceiving flavor; flavor; small quantity; liking; sense of what is proper, beautiful.

tat·ter, n. torn piece. pl. ragged clothing. **tat·tered,** a.

tat·tle, v. gossip; let out secrets.

tat·too, n. pl., -toos. marking skin with indelible patterns. v. mark with tattoos.

taunt, v., n. (reproach, provoke with) insulting words.

taut, a. tight; tense.

tav·ern, n. place where liquor is sold by the drink; inn.

taw·dry, a. cheap; gaudy.

taw·ny, a. yellowish-brown.

tax, n. charge imposed by governmental authority; burden. v. impose a tax upon; subject to a strain.

tax·i, n. pl., -is, -ies. taxicab. v. -ied, -i·ing or -y·ing. travel by taxicab; move over the ground under its own power.

tax·i·cab, n. public vehicle for hire.

tea, n. beverage made by infusion of aromatic leaves in hot water; service of tea. **tea bag, tea·cup,** n.

teach, v., taught, teach·ing. give instruction to. **teach·er,** n.

tea·ket·tle, n. kettle with cover, spout, handle, for boiling water.

team, n. persons in a joint endeavor; animals harnessed together. **team·mate,** n. **team·**
work,

team·ster, n. truck driver.

tea·pot, n. vessel with lid, spout, handle, for brewing, serving tea.

tear, n. droplike liquid secretion of the eye. **tear·y,** a.

tear, v., tore, torn, tear·ing. pull apart by force; distress greatly; move with violence, haste. n. fissure; place torn.

tease, v. raise a nap on; irritate by persistent petty annoyance. n. act of teasing; one who teases.

tea·spoon, n. small spoon. **tea·spoon·ful,** n. pl., -fuls.

teat, n. nipple.

tech·ni·cal, a. of a particular art, science, profession.

tech·ni·cal·i·ty, n. technical point or detail.

tech·ni·cian, n. one skilled in a technique.

tech·nique, n. method of performance.

tech·nol·o·gy, n. study of industrial arts and sciences.

te·di·ous, a. tiresome; monotonous. **te·di·um,** n.

tee, n. starting place, holder from which golf ball is driven. v. place on a tee.

teem, v. to be overflowing, prolific.

teens, n. pl. years, age from 13 through 19. **teen·ag·er,** n. **teen·age,** a.

tee·ter, v. seesaw; move unsteadily.

teethe, v., teethed, teeth·ing. grow teeth. **teeth·ing,** n.

tel·e·cast, v. broadcast by television. n. televised broadcast.

tel·e·gram, n. message sent by telegraph.

tel·e·graph, v., n. (transmit a message by) a device for sending signals long-distance over a wire. **te·leg·ra·phy,** n.

te·lep·a·thy, n. direct communication between two minds.

tel·e·phone, v., n. (speak by) a device for transmission of sound to a distant point.

tel·e·scope, n. optical instrument to make distant objects appear nearer, larger. v. slide one into another; shorten. **tel·e·scop·ic,** a.

tel·e·vise, v. transmit by television.

tel·e·vi·sion, n. transmission of scenes by converting light rays to electrical waves, then reconverting them to give original image; receiver set.

tell, v., **told, tell-ing.** narrate; utter; discern; command.

tell-er, n. bank cashier.

tell-tale, a. revealing.

tem-per, v. soften, tone down, modify. n. mental balance; frame of mind; anger.

tem-per-a-ment, n. disposition; irritable disposition.

tem-per-a-ment-al, a. moody.

tem-per-ance, n. moderation.

tem-per-ate, a. moderate.

tem-per-a-ture, n. degree of heat or cold; fever.

tem-pest, n. violent wind, storm; commotion. **tem-pes-tu-ous,** a.

tem-ple, n. building for worship or for public use; area on either side of forehead.

tem-po, n. pl., **-pos, -pi,** speed, pace at which music is played; rate of activity.

tem-po-ral, a. of limited time.

tem-po-rar-y, a. for a limited time. **tem-po-rar-i-ly,** adv.

tempt, v. entice. **temp-ta-tion,** n. **tempt-ing,** a.

ten, n. cardinal number between nine and eleven.

ten-a-ble, a. capable of being held, maintained.

te-na-cious, a. holding fast. **te-nac-i-ty,** n.

ten-ant, n. rent-paying occupant.

tend, v. incline, be directed toward; look after.

ten-den-cy, n. inclination; bent.

ten-der, a. soft; yielding; fragile; young; kind; loving; sensitive. n. one who tends; offer. v. make an offer. **ten-der-ly,** adv.

ten-don, n. cord fibers attaching a muscle to a bone.

ten-dril, n. threadlike part of climbing plant.

ten-e-ment, n. dwelling house.

ten-et, n. opinion; doctrine.

ten-nis, n. game in which ball is hit by rackets over a net.

ten-or, n. prevailing course; highest adult male voice.

tense, a. taut; in a strained nervous state. v. make, become tense; stiffen. n. verb form expressing time.

ten-sion, n. act of stretching; stiffness; mental strain.

tent, n. portable canvas shelter.

ten-ta-cle, n. appendage on head of some animals, used as a feeler.

ten-ta-tive, a. provisional.

ten-u-ous, a. thin; weak.

ten-ure, n. right of holding property, a position.

te-pee, n. cone-shaped tent.

tep-id, a. lukewarm.

term, n. word or phrase; time limit; school year period; pl. language; stated conditions; relative position. v. name.

ter-mi-nal, n. extremity; station. a. of or at the end; causing death.

ter-mi-nate, v. end; complete.

ter-mi-nol-o-gy, n. particular set of words, phrases.

ter-mi-nus, n. pl., **-nus-es, -ni.** end or limit.

ter-mite, n. wood-eating insect.

ter-race, n. raised level with vertical or sloping front, sides; open platform; patio.

ter-rain, n. tract of land.

ter-res-tri-al, a. of the earth; wordly.

ter-ri-ble, a. causing fear; dreadful. inf. very bad.

ter-ri-er, n. breed of dog.

ter-rif-ic, a. terrifying. inf. extraordinary; splendid.

ter-ri-fy, v., **-fied, -fy-ing.** frighten; shock.

ter-ri-to-ry, n. region; land, waters under jurisdiction of a state; region not admitted to U.S. as a state.

ter-ror, n. intense fear (cause of).

ter-ror-ism, n. systematic use of terror to intimidate. **ter-ror-ist,** n. **ter-ror-ize,** v.

terse, a. to the point.

ter-ti-ar-y, a. third.

test, n. trial, examination. v. subject to examination.

tes-ta-ment, n. a will; (cap.) either division of the Bible.

tes-ti-fy, v. indicate; give evidence under oath. **tes-ti-mo-ny,** n.

tes-ti-mo-ni-al, n. statement of recommendation; thing given in appreciation.

tes-ty, a. touchy; irritable.

teth-er, n. rope, chain confining animal. v. confine with a tether.

text, n. main part of a printed work; exact or original wording; subject; textbook; passage of Scripture.

text-book, n. book of instruction.

tex·tile, *a.* woven; formed by weaving. *n.* fabric made by, used for weaving.

tex·ture, *n.* characteristic disposition of constituent parts.

than, *conj.* compared to.

thank, *v.* express gratitude.

thank·ful, *a.* appreciative.

thank·less, *a.* not appreciated.

thanks, *n. pl.* expression of gratitude.

thanks·giv·ing, *n.* thanks; (*cap.*) national U.S. holiday.

that, *pron. pl.,* those. the one mentioned; the one more remote; unspecified, unknown quality, object; who, whom, or which. *a.* being that one; so. *conj.* used to connect clauses.

thatch, *v., n.* (cover with) straw roofing.

thaw, *v.* (cause to) melt; *n.* process of thawing.

the, *def. art.* used before nouns with a specifying or particularizing effect. *adv.* in or by that (much).

the·a·ter, *n.* building, place for presentation of entertainment; dramatic representation; locality of events. **the·at·ri·cal,** *a.*

thee, *pron.* objective and dative case of *thou.*

theft, *n.* act of stealing.

their, *a.* possessive case of *they.*

theirs, *pron.* them, *pron.* objective case of *they.*

theme, *n.* subject of discourse; short essay; leading melody.

them·selves, *pron. pl.* reflexive or emphatic form of *they.*

then, *adv.* at that time; next in addition; in that case.

thence, *adv.* from that place, time.

thence·forth, *adv.* from that time or place. Also **thence·for·ward.**

the·ol·o·gy, *n.* study of God, religious doctrine.

the·o·rem, *n.* position to be proved or accepted as a truth.

the·o·ry, *n.* systematic arrangement of facts; hypothesis; suggested plan of action. **the·o·ret·i·cal,** *a.* **the·o·rize,** *v.*

ther·a·py, *n.* curative process of treating disease, disability. **ther·a·peu·tic,** *a.* **ther·a·pist,** *n.*

there, *adv.* in that place, at, to. *n.* that state, position, point.

there·a·bout, *adv.* approximate-ly.

there·af·ter, *adv.* afterward.

there·by, *adv.* by that means.

there·fore, *adv., conj.* for that or this reason.

there·in, *adv.* into or in that place, time, thing; in that respect.

there·of, *adv.* of that, this, or it; because of that cause.

there·up·on, *adv.* in consequence of that; at once.

ther·mal, *a.* of, caused by, heat.

ther·mom·e·ter, *n.* instrument for measuring temperature.

ther·mo·nu·cle·ar, *a.* of nuclear reactions, processes.

ther·mos bot·tle, *n.* vacuum bottle.

ther·mo·stat, *n.* automatic device for regulating temperature.

the·sau·rus, *n.* book of synonyms and antonyms.

the·sis, *n. pl.,* -ses. statement to be discussed and proved; scholarly paper.

they, *pron.* people in general; the ones mentioned.

thi·a·mine, *n.* vitamin B₁.

thick, *a.* of great extent from side to side; placed close together; dense. *n.* most active part.

thick·et, *n.* dense shrubbery.

thief, *n. pl.,* thieves. one who steals. **thieve,** *v.*

thigh, *n.* leg between hip and knee.

thim·ble, *n.* cap worn to protect finger in sewing.

thin, *a.* not thick; slender; transparent; not dense; fluid; unsubstantial. *v.* (make, become) thin.

thine, *pron.* possessive form of *thou.*

thing, *n.* an entity; a matter of occurrence; *pl.* personal possessions.

think, *v.,* thought, think·ing. form or conceive mentally; ponder; believe; remember.

third, *n., a.* (the one) following the second; (one) of three equal parts.

thirst, *n.* need of fluids; strong desire. *v.* feel thirst. **thirst·y,** *a.*

thir·teen, *n.* number between 12 and 14. **thir·teenth,** *a., n.*

thir·ty, *n.* number between 29 and 31. **thir·ti·eth,** *a., n.*

this, *a., pron. pl.,* these. person, thing, idea, or condition pre-

thistle, *n.* prickly plant.

this·tle, *n.* prickly plant.

thith·er, *adv.* to that place; toward.

thong, *n.* leather strap.

tho·rax, *n.* chest; portion of an insect between head and abdomen.

thorn, *n.* sharp-pointed growth from a branch. **thorn·y**, *a.*

thor·ough, *a.* complete or perfect; careful.

thor·ough·bred, *n., a.* (animal) of pure breed.

thor·ough·fare, *n.* unobstructed road.

thou, *pron.* (Poetic, Biblical) you.

though, *conj.* although; yet. *adv.* however.

thought, *n.* act or power of thinking; idea; deliberation.

thought·ful, *a.* meditative; considerate.

thought·less, *a.* heedless; inconsiderate.

thou·sand, *a., n.* ten hundred. **thou·sandth**, *a., n.*

thrash, *v.* beat; thresh; toss about violently.

thread, *n.* fine cord; spiral part of a screw. *v.* pass a thread through.

thread·bare, *a.* poor; shabby.

threat, *n.* menace; warning of impending danger; damage. **threat·en**, *v.*

three, *a., n.* number between 2 and 4.

three-score, *a.* sixty.

thresh, *v.* beat out grain from the husk.

thresh·old, *n.* doorsill; beginning.

thrice, *adv.* three times.

thrift, *n.* economical management; frugality. **thrift·y**, *a.*

thrill, *v., n.* (cause) a keen emotion of delight, excitement; produce a tingling sensation; quiver.

thrive, *v.*, **thrived** or **throve**, **thrived** or **thriv·en**, prosper; increase.

throat, *n.* passage from nose and mouth to lungs and stomach; front of neck.

throb, *v.* beat with force; rapidity.

throne, *n.* (chair, office of a) sovereign.

throng, *n., v.* crowd.

throt·tle, *v.* choke. *n.* lever to control fuel or steam volume in engine.

through, **thru**, *prep.* from one end to the other; from beginning to end; having reached the end of; by means of. *adv.* from one end to the other; completely. *a.* extending without interruption; finished.

through·out, *prep.* in or to every part of. *adv.* in or to every part; at every moment.

throw, *v.*, **threw**, **thrown**, propel through air by a sudden jerk of the arm; direct; put on hastily; move to connect or disconnect. *n.* act of throwing.

throw·back, *n.* reversion to an ancestral type.

thru, *prep., adv., a.* through.

thrush, *n.* a songbird.

thrust, *v.*, **thrust**, **thrust·ing**. push forcibly. *n.* forcible push; stab; outward or sidewise stress.

thud, *v.* strike with a dull sound. *n.* (blow causing a) dull sound.

thumb, *n.* short, thick, inner digit of hand.

thump, *n.* (sound made by) a heavy blow. *v.* beat with a heavy blow.

thun·der, *n.* sound which follows lightning flash; *v.* emit thunder.

thun·der·bolt, *n.* lightning followed by thunder.

Thurs·day, *n.* fifth day of week.

thus, *adv.* in this way; to this degree; so.

thwart, *v.* oppose successfully.

thy, *a. archaic.* your.

thy·roid gland, *n.* gland which affects growth and metabolism.

thy·self, *pron. archaic.* yourself.

tib·i·a, *n.* shinbone.

tic, *n.* habitual muscle spasm.

tick, *n.* light tap; recurring click; checkmark; insect.

tick·et, *n.* card entitling holder to some service or right; label or tag; list of candidates. *v.* attach a ticket to.

tick·le, *v.* stroke lightly to excite tingling or itching; excite agreeably.

tick·lish, *a.* sensitive to tickling; unsteady; difficult.

tid·bit, *n.* delicious morsel.

tide, *n.* periodical rise and fall of ocean waters. **ti·dal**, *a.*

ti·dings, *n. pl.* news.

ti·dy, *a.* neat. *inf.* considerable. *v.* make tidy.

tie, *v.*, **tied**, **ty·ing.** bind with a cord; draw into a knot; confine; make the same score. *n.* cord that ties; necktie; link; equality of scores in a contest.

tier, *n.* one of a series of rows rising one behind, above another.

ti·ger, *n.* large, carnivorous, jungle feline.

tight, *a.* fitting closely; taut; difficult to manage; packed full; impervious to water, steam, air. *adv.* closely. **tight·en**, *v.*

tights, *n. pl.* stretchable garment worn over hips and legs.

tile, *n.* thin slab of baked clay for covering roofs, floors, etc.

till, *prep., conj.* to the time of, when. *v.* cultivate the soil. *n.* drawer where cash is kept.

till·er, *n.* lever fitted to boat rudder for steering.

tilt, *v.* slope or slant; rush at or charge. *n.* act of tilting; sloping position; joust.

tim·ber, *n.* wood for building trees; wooden beam.

tim·bre, *n.* distinctive quality in a sound.

time, *n.* (system of measuring) relations past, present, future; duration; particular period; right moment; each occasion; beats in music. *v.* appoint the time of; regulate, as to time, measure. *a.* of a certain time.

time-keep·er, *n.* one who records, announces time of occurrence, time occupied.

time-less, *a.* eternal.

time-ly, *a.* opportune; well-timed.

time-piece, *n.* clock; watch.

tim·er, *n.* one who or device that measures or records time.

time-ta·ble, *n.* schedule of arrival, departure times.

tim·id, *a.* fearful; shy. **tim·id·i·ty**, *n.*

tim·or·ous, *a.* timid.

tin, *n.* silver-white, malleable, ductile metallic element; tin container.

tinc·ture, *n.* tinge; slight taste; solution of some substance in a solvent.

tin·der, *n.* inflammable substance for kindling fire.

tine, *n.* prong (of a fork).

tinge, *v.*, *n.* (give a) slight degree of color, taste to.

tin·gle, *v.*, *n.* (have a) sensation of slight stings, quivers.

tink·er, *n.* mender of metal household articles. *v.* work unskillfully.

tin·kle, *v.*, *n.* (make) small, quick, sharp, ringing sounds.

tin·sel, *n.* thin strips, sheets of glittering metal; anything showy, superficial.

tint, *n.*, *v.* (give) a slight coloring (to).

ti·ny, *a.* very small.

tip, *n.* pointed extremity or end; top; small gift of money; useful, oft. private, information; tap. *v.* slant; overturn; give a gratuity to; strike lightly.

tip·ple, *v.* drink liquor.

tip·sy, *a.* mildly intoxicated.

tip·toe, *n.* tips of the toes. *v.* move about on tiptoe.

ti·rade, *n.* long, violent speech.

tire, *v.* exhaust the strength, patience of; become weary. **tired**, *a.* *n.* hoop of rubber around a wheel.

tire·some, *a.* boring; tedious.

tis·sue, *n.* group of cells usu. of similar structure; light-textured material.

ti·tan, *n.* person, thing of enormous size, strength. **ti·tan·ic**, *a.*

tithe, *n.* tenth part of income paid as tax to religious institutions.

ti·tle, *n.* descriptive or distinctive name; name given to show rank, office, respect; legal right to possession.

tit·mouse, *n. pl.*, **-mice**, crested bird.

tit·ter, *v.* laugh nervously.

tit·u·lar, *a.* having the title or name only.

TNT, T.N.T., *n.* an explosive.

to, *prep.* toward; to the degree that; in contact with; until; for the purpose of; causing; in. *adv.* toward.

toad, *n.* tailless, warty-skinned, land amphibian.

toad-stool, *n.* oft. poisonous fungi with stalk and umbrella-like cap.

toad·y, *n.* servile flatterer.

toast, *v.* brown by exposure to heat; salute with a drink. *n.* browned bread; sentiment to which one drinks.

to·bac·co, *n.* plant whose leaves are prepared for smoking or chewing.

to·bog·gan, *n*. flat-bottomed sled.

to·day, to-day, *adv*. on this present day; in these days. *n*. this present day or age.

tod·dle, *v*., *n*. (walk with) an unsteady gait.

toe, *n*. one of the terminal digits of foot. **toe·nail**, *n*.

tof·fee, tof·fy, *n*. hard, chewy candy.

to·ga, *n*. loose outer garment of ancient Roman citizens.

to·geth·er, *adv*. in one gathering, mass; in unison; in cooperation.

toil, *v*. labor arduously. *n*. hard, continuous work.

toi·let, *n*. bathroom; bathroom fixture for disposing of body waste; process of dressing.

toi·let·ry, *n*. grooming article.

to·ken, *n*. symbol; sign; atonement; stamped metal disk used for fares, etc. *a*. symbolic.

tol·er·a·ble, *a*. endurable, moderately good. **tol·er·a·bly**, *adv*.

tol·er·ance, *n*. act of, or capacity to endure (a drug, poison). **tol·er·ant**, *a*.

tol·er·ate, *v*. to put up with; to permit.

toll, *n*. payment exacted for some right, privilege, service; cost, as in damage or loss. *v*. cause to ring slowly and regularly.

tom·a·hawk, *n*. light ax used by N. American Indians.

to·ma·to, *n*., *pl*. -**toes**. plant bearing a red, pulpy fruit, used as a vegetable; the fruit itself.

tomb, *n*. grave.

tomb·stone, *n*. inscribed grave marker.

tome, *n*. large book.

to·mor·row, to-mor·row, *n*., *adv*. day after this day.

tom-tom, *n*. smallheaded drum.

ton, *n*. 2,000 pounds.

tone, *n*. any sound of distinctive character; vocal inflection; fundamental note; prevailing character; healthy body condition; shade. **ton·al**, *a*.

tongs, *n*. *pl*. metal instrument with hinged arms, for grasping.

tongue, *n*. freely moving organ within mouth for tasting, swallowing; speech; power, act of speech; language.

ton·ic, *n*. medicine, treatment to restore healthy body condition.

to·night, to-night, *adv*, *n*. (on) the present night; (on) the night after the present day.

ton·nage, *n*. carrying capacity of merchant ship in tons of 100 cubic feet; ships collectively.

ton·sil, *n*. one of two oblong masses of soft tissue on sides of throat.

ton·sil·lec·to·my, *n*. removal of tonsils.

ton·sil·li·tis, *n*. inflammation of tonsils.

too, *adv*. likewise; also; more than enough; very.

tool, *n*. implement used for work. *v*. shape with a tool.

toot, *v*., *n*. (make) a brief blasting noise.

tooth, *n*. *pl*., **teeth**. one of the bony structures attached in a row to each jaw; toothlike projection. **tooth·ache, tooth·brush**, *n*.

tooth·some, *a*. agreeable to the taste.

top, *n*. highest or uppermost point, part, surface; lid; beginning; choicest part; child's spinning toy. *a*. highest; uppermost; greatest. *v*. put on, as a top; be at the top of; rise above; finish.

to·paz, *n*. yellow gem.

top·coat, *n*. light overcoat.

top hat, *n*. man's tall, cylindrical, dress hat.

top·ic, *n*. subject of speech or writing.

top·i·cal, *a*. of matters of current or local interest.

top·most, *a*. uppermost.

to·pog·ra·phy, *n*. accurate, detailed description of any region.

top·ple, *v*. fall forward; overturn.

top·sy-tur·vy, *adv*., *a*. upside down; confused, disorderly.

torch, *n*. hand-carried light; device for emission of hot flame.

tor·e·a·dor, *n*. bullfighter.

tor·ment, *v*., *n*. put to extreme pain, anguish.

tor·na·do, *n*. destructive rotatory windstorm with funnellike cloud.

tor·pe·do, *n*. *pl*., -**does**. underwater explosive device. *v*. attack with a torpedo.

tor·pid, *a*. numb; sluggish. **tor·por**, *n*.

tor·rent, *n*. rushing, violent,

abundant stream.

tor·rid, *a.* parching or burning; passionate.

tor·sion, *n.* twisting; twisted state.

tor·so, *n.* trunk of human body.

tor·til·la, *n.* thin, round, cornmeal cake.

tor·toise, *n.* turtle, esp. a terrestrial one.

tor·tu·ous, *a.* twisting, winding, crooked; indirect.

tor·ture, *v., n.* (subject to, inflict) severe pain, physical or mental.

toss, *v.* throw lightly or carelessly; jerk upward suddenly; discuss freely; mix gently. *n.* a tossing.

toss-up, *n. inf.* tossing of coin to decide something by its fall; even chance.

tot, *n.* young child.

to·tal, *a.* entire; complete; absolute. *n.* total amount; the whole. *v.* add up; amount to. **to·tal·i·ty,** *n.* **to·tal·ly,** *adv.*

to·tal·i·tar·i·an, *a.* of a centralized form of government with controlling party not tolerating opposition.

tote, *v. inf.* carry.

to·tem, *n.* token or emblem of a group. **to·tem·ic,** *a.*

to·tem pole, *n.* post carved and painted with totemic figures.

tot·ter, *v.* walk with faltering steps.

touch, *v.* come into contact with by feeling with hand; be adjacent to; compare with; mark slightly; affect with emotion. *n.* act of touching; sense by which matter is perceived through contact; slight bit.

touch·down, *n.* football play scoring six points.

touch·stone, *n.* criterion.

touch·y, *a.* irritable; precarious.

tough, *a.* strong; durable; difficult to cut or chew, difficult. **tough·en,** *v.*

tou·pee, *n.* wig to cover bald spot.

tour, *n.* lengthy trip, excursion; period of service. *v.* make a tour. **tour·ism,** **tour·ist,** *n.*

tour·na·ment, *n.* series of games testing a skill.

tour·ni·quet, *n.* bandage tightened around bleeding wound.

tou·sle, *v.* dishevel; rumple. **tou·sled,** *a.*

tow, *v.* drag, pull by rope, etc. *n.*

a towing (device).

to·ward, *prep.* in the direction of; close to; near in time; in regard, with respect to. Also **to·wards.**

tow·el, *n.* cloth, soft paper for drying, wiping.

tow·er, *n.* tall, narrow structure. *v.* rise high; surpass.

town, *n.* urban center larger than a village; central city area.

town·ship, *n.* administrative division of county; region six miles square.

tox·in, *n.* poison produced by bacteria. **tox·ic,** *a.*

toy, *n.* plaything; *a.* petty; small. *v.* act idly (with).

trace, *n.* mark left when thing itself is gone; minute quantity. *v.* follow by traces left; copy by following lines.

trac·er·y, *n.* ornamental work of intersecting lines.

tra·che·a, *n.* windpipe; tube that carries air to and from lungs.

track, *n.* pairs of rails for railroad cars; mark(s) left by something that has passed; path; course of action; course for running, racing; pursue by traces left; make footprints on.

tract, *n.* stretch of land, water; particular area of body; brief treatise.

trac·ta·ble, *a.* easily trained or managed.

trac·tion, *n.* pulling; a body's friction on a surface.

trac·tor, *n.* motorized vehicle for pulling heavy equipment.

trade, *n.* business, esp. skilled mechanical work; buying and selling of commodities; patronage; purchase, sale, or exchange. *v.* buy, sell; exchange.

trade-mark, *n.* mark, wording, device to distinguish one product from others.

trade un·ion, *n.* labor union.

trade wind, *n.* wind over the oceans blowing toward equator.

tra·di·tion, *n.* handing down of opinions, practices from generation to generation; custom. **tra·di·tion·al,** *a.*

tra·duce, *v.* misrepresent willfully.

traf·fic, *n.* movement of goods, vehicles, persons; business flow. *v.*, **-ficked, -fick·ing.** do business, esp. illegally.

tra-ge-di-an, *n*. writer, actor of tragedy.

trag-e-dy, *n*. drama culminating in disaster; any disaster, misfortune, death. **trag-ic**, *a*.

trail, *v*. draw behind or along ground; follow; dwindle. *n*. path or route; evidence of passage left behind.

trail-er, *n*. vehicle drawn by car, tractor, truck; house on wheels.

train, *n*. series of railway cars; procession; of something from a moving object. *v*. discipline and instruct; make fit; aim, direct.

trait, *n*. characteristic.

trai-tor, *n*. one guilty of betrayal.

tra-jec-to-ry, *n*. curve in vertical plane traced by object moving through space.

tramp, *v*. walk heavily; vagabond. *n*. hobo.

tram-ple, *v*. tread heavily on or over.

trance, *n*. dazed or sleep-like condition.

tran-quil, *a*. quiet; calm. **tran-quil-li-ty**, *n*. **tran-quil-ize**, *v*. **tran-quil-iz-er**, *n*.

trans-act, *v*. conduct or carry through (business). **trans-ac-tion**, *n*.

tran-scend, *v*. exceed. **tran-scend-ent**, *a*.

tran-scribe, *v*. make a handwritten or typed copy of. **tran-scrip-tion**, *n*.

tran-script, *n*. written or typed copy.

trans-fer, *v*., **-ferred**, **-fer-ring**. convey from one place or person to another. *n*. act of transferring; thing transferred. **trans-fer-a-ble**, *a*. **trans-fer-ence**, *n*.

trans-fig-ure, *v*. change outward form of; idealize.

trans-form, *v*. change in form, appearance, condition. **trans-for-ma-tion**, *n*.

trans-form-er, *n*. appliance for changing current to lower or higher voltage.

trans-fuse, *v*. instill or impart; transfer blood. **trans-fu-sion**, *n*.

trans-gress, *v*. overpass; break or violate. **trans-gres-sor**, **trans-gres-sion**, *n*.

tran-sient, *a*., *n*. (temporary, passing) person or thing.

tran-sis-tor, *n*. device using a semi-conductor that performs as an electron tube.

trans-it, *n*. passing over or through; process of conveying.

tran-si-tion, *n*. passage from one place or state to another. **tran-si-tion-al**, *a*.

tran-si-tive, *a*. of a verb that takes a direct object.

tran-si-to-ry, *a*. fleeting.

trans-late, *v*. render into another language. **trans-la-tion**, *n*.

trans-lu-cent, *a*. allowing light to pass through, but not transparent.

trans-mis-sion, *n*. act of transmitting; device that transmits power from engine to wheels.

trans-mit, *v*., **-mit-ted**, **-mit-ting**. cause to pass from one point to another; communicate by sending; send out electrical energy in a signal. **trans-mit-ter**, *n*.

tran-som, *n*. small window above door or larger window.

trans-par-ent, *a*. easily seen through.

tran-spire, *v*. excrete through skin pores; take place.

trans-plant, *v*. remove, transfer from one place to another. *n*. act of transplanting; thing transplanted.

trans-port, *v*. carry or convey from one place to another; carry away with emotion. *n*. vessel for transporting. **trans-por-ta-tion**, *n*.

trans-pose, *v*. change places; change musical key.

trans-verse, *a*. being in a cross direction.

trap, *n*. device that shuts suddenly for catching game; plan to catch one unaware; golf course hazard; trap door. *v*. catch in a trap.

trap door, *n*. door flush with surface of floor, ceiling, roof.

tra-peze, *n*. swing for acrobatic feats.

trap-e-zoid, *n*. four-sided plane figure with two opposite sides parallel.

trap-pings, *n. pl*. ornamental accessories.

trash, *n*. worthless matter. **trash-y**, *a*.

trau-ma, *n*. wound; disturbed state resulting from stress, injury. **trau·mat·ic**, a.

tra·vail, n. difficult, strenuous work; pain, suffering.

trav·el, v., **-eled** or **-elled**, **-el·ing** or **-el·ling**. make a journey; go from place to place. n. act of traveling; pl. trips.

trav·erse, v. go across, over, through, or along. a. going, reaching across; of cord-pulled draperies.

trav·es·ty, n. grotesque or debased imitation.

tray, n. shallow receptacle with rimmed edge.

treach·er·ous, a. faithless; deceptive; risky. **treach·er·y**, n.

tread, v., **trod**, **trod·den** or **trod**, **tread·ing**. walk on, along, in or over; crush under the feet; n. act, sound, or way of walking; a step; tire pattern.

trea·dle, n. foot lever.

tread·mill, n. endless belt to operate a mill; monotonous, futile routine.

trea·son, n. disloyalty to one's country.

treas·ure, n. accumulated wealth; valued thing, person. v. hoard; cherish.

treas·ur·y, n. place where government money or valuables are kept. **treas·ur·er**, n.

treat, v. actor behave toward; give remedies to; handle in writing, speaking, etc. entertain without expense to guest. n. thing that gives pleasure; process of treating. **treat·ment**, n.

trea·tise, n. formal essay.

trea·ty, n. formally negotiated agreement between nations.

tre·ble, a. triple; of the highest musical sounds. n. high-pitched sound. v. triple.

tree, n. perennial plant with woody trunk, branches.

trek, v., **trekked**, **trek·king**. travel slowly. n. slow, difficult journey.

trel·lis, n. latticework to support vines.

trem·ble, v. shake; quiver.

tre·men·dous, a. inf. able to astonish by size, greatness, etc.

trem·or, n. involuntary shaking of body, limbs. **trem·u·lous**, a.

trench, n. ditch.

trench·ant, a. incisive.

trend, v., n. (have) a general tendency.

trep·i·da·tion, n. fear; dread.

tres·pass, v. commit an offense; encroach or infringe. n. offense; sin; intrusion.

tress, n. lock of hair.

tres·tle, n. supporting framework.

tri·ad, n. group of three.

tri·al, n. examination of a controversy before a tribunal; a testing; an attempt; trouble, pain.

tri·an·gle, n. polygon with three sides and three angles. **tri·an·gu·lar**, a.

tribe, n. division, class, or group under a leader. **trib·al**, a.

trib·u·la·tion, n. distress; trouble.

tri·bu·nal, n. court of justice.

trib·u·tar·y, n., a. (stream) flowing into larger stream.

trib·ute, n. thing said or done as token of gratitude, esteem; rent or tax.

trick, n. crafty device; artifice, ruse; prank; clever feat; cards played and won in one round. v. deceive by trickery. **trick·er·y**, n. **trick·y**, a.

trick·le, v. flow by drops or in a broken stream. n. slow, broken flow.

tri·cy·cle, n. three-wheeled vehicle.

tried, a. tested; proved; dependable.

tri·fle, n. insignificant thing, matter. v. deal lightly (with).

tri·fling, a. of slight importance.

trig·ger, n. lever pressed to make a weapon fire. v. start or set off.

trig·o·nom·e·try, n. mathematics of triangles.

trill, v., n. (sing or play with) a vibratory effect.

tril·lion, n. a million times a million; 1,000 billions; 1,000,000,000,000.

trim, v., **trimmed**, **trim·ming**. make neat by removing waste or used parts; decorate. n. proper conditions; decorations; building woodwork. a. neat; in good condition. **trim·ming**, n.

trin·ket, n. small ornament.

tri·o, n. pl. **-os**. musical composition for three players; group of three.

trip, n. journey; stumbling; light quick tread; mistake. v. make a trip; to stumble; step lightly; make or cause a mistake.

tri-ple, *a.* threefold; three times as great. *n.* triad. *v.* make or become triple.

tri-plet, *n.* one of three offspring born at same time.

trip-li-cate, *v.* make or produce a third time or in units of three. *a.* threefold.

tri-pod, *n.* three-legged vessel, frame, stand.

trite, *a.* commonplace; stale.

tri-umph, *v., n.* (gain) a victory. **tri-um-phal, tri-um-phant,** *a.*

triv-et, *n.* metal stand for hot dishes.

triv-i-a, *n. pl.* insignificant matters. **triv-i-al, triv-i-al-i-ty,** *n.*

tro-che, *n.* small medicinal lozenge.

trog-lo-dyte, *n.* cave dweller.

troll, *v.* sing in a full, rolling voice; fish by dragging hook and line; to cause to turn round and round. *n.* supernatural cave-dwellers.

trol-ley, *n.* electric streetcar.

trom-bone, *n.* brass musical instrument with sliding tube.

troop, *n.* soldier(s); cavalry unit; group. *v.* gather, move in a group.

troop-er, *n.* cavalryman; policeman.

tro-phy, *n. pl.,* **-phies.** token of victory, valor, skill.

trop-ic, *n.* one of two parallels of latitude N. and S. of equator; *pl.* regions near these parallels. **trop-i-cal,** *a.*

trot, *v.* go at a quick, steady gait. *n.* horse's gait between walk and canter.

trou-ba-dour, *n.* writer, singer of love songs.

trou-ble, *v.* disturb; distress. *n.* difficult; unfortunate condition. **trou-ble-some,** *a.*

trough, *n.* long, shallow vessel holding water, food for animals; narrow channel.

troupe, *n.* touring band of players, etc. **troup-er,** *n.*

trou-sers, *n. pl.* man's outer garment covering each leg separately.

trous-seau, *n.* bride's clothes, linens.

trout, *n.* fresh-water food and game fish.

trow-el, *n.* small smoothing or garden tool.

tru-ant, *n.* one who neglects duties; child absent from school without leave. **tru-an-cy,** *n.*

truce, *n.* agreement to suspend hostilities.

truck, *n.* vehicle for transporting goods; vegetables raised for market. *v.* convey by truck; drive a truck.

trudge, *v.* walk wearily.

true, *a.* loyal; trusty; honest, sincere; not false; sure; genuine. *n.* exact fact. *adv.* in a true manner. **tru-ly,** *adj.*

trump, *v., n.* (take with) a high-ranking card.

trum-pet, *n.* musical instrument with long, curved tube and bell-shaped end.

trun-cate, *v.* shorten by cutting abruptly.

trun-dle, *v.* cause to roll. *n.* little wheel; small carriage; truck with low wheels.

trun-dle bed, *n.* low bed on casters.

trunk, *n.* main stem of a tree; large box, case; automobile storage compartment; torso; main line; elephant's long snout.

truss, *v.,* tie, bind, or fasten; support. *n.* supporting framework.

trust, *n.* reliance on some quality of a person, thing; obligation; custody. *v.* have confidence in; hope; rely on; believe. **trust-ful, trust-wor-thy,** *a.*

trus-tee, *n.* one entrusted with another's property, funds.

trust-y, *a.* reliable.

truth, *n.* conformity to fact, reality. **truth-ful,** *a.*

try, *v.,* **tried, try-ing.** attempt; test the effect, quality of; strain the endurance; determine judicially. *n.* attempt; effort.

try-ing, *a.* hard to endure.

try-out, *n.* test of fitness.

tryst, *n.* appointment to meet; meeting place.

T-shirt, *n.* collarless, short-sleeved pullover shirt. Also **tee shirt.**

T-square, *n.* T-shaped ruler.

tub, *n.* round, open, wide vessel; bathtub.

tu-ba, *n.* large brass musical instrument of low pitch.

tube, *n.* hollow, slender cylinder; cylindrical container.

tu-ber, *n.* fleshy thickening of underground stem.

tu-ber-cu-lo-sis, *n.* infectious

disease of various body tissues, esp. the lungs.

tuck, *v.* pull up into a fold; thrust between retaining parts or in a safe place.

tuck-er, *v. inf.* tire (out).

Tues-day, *n.* third day of week.

tuft, *n.* bunch of small things fixed at base with upper ends loose.

tug, *v.* pull forcibly; drag. *n.* strong pull; tugboat.

tug-boat, *n.* small powerful boat for pulling, pushing other boats.

tu-i-tion, *n.* amount charged for instruction.

tu-lip, *n.* cup-shaped flower grown from bulbs.

tum-ble, *v.* perform acrobatics; toss; stumble or fall over. *n. a* tumble; confused heap.

tum-bler, *n.* acrobat; flat-bottomed drinking glass.

tu-mor, *n.* abnormal growth in any part of body.

tu-mult, *n.* uproar; confused motion. **tu-mul-tu-ous,** *a.*

tu-na, *n.* ocean game and food fish.

tun-dra, *n.* treeless arctic plain.

tune, *n.* melody; agreement in pitch; accord in relationships. *v.* adjust to correct pitch; adjust mechanisms.

tune-ful, *a.* full of melody.

tung-sten, *n.* gray, lustrous metallic element with high melting point.

tu-nic, *n.* shirt-like or gown-like garment.

tun-nel, *v., n.* (make) an underground passage.

tur-ban, *n.* long scarf wound around head.

tur-bid, *a.* muddy; not clear.

tur-bine, *n.* engine powered by flow of steam, air, water against curved rotor blades.

tur-bu-lent, *a.* disordered; agitated. **tur-bu-lence,** *n.*

tu-reen, *n.* vessel for holding, serving soup, etc.

turf, *n.* grassy surface layer of land.

tur-gid, *a.* swollen.

tur-key, *n.* large bird eaten as food.

tur-moil, *n.* extreme commotion.

turn, *v.* rotate; revolve; shift about; change direction; direct thought, attention, desire toward or away from something; depend on; become hostile; change in nature, character, appearance; reach or pass; shape material into rounded form. *n.* total or partial rotation; change in direction; place where such a change occurs; opportunity; change in condition, character; direction. **in turn,** in order of succession. **turn down,** fold down; decrease; reject. **turn out,** send away; produce.

turn-a-bout, *n.* facing another direction; taking a new opinion.

turn-coat, *n.* traitor.

tur-nip, *n.* plant with thick, fleshy edible root.

turn-out, *n.* number of persons present; output.

turn-o-ver, *n.* overthrow; employee replacement rate.

turn-pike, *n.* highway maintained by toll charges.

turn-stile, *n.* revolving gateway.

turn-ta-ble, *n.* circular revolving platform.

tur-pen-tine, *n.* oily resin.

tur-pi-tude, *n.* vileness.

tur-quoise, *n.* greenish-blue gemstone, color.

tur-ret, *n.* small tower on a building.

tur-tle, *n.* aquatic reptile whose body is enclosed in a shell.

tusk, *n.* long protruding tooth.

tus-sle, *n., v.* struggle.

tu-te-lage, *n.* guardianship; instruction.

tu-tor, *n.* private instructor. *v.* teach. **tu-to-ri-al,** *a.*

tux-e-do, *n.* suit of semi-formal clothing.

TV, *n. pl.,* **TVs, TV's.** television.

twang, *v., n.* (make) a quick, sharp, vibrating noise; harsh, nasal tone.

tweak, *v.* pinch with a sudden twist. *n.* abrupt, twisting pinch.

tweed, *n.* coarse, twilled woolen fabric.

tweez-ers, *n. pl.* small pincers. **tweeze,** *v.*

twelve, *n., a.* number between 11 and 13; a dozen. **twelfth,** *a.*

twen-ty, *n.* number between 19 and 21. **twen-ti-eth,** *a.*

twice, *adv.* two times; two times as much.

twid-dle, *v.* twirl with the fingers; play with idly.

twig, *n.* slender shoot of a tree,

plant.

twi-light, *n.* dim evening light.

twill, *n.* fabric woven in parallel diagonal lines. **twilled,** *a.*

twin, *n.* one of two born together or resembling each other. *a.* being born together; closely related, much alike.

twine, *n.* strong twisted thread. *v.* twist together; wind around.

twinge, *n.* sudden, sharp pain.

twin-kle, *v.* sparkle; give off light in flashes. *n.* a gleam.

twirl, *v.*, *n.* spin.

twist, *v.* combine by winding together; wind around; wring out of shape or place; bend tortuously; cause to rotate. *n.* deviation, curve, turn, or bend; a twisting action.

twitch, *v.* pull abruptly. *n.* a jerk.

twit-ter, *v.*, *n.* (utter) series of small chirps.

two, *n.* number between one and three.

two-faced, *a.* deceitful; hypocritical.

two-fold, *a.*, *adv.* double; multiplied by two.

ty-coon, *n.* *inf.* wealthy, powerful businessman.

tyke, *n.* *inf.* small child.

tym-pan-ic mem-brane, *n.* eardrum.

type, *n.* a kind, class, or group; metal piece(s) with letter, character for printing; printed characters. *v.* typewrite; designate the type of.

type-write, *v.*, **-wrote, -writ-ten, -writ-ing.** print by a typewriter. Also **type.**

type-writ-er, *n.* keyboard machine for producing, type-like writing.

ty-phoid, *n.* infectious intestinal disease. Also **ty-phoid fe-ver.**

ty-phoon, *n.* hurricane.

ty-phus, *n.* acute infectious disease with fever, rash.

typ-i-cal, *a.* representative; conforming to some type.

typ-i-fy, *v.* be the typical specimen of.

typ-ist, *n.* typewriter operator.

ty-pog-ra-phy, *n.* setting and arranging types and printing from them; general appearance of printed matter.

tyr-an-ny, *n.* government by absolute rule; oppressive, unjust government. **ty-rant,** *n.* **ty-ran-ni-cal,** *a.* **tyr-an-nize,** *v.*

ty-ro, *n.* novice.

U

u-biq-ui-tous, *a.* being everywhere simultaneously. Also **u-biq-ui-tar-y.**

u-biq-ui-ty, *n.* omnipresence.

ud-der, *n.* baggy mammary gland with more than one teat.

ugh, *int.* exclamation of disgust.

ug-ly, *a.*, **-li-er, -li-est.** repulsive; vile; troublesome. *inf.* ill-natured. **ug-li-ly,** *adv.* **ug-li-ness,** *n.*

u-ku-le-le, *n.* small guitar-like instrument.

ul-cer, *n.* open sore.

ul-te-ri-or, *a.* being or situated beyond.

ul-ti-mate, *a.* extreme; final and decisive; fundamental. *n.* conclusion. **ul-ti-mate-ly,** *adv.*

ul-ti-ma-tum, *n. pl.,* **-tums, -ta.** final proposal.

ul-tra, *a.* excessive.

ul-tra-con-serv-a-tive, *a.* overly conservative.

ul-tra-son-ic, *a.* frequencies above the range of human audibility.

ul-tra-vi-o-let, *a.* of light rays with very short wavelengths.

um-ber, *n.* brown pigment.

um-bil-i-cal, *a.* referring to the navel.

um-bra, *n. pl.,* **-bras, -brae,** area of total shadow.

um-brage, *n.* resentment; offense.

um-brel-la, *n.* portable canopy on a collapsible frame used for shelter from sun or rain.

u-mi-ak, *n.* Eskimo boat.

um-laut, *n.* mark (¨) over a vowel, as *äu ö ü,* used to mark a vowel sound.

um-pire, *n.* official who enforces the game rules in some sports.

ump-teen, *a.* *inf.* many.

un-a-bashed, *a.* not embarrassed. **un-a-bash-ed-ly,** *adv.*

un-a-ble, *a.* not able.

un-a-bridged, *a.* comprehensive.

un-ac-count-a-ble, *a.* not explicable; strange. **un-ac-count-a-bly,** *adv.*

un-ac-cus-tomed, *a.* uncommon.

un-af-fect-ed, *a.* natural; sincere. **un-af-fect-ed-ly,** *adv.*

u-nan-i-mous, *a.* showing complete accord. **u-na-nim-i-ty,** *n.*

u·nan·i·mous·ly, *adv*.

un·ap·proach·a·ble, *a*. inaccessible; aloof.

un·armed, *a*. not having weapons. *a*.

un·as·sum·ing, *a*. modest; unpretentious.

un·at·tached, *a*. unmarried; not associated with.

un·a·void·a·ble, *a*. inevitable.

un·a·ware, *a*. not cognizant.

un·a·wares, *adv*. unknowingly; unexpectedly.

un·bal·anced, *a*. not balanced; mentally disordered.

un·be·com·ing, *a*. unattractive; improper.

un·be·liev·a·ble, *a*. incredible.

un·be·liev·er, *n*. skeptic; one who lacks religious faith.

un·bend, *v*., **-bent** or **-bend·ed**, **-bend·ing**. relax.

un·bend·ing, *a*. stiff; resolute.

un·bi·ased, *a*. free from prejudice.

un·blem·ished, *a*. untarnished; pure.

un·born, *a*. not yet born.

un·bos·om, *v*. disclose; reveal.

un·break·a·ble, *a*. not breakable.

un·bri·dled, *a*. unrestrained; unruly.

un·called-for, *a*. unwarranted; gratuitous.

un·can·ny, *a*. eerie, mysterious; superhuman.

un·ceas·ing, *a*. perpetual; continual. **un·ceas·ing·ly**, *adv*.

un·cer·e·mo·ni·ous, *a*. informal; abrupt; rude.

un·cer·tain, *a*. not sure; unreliable.

un·char·i·ta·ble, *a*. unforgiving; harsh.

un·cle, *n*. brother of one's father or mother; husband of one's aunt.

un·clean, *a*. filthy; unchaste.

un·clear, *a*. clouded; indistinct.

un·coil, *v*. unwind.

un·com·fort·a·ble, *a*. ill at ease; disquieting.

un·com·mon, *a*. not usual; extraordinary. **un·com·mon·ly**, *adv*. **un·com·mon·ness**, *n*.

un·com·mu·ni·ca·tive, *a*. reserved.

un·com·pro·mis·ing, *a*. inflexible; unyielding. **un·com·pro·mised**, *a*. **un·com·pro·mis·ing·ly**, *adv*.

un·con·cern, *n*. indifference; cool. **un·con·cerned**, *a*.

un·con·di·tion·al, *a*. absolute. **un·con·di·tion·al·ly**, *adv*.

un·con·scion·a·ble, *a*. unscrupulous; unprincipled. **un·con·scion·a·ble·ness**, *n*. **un·con·scion·a·bly**, *adv*.

un·con·scious, *a*. not aware; not known to; unintentional.

un·con·sti·tu·tion·al, *a*. not in accordance with the constitution.

un·con·strained, *a*. voluntary.

un·con·trol·la·ble, *a*. ungovernable.

un·con·ven·tion·al, *a*. out of the ordinary.

un·count·ed, *a*. innumerable.

un·cou·ple, *v*., **-pled**, **-pling**. unfasten; become loose.

un·couth, *a*. lacking in manners; crude. **un·couth·ness**, *n*.

un·cov·er, *v*. disclose; remove a cover from.

unc·tion, *n*. act of anointing; ointment.

unc·tu·ous, *a*. greasy; suave. **unc·tu·ous·ly**, *adv*.

un·daunt·ed, *a*. fearless; intrepid.

un·de·cid·ed, *a*. not settled; irresolute.

un·de·mon·stra·tive, *a*. reserved.

un·de·ni·a·ble, *a*. indisputable.

un·de·pend·a·ble, *a*. unreliable; untrustworthy.

un·der, *prep*. beneath; below; lower than; subject to. *adv*. below or beneath; in a lower degree. *a*. lower; subordinate.

un·der·act, *v*. perform inadequately; underplay.

un·der·brush, *n*. undergrowth.

un·der·class·man, *n. pl*., **-men**. freshman or sophomore.

un·der·clothes, *n. pl*. underwear.

un·der·coat, *n*. surface-sealing compound.

un·der·cov·er, *a*. acting in secret.

un·der·cur·rent, *n*. current below the surface; underlying tendency.

un·der·dog, *n*. predicted loser; victim of oppression.

un·der·es·ti·mate, *v*., **-mat·ed**, **-mat·ing**. estimate at too low a rate.

un·der·foot, *adv*., *a*. in the way.

un·der·go, *v*., **-went**, **-gone**, **-go·ing**. experience; endure.

un·der·grad·u·ate, *n*. nondegreed student.

un·der·ground, *adv*. below ground; not openly. *a*. hidden.

n. clandestine movement.

un·der·hand, *a.* covert; not open. *adv.* secretly.

un·der·hand·ed, *a.* covert; sly.

un·der·lie, *v.,* **-lay, -lain, -ly·ing.** be at the basis of.

un·der·line, *v.,* **-lined, -lin·ing.** underscore; stress.

un·der·ling, *n.* subordinate.

un·der·ly·ing, *a.* fundamental.

un·der·mine, *v.,* **-mined, -min·ing.** wear away; weaken.

un·der·neath, *prep.* below. *adv.* in or at a lower place. *a.* lower. *n.* lower part.

un·der·priv·i·leged, *a.* poor.

un·der·rate, *v.,* **-rat·ed, -rat·ing.** undervalue.

un·der·score, *v.,* **-scored, -scor·ing.** accentuate.

un·der·sell, *v.,* **-sold, -sell·ing.** sell for less.

un·der·side, *n.* surface underneath.

un·der·stand, *v.,* **-stood, -stand·ing.** comprehend; gain knowledge of; accept. *n.* **un·der·stand·a·ble,** *a.* **un·der·stand·a·bly,** *adv.*

un·der·stand·ing, *n.* comprehension; tolerance; mutual agreement. *a.*

un·der·state, *v.,* **-stat·ed, -stat·ing.** state in a restrained manner. **un·der·state·ment,** *n.*

un·der·stood, *a.* agreed upon; assumed.

un·der·stud·y, *v.,* **-ied, -y·ing.** be ready to replace. *n. pl.,* **-ies.** substitute.

un·der·take, *v.,* **-took, -tak·en, -tak·ing.** attempt; guarantee.

un·der·tak·er, *n.* mortician.

un·der·tak·ing, *n.* task; pledge.

un·der·tone, *n.* subdued tone; underlying quality.

un·der·tow, *n.* forceful undercurrent.

un·der·wear, *n.* garments worn nearest the skin.

un·der·world, *n.* organized criminals; Hades.

un·der·write, *v.,* **-wrote, -writ·ten, -writ·ing.** subscribe; assume liability; sign; insure.

un·do, *v.,* **-did, -done, -do·ing.** reverse, annul; open up; destroy.

un·doubt·ed, *a.* indisputable. **un·doubt·ed·ly,** *adv.*

un·dress, *v.,* **-dressed** or **-drest, -dress·ing.** divest of clothes.

un·due, *a.* improper; excessive.

un·du·late, *v.,* **-lat·ed, -lat·ing.**

move in curving lines; wave.

un·du·ly, *adv.* unjustifiably.

un·earth, *v.* dig up; discover.

un·earth·ly, *a.* supernatural; unreal.

un·eas·y, *a.,* **-i·er, -i·est.** uncomfortable; disturbed. **un·ease,** *n.* **un·eas·i·ly,** *adv.* **un·eas·i·ness,** *n.*

un·em·ployed, *a.* out of work. **un·em·ploy·ment,** *n.*

un·e·quiv·o·cal, *a.* clear; not ambiguous. **un·e·quiv·o·cal·ly,** *adv.*

un·e·ven, *a.* not smooth; odd; rough.

un·ex·pect·ed, *a.* unforeseen. **un·ex·pect·ed·ly,** *adv.*

un·faith·ful, *a.* disloyal; violating a vow.

un·fa·mil·iar, *a.* not well known; strange. **un·fa·mil·i·ar·i·ty,** *n.*

un·fath·om·a·ble, *a.* immeasurable.

un·feigned, *a.* real; sincere. **un·feign·ed·ly,** *adv.*

un·fin·ished, *a.* incomplete.

un·flinch·ing, *a.* not shrinking. **un·flinch·ing·ly,** *adv.*

un·fold, *v.* open; expand; disclose.

un·for·get·ta·ble, *a.* never to be forgotten. **un·for·get·ta·bly,** *adv.*

un·for·giv·a·ble, *a.* unpardonable.

un·for·tu·nate, *a.* unlucky; sad. *n.* unlucky person.

un·found·ed, *a.* groundless; unconfirmed.

un·furl, *v.* spread out; unfold.

un·gain·ly, *a.* clumsy; uncouth.

un·god·ly, *a.,* **-li·er, -li·est.** godless; impious. *inf.* outrageous. **un·god·li·ness,** *n.*

un·gra·cious, *a.* rude; offensive.

un·guent, *n.* salve; ointment.

un·ham·pered, *a.* unimpeded.

un·hand, *v.* let go.

un·hap·py, *a.,* **-pi·er, -pi·est.** not gay; wretched. **un·hap·pi·ly,** *adv.* **un·hap·pi·ness,** *n.*

un·harmed, *a.* unscathed.

un·health·y, *a.,* **-i·er, -i·est.** sickly; unwholesome.

un·heard-of, *a.* unprecedented; unknown.

un·ho·ly, *a.,* **-li·er, -li·est.** not sacred; evil. *inf.* dreadful.

un·hur·ried, *a.* leisurely.

un·hurt, *a.* unharmed.

u·ni·cel·lu·lar, *a.* consisting of one cell.

u·ni·corn, *n.* legendary horselike animal.

u·ni·form, *a.* unchanging; invariable. **u·ni·form·i·ty**, *n.*

u·ni·fy, *v.*, **-fied**, **-fy·ing**. form into one; consolidate. **u·ni·fi·ca·tion**, *n.*

u·ni·lat·er·al, *a.* one-sided.

un·im·ag·i·na·ble, *a.* inconceivable.

un·im·peach·a·ble, *a.* irreproachable.

un·in·hib·it·ed, *a.* heedless of convention.

un·in·ter·est·ed, *a.* indifferent.

un·ion, *n.* united; junction; a joining.

un·ion·ize, *v.*, **-ized**, **-iz·ing**. form into a union.

u·nique, *a.* without equal; unmatched. *n.*

u·ni·son, *n.* coincidence in pitch. **in u·ni·son**, in accord.

u·nit, *n.* single thing; whole; one.

u·nite, *v.*, **-nit·ed**, **-nit·ing**. join; incorporate.

u·nit·ed, *a.* combined.

u·ni·ty, *n. pl.*, **-ties**. oneness; harmony.

u·ni·ver·sal, *a.* of the whole; involving all. **u·ni·ver·sal·i·ty**, *n.* **u·ni·ver·sal·ize**, *v.*

u·ni·verse, *n.* cosmos; whole world.

u·ni·ver·si·ty, *n. pl.*, **-ties**. institution of higher learning.

un·just, *a.* unfair. **un·just·ly**, *adv.*

un·kempt, *a.* disheveled.

un·known, *a.* unfamiliar; not discovered.

un·law·ful, *a.* illegal.

un·learn·ed, *a.* illiterate.

un·leash, *v.* to let go of.

un·less, *conj.* if not. *prep.* except.

un·let·tered, *a.* without education.

un·like, *a.* different. *prep.* different from.

un·like·ly, *a.*, **-li·er**, **-li·est**. improbable. *adv.*

un·lim·it·ed, *a.* boundless; infinite.

un·load, *v.* remove the burden; get rid of.

un·looked-for, *a.* unforeseen.

un·luck·y, *a.*, **-i·er**, **-i·est**. inauspicious.

un·man, *v.*, **-manned**, **-man·ning**. emasculate.

un·mask, *v.* expose.

un·men·tion·a·ble, *a.* unfit to be noticed. *n.*

un·mer·ci·ful, *a.* relentless. **un·mer·ci·ful·ly**, *adv.*

un·mis·tak·a·ble, *a.* clear.

un·mit·i·gat·ed, *a.* not toned down; unmodified.

un·nat·u·ral, *a.* abnormal; cruel.

un·nec·es·sar·y, *a.* needless.

un·num·bered, *a.* countless.

un·pack, *v.* unload.

un·par·al·leled, *a.* matchless.

un·pleas·ant, *a.* disagreeable. **un·pleas·ant·ness**, *n.*

un·pop·u·lar, *a.* generally disapproved.

un·prec·e·dent·ed, *a.* unheard of.

un·prin·ci·pled, *a.* unscrupulous.

un·print·a·ble, *a.* offensive. *a.*

un·ques·tion·a·ble, *a.* beyond doubt; indisputable.

un·ques·tioned, *a.* undisputed.

un·quote, *v.*, **-quot·ed**, **-quot·ing**. end a quotation.

un·rav·el, *v.*, **-eled**, **-el·ing**. untangle.

un·re·al, *a.* imaginary.

un·rea·son·a·ble, *a.* immoderate.

un·re·lat·ed, *a.* having no connection.

un·re·lent·ing, *a.* pitiless.

un·re·mit·ting, *a.* continuous.

un·rest, *n.* uneasiness; anxiety.

un·ri·valed, *a.* peerless.

un·roll, *v.* uncoil.

un·ruf·fled, *a.* calm; smooth.

un·ru·ly, *a.*, **-i·er**, **-i·est**. turbulent; ungovernable. **un·ru·li·ness**, *n.*

un·sa·vor·y, *a.* disagreeable; offensive.

un·scathed, *a.* uninjured.

un·scru·pu·lous, *a.* having no principles.

un·seem·ly, *a.* indecent.

un·set·tle, *v.*, **-tled**, **-tling**. disrupt; upset.

un·sight·ly, *a.*, **-li·er**, **-li·est**. repulsive.

un·skilled, *a.* untrained.

un·snarl, *v.* disentangle.

un·so·phis·ti·cat·ed, *a.* naïve; plain. **un·so·phis·ti·ca·tion**, *n.*

un·sound, *a.* defective.

un·speak·a·ble, *a.* very bad.

un·sta·ble, *a.* irresolute.

un·stead·y, *a.*, **-i·er**, **-i·est**. shaky; fickle.

un·strung, *a.* nervous; weak.

un·sung, *a.* unacclaimed.

un·taught, *a.* not educated.

un·think·a·ble, *a.* inconceivable.

un·think·ing, *a.* inconsiderate.

un·til, *conj.* before. *prep.* onward to.

un·time·ly, *a.* inopportune; premature. *adv.* unseasonably.

un·to, *prep.* Archaic. to.

un·told, *a.* not related; very great.

un·truth, *n.* false assertion. **un·truth·ful**, *a.*

un·used, *a.* not used; unaccustomed.

un·u·su·al, *a.* rare.

un·ut·ter·a·ble, *a.* unspeakable.

un·var·nished, *a.* plain.

un·veil, *v.* disclose; reveal.

un·war·y, *a.* careless.

un·whole·some, *a.* unhealthy.

un·wield·y, *a.* bulky; clumsy.

un·will·ing, *a.* reluctant.

un·wit·ting, *a.* unaware; accidental. **un·wit·ting·ly**, *adv.*

un·wont·ed, *a.* not habitual. **un·wont·ed·ness**, *n.*

un·wor·thy, *a.* undeserving.

un·wrap, *v.*, **-wrapped**, **-wrapping**. open or undo.

un·yield·ing, *a.* stiff; obstinate.

up, *adv.* to, toward, or in a more elevated position; erect; at a center; into or in activity; to or at an end. *a.* tending or inclining upward. *inf.* aware; abreast; happening. *prep.* to, toward, or at. *n.* ascent. *v.*, **upped**, **up·ping**. *inf.* increase.

up·beat, *a. inf.* lively.

up·braid, *v.* scold; chide.

up·bring·ing, *n.* training.

up·date, *v.*, **-dat·ed**, **-dat·ing**. make modern.

up·grade, *n.* ascending road; increase. *v.*, **-grad·ed**, **-grad·ing**. elevate.

up·heav·al, *n.* abrupt change.

up·heave, *v.*, **-heaved** or **up·heaved** or **up·hove**, **up·heav·ing**.

up·hill, *adv.* upward. *a.* going up.

up·hold, *v.*, **-held**, **-hold·ing**. sustain.

up·hol·ster, *v.* cover furniture with fabric. **up·hol·ster·y**, *n. pl.*, **-ies**.

up·keep, *n.* maintenance.

up·on, *prep.* on. *adv.* on.

up·per, *a.* higher; *n.* shoe above the sole. *inf.* berth; stimulating drug.

up·per·most, *a.* highest in place. *adv.* first.

up·pish, *a. inf.* arrogant.

up·pi·ty, *a. inf.* snobbish.

up·raise, *v. inf.*, **-raised**, **-rais·ing**. lift up.

up·right, *a.* vertical; erect; of

inflexible honesty. *n.* something standing erect.

up·ris·ing, *n.* rebellion.

up·roar, *n.* commotion.

up·roar·i·ous, *a.* noisy; comical.

up·root, *v.* eradicate; tear away.

up·set, *v.*, **-set**, **-set·ting**. overturn; disturb; defeat unexpectedly. *n.* overthrow; disturbance. *a.* disordered.

up·shot, *n.* conclusion.

up·side down, *adv.* in complete disorder. **up·side-down**, *a.*

up·stage, *v.*, **-staged**, **-stag·ing**. steal the scene.

up·stairs, *a.* pertaining to an upper floor. *n. pl., usu. sing. in constr.* upper story.

up·stand·ing, *a.* erect and tall; honorable.

up·swing, *n.* increase; rise.

up-to-date, *a.* including the latest facts; abreast of the times.

up·turn, *v.* turn upward. *n.* increase or rise.

up·ward, *adv.* toward a higher place. **up·ward** or **up·wards of**, more or higher than.

u·ra·ni·um, *n.* metallic element. Sym. U.

U·ra·nus, *n.* major planet.

ur·ban, *a.* characteristic of cities.

ur·bane, *a.* sophisticated; polished. **ur·ban·i·ty**, *n.*

ur·chin, *n.* roguish child.

urge, *v.*, **urged**, **urg·ing**. impel; stimulate; persuade. *n.* impulse.

ur·gent, *a.* earnestly insistent. **ur·gen·cy**, *n. pl.*, **-cies**. **ur·gent·ly**, *adv.*

u·ri·nate, *v.*, **-nat·ed**, **-nat·ing**. pass urine. **u·ri·na·tion**, *n.*

u·rine, *n.* liquid secretion of the kidneys.

urn, *n.* large vase.

us, *pron.* objective case of *we*.

us·a·ble, **use·a·ble**, *a.* in suitable condition. **us·a·bly**, **use·a·bly**, *adv.* **us·a·bil·i·ty**, **use·a·bil·i·ty**, *n.*

us·age, *n.* habitual practice; custom.

use, *v.*, **used**, **us·ing**. put into service; utilize; treat; consume. *n.* purpose; function; power. **of no use**, of no help. **use up**, exhaust.

used, *a.* secondhand.

use·ful, *a.* valuable; helpful. **use·ful·ness**, *n.*

use·less, *a.* futile.

ush·er, *n.* one who guides peo-

ple to seats. *v.* escort.
u·su·al, *a.* ordinary. **u·su·al·ly,** *adv.*

u·surp, *v.* seize unlawfully.

u·su·ry, *n. pl.,* **-ries.** taking exorbitant interest for the use of money.

u·ten·sil, *n.* tool for domestic use.

u·ter·us, *n. pl.,* **-i.** womb.

u·til·i·ty, *n. pl.,* **-ties.** usefulness; beneficial service to the public. **u·til·i·tar·i·an,** *n.*

u·ti·lize, *v.,* **-lized, -liz·ing.** make useful. **u·ti·li·za·tion,** *n.*

ut·most, *a.* of the greatest degree. *n.* extreme extent.

u·to·pi·a, *n.* ideally perfect situation.

ut·ter, *a.* absolute. *v.* pronounce. **ut·ter·ance,** *n.*

ut·ter·most, *a., n.* utmost.

V

va·can·cy, *n. pl.,* **-cies.** unoccupied place or empty space. **va·cant,** *a.* **va·cant·ly,** *adv.*

va·cate, *v.,* **-cat·ed, -cat·ing.** make empty.

va·ca·tion, *n.* rest from regular duty. *v.*

vac·cine, *n.* preparation used for preventive inoculation. **vac·ci·nate,** *v.,* **vac·ci·na·tion,** *n.*

vac·il·late, *v.,* **-lat·ed, -lat·ing.** fluctuate; to be indecisive. **vac·il·lat·ing,** *a.* **vac·il·la·tion,** *n.*

va·cu·i·ty, *n. pl.,* **-ties.** emptiness; lack of thought.

vac·u·ous, *a.* unintelligent; showing mental vacancy.

vac·u·um, *n. pl.,* **-ums.** empty, enclosed space. *v.* clean with a vacuum cleaner.

vag·a·bond, *a.* nomadic; vagrant. *n.* **vag·a·bond·age,** *n.,* **vag·a·bond·ish,** *a.*

va·gar·y, *n. pl.,* **-ies.** odd notion or action. **va·gar·i·ous,** *a.*

va·grant, *n.* homeless wanderer. **va·gran·cy,** *n.*

vague, *a.* unclear; indefinite; hazy. **vague·ness,** *n.*

vain, *a.* conceited; ineffectual. **in vain,** unsuccessful; profanely. **vain·ly,** *adv.*

val·ance, *n.* short, decorative drapery. **val·anced,** *a.*

vale, *n.* valley.

val·e·dic·to·ry, *n. pl.,* **-ries.** farewell oration. **val·e·dic·to·ri·an,** *n.*

val·en·tine, *n.* sweetheart on St. Valentine's Day.

val·et, *n.* manservant.

val·iant, *a.* brave.

val·id, *a.* supported by fact; having sufficient legal force. **val·id·ly,** *adv.* **val·i·date,** *v.*

va·lid·i·ty, *n. pl.,* **-ties.** soundness.

va·lise, *n.* small suitcase.

val·ley, *n. pl.,* **-leys.** land between hills or mountains; land drained by a river.

val·or, *n.* personal bravery. **val·or·ous,** *a.*

val·u·a·ble, *a.* having great worth. *n. Usu. pl.* valuable articles.

val·u·a·tion, *n.* appraisal; estimated worth of something. **val·u·a·tion·al,** *a.*

val·ue, *n.* worth, merit, or importance. *pl.* principles. *v.,* **-ued, -u·ing.** appraise; esteem. **val·ued,** *a.*

valve, *n.* device used to regulate fluid flow.

vamp, *n. inf.* seductive woman.

vam·pire, *n.* blood-sucking bat.

van, *n.* vanguard; large closed truck.

van·dal, *n.* willful damager of property. **van·dal·ism,** *n.* **van·dal·ize,** *v.,* **-ized, -iz·ing.**

vane, *n.* device used to show wind direction.

van·guard, *n.* front division of an army.

va·nil·la, *n.* flavoring from pods of an orchid.

van·ish, *v.* disappear.

van·i·ty, *n. pl.,* **-ties.** excessive pride; futility; a dressing table.

van·quish, *v.* conquer.

van·tage, *n.* advantage.

vap·id, *a.* insipid; dull. **va·pid·i·ty, vap·id·ness,** *n.*

va·por, *n.* gaseous form of any heated solid or liquid; thick mist. **va·por·ous,** *a.*

va·por·ize, *v.,* **-ized, -iz·ing.** convert into vapor.

var·i·a·ble, *a.* changeable; diverse. *n.* something variable. **var·i·a·bil·i·ty, var·i·a·ble·ness,** *n.*

var·i·ance, *n.* difference; discord.

var·i·ant, *a.* varying; different. *n.* a variant form.

var·i·a·tion, *n.* diversity; alteration; deviation.

var·i·cose, *a.* swollen.

var·ied, *a.* diversified.

var·i·e·gate, *v.,* **-gat·ed, -gat·ing.** give variety to. **var·i·e·gat·ed,** *a.*

va·ri·e·ty, *n. pl.,* **-ties.** diversity; varied assortment. **va·ri·e·tal,** *a.*

var·i·ous, *a.* of different kinds; marked by variety; several or many.

var·nish, *n.* glossy, resinous coating. *v.* spread varnish on.

var·si·ty, *n. pl.,* **-ties.** principal school team.

var·y, *v.,* **-ied, -y·ing.** differ; change.

vase, *n.* flower container.

vas·ec·to·my, *n. pl.,* **-mies.** excision of the sperm-transferring duct.

vas·sal, *n.* subject; serf.

vast, *a.* immense.

vat, *n.* tank; tub; cistern. *v.,* **-vat·ed, vat·ting.**

vaude·ville, *n.* variety show.

vault, *v.* leap over. *n.* arched roof; burial chamber; storage room.

vaunt, *v.* boast. *n.* a brag. **vaunt·ing·ly,** *adv.*

veal, *n.* meat from a calf.

vec·tor, *n.* entity having direction and magnitude.

veer, *v.* shift; turn around. **veer·ing·ly,** *adv.*

veg·e·ta·ble, *n.* edible plant.

veg·e·tar·i·an, *n.* one who does not eat meat. **veg·e·tar·i·an·ism,** *n.*

veg·e·tate, *v.,* **-tat·ed, -tat·ing.** grow as a plant; to be inactive. **veg·e·ta·tion,** *n.* **veg·e·ta·tive,** *a.*

ve·he·ment, *a.* passionate; violent. **ve·he·mence, ve·he·men·cy,** *n.*

ve·hi·cle, *n.* device on wheels used for conveyance; means of communication. **ve·hic·u·lar,** *a.*

veil, *n.* thin material worn over the head or face; something that conceals.

vein, *n.* blood vessel to the heart; mineral deposit; streak or marking, as in marble. *v.* to streak. **veined,** *a.* **vein·ing,** *n.*

veld, veldt, *n.* grassland.

vel·lum, *n.* fine parchment.

ve·loc·i·ty, *n. pl.,* **-ties.** speed.

vel·ours, vel·our, *n. pl.,* **ve·lours,** velvety fabric.

vel·vet, *n.* fabric having a thick, soft pile; softness. **vel·vet·y,** *a.*

vel·vet·een, *n.* cloth having a short pile in imitation of velvet. *a.* made of velveteen.

ve·nal, *a.* corrupt. **ve·nal·i·ty,** *n.*

ve·na·tion, *n.* system of veins. **ve·na·tion·al,** *a.*

vend, *v.* sell. **vend·or,** *n.*

ven·det·ta, *n.* blood feud.

vend·i·ble, *a.* salable. *n. usu. pl.* vendible article.

ve·neer, *n.* overlay of fine wood; superficial.

ven·er·a·ble, *a.* worthy of reverence. **-a·bil·i·ty,** *n.*

ven·er·ate, *v.,* **-at·ed, -at·ing.** revere. **-a·tion,** *n.*

ve·ne·re·al, *a.* of or from sexual intercourse.

ven·geance, *n.* retribution.

venge·ful, *a.* vindictive.

ve·ni·al, *a.* pardonable. **ve·ni·al·i·ty,** *n.*

ven·i·son, *n.* deer meat.

ven·om, *n.* poisonous fluid; malice. **ven·om·ous,** *a.*

ve·nous, *a.* of, pertaining to, or full of veins.

vent, *n.* outlet. *v.,* **vent·ed, vent·ing.** express.

ven·ti·late, *v.,* **-lat·ed, -lat·ing.** supply with fresh air; discuss freely. **ven·ti·la·tion,** *n.*

ven·tral, *a.* abdominal.

ven·tri·cle, *n.* cavity of the heart.

ven·tril·o·quism, *n.* art of speaking with barely visible lip movement. **ven·tril·o·quist,** *n.*

ven·ture, *n.* risk; hazard. *v.* expose to hazard; dare. **ven·ture·some,** *a.* **ven·tur·ous,** *a.*

Ve·nus, *n.* second planet from the sun; goddess of love.

ve·ra·cious, *a.* truthful. **ve·rac·i·ty,** *n.*

ve·ran·da, ve·ran·dah, *n.* open porch.

verb, *n.* part of speech expressing existence, action, occurrence.

ver·bal, *a.* oral. *n.* word derived from a verb. **ver·bal·ly,** *adv.*

ver·bal·ize, *v.,* **-ized, -iz·ing.** articulate. **ver·bal·i·za·tion,** *n.*

ver·ba·tim, *adv.* word for word. *a.*

ver·bi·age, *n.* wordiness.

ver·bose, *a.* wordy. **-bos·i·ty,** *n.*

ver·dant, *a.* green. **ver·dan·cy,** *n.*

ver·dict, *n.* judgment; decision.

ver·di·gris, *n.* green or bluish patina.

ver·dure, *n.* greenness; vigor.

verge, *n.* edge, margin. *v.*

verged. verg·ing. border, approach; incline.

ver·i·fy, *v.,* **-fied, -fy·ing.** confirm. **-fi·ca·tion,** *n.*

ver·i·si·mil·i·tude, *n.* appearance of truth.

ver·i·ta·ble, *a.* true; actual. **ver·i·ta·bly,** *adv.*

ver·i·ty, *n. pl.,* **-ties.** truth.

ver·mic·u·lar, *a.* wormlike.

ver·mi·fuge, *n.* medicine that expels worms.

ver·mil·ion, ver·mil·lion, *n.* bright red pigment. *a.* bright red.

ver·min, *n. pl.,* **ver·min.** noxious small mammals; parasitic insects. **ver·min·ous,** *a.*

ver·mouth, *n.* white, herbed wine.

ver·nac·u·lar, *a.* peculiar to a place. *n.* native speech. **ver·nac·u·lar·ism,** *n.*

ver·nal, *n.* of spring; of youth. **ver·nal·ly,** *adv.*

ver·sa·tile, *a.* having many uses. **ver·sa·til·i·ty,** *n.*

verse, *n.* line of a poem.; poem.

versed, *a.* experienced.

ver·si·fy, *v.,* **-fied, -fy·ing.** turn into verse. **ver·si·fi·ca·tion,** *n.*

ver·sion, *n.* translation; account. **ver·sion·al,** *a.*

ver·sus, *prep.* against.

ver·te·bra, *n. pl.,* **-brae.** bone or segment of the spinal column. **ver·te·bral,** *a.*

ver·te·brate, *a.* having vertebrae. *n.* vertebrate animal.

ver·tex, *n. pl.,* **-tex·es, -ti·ces.** apex; summit.

ver·ti·cal, *a.* perpendicular to the horizon. *n.* vertical line or plane.

ver·ti·go, *n. pl.,* **-ti·goes, -tig·i·nes.** dizziness.

verve, *n.* vitality.

ver·y, *adv.* extremely. *a.,* **-i·er, -i·est.** same; actual; true; mere.

ves·i·cant, *n.* blistering agent.

ves·i·cate, *v.,* **-cat·ed, -cat·ing.** blister.

ves·i·cle, *n.* cavity; small sac. **ve·sic·u·lar,** *a.*

ves·per, *a.* of or relating to evening.

ves·pers, *n.* religious evening service.

ves·sel, *n.* ship; receptacle; tube or duct.

vest, *n.* waistcoat. *v.* clothe; endow.

ves·ti·bule, *n.* lobby.

ves·tige, *n.* trace; surviving evidence. **ves·tig·i·al,** *a.*

vest·ment, *n.* garment; robe.

vest-pock·et, *a.* conveniently small.

ves·try, *n. pl.,* **-tries.** vestment room; church room for meetings.

vet, *n. inf.* veterinarian; vet. *a.*

vetch, *n.* twining legumes.

vet·er·an, *n.* one who has seen service. *a.* experienced.

vet·er·i·nar·i·an, *n.* one who treats animals.

vet·er·i·nar·y, *n. pl.,* **-ies.** veterinarian. *a.* referring to veterinary medicine.

ve·to, *n.* power to refuse or prohibit. *v.,* **-toed, -to·ing.** interdict.

vex, *v.* annoy; worry. **vex·a·tion,** *n.* **vex·a·tious,** *a.* **vexed,** *a.*

vi·a, *prep.* by way of.

vi·a·ble, *a.* capable of living; workable. **vi·a·bil·i·ty,** *n.* **vi·a·bly,** *adv.*

vi·a·duct, *n.* bridge over a valley, ravine, etc.

vi·al, *n.* small glass vessel.

vi·and, *n.* item of food.

vibes, *n. pl. inf.* vibrations; reactions.

vi·brant, *a.* resonant; vigorous. **vi·bran·cy,** *n.*

vi·brate, *v.,* **-brat·ed, -brat·ing.** oscillate; quiver. **vi·bra·tion,** *n.* **vi·bra·tor,** *n.* **vi·bra·to·ry,** *a.*

vic·ar, *n.* parish clergyman. **vic·ar·ship,** *n.*

vic·ar·age, *n.* benefice of a vicar; vicar's house.

vi·car·i·ous, *a.* substitute. **vi·car·i·ous·ly,** *adv.* **vi·car·i·ous·ness,** *n.*

vice, *n.* evil habit.

vi·ce, *prep.* instead of.

vice pres·i·dent, *n.* officer next in rank to president. **vice-pres·i·den·cy,** *n.*

vice·roy, *n.* ruler of country as deputy of the sovereign. **vice·roy·al,** *a.*

vice ver·sa, *adv.* conversely.

vi·cin·i·ty, *n. pl.,* **-ties.** proximity.

vi·cious, *a.* depraved; evil; spiteful. **vi·cious·ness,** *n.*

vi·cis·si·tude, *n.* change.

vic·tim, *n.* one hurt by an action; dupe; sacrifice. **vic·tim·ize,** *v.,* **-ized, -iz·ing. vic·tim·iz·er,** *n.*

vic·tor, *n.* conqueror. **vic·to·ri·ous,** *a.*

vic·to·ry, *n. pl.,* **-ries.** success in a contest.

vict·ual, *n. (usu. pl.)* food. *v.,* **-ualed, -ual·ing.** supply with victuals.

vid·e·o, *a.* of television. *n.* television.

vie, *v.,* **vied, vy·ing.** contend for or with. **vi·er,** *n.*

view, *n.* sight; scene; opinion; purpose. *v.* see; consider. **view·er,** *n.*

view·less, *a.* having no opinion.

view·point, *n.* opinion.

vig·il, *n.* nightwatch.

vig·i·lance, *n.* watchfulness. **vig·i·lant,** *a.*

vi·gnette, *n.* small running design; short literary sketch.

vig·or, *n.* energy; vitality. **vig·or·ous,** *a.* **vig·or·ous·ly,** *adv.*

vile, *a.,* **vil·er, vil·est.** very bad; offensive.

vil·i·fy, *v.,* **-fied, -fy·ing.** malign. **vil·i·fi·ca·tion,** *n.*

vil·la, *n.* sizeable country residence.

vil·lage, *n.* small town.

vil·lain, *n.* scoundrel. **vil·lain·ous,** *a.* **vil·lain·y,** *n. pl.,* **-ies.**

vim, *n.* vigor.

vin·ci·ble, *a.* conquerable. **vin·ci·bil·i·ty,** *n.*

vin·di·cate, *v.,* **-cat·ed, -cat·ing.** clear from suspicion. **vin·di·ca·tion,** *n.* **vin·di·ca·tor,** *n.*

vin·dic·tive, *a.* revengeful. **vin·dic·tive·ness,** *n.*

vine, *n.* trailing or creeping plant.

vin·e·gar, *n.* sour liquid used as a condiment. **vin·e·gar·y,** *a.*

vine·yard, *n.* plantation of grapevines.

vi·nous, *a.* resembling or referring to wine.

vin·tage, *n.* grape harvest. *a.* outmoded; classic.

vint·ner, *n.* wine merchant.

vi·nyl, *n.* type of plastic.

vi·ol, *n.* stringed musical instrument.

vi·o·la, *n.* instrument of violin class.

vi·o·la·ble, *a.* capable of being violated.

vi·o·late, *v.,* **-lat·ed, -lat·ing.** transgress; desecrate; injure. **vi·o·la·tor,** *n.* **vi·o·la·tion,** *n.*

vi·o·lence, *n.* destructive force.

vi·o·lent, *a.*

vi·o·let, *n.* bluish purple color. *a.*

vi·o·lin, *n.* stringed musical instrument, played with a bow.

vi·o·lin·ist, *n.*

vi·o·lon·cel·lo, *n.* cello. **vi·o·lon·cel·list,** *n.*

vir·tu·o·so, *n. pl.,* **-sos, -si.** one of special skill, esp. in music. **vir·tu·os·ic,** *a.* **vir·tu·os·i·ty,** *n. pl.,* **-ties.**

vir·u·lent, *a.* poisonous; hostile. **vir·u·lence,** *n.*

vi·rus, *n. pl.,* **-rus·es.** infective organism; corruption.

vi·sa, *n.* passport endorsement.

vis·age, *n.* face; aspect.

vis·cer·a, *n. pl.* soft interior organs. **vis·cer·al,** *a.*

vis·cid, *a.* sticky; gluelike. **vis·cid·i·ty,** *n.* **vis·cos·i·ty,** *n.*

vis·count, *n.* nobleman. **vis·count·ess,** *n.*

vi·per, *n.* snake; spiteful person.

vi·ra·go, *n. pl.,* **-goes, -gos.** shrew.

vi·ral, *a.* relating to a virus.

vir·gin, *n.* chaste woman; maiden. *a.* chaste; untouched. **vir·gin·al,** *a.* **vir·gin·i·ty,** *n.*

vir·ile, *a.* manly. **vi·ril·i·ty,** *n.*

vir·tu·al, *a.* in essence; equivalent. **vir·tu·al·ly,** *adv.*

vir·tue, *n.* moral goodness. **vir·tu·ous,** *a.*

vise, *n.* device used to hold an object firmly.

vis·i·ble, *a.* open to sight; perceivable; conspicuous. **vis·i·bil·i·ty,** *n.*

vi·sion, *n.* sight; foresight; anticipation.

vi·sion·ar·y, *a.* utopian. *n. pl.,* **-ies.** dreamer.

vis·it, *v.* go to see a person, place, etc. *n.* a stay or sojourn as a guest. **vis·i·tant,** *n.* **vis·i·tor,** *n.*

vis·it·a·tion, *n.* formal visit.

vi·sor, *n.* shield, usu. projecting from a cap.

vis·ta, *n.* view, as through an avenue.

vis·u·al, *a.* referring to vision. **vis·u·al·ly,** *adv.*

vis·u·al·ize, *v.,* **-ized, -iz·ing.** make visual; form a mental image. **vis·u·al·i·za·tion,** *n.*

vi·tal, *a.* of life; necessary to life; essential.

vi·tal·i·ty, *n. pl.,* **-ties.** vital force; vigor; animation.

vi·tal·ize, *v.,* **-ized, -iz·ing.** invigorate. **-i·za·tion,** *n.*

vi·tals, *n. pl.* internal organs.

vi·ta·min, *n.* essential food factor.

vi·ti·ate, *v.,* **-at·ed, -at·ing.** impair; invalidate. **vi·ti·a·tion**, *n.*

vit·re·ous, *a.* resembling glass. **vit·re·os·i·ty**, *n.*

vit·ri·fy, *v.*, **-fied, -fy·ing.** convert into glass. **vit·ri·fi·a·ble**, *a.* **vit·ri·fi·ca·tion**, *n.*

vit·ri·ol, *n.* glassy metallic sulfates; sulfuric acid; caustic criticism. **vit·ri·ol·ic**, *a.*

vi·tu·per·ate, *v.*, **-at·ed, -at·ing.** berate. **vi·tu·per·a·tion**, *n.*

vi·va·cious, *a.* animated. **vi·vac·i·ty**, *n. pl.*, **-ties.**

viv·id, *a.* bright; intense; lively. **viv·i·fy**, *v.*, **-fied, -fy·ing.** animate. **-fi·ca·tion**, *n.*

viv·i·sec·tion, *n.* dissection of a living organism.

vix·en, *n.* quarrelsome woman; female fox.

vi·zor, *n.* visor.

vo·cab·u·lar·y, *n. pl.*, **-ies.** stock of words used; list of words.

vo·cal, *a.* of the voice; for singing; articulate. **vo·cal·ize**, **-ized, -iz·ing. vo·cal·i·za·tion**, *n.*

vocal cords, *n. pl.* membranes that produce vocal sound.

vo·cal·ist, *n.* singer.

vo·ca·tion, *n.* occupation; calling. **vo·ca·tion·al**, *a.*

vo·cif·er·ous, *a.* noisy.

vod·ka, *n.* colorless liquor.

vogue, *n.* mode.

voice, *n.* uttered sound; speaking or singing; expression; choice; verb forms. *v.*, **voiced, voic·ing.** express; utter.

voice·less, *a.* mute; silent.

voiced, *a.* expressed; spoken.

void, *a.* null; devoid. *n.* vacuum. *v.* nullify. **void·a·ble**, *a.*

voile, *n.* sheer fabric.

vol·a·tile, *a.* able to vaporize freely; fickle; explosive. **vol·a·til·i·ty**, *n.*

vol·ca·no, *n. pl.*, **-noes, -nos.** eruption on earth's surface. **vol·can·ic**, *a.* **vol·can·i·cal·ly**, *adv.*

vole, *n.* small rodent.

vo·li·tion, *n.* will.

vol·ley, *n. pl.*, **-leys.** flight of missiles; return of the ball before it touches the ground. *v.*, **-leyed, ley·ing.** discharge with a volley; return a ball.

volt, *n.* unit of electromotive force. **volt·age**, *n.*

vol·u·ble, *a.* glibly fluent. **vol·u·bly**, *adv.* **vol·u·bil·i·ty**, *n.*

vol·ume, *n.* book; size in three dimensions; mass; loudness.

vo·lu·mi·nous, *a.* of great vol-

ume; ample. **vo·lu·mi·nous·ly**, *adv.*

vol·un·tar·y, *a.* of or by free choice. **vol·un·tar·i·ly**, *adv.*

vol·un·teer, *n.* one who offers service willingly. *v.* offer service.

vo·lup·tu·ar·y, *n. pl.*, **-ies.** sensualist. *a.*

vo·lup·tu·ous, *a.* sensuous; luxurious.

vom·it, *v.* eject food; throw up; spew. *n.* vomited matter.

voo·doo, *n. pl.*, **-doos.** sorcery. **voo·doo·ism**, *n.* **voo·doo·ist**, *n.*

vo·ra·cious, *a.* greedy; ravenous. **vo·rac·i·ty**, *n.*

vor·tex, *n. pl.*, **-tex·es, -ti·ces.** whirlpool; whirlwind.

vote, *n.* formal expression of choice. *v.*, **vot·ed, vot·ing.** cast a vote. **vot·er**, *n.*

vouch, *v.* assert; give warrant; attest; assure.

vouch·er, *n.* that which vouches; receipt.

vouch·safe, *v.*, **-safed, -saf·ing.** grant; permit.

vow, *n.* solemn promise. *v.* make a vow.

vow·el, *n.* more or less open speech sounds; letter representing such a sound.

voy·age, *n.* journey. *v.*, **-aged, -ag·ing. voy·ag·er**, *n.*

vo·yeur, *n.* peeping Tom. **vo·yeur·ism**, *n.* **voy·eur·is·tic**, *a.*

vul·can·ize, *v.*, **-ized, -iz·ing.** treat rubber with sulfur and heat. **vul·can·i·za·tion**, *n.*

vul·gar, *a.* crude; obscene; the vernacular. **vul·gar·ism**, *n.*

vul·gar·i·ty, *n. pl.*, **-ties. vul·gar·ize**, *v.*, **-ized, -iz·ing.**

vul·ner·a·ble, *a.* open to attack. **vul·ner·a·bil·i·ty**, *n.* **vul·ner·a·bly**, *adv.*

vul·pine, *a.* of the fox; cunning.

vul·ture, *n.* large bird of prey.

vul·va, *n. pl.*, **-vae, -vas.** external female genitals.

W

wack·y, *a.*, **-i·er, -i·est.** *inf.* eccentric; crazy.

wad, *n.* soft mass; plug. *v.*, **wad·ded, wad·ding.** mold into a wad; plug; stuff.

wad·dle, *v.*, **-dled, -dling.** walk in a tottering manner.

wade, *v.*, **wad·ed, wad·ing.** move with difficulty; ford. **wad·er**, *n.*

wa·fer, *n.* small, crisp cracker;

thin coating of dried paste.

waf·fle, *n.* crisp, latticed, batter cake.

waft, *v.* sail or float through air. *n.* anything conveyed gently through the air.

wag, *v.*, **wagged, wag·ging.** move rapidly and repeatedly. *n.* joker.

wage, *n. Often pl.* money paid for labor. *Pl. sing. or pl. in constr.* recompense. *v.*, **waged, wag·ing.** carry on.

wa·ger, *n.* bet. *v.* stake; bet.

wag·on, *n.* four-wheeled vehicle.

waif, *n.* homeless child; wanderer.

wail, *v.* utter a mournful cry. *n.* lament.

wain·scot, *n.* wood paneling.

waist, *n.* part of the human body between the ribs and the hips.

waist·coat, *n. Chiefly Brit.* vest.

waist·line, *n.* line of the waist.

wait, *v.* stay; be in readiness; defer. *n.* delay.

wait·er, *n.* male who waits on tables. **wait·ress**, *n. fem.*

wait·ing, *a.* expecting.

waive, *v.*, **waived, waiv·ing.** relinquish; dismiss.

waiv·er, *n.* written statement of relinquishment.

wake, *v.*, **waked** or **woke, waked, wak·ing.** become roused from sleep; become aware. *n.* vigil; track.

wake·ful, *a.* sleeplessly alert.

wak·en, *v.* wake.

walk, *v.* travel on foot. *n.* time of walking; distance walked; profession.

walk·er, *n.* device which aids someone in walking.

walk·ie-talk·ie, *n.* portable two-way radio-telephone system.

walk·out, *n.* workers' strike.

walk·o·ver, *n. inf.* easy victory.

walk·up, *n. inf.* apartment in which there is no elevator.

wall, *n.* vertical structure which encloses or divides. *v.* separate with a wall.

wal·la·by, *n. pl.*, **-bies, -by.** small kangaroo.

wall·board, *n.* substitute for wooden boards or plaster.

wal·let, *n.* small, pocket case.

wal·lop, *v. inf.* thrash; defeat thoroughly. *n. inf.* forceful blow.

wal·low, *v.* roll in mud; live self-indulgently.

wall·pa·per, *n.* paper covering the walls.

wal·nut, *n.* nut-bearing tree.

wal·rus, *n. pl.*, **-rus·es, -rus.** large marine mammal.

waltz, *n.* ballroom dance. *v.* dance to waltz time.

wam·pum, *n.* small beads used for barter.

wan, *a.*, **wan·ner, wan·nest.** pallid. **wan·ness**, *n.*

wand, *n.* long, slender rod.

wan·der, *v.* roam; stray; err. *n.* stroll.

wan·der·lust, *n.* desire to wander.

wane, *v.*, **waned, wan·ing.** diminish; grow less. *n.* decline.

wan·gle, *v.*, **-gled, -gling.** *inf.* accomplish by devious means.

want, *v.* need; lack; desire. *n.* lack; poverty; desire.

want·ing, *a.* lacking; deficient. *prep.* without; minus.

wan·ton, *a.* lustful; unprovoked; excessive. *n.* lustful person. *v.* waste recklessly; carouse.

wap·i·ti, *n. pl.*, **-ties, -ti.** elk.

war, *n.* military conflict. **warred, war·ring.** make war.

war·ble, *v.*, **-bled, -bling.** sing in a trilling manner. *n.* flow of melodious sounds.

war cry, *n.* battle slogan.

ward, *v.* fend off. *n.* minor under one's care; voting district; prison or hospital division.

war·den, *n.* guardian; custodian; chief official of a prison.

ward·robe, *n.* cabinet for clothes; wearing apparel.

ware, *n. Usu. pl.* articles of merchandise; pottery.

ware·house, *n.* building in which goods are kept.

war·fare, *n.* military struggle.

war·head, *n.* explosive part of a bomb.

war·lock, *n.* male witch.

warm, *a.*, **warm·er, warm·est.** moderately warm; sympathetic; intimate; lively. *v.* make warm; excite.

warm-heart·ed, warm·heart·ed, *a.* cordial.

war·mon·ger, *n.* one who advocates war.

warmth, *n.* gentle heat; hearty kindness; zeal; slight anger.

warn, *v.* give caution.

warn·ing, *n.* admonishment.

warp, *v.* change the shape; pervert; deviate. *n.* twist; mental quirk; towline.

war-rant, *n.* authorization; security. *v.* authorize; justify; guarantee.

war-ran-ty, *n. pl.*, **-ties.** guarantee.

war-ren, *n.* buildings containing many tenants in limited quarters.

war-ri-or, *n.* soldier.

wart, *n.* small nonmalignant lesion.

wart hog, *n.* wild swine.

war-y, *a.*, **-i-er**, **-i-est.** on one's guard; careful. **war-i-ly**, *adv.* **war-i-ness**, *n.*

was, past tense of the first and third person singular of the verb *to be*.

wash, *v.* clean with water or other liquid; flow against or through; remove by the flow of water. *n.* items washed; liquid used for wetting; rush of water; wake. **wash-cloth**, *n.*

wash-er, *n.* washing machine; flat ring used to give tightness to a joint.

wash-ing, *n.* articles washed at one time; material obtained after washing soil.

wash-out, *n.* loss of earth by heavy rains. *inf.* failure.

wash-room, *n.* room containing washbowls and other toilet facilities.

wash-stand, *n.* piece of furniture which holds toiletry articles.

wash-tub, *n.* tub for use in washing clothes.

was-n't, contraction of was not.

wasp, *n.* stinging insect.

was-sail, *n.* drinking toast; spiced ale.

Was-ser-mann test, *n.* syphilis detection test.

wast-age, *n.* loss by use.

waste, *v.*, **wast-ed, wast-ing.** consume foolishly; fail to use; consume gradually; wear down. *n.* useless consumption; neglect; ruin; anything left over. *pl.* excrement. *a.* not used; uninhabited; left over.

waste-land, *n.* barren area.

wast-rel, *n.* spendthrift.

watch, *v.* keep vigil; guard; wait; tend; to look for. *n.* vigil; guards; time; on guard; small timepiece; period of duty for a ship's crew.

watch-ful, *a.* alert.

watch-man, *n. pl.*, **-men.** guardi-

an.

watch-word, *n.* password.

wa-ter, *n.* liquid which constitutes rain, lakes, etc.; particular body of water; aqueous organic secretion. *v.* moisten; supply with water; dilute.

wa-ter chest-nut, *n.* aquatic plants with nutlike fruit.

wa-ter clock, *n.* device which measures time by water flow.

wa-ter-col-or, *n.* paint in which the pigment is mixed with water.

wa-ter-course, *n.* stream of water; natural channel.

wa-ter-cress, *n.* perennial of the mustard family used for salad.

wa-ter-fall, *n.* perpendicular cascade of the water.

wa-ter-fowl, *n. pl.*, **-fowls, -fowl.** swimming game bird.

wa-ter-front, *n.* land abutting on a body of water.

wa-ter lil-y, *n. pl.*, **lil-ies**, aquatic plant with showy flowers.

wa-ter-logged, *a.* excessively saturated with water.

wa-ter main, *n.* principal pipe which conveys water.

wa-ter-mark, *n.* mark indicating the height to which water rises; faint letter on paper.

wa-ter-mel-on, *n.* large edible fruit.

wa-ter moc-ca-sin, *n.* large venomous viper.

wa-ter pow-er, *n.* power of water used to drive machinery.

wa-ter-proof, *a.* impervious to water. *n.* waterproof material.

wa-ter-side, *n.* bank of a river.

wa-ter sof-ten-er, *n.* chemical substance used in the treatment of hard water.

wa-ter-spout, *n.* tornadolike storm over the sea; drainpipe.

wa-ter-tight, *a.* foolproof.

wa-ter va-por, *n.* water in a gaseous state.

wa-ter-way, *n.* body of water as a way of transport.

wa-ter-works, *n. pl.* city sanitation plant.

wa-ter-y, *a.* full of water; resembling water; vapid.

watt, *n.* unit of electric power.

watt-age, *n.* amount of power.

watt-hour, *n.* unit of energy.

wave, *n.* moving swell; surge of emotion; undulation; spell of extreme weather; a waving. *v.*, **waved, wav-ing.** flutter; undulate; beckon.

wa·ver, v. sway; flutter; hesitate; totter. n. act of wavering.

wav·y, a., **-i·er, -i·est.** swelling in waves; undulation.

wax, n. pl., **wax·es.** solid, yellowish secretion discharged by bees; paraffin. v., **waxed, wax·ing.** coat with wax; increase in size. **wax·y**, a., **-i·er, -i·est.**

wax·en, a. made of wax; pale.

wax myr·tle, n. tree that bears small waxy berries.

wax·wing, n. crested bird.

wax·work, n. paraffin figures.

way, n. manner; respect; direction; distance; path; condition. **un·der way**, in motion.

way·far·er, n. traveler.

way·lay, v., **-laid, -lay·ing.** intercept; ambush.

way·side, n. edge of a road. a. situated near the side.

way·ward, a. forward; disobedient.

we, pron. nominative pl. of 'I'.

weak, a. not strong; deficient; wanting; ineffectual.

weak·en, v. make weak.

weak-kneed, a. yielding to intimidation.

weak·ling, n. ineffectual person.

weak·ly, a., **-li·er, -li·est.** feeble.

weak-mind·ed, a. irresolute.

weak·ness, n. feebleness; failing.

wealth, n. affluence; material possessions.

wealth·y, a., **-i·er, -i·est.** affluent. **wealth·i·ness**, n.

wean, v. stop suckling; alienate.

weap·on, n. instrument of offense or defense.

weap·on·ry, n. assorted weapons.

wear, v. past **wore**, pp. **worn**, ppr. **wear·ing.** have on the body; use habitually; waste; exhaust. n. clothing; diminution; durability.

wear·ing, a. fatiguing.

wea·ri·some, a. tiresome; irksome.

wea·ry, a., **-ri·er, -ri·est.** tired; impatient; boring. v., **-ried, -ry·ing.** exhaust; harass. **wea·ri·ness**, n.

wea·sel, n. pl., **-sels, -sel.** small carnivorous mammal. v. be deceptive.

weath·er, n. state of the atmosphere with respect to temperature. v. expose to the effects of; bear up.

weath·er-beat·en, a. worn by the weather.

weath·er·glass, n. barometer.

weath·er·man, n. pl., **-men.** weather forecaster.

weath·er-proof, a. able to withstand exposure to weather.

weave, v. past **wove** or **weaved**, pp. **wov·en** or **wove**, ppr. **weav·ing.** form fabric by interlacing threads; zigzag. n. style of weaving.

web, n. woven fabric; cobweb; network. v., **webbed, web·bing.** ensnare; form a web.

web·bing, n. woven material of hemp.

wed, v., **wed·ded** or **wed, wed·ding.** marry; unite closely.

we'd, contraction of we should, we had, or we would.

wed·ding, n. marriage ceremony.

wedge, n. piece of wood tapering to a thin edge; breach. v., **wedged, wedg·ing.** split with a wedge; compress.

wed·lock, n. matrimony.

Wednes·day, n. fourth day of the week.

wee, a. **we·er, we·est.** tiny; extremely early.

weed, n. troublesome plant. v. free from weeds; remove as undesirable.

weed·y, a., **-i·er, -i·est.** abounding with weeds. inf. scrawny.

week, n. period of seven consecutive days; workweek.

week·day, n. any day of the week except Saturday and Sunday.

week·end, n. period from Friday night to Sunday night.

week·ly, a. happening once a week. adv. once a week.

weep, v., **wept, weep·ing.** shed tears.

wee·vil, n. various destructive beetles.

weigh, v. measure the gravitational pull on; compare; measure by weight.

weight, n. amount of heaviness; object used for holding something down; burden; pressure. v. add weight to; burden with.

weight·y, a., **-i·er, -i·est.** ponderous.

weir, n. dam.

weird, a., **weird·er, weird·est.** unearthly; eerie; odd.

wel·come, *a.* received happily; pleasing. *n.* warm salutation. *v.,* **-comed, -com·ing.** receive hospitably.

weld, *v.* fuse by heating.

wel·fare, *n.* condition of well-being.

well, *n.* spring; shaft reservoir. *v.* gush from. *adv.,* **bet·ter, best.** advantageous; sufficiently; intimately. *a.* satisfactory; proper. *int.* expression of surprise.

we'll, contraction of we will or we shall.

well-be·ing, *n.* happiness and good health.

well-bred, *a.* polite.

well-dis·posed, *a.* favorably inclined.

well-groomed, *a.* neat.

well-known, *a.* famous.

well-nigh, *adv.* almost.

well-off, *a.* financially secure.

well-read, *a.* knowledgeable.

well-spring, *n.* stream's source; unflagging source.

well-thought-of, *a.* highly regarded.

well-timed, *a.* opportune.

well-to-do, *a.* prosperous.

welt, *n.* decorative seam; stripe raised on the skin.

wel·ter, *v.* wallow. *n.* turmoil.

wench, *n.* young woman.

wend, *v.* direct.

were, past indicative plural and second person singular of be.

we're, contraction of we are.

weren't, contraction of were not.

were·wolf, wer·wolf, *n.* man transformed into a wolf.

west, *n.* point where the sun is seen to set at the equinox. *a.* lying toward the west. *adv.* westward. **west·er·ly,** *a.*

west·ern, *a.* being in, or of the west.

west·ern·er, *n.* inhabitant of the West.

west·ern·ize, *v.,* **-ized, -iz·ing.** render western in character. **west·ern·i·za·tion,** *n.*

west·ward, *adv.* toward the west.

wet, *a.,* **wet·ter, wet·test.** soaked with water; not totally dry. *n.* moisture; rain. *v.,* *past* wet or **wet·ted,** moisten; drench.

wet·back, *n. inf.* person who illegally enters the U.S.

we've, contraction of we have.

whack, *v. inf.* give a hearty blow

to. *n. inf.* hearty blow.

whale, *n.* very large, fishlike mammal. *v.,* **whaled, whal·ing.** hunt for whales; thrash soundly.

whale·bone, *n.* horny substance in whale's palate.

wharf, *n. pl.,* **wharves, wharfs.** docking structure for boats.

what, *pron., pl.,* **what.** used in asking for; that which; how much? *a.* whatever; how much? *adv.* to what extent or degree. *int.* used to express surprise. **what if,** supposing. **what's what,** true nature of things.

what·ev·er, *pron.* anything that; what not; any amount; what. *a.* any; that no matter.

what-not, *n.* bric-a-brac cabinet.

what·so·ev·er, *pron., a.* whatever.

wheat, *n.* grain of cereal grass.

whee·dle, *v.,* **-dled, -dling.** coax; cajole. **whee·dler,** *n.*

wheel, *n.* circular disk which turns on an axis. *inf.* important person. *v.* rotate; roll along on wheels.

wheel·bar·row, *n.* single wheeled box with handles.

wheel-chair, *n.* chair mounted on wheels.

wheeze, *v.,* **wheezed, wheez·ing.** breathe with difficulty and a whistling sound. **wheez·y,** *a.*

whelk, *n.* sea mollusk.

whelp, *n.* puppy; cub.

when, *adv.* at what time. *conj.* at what time; if; after which. *pron.* what time. *n.* time of anything.

whence, *adv.* from what cause. *conj.* from what place.

when·ev·er, *conj.* at whatever time. *adv. inf.* when.

where, *adv.* in or at what place; in what part; in what position; *conj.* in or at what place; in or at the place at which; to what place. *n.* the place of something.

where·a·bouts, *adv.* where. *conj.* near. *n. pl., sing. or pl. in constr.* locality.

where·as, *conj.* when in fact.

where·by, *adv., conj.* by; by what.

where·in, *adv.* in what; how. *conj.* in what or which.

where·to, *adv.* whither.

where·up·on, *adv.* whereon. *conj.* at which.

wher·ev·er, *adv.* where. *conj.* in, at, or to.

where·with·al, *n.* resources.

whet, *v.,* **whet·ted, whet·ting.** sharpen; stimulate.

wheth·er, *conj.* term introducing alternatives.

whew, *interj.* whistling exclamation.

whey, *n.* watery part of milk.

which, *pron.* what one; that or which. *a.* what one; whichever.

which·ev·er, *a.* no matter which. *pron.* anyone.

whiff, *n.* puff.

while, *n.* space of time. *conj.* during or in the time that. *v.,* **whiled, whil·ing.** cause time to pass.

whim, *n.* capricious notion.

whim·per, *v.* cry with a low, whining voice. *n.* peevish cry.

whim·si·cal, *a.* capricious; odd. **whim·sy,** *n.*

whine, *v.,* **whined, whin·ing.** whimper. *n.* petty complaint.

whin·ny, *v.,* **-nied, -ny·ing.** neigh. *n. pl.* **-nies.** cry of a horse.

whip, *v.,* **whipped** or **whipt, whip·ping.** flog; drive on; defeat; beat into a froth; overcast; start suddenly. *n.* rod with a lash; type of dessert.

whip·lash, *n.* injury to the neck.

whip·per·snap·per, *n.* impertinent person.

whip·poor·will, *n.* bird of the goatsucker family.

whir, whirr, *v.,* **whirred, whir·ring.** whiz with a buzzing sound. *n.* buzzing sound.

whirl, *v.* spin rapidly. *n.* rapid rotation.

whirl·i·gig, *n.* something that revolves.

whirl·pool, *n.* circular eddy.

whirl·wind, *n.* spiraling mass of air; violent activity.

whisk, *v.* move with a rapid, sweeping stroke.

whisk broom, *n.* short-handled, small broom.

whisk·er, *n. pl.* hair on a man's face; bristly hairs growing about an animal's mouth.

whis·key, whis·ky, *n., pl.,* **-keys, -kies.** alcoholic liquor made from grain.

whis·per, *v.* talk softly. *n.* soft, rustling sound.

whist, *n.* card game.

whis·tle, *v.,* **-tled, -tling.** make a

clear musical sound through the teeth. *n.* instrument for producing whistling sounds.

whit, *n.* iota.

white, *a.,* **whit·er, whit·est.** of the color of pure snow; pale; pure. *n.* achromatic color without hue.

white-col·lar, *a.* of clerical or professional employees.

white flag, *n.* token of truce.

white lie, *n.* harmless falsehood.

whit·en, *v.* bleach; blanch.

white·wash, *n.* liquid of lime used for whitening walls. *v. inf.* cover up errors.

white wa·ter, *n.* water in rapids.

whith·er, *adv.* where. *conj.* to which place.

whit·ing, *n.* material made from chalk.

whit·tle, *v.,* **-tled, -tling.** cut wood by removing small chips.

whiz, whizz, *v.,* **whizzed, whiz·zing.** make a humming sound; rush. *n. pl.,* **-zes.** sound between hissing and humming.

who, *pron., nom.* **who,** *poss.* **whose,** *obj.* **whom.** what person; of a person; that.

whoa, *int.* stop!

who·ev·er, *pron., nom.* **who·ev·er,** *poss.* **whos·ev·er,** *obj.* **whom·ev·er.** anyone who; whatever person.

whole, *a.* well; entire; intact. *n.* entire thing; total.

whole-heart·ed, *a.* hearty.

whole-num·ber, *n.* integer.

whole·sale, *n.* sale of large quantities to retailers. *a.* indiscriminate. *adv.* in bulk.

whole·some, *a.* healthful; morally good.

whole·wheat, *a.* made with the entire wheat grain.

whol·ly, *adv.* totally; quite.

whom, *pron.* objective case of *who.*

whom·ev·er, *pron.* objective case of *whoever.*

whoop, *n.* loud cry. *v.* utter a loud cry.

whop·per, *n. inf.* big lie.

whop·ping, *a. inf.* thumping; huge.

whore, *n.* prostitute.

whorl, *n.* anything having the shape or appearance of a coil.

whose, *pron.* possessive case of *who.*

why, *adv.* for what cause; wherefore. *n. pl.,* **whys.** reason. *conj.* reason for which.

wick, *n.* piece of cord for burning in a candle, etc.

wick·ed, *a.* evil; malicious.

wick·er, *n.* small pliant twig. *a.* made of plaited twigs.

wide, *a.,* **wid·er, wid·est.** broad; of a limited width; vast. *adv.* over a specified distance.

wide-a·wake, *a.* alert.

wide-eyed, *a.* naive.

wid·en, *v.* extend in breadth.

wide·spread, *a.* broadly accepted.

wid·ow, *n.* woman who's husband has died.

wid·ow·er, *n.* man who's wife has died. **wid·ow·hood,** *n.*

width, *n.* measure taken from side to side.

wield, *v.* exert influence; use with skill.

wie·ner, *n.* frankfurter.

wife, *n. pl.,* **wives.** married woman.

wig, *n.* artificial hair.

wig·gle, *v.,* **-gled, -gling.** move quickly and irregularly. **wig·gly,** *a.*

wig-wag, *v.,* **-wagged, -wag·ging.** move to and fro.

wig·wam, *n.* American Indian hut.

wild, *a.* in its natural state; uninhabited; unruly; fantastic. *adv.* in a wild manner. *n.* Often pl. wilderness.

wild boar, *n.* old-world hog.

wild·cat strike, *n.* unauthorized walk-out.

wil·der·ness, *n.* wild region.

wild·fire, *n.* highly inflammable composition; something that spreads with great rapidity.

wild-goose chase, *n.* earnest pursuit of the unattainable.

wild·wood, *n.* forest land.

wile, *n.* guile. *v.,* **wiled, wil·ing.** turn away.

will, *aux. v., past* **would.** used before the infinitive to show: futurity; inevitability; willingness; capability.

will, *n.* choice; wish; determination; legal declaration of a person's disposition of property. *v.* decide; bequeath.

will·ful, wil·ful, *a.* obstinate; intentional.

wil·lies, *n. pl. inf.* jitters.

will·ing, *a.* not averse; ready.

wil·low, *n.* various shrubs with pliable branches.

wil·low·y, *a.* slender and graceful.

will pow·er, *n.* self-control.

wil·ly-nil·ly, *adv.* willingly or unwillingly.

wilt, *v.* wither. *n.* plant disease.

win, *v.,* **won, win·ing.** gain the victory; get by effort; persuade. *n.* success.

wince, *v.,* **winced, winc·ing.** recoil; shrink back. *n.* sudden start.

winch, *n.* hoisting machine. *v.* move with a winch.

wind, *n.* air in motion; gale; breath; idle talk. *pl.* wind instruments. *v.* make short of breath.

wind, *v.,* **wound, wind·ing.** change direction; meander; coil; turn. *n.* bend or turn.

wind·ed, *a.* out of breath.

wind·fall, *n.* unexpected legacy.

wind·ing, *n.* bend; coiling.

wind in·stru·ment, *n.* instrument played by breath.

wind·lass, *n.* hauling apparatus.

wind·mill, *n.* machine operated by the wind.

win·dow, *n.* opening in the wall.

win·dow-pane, *n.* plate of glass in a window.

wind·pipe, *n.* trachea.

wind·shield, *n.* framed shield of glass.

wind-up, *n.* concluding part.

wind·ward, *n.* direction from which the wind blows. *adv.* toward the wind.

wind·y, *a.,* **-i·er, -i·est.** windswept; verbose.

wine, *n.* fermented juice of the grape.

win·er·y, *n. pl.,* **-ies.** establishment for making wine.

wine·skin, *n.* vessel made of animal skin, used for holding wine.

wing, *n.* appendages adapted for flight.

wink, *v.* close and open one eyelid rapidly; blink; twinkle. *n.* winking; instant.

win·ner, *n.* victor.

win·ning, *n.* victory. *Usu. pl.* sum won by victory. *a.* successful; engaging.

win·now, *v.* analyze; sift.

win·some, *a.* agreeable; engaging.

win·ter, *n.* cold season of the year. *a.* relating to winter. *v.* spend the winter.

win·ter·ize, *v.,* **-ized, -iz·ing.** put in readiness for cold winter weather.

win·try, *a.*, **-tri·er**, **-tri·est.** cold; bleak.

wipe, *v.*, **wiped**, **wip·ing.** rub lightly; blot out. *n.* act of wiping; rub.

wire, *n.* flexible thread of metal; cable. *inf.* telegram. *a.* of a wire. *v.*, **wired**, **wir·ing.** bind with wire; equip with wire.

wire-tap, *v.*, **-tapped**, **-tap·ping.** monitor secretly. *n.* concealed device to intercept information.

wir·ing, *n.* system of wires.

wir·y, *a.*, **-ri·er**, **-ri·est.** tough; sinewy.

wis·dom, *n.* being wise; sound judgment.

wise, *a.*, **wis·er**, **wis·est.** judicious; sage; learned. *n.* manner; method.

wise-crack, *n.* *inf.* facetious remark.

wish, *v.* long for; desire; invoke upon. *n.* desire; a longing.

wish·ful, *a.* desirous.

wish·y-wash·y, *a.* diluted; unsubstantial.

wisp, *n.* something delicate or tiny. **wisp·y**, *a.*

wis·te·ri·a, *n.* various climbing shrubs. *Also* **wis·tar·i·a**, *a.*

wist·ful, *a.* pensive.

wit, *n.* intelligence; keen perception; one having a talent for clever conversation. **at one's wits' end**, befuddled.

witch, *n. pl.*, **witch·es.** sorceress; hag. *v.* bewitch; enchant. **witch·craft**, *n.*

with, *prep.* accompanying; in some particular relation to; by means or use of; in proportion to; in regard to; in the course of; current; in spite of; from; against; on the side of.

with·draw, *v.*, *past.* **-drew**, *pp.* **-drawn**, *ppr.* **-draw·ing.** pull out; retreat; remove; recall. **with·draw·n**, *a.* **with·draw·al**, *n.*

with·er, *v.* dry and shrivel up; embarrass. **with·ered**, *a.* **with·er·ing**, *a.*

with·hold, *v.*, **-held**, **-hold·ing.** restrain; refuse to grant.

with·in, *prep.* inside of; not beyond. *adv.* inwardly; internally. *n.* inside part.

with·out, *prep.* out of; beyond; not having. *adv.* externally; lacking. *n.* outer place.

with·stand, *v.*, **-stood**, **-stand·ing.** resist; oppose.

wit·less, *a.* senseless; silly.

wit·ness, *n.* personal observer; testimony. *v.* give evidence; testify.

wit·ti·cism, *n.* clever phrase.

wit·ting, *a.* aware.

wit·ty, *a.*, **-ti·er**, **-ti·est.** cleverly facetious; amusing.

wiz·ard, *n.* magician; enchanter. **wiz·ard·ry**, *n.*

wiz·en, *a.* shriveled. *v.* wither. **wiz·ened**, *a.*

wob·ble, *v.*, **-bled**, **-bling.** vacillate; tremble or falter. *n.* wavering. **wob·bly**, *a.*

woe, *n.* grief. *int.* expression of sorrow.

woe·ful, **wo·ful**, *a.* piteous.

wolf, *n. pl.*, **wolves.** wild carnivorous mammal. *v.* gulp down.

wom·an, *n. pl.*, **-en.** female of the human race. **wom·an·hood**, *n.*

wom·an·kind, *n.* female sex.

womb, *n.* uterus.

wom·bat, *n.* marsupial mammal.

wom·en's rights, *n. pl.* legal rights of women, equal to men. *Also* **wom·an's rights.**

won·der, *v.* think with curiosity; speculate. *n.* surprising thing; feeling of surprise.

won·der·ful, *a.* astonishing.

won·der·ment, *n.* surprise.

wont, *a.* accustomed. *n.* habit.

won't, contraction of will not.

woo, *v.*, **wood**, **woo·ing.** court; solicit.

wood, *n.* hard fibrous substance under a tree's bark.

wood·bine, *n.* honeysuckle.

wood·chuck, *n.* burrowing marmot.

wood·craft, *n.* skill in anything which pertains to woods.

wood·cut, *n.* engraved wood block used for making prints.

wood·en, *a.* made of wood; without expression.

wood·land, *n.* land covered with trees.

wood·peck·er, *n.* bird that bores holes into wood.

wood·pile, *n.* stack of cut wood.

wood·wind, *n.* wind instrument.

wood·work, *n.* part of any structure that is made of wood.

wood·y, *a.*, **-i·er**, **-i·est.** abounding with wood. **wood·i·ness**, *n.*

woof, *n.* weft; texture.

wool, *n.* fleece of sheep; cloth made of wool. **wool·en**, **wooll·en**, *a.*

wool·gath·er·ing, *n.* indulgence

in idle fancies.

wool·ly, wool·y, *a.,* **-li·er, -li·est.** fleecelike; wool-bearing.

wooz·y, *a.,* **-i·er, -i·est.** muddled.

word, *n.* speech sound or sounds as a unit; something said; command; promise. *v.* express in words; phrase.

word-book, *n.* lexicon.

word for word, *adv.* verbatim.

word·ing, *n.* phraseology.

word·less, *a.* silent; unexpressed. **word·less·ly,** *adv.*

word·y, *a.,* **-i·er, -i·est.** verbose.

word·i·ly, *adv.* **word·i·ness,** *n.*

work, *n.* labor; employment; task; act. *pl. but usu. sing. in constr.* place of employment. *v.* labor; be employed; operate effectively; cause; achieve by effort. **the works,** *inf.* everything possible.

work·a·ble, *a.* possible.

work·a·day, *a.* commonplace.

work-book, *n.* consumable textbook.

worked-up, *a.* excited.

work·er, *n.* laborer.

work·ing, *a.* engaged in work. *n.* operation; movement.

work·ing class, *n. pl.,* **class·es.** proletariat. **work·ing-class,** *a.*

work·man, *pl.,* **-men.** manual laborer.

work·man·like, *a.* skillful.

work·man·ship, *n.* skill of a workman.

work·out, *n. inf.* rigorous activity.

work·shop, *n.* place one works; discussion group.

world, *n.* planet earth; sphere of existence; mankind; realm. *Often pl.* great quantity.

world·ly, *a.,* **-li·er, -li·est.** secular; earthly. **world·li·ness,** *n.*

world·ly-wise, *a.* wise as to the affairs of this world.

world-wide, *a.* spread throughout the world.

worm, *n.* small slim invertebrate. wretch. *v.* insinuate; grovel.

worm-eat·en, *a.* decayed.

worm·y, *a.,* **-i·er, -i·est.** infested with worms; groveling.

worn, *a.* exhausted; impaired by wear.

worn-out, *a.* wearied.

wor·ri·some, *a.* annoying; anxious.

wor·ry, *v.,* **-ried, -ry·ing.** torment; fret; trouble. *n. pl.,* **-ries.** uneasiness; anxiety.

worse, *a., irreg. compar.* of **bad** and **ill.** more unsatisfactory; in poorer health. *n.* that which is worse; *adv.* more evil; with greater intensity.

wors·en, *v.* become worse.

wor·ship, *n.* religious exercises; reverence; loving devotion. *v.* pay divine honors to; idolize.

wor·ship·ful, *a.* honorable.

worst, *a., irreg. superl.* of **bad** and **ill.** most faulty; most wicked; most injurious; in the poorest condition. *n.* worst state. *adv.* in the worst manner; greatest intensity.

wor·sted, *n.* firmly twisted yarn.

worth, *n.* value; wealth; sum in money. *a.* equal in value; deserving of. **worth·less,** *a.*

worth·while, *a.* such as to repay one's time, trouble.

wor·thy, *a.,* **-thi·er, -thi·est.** valuable; deserving praise. **wor·thi·ly,** *adv.* **wor·thi·ness,** *n.*

would, *aux. v.* past and pp. of *will.* used to convey: mood; intent; condition; uncertainty; future statement.

would-be, *a.* wishing; pretending.

would·n't contraction of would not.

wound, *n.* cut in the skin; injury. *v.* inflict a wound; hurt the feelings of.

wow, *int. inf.* exclamation of surprise. *v. inf.* please greatly.

wraith, *n.* ghost.

wran·gle, *v.,* **-gled, -gling.** brawl; altercate. *n.* noisy quarrel.

wran·gler, *n.*

wrap, *v.,* **wrapped, wrap·ping.** fold about; enclose. *n. pl.* outdoor garments. **wrapped up in,** *inf.* involved in. **keep un·der wraps.** *inf.* keep secret.

wrath, *n.* violent anger.

wreak, *v.* cause to take effect; give vent to.

wreath, *n. pl.,* **wreaths.** garland.

wreck, *n.* something in a state of ruin. someone in poor health. *v.* cause the ruin of.

wreck·age, *n.* anything demolished.

wreck·er, *n.* machine or person which wrecks; plunderer.

wren, *n.* small bird.

wrench, *n.* violent twist; emotional shock; tool for turning nuts or bolts.

wrest, *v.* twist; extort.

wres·tle, *v.,* **-tled, -tling.** contend

by grappling; struggle.

wretch, *n.* miserable person.

wretch·ed, *a.* miserable; very poor.

wrig·gle, *v.,* **-gled, -gling.** move by writhing. *n.* quick twisting motion.

wring, *v.,* **wrung, wring·ing.** twist and squeeze; torture. *n.* twisting.

wrin·kle, *n.* small crease or fold. *v.,* **-kled, -kling.** crease.

wrist, *n.* joint by which the hand is united to the arm.

writ, *n.* written order.

write, *v. past* **wrote,** *pp.* **written,** *ppr.* **writ·ing.** form or trace words; work as a writer.

writ·er, *n.* author.

writhe, *v.,* **writhed, writh·ing.** twist the body about; distort. *n.* twisted shape.

writ·ing, *n.* written form; inscription; literary work.

wrong, *a.* not right; inaccurate. *n.* anything unjust; injury. *adv.* in a wrong manner. *v.* treat with injustice; deal harshly.

wronged, *a.* harmed.

wroth, *a.* very angry.

wrought, *a.* not rough; beaten and shaped with a hammer.

wrought-up, *a.* excited.

wry, *a.,* **wri·er, wri·est.** twisted; ironically humorous.

X-Y-Z

X-chro·mo·some, *n.* female sex chromosome.

xe·non, *n.* colorless, inert gaseous element.

xen·o·pho·bi·a, *n.* hatred, fear of foreigners.

Xmas, *n.* Christmas.

x-ray, *n.* electromagnetic ray used in medical diagnosis. *v.* examine or treat with x-rays.

xy·lem, *n.* woody conductive tissue of plants.

xy·lo·phone, *n.* musical instrument. **xy·lo·phon·ist,** *n.*

yacht, *n.* pleasure ship. **yacht·ing,** *n.* **yachts·man,** *n.*

yak, *n. pl.,* **yaks, yak.** Tibetan ox.

yam, *n.* sweet potato.

yank, *v.* jerk.

Yan·kee, *n.* native of northern U.S. states; northern soldier in the American Civil War; native of the U.S.

yap, *v.,* **yapped, yap·ping.** yelp.

yard, *n.* linear unit of measure (3 feet); enclosed area outdoors.

yard·age, *n.* amount in yards.

yard goods, *n.* fabrics.

yard·stick, *n.* measuring stick a yard long.

yarn, *n.* thread spun from wool. *inf.* story or tale.

yar·row, *n.* perennial plant.

yaw, *v.* deviate. *n.* deviation.

yawn, *v.* open mouth involuntarily with a long inhalation of air.

Y-chro·mo·some, *n.* male sex chromosome.

ye, *def. art.* old printed form of 'the'; *pron.* you.

yea, *adv.* yes.

year, *n.* period of 365 or 366 days. **year·ly,** *adj. adv.*

year·ling, *n.* animal one year old.

yearn, *v.* desire. **yearn·ing,** *n.*

yeast, *n.* yellowish substance used to ferment liquor, leaven bread, etc. **yeast·y,** *a.,* **-i·er, -i·est.**

yell, *v.* shout loudly.

yel·low, *a.* color of butter, lemons, etc. *inf.* cowardly. **yel·low·ish,** *a.*

yel·low·bird, *n.* goldfinch.

yel·low·fe·ver, *n.* infectious tropical disease. Also **yel·low·jack.**

yel·low·jack·et, *n.* yellow-striped wasp.

yelp, *v.* cry out sharply. *n.* sharp bark or cry.

yen, *n. inf.* intense desire.

yeo·man, *n. pl.,* **-men.** petty officer in the Navy; independent farmer.

yes, *adv.* expression of affirmation.

ye·shi·va, *n. pl.,* **-vas.** Jewish education institution.

yes·ter·day, *n.* day before today.

yet, *adv.* still; in addition; further; nevertheless. *conj.* however.

yet·i, *n.* abominable snowman.

yew, *n.* evergreen tree.

yield, *v.* produce; give up; surrender. *n.* that which is yielded.

yield·ing, *a.* unresisting.

yip, *v.,* **yipped, yip·ping.** yelp.

yo·del, *v.,* **-deled, -del·ing.** sing, changing to and from falsetto. **yo·del·er,** *n.*

yo·ga, *n.* system of physical and mental exercises based on

Hindu theistic philosophy.

yo·gi, *n. pl.*, *-gis.* one who practices or teaches yoga.

yo·gurt, *n.* fermented milk product.

yoke, *n.* crosspiece for joining two oxen. *v.*, yoked, yok·ing. couple; unite.

yo·kel, *n.* rustic.

yolk, *n.* yellow of an egg.

yon·der, *adv.* there. *a.*

yore, *n.* distant past.

you, *pron.* person or persons addressed.

young, *a.* in early stages of life; new. *n.* youth, collectively.

young·ster, *n.* child.

your, *pronominal a.* possessive of *you*. yours, *pron.*

your·self, *pron. pl.*, *-selves.* emphatic or reflexive form of *you*.

youth, *n. pl.*, youth, youths. youthfulness; a young individual; young persons collectively. youth·ful, *a.*

yowl, *v.* howl. *n.*

yuc·ca, *n.* tropical American plant.

yule, *n.* Christmas.

yule·tide, *n.* Christmas season.

yum·my, *a.*, *-mi·er*, *-mi·est. inf.* delicious.

za·ny, *n. pl.*, *-nies.* clown; *a.*, *-ni·er*, *-ni·est.* silly. za·ni·ly, *adv.* za·ni·ness, *n.*

zeal, *n.* passionate ardor; earnestness. zeal·ous, *a.*

zeal·ot, *n.* fanatic.

ze·bra, *n. pl.*, *-bras*, *-bra.* wild, striped, horselike animal.

Zen, *n.* form of Buddhism.

ze·nith, *n.* vertical point of the heavens; highest point.

zeph·yr, *n.* mild breeze.

zep·pe·lin, *n.* large, rigid dirigible.

ze·ro, *n. pl.*, *-ros*, *-roes.* number

that indicates the absence of quantity; origin; nonentity; nil. *a.* nonexistent; lacking.

ze·ro hour, *n.* starting time.

zest, *n.* relish; enjoyment; gusto, zest·y, *a.*

zig·zag, *n.* line going sharply back and forth. *a. adv.* in a zigzag manner. *v.*, zagged, zag·ging. proceed in a zigzag course.

zinc, *n.* bluish metallic element.

zinc ox·ide, *n.* salve of zinc and oxygen.

zing, *n.* sharp, high-pitched whining sound.

zin·ni·a, *n.* bright, flowering plant.

Zi·on·ism, *n.* Hebrew colonization of Palestine.

zip, *n. inf.* vim. *v.*, zipped, zip·ping. *inf.* move speedily.

zip·per, *n.* fastener with interlocking edges. zip, *v.*, zipped, zip·ping.

zip·py, *a.*, *-pi·er*, *-pi·est.* energetic; peppy.

zith·er, *n.* stringed, musical instrument.

zo·di·ac, *n.* imaginary belt of the heavens.

zom·bie, zom·bi, *n.* reanimated corpse.

zone, *n.* area. *v.*, zoned, zon·ing. divide into zones. zon·al, *a.*

zoo, *n. pl.*, zoos. living animal display.

zo·ol·o·gy, *n.* science of animals. zo·ol·o·gist, *n.* zo·o·log·i·cal, *a.*

zoom, *v.i.* speed sharply upward.

zuc·chi·ni, *n. pl.*, *-ni*, *-nis.* slender summer squash.

zwie·back, *n.* kind of dried bread.

zy·gote, *n.* cell formed by the union of two gametes.

METRIC SYSTEM

Linear Measure

Unit	U.S. equivalent
square millimeter (mm²)	0.00155 square inch
square centimeter (cm²)	0.155 square inch
centare (ca) or square meter (m²)	10.76 square feet
deciare (da)	11.96 square yards
aretare (a) or square dekameter (dkm²)	119.60 square yards
dekare (dka)	0.247 acre
hectare (ha) or square hectometer (hm²)	2.471 acres
square kilometer (km²)	0.386 square mile

Area

Unit	U.S. equivalent
micron (μ)	0.00003937 inch, 0.03937 mil
millimeter (mm)	0.03937 inch, 39.37 mils
centimeter (cm)	0.3937 inch
decimeter (dm)	3.937 inches
meter (m)	39.37 inches
dekameter (dkm)	10.93 yards, 32.81 feet
hectometer (hm)	109.36 yards, 328.1 feet
kilometer (km)	0.6214 mile

Capacity

Unit	U.S. equivalent dry	U.S. equivalent liquid
milliliter (ml)	0.0018 pint	0.034 fluidounce
centiliter (cl)	0.018 pint	0.338 fluidounce
deciliter (dl)	0.18 pint	3.381 fluidounces
liter (l)	0.908 quart	1.057 quarts
dekaliter (dkl)	1.14 pecks	2.643 gallons
hectoliter (hl)	2.84 bushels	26.425 gallons
kiloliter (kl)	28.38 bushels	264.25 gallons

Volume

Unit	U.S. equivalent
cubic millimeter (mm³)	0.000061 cubic inch, 0.016 minim
cubic centimeter (cm³ or cc)	0.061 cubic inch
cubic decimeter (dm³)	61.02 cubic inches
decistere (ds)	3.53 cubic feet
stere (s) or cubic meter (m³)	1.308 cubic yards, 35.31 cubic feet
dekastere (dks)	13.079 cubic yards
cubic dekameter (dkm³)	1,307.943 cubic yards

Mass and Weight

Unit	U.S. equivalent (Avoirdupois weight)
milligram (mg)	0.0154 grain
centigram (cg)	0.154 grain
decigram (dg)	1.543 grains
gram (g or gm)	0.0353 ounce, 15.43 grains
dekagram (dkg)	0.353 ounce
hectogram (hg)	3.527 ounces
kilogram (kg)	2.205 pounds
metric ton (MT or t)	1.102 tons, 2,204.6 pounds

MEASURES AND WEIGHTS

UNIT		
		Avoirdupois
short ton		20 short hundredweight, 2000 lbs.
long ton		20 long hundredweight, 2240 lbs.
short hundredweight		100 lbs., 0.05 short tons
long hundredweight	WEIGHT	112 lbs., 0.05 long tons
pound (lb.)		16 oz., 7000 gr.
ounce (oz.)		16 drams, 437.5 gr.
pennyweight		
dram		27.343 gr., 0.0625 oz.
scruple		
grain (gr.)		0.036 drams, 0.002285 oz.
		U.S. liquid measure
bushel		
peck		
gallon		4 quarts (231 in.³)
quart		2 pints (57.75 in.³)
pint	CAPACITY	4 gills (28.875 in.³)
gill		4 fluidounces (7.218 in.³)
fluidounce		8 fluidrams (1.804 in.³)
fluidram		60 minims (0.225 in.³)
minim		1/60 fluidram (0.003759 in.³)
		Volume
cubic yard		27 ft.³, 46,656 in.³
cubic foot		1728 in.³, 0.0370 yd.³
cubic inch		0.00058 ft.³, 0.000021 yd.³
square mile		
acre		
square rod		
square yard	DIMENSION	
square foot		
square inch		
mile		
rod		
yard		
foot		
inch		

MEASURES AND WEIGHTS

UNIT		
		Troy
short ton		
long ton		
short hundredweight		
long hundredweight		
pound (lb.)	**WEIGHT**	12 oz., 240 pennyweight, 5760 gr.
ounce (oz.)		20 pennyweight, 480 gr.
pennyweight		24 gr., 0.05 oz.
dram		
scruple		0.042 pennyweight, 0.002083 oz.
grain (gr.)		
		U.S. dry measure
bushel		4 pecks (2150.42 in.³)
peck		8 quarts (537.605 in.³)
gallon		
quart	**CAPACITY**	2 pints (67.200 in.³)
pint		½ quart (33.600 in.³)
gill		
fluidounce		
fluidram		
minim		
		Area
cubic yard		
cubic foot		
cubic inch		
square mile		640 acres, 102,400 rods²
acre		4840 yd.², 43,560 ft.²
square rod	**DIMENSION**	30.25 yd.², 0.006 acres
square yard		1296 in.², 9 ft.²
square foot		144 in.², 0.111 yd.²
square inch		0.007 ft.², 0.00077 yd.²
mile		
rod		
yard		
foot		
inch		

UNIT		
		Apothecaries'
short ton		
long ton		
short hundredweight		
long hundredweight		
pound (lb.)	WEIGHT	12 oz., 5760 gr.
ounce (oz.)		8 drams, 480 gr.
pennyweight		
dram		3 scruples, 60 gr.
scruple		20 gr., 0.333 drams
grain (gr.)		0.05 scruples, 0.002083 oz.
		British liquid and dry measure
bushel		4 pecks (2219.36 in.³)
peck		2 gallons (554.84 in.³)
gallon		4 quarts (277.420 in.³)
quart	CAPACITY	2 pints (69.355 in.³)
pint		4 gills (34.678 in.³)
gill		5 fluidounces (8.669 in.³)
fluidounce		8 fluidrams (1.7339 in.³)
fluidram		60 minims (0.216734 in.³)
minim		1/60 fluidram (0.003612 in.³)
		Length
cubic yard		
cubic foot		
cubic inch		
square mile		
acre		
square rod	DIMENSION	
square yard		
square foot		
square inch		
mile		320 rods, 1760 yd., 5280 ft.
rod		5.50 yd., 16.5 ft.
yard		3 ft., 36 in.
foot		12 in., 0.333 yd.
inch		0.083 ft., 0.027 yd.

TABLE OF SQUARES, CUBES, SQUARE ROOTS, AND CUBE ROOTS

No.	Square	Cube	Square Root	Cube Root
1	1	1	1.000	1.000
2	4	8	1.414	1.260
3	9	27	1.732	1.442
4	16	64	2.000	1.587
5	25	125	2.236	1.710
6	36	216	2.449	1.817
7	49	343	2.646	1.913
8	64	512	2.828	2.000
9	81	729	3.000	2.080
10	100	1,000	3.162	2.154
11	121	1,331	3.317	2.224
12	144	1,728	3.464	2.289
13	169	2,197	3.606	2.351
14	196	2,744	3.742	2.410
15	225	3,375	3.873	2.466
16	256	4,096	4.000	2.520
17	289	4,913	4.123	2.571
18	324	5,832	4.243	2.621
19	361	6,859	4.359	2.668
20	400	8,000	4.472	2.714
21	441	9,261	4.583	2.759
22	484	10,648	4.690	2.802
23	529	12,167	4.796	2.844

No.	Square	Cube	Square Root	Cube Root
24	576	13,824	4.899	2.884
25	625	15,625	5.000	2.924
26	676	17,576	5.099	2.962
27	729	19,683	5.196	3.000
28	784	21,952	5.292	3.037
29	841	24,389	5.385	3.072
30	900	27,000	5.477	3.107
31	961	29,791	5.568	3.141
32	1,024	32,768	5.657	3.175
33	1,089	35,937	5.745	3.208
34	1,156	39,304	5.831	3.240
35	1,225	42,875	5.916	3.271
36	1,296	46,656	6.000	3.302
37	1,369	50,653	6.083	3.332
38	1,444	54,872	6.164	3.362
39	1,521	59,319	6.245	3.391
40	1,600	64,000	6.325	3.420
41	1,681	68,921	6.403	3.448
42	1,764	74,088	6.481	3.476
43	1,849	79,507	6.557	3.503
44	1,936	85,184	6.633	3.530
45	2,025	91,125	6.708	3.557
46	2,116	97,336	6.782	3.583
47	2,209	103,823	6.856	3.609
48	2,304	110,592	6.928	3.634
49	2,401	117,649	7.000	3.659
50	2,500	125,000	7.071	3.684
51	2,601	132,651	7.141	3.708

No.	Square	Cube	Square Root	Cube Root
52	2,704	140,608	7.211	3.732
53	2,809	148,877	7.280	3.756
54	2,916	157,464	7.348	3.780
55	3,025	166,375	7.416	3.803
56	3,136	175,616	7.483	3.826
57	3,249	185,193	7.550	3.848
58	3,364	195,112	7.616	3.871
59	3,481	205,379	7.681	3.893
60	3,600	216,000	7.746	3.915
61	3,721	226,981	7.810	3.936
62	3,844	238,328	7.874	3.958
63	3,969	250,047	7.937	3.979
64	4,096	262,144	8.000	4.000
65	4,225	274,625	8.062	4.021
66	4,356	287,496	8.124	4.041
67	4,489	300,763	8.185	4.061
68	4,624	314,432	8.246	4.082
69	4,761	328,509	8.307	4.101
70	4,900	343,000	8.367	4.121
71	5,041	357,911	8.426	4.141
72	5,184	373,248	8.485	4.160
73	5,329	389,017	8.544	4.179
74	5,476	405,224	8.602	4.198
75	5,625	421,875	8.660	4.217
76	5,776	438,976	8.718	4.236
77	5,929	456,533	8.775	4.254
78	6,084	474,552	8.832	4.273
79	6,241	493,039	8.888	4.291
80	6,400	512,000	8.944	4.309

No.	Square	Cube	Square Root	Cube Root
81	6,561	531,441	9.000	4.327
82	6,724	551,368	9.055	4.344
83	6,889	571,787	9.110	4.362
84	7,056	592,704	9.165	4.379
85	7,225	614,125	9.219	4.397
86	7,396	636,056	9.274	4.414
87	7,569	658,503	9.327	4.431
88	7,744	681,472	9.381	4.448
89	7,921	704,969	9.434	4.465
90	8,100	729,000	9.487	4.481
91	8,281	753,571	9.539	4.498
92	8,464	778,688	9.592	4.514
93	8,649	804,357	9.644	4.531
94	8,836	830,584	9.695	4.547
95	9,025	857,375	9.747	4.563
96	9,216	884,736	9.798	4.579
97	9,409	912,673	9.849	4.595
98	9,604	941,192	9.899	4.610
99	9,801	970,299	9.950	4.626
100	10,000	1,000,000	10.000	4.642